FOUNDATIONS *of*

Mac®
PROGRAMMING

FOUNDATIONS *of* Mac® PROGRAMMING

FIFTH
5
ANNIVERSARY
IDG
BOOKS
WORLDWIDE

DAN PARKS SYDOW

Foundations of Mac® Programming

Published by

IDG Books Worldwide, Inc.

An International Data Group Company

919 E. Hillsdale Blvd.

Foster City, CA 94404

Library of Congress Catalog Card No.: 95-81091

ISBN: 1-56884-349-6

Printed in the United States of America

10 9 8 7 6 5 4 3 2 1

1A/SZ/RR/ZV

Distributed in the United States by IDG Books Worldwide, Inc.

Distributed by Macmillan Canada for Canada; by Computer and Technical Books for the Caribbean Basin; by Contemporanea de Ediciones for Venezuela; by Distribuidora Cuspide for Argentina; by CITEC for Brazil; by Ediciones ZETA S.C.R. Ltda. for Peru; by Editorial Limusa SA for Mexico; by Transworld Publishers Limited in the United Kingdom and Europe; by Al-Maiman Publishers & Distributors for Saudi Arabia; by Simron Pty. Ltd. for South Africa; by IDG Communications (HK) Ltd. for Hong Kong; by Toppan Company Ltd. for Japan; by Addison Wesley Publishing Company for Korea; by Longman Singapore Publishers Ltd. for Singapore, Malaysia, Thailand, and Indonesia; by Unalis Corporation for Taiwan; by WS Computer Publishing Company, Inc. for the Philippines; by WoodsLane Pty. Ltd. for Australia; by WoodsLane Enterprises Ltd. for New Zealand.

For general information on IDG Books Worldwide's books in the U.S., please call our Consumer Customer Service department at 800-762-2974. For reseller information, including discounts and premium sales, please call our Reseller Customer Service department at 800-434-3422.

For information on where to purchase IDG Books Worldwide's books outside the U.S., contact IDG Books Worldwide at 415-655-3021 or fax 415-655-3295.

For information on translations, contact Marc Jeffrey Mikulich, Director, Foreign & Subsidiary Rights, at IDG Books Worldwide, 415-655-3018 or fax 415-655-3295.

For sales inquiries and special prices for bulk quantities, write to the address above or call IDG Books Worldwide at 415-655-3200.

For information on using IDG Books Worldwide's books in the classroom, or ordering examination copies, contact Jim Kelly at 800-434-2086.

For authorization to photocopy items for corporate, personal, or educational use, please contact Copyright Clearance Center, 222 Rosewood Drive, Danvers, MA 01923, or fax 508-750-4470.

 is a trademark under exclusive license to IDG Books Worldwide, Inc., from International Data Group, Inc.

About the Author

Since graduating from the Milwaukee School of Engineering, Dan Parks Sydow has worked on software in areas as diverse as the control of nuclear reactors for defense purposes and the display of heart images for medical purposes. He is currently a consultant and free-lance writer. Dan is the author of several books on programming the Macintosh, including Programming the PowerPC and the IDG title *Mac Programming For Dummies*.

You can contact Dan at danparks@aol.com

Welcome to the world of IDG Books Worldwide.

IDG Books Worldwide, Inc., is a subsidiary of International Data Group, the world's largest publisher of computer-related information and the leading global provider of information services on information technology. IDG was founded more than 25 years ago and now employs more than 7,700 people worldwide. IDG publishes more than 250 computer publications in 67 countries (see listing below). More than 70 million people read one or more IDG publications each month.

Launched in 1990, IDG Books Worldwide is today the #1 publisher of best-selling computer books in the United States. We are proud to have received 8 awards from the Computer Press Association in recognition of editorial excellence and three from Computer Currents' First Annual Readers' Choice Awards, and our best-selling ...*For Dummies*® series has more than 19 million copies in print with translations in 28 languages. IDG Books Worldwide, through a joint venture with IDG's Hi-Tech Beijing, became the first U.S. publisher to publish a computer book in the People's Republic of China. In record time, IDG Books Worldwide has become the first choice for millions of readers around the world who want to learn how to better manage their businesses.

Our mission is simple: Every one of our books is designed to bring extra value and skill-building instructions to the reader. Our books are written by experts who understand and care about our readers. The knowledge base of our editorial staff comes from years of experience in publishing, education, and journalism — experience which we use to produce books for the '90s. In short, we care about books, so we attract the best people. We devote special attention to details such as audience, interior design, use of icons, and illustrations. And because we use an efficient process of authoring, editing, and desktop publishing our books electronically, we can spend more time ensuring superior content and spend less time on the technicalities of making books.

You can count on our commitment to deliver high-quality books at competitive prices on topics you want to read about. At IDG Books Worldwide, we continue in the IDG tradition of delivering quality for more than 25 years. You'll find no better book on a subject than one from IDG Books Worldwide.

John J. Kilcullen

John Kilcullen
President and CEO
IDG Books Worldwide, Inc.

Acknowledgments

Most importantly, I'd like to thank Nadine and Taylor for their patience and support. Without knowing it, you've helped write this book!

Thanks to Ken Brown, Developmental Editor, IDG Books, for keeping things running smoothly, and to Felicity O'Meara, who brought her keen copy editor's eyes to the manuscript. As always, Peter Ferrante, Apple Computer, gains my appreciation for another helpful technical edit. Thanks also to Carole McClendon, Waterside Productions, for making this book happen.

Many thanks to the software authors who granted permission to allow their programs and utilities to appear on this book's CD. A special thanks to Ambrosia Software — their handy, easy to use shareware products helped with this book's figures. The ColorSwitch color-setting control panel made it easy to quickly change monitor color levels, and the Snapz screen-capture control panel allowed screen dumps to be made while menus were dropped. Contact Ambrosia Software at AmbrosiaSW@aol.com.

(The Publisher would like to give special thanks to Patrick J. McGovern, without whom this book would not have been possible.)

Credits

**Senior Vice President
and Group Publisher**
Brenda McLaughlin

Acquisitions Editor
Nancy E. Dunn

Brand Manager
Pradeepa Siva

Developmental Editor
Kenyon Brown

Editorial Assistant
Suki Gear

Production Director
Beth Jenkins

Production Assistant
Jacalyn L. Pennywell

**Supervisor of
Project Coordination**
Cindy L. Phipps

Supervisor of Page Layout
Kathie S. Schnorr

Production Systems Specialist
Steve Peake

Pre-Press Coordination
Tony Augsburger
Patricia R. Reynolds
Theresa Sánchez-Baker

Media/Archive Coordination
Leslie Popplewell
Kerri Cornell
Michael Wilkey

Copy Editor
Felicity O'Meara

Technical Reviewer
Peter Ferrante

Project Coordinator
Valery Bourke

Graphics Coordination
Shelley Lea
Gina Scott
Carla Radzikinas

Production Page Layout
Dominique DeFelice
Angela Hunckler
Drew R. Moore

Proofreaders
Sandra Profant
Gwenette Gaddis
Dwight Ramsey
Carl Saff
Robert Springer

Indexer
Richard T. Evans

Cover Design
Draper and Liew

Cover Image
Draper and Liew

Contents Overview

If you're new to Macintosh programming, or have only compiled a few trivial example programs, you'll want to read the chapters in Part I to get an overview of what Mac code looks like, how it works, and how it interacts with resources and memory.

This chapter covers the topics, techniques, and terminology that are of importance to all Mac programmers, and introduces you to the purpose of resources and the Macintosh Toolbox. Here you'll find a very short, well-documented first look at a Macintosh source code listing for a program that plays a QuickTime movie.

This chapter takes a look at how a programmer uses resources to easily define the elements of the Mac's graphical user interface — elements such as menus, windows, dialog boxes. The chapter describes how a Mac program loads resource data into memory for use by your program's code.

Each program that runs on a Macintosh is given its own private area of RAM. This chapter shows how your program will make use of this memory.

The topics covered in Part II are the true fundamentals of Macintosh programming. All but the most trivial Mac applications make use of the topics covered here.

Much of the work of drawing graphics to a window is taken care of for you by QuickDraw. QuickDraw is the name for the hundreds of built-in drawing routines that are a subset of the thousands of Toolbox routines. This chapter shows how simple shapes such as rectangles and ovals can be drawn with just a function call or two.

Macintosh programs respond to actions, or events, initiated by the user. A click of the mouse button or a press of a key on the keyboard are each considered an event. This chapter shows how to write an event-driven program — an application that handles such events.

Users of a Macintosh program make their wishes known to a program through menu selections. All but the simplest of example programs display a menu bar and menus, and respond to user's selection from these menus. This chapter describes how menus are added to a program, and how that program takes the correct action in response to a user's menu choice.

Everything that is displayed by a Mac program is done so in a window. Whether it's graphics, text, or a movie, a programmer needs to first display a window to be used as the drawing board. This chapter shows how to not only open windows, but to allow the user to drag, grow, zoom, and close them as well.

A dialog box is a window with a few "extras" thrown in. These extras, called dialog items, consist of buttons, check boxes, radio buttons, text items, and more. This chapter demonstrates how a dialog box is displayed and how your program properly handles user mouse button clicks on any of the dialog box items. Both stationary and movable dialog boxes are covered in detail.

Getting text from the keyboard into a window of your program is the topic of this chapter. Here you'll learn how typed text can be displayed in any part of a window, and how that text can be edited by the user.

The topics covered in Part I and Part II provide an important base for writing a Macintosh application — each topic is essential to writing a program that looks and behaves as expected of a Mac program. Now it's time for the fun stuff!

Chapter 4 provided an introduction to drawing. This chapter shows how QuickDraw can be used to draw much more than just circles and squares. This chapter discusses the drawing of more complex shapes. It also describes how these shapes can be filled with any pattern of your choosing.

A monitor connected to a Mac can display hundreds of colors. Some models can display thousands or even millions of colors. This chapter discusses the system the Macintosh uses for defining colors. You'll read how to select a color from within your code and how to give users the ability to make color selections of their own choosing. Once a color is selected, your program can use that color to fill a shape or the entire window with it.

Chapter 11 described how you can draw in color in a Window. In this chapter you'll learn how to add color to a window. Through the use of a window color table resource you'll be able to add color to a window's frame, title, or content area. As you'll see in this chapter, the same holds true for dialog boxes. Finally, this chapter shows how you can add a little — or a lot — of color to a program's menus.

The Mac has always been known for its graphics capabilities. But from its inception it has also been capable of producing sound. In this chapter you'll see how to store digitized sounds in both resources and sound files. You'll then learn how your program can play back these sounds at any time.

QuickTime may very well be the embodiment of multimedia. Sound, graphics, animation — all contained in a single file that is easily playable from any of your own Mac programs. In this chapter you'll see how your program can open and play any existing QuickTime movie.

Your program should be able to allow users to create interesting things. It should also allow users to save and print the results of their work. After you've implemented the features that have been described in the other parts of this book, you'll want to add the two features covered in Part IV: file handling and printing.

A program that makes use of user-supplied data usually makes use of files. In this chapter you'll learn how your program can create a new file and then save data to it. This chapter also describes how to reopen this saved file at any time in order to access the data in it.

Saving data to a file may not be enough for some users — they may want to also save it on paper. In this chapter you'll learn how to send both text and graphics to the user's printer. The printing techniques described here will work regardless of the type of printer users have connected to their Macs.

Table of Contents

PART II: PROGRAMMING FUNDAMENTALS 133

Chapter 4: Drawing 135

Chapter 5: Events 167

PART IV: FILES AND PRINTING 593

Chapter 15: Files 595

Foreword

It has long been Metrowerks' philosophy to promote and support the Macintosh as a programming platform. As you make your way through this book, you, too, will discover Mac programming and make it your own.

The Macintosh is incredibly easy to use, its interface elegant. No one will argue with that. On the other hand, the Mac has a reputation as a difficult machine to program. Part of this stems from the more than 27 volumes of *Inside Macintosh* that describe the inner workings of the Mac.

Truth is, with CodeWarrior and a few Mac programming books, you can have your first Mac application up and running in pretty short order. Foundations of Macintosh Programming begins by covering general Mac programming concepts and moves into more specific topics — including the fun stuff that attracts people to the Mac — like QuickTime movies and sound.

One of the best ways to learn a concept is to see sample source code demonstrating the concept. Foundations of Macintosh Programming serves as both a reference book with syntax references and a tutorial book with sample code that can be compiled using CodeWarrior. Dan has taken Niklaus Wirth's phrase "Programming is a constructive art" and turned it into this wonderful book.

With Foundations of Macintosh Programming, the new Mac developer can take the first step into becoming a true code warrior. We're real happy to be part of that first step and wish you well in your trip.

If you want to send Metrowerks comments or flames, send email to prez@metrowerks.com. It will find me.

Greg Galanos
President and CEO
Metrowerks, Inc.
Austin, Texas
October 10, 1995

Introduction

Welcome to *Foundations of Mac Programming!* This book exists to get potential Mac programmers started and to supply intermediate-level Mac programmers with the information needed to write more sophisticated applications. More advanced Mac developers will also benefit — the sheer size of this text guarantees there'll be at least a few tips and techniques not encountered elsewhere! Whatever your current programming skill level, the goal of this book remains the same: to provide a firm foundation on which all your Mac programs can be built and to move you on to the next level of application development.

Foundations of Mac Programming includes chapters that cover all the basics of Mac programming — topics such as using windows, menus, dialog boxes, graphics, and more. Additionally, there's plenty of material devoted to the fun stuff — topics such as programming with color and adding sound-playing and movie-playing capabilities to any of your programs. You'll find that the emphasis of each chapter isn't on writing programs from scratch. Instead, the focus of a chapter is on achieving programming goals by using the Macintosh Toolbox — the rich, expansive set of Apple-supplied functions built into every Mac. Each chapter ends with a handy reference section that provides a summary of the Toolbox functions used in the chapter.

This book includes a CD-ROM that contains all the example code included in the book. If you use a Symantec compiler, you'll make use of the Symantec folder. There you'll find a Symantec project and source code file for each and every example. If your compiler happens to match the author's compiler of choice — Metrowerks CodeWarrior — you'll be pleased to find that the CD also houses a Metrowerks version of each project and source file. Regardless of the compiler you choose, you'll find the numerous public domain and shareware programs and utilities that are also included on the CD of great help in your programming endeavors.

Four Parts Make a Whole

This Foundations book is divided into four parts. Part I covers the very basics of Mac programming: topics such as Mac programming terminology, C data types specific to the Mac, and a look at a Mac source code listing. Part II covers the interface elements that just about any Mac program requires: windows, menus, and the like. After mastering the basics, you're ready to diversify a little and move on to more exciting topics. Part III shows you how to add multimedia features such as sound playing and movie playing to your programs. Finally, Part IV describes how to complete a program by adding data-saving and printing capabilities to it.

PART I: INTRODUCTION TO MAC PROGRAMMING CONCEPTS

Part I introduces the basic concepts, data types, and terminology used by programmers of Macintosh applications. It begins with an overview of just what a Mac program consists of. Chapter 1 includes source code listings for two short, simple Mac programs — each requires less than 50 lines of code. The first program opens a window and writes some text to it. The second program is a little more ambitious and a little more useful — it opens a window and plays a QuickTime movie in it. Chapter 1 takes a long, detailed look at each of these programs so that you'll feel comfortable with the format of Macintosh C language code.

Part I also covers two topics every Mac programmer becomes intimate with: resources and memory. A resource is a special type of code used to define an element of the interface, such as a window or menu. Resources make it easy to create and edit these elements — as Part I points out. Like any type of code, resource code eventually makes its way into RAM. When your program runs, it loads resource code and your application's code into memory. Part I provides all the details of how this happens and why it's of importance to you.

PART II: PROGRAMMING FUNDAMENTALS

Part II provides you with the information you need to write real Mac applications. How to display a window, a dialog box, menus, and the menu bar — it's all covered here. Displaying these interface elements isn't enough, of course — your program needs to be able to work with them. A Mac program allows the user to drag and close a window, click on items in a dialog box, and make menu selections from a menu. In Part II you'll learn to do all of that.

Opening a window and allowing the user to move it, resize it, and close it will give you a sense of accomplishment. But it won't cut it as a program — for that you need to add a little content! In Part II you'll learn how to add both graphics and text to a window.

PART III: MULTIMEDIA: GRAPHICS, SOUND, AND MOVIES

The basics are out of the way, the foundation has been laid — now its on to more interesting and more challenging topics! Part III covers multimedia programming topics such as graphics, color, sound, and movies. Programmers who write programs for platforms other than the Mac might consider these topics as advanced, but developers of Macintosh applications would consider even these more diverse topics as the foundations of programming. That's because Mac users *expect* and *demand* interesting, exciting, feature-laden applications. The chapters that comprise Part III prove that on the Mac even multimedia programming techniques are well within the grasp of beginner and intermediate programmers.

PART IV: FILES AND PRINTING

Part IV covers a couple of topics that serve to round out a Macintosh application. While a Mac program may do exciting things for the user here and now — what does it do for the user later? A program should allow the user to save the results of his or her efforts — to be used or viewed at a later time. In Part IV you'll learn how to save user-supplied data in files. That allows the user to recall data at a later running of your program. In Part IV you'll also see how to add printing capabilities to your program. That allows users to show off their work to people who don't have access to a Mac!

How to Use This Book

If you're new to Mac programming, it's strongly recommended that you begin at Part I and read the chapters in that part in their entirety. Part I — and Chapter 1 in particular — will get you in the Mac programmer frame of mind! After Part I, move on to Part II. The topics in this part are essential reading if you hope to accomplish anything beyond a very trivial program. After Part II you're free to pick and choose topics from the remainder of the book.

If you're an intermediate-level Mac programmer, you'll probably want to skim the chapters that make up Part I. You might want to skip Chapter 1 altogether — though a good programming refresher never hurts! You may be familiar with many of the topics described in Part II — but undoubtedly you'll find a few tidbits of interest. In particular, you may not be familiar with using TextEdit. If that is in fact the case, make sure to read and follow the examples in Chapter 9. The chapters in Parts III and IV should provide a wealth of material of interest to you. Even if you do find yourself skipping a chapter here and there, don't forget that every chapter after Chapter 1 ends with a reference section that describes the API — the application programming interface — for the Toolbox routines discussed in the chapter. That makes *Foundations of Mac Programming* a good reference book for looking up the calling conventions of a couple of hundred of the most commonly used Toolbox functions.

If you're an advanced-level Mac programmer, you may still find some points of interest in this text. In particular, you should find yourself thumbing through the back of each chapter whenever you can't recall exactly which Toolbox routine you need to call in order to achieve a specific task.

Regardless of your programming skill level, you'll be happy to know that every example program in this text — over 50 in all — can be found on the included CD-ROM. In an attempt to cater to every reader's choice of compiler and choice of target computer, there's actually a few versions of each example. Whether you use a Symantec compiler or a Metrowerks CodeWarrior compiler, you'll find a project for you — and for each example. And no matter which type of machine you expect your example to run on (that is, whether the *target* will be a new Power Mac or an older Mac that doesn't use the PowerPC chip), you'll find a project suited for you.

Conventions Used in This Book

I've tried to be clear and consistent about what's what in this book. This can get tricky, so I used the following typographical conventions to distinguish among a variety of elements that you're likely to encounter while programming.

CODE

When I include fragments of code or whole programs, I set them off from the rest of the text, like this:

```
OSErr    theError;
FSSpec   MooVFSSpec;

theError = FSMakeFSSpec( 0, 0, "\pMyTestMovie", &MooVFSSpec );
```

When I quote an element of code in running text, you'll see a different typeface used to set it off, as in "The Movie Toolbox function `EnterMovies()` allocates a block of memory that the Movie Toolbox will use exclusively for your program."

ICONS

 This icon highlights short, to-the-point time-savers or quick techniques that will help you work smarter.

 This icon highlights a special point of interest about the topic under discussion — information you might not need if you're just skimming a chapter but that might be valuable when you need more details about a particular topic.

 This icon alerts you that the action or operation being described can cause problems if you're not careful.

This icon highlights concerns or issues that are peripheral to the main topic or provide additional background information like the example shown below:

> Not just any compiler will generate fast PowerPC code. When the Macs based on the new PowerPC microprocessor became available in 1994, each compiler vendor had to design a new version of their Macintosh compiler. The new compiler had to be one that would produce *native* code — code consisting of instructions that were a part of the PowerPC instruction set. Metrowerks managed to accomplish this feat before Symantec and won quite a few converts in doing so. Refer to Appendix A for more information.

Onward!

Enough of the preliminaries — it's time to start coding! As you do, feel free to take a break at any time to share your thoughts and opinions, pro or con, about the way this text presents material to you. You can contact the author at the email address listed in the "About the Author" section.

I

Introduction to Mac Programming Concepts

*I*f you're new to Macintosh programming or have only compiled a few trivial example programs, you'll want to read the chapters in Part I to get an overview of what Mac code looks like, how it works, and how it interacts with resources and memory.

1

Overview of Mac Programming

*I*f you've never programmed on a Macintosh, this chapter provides an overview of the topics, techniques, and terminology that are of importance to all Mac programmers. If you have written Mac programs, you might want to at least browse this chapter — it serves as a good review of Macintosh programming basics.

You'll learn how a Macintosh program relies on resources and the Macintosh Toolbox to implement the elements of a graphical user interface — elements such as windows, menus, and dialog boxes. You'll see how a Mac program watches for, and responds to, events — user actions such as a click of the mouse button or a press of a keyboard key. A short, simple source code listing demonstrates these concepts, and a thorough explanation of the code reinforces these topics.

The chapter explains the conventions the book uses for naming local variables, global variables, and constants. It also describes how to make proper use of the universal interface files, which are an important set of header files that Apple supplies. You'll learn to add simple error-checking to your code to help ensure that your program won't come to a quick, unexpected halt. All of this information is then summed up and demonstrated in the chapter's second complete source code listing, a one-page program that plays a QuickTime movie. The chapter ends with a discussion of the differences between code written for pre-PowerPC Macs and code written for the newer Macs that are driven by the PowerPC chip.

Macintosh Programming Basics

Macintosh programmers are familiar with bitmapped graphics, resources, the Macintosh Toolbox, events, and data types unique to the Macintosh. This section provides an overview of these important Macintosh topics.

PIXELS AND BITMAPPED GRAPHICS

Each dot, or *pixel,* on an older monochrome Macintosh screen is always in one of two states — on or off. The computer turns some pixels on and others off to display images on screen. Images can be as simple as a dot, a line, or an icon, or as complex as a full-screen digitized image. To keep track of these images, a Macintosh must keep track of the state of each pixel. This pixel information is stored in memory. On a monochrome Mac, each pixel has a corresponding bit in memory. Since a single bit can have a value of 0 or 1, it is the perfect unit of memory for keeping track of a two-state pixel. This mapping, or relationship, between pixels and bits gives rise to the term bitmapped graphics. Color monitors also use bitmapped graphics. For a color system, however, each pixel requires more than a single bit of memory. To keep track of which of many states — or colors — a single pixel currently is in, color systems use 8, 16, or 24 bits.

To draw an image, a Macintosh program alters the state of some of the screen's pixels. To draw at a desired location, a program needs a means of specifying which pixels to alter, so it uses a coordinate system that assigns each pixel a horizontal and vertical value. Since a program always draws to a window, each window has its own coordinate system. The pixel in the upper left corner of the window's content area (the area excluding the title bar) is pixel (0, 0) and serves as the reference point for all of the other pixels in that window. Consider a rectangle that is to be drawn in a window. If the upper left corner of the rectangle is supposed to appear 60 pixels from the left edge of the window and 150 pixels down from the top of the window, then that corner will be at point (60, 150). Figure 1-1 illustrates this.

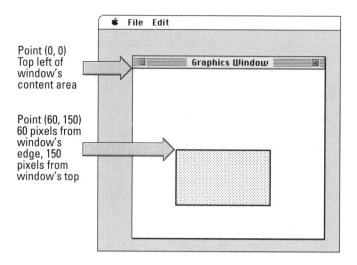

Figure 1-1

Graphics are drawn to a window using a pixel coordinate system as a reference.

RESOURCES

The Macintosh graphical user interface is achieved through the use of resources. A resource is code that describes a part of the interface — there's a resource for each menu, icon, dialog box, and window that you see on the Mac screen. Because resource code describes a visual element of a program, the code lends itself to being viewed visually as well. Instead of a text editor, a Mac programmer uses a resource editor to create, edit, and view resource code. Far and away the most popular resource editor is ResEdit, a program that is freely distributed by Apple. The other leading resource editor is Mathemaesthetics Resorcerer. Resorcerer has the advantage of being a more powerful editor than ResEdit, but at a cost. Because it is a third-party product, you'll of course have to pay for this editor.

As an example of how a resource is viewed in a resource editor, consider the WIND resource. A WIND resource holds the information that describes what a window looks like. By making changes to a WIND resource, a programmer can alter the size, initial placement on the screen, and the overall look of a window. Figure 1-2 shows how a WIND resource looks as viewed in ResEdit. Figure 1-3 shows that same resource as viewed in Resorcerer.

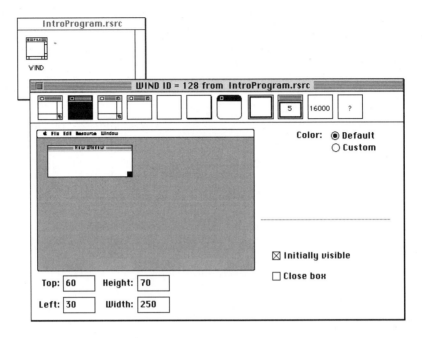

Figure 1-2

A WIND *resource, as viewed in the resource editor ResEdit.*

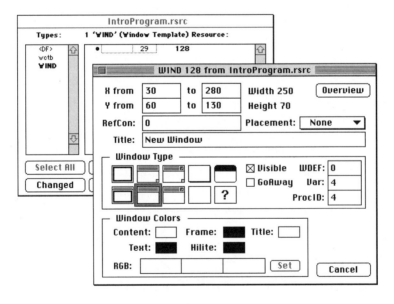

Figure 1-3

A WIND *resource, as viewed in the resource editor Resorcerer.*

The ability to graphically edit resources is one advantage to using them. A second advantage is that a single resource can be used as a template from which any number of interface elements can be created. For instance, a WIND resource can be used to define the look of a window used by a text editing program. That program will use the same resource every time the user selects New from the program's File menu. As Figure 1-4 shows, the data that makes up a WIND resource gets loaded into memory. From there, the program that loaded the data uses that data to create as many windows as needed.

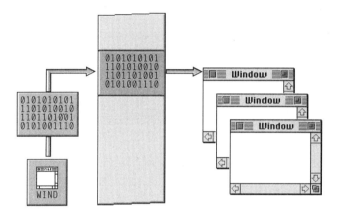

Figure 1-4
A resource holds data that gets loaded into memory and used by an application.

You saw in Figures 1-2 and 1-3 that a WIND resource displayed in a resource editor is very "human-readable." Yet in Figure 1-4, the WIND resource data is shown as nothing but a group of 1s and 0s. That's because resource data is in fact code that's ready to be linked with compiled source code. A resource editing program, through the use of a number of individual resource type editors (such as a WIND editor), presents this code to the user in a graphical manner.

What Mac programmers call a *compiler* is actually both a compiler and a linker. When a programmer builds, or makes, a Macintosh application, the compiler compiles source code. The result is object code. The linker then combines this object code with the code that makes up the resources that are to be used with the program. The result is a Macintosh application that contains both compiled source code and resource code, as shown in Figure 1-5.

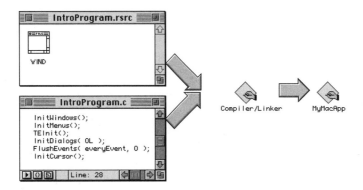

Figure 1-5
A Macintosh program consists of code that comes from source code and from resources.

THE MACINTOSH TOOLBOX

In a graphical user interface environment such as that of the Macintosh, most programs share many similar programming tasks. Tracking the movement of the cursor as the user moves the mouse, dropping menus down in response to a mouse-click in the menu bar, displaying a new window when the user selects New from the File menu — these are all examples of situations that almost every Mac programmer must write code for. Apple anticipated this and wrote all of the code necessary to handle such program tasks. This code was then added to the ROM chips of each Macintosh. Finally, an application programming interface, or API, was developed to give all Mac programmers access to this code. The API is commonly called the Macintosh Toolbox, or simply the Toolbox, and is a set of several thousand routines that any Macintosh programmer can make use of in any Mac program he or she writes.

Having Apple engineers pour thousands of man-hours into the writing of code that is given away may seem too good to be true. But as you'll see in the points below, Apple had good reason for doing so. Here's why the Toolbox exists and why it is free:

- It forces Mac programs to have a similar "look and feel" — which is a key part of the Macintosh philosophy.

- It saves programmers the effort of "reinventing the wheel," or spending time solving programming problems that have been solved by others.

- It is a good selling point of Macintosh computers to developers.

How does a programmer make use of one of the many Toolbox routines? By simply making a call to the function from within the source code of a program. Earlier the idea that the data that makes up a WIND resource could be loaded into memory was discussed. Because almost every Mac program displays at least one window, this scenario is a perfect example of why a particular Toolbox routine exists. Rather than force each programmer to determine the format of the data in a WIND resource and then devise a way to move that data from a resource on disk to an area in RAM that a program can access, Apple has supplied a Toolbox routine to handle these tasks. The Toolbox function is named GetNewWindow(), and a call to it looks like this:

```
theWindow = GetNewWindow( 128, nil, (WindowPtr)-1L );
```

After adding the above line of code to a source code file, a programmer can assume that the data that describes a window is loaded into memory and can be accessed by the variable named theWindow. From that point on, theWindow can be used to work with that one particular window — to move it, resize it, draw to it, and so forth.

 There'll be WIND resource data in memory only if the programmer remembered to add a WIND resource, of course. In Chapter 2 you'll see how to verify the success of a call to a Toolbox routine that works with re-sources. Later in this chapter, and then in Chapter 7, you'll read about the parameters to GetNewWindow().

Of the several thousand Toolbox routines, the average programmer typically uses only a few hundred. A very small Macintosh program (like the one shown a little later in this chapter) might contain a dozen or so Toolbox calls. A somewhat larger program, such as a simple text editor, would make use of a couple of hundred or more Toolbox calls. You'll find that this book thoroughly documents more than 200 Macintosh Toolbox functions.

RESPONDING TO EVENTS

Older computer programs used to run sequentially. You would have to traverse through menus to get to a particular screen of information. You wouldn't use the pull-down menus you now find in Macintosh programs to execute commands; you'd select items from menus to take specific actions. For example, you might see a menu like the one in Figure 1-6.

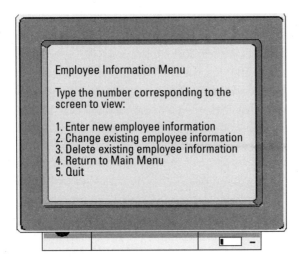

Figure 1-6
Menus in older computer programs allowed you to select items and take specific actions.

While the above system worked, it had the severe limitation of forcing the user to travel in only set directions — directions established by the computer. The Macintosh operating system, as well as other graphical user interface operating systems, gives program control to the user. Instead of providing the user with a strictly defined set of choices and forcing the user to accept one before continuing, the Macintosh program waits for the user to select any one of perhaps dozens of menu selections. Further, the user often has access to numerous unrelated menu choices rather than a screen of narrowly defined options. Further still, before a user makes a choice, he or she is free to perform other actions, such as moving windows, scrolling through information in any one of perhaps several open windows, or even changing to a different application. The mechanism that makes this type of program possible is the *event*.

When the user clicks the mouse, a mouse-down event occurs. When the user presses a key on the keyboard, a key-down event occurs. When the user moves a window that was partially off screen back on screen, a window update event occurs. When . . . well, you get the point. User actions generate events. If a program is written in such a way that it watches for events and responds to events, then the program is said to be *event-driven*. Macintosh programs, of course, are event-driven.

Because the search for events is one of those tasks common to just about any Mac program, the Macintosh Toolbox has a routine that provides assistance in this area. That routine is named WaitNextEvent(). Here's a typical call to WaitNextEvent():

```
WaitNextEvent( everyEvent, &theEvent, 15L, nil );
```

If WaitNextEvent() comes across an event, it supplies the program with information about the event by placing that information in the theEvent parameter. Next, it's up to the programmer to examine the theEvent variable to see what type of event occurred. After that, some action should be taken. The action taken will depend on the type of event and on the requirements of a particular program. The following snippet provides a general look at event-handling for a program that watches for a click of the mouse button or a press of a key. Because this overview omits the details of event processing, comments have been used in place of much of the necessary code.

```
WaitNextEvent( everyEvent, &theEvent, 15L, 0Lnil);
switch ( theEvent.what )
{
   // case mouse click event:
   //    handle mouse click event
         break;

   // case key press event:
   //    handle key press event
         break;
}
```

The above snippet — and many others in this book — use C++-style comments. For you C programmers, a double slash (//) can be used to create a single-line comment. Most C compilers now recognize this style of comment and allow you to use them in your source code.

NOTE

The details of events, event-handling, and event-driven programming can be found in Chapter 5.

When `WaitNextEvent()` is called, it checks the current status of the Mac. In other words, at the moment `WaitNextEvent()` is invoked, the Macintosh Toolbox checks things over. Is the user pressing the mouse button right now? Is the user pressing a key on the keyboard right now? If such an action is being taken, an event is occurring and needs to be handled. That's all well and good for the moment — but what about a minute later? Or a second later? Or even a fraction of a second later? The one call to `WaitNextEvent()` can't foresee what will happen next. So apparently one call to this routine isn't enough. As it turns out, it isn't *close* to being enough. A Macintosh program calls `WaitNextEvent()` continuously as the program runs — a couple of thousand times or more a minute. For the programmer, this isn't as frightening of a job as you might think. Simply wrapping the call to `WaitNextEvent()` in a loop takes care of this repetitive task.

```
// loop until user quits
   {
      WaitNextEvent( everyEvent, &theEvent, 15L, 0Lnil );
      switch ( theEvent.what )
      {
         // case mouse click event:
         //    handle mouse click event
            break;

         // case key press event:
         //    handle key press event
            break;
      }
   }
```

Because the call to `WaitNextEvent()` is found in a loop, the section of code that holds the loop and the `WaitNextEvent()` call is referred to as a program's *main event loop,* or simply its *event loop.*

MACINTOSH DATA TYPES

If you've programmed in C but not on a Macintosh, you're acquainted with only a subset of the C data types that you'll need to be familiar with. You'll find the ANSI C data types such as `void`, `float`, `double`, `int`, `short`, and long useful in Mac programming — but you'll also find that these data types aren't enough. That's because ANSI C makes no provisions for working with data that is unique to a particular operating system. For instance, because all computer operating systems don't make use of windows, you won't find an ANSI C data type that serves as a pointer to a window. When you write a program that is to be compiled with a Macintosh compiler, however, you will make use of such a data type — the WindowPtr type. After loading WIND resource data into memory, the Toolbox function GetNewWindow() creates a pointer to this data and returns that pointer to your program. It returns this pointer in the form of a WindowPtr variable.

```
WindowPtr  theWindow;
theWindow = GetNewWindow( 128, nil, (WindowPtr)-1L );
```

There are hundreds of other data types that are used by Macintosh programmers but not by developers of programs written for other operating systems. You'll encounter a couple more of these types in this chapter, and many others throughout the remaining chapters of this book.

A SIMPLE MACINTOSH SOURCE CODE LISTING

On the CD that accompanies this book, you'll find a folder named IDG Sydow Book Examples. This folder holds two additional folders. One contains book examples in a format ready to be compiled by a Symantec compiler; the other has the same examples in Metrowerks format. If you look in either of these two folders, you'll find one folder per book chapter. Within the one named C01 Overview, you'll find a folder named P01 Intro Program. This folder holds the code for this chapter's IntroProgram example. Figure 1-7 shows the folder hierarchy that leads to the Metrowerks version of this example.

The IntroProgram is a short, simple program designed simply to serve as a demonstration of the very basics of Macintosh programming. When you compile and run the IntroProgram (or when you double-click on the application icon), you'll see a window like the one shown in Figure 1-8. To quit the program, click the mouse button.

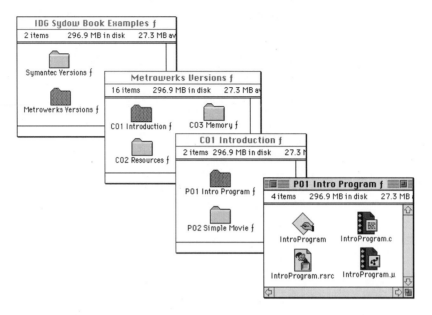

Figure 1-7
This book's CD contains two versions of every program — a Symantec version and a Metrowerks version.

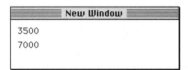

Figure 1-8
The result of running the IntroProgram example application.

The following listing is the contents of the IntroProgram.c file — the complete source code listing for the IntroProgram example. A walk-through of the listing's key points follows.

```
void  main( void )
{
    EventRecord    theEvent;
    WindowPtr      theWindow;
    Str255         theString = "\p3500";
    long           theNumber;
```

```
    InitGraf( &qd.thePort );
    InitFonts();
    InitWindows();
    InitMenus();
    TEInit();
    InitDialogs( 0L );
    FlushEvents( everyEvent, 0 );
    InitCursor();

    theWindow = GetNewWindow( 128, nil, (WindowPtr)-1L );
    SetPort( theWindow );
    MoveTo( 10, 20 );
    DrawString( theString );

    StringToNum( theString, &theNumber );
    theNumber *= 2;
    NumToString( theNumber, theString );

    MoveTo( 10, 40 );
    DrawString( theString );
    for (;;)
    {
        WaitNextEvent( everyEvent, &theEvent, 15L, 0Lnil );
        switch ( theEvent.what )
        {
            case mouseDown:
                ExitToShell();
                break;
        }
    }
}
```

The main ( ) Function

Like any C program, a Macintosh program must have a main() function.
The beginning of the main() function is the starting point for the execution
of the program. Because main() has no return value and no parameters, its
return type is void and its parameter list is void.

```
    void  main( void )
```

Variables

The IntroProgram declares these four variables:

```
    EventRecord   theEvent;
    WindowPtr     theWindow;
    Str255        theString = "\p3500";
    long          theNumber;
```

The first three variables are of data types that you won't find in ANSI C. A variable of type `EventRecord` is used to hold information about one event. A variable of type `WindowPtr` is used as a pointer to a window. A variable of type `Str255` is a string that can consist of up to 255 characters. The last variable is of the ANSI C data type `long`. A variable of this type can hold a number in the range of –2,147,483,648 to +2,147,483,647.

A Macintosh string stored in a `Str255` variable always starts with the "\p" characters. The backslash and the letter *p* tell the C compiler that the string should be in the format of a Pascal string — the original language of the Macintosh operating system. The Toolbox will be expecting a `Str255` to be in this Pascal format, so the inclusion of these two characters is an important and necessary step. The "\p" characters, by the way, won't show up when the string is drawn to a window.

 You C programmers who are familiar with ANSI C know that C strings end with, or are terminated by, the "\0" characters. A Pascal string doesn't need these characters to signal where it ends. Instead, the first character of a Pascal string holds the length of the string.

Initializations

Before a program works with the Macintosh Toolbox, some parts of the Toolbox need to be initialized. This initialization of the Toolbox can be performed by the Toolbox itself. These eight Toolbox function calls take care of this task:

```
InitGraf( &qd.thePort );
InitFonts();
InitWindows();
InitMenus();
TEInit();
InitDialogs( 0L );
FlushEvents( everyEvent, 0 );
InitCursor();
```

The Toolbox routines are grouped by topic, and each group of routines is referred to as a manager. Some of the various managers, such as the Menu Manager and the Window Manager, need a one-time initialization at the start of a program. Initialization consists of different things for different managers. For the Window Manager, for example, a call to `InitWindows()` draws the desktop and an empty menu bar.

It's a good idea to call the above eight routines at the start of *every* Mac program. A program that fails to initialize a manager and later attempts to use a routine from that manager will crash. A program that initializes a manager and doesn't make use of any of that manager's functions will not be adversely affected. Thus, even though each Mac application you write might not make use of Toolbox routines found in all of the managers, it is a good idea to get in the habit of playing it safe and initialize the managers anyway.

In the next example program in this chapter, SimpleMovie, these eight Toolbox functions will be grouped together in a single function defined by the application.

Opening a Window

After the Toolbox completes its initialization, the program calls the Toolbox function GetNewWindow() to load the data from a WIND resource into memory.

```
theWindow = GetNewWindow( 128, nil, (WindowPtr)-1L );
```

The resource file used to hold this WIND resource was pictured back in Figures 1-2 and 1-3. Windows and the GetNewWindow() function are discussed at length in Chapter 7. For now, take a look at the first parameter to GetNewWindow(). The number that is used for this parameter should be the resource ID of the WIND resource that holds the data to load. If you page back to Figure 1-2 or 1-3 you'll see that the WIND resource pictured in these figures does in fact have an ID of 128.

Drawing in a Window

In a Macintosh application, graphics are always drawn to a window. But a Macintosh program may have several windows open at the same time — so which window receives the drawing? To specify the window that is to be the recipient of future drawing commands, call the Toolbox function SetPort(). Pass SetPort() the window pointer that was returned by the call to GetNewWindow().

```
SetPort( theWindow );
```

Two of the many drawing-related Toolbox routines a program can use are the `MoveTo()` and `DrawString()` functions.

```
MoveTo( 10, 20 );
DrawString( theString );
```

Here the effect of `MoveTo()` is to prepare for the drawing of a string by telling the application where in a window the drawing of the string will start. In this example the string will start 10 pixels from the left edge of the window and 20 pixels down from the top. The call to `DrawString()` will draw the current value of the string `theString` to the window — the string *3500* will appear near the top left of the window, as shown back in Figure 1-8.

A string can represent a number, as `theString` does, but the string value can't be *treated* as a number. To convert a string to a number, use the Toolbox routine `StringToNum()`.

```
StringToNum( theString, &theNumber );
```

Pass this function a string and the address of a `long` variable, and the routine will determine the number that the string represents and place that value in the `long` variable. After that, your program can use the `long` variable as it would any number. In this example the value 3500 is multiplied by 2.

```
theNumber *= 2;
```

Just as a string can't be treated as a number, a number can't be treated as a string. Thus, to write a number to a window, it must first be converted to a string. `StringToNum()` has a companion Toolbox routine named `NumToString()` that takes care of this task.

```
NumToString( theNumber, theString );
```

Pass this function a long variable (*not* its address) and a string, and the function will convert the number to a string and store the result in the string variable.

After the call to `NumToString()`, `theString` has a value of "\p7000" rather than "\p3500." This string can be drawn to the window as done previously — by calling `MoveTo()` and `DrawString()`.

```
MoveTo( 10, 40 );
DrawString( theString );
```

The parameters passed in this second call to MoveTo() tell the program that this string will line up with the first string but will appear 20 pixels below it — both strings start 10 pixels from the left edge of the window, but the first starts 20 pixels from the top, while the second appears 40 pixels from the top.

Main Event Loop

The Macintosh main event loop was discussed earlier in the chapter. Here's the IntroProgram version of a main event loop:

```
for (;;)
{
    WaitNextEvent( everyEvent, &theEvent, 15L, 0Lnil );
    switch ( theEvent.what )
    {
        case mouseDown:
            ExitToShell();
            break;
    }
}
```

The main event loop in this program relies on a standard for loop. Because no conditions are specified in the loop statement, the loop will repeat indefinitely. Once the program opens a window and draws to it, the event loop starts, and it doesn't stop until the program terminates. In this simple example, that's accomplished by the user clicking the mouse. In a more sophisticated program — one that makes use of menus — the user would end the program by selecting the Quit item from the File menu.

As discussed earlier, an event loop is centered around a call to WaitNextEvent(). This Toolbox function gets called over and over, checking for the occurrence of an event each time it is invoked. Mac programs can look for, and handle, a number of different kinds of events. The IntroProgram only acknowledges one event type, a mouse-down event. The case label mouseDown is an Apple-defined constant that is used in a comparison of the what field of the EventRecord variable theEvent. When a mouse-click occurs, WaitNextEvent() becomes aware of it and fills the what field of theEvent with the value mouseDown. Then the code under the `mouseDown` case label executes. The IntroProgram chooses to handle a `mouseDown` event by calling the Toolbox function `ExitToShell()`. This function tells the program to exit, or quit.

Macintosh Code and Code Conventions

An application consists of calls to both Toolbox functions and functions defined by the application. It also consists of variables of different scope (local and global) and constants that represent resource IDs and nonresource-related values. To increase the readability of a Mac source code listing, this book uses a few naming conventions.

APPLICATION-DEFINED ROUTINES AND TOOLBOX ROUTINES

The Macintosh Toolbox consists of several thousand routines. The more you program, the more of them you'll recognize. No matter how much time you spend programming the Mac, however, you'll find that there are far more Toolbox functions than can ever be memorized. When looking over source code written by someone other than yourself, this can present a problem: How can you tell which functions are defined by Apple as part of the Toolbox and which are defined by the programmer who wrote the example code? Consider this snippet:

```
StopAlert( 128, nil );
SoundAlert( 128 );
```

The first function call is to a Toolbox function named `StopAlert()`. The second function, `SoundAlert()`, is a routine defined by the application from which the snippet came. To some readers it may not be obvious which routine is a Toolbox routine and which isn't. To clear this up, in the body of text that describes a snippet, the Toolbox function will always be referred to as just that — a *Toolbox function.* On the other hand, a function that is defined by an application will be referred to as an *application-defined function.* For instance, a textual description of the above snippet might read as follows: The Toolbox function `StopAlert()` displays an alert with a stop

sign icon in its upper left corner. The application-defined function
SoundAlert() posts an alert and broadcasts a warning sound from the
Mac's speaker.

Before your program calls an application-defined function, the compiler
needs to be informed of the function's format. That is, the compiler needs to
be aware of what types of parameters the function accepts and what type of
value, if any, the function will be returning to the program. The application-
defined SoundAlert() function has one parameter — of type short — and
no return value. Its prototype would look like this:

```
void  SoundAlert( short );
```

Typically, each application-defined function has a function prototype, and
all of the prototypes are grouped together and listed either at the top of a
source code file or in a header file that can be included in a source code file.

LOCAL AND GLOBAL VARIABLE NAMES

Different programmers use different conventions to make the scope of
variables easily recognizable. Some start the name of a global variable with
an uppercase character, as in GrandTotal or Grand_Total, and that of a
local variable with a lowercase character, as in bonusPoints or
bonus_points. In this text you'll find that all global variable names have a
leading lowercase g, which stands, of course, for global. Each word in the
name will begin with an uppercase character. An example of a global
variable name that follows this convention is gGrandTotal. The name of
each local variable in this text will always begin with a lowercase character;
only the first character of the second and subsequent words in a local
variable name will be capitalized. An example of such a local variable name
is bonusPoints.

Because function parameters act as variables local to the function in
which they appear, in this text, parameters will follow the same naming
convention as local variables. The following snippet from part of a
Macintosh program defines one global variable (gGrandTotal), one local
variable (bonusPoints), and one passed parameter (baseScore):

```
//_____
//  Define global variables
long  gGrandTotal;
//_____
//  Application-defined function
void  DetermineGrandTotal( long baseScore )
{
   long  bonusPoints;
   bonusPoints = 5;
   gGrandTotal = baseScore + bonusPoints;
}
```

CONSTANT DEFINITIONS

Like variable names, the first character in a constant name will be the indicator of a constant's type. You'll find that most constants in this book begin with a lowercase *k,* as in the kSalesTaxRate constant defined here:

```
#define     kSalesTaxRate     0.05
```

Here's a snippet that is a rewrite of the previous one. This version uses a constant rather than a variable to hold the bonus point value.

```
//_____
//  Define global variables
long  gGrandTotal;
//_____
//  Define global constants
#define     kBonusPoints     5
//_____
//  Application-defined function
void  DetermineGrandTotal( long baseScore )
{
   gGrandTotal = baseScore + kBonusPoints;
}
```

To identify constants as resource-related, some constants will begin with a lowercase *m* for menu resource, *i* for item in a menu resource, and *r* for resource — other resource types. The following shows an example of each constant definition:

```
#define     mFile          128    // MENU resource with ID 128
#define     iNew             1    // 1st item in the menu
```

```
#define    iOpen             2    // 2nd item in the menu
#define    iQuit             3    // 3rd item in the menu
#define    rScoreDialog    200    // DLOG resource with ID 200
```

 You'll find more examples of menu constants, and example programs that use them, in the chapters that cover resources and menus — Chapters 2 and 6, respectively.

Apple's Universal Interface Files

Regardless of the compiler you use, it will make use of Apple's *universal interface files* — also called the *universal header files.* Your Macintosh compiler came with a folder that contains more than 100 such files. That folder should be similar to the one pictured in Figure 1-9.

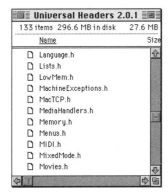

Figure 1-9
Some of the more than 100 universal header files.

 Your compiler may have come with more or fewer header files. Different compilers, and different versions of compilers, include different versions of the universal header files. By the way, the word *universal* in "universal header files" refers to the fact that a set of these header files will work for code being compiled for either an older Macintosh or a newer Mac that uses the PowerPC chip. Differences between Macintosh models are discussed later in this chapter.

Just as each application-defined function must have a function proto-type, so must each Toolbox routine used by your program. The function prototypes for *all* of the Toolbox functions appear in these universal interface files. For example, the prototype for the NumToString() Toolbox function used in the IntroProgram example can be found in the TextUtils.h universal interface file — it appears on the top line of the file shown in Figure 1-10.

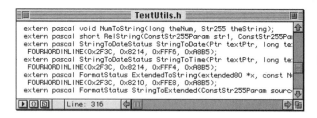

Figure 1-10
A universal header file holds the function prototypes for several Toolbox functions.

 Pascal is the original language of the Macintosh operating system. You'll see that the universal interface files define Toolbox routines using the pascal keyword. This tells the compiler to use Pascal conventions rather than C conventions. One example is in the compiler's ordering of function parameters. Pascal and C specify a different placement of function param-eters on the stack.

Figure 1-10 shows that the TextUtils.h universal header file defines NumToString() as a Toolbox function that accepts two parameters, one of type long and one of type Str255. While the NumToString() returns a value in the Str255 variable (a string version of the number passed as the first parameter), the function has no return type — the void keyword tells you that. From earlier in this chapter you can see that in the IntroProgram source code listing properly called NumToString()— the function call from that program is repeated in the following snippet:

```
Str255  theString = "\p3500";
long    theNumber;
...
...
theNumber *= 2;
NumToString( theNumber, theString );
```

To make your program aware of a particular universal header file, you can use an #include directive at the top of a source code file. If your program uses the NumToString() function, for instance, you can include the TextUtils.h header file that holds this function's prototype by using the following line:

```
#include <TextUtils.h>
```

If you're observant, you may have noticed that the source code listing for the IntroProgram that appeared earlier in this chapter didn't use such an #include directive — even though the program used the NumToString() Toolbox function. This was possible because compilers like those made by Symantec and Metrowerks automatically include dozens of the many universal header files in any program you write.

Figure 1-9 shows that more than 100 universal header files exist — 133 at this writing. Rather than include every one of these files in a program, Symantec and Metrowerks each use a single *precompiled header file* that holds the compiled header file information found in many of the most commonly used header files.

Precompiled header files are discussed later in this chapter, on the pages that deal with Symantec and Metrowerks projects.

You'll find that the source code listings for many Macintosh programs don't use any #include directives. That means that all of the Toolbox functions used by such a program are defined in the universal header files that are automatically included in each program. Other Mac programs, however, include one or more universal header files. When a source code listing includes universal header files, it tells you that program makes calls to Toolbox functions not found in the header files automatically included in a program. Here's one example:

```
#include <Movies.h>
```

The Movies.h header file holds the definitions for Toolbox routines that work with QuickTime. Since the majority of programs don't make use of QuickTime movies, Symantec has decided not to include the Movies.h header file in its group of header files that get turned into a precompiled header file. The same holds true for Metrowerks. Because the Movies.h header file isn't automatically a part of your program, you'll need to manually include it (as shown above) if your program uses QuickTime movies.

If you're new to Macintosh programming, you may be wondering how to determine which — if any — universal header files need to be included in your program. To find out, try compiling your source code. If it compiles successfully, you needn't add any universal header files. If you get error messages that say "function has no prototype," or some similarly worded messages, you'll know that you need to add at least one of the header files. Figure 1-11 shows such messages as displayed by the Metrowerks compiler. To determine which header file or files to include in your source code, search for a function by name in the files in the universal header files folder. Using the error messages in Figure 1-11, for example, you could search for EnterMovies. The result of that search would show that this routine is found in the Movies.h header file. Including that file in the source code listing and recompiling would eliminate the error messages shown in the figure.

Your compiler enables you to look through multiple files in a single search. Refer to your compiler's documentation to see how this is done.

Figure 1-11
Compiler errors can be caused by a failure to use one or more of the header files.

CHECKING FOR ERRORS

One of the many Macintosh data types you may not be familiar with is the OSErr type. A value of this operating system error type is returned by many Toolbox functions to let your program know if a Toolbox function call was successfully executed. What might cause a Toolbox routine to not execute properly? There are many possible reasons. If a routine is to perform some initialization, and the thing to initialize is not found, an operating system error will occur. If a routine is to open a file, and the file is not found, an operating system error will occur. An example of the latter is the Toolbox function `OpenMovieFile()`. This routine is called to open a QuickTime movie file in preparation for playing. The Movies.h universal header file lists the prototype for `OpenMovieFile()` as follows:

```
extern pascal OSErr OpenMovieFile(const FSSpec *fileSpec,
                                  short *resRefNum, SInt8 permission)
```

From the function prototype you can see that `OpenMovieFile()` is a function that requires three parameters and returns a value of type `OSErr`. Here our concern won't be with the parameters and what they're used for, but rather the fact that the function returns an `OSErr` value. Here's what a call to `OpenMovieFile()` might look like in a Macintosh source code listing:

```
OSErr   theError;
short   moovRefNum;
FSSpec  theFSSpec;
theError = OpenMovieFile( &theFSSpec, &moovRefNum, fsRdPerm );
```

If an error occurs, `OpenMovieFile()` returns a value that corresponds to one of several Apple-defined constants. For instance, if the QuickTime movie file that `OpenMovieFile()` is attempting to open can't be found — perhaps the user deleted it from his or her hard drive — no file will be opened and `theError` will be assigned a value of `fnfErr`. Each operating system error has a numerical value, but your code should refer to an error by its Apple-defined names rather than by its number. For instance, after calling `OpenMovieFile()`, your code could compare the value of `theError` with one or more Apple-defined constants.

```
theError = OpenMovieFile( &theFSSpec, &moovRefNum, fsRdPerm );
if ( theError == fnfErr )
   // post an alert that says "QuickTime movie file not found"
else
   // assume file has been opened and carry on...
```

Rather than handle specific errors, as shown above, your code can compare the returned `OSErr` value with the Apple-defined constant `noErr`. If a Toolbox routine that returns an `OSErr` returns a value of `noErr`, you can assume the function executed properly. Following is another snippet that calls `OpenMovieFile()`. After the call, the code compares the value of `theError` with the value of the Apple-defined constant `noErr`. If the two aren't equal, the program knows that an error of some sort occurred. Your program can then handle the error as it sees fit — usually by displaying an error message in an alert and, possibly, terminating the program.

```
theError = OpenMovieFile( &theFSSpec, &moovRefNum, fsRdPerm );
if ( theError != noErr )
    // post a general "Sorry, error" alert and/or quit the program
else
    // assume file has been opened and carry on...
```

You'll find Apple-defined operating system error constants described in their appropriate chapters. For instance, the `fnfErr` is mentioned in Chapter 15.

Toolbox routines aren't the only type of function that can return an `OSErr`. You can write any application-defined function in such a way that it too returns an error code. The following snippet shows part of an application-defined routine named `MyOpenAndPlayMovie()`.

```
OSErr  MyOpenAndPlayMovie( Str255 theMovieName )
{
    OSErr    theError;
    short    moovRefNum;
    FSSpec   theFSSpec;

    theError = FSMakeFSSpec( 0, 0L, theMovieName, &theFSSpec );
    if ( theError != noErr )
        return ( theError );
    theError = OpenMovieFile( &theFSSpec, &moovRefNum, fsRdPerm );
    if ( theError != noErr )
        return ( theError );
    ...
    ...
    return ( noErr );
}
```

Again, it isn't important to understand how Toolbox functions such as `FSMakeFSSpec()` and `OpenMovieFile()` work — you'll find all the details pertaining to these routines in Chapter 14. Instead, just examine the code and read the following text to gain an understanding of the general technique of implementing a function that returns an error code.

The `MyOpenAndPlayMovie()` routine makes several calls to Toolbox functions that each return an `OSErr` value — two of the calls are shown. After each call, the returned `OSErr` value is compared to the Apple-defined constant noErr. If the value of variable `theError` doesn't match the value of noErr, the function immediately exits and returns the value of theError. If the function executes without an error, the value of noErr is returned to signal this fact.

Notice that the MyOpenAndPlayMovie() function doesn't actually handle any errors; it just returns the error code and leaves the task of error-handling to the routine that calls MyOpenAndPlayMovie(). The MyOpenAndPlayMovie() function has an advantage over a similar function that presupposes how a program will handle errors. By leaving specific error-handling chores to the program, a function such as MyOpenAndPlayMovie() is a likely candidate to be used as-is in another program — a simple copy and paste, and the code is reused. If, on the other hand, the function itself determined how errors should be handled, then the potential would exist for errors to be handled in a way contrary to how a program expects that to be done.

The following snippet shows one way that a program could handle an error code returned by the application-defined routine MyOpenAndPlayMovie(). In this code it is assumed that PostErrorAlert() is an application-defined routine that posts an alert that displays the passed-in string.

```
OSErr  theError;
theError = MyOpenAndPlayMovie( "\pGambling Movie" );
if ( theError == fnfErr )
    PostErrorAlert( "\pFile not found" );
else
    PostErrorAlert( "\pUnknown error" );
```

DETERMINING THE FEATURES OF A USER'S MACINTOSH

If the Macintosh application that you write is a simple one, you're pretty much assured that it will run on just about any Macintosh model that is currently being sold. As your programs become more sophisticated, though, this assumption shouldn't be made. Why? Because programs that do more require more. The more that's referred to here is usually a *system software extension.*

Most of the operating system functionality on a user's Mac is supplied by the System file found in the user's System Folder. An extension is software that adds capabilities to the system software found in the System file. The Speech Manager extension, for example, enables a Mac owner to add speech capabilities to his or her Macintosh. QuickTime, another extension, adds movie-playing capabilities to a user's Macintosh.

Whenever a Mac program makes a call to a function that makes use of an extension, that program relies on the extension's being in the System folder of every Macintosh the program runs on. For instance, if a program calls a Toolbox routine such as OpenMovieFile() in preparation for the playing of a movie, that program expects the Mac it is currently running on to have the QuickTime extension installed. Because an extension is an optional piece of software, any program that relies on an extension must first verify the presence of that extension.

The Gestalt ( ) Function

The Toolbox provides a powerful function that any Mac program can use to check for the availability of an extension such as the Speech Manager or QuickTime. That function is Gestalt(). Gestalt() accepts two parameters. The first parameter is a *selector code* that tells Gestalt() what type of information is being sought. The second parameter is a *response parameter* that Gestalt() uses to turn information to a program. There are dozens of Apple-defined selector codes and hundreds of Apple-defined response parameter values. The following snippet uses the gestaltQuickTime selector code to determine whether the QuickTime extension is installed on the user's Macintosh.

```
OSErr   theError;
long    theResult;
theError = Gestalt( gestaltQuickTime, &theResult );
if ( theError != noErr )
   ExitToShell();
```

Recall that in C, passing a function the address of a variable allows the function to make a lasting change to the value of that variable. The same holds true for Toolbox routines. Passing a Toolbox routine a pointer — the address of a variable — lets the Toolbox fill the variable with information that can then be used by your program.

When Gestalt() receives a gestaltQuickTime select code, the function checks the user's machine to see if QuickTime is installed. If it is, Gestalt() uses the response parameter — the long variable theResult — to pass back the version number of the QuickTime extension. If any version of QuickTime is on the user's machine, Gestalt() also returns a value of `noErr` as the function's `OSErr` return value. If your program is only interested in whether the user's machine has QuickTime installed, it can simply check to see if the `OSErr` return value is `noErr`. If your program also needs to know the version number of the QuickTime extension, it can go on to examine the value in `theResult`.

Gestalt() isn't used exclusively for determining the presence of system software extensions. It can be used to gather all sorts of information about the user's software and hardware. You can see the power of `Gestalt()` by opening and scrolling through the Gestalt.h universal header file. In that file you'll find the definitions for all of the `Gestalt()` selector codes and response parameters. Figure 1-12 shows that a selector code has a value surrounded by single quotes. Underneath a selector code you'll find the response parameters for that code.

At the time of this writing, Symantec uses a set of universal header files that includes a GestaltEqu.h file rather than the Gestalt.h file. If you're using a Symantec compiler and you can't find a file named Gestalt.h, look for this GestaltEqu.h file.

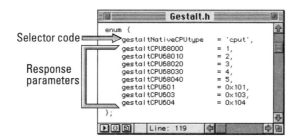

Figure 1-12
The Gestalt.h universal header file holds Gestalt selector code and response parameter values.

In Figure 1-12 you can see that the type of CPU the user's Mac has can be determined by using `Gestalt()` and a selector code of `gestaltNativeCPUtype`. `Gestalt()` will return one of eight response parameters for this selector code. If you include response parameter constants in your code, as recommended, you can ignore their numerical values. The following snippet shows how the `gestaltNativeCPUtype` selector code can be used with `Gestalt()`. The snippet also shows one way to check the response parameter value returned by `Gestalt()`.

```
theError = Gestalt( gestaltNativeCPUtype, &theResult );
switch ( theResult )
{
   case gestaltCPU68000:
      DrawString( "\pYour 68000 CPU is outdated - upgrade!" );
      break;
   case gestaltCPU68020:
   case gestaltCPU68030:
   case gestaltCPU68040:
      DrawString( "\pConsider moving to PowerPC!" );
      break;
   default:
      DrawString( "\pYou're enjoying the power of PowerPC!" );
      break;
}
```

The above snippet writes out a message regarding the CPU in the user's machine. The 68000 CPU is the original Macintosh processor found only in older models such as the Mac Plus, as pointed out in the case section for the gestaltCPU68000 response parameter value. The 68010 was never used in any Mac, so that response parameter isn't given a case label. If theResult *doesn't* have one of the gestaltCPU680x0 values, then it *must* have one of the gestaltCPU60x values. The 601, 603, and 604 are PowerPC chip numbers, so the message reflects that fact.

THE SIMPLEMOVIE SOURCE CODE LISTING

Many of the topics covered in this chapter have been supported by example snippets and discussions that used QuickTime movies, so it should come as no surprise to you that the next example program also uses QuickTime. When run, the SimpleMovie program opens a window, plays a short QuickTime movie, and then quits. One frame from the movie — which is a waving flag — can be seen in Figure 1-13.

Like the IntroProgram, the SimpleMovie application requires only a single WIND resource, pictured in Figure 1-14. Rather than use a window with a title bar, SimpleMovie uses a window frame like that found on a modal, or fixed, dialog box. This information is set in the WIND resource. In ResEdit, a click on one of the small window icons in the window editor changes the look of the window.

Figure 1-13
The result of running the SimpleMovie example application.

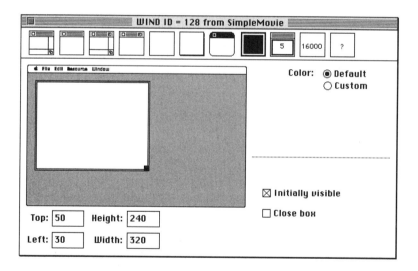

Figure 1-14
The WIND *resource used by the SimpleMovie example program.*

As with the previous example program, the entire source code listing is given first, followed by a detailed explanation. Here's the listing from the SimpleMovie.c file:

```
//_____
#include <Movies.h>
//_____
void    InitializeToolbox( void );
//_____
Movie   gTheMovie;
//_____
#define     kMovieFileName      "\pFlag"
#define     rMovieWindow              128
//_____
void   main( void )
{
   WindowPtr   theWindow;
   OSErr       theError;
   long        theResult;
   short       moovRefNum;
   short       moovResID = 0;
   Str255      movieName;
   Boolean     wasChanged;
   FSSpec      theFSSpec;
   InitializeToolbox();
   theError = Gestalt( gestaltQuickTime, &theResult );
   if ( theError != noErr )
      ExitToShell();
   theError = EnterMovies();

   theError = FSMakeFSSpec( 0, 0L, kMovieFileName, &theFSSpec );
   theError = OpenMovieFile( &theFSSpec, &moovRefNum, fsRdPerm );
   theError = NewMovieFromFile( &gTheMovie, moovRefNum, &moovResID,
                                movieName, newMovieActive,
                                &wasChanged );
   CloseMovieFile( moovRefNum );

   theWindow = GetNewWindow( rMovieWindow, nil, (WindowPtr)-1L );
   SetMovieGWorld( gTheMovie, (CGrafPtr)theWindow, nil );
   StartMovie( gTheMovie );
   do
      MoviesTask( gTheMovie, 0 );
   while ( IsMovieDone( gTheMovie ) == false );
}
//_____
void  InitializeToolbox( void )
{
   InitGraf( &qd.thePort );
   InitFonts();
   InitWindows();
   InitMenus();
   TEInit();
   InitDialogs( 0L );
   FlushEvents( everyEvent, 0 );
   InitCursor();
}
```

Universal Header Files

Because IntroProgram was such a simple application, its source code got away without including any of the universal header files. SimpleMovie uses some Toolbox functions not called by most applications, so it needs to add one of the universal header files that isn't a part of the precompiled header file found in all applications. The prototypes for all of the nonstandard Toolbox routines used by SimpleMovie can be found in Movies.h, so that's the only universal header file that needs to be included in the listing.

```
#include <Movies.h>
```

Function Prototypes

All application-defined functions other than `main( )` require a function prototype. SimpleMovie defines just one function — it's called `InitializeToolbox( )`.

```
void  InitializeToolbox( void );
```

Global Variables

This book's variable-naming convention states that all global variables begin with a lowercase *g*. SimpleMovie declares one global variable, a variable of the Macintosh type `Movie`.

```
Movie  gTheMovie;
```

Constants

In this book you'll find that an application-defined constant that is used for a resource begins with a lowercase *r*. SimpleMovie defines a constant named `rMovieWindow` to hold the value of the `WIND` resource. Other application-defined constants that aren't resource-related begin with a lowercase *k*. SimpleMovie defines a constant named `kMovieFileName` to store the name of the QuickTime movie file that is to be played.

```
#define    kMovieFileName    "\pFlag"
#define    rMovieWindow            128
```

In a large application, the movie file name could appear in numerous places throughout the source code listing. If it's decided to use a different movie in a later version of the program, only the constant definition would have to be changed. All of the source code, which uses the name kMovieFileName rather than the string, remains untouched. The same applies to the WIND resource ID.

Local Variables

SimpleMovie declares a host of variables local to main( ). Each variable follows this book's convention of using lowercase for the first word of each local variable name.

```
WindowPtr   theWindow;
OSErr       theError;
long        theResult;
short       moovRefNum;
short       moovResID = 0;
Str255      movieName;
Boolean     wasChanged;
FSSpec      theFSSpec;
```

Initializations

The main( ) function begins by calling the application-defined routine InitializeToolbox( ). Recall that the Toolbox initialization should be the first thing your application does.

```
InitializeToolbox();
```

The InitializeToolbox() function consists of nothing more than calls to the same eight Toolbox functions made at the start of the IntroProgram's main( ) routine.

```
void  InitializeToolbox( void )
{
   InitGraf( &qd.thePort );
   InitFonts();
   InitWindows();
   InitMenus();
   TEInit();
   InitDialogs( 0L );
   FlushEvents( everyEvent, 0 );
   InitCursor();
}
```

The `InitializeToolbox()` function is used in every example program in this book. To save a little ink, the listing for this function is not included in the rest of the book's source code listings. You will, of course, find its listing in every example source code file that appears on this book's CD.

Checking for QuickTime

Because SimpleMovie relies on QuickTime, the program needs to verify that this system extension is present on the user's machine. A call to `Gestalt()`, using the `gestaltQuickTime` selector code, provides this verification. SimpleMovie demonstrates error checking by examining the returned `OSErr` value. If it is anything other than `noErr`, the program will realize that QuickTime isn't available. A call to the Toolbox function `ExitToShell()` will then terminate the program.

```
theError = Gestalt( gestaltQuickTime, &theResult );
if ( theError != noErr )
   ExitToShell();
```

Playing a Movie

Next, SimpleMovie calls four Toolbox functions that each return an `OSErr` value. Error handling has already been demonstrated in the call to `Gestalt()`, so in this abbreviated program, no error-checking is performed on these returned values. In a full-featured application, it would be wise to examine the value of `theError` after each call. If at any time `theError` takes on a value other than `noErr`, a problem has occurred and should be dealt with.

```
theError = EnterMovies();
theError = FSMakeFSSpec( 0, 0L, kMovieFileName, &theFSSpec );
theError = OpenMovieFile( &theFSSpec, &moovRefNum, fsRdPerm );
theError = NewMovieFromFile( &gTheMovie, moovRefNum, &moovResID,
                             movieName, newMovieActive, &wasChanged
);
```

The details of the above four Toolbox functions are provided in Chapter 14. Suffice it to say, these functions do the following:

- Initialize the movie-related Toolbox functions.
- Create a record that tells where the movie file can be found on disk.
- Open the movie file.
- Create a movie in memory based on the data in the movie file.

After the movie is loaded in memory, the file from which the movie data came from can be closed. Another Toolbox function takes care of this chore.

```
CloseMovieFile( moovRefNum );
```

A movie is played in a window. A call to the Toolbox function GetNewWindow() loads the WIND resource data into memory. Rather than using the numerical value of the WIND resource ID as a parameter, SimpleMovie uses an application-defined constant. After the window is opened, a call to the Toolbox routine SetMovieGWorld() associates the QuickTime movie with the new window.

```
theWindow = GetNewWindow( rMovieWindow, nil, (WindowPtr)-1L );
SetMovieGWorld( gTheMovie, (CGrafPtr)theWindow, nil );
```

SimpleMovie plays the QuickTime movie by calling the Toolbox routines StartMovie(), MoviesTask(), and IsMovieDone().

```
StartMovie( gTheMovie );
do
    MoviesTask( gTheMovie, 0 );
while ( IsMovieDone( gTheMovie ) == false );
```

Each of these routines is covered in Chapter 14, the QuickTime chapter.

SimpleMovie has no event loop. When the movie completes playing, the do-while loop will end — and so will the program.

SimpleMovie makes 21 function calls — 20 calls to Toolbox routines and 1 call to an application-defined routine. SimpleMovie makes it apparent that the power of Macintosh programming lies in the Toolbox. Your ability to exploit that power comes from gaining a knowledge of the routines that make up the Toolbox.

Writing Code for Old and New Macs

Before 1994, all Macintosh computers used one of the microprocessors from the Motorola 680x0 family of CPUs. Now, there are millions of Macintosh computers with these Motorola chips and millions of Macintosh computers based on the newer PowerPC microprocessor. These two microprocessors use different instructions, and a compiler that generates Macintosh applications can't compile code using two different instruction sets. While there may soon be dual-processor machines that hold both types of processors, those Macintosh computers will be the exception rather than the norm.

68K AND PPC COMPUTERS

As noted, all Macintosh computers used a version of the Motorola 680x0 microprocessor until recently. The *x* in 680x0 means that there are several different CPUs in this family of microprocessors — including the 68000, 68020, 68030, and 68040 versions. Now Apple is phasing out the 680x0 family of processors and bringing in the PowerPC family of microprocessors.

Since some current Macs use the 680x0 processor and some use the PowerPC processor, a distinction needs to be made when one discusses the type of machine a Mac program will be running on. A Macintosh that is driven by one of the 680x0 family of processors is said to be a *680x0-based Macintosh*, or a *68K-based Macintosh*. A Mac that uses one of the PowerPC family of chips is referred to as a *PowerPC-based Macintosh,* or a *PPC-based Macintosh*. This book uses the phrases 68K-based and PPC-based.

68K AND PPC APPLICATIONS

The 680x0 chips and the PowerPC chips use different instruction sets. Compiled code that is recognized by one chip is not recognized by the other. Because of this, companies such as Symantec and Metrowerks that make Mac compilers each distribute two separate compilers, one that generates 68K applications and one that generates PPC applications.

The above statement is subject to change. Both Symantec and Metrowerks will each soon have a single environment that allows the creation of either a 68K or PPC application. Even as you read this note, one or both may be available!

A 68K-based Macintosh cannot run a program that was designed to run on a PPC-based Macintosh because of the different instruction set the PowerPC chips use. A PPC-based Macintosh, on the other hand, can run both types of programs — those designed for PPC-based Macs and those designed for 68K-based Macs. There's a simple explanation for this apparent contradiction — a PPC-based Mac contains code that enables the computer to emulate 68K code. That is, when a PPC-based Macintosh encounters a program designed to run on a 68K-based Mac, it knows how to interpret the 68K instructions and convert them to recognizable PPC instructions. Figure 1-15 illustrates this.

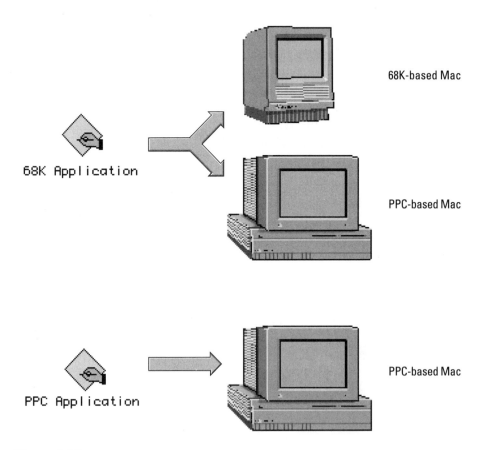

Figure 1-15

A 68K application can run on either a 68K-based Mac or a PPC-based Mac, while a PPC application can run only on a PPC-based Mac.

If a PPC application only runs on PPC-based Macs while a 68K application can run on both 68K-based and PPC-based Macs, why write a PPC application? Because while a 68K application will run on a PPC-based Macintosh, it won't run in native mode; that is, it won't take advantage of the faster processing speed of the PowerPC chip. Instead, the 68K code that makes up the 68K application will have to be converted to PowerPC instructions by the PPC-based Macintosh. That significantly slows down the execution of the 68K program.

To create the fastest program, you'll want to create a PPC application. The drawback to this is that owners of 68K-based Macs can't use your program. The solution to that dilemma is to create two versions of the same program. One is generated by a 68K compiler and consists of 68K code for 68K-based Mac owners, and the other is generated by a PPC compiler and consists of faster PPC code for PPC-based Mac owners.

Distributing two versions of the same program could cause confusion for some Mac owners — they might not understand why they have two copies of the same program, or they might feel that they're paying extra money for a second program that they'll never use. To make things more convenient for the end user, a developer has the option of combining the two versions of a program into one single program. This *fat binary application,* or *fat app,* is the perfect solution. When an owner of a 68K-based Mac double-clicks on the application icon, the Macintosh is smart enough to determine which of the two sets of code should be executed. The same holds true when the owner of a PPC-based Mac double-clicks on the same application icon — only the PPC code will be executed.

COMPILERS AND THE INTEGRATED DEVELOPMENT ENVIRONMENT (IDE)

Your compiler of choice is really much more than just a compiler — it's a source code editor, compiler, linker, and debugger. When an assortment of program development utilities are packaged together, this is often referred to as an *integrated development environment,* or *IDE.* If you use Symantec's THINK C, the Think Project Manager is your IDE. If you use Symantec C++, the Symantec Project Manager is your IDE. If you're a Metrowerks fan, than you're using the Code Warrior IDE as your IDE. Since the phrase *integrated development environment* is a bit wordy and *IDE* is a little too brief, this book compromises and refers to your development package as the *development environment*.

Macintosh compilers such as the ones from Symantec and Metrowerks are project-based. A project is a file that serves as an organizer of the files that make up the Macintosh program under development. A single project may hold one or more source code files, one or more resource files, and one or more library files. A library is a file that holds code that has already been compiled. Compilers come with libraries of code that provide your project with support for the Toolbox routines. Symantec's MacTraps and Metrowerks' MacOS.lib are two commonly used libraries. Figure 1-16 shows how a project typically consists of three types of files and how the IDE turns these three files into a single application.

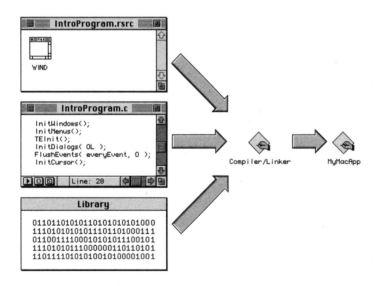

Figure 1-16
A Macintosh project holds source code, resource, and library files that together will become a Macintosh application.

Figure 1-16 uses a resource window from the ResEdit resource editor to represent a resource file and a source code window from the Metrowerks editor to represent a source code file. A library has no such editor that can be used to view its contents, so Figure 1-16 uses a host of 1s and 0s to represent a library. A library file consists of compiled code, so its contents can't be viewed in the way that a resource file or source code file can be.

Source code that is to become a 68K application needs to be compiled differently than source code that is to become a PPC application. If you want to create both a 68K version and a PPC version of the same program, an IDE will typically require that you create two separate projects. Each project might hold the same source code file and the same resource file, but the two projects will be compiled differently. The details of these differences are generally left to the compiler. Because you'll be more concerned with generating a working application rather than understanding the details of different CPU instruction sets, this should set well with you!

All source code listings in this book compile using either a 68K or PPC compiler, so you can generate either a 68K or a PPC version of any example. In each folder that holds an example you'll find a source code file, a resource file, and two projects — one project to be used with a 68K compiler and one to be used with a PPC compiler. Both projects share the same source code file and resource file, but each uses different supporting libraries.

2

Resources

A Macintosh program is composed of resources: a few, dozens, or even hundreds. In this chapter you will learn how all interface elements start as resources. You'll also learn how some of the more common resource types are created and used.

When you launch a Mac application, many of its resources remain on disk; they don't get loaded into memory. Before a program can use certain resources, though, the program must load them into memory. This chapter describes both a specific approach you can use to load specific types of resources and a more general approach that you can use to load any type of resource. Because loading a resource success-fully is dependent on the availability of free memory, this chapter describes a simple method for handling resource-related errors.

A program's resources are usually all stored within the program itself. A program may, however, also use resources that are stored outside the application — resources that reside in external resource files. In this chapter you'll see how a program can do this, as well as *why* a program might do this.

About Resources

Resources, resources, resources. If you're programming the Mac, you can't escape this topic. Here's why resources are of such importance to Macintosh programmers.

RESOURCES AND THE MACINTOSH INTERFACE

In Chapter 1, you learned that the Macintosh graphical user interface is created by using resources. Almost anything you see on your Macintosh screen starts out as a resource. A window is defined by a WIND resource; the menu bar is defined by a MBAR resource; each menu in the menu bar is described by a MENU resource; each icon on the desktop is identified by an ICON or similar resource.

The Macintosh views a resource as just more computer code. For programmers, though, the Mac displays this code in a graphical manner that makes for easy viewing and editing.

EDITING RESOURCES

Computer programs usually keep track of numbers. For example, programs calculate the population of cities, update the number of items in a store's inventory, and measure the distance between planets. Computer programs that display a graphical user interface also keep track of, obviously, graphics. While numbers don't lend themselves to an editing process that is primarily visual, graphics do. So it's natural that interface elements such as windows, menus, dialog boxes, and icons can be edited in a manner that deals with graphics rather than numbers. While text is treated as text in a text editor, resources are treated as graphics in a resource editor.

Mac programmers have a choice when it comes to using a resource editor. ResEdit, an Apple product, is by far the most popular resource editor. It is freely available from online services and is included with most development environments. Symantec and Metrowerks include it on their CDs. Resorcerer, a third-party product, can be purchased directly from the company that makes it, Mathemaesthetics, Inc.

Most programmers use ResEdit. Books like this one show most resource-related screen dumps from a ResEdit perspective. So ResEdit must be the best choice of the resource editors, right? Consider the following before drawing that conclusion. Most programmers use ResEdit because it's free. And most books use ResEdit in screen shots because most programmers are using ResEdit. Remember, *free* means just that — free. It doesn't mean better. If you are a beginner to intermediate Macintosh programmer,

ResEdit should work just fine. Should you begin to take Mac programming very seriously, you might consider investing in Resorcerer. It offers numerous resource-editing features not found in ResEdit.

Resources are stored in resource files. A single resource file may contain several different types of resources, and several resources of any given type of these different types. Because more than one resource of a type can be saved in a single file, each resource has a resource ID. Figure 2-1 shows a file that contains two WIND resources. The figure shows that the WIND resource with an ID of 128 is being edited.

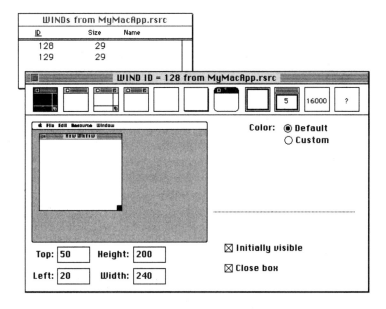

Figure 2-1
A resource file may contain more than one resource of a resource type.

Figure 2-1 shows how you can edit a resource graphically. At the top of the WIND editor is a row containing icons that represent the different looks a window can have. By clicking on one of these icons, you can change the look of the window that this WIND resource will be used to create.

While a resource editor provides a programmer the comfort of editing resources in a visual manner, underneath it all, numbers are still involved. When you use a resource editor to change a characteristic of a resource, such as the look of a window, you are really just changing numbers that get stored as information in a window definition. You can confirm this by using your resource editor to view any resource in a format other than the graphical one that the editor usually presents to you. If you're using ResEdit, open a resource file (any resource file with a WIND will do — the resource file for this chapter's ResourceLoader program includes one). Double-click on the WIND icon in the *type picker* (the main ResEdit window), and then click once on a WIND resource to select it. Don't double-click on it as you would to view it in the WIND editor. Next, select Open Using Hex Editor from the Resource menu. When you do that, you'll see the WIND resource shown as hexadecimal numbers rather than as it looks with a fancy graphical front end. Figure 2-2 shows how the WIND resource pictured in Figure 2-1 looks when viewed in this way.

If you're using Resorcerer, open a resource file. Then click on WIND on the left side of the File window — the main Resorcerer window. That displays a list of all the WIND resources in the file (depending on which resource file you use, there may, of course, be only one — or perhaps none at all). Click once on one of these WIND resources. Then click on the Hex button in the File window.

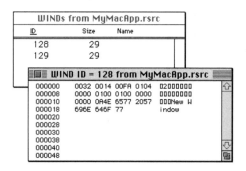

Figure 2-2
A WIND resource, as viewed using the hex editor in ResEdit.

RESOURCES AND THEIR ROLE IN MAC PROGRAMS

Because Macintosh programs are graphical, consisting of menus, windows, dialog boxes, pictures, sounds, movies, and more, you might expect that a typical Mac application holds a number of resources. If that was your guess, go ahead and award yourself a prize. Macintosh programs contain dozens — even hundreds — of resources.

To see the resources that any Mac program contains, launch your resource editor. Then select Open from the File menu and open the application. Remember, when an application is built using a development environment, compiled source code and resources are combined into a single file, the application file. Programs such as ResEdit and Resorcerer can open any file that contains resources, and that includes applications.

Several software companies distribute program documentation on disk rather than in hardcopy form. Some of those companies also distribute Apple's DocViewer as the application with which users view their documentation. For an example of the types of resources you can expect to find in a program, refer to Figure 2-3. This figure shows how Apple's DocViewer program looks when opened with ResEdit.

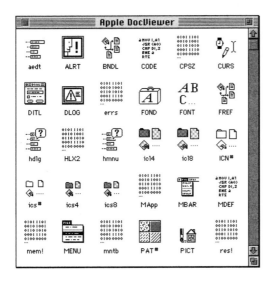

Figure 2-3
Some of the many resource types found in a typical commercial application.

There are far too many resource types to describe in detail in this book. Knowledge of the more than 100 resource types isn't important; only a handful are used by most programmers. The other, more esoteric, resource types are used by large applications that include a vast multitude of features. Table 2-1 provides a good summary of the most common resource types — the types you're likely to encounter as you program the Macintosh.

Table 2-1

Some of the Common Resource Types

Four-character name	Description
ALRT	Alert box
BNDL	Bundle, groups together icon information
CNTL	Control, defines a control for a window or dialog box
CODE	Code segment, holds 68K executable code
DITL	Dialog item list, the items that appear in a dialog box
DLOG	Dialog box
FREF	File reference, relates icons to file types
ICN#	Large black and white icon (32 by 32 pixels)
ics#	Small black and white icon (16 by 16 pixels)
icl4	Large 4-bit color icon (32 by 32 pixels)
ics4	Small 4-bit color icon (16 by 16 pixels)
icl8	Large 8-bit color icon (32 by 32 pixels)
ics8	Small 8-bit color icon (16 by 16 pixels)
MBAR	Menu bar
MENU	Menu
PICT	Picture
snd	Sound (note: last character in resource name is a space)
STR	String (note: last character in resource name is a space)
STR#	String list, holds one or more strings
WIND	Window

Loading Resources

When you start up a Mac application, only some of its resources get loaded into memory. Before your program can use the other resources, it must load them into memory.

RESOURCES AND MEMORY

When a Macintosh program is launched, or started, a copy of a part of the program is loaded into a partition, or area, in RAM. Chapter 3 provides details of this *application partition*. The part of the program that gets loaded into RAM is the program's *executable code* — the compiled code.

So, as a program runs, it will load more and more resources and will eventually use up more and more RAM, right? Partially right. More and more resources will get loaded. But resources have a purgeable attribute that can be set. That means that when a program is finished with a resource, it lets the Memory Manager know that it's okay to deallocate the memory that resource uses. So while one resource is getting loaded into memory, another one may be getting thrown out.

Loading a resource consists of making a copy of the resource's data, finding a free area in memory that is large enough to hold that data, and then moving the data into that area. Fortunately, the details of this process are handled by the Resource Manager and the Memory Manager — you only need to make a single Toolbox call to accomplish all of this. One such Toolbox call is `GetNewWindow()`. Figure 2-4 shows that a call to this function results in the copying of the data from a `WIND` resource and the loading of that data into RAM.

Earlier in this chapter you saw that the storage of a program's executable code varies depending on whether the application was compiled with a 68K compiler or a PowerPC compiler (refer to Chapter 1 for a definition of these types of compilers). This leads to a difference in the loading of the code as well:

- A program compiled with a 68K compiler has some of its `CODE` resources loaded at application launch (those `CODE` resources with a preload attribute set), while other `CODE` resources are loaded as need arises during program execution.

- A program compiled with a PowerPC compiler has all its executable code loaded from the data fork at application launch.

When you launch a program, a copy of the executable code gets loaded into memory — but most of the application's resources don't. Instead, resources remain on disk until needed. Only when a program requires the data that makes up a particular resource does a copy of that data get loaded into memory. Some programs occupy several megabytes of disk space, yet they require far less RAM than that in order to execute. Keeping resources on disk and loading them only on demand makes this possible.

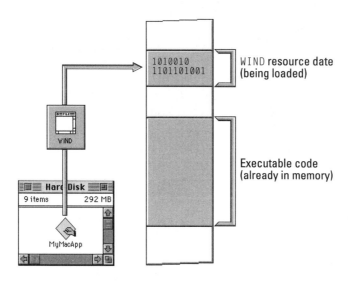

WIND resource date
(being loaded)

Executable code
(already in memory)

Figure 2-4
A resource holds data that gets loaded into memory and used by an application.

Once in memory, a resource is usually treated as an object rather than as the collection of data that it is. Instead of directly accessing the resource data in memory, Toolbox routines are called to act on the object. For example, the data of a WIND resource is thought of as a window, and is treated as a window object. To move the window on the screen, the Toolbox routine DragWindow() is used. To change the window's size, the Toolbox routine GrowWindow() is called.

In Chapter 1 it was mentioned that a resource serves as a template from which any number of instances, or elements, can be created. Now that you know that the loading of a resource means the loading of a copy of the resource data, this concept should make sense. A program can call GetNewWindow() any number of times using the same WIND resource ID. Each call will result in a new window (and a new pointer to that window) in memory. If each window is based on the same WIND resource, each will have the same characteristics (such as the same window type, or look, the same size, the same initial location on the screen, and so forth).

LOADING A WIND RESOURCE

In Chapter 1 you were introduced to the WIND resource type. The WIND is the most common of the more than 100 resource types. Because the loading of some resource types is such a common programming task, the Toolbox contains routines that are each designed to load a specific resource type. You've already seen one such routine, GetNewWindow().

In a call to GetNewWindow(), you don't need to specify which resource type should be loaded. The Toolbox knows what you're after. However, because a resource file can hold more than one resource of a resource type, you will need to specify the resource ID of the WIND resource to load. The following snippet loads a WIND resource with an ID of 500:

```
#define      rMessageWindow      500
theWindow = GetNewWindow( rMessageWindow, nil, (WindowPtr)-1L );
```

LOADING A PICT RESOURCE

Another Toolbox routine designed to load a particular type of resource is GetPicture(). In Macintosh programming, you can paste a clip-art picture (or one you have created using a paint or draw program) into a resource file, where it will automatically be saved as a PICT resource. If a program is to make use of a PICT resource, it should call the Toolbox routine GetPicture() to load the picture data into memory. The following snippet will load a PICT resource with an ID of 300:

```
#define      rEinsteinPicture      300
PicHandle    thePicture;
thePicture = GetPicture( rEinsteinPicture );
```

As is the case with GetNewWindow() and window data, GetPicture() only loads the picture data into memory — it doesn't do anything with the data. Just as you call other Toolbox routines (such as SetPort(), as mentioned in Chapter 1) to take some action with window data, you call other Toolbox routines to take some action with picture data. A call to DrawPicture(), for instance, draws the picture data to the frontmost window:

```
DrawPicture( thePicture, &theRect );
```

The second parameter to `GetNewWindow()` is used to optionally specify a memory location for the `WIND` resource. Pass `nil` to let the Window Manager locate a free area in memory.

The awkward-looking third parameter is used to indicate whether the window should appear in front of any other open windows. A value of −1 places the window in front, a value of `nil` places it behind all others. Because the Toolbox defines this parameter to be of type `WindowPtr`, you will need to typecast a value of −1. To typecast, or force, a value to a different data type, precede the value with the data type, enclosed in parentheses. In this case, precede the number −1 with (`WindowPtr`). Because all Macintosh pointers (including the `WindowPtr`) are 4 bytes in size, append an uppercase letter *L* to the numerical value that is to be typecast. That guarantees that the number will occupy the 4-byte memory size of a `long` type, which is the same size as a pointer.

The second parameter to `DrawPicture()` is a rectangle that defines the coordinates at which the picture will be drawn in the frontmost window. Pictures and `DrawPicture()` are discussed in detail in Chapter 10.

LOADING OTHER RESOURCE TYPES

There isn't a Toolbox routine written to specifically load each type of resource. But there is a generic resource-loading Toolbox function you can use to load any type of resource: `GetResource()`. The `GetResource()` function is used to get a *handle* to a resource. Here's an example of a call to this function:

```
Handle   theHandle;

theHandle = GetResource( 'snd ', 9000 );
```

As you'll see in Chapter 3, a pointer holds the address of an object in memory, while a handle holds the address of a pointer. This somewhat confusing memory management scheme actually has a very practical purpose, as you'll see in the next chapter. For now, Figure 2-5 illustrates how a handle variable named theHandle indirectly leads to an object in memory. In this figure a sound resource (a resource of type snd) is loaded into memory using a call to `GetResource()`. After loading the sound data, `GetResource()` returns to the program a handle to this data. When the program needs to access the sound data, it will use this handle.

```
Handle  theHandle
theHandle = GetResource( 'snd ', 9000 );
```

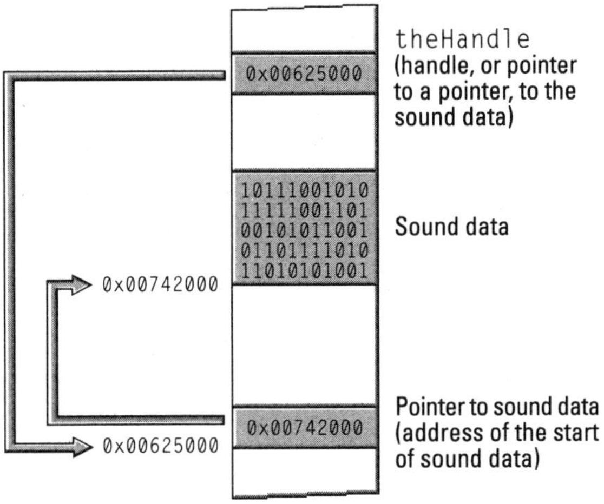

theHandle
(handle, or pointer
to a pointer, to the
sound data)

0x00625000

10111001010
11111001101
00101011001   Sound data
01101111010
11010101001

0x00742000

Pointer to sound data
(address of the start
of sound data)

0x00742000

0x00625000

Figure 2-5
*A handle holds the address of a pointer, while the pointer holds the address
of data.*

The GetResource() function requires two parameters. The first is the
type of resource that is to be loaded. The type is the four-character resource
name — WIND and PICT are examples. Because you can use
GetNewWindow() and GetPicture() to load resources of these types, you
won't need to call GetResource() to load window or picture data. Instead,
you'll use GetResource() for loading resource types such as the sound
resource.

The second parameter to GetResource() is the ID of the resource to be
loaded. Because a resource file may have more than one sound (or more
than one of whatever other type of resource is being loaded), you need to
specify which is to be loaded. In the above snippet a snd resource with an
ID of 9000 is being loaded into memory.

Chapter 13 discusses sound resources, sound files, and the playing of
sounds. This book's CD contains several sounds you can experiment with in
your own programs.

You can record sounds with your Macintosh and save them as resources, or you can purchase collections of sound resources. In either case,
a sound that is in a resource file has a type of snd . That space that appears

between the *d* of snd and the period isn't a typo — the snd resource type
ends with a space. Remember, resources all have a type that must be four
characters long. To meet this four-character requirement, the sound resource
type ends with a space.

After calling GetResource(), your program will have a handle that can
be used to reference the resource data that has been loaded into memory.
Continuing with the sound example, the sound data in memory can be
played by calling the Toolbox function SndPlay(). You'll see an example of
how this function works in the ResourceLoading program.

Example Program: ResourceLoading

ResourceLoading is a simple program that serves to demonstrate how to
load three different types of resources: a window resource, a picture
resource, and a sound resource. When you run ResourceLoading, you'll see
a window like the one pictured in Figure 2-6. You'll also hear the whinny of
a horse. After several seconds the program will quit on its own.

Figure 2-6
The window displayed by the ResourceLoading program.

RESOURCES FOR THE EXAMPLE PROGRAM

The ResourceLoading project uses three resources: a WIND, a PICT, and a snd . Figure 2-7 uses ResEdit to show the ID and size of each of these resources.

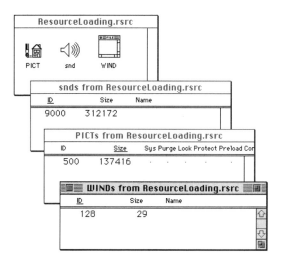

Figure 2-7
The resources used in the ResourceLoading project.

 Resource editors let you view resources in different ways. If you're using ResEdit, double-click on the PICT icon to see a reduced-size version of the picture used by ResourceLoading. To view this picture by its size, as shown in Figure 2-7, select the By Size menu item from the View menu. If you're using Resorcerer as your resource editor, you won't need to take this extra step — the size of the picture will be displayed next to the reduced-size view of the picture resource.

Why *are* the resources shown by size in Figure 2-7? To introduce a new, only slightly related topic, of course! At some point in the running of ResourceLoading, all three of its resources will be in memory at the same time: The window will be open with the picture drawn in it, and the sound will be playing. If you refer to Figure 2-7, you can add up the sizes of these resources to see that they total about 450,000 bytes, or roughly 450K. Because these resources will all be in memory at the same time, you now know that ResourceLoading will need at *least* this much memory in order to run.

Your development environment assigns a preset, or default, size for new applications — one typical value is 384K. That's good enough for many programs but not good enough for ResourceLoading. A size of 1024K (1MB) is more appropriate. You can increase this application partition size from within your development environment. Then, when you build, or make, a new version of the ResourceLoading program, it will be assigned a new, larger, memory partition size.

The different development environments provide slightly different means of changing the partition size for a program that is to be built from a project. Figure 2-8 shows that the Project panel in the Preferences dialog box is the place to make this change when using a Metrowerks compiler. Figure 2-9 shows that the Project Type panel in the Options dialog box is where you set the partition size when using a Symantec compiler.

Figure 2-8 shows the dialog box that appears when you select Preferences from the Edit menu of version 6 of the CodeWarrior compiler. Figure 2-9 shows the dialog box that appears when you select Options from the Project menu of version 8.0 of the Symantec compiler. Earlier versions of the Symantec compiler let you make the partition size change from a dialog box brought up by selecting Set Project Type from the Project menu. Regardless of the compiler, or version of compiler, that you use, a little menu searching will enable you to find a way to change the partition size.

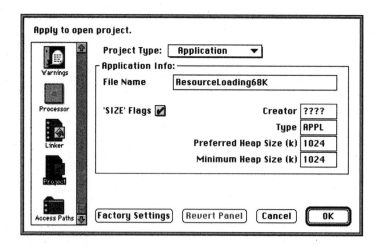

Figure 2-8

For a Metrowerks CodeWarrior project, the partition size is set from the Project panel of the Preferences dialog box.

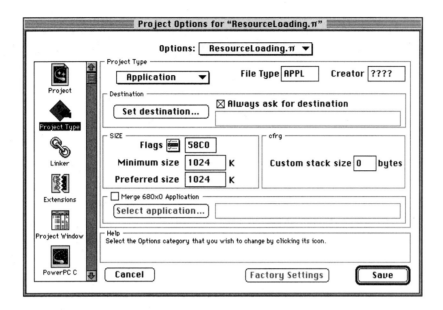

Figure 2-9

For a Symantec 8.x project, the partition size is set from the Project Type panel of the Options dialog box.

In the versions of the compilers being examined here, Symantec uses a default partition size of 1024K, or 1MB, while Metrowerks uses 384K. Both compilers allow you to set both a minimum partition size and a preferred partition size. If there is sufficient free memory on the user's Mac when ResourceLoader is launched, the preferred size will be used. If there isn't that much memory available, an amount as low as the minimum value will be used. If there isn't even *that* much free memory, the application won't launch and an alert will inform the user of this memory shortage.

The PICT resource used in the ResourceLoading project is a digitized picture of two horses. The picture started as a TIFF file (a file format commonly used to hold digitized pictures) that was opened in a paint program. From the paint program, a large section of the picture was selected and copied. Creating a PICT resource was a simple matter of opening the ResourceLoading resource file and pasting the contents of the clipboard to the resource file. Both ResEdit and Resorcerer will turn a copied picture into a PICT resource in this manner. Figure 2-10 shows this PICT resource.

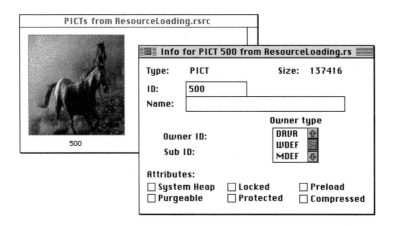

Figure 2-10
Using ResEdit to change the ID of the PICT *resource used in the*
ResourceLoading project.

Figure 2-10 shows how ResEdit displays reduced-size versions of PICT
resources. It also shows how to change the resource ID of a resource. To
display the Info dialog box for a resource, click on the resource once, and
then select Get Resource Info from the Resource menu. Type in an ID of
your choosing. If you're using Resorcerer, click on a resource and then click
on the Info button in the File window — the main Resorcerer window.

Figure 2-11 shows the last of the three ResourceLoading resources, the
WIND resource. Using ResEdit, the look of the window was set by clicking
on one of the icons in the row of window icons found at the top of the
WIND editor window. If you're using Resorcerer, first click once on the WIND
type in the column of resource types on the left of the File window. Then
double-click on the WIND displayed on the right of the File window. Next,
select Set Window Info from the window menu. That will open a dialog
box that lets you specify the window type, its size, and other information.

When creating the WIND resource for ResourceLoading, make sure the
Initially visible checkbox is unchecked. And don't be concerned with the
size of the window — any values can be used for this program. That's
because the final size of the window will be determined and set from within
the source code, as described next.

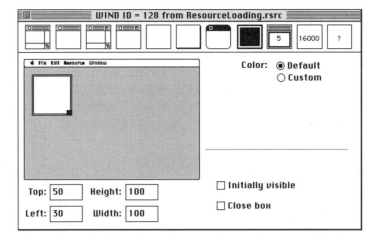

Figure 2-11
The WIND *resource used by the ResourceLoading project, as viewed in ResEdit.*

SOURCE CODE FOR THE EXAMPLE PROGRAM

The ResourceLoading program starts, as do all programs in this book, by making a call to InitializeToolbox() to initialize the various Toolbox managers. After that, calls to GetNewWindow(), GetPicture(), and GetResource() are made to load each of the three resources:

```
#define      rMovieWindow       128
#define      rHorsePicture      500
#define      rHorseSound        9000
WindowPtr  theWindow;
PicHandle  thePicture;
Handle     theSound;
theWindow  = GetNewWindow( rMovieWindow, nil, (WindowPtr)-1L );
thePicture = GetPicture( rHorsePicture );
theSound   = GetResource( 'snd ', rHorseSound );
```

When picture data is in memory, it appears there in a specific order. That means that a program can easily access particular pieces of information about the picture. For instance, the second piece of information in a block of memory that holds picture data is always the pixel coordinates of the picture. This information is held in the form of a rectangle. The four values of the rectangle represent the four coordinates of the picture. This information is given the name picFrame and will be of use to the ResourceLoading program in just a bit. Figure 2-12 shows that picture data always appears in memory as a value that holds the size of the picture, the picture's boundary rectangle, and finally the data that makes up the picture itself.

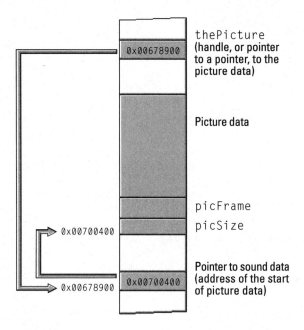

Figure 2-12
PICT resource data gets loaded into memory in a predictable order.

 This concept of resource data matching a particular known format in memory isn't limited to `PICT` resources; it applies to any resource type. It's not enough that resource data gets loaded into memory — a program needs to be able to access the different fields of information held in a resource. Chapter 3 provides some detail about the format that `WIND` resource data takes when loaded into memory.

To find out how large a picture is, in pixel dimensions, a program can examine the `picFrame` data. The four values found in this rectangle data appear in the order top, left, bottom, right; so if these values happen to be 0, 0, 309, and 480, you know that the picture is 309 pixels in height and 480 pixels across. You also know that because the top and left values are each 0, the picture, if drawn now, would fit snugly in the top left corner of whatever window it was drawn to.

Figure 2-12 shows that the `picFrame` information appears as the second group of data in a picture resource loaded into memory. Fortunately, you don't have to keep track of the order of different fields of information for resources in memory. Instead, you can just use the field's name in an assignment statement. In the following snippet the rectangle information is being assigned to a rectangle, or `Rect`, variable:

```
PicHandle   thePicture;
Rect        theRect;
thePicture = GetPicture( rHorsePicture );
theRect = (**thePicture).picFrame;
```

In the above code the `PicHandle` variable `thePicture` is dereferenced twice before the `picFrame` data is accessed. Dereferencing one time leads to the pointer to the picture data; dereferencing a second time leads to the picture data itself. Then it's a matter of naming the field of interest — `picFrame`.

After the above code executes, the ResourceLoading program will have a `Rect` variable that holds the boundaries of the picture that `thePicture` references in memory. While there is the possibility that this rectangle may have top and left boundaries of 0, there is no guarantee that this will be the case. Calling the Toolbox routine `OffsetRect()` with the parameters shown shifts the four coordinates of the rectangle in such a way that the boundaries are forced to include 0 as the top coordinate and 0 as the left coordinate.

```
theRect = (**thePicture).picFrame;
OffsetRect( &theRect, -theRect.left, -theRect.top );
```

The first parameter to `OffsetRect()` is the rectangle to shift. The second parameter is the number of pixels to shift the rectangle in the horizontal direction, while the third parameter is the number of pixels to shift the rectangle in the vertical direction. To verify that this technique works, plug in some example values. Keeping in mind that a variable of type `Rect` has four fields (`top`, `bottom`, `left` and `right`), let's say that `picFrame` looks like this before the offset:

```
picFrame.left      50
picFrame.right    530
picFrame.top       30
picFrame.bottom   339
```

After assigning theRect the value of `picFrame`, this variable will have the same values:

```
theRect.left       50
theRect.right     530
theRect.top        30
theRect.bottom    339
```

Now the call to `OffsetRect()`:

```
OffsetRect( &theRect, -theRect.left, -theRect.top );
```

The amount to shift horizontally is `-theRect.left`, or -50. The amount to shift vertically is `-theRect.top`, or 30. After shifting the rectangle by these amounts, the new `theRect` values will be as follows:

```
theRect.left       50 - 50  =   0
theRect.right     530 - 50  = 480
theRect.top        30 - 30  =   0
theRect.bottom    339 - 30  = 309
```

The rectangle has been shifted so that its upper left corner is at point (0, 0), as desired. And the rectangle has kept its same dimensions — before and after the shift it is 480 pixels across by 309 pixels high.

At this point (or perhaps at a much earlier point), you may be wondering what benefits have been derived from this whole business of rectangle shifting. The first benefit of the call to `OffsetRect()` is that it is now very easy to determine the size of the picture. Because the rectangle `theRect` is the size of the picture (recall that it obtained its original values from `picFrame`) and because `theRect` has been shifted so that its left and top coordinates are each at 0, the bottom of `theRect` represents the rectangle's height and the right of `theRect` represents the rectangle's width. ResourceLoading takes advantage of these facts when it resizes the program's window using a call to the Toolbox function `SizeWindow()`.

```
SizeWindow( theWindow, theRect.right, theRect.bottom, true );
```

After the above call, the window referenced by variable `theWindow` will have a width of `theRect.right` (480 pixels) and a height of theRect.bottom (309 pixels). The last parameter to SizeWindow(), incidentally, tells the Window Manager that the window has been altered and needs to be redrawn.

 Determining the picture boundary rectangle using the picFrame field of the resource data means the program is directly accessing a field of resource information. In Macintosh programming, this isn't the norm. More often then not, the Toolbox provides a function that can be used to do this dirty work. Consider the resizing of a window. This task is accomplished by changing the values in the portRect field of a window's resource information. Notice, though, that this field isn't mentioned in the source code. Instead, it's left up to the SizeWindow() function to take care of accessing this field.

The call to SizeWindow() explains why the size of the window established by the WIND resource was unimportant: The ResourceLoading program resizes it to match whatever size the picture has. There was one other point emphasized in the creation of the WIND resource — the window was set to be initially invisible. That was done so that while a call to GetNewWindow() would still load the WIND resource into memory, it wouldn't display the window on the screen. That prevents the user from seeing the window and then seeing it change size. Instead, this size finagling takes place behind the scenes. After resizing, a call to the Toolbox function ShowWindow() finally displays the window. A call to SetPort() ensures that subsequent drawing will take place in this window.

```
ShowWindow( theWindow );
SetPort( theWindow );
```

The second benefit of the rectangle shifting is that the rectangle now has a top left corner coordinate of (0, 0). That's important if the picture is to be drawn in such a way that it starts in the upper left corner of a window. Here's the Toolbox call that ResourceLoading uses to do just that:

```
DrawPicture( thePicture, &theRect );
```

The above call draws the picture referenced by thePicture (the horse picture that was loaded to memory earlier) at the coordinates specified by the rectangle theRect.

At this point the window is open, resized, and has the picture of the horses drawn in it. There is only one task left to perform: The sound needs to be played. A call to the Toolbox function SndPlay() does that.

```
SndPlay( nil, (SndListHandle)theSound, false );
```

The SndPlay() function plays sound data that is in memory and that is referenced by the handle specified in the second parameter. You'll find all the details concerning sounds and the SndPlay() function in Chapter 13.

Finally, here's the complete source code listing for the ResourceLoading program. You've just taken a long walk through the listing of a very short program. It's only Chapter 2, so it's not a bad idea to take things slow. As you progress through the book, you'll be exposed to more code and a little less talk.

```
//_____
#define      rMovieWindow        128
#define      rHorsePicture       500
#define      rHorseSound        9000
//_____
void  main( void )
{
    WindowPtr   theWindow;
    PicHandle   thePicture;
    Handle      theSound;
    Rect        theRect;

    InitializeToolbox();
    theWindow  = GetNewWindow( rMovieWindow, nil, (WindowPtr)-1L );
    thePicture = GetPicture( rHorsePicture );
    theSound   = GetResource( 'snd ', rHorseSound );
    theRect = (**thePicture).picFrame;
    OffsetRect( &theRect, -theRect.left, -theRect.top );
    SizeWindow( theWindow, theRect.right, theRect.bottom, true );
    ShowWindow( theWindow );
    SetPort( theWindow );

    DrawPicture( thePicture, &theRect );

    SndPlay( nil, (SndListHandle)theSound, false );
}
```

Resource-Related Errors

Your program can often make a call to a Toolbox function without regard as to whether or not the call will execute properly. Calls to a resource-loading function such as GetNewWindow() or GetResource() are a little different. Before continuing on, a program that makes such a call should verify that the routine executed as desired.

Two factors enter into the precautionary tactic mentioned above. First, the success of a resource-loading call is dependent on supplemental data, the data being the resource that is to be loaded. If you've forgotten to add, say, a WIND resource to a resource file, a call to GetNewWindow() will fail. Second, the success of a resource-loading call is dependent on the amount of free memory that is available. As you saw in the ResourceLoading example, some resources can be quite large. If there isn't enough free memory to hold a resource that is to be loaded, the Toolbox function that is attempting to perform the load will fail.

VERIFYING THAT A RESOURCE HAS BEEN LOADED

Verifying the success of a call to a Toolbox routine that loads a resource is a straightforward process: Load the resource, and then compare the returned pointer or handle to nil. If the returned address is a value other than nil, the call was successful.

Routines such as GetNewWindow(), GetPicture(), and GetResource() all return a reference to the newly loaded resource data. GetNewWindow() returns a pointer (type WindowPtr) to the data. GetPicture() returns a handle (type PicHandle) to the data. The GetResource() function returns a handle (type Handle) to the data. If any of these routines is successful, a valid pointer or handle will be returned to the program. That is, a valid address, or nonzero address, will be returned. If any of these routines fails — that is, if a resource can't be loaded for one reason or another — an invalid, or nil, pointer or handle will be returned. A nil pointer or handle has a value of 0.

The following snippet shows how the result of a call to GetNewWindow() can be verified. If the returned WindowPtr variable has a value of nil, it can be assumed that the attempt to load the window resource data has failed and that the program should exit.

```
#define    rMovieWindow    128
WindowPtr  theWindow;
theWindow = GetNewWindow( rMovieWindow, nil, (WindowPtr)-1L );
if ( theWindow == nil )
   ExitToShell();
```

You'll find many examples of programs that don't perform the above test following a call to GetNewWindow(). That's because the primary reason for a resource's failing to load is a memory shortage, and windows occupy very little memory. For example, the WIND resource shown back in Figure 2-7 occupies only 29 bytes. While a window occupies more memory than this (GetNewWindow() reserves space for more information than is specified in the WIND resource), it still occupies relatively little memory. Again looking at Figure 2-7 you can see that it is much more likely that an attempt to load a picture or sound resource will fail. The PICT resource in Figure 2-7 is about 135K in size, while the snd resource is over 300K in size. The following snippet is an example of how your program can verify the success of an attempt to load a PICT resource and a snd resource:

```
#define      rHorsePicture      500
#define      rHorseSound        9000
PicHandle    thePicture;
Handle       theSound;

thePicture = GetPicture( rHorsePicture );
if ( thePicture == nil )
   ExitToShell();
theSound = GetResource( 'snd ', rHorseSound );
if ( theSound == nil )
   ExitToShell();
```

For the sake of brevity, most of the examples in this book omit some error-checking code. When you decide to write a full-featured Macintosh program, make liberal use of error-checking code.

While low-memory situations are the most common cause of a failed attempt to load a resource, there are other reasons. If a program that uses resources quits unexpectedly, check for each of these situations:

- A resource file wasn't created.

- A resource file was created but was inadvertently left out of the project.

- A resource file was created, but the resource in question wasn't added to it.

- A resource file was created, and the resource in question was added, but the resource was misnumbered.

- A resource file was created, and the resource in question was added and properly numbered, but the program doesn't have enough free memory to load the resource.

USING AN ERROR-HANDLING ROUTINE

Calling the Toolbox routine ExitToShell() is a quick-and-dirty way to respond to an error. Terminating a program in response to an error makes for easy programming (and helps keep example programs short and to the point), but it isn't very user-friendly. In fact, it can be downright disconcerting to the user. Instead of simply quitting, you'll want to post an alert that holds a message that's at least somewhat informative. If the error is severe enough, your program can then exit. If the error is relatively harmless, your program may be able to proceed despite the fact that some resource data is now missing from the program.

Don't just assume that a failed loading of a resource spells disaster for your program. Examine each case individually. For example, if a sound resource fails to load, it may just mean that a user of your program misses out on an interesting sound effect that serves to supplement a more important on-screen action. In a case like this, the program shouldn't terminate.

The following application-defined function can be called in response to a variety of errors. When called, ErrorAlert() displays an alert like the one pictured in Figure 2-13. The message in the alert will vary depending on the type of error that occurred:

```
#define       rErrorStringList      128
#define       rErrorAlert           128
void  ErrorAlert( short theErrorCode, Boolean fatalError )
{
   Str255  theErrorStr;

   GetIndString( theErrorStr, rErrorStringList, theErrorCode );
   ParamText( theErrorStr, "\p", "\p", "\p" );

   StopAlert( rErrorAlert, nil );

   if ( fatalError == true )
      ExitToShell();
}
```

The ErrorAlert() function accepts two parameters. The first parameter is an application-defined constant that tells the routine what type of error occurred. The second parameter is a Boolean value that tells the routine whether the error was severe enough to warrant terminating the program (true) or whether the program should proceed (false).

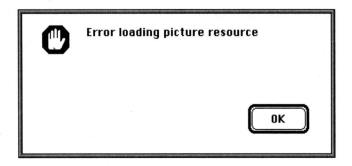

Figure 2-13
The alert displayed by the application-defined routine ErrorAlert().

When called, ErrorAlert() invokes the Toolbox function GetIndString() to get one string from a resource that holds a list of strings — a STR# resource. The first parameter to GetIndString() is a Str255 variable that will hold the string once the call to GetIndString() has completed. The second parameter is the resource ID of the STR# resource to use. The final parameter is an index into the string list. A value of 1 retrieves the first string in the list, a value of 2 returns the second string, and so forth. Figure 2-14 shows how ResEdit displays a STR# resource with an ID of 128. This resource holds four strings.

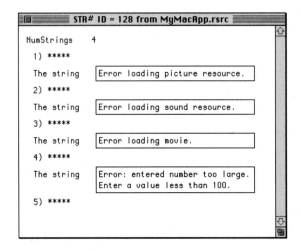

Figure 2-14
A STR# *string list resource, as viewed in ResEdit.*

After GetIndString() fills variable theErrorStr with an error message string, a call to the Toolbox function ParamText() prepares for the writing of the string into an alert that is about to be displayed. The ParamText() routine accepts up to four strings (\p can be used for empty strings). These four strings will be written to dialog boxes or alerts that contain static text items with the following values already in place: ^0, ^1, ^2, ^3. Figure 2-15 provides an example. In this figure, the DITL resource has a single static text item that will display a single string, ^0. When this DITL is used by a program, this ^0 string will be replaced by the first of four strings provided in a call to ParamText().

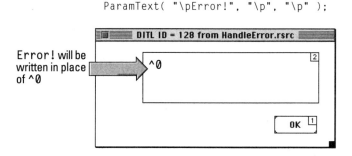

```
ParamText( "\pError!", "\p", "\p" );
```

Figure 2-15
A DITL resource that holds a static text item with a marker that will be replaced by text defined in a program.

The ALRT and DITL resources used to hold the information that defines an alert are discussed in detail in Chapter 8.

After making calls to GetIndString() and ParamText() to set up the string to use in the error alert, ErrorAlert() calls the Toolbox function StopAlert() to display a simple alert. After the user dismisses this alert, ErrorAlert() checks to see if the program should be terminated using a call to ExitToShell(). The following snippet provides an example of the use of ErrorAlert():

```
#define      kErrLoadingPicture      1
#define      kErrLoadingSound        2
#define      kErrLoadingMovie        3
#define      kErrNumberTooBig        4
thePicture = GetPicture( rHorsePicture );
if ( thePicture == nil )
   ErrorAlert( kErrLoadingPicture, true );
```

If the STR# shown in Figure 2-14 were used in the program that included the above snippet, the first string (string number kErrLoadingPicture) would appear in the error alert. That is, the ^0 would be replaced by "Error loading picture resource."

The above snippet shows that an application-defined constant should be defined for each error string that might be displayed. The names of these constants in this same snippet hint that error messages aren't used only for errors related to resource loading. If a program saves a user-entered value in a variable named theTestScore, for example, a check could be made to verify that a valid number has been entered.

```
#define        kErrLoadingPicture      1
#define        kErrLoadingSound        2
#define        kErrLoadingMovie        3
#define        kErrNumberTooBig        4
if ( theTestScore > 100 )
   ErrorAlert( kErrNumberTooBig, false );
```

EXAMPLE PROGRAM: HANDLEERROR

This chapter's HandleError program is a modification of this chapter's ResourceLoading program. In short, HandleError adds error-checking to ResourceLoading.

The HandleError program verifies that both the picture resource and the sound resource get loaded. If there is a problem with either resource, the ErrorAlert() function described earlier gets called. If the picture fails to load, the program will post the error alert and then exit. If the sound fails to load, the program will post the error alert but continue.

```
thePicture = GetPicture( rHorsePicture );
if ( thePicture == nil )
   ErrorAlert( kErrLoadingPicture, true );
theSound = GetResource( 'snd ', rHorseSound );
if ( theSound == nil )
   ErrorAlert( kErrLoadingSound, false );
```

Later in the program the picture is drawn to the window with a call to DrawPicture(), just as it was in the ResourceLoading program.

```
DrawPicture( thePicture, &theRect );
```

What happens if the attempt to load the picture fails, and the variable thePicture doesn't hold a valid handle to picture data? If DrawPicture() executes under those circumstances, the call will fail. In the HandleError program, this scenario will never happen. If the attempt to load the picture fails, ErrorAlert() is called with a value of true as its second parameter. That tells ErrorAlert() to exit — and that of course means that the DrawPicture() call will never be reached.

The playing of the sound data is handled differently than the drawing of the picture data. The HandleError program assumes that the playing of the sound is less important than the drawing of the picture. As such, the program will continue even if the sound data can't be loaded. This necessitates a check before the call to SndPlay(). If sound loading failed, the handle theSound will have a value of nil. If that is the case, the call to SndPlay() gets skipped. Any other theSound value — any non-nil value — results in SndPlay() getting called.

```
if ( theSound != nil )
   SndPlay( nil, (SndListHandle)theSound, false );
```

You can test the effectiveness of this chapter's error-handling technique by varying the size of the HandleError application partition. First, use your development environment to specify a large partition size such as 1024K. Then build the program and run it to verify that the program works as expected. The HandleError program includes a while loop that causes the program to run until you click the mouse button. Now, from the Finder, click once on the HandleError icon. Now select Get Info from the File menu. The dialog box that opens, shown in Figure 2-16, lets you change the size of the HandleError memory partition.

For a first test, change both memory values to 100K, as shown in Figure 2-16. Close the Get Info window, and run the HandleError program. Because the partition size for HandleError is less than the 135K needed for the PICT resource, the error alert will appear. Once you dismiss the alert the application will quit.

As a second test, again select Get Info for the HandleError program. This time enter a value of 200K. Then run HandleError. Now there is enough memory to load the 135K picture. But there isn't enough free

Figure 2-16
The Finder's Get Info dialog box lets you change the partition size for an application.

memory to load the 300K sound resource. The program will display the error alert with the sound-loading error message. When you dismiss the alert, the picture will be drawn in the window, but the sound won't play. Notice that the program won't quit. Instead, the code continues to execute, entering the `while` loop. Click the mouse button once to end the program.

```
//_____
#include <sound.h>
//_____
#define      rMovieWindow          128
#define      rHorsePicture         500
#define      rHorseSound           9000
#define      rErrorStringList      128
#define      rErrorAlert           128
#define      kErrLoadingPicture    1
#define      kErrLoadingSound      2
//_____
void  main( void )
{
    WindowPtr   theWindow;
    PicHandle   thePicture;
    Handle      theSound;
    Rect        theRect;
```

```
    InitializeToolbox();
    theWindow = GetNewWindow( rMovieWindow, nil, (WindowPtr)-1L );
    thePicture = GetPicture( rHorsePicture );
    if ( thePicture == nil )
        ErrorAlert( kErrLoadingPicture, true );
    theSound = GetResource( 'snd ', rHorseSound );
    if ( theSound == nil )
        ErrorAlert( kErrLoadingSound, false );

    theRect = (**thePicture).picFrame;
    OffsetRect( &theRect, -theRect.left, -theRect.top );
    SizeWindow( theWindow, theRect.right, theRect.bottom, true );
    ShowWindow( theWindow );
    SetPort( theWindow );

    DrawPicture( thePicture, &theRect );

    if ( theSound != nil )
        SndPlay( nil, (SndListHandle)theSound, false );
    while ( !Button() )
        ;
}
//_____
void  ErrorAlert( short theErrorCode, Boolean fatalError )
{
    Str255  theErrorStr;

    GetIndString( theErrorStr, rErrorStringList, theErrorCode );
    ParamText( theErrorStr, "\p", "\p", "\p" );

    StopAlert( rErrorAlert, nil );

    if ( fatalError == true )
        ExitToShell();
}
```

Resource Files

You've seen that resources reside in a resource file. Your development environment then merges the resources from a resource file with your compiled source code to create a stand-alone application. That fact tells you that resources don't *have to* exist alone in a resource file — they can be a part of an application file.

Resource Files and Resource Forks

Macintosh files consist of two forks — two areas that hold data in different manners. You may not know it by name, but you're already familiar with the *resource fork* of a file. A resource fork always holds — you guessed it — resources. The second type of fork is named the data fork and, unsurprisingly, holds data other than resource-related data. In a resource file, such as the one you use to hold resources for a programming project, the resource fork holds one or more resources. The data fork is empty. Figure 2-17 illustrates this.

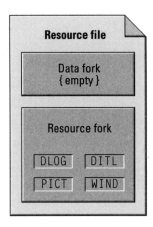

Figure 2-17
A resource file has a resource fork with resources, and an empty data fork.

When you use your development environment to build an application, the resources in the project's resource file get merged with your compiled source code. The result is a single application file. If a compiler that generates 68K applications was used, the application file will have an empty data fork and a resource fork that holds all the resources that were in the project's resource file, along with CODE resources that hold the application's compiled, or executable, code. These CODE resources will have been generated by your development environment. The file on the left side of Figure 2-18 shows the forks of a 68K application.

If you use a compiler that generates native PowerPC applications, the resulting application file will have a data fork that isn't empty. Instead, the data fork will hold the application's executable code. The PowerPC doesn't use CODE resources; it instead looks for executable code in an application's data fork. The resource fork of the PowerPC application will hold all of the resources originally found in the project's resource file. The file shown on the right side of Figure 2-18 illustrates the forks in a PowerPC application.

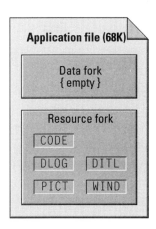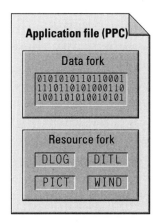

Figure 2-18
The contents of the forks in a 68K and a PowerPC application differ.

Not all Macintosh files hold resources. Many document files (files created by an application) store all their information in the file's data fork. Figure 2-19 shows a typical document file.

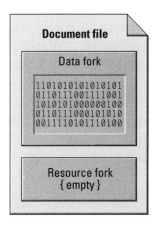

Figure 2-19
A document file usually has document data stored in its data fork, and an empty resource fork.

USING MULTIPLE RESOURCE FILES

This topic's heading may cause you to think of using more than one resource file to hold the resources for your project. Development environments let you use more than one resource file to hold a project's resources. Some large projects take advantage of this feature in order to better organize the project's resources while working on them. This topic, however, is about stand-alone applications that rely on external resource files to hold some or all of their resources.

The examples you've seen so far have all had their resources stored in the application's resource fork. The resources started out in a resource file that was added to a project. From there, the resources were merged with compiled code to become part of the application. The three files shown on the left of Figure 2-20 are typical of the three files used to build an application with a Metrowerks IDE. After performing a build, an application is created. This application needs no other files in order to run.

Rather than storing all the resources used by a program in the program itself, an application can keep none or some resources within its own resource fork and store other resources in external resource files. As the program runs, it will access these external resources and use them just as if they resided in the application's resource fork. Because some or all of the resources used by the program are stored in external files, these external files must accompany the application file. If a user obtains just the application file and attempts to run the program, the program will terminate when it attempts to load a missing file. The three files on the right of Figure 2-20 provide an example of a program that uses resources from two resource files.

Why store resources in external files? In most instances you won't need to. For large applications that are heavily resource-dependent, however, this approach might be advantageous. For example, consider a program that uses a few PICT resources that you know will be changed in the near future (perhaps you'll be replacing some black-and-white PICT resources with color ones). Instead of changing the resources in the application and distributing your large application (perhaps on several disks) to each user, you could just make the changes to a small resource file and distribute only that small file. Users could then replace the old resource file with the new version.

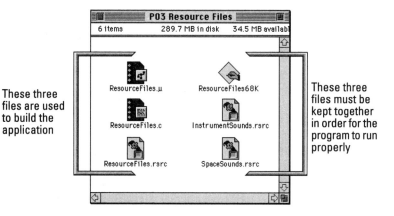

These three files are used to build the application

These three files must be kept together in order for the program to run properly

Figure 2-20
An example of how resource files are used by both a project and an application.

Creating additional resource files is easy — you use ResEdit or Resorcerer to create new files and add the desired resources to the files. Using external resources from within your application is relatively easy too — you just have to make sure that your application knows where to look to find each resource.

Resources that reside in the resource fork of an application are always available to the application. You know this because none of your programs have made any special effort to make sure that an application's resource fork was accessible. When you launch an application, the system opens the application's resource fork. Before an application can make use of a resource located in an external resource file, though, the application has to open that file's resource fork.

The Toolbox routine OpenResFile() can be used to open the resource fork of a file. The parameter to this routine is the name of the resource file to be opened. After the call to OpenResFile() is complete, a file reference number is returned. This reference number will be used when it comes time to access a resource from the opened file. Remember, a program can open the resource fork of more than one file — the reference number allows your program to distinguish between these open files. The following snippet opens the resource fork of a resource file named SpaceSounds.rsrc and returns a file reference number in the variable theFileRefNum:

```
short  theFileRefNum;
theFileRefNum = OpenResFile( "\pSpaceSounds.rsrc" );
```

Refer to Chapter 15 for a more sophisticated way of opening a resource fork — one that involves first creating a *file system specification* for the file to open and then a call to FSpOpenResFile(). Here, the call to OpenResFile() will suffice just fine.

Different resource files can hold the same type of resource. Not only that, different resource files can even hold resources of the same type and resource ID. For example, two resource files could have different sound resources (type snd), both with an ID of, say, 9500. Knowing this, it should make sense that when multiple resource forks are open, a program should make sure to specify which file a particular resource is to come from. That is, before loading a resource, a program should be informed of which file the resource resides in. Figure 2-21 emphasizes this point.

Because a resource fork is treated as a file, you will see the terms *resource file* and *resource fork* used interchangeably in this and other texts.

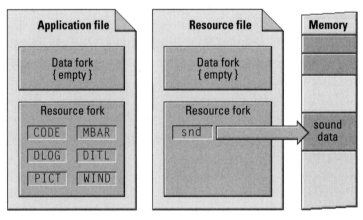

Both resource forks have snd resources, and both forks may even have snd resources with the same ID

Figure 2-21
When multiple resource forks are open, an application must be made aware of which file a resource is to be loaded from.

The Toolbox routine UseResFile() is used to tell an application which file to use. Pass UseResFile() a file reference number, and the application will search for the resource in the file specified by that reference number.

The following snippet opens the resource fork of a file named
SpaceSounds.rsrc and then tells the application to use that file for any
subsequent call that loads a resource:

```
short  theFileRefNum;
theFileRefNum = OpenResFile( "\pSpaceSounds.rsrc" );
UseResFile( theFileRefNum);
```

Calling `OpenResFile()` returns a file reference number for a newly
opened file. What about the resource fork of the application itself? That fork
is always open, so how does an application get a reference number for it? A
call to the Toolbox routine `CurResFile()` takes care of that. This routine
returns a file reference number to whichever resource file is currently in use.
If you call this routine shortly after your application launches, when the
application's resource fork is the only resource fork open, you'll be guaranteed a reference number to the application resource fork.

```
short  theAppRefNum;
theAppRefNum = CurResFile();
```

The following snippet begins by getting a reference number to the
application's resource fork. Then, the resource fork of a resource file named
SpaceSounds.rsrc is opened and a reference number to it is returned. This
file holds a sound resource that the application needs to play, so
`UseResFile()` is called to let the application know that the snd resource
that is about to be loaded can be found in the newly opened resource fork.
Then, calls to `GetResource()` and `SndPlay()` load the sound and play it.
Finally, another call to `UseResFile()` is made. This call reestablishes the
application's resource fork as the current resource fork. That means that the
next resource that gets loaded will come from the application, not the
external file.

```
short    theAppRefNum;
short    theSpaceFileRefNum;
Handle   theSound;

theAppRefNum = CurResFile();
theSpaceFileRefNum = OpenResFile( "\pSpaceSounds.rsrc" );
UseResFile( theSpaceFileRefNum );
theSound = GetResource( 'snd ', 9500 );
SndPlay( nil, (SndListHandle)theSound, false );
UseResFile( theAppRefNum );
```

EXAMPLE PROGRAM: RESOURCEFILES

When you run the ResourceFiles program, you won't see any evidence of a running program on your screen. Instead, you'll hear several sounds. ResourceFiles simply plays the sounds and then quits. You'll hear the sound of horses used in previous programs, followed by the sound of a UFO, and then drums. Next, you'll hear a sound like the one the "Star Trek" transport makes, followed by the sound of bells. Finally, the program finishes by again playing the sound of horses.

The ResourceFiles program uses five sound resources to play the sounds. Only one of these sound resources is found in the project's resource file. Figure 2-22 shows that the ResourcesFiles.rsrc file holds a single resource — a snd resource with an ID of 9000.

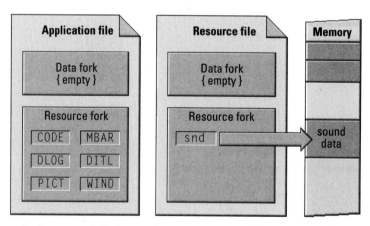

Both resource forks have snd resources, and both forks may even have snd resources with the same ID

Figure 2-22
The single resource used by the ResourceFiles project.

When you examine the project used to build the ResourceFiles program, you'll see that it uses only one resource file, the one pictured in Figure 2-22. When you run the ResourceFiles program, however, you will notice that the program uses several resources. The other resources are found in two external resource files — a file named SpaceSounds.rsrc and a file named InstrumentSounds.rsrc. Figure 2-23 provides a ResEdit view of the application's resource fork and the resource forks of the two files that the ResourceFiles program uses. Take particular note of the fact that both the SpaceSounds.rsrc file and the InstrumentSounds.rsrc file hold a sound resource with the same ID, 10001.

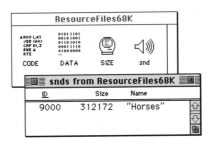

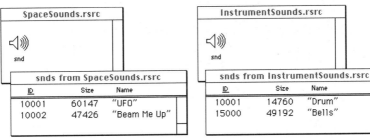

Figure 2-23
The ResourceFiles application uses snd resources from three resource forks.

 The top file pictured in Figure 2-23 is the application itself. When an application is built, your development environment merges the resources from the project's resource file (here, a single snd resource) with code, data, and a SIZE resource. Your development environment is responsible for adding these other resources to the application.

ResourceFiles begins by initializing the Toolbox and then obtaining and saving a reference number to the application's resource fork. Next, the two external resource files are opened. At this point the application has three reference numbers saved, one for each resource fork. Whenever a resource is loaded, the application first calls UseResFile(). This serves two purposes. First, it guarantees that the resource comes from the proper file. Second, it eliminates the need to keep track of which resource fork is current. There is never a need to examine the value of the reference number of the current resource fork to see if it's the correct one. Instead, the program just sets the current fork to the one that holds the resource and then performs the load. Finally, when the program is through with a resource fork, the Toolbox routine CloseResFile() is called to close the fork.

Now that you know how to handle resource-related errors, you may want to add error-handling to the ResourceFiles source code as an exercise.

```c
//_____
#include <sound.h>
//_____
#define      rHorseSound        9000   // in application
#define      rUFOSound          10001  // in SpaceSounds.rsrc
#define      rBeamMeUpSound     10002  // in SpaceSounds.rsrc
#define      rDrumSound         10001  // in InstrumentSounds.rsrc
#define      rBellsSound        15000  // in InstrumentSounds.rsrc
#define      kSpaceFileName         "\pSpaceSounds.rsrc"
#define      kInstrumentFileName    "\pInstrumentSounds.rsrc"
//_____
void  main( void )
{
    short   theAppRefNum;
    short   theSpaceFileRefNum;
    short   theInstrumentFileRefNum;
    Handle  theSound;

    InitializeToolbox();
    theAppRefNum = CurResFile();
    theSpaceFileRefNum = OpenResFile( kSpaceFileName );
    theInstrumentFileRefNum = OpenResFile( kInstrumentFileName );
    UseResFile( theAppRefNum );
    theSound = GetResource( 'snd ', rHorseSound );
    SndPlay( nil, (SndListHandle)theSound, false );
    UseResFile( theSpaceFileRefNum );
    theSound = GetResource( 'snd ', rUFOSound );
    SndPlay( nil, (SndListHandle)theSound, false );
    UseResFile( theInstrumentFileRefNum );
    theSound = GetResource( 'snd ', rDrumSound );
    SndPlay( nil, (SndListHandle)theSound, false );
    UseResFile( theSpaceFileRefNum );
    theSound = GetResource( 'snd ', rBeamMeUpSound );
    SndPlay( nil, (SndListHandle)theSound, false );
    UseResFile( theInstrumentFileRefNum );
    theSound = GetResource( 'snd ', rBellsSound );
    SndPlay( nil, (SndListHandle)theSound, false );

    UseResFile( theAppRefNum );
    theSound = GetResource( 'snd ', rHorseSound );
    SndPlay( nil, (SndListHandle)theSound, false );
    CloseResFile( theSpaceFileRefNum );
    CloseResFile( theInstrumentFileRefNum );
}
```

Resource Reference

This section summarizes the Toolbox functions that work with resources and resource files.

LOADING RESOURCES

Before working with a resource, a copy of its data needs to be loaded from disk to memory.

GetNewWindow( )

To bring a new window to the screen, first call `GetNewWindow()` to load a `WIND` resource into memory. If the `WIND` resource has its visible field set to false, follow the call to `GetNewWindow()` with a call to `ShowWindow()` (described later) to display the window.

```
#define     rMyWindow     128
WindowPtr   theWindow;
Ptr         theStorage = nil;
theWindow = GetNewWindow( rMyWindow, theStorage, (WindowPtr)-1L );
```

Pass `GetNewWindow()` the resource ID of the `WIND` resource that holds the window information. Pass a `nil` pointer to let the Toolbox allocate memory for the window (as opposed to your supplying a pointer to a memory block — refer to Chapter 7 for more information). Typecast -1L to a `WindowPtr` as the last parameter to tell the Toolbox to place the window in front of all others. `GetNewWindow()` will return a pointer to the window data that gets loaded into memory.

GetPicture( )

To draw a picture, first call `GetPicture()` to load a `PICT` resource into memory. To draw the picture, call `DrawPicture()` (described later).

Pass `GetPicture()` the ID of the `PICT` to load. `GetPicture()` will return a handle to the picture data that gets loaded into memory.

GetResource( )

Some resource types have Toolbox routines specifically written to load that type of resource. `GetNewWindow()` loads a `WIND`; `GetPicture()` loads a `PICT`. Other resource types don't have such a routine. For those types, call `GetResource()`.

```
Handle   theHandle;
ResType  theResourceType = 'snd ';
short    theResID = 9000;

theHandle = GetResource( theResourceType, theResID );
```

Pass `GetResource()` the four-character resource type of the resource that is to be loaded. The second parameter should be the resource ID of the resource to load. In return, `GetResource()` will load the resource data into memory and return a handle to the block of memory that holds the data.

WORKING WITH RESOURCES

Once resource data is loaded into memory, the data can be treated as an object and worked with. For instance, sound data can be treated as a sound and played back on the speakers of the user's Mac.

ShowWindow( )

Once `GetNewWindow()` is called to load `WIND` resource data into memory, other Toolbox routines can be called to act on that window. `ShowWindow()` is such a function. If the `WIND` resource marked the window to be invisible, `ShowWindow()` will now make the window visible.

```
WindowPtr  theWindow;
// load the window data with GetNewWindow()
ShowWindow( theWindow );
```

Note that there are numerous Toolbox functions that work with windows. See Chapter 7 for more information.

DrawPicture( )

Once `GetPicture()` is called to load `PICT` resource data into memory, other Toolbox routines can be called to act on that picture. `DrawPicture()` is such a function. This routine will draw the picture to the active, or frontmost, window:

```
PicHandle   thePicture;
Rect        theRect;
// load the picture data with GetPicture()
// establish the rectangle to which the picture should be drawn
DrawPicture( thePicture, &theRect );
```

The first parameter to `DrawPicture()` is a handle (type `PicHandle`) to the picture data loaded into memory by a call to `GetPicture()`. The second parameter is the destination rectangle to which the picture should be drawn. Refer to Chapter 10 for more information about pictures.

SndPlay( )

Once `GetResource()` is called to load snd resource data into memory, other Toolbox routines can be called to act on that sound. `SndPlay()` is one such function. This routine will play the sound on the speakers of the user's Macintosh.

```
Handle          theSound;
SndChannelPtr   theSndChan = nil;
Boolean         asynch = false;
// load the picture data with GetResource()
SndPlay( theSndChan, (SndListHandle)theSound, asynch );
```

The first parameter to `SndPlay()` is a pointer to a sound channel. If you'd like the Sound Manager to take care of the allocation of a sound channel, pass a `nil` pointer here. The second parameter is a handle to the sound data in memory. The third parameter to `SndPlay()` is a `Boolean` that tells the Sound Manager whether this sound will be played asynchronously (`true`, other actions can take place simultaneously) or synchronously (`false`, no other actions can take place until the sound has completed playing). For information about sound channels and asynchronous sound play, refer to Chapter 13.

RESOURCE ERRORS

If a resource or resource file is missing, a resource cannot be loaded into memory. If there is limited free memory, an attempt to load a large resource may fail. Your application should include a function that handles resource-loading errors. If it does, that function will make use of the Toolbox routines listed here.

GetIndString( )

Strings can be stored in groups within a single STR# resource. To retrieve an individual string from a STR# resource, call GetIndString():

```
#define      rErrorStringList      128
Str255       theErrorStr;
short        theErrorCode;

GetIndString( theErrorStr, rErrorStringList, theErrorCode );
```

The first parameter to GetIndString() is a Str255 variable that will hold the desired string once the call to GetIndString() has completed. The second parameter is the ID of the STR# resource to use; a resource file may hold more than one collection of strings, each held in a STR# resource. The final parameter is an index into the string list. A value of 1 retrieves the first string in the list, a value of 2 returns the second string, and so forth.

ParamText( )

An alert or dialog box has a DITL resource that defines items that will appear in the alert of dialog box. One such item can be a static text item. The static text item can define the text that will appear in the alert or dialog box, or it can use a *marker* that will be filled in with text as a program executes. This allows the text of an item to be dynamic — to change as program conditions warrant. Call ParamText() to define up to four strings that will be used to fill in the text items that have markers.

```
Str255  theString1 = "\pName:";
Str255  theString2 = "\pRank:";
Str255  theString3 = "\pSerial Number:";
Str255  theString4 = "\p";
ParamText( theString1, theString2, theString3, theString4 );
```

The four possible markers that may appear in static items in a DITL are: ^0, ^1, ^2, and ^3. That means any one DITL can hold up to four static text items that will each display a string defined by the program that uses the DITL. If an alert or dialog box opens and there is a static text item with the marker ^0 in it, that marker will be replaced by whatever string was used as the first of the four strings that are the parameters to the most recent call to ParamText(). The marker ^1 will be replaced by the second string used in a call to ParamText(), and so forth.

ParamText() doesn't bind the four strings to any one alert or dialog box. Any alert or dialog box that uses a text item with one of the markers will have that marker replaced by a string used in the most recent call to ParamText().

StopAlert( )

A program can post an alert by calling StopAlert(). An alert always includes an OK or Done button as the first item in its dialog item list (DITL item number 1).

```
#define        rErrorAlert     128
ModalFilterUPP  theFilter = nil;
StopAlert( rErrorAlert, theFilter );
```

The first parameter to StopAlert() is the ID of the DITL resource that holds the items that are to appear in the alert. The second parameter is a universal procedure pointer, or UPP, that points to an optional filter function. The purpose of a filter function is to add functionality to an alert. In most cases you'll pass a value of nil to signify that your alert uses no filter function.

RESOURCE FILES

A program normally stores all its resources in a single resource fork, the resource fork that is a part of the application itself. However, a program does have the power to use resources stored in external resource files.

OpenResFile( )

A resource file on disk needs to be opened before a program can access any of its resources. Call OpenResFile() to do this.

```
#define      theResFileName      "\pMyResourceFile"
short        theFileRefNum;
theFileRefNum = OpenResFile( theResFileName );
```

The parameter to OpenResFile() is the name of the resource file to open. The file should reside in the same folder as the application that uses it. For more sophisticated file-handling techniques, refer to Chapter 15. After opening the resource file, OpenResFile() returns a file reference number, an identifier that can be used in other Toolbox calls to specify which resource file is to be worked with.

CloseResFile( )

When your program is through with an open resource file, call CloseResFile() to close it.

```
short  theFileRefNum;
CloseResFile( theFileRefNum );
```

The parameter to CloseResFile() is a file reference number that specifies which resource file is to be closed. This reference number is the one returned by the call to OpenResFile() that opened the file.

CurResFile( )

When more than one resource fork is open, only one will be the current resource fork. To determine the file reference number of the resource file that is currently being used, call CurResFile(). This routine is of use when determining the reference number of the application's resource fork. The application's resource fork, like other resource forks, is treated as a file and has its own reference number.

```
short  theFileRefNum;
theFileRefNum = CurResFile();
```

UseResFile( )

When more than one resource fork is open, only one will be the current resource fork. To set a particular fork to be the current fork, call UseResFile():

```
short   theFileRefNum;
UseResFile( theFileRefNum );
```

The parameter to UseResFile() is the file reference number for the resource fork to make current. This reference number is the one returned by the call to OpenResFile() that opened the file.

3

Memory

*I*n order to write programs that don't crash and display the feared "bomb alert" (the alert a user sees when the Mac seizes up), you'll need to know a little about how the Macintosh manages and allocates memory. While the subject of memory can be very involved and more than a little confusing, you'll discover that understanding only a small subset of this detailed topic is enough to help you write stable programs.

In this chapter, you'll learn that each program that is currently running on a Mac is given its own private area in RAM — its own *application partition*. You'll also see that each partition consists of a *stack* and a *heap*. You'll learn that pointer and handle variables are stored on the stack and are used to access data that is stored in the heap.

Memory Overview

If you're new to Macintosh programming, you'll discover that you can't get too far without at least a rudimentary knowledge of how memory is organized.

THE APPLICATION PARTITION

To the user, double-clicking on a Macintosh application icon starts that program. To the programmer, the launching of a program means that a section of free RAM — an application partition — has been reserved for some or all of the program's code and that this code has been loaded into that partition. An application partition consists of an application stack, an application heap, and an area of free memory between the stack and heap, as shown in Figure 3-1.

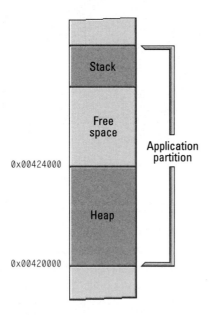

Figure 3-1

An application partition consists of a stack and a heap, and the amount of free space between them.

 Figure 3-1 shows a couple of addresses simply to indicate that, by convention, low memory or a smaller address appears at the bottom of a figure.

A Macintosh computer is capable of running more than one application at a time. When it does so, each executing application is given its own private area in RAM — its own application partition. Each partition consists of its own stack, free memory area, and heap. Figure 3-2 shows a section of memory that has three applications running on a Mac at the same time.

The application heap, often called simply the heap, is used to hold an application's executable code. If the application is a native PowerPC program (compiled using a PowerPC compiler), then the entire application code is loaded into the heap. If the application is a 68K application (compiled using a 68K compiler), some or all of the code is loaded into the heap. If the heap size for a 68K application (which is established by the programmer at the time the program is built) is set large enough, all of the code may end up in the heap. If the heap isn't large enough to hold all of the code at one time, blocks of code will be loaded and unloaded as needed.

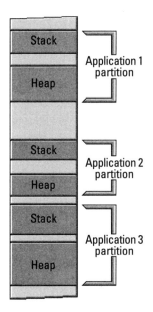

Figure 3-2

RAM holds an application partition for each program that is currently running on a Mac.

     These blocks of code are CODE resources. When you build a 68K application, your compiler will divide the executable code into a number of these CODE resources and store them in the resource fork of the application. The compiler does the work of creating CODE resources and you won't ever have to manually create them. And when the application is executing, the operating system does the work of loading and unloading these CODE resources.

     Your development environment lets you set the application heap size for any program you write. Refer back to Chapter 2 for more details.

Besides holding executable code, the heap holds data structures that are created by the application and by calls to the Toolbox. Application-created data is described later in this chapter. An example of data created by calls to the Toolbox is window data that gets loaded into the heap in response to a call to the Toolbox function GetNewWindow().

The *application stack*, or *stack*, contains data that is local to routines in the program. When an application-defined function is called, the parameters that are passed to the function get stored on the stack. As the program calls enters that function, the variables that are declared local to the function also get stored on the stack.

The application partition for a 68K application includes an area called the A5 World. This area, located just above the stack, holds the global variables for an application. PowerPC applications store global variable information without the need for an A5 World. If you need information about the A5 World (or the A5 CPU register after which this section of the partition is named), refer to a more advanced text than this book.

Both the stack and the heap grow and shrink in size as items are added and removed from them. In Figure 3-1 you saw that between the stack and the heap lies an area of free memory. This area is used by both the stack and heap. As items are added to the stack, it grows downward toward the heap. This can be a source of confusion to programmers, as it means that the *top* of the stack is figuratively shown at the *lower end* of the stack. Conversely, as items are added to the heap, it grows upward toward the stack. Figure 3-3 shows the same application partition that's shown in Figure 3-1. In this new figure, the free space between the stack and heap has been reduced by the addition of a stack item and a heap item.

An item can be any number of things. If an application calls a function, and that function includes two local variables, those two variables become the items that get added to the top of the stack. If a resource (such as a WIND or MENU) is loaded into memory, its data will be an item that is added to the heap. If your application is, say, a program that catalogs a person's music CDs, information the person enters for a each CD can be a data structure that's added to the heap.

THE APPLICATION HEAP

As mentioned earlier, a program has blocks of memory allocated and deallocated to its application heap as the application executes. Each block is a series of contiguous (adjacent) bytes that hold resource data or an application data structure. When an application doesn't need a block, it may deallocate, or purge, that block from the heap. If the purged block isn't at one end or the other of the heap, a gap of free memory forms in the heap. Each time such a block is purged, a new gap forms. These free blocks can lead to *fragmentation*.

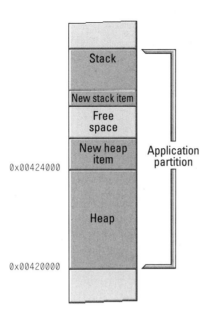

Figure 3-3
The stack grows downward as items are added, while the heap grows upward.

Figure 3-3 shows a new block that's been added to the top of an application heap. As you've just read, however, a block isn't always added to the top. If the heap contains a block of free memory that's of sufficient size, the block will be allocated within this free area.

When a new block is to be allocated, there must be enough contiguous heap memory to hold the entire block. While the total amount of free heap memory may be large enough to hold this block, if the free memory isn't contiguous, it can't hold the block. Thus the fragmented memory can become wasted memory. To eliminate fragmentation, the operating system occasionally compacts the heap, moving blocks so that free memory gaps are eliminated. Figure 3-4 illustrates this. At the left of this figure is an application heap that holds five blocks. Pictured in the center of the figure is this same heap after two of the blocks have been purged. To eliminate the two free memory gaps, the heap is compacted. While compaction doesn't increase the amount of free memory, it does make the free memory usable. After compaction there is a single, larger block of free memory that is capable of holding a much larger item than the heap could hold before compaction.

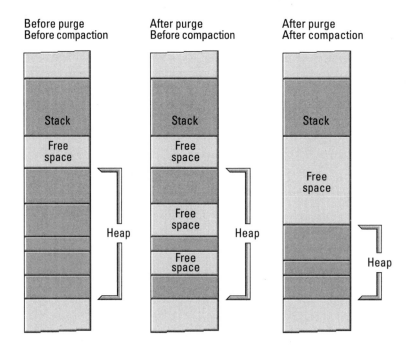

Figure 3-4
Memory compaction reduces unusable free space in the heap.

Not all blocks in the application heap are affected by compaction. A block can have the attribute of being relocatable or nonrelocatable. As the terms suggest, a relocatable block can be moved about within the heap and a nonrelocatable block cannot be moved. If you understand the concept of compaction, it makes sense that the system prefers to deal with relocatable blocks. Nonrelocatable blocks hinder compaction because they form immovable barriers that can trap pockets of free space.

NONRELOCATABLE BLOCKS AND POINTERS

The heap can contain blocks that are relocatable and blocks that are nonrelocatable. Relocatable blocks — the topic of the next section — are referenced by handles. Nonrelocatable blocks are referenced by pointers.

When you declare a local variable that is a pointer, the pointer variable is created on the stack. The block that the pointer points to, however, may be allocated in the heap. A WindowPtr variable, for example, is a pointer.

Keeping in mind that a variable declared in main() is a local variable, the following snippet creates a variable named theWindow that appears the stack. The snippet also allocates a block of window-descriptive data on the heap.

```
void  main( void )
{
   WindowPtr  theWindow;
   theWindow = GetNewWindow( 128, nil, (WindowPtr)-1L );
   ...
}
```

As shown in Figure 3-5, the WindowPtr variable will hold the address of this heap block.

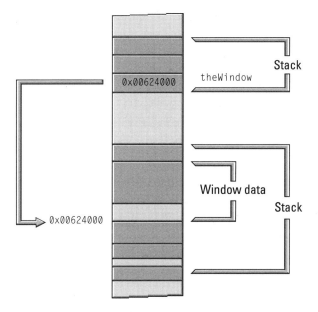

Figure 3-5
A pointer variable on the stack holds the address of a block of data in the heap.

You'll notice in Figure 3-5 that the pointer appears to point to the bottom of the window data. Actually, it's pointing to the first byte in the block of data — as pointers always do. You should keep in mind that smaller addresses are shown lower in memory; therefore, a block is pictured as starting at the lower end of a figure and ending higher up in the figure.

Here's something else to notice about Figure 3-5. Pointers point to nonrelocatable blocks; thus the window data block pictured in Figure 3-5 cannot be moved. Below the window data block is a block of free memory. If the block *below* the free memory block happens to be nonrelocatable, then the Memory Manager won't be able to do anything with that free block during compaction. The free block will be trapped, and potentially unusable (it will be unusable if the Memory Manager needs to allocate a block any larger than this free block).

Because a heap block referenced by a pointer can cause heap fragmentation, it's better to use a block referenced by a handle. Because some Toolbox routines only use pointers (for example, GetNewWindow(), which uses a WindowPtr pointer), it isn't always possible to satisfy this preference.

RELOCATABLE BLOCKS AND HANDLES

The heap can hold relocatable blocks, which are referenced by handles, in addition to nonrelocatable blocks (referenced by pointers). Declaring a local variable that is a handle creates a handle variable on the stack. The block that the handle leads to will be allocated in the heap. This is the same as it is for a pointer variable. The difference between the two is in the path that is taken from the variable to the heap block.

A pointer variable holds the address of the heap data block — the pointer leads directly to the block. A handle variable holds the address of a *master pointer*. The master pointer in turn holds the address of the heap data block. Like all pointers, a master pointer is nonrelocatable — it's fixed in memory. Unlike a pointer variable that your program declares in an application-defined function, a master pointer is found in the heap, not on the stack.

When an application is launched, a number of master pointers are created near the bottom of the heap. These pointers remain in the heap until the program terminates. While pointers are generally shunned by programmers because they block the movement of relocatable heap blocks, master pointers don't share this bad reputation. Because they reside at the bottom of the heap, they don't interfere with compaction, as pointers in the middle of the heap do.

Having to traverse through a master pointer to reach a data block in the heap seems a roundabout means of accessing data. Why is this extra step necessary for a handle but not for a pointer? The answer lies in relocation. Because a handle leads to a block that can be moved by the Memory Manager, extra precautions must be taken to keep track of the block.

There are several situations in which your code will rely on a handle. Loading a resource is one of them. The following snippet loads a sound resource with an ID of 128 into memory, then returns a handle to the loaded sound data.

```
void   main( void )
{
   Handle  theHandle;
   theHandle = GetResource( 'snd ', 128 );
   ...
}
```

Sounds and sound resources are discussed in detail in Chapter 13. Here, it is sufficient to know that a sound — such as a digitized sound — can be stored as a resource of type snd in the resource fork of an application. Loading the sound resource into memory readies it for playing on the Mac's speakers.

A call to the Toolbox function GetResource() loads resource data into memory. The call also sets a master pointer to point to this loaded data. Finally, the call returns the address of the master pointer (*not* the loaded resource data) and assigns it to the handle. Figure 3-6 illustrates this.

As in all of this chapter's figures that include addresses, the particular addresses shown here aren't of importance — they're in the figure merely to give you something concrete to reference. You can't predict at what address the Memory Manager will place a new block. And because the Memory Manager is responsible for its placement, you won't care which address a block is at!

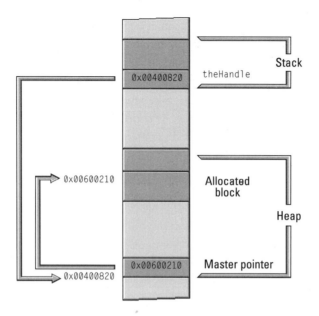

Figure 3-6
A handle variable on the stack holds the address of a master pointer in the heap. The master pointer in turn holds the address of a block of data in the heap.

Examine Figure 3-6 closely. Notice that the handle holds the address of the master pointer, while the master pointer holds the address of the allocated block — the address of the sound data, in this example. Now consider what will happen when memory compaction takes place. The allocated block, which is relocatable, may be moved by the Memory Manager. If that happens, the Memory Manager will update the address of the block in the master pointer. That is, the current address (0x00600210 in the figure) will be replaced with the new block address. And the address in the handle? That won't change. The handle holds the address of the master pointer. The master pointer itself never moves in memory. In the example, it will always appear at address 0x00400820.

Because of how the memory management technique of handles works, the Memory Manager is only responsible for changing the address that appears in a master pointer. The Memory Manager doesn't ever need to attempt to change the address found in a handle variable in your program.

Working with Pointers

To avoid fragmentation, it's preferable to work with handles rather than pointers (handles work with relocatable blocks, and pointers don't). Occasionally, however, a program will need to allocate a nonrelocatable block of memory.

THE TOOLBOX AND CALLS TO NEWPTR( )

Sometimes your program will explicitly make a call to the Toolbox function NewPtr(), and at other times the call will be made implicitly — a Toolbox function that your program calls will in turn call NewPtr(). In either case, a nonrelocatable block of memory will be allocated in memory, and a pointer to that block will be returned to your program.

A call to GetNewWindow() is an example of a Toolbox function that calls NewPtr() and returns a pointer. Specifically, GetNewWindow() returns a WindowPtr:

```
WindowPtr  theWindow;
theWindow = GetNewWindow( 128, nil, (WindowPtr)-1L );
```

When a Toolbox routine like GetNewWindow() makes a call to NewPtr(), the Toolbox is responsible for taking care of memory allocation. As you'll soon see, when your program calls NewPtr() directly, then your program is responsible for allocating a block of memory of the proper size.

THE APPLICATION AND CALLS TO NEWPTR( )

A specific pointer type always points to the same specific data structure in memory. For instance, a WindowPtr points to a WindowRecord — the data structure that defines what a window looks like. A DialogPtr points to a DialogRecord — the data structure that defines the look of, and the items in, a dialog box. On the other hand, the Macintosh data type Ptr is used to create a generic pointer; that is, a variable of type `Ptr` can point to any block of memory that your program wishes it to. The following is a declaration of a `Ptr` variable named `thePtr`:

```
Ptr  thePtr;
```

Just as declaring a `WindowPtr` variable named `theWindow` doesn't automatically create a pointer that points to a `WindowRecord` in memory, the declaration of a `Ptr` variable doesn't tell your program what memory is being pointed to. Figure 3-7 shows that a `Ptr` declaration creates a pointer variable on the stack, but it doesn't create a variable that is immediately of use by your program.

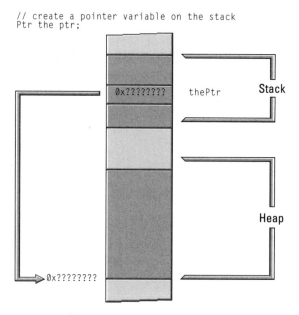

Figure 3-7

Declaring a pointer adds a pointer variable to the stack.

BY THE WAY

Where will the pointer variable be on the stack? If no other variable is declared after the pointer, it will be at the top of the stack (which, remember, is pictured in figures at the lower end of the stack). If a function declares a few variables, then the pointer may not be at the top of the stack:

```
short   theValue;
Ptr     thePtr;
long    theTotal;
```

In any case, the exact stack location of a variable won't be of concern to you or to your program.

Just as your program needs to make a call to the Toolbox function GetNewWindow() to assign a WindowPtr something to point to, your program needs to make a call to a Toolbox function to set a Ptr variable pointing to something. The Toolbox call that you'll use is NewPtr(), and the thing that the new pointer will point to is specified as the parameter to NewPtr():

```
Ptr  thePtr;
thePtr = NewPtr( sizeof( long ) );
```

The above call to NewPtr() tells the Toolbox to allocate a block of memory the size of a long variable and return a pointer to that block to the calling program. Including sizeof() as a part of the parameter to NewPtr() is necessary because NewPtr() is expecting a number as its parameter. The number is the size of the memory block to allocate, in bytes. Because the long data type always occupies 4 bytes of memory, the above snippet will allocate a 4-byte block of memory in the heap and return a pointer to that block. Figure 3-8 shows that the call to NewPtr() assigns Ptr variable thePtr the address of the newly allocated memory block. The figure also shows that the new block starts at address 0x00600010. The block that follows the new block begins at address 0x00600014, making the size of the new block 4 bytes in size (that is, bytes found at addresses 0x00600010, 0x00600011, 0x00600012, and 0x00600013).

```
// allocate a block of memory the size of a
// long and return that block's address
thePtr = NewPtr( sizeof( long) );
```

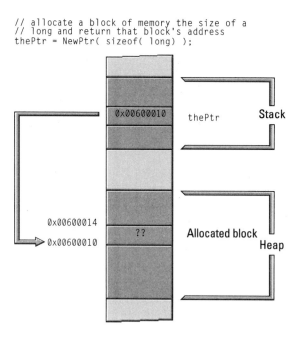

Figure 3-8

Calling NewPtr() *allocates a block of memory and sets the pointer variable to point to it.*

In Figure 3-8 you can see that the call to NewPtr() turns variable thePtr from an invalid pointer (a pointer that pointed to an unknown address) to a valid pointer (a pointer that points to a particular block of memory). While the pointer points to a valid block, the contents of the block are unknown. To store a value in the contents of the block, you may be tempted to try the following:

```
thePtr = 50;    // this WON'T work
```

The above line of code doesn't work because a pointer holds an address. The above line sets thePtr to point to memory address 50 — which isn't the desired result. To instead assign the contents of the block of memory a value of 50, use the * operator (the *indirection* operator, or *dereferencing* operator):

```
*thePtr = 50;    // this WILL work
```

In the above line of code, the * operator tells the compiler to assign the value on the right of the assignment operator (the = sign) to the block pointed to by the pointer variable on the left of the assignment operator. Figure 3-9 shows how dereferencing the pointer variable thePtr allows a program to access the memory block that thePtr points to.

```
// dereference the pointer to assign a value
// to the block of memory
*thePtr = 50;
```

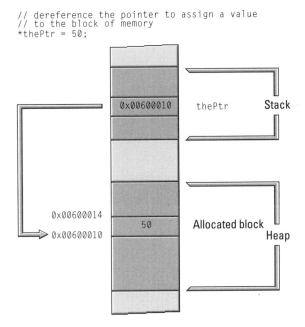

Figure 3-9
Dereferencing a pointer lets a program assign a value to the object that the pointer points to.

POINTERS AND APPLICATION-DEFINED DATA STRUCTURES

For simplicity, the previous discussion used a pointer to a block of memory the size of a long variable. In practice, it's unlikely that you'll need to create a pointer to a block of memory that holds a single long value. Instead, it's more likely that your program will define a data structure and then use a pointer to point to the entire data structure. Consider the following data structure definition:

```
typedef  struct
{
   short  length;
   short  width;
   long   area;

}  MyRecord, *MyRecordPtr;
```

The above definition creates two application-defined data types. The first, MyRecord, is a data structure with three fields. The second, MyRecordPtr, is a pointer to a struct of type MyRecord.

To create a variable of type MyRecord, declare one as you would any other type of variable. To assign a value to one of the fields of the structure variable, use the dot operator (the structure member operator):

```
MyRecord  theRec;
theRec.length = 5;
```

To instead create a variable that is a pointer to a MyRecord structure, declare a MyRecordPtr variable:

```
MyRecordPtr  theRecPtr;
```

Unlike the MyRecord variable, you can't immediately use the MyRecordPtr variable in an assignment statement. Instead, you need to allocate a block of memory for variable theRecPtr to point at. As you've seen, a call to NewPtr() takes care of that task:

```
theRecPtr = (MyRecordPtr)NewPtr( sizeof( MyRecord ) );
```

In the above line the parameter to NewPtr() is the size of a MyRecord data structure. Because each of the two short fields occupies two bytes and the one long field occupies four bytes, the Memory Manager will allocate a block of memory 8 bytes in size. The Memory Manager will then assign the first address of this block to the variable theRecPtr. Figure 3-10 illustrates this example.

```
// allocate a block of memory the size of a
// MyRecord data structure
theRecPtr = (MyRecordPtr)NewPtr( sizeof (MyRecord) );
```

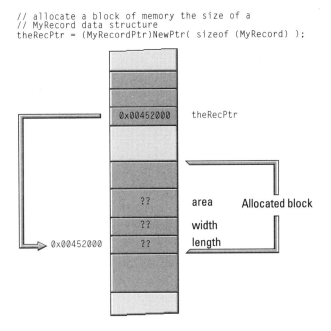

Figure 3-10
NewPtr() can be used to allocate a block of memory the size of a data structure.

You can use either of two methods to assign a value to one of the fields of the data structure that theRecPtr points to. One way is to use the * operator to dereference the pointer. Once you do that, you need to use the dot operator — the structure member operator —to access a particular field of the pointed-to structure. In the following example the length field of a MyRecord structure is assigned a value of 3. Notice that the pointer variable name is enclosed in parentheses to tell the compiler that the * operator is to be used to dereference the pointer variable theRecPtr. Without the parentheses, the compiler would assume that theRecPtr.length was the pointer to dereference.

```
(*theRecPtr).length = 3;
```

The second method of assigning a value to a structure member via a pointer to that structure is through the use of the -> operator (a hyphen (–) followed by the greater-than symbol (>)):

```
theRecPtr->length = 3;
```

The above two methods of accessing a structure member via a pointer variable both accomplish the same task. The method you use will be strictly a matter of personal preference. In this book the first method is used.

EXAMPLE PROGRAM: POINTERS

The Pointers example program demonstrates the use of NewPtr() with an application-defined data type. The Pointers program uses the same MyRecord structure that was shown earlier in this chapter:

```
typedef  struct
{
    short   length;
    short   width;
    long    area;

}  MyRecord, *MyRecordPtr;
```

The program declares two variables that make use of the MyRecord data structure. The first is a MyRecord variable; the second is a pointer to an area in memory that holds a MyRecord structure:

```
MyRecord     theRec;
MyRecordPtr  theRecPtr;
```

BY THE WAY

What's so special about using a pointer to a data structure rather than just using a variable of that data structure type? Altering the value of a variable from within a function is one reason to use a pointer. Remember, in C, when a function makes a change to the value of a variable that is passed as a parameter, that change doesn't last beyond the time that function executes. When the function ends, the variable's value goes back to the value it had when passed in. Passing an address of a data structure rather than the structure itself enables a function to change the value of the structure — and the change will last even when the function ends.

After the variable declarations, the program assigns values to each of the members of the `MyRecord` variable:

```
theRec.length = 5;
theRec.width  = 4;
theRec.area   = theRec.length * theRec.width;
```

Next, memory is allocated for one `MyRecord` data structure. That gives the `MyRecordPtr` variable `theRecPtr` something to point to:

```
theRecPtr = (MyRecordPtr)NewPtr( sizeof( MyRecord ) );
```

With a block of memory allocated, the program uses the * operator with the pointer to fill each of the three fields of the memory block:

```
(*theRecPtr).length = 3;
(*theRecPtr).width  = 2;
(*theRecPtr).area   = (*theRecPtr).length * (*theRecPtr).width;
```

If you're familiar with your development environment's debugger, you might want to step through this short program to see the members getting assigned values. Otherwise, you can use a call to the Toolbox function `NumToString()` to convert to a string any member of either variable. Then draw the result to the window that the Pointers program displays. The Pointers program does that with the area field for both the `theRec` variable and the pointer variable `theRecPtr`. The result is shown in Figure 3-11. To end the Pointers program, press the mouse button.

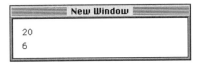

Figure 3-11
The result of running the Pointers program.

After compiling and running Pointers, you can try a simple test to see if the call to `NewPtr()` is really necessary. Move to the `NewPtr()` line in the Pointers.c source code file and comment out that line. Then build, or make, an application from the project. What happens next depends on which development environment you're using and on what preferences settings you have set. You may end up with a compilation error — Figure 3-12 shows the commented-out line in the source code window and such an error in the Metrowerks Message Window. Or, the source code might just compile — but don't be too pleased. If you double-click on the standalone application's icon, the program may very well start, then quit. Figure 3-13 shows one possible alert the Finder could report — a type 1, or bus error. Regardless of what goes wrong, something certainly *is* wrong. The lesson here is that when declaring a pointer variable that is to be used with application-defined data, make sure to provide your program with memory to point to.

Keep in mind that you don't have to allocate memory for Macintosh pointer types such as a `WindowPtr` or `DialogPtr`. The Toolbox will take care of memory management when you use a variable of one of these types.

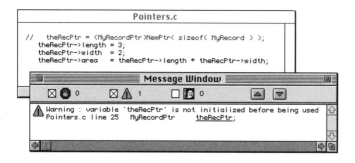

Figure 3-12
Some compilers report an error if a pointer is used before it is assigned a block to point to.

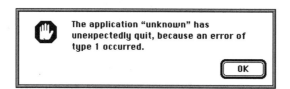

Figure 3-13
A program that doesn't allocate memory properly may not run properly.

The Pointers project requires a single resource — a `WIND` — with an ID of 128. Figure 3-14 shows the type and size of the window used by the program.

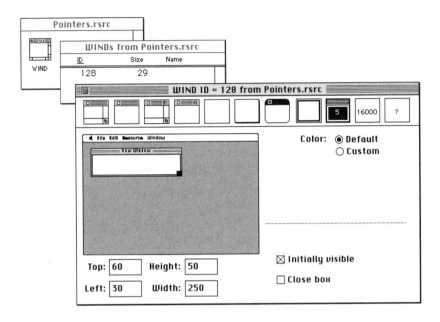

Figure 3-14
The Pointers project uses a single WIND *resource.*

The source code for Pointers appears next. There's only one thing that happens that hasn't been mentioned yet. When your program is finished with a pointer variable, it should dispose of the memory block that the pointer referenced. The last line of main() does that with a call to the Toolbox function DisposePtr(). You pass DisposePtr() a pointer to the block that is to be freed. This routine requires a generic pointer — a variable of type Ptr. Since the program uses an application-defined pointer type — the MyRecordPtr type — it is necessary to typecast the application-defined pointer type to a Ptr pointer type. Typecasting a variable temporarily converts the variable to a different type. Here, preceding the variable named theRecPtr with (Ptr) does that.

```
//_____
void    InitializeToolbox( void );
//_____
typedef  struct
{
   short   length;
   short   width;
   long    area;
```

```
}  MyRecord, *MyRecordPtr;
//_____

void  main( void )
{
    MyRecord        theRec;
    MyRecordPtr     theRecPtr;
    WindowPtr       theWindow;
    Str255          theString;

    InitializeToolbox();

    theRec.length = 5;
    theRec.width  = 4;
    theRec.area   = theRec.length * theRec.width;

    theRecPtr = (MyRecordPtr)NewPtr( sizeof( MyRecord ) );
    (*theRecPtr).length = 3;
    (*theRecPtr).width  = 2;
    (*theRecPtr).area   = (*theRecPtr).length * (*theRecPtr).width;
    theWindow = GetNewWindow( 128, nil, (WindowPtr)-1L );
    SetPort( theWindow );

    NumToString( theRec.area, theString );
    MoveTo( 10, 20 );
    DrawString( theString );

    NumToString( (*theRecPtr).area, theString );
    MoveTo( 10, 40 );
    DrawString( theString );
    while ( !Button() );
        ;

    DisposePtr( (Ptr)theRecPtr );
}
```

Working with Handles

Just as the Toolbox and an application can both allocate memory and create a pointer that references that memory, so too can the Toolbox and an application allocate memory and then create a handle that references the new memory block.

NOTE   A pointer points to a block of memory. A handle also does, but indirectly. A handle points to a master pointer, and the master pointer in turn points to the memory block. Rather than say that a handle indirectly points to a block, this book will just say that a handle *references* a block.

THE TOOLBOX AND CALLS TO NEWHANDLE( )

Toolbox routines that allocate memory may return either a pointer or a handle to that memory. You've seen that GetNewWindow( ) allocates a nonrelocatable block of heap memory and returns a pointer to that memory — a WindowPtr. There are other Toolbox routines that allocate a relocatable block and return a handle to that memory. When a program calls the Toolbox routine GetPicture( ) to load a picture (a PICT resource) into memory, for example, the Toolbox allocates a relocatable block of memory to hold the picture data in, loads the data into that memory, and then returns a PicHandle to the program. Anytime the program needs to access the picture data (to draw the picture in a window, for instance), the PicHandle can be used.

When a Toolbox routine like GetPicture( ) allocates memory, it calls another Toolbox routine to do the allocation — NewHandle( ). GetPicture( ) uses NewHandle( ) to allocate a block of memory the size of a Picture — a Macintosh data type that holds information about a picture. When a Toolbox routine calls NewHandle( ), it is the Toolbox routine that is responsible for memory allocation. When your program calls NewHandle( ), your program must specify the size of the block to allocate. As you've seen, this is how NewPtr( ) and memory allocation work.

THE APPLICATION AND CALLS TO NEWHANDLE( )

A Toolbox routine like GetPicture( ) returns a handle that always references a particular type of data structure, the Picture structure. When your application calls NewHandle( ), it can specify that a block of memory be allocated for any type of structure. Before calling NewHandle( ), your program will declare a Handle variable:

```
Handle  theHand;
```

As Figure 3-15 illustrates, the declaration creates a new variable on the stack, but it doesn't give that variable the address of a master pointer.

```
// create a handle variable on the stack
Handle theHand;
```

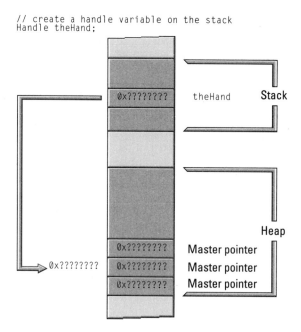

Figure 3-15
Declaring a handle adds a handle variable to the stack.

After declaring the Handle variable, your program will call NewHandle()
to allocate a block of memory, set a master pointer pointing to that block,
and return a handle to your program. Just as it was for NewPtr(), the one
parameter to NewHandle() is the size, in bytes, of the block to allocate.

```
Handle  theHand;
theHand = NewHandle( sizeof( long ) );
```

The above snippet allocates a block of memory the size of a long — 4
bytes. Figure 3-16 shows how memory now looks.

In Figure 3-16 you can see that the variable theHand holds the address
of a master pointer. The master pointer, in turn, holds the address of the
new block of memory. To assign a value to the contents of this block, the
handle variable needs to be dereferenced twice:

```
Handle  theHand;
theHand = NewHandle( sizeof( long ) );
**theHand = 50;
```

```
// allocate heap memory for the master
// pointer to point up to
theHand = NewHandle( sizeof( long) );
```

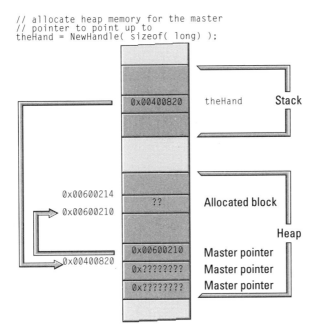

Figure 3-16

Calling NewHandle() *allocates a block of memory and sets up the handle variable to reference it.*

The above snippet fills the new block of memory with the number 50. Figure 3-17 shows this.

Why does a handle variable need to be dereferenced twice in order to get to the value in memory? A handle holds the address of a master pointer. A master pointer holds the address of a block of memory. The block of memory holds a value. Dereferencing a handle a single time yields the contents of the master pointer (which is an address — the address of the heap block). Dereferencing a second time yields the contents of the block. Figure 3-18 illustrates the values the handle has — as a handle, as a handle dereferenced once, and as a handle dereferenced twice.

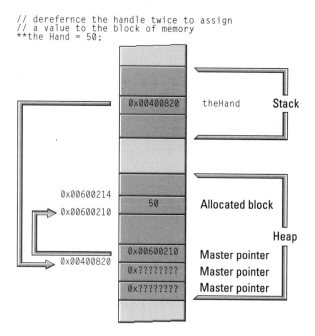

```
// derefernce the handle twice to assign
// a value to the block of memory
**the Hand = 50;
```

Figure 3-17
Dereferencing a handle lets a program assign a value to the object that the handle refers to.

HANDLES AND APPLICATION-DEFINED DATA STRUCTURES

You've seen that a pointer can be used to keep track of a data structure in memory. A handle can be used in the same way. And because a handle references a block of memory that the system can relocate, a handle is the preferred way of allocating memory. The following application-defined data structure expands upon the MyRecord struct that was introduced earlier in this chapter:

```
typedef  struct
{
   short  length;
   short  width;
   long   area;

}  MyRecord, *MyRecordPtr, **MyRecordHandle;
```

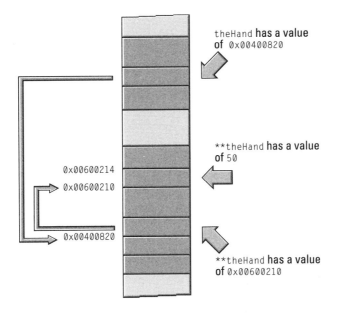

Figure 3-18
A handle holds the address of a master pointer; the master pointer holds the address of a block of memory.

To create a variable that is a handle to a MyRecord structure, declare a MyRecordHandle variable:

```
MyRecordHandle  theRecHand;
```

Next, allocate a block of memory the size of one MyRecord structure and get a handle to that block:

```
theRecHand = (MyRecordHandle)NewHandle( sizeof( MyRecord ) );
```

As is the case for a pointer variable, you can use either of two methods to access a member of the structure a handle references. You can use the * operator to dereference the handle once (which results in a pointer), and then use the -> operator to access a member of the pointed-to structure:

```
(*theRecHand)->length = 7;
```

A second means of accessing a field of a structure referenced by a handle is to dereference the handle twice and then use the dot operator:

```
(**theRecHand).length = 7;
```

As in working with pointers, the method of member access is at the discretion of the programmer. In this book the second method is used.

EXAMPLE PROGRAM: HANDLES

The Handles example program is a demonstration of the use of NewHandle() with an application-defined data type. The Handles program uses the same MyRecord structure that was shown earlier in this chapter and in the Pointers example. Here the MyRecordHandle type has been added to the structure definition:

```
typedef  struct
{
   short  length;
   short  width;
   long   area;

}  MyRecord, *MyRecordPtr, **MyRecordHandle;
```

The program declares a handle to an area in memory that holds a MyRecord structure:

```
MyRecordHandle  theRecHand;
```

Next, memory is allocated for one MyRecord data structure. That gives the MyRecordPtr variable theRecPtr something to point to:

```
theRecPtr = (MyRecordPtr)NewPtr( sizeof( MyRecord ) );
```

With a block of memory allocated, the program uses the * operator with the handle to fill the three members of the structure in the memory block:

```
(**theRecHand).length = 7;
(**theRecHand).width  = 6;
(**theRecHand).area   = (**theRecHand).length *
(**theRecHand).width;
```

The Handles program uses a call to the Toolbox function NumToString() to convert the area member to a string. That string is drawn to a window — just as was done in the Pointers program. Figure 3-19 shows the results you should expect to see when you run the Handles program. To quit the program, press the mouse button.

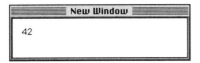

Figure 3-19
The result of running the Handles program.

Here's one last reminder. Remember that you don't have to allocate memory for Macintosh handle types like the PicHandle — the Toolbox takes care of memory allocation for Macintosh data types. You only need to call NewHandle() when you're working with application-defined data types and handles to these types.

The Handles project requires the same resource used in the Pointers program — a WIND with an ID of 128. The project's source code is shown next. Take note of the last line of code in the listing. When your program is finished with a handle variable, it should free up the block the handle references, just as is done with a pointer variable. A call to the Toolbox function DisposeHandle() takes care of that task. Make sure to typecast whatever handle type you pass to DisposeHandle() — this function requires a generic Handle data type as its one parameter.

```
//_____
void  InitializeToolbox( void );
//_____
typedef  struct
{
   short  length;
   short  width;
   long   area;

}  MyRecord, *MyRecordPtr, **MyRecordHandle;
//_____
void  main( void )
```

```
{
    MyRecordHandle   theRecHand;
    WindowPtr        theWindow;
    Str255           theString;

    InitializeToolbox();

    theRecHand = (MyRecordHandle)NewHandle( sizeof( MyRecord ) );
    (**theRecHand).length = 7;
    (**theRecHand).width  = 6;
    (**theRecHand).area    = (**theRecHand).length * (**theRecHand).width;
    theWindow = GetNewWindow( 128, nil, (WindowPtr)-1L );
    SetPort( theWindow );

    NumToString( (**theRecHand).area, theString );
    MoveTo( 10, 20 );
    DrawString( theString );

    while ( !Button() );
        ;

    DisposeHandle( (Handle)theRecHand );
}
```

Memory Reference

This section summarizes the Toolbox functions that work with pointers and handles.

POINTERS

Toolbox functions that work with pointers will take care of memory allocation without help from you. If your program creates pointers to its own data structures, however, your program will need to allocate memory to hold the structure.

NewPtr( )

A call to NewPtr() allocates a block of memory in the application heap and returns a pointer to that block. The pointer holds the first address of the block.

```
Ptr    thePtr;
Size   numBytes;
thePtr = NewPtr( numBytes );
```

NewPtr() accepts a parameter of type Size. The Size data type is defined to be a long. This parameter is the size, in bytes, of the block of memory that is to be allocated. After NewPtr() allocates the block, it returns a pointer to that block.

If the exact number of bytes to allocate is unknown — as is often the case — use the sizeof() operator as part of the parameter to NewPtr(). The sizeof() operator accepts a data type as its parameter and returns the number of bytes that one instance of that data type would occupy. For example, because the short data type always occupies 2 bytes of memory and the long data type always occupies 4 bytes, sizeof(short) returns two, sizeof(long) returns four. This technique can be used to easily allocate memory for one instance of an application-defined data structure. The following snippet allocates a block of memory the size of a single AutoStruct data structure and returns a pointer to it:

```
typedef  struct
{
    Str255  model;
    Str255  make;
    short   year;
}  AutoStruct, *AutoStructPtr;
AutoStructPtr  theAutoPtr;
theAutoPtr = NewPtr( sizeof( AutoStruct ) );
```

DisposePtr( )

When your program is through with a pointer, it should free the block of memory that the pointer referenced. To do that, call DisposePtr(). DisposePtr() accepts a pointer of type Ptr as its one parameter. The following snippet allocates memory for an application-defined structure and then frees that same memory.

```
typedef  struct
{
    Str255  model;
    Str255  make;
    short   year;
}  AutoStruct, *AutoStructPtr;
```

```
AutoStructPtr   theAutoPtr;
theAutoPtr = NewPtr( sizeof( AutoStruct ) );
...
...
DisposePtr( (Ptr)theAutoPtr );
```

HANDLES

Toolbox functions that allocate memory and return a handle to that memory take care of memory management chores for you. If your program creates handles to its own data structures, your program will be responsible for allocating memory to hold the structure.

NewHandle( )

A call to NewHandle() allocates a block of memory in the application heap and returns a handle to that block. The handle holds the address of a master pointer. The master pointer holds the first address of the block.

```
Handle  theHand;
Size    numBytes;
theHand = NewHandle( numBytes );
```

NewHandle() accepts a parameter of type Size. The Size data type is defined to be a long. The numBytes parameter is the size, in bytes, of the block of memory that is to be allocated. After NewHandle() allocates the block, it returns a handle to that block.

If the block is to be the size of an application-defined data type, the number of bytes to allocate may be unknown — especially if the data type consists of several members. To let the compiler calculate the size of a data type, pass the data type name to the sizeof() operator. This can be done from within the call to NewHandle(), as demonstrated below. The following snippet allocates a block of memory the size of a single AutoStruct data structure and returns a handle to it:

```
typedef  struct
{
   Str255   model;
   Str255   make;
   short    year;
```

```
}  AutoStruct, *AutoStructPtr, **AutoStructHandle;
AutoStructHandle   theAutoHand;
theAutoHand = NewHandle( sizeof( AutoStruct ) );
```

DisposeHandle( )

When your program is through with a handle, it should free the block of memory that the handle referenced. The Toolbox routine `DisposeHandle()` will do that. Pass this function a handle of type `Handle`. The following example allocates memory for an application-defined structure and then frees that memory block.

```
typedef  struct
{
   Str255   model;
   Str255   make;
   short    year;
}  AutoStruct, *AutoStructPtr, **AutoStructHandle;
AutoStructHandle   theAutoHand;
theAutoHand = NewHandle( sizeof( AutoStruct ) );
...
...
DisposeHandle( (Handle)theAutoHand );
```

Programming Fundamentals

*T*he topics covered in Part II are the true fundamentals of Macintosh programming. All but the most trivial Mac applications make use of the topics covered in this section.

4

Drawing

*T*he Macintosh Toolbox, described in Chapter 1, holds the myriad functions that enable you to add interface elements such as windows, menus, and dialog boxes to your programs. The Toolbox also enables you to add graphics. It consists of hundreds of drawing routines. In this introductory drawing chapter, you'll learn about several of these functions. You'll learn more about QuickDraw graphics functions in Chapter 10.

The routines in the Macintosh Toolbox are divided conceptually into separate areas, each area consisting of functions that work with a single interface topic. Each of these areas has a name, and most of the names end with the word *Manager*. There's the Window Manager, the Menu Manager, the Dialog Manager, and others. There's also an area that for one reason or another doesn't end with *Manager*. Instead, it's just known as QuickDraw. QuickDraw includes the Toolbox drawing routines that enable programmers to draw simple objects such as lines, rectangles, and circles. Those are the types of shapes you'll see described in this chapter. QuickDraw also holds Toolbox functions that are used to create more sophisticated shapes such as polygons, regions, and pictures. Those shapes are discussed in Chapter 10.

Drawing Basics

Before drawing, you will need to know where you're drawing to and what you're drawing with. That is, you'll need to specify both the location at which drawing is to take place and the characteristics of the "pen" that is to be doing the drawing.

THE COORDINATE SYSTEM

Before delving into the details of *how* to draw, a quick look at *where* to draw is in order. QuickDraw easily allows you to draw lines, shapes, and text anywhere you want in a window. You specify where by using a coordinate grid system. As shown in Figure 4-1, in the horizontal direction the coordinate system starts at 0 at the left edge of a window and increases to the right. The numbering refers to pixels, or dots on the screen. The distance between any two consecutive horizontal values, such as 30 to 31, is the width of a single pixel. Monitors typically have about 70 pixels per linear inch, so the width of a pixel is about 1/70 inch. In the vertical direction the system starts at 0 at the top of a window and increases downward. Again, the distance between any two consecutive values is the distance between two consecutive pixels. In Figure 4-1, notice that because the window's title bar isn't part of the window's drawing area, it isn't included in the coordinate system.

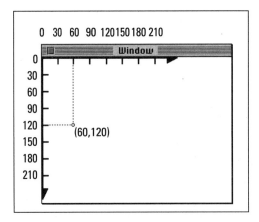

Figure 4-1
The pixel located at (60, 120) in a window's coordinate system.

Figure 4-1 shows how any one point — any one pixel — in a window is referred to. A point is specified by first giving the horizontal, or *x*, value, then the vertical, or *y*, value. In Figure 4-1 the point that lies 60 pixels from the left edge of a window and 120 pixels down from the window's top is referred to by the coordinate system pair of values (60, 120).

In past chapters you have seen that before calling the Toolbox function DrawString() to draw a string of text, a program calls the Toolbox function MoveTo(). The MoveTo() function establishes where subsequent drawing will begin. The following snippet shows how a sentence could be started 60 pixels from the left edge of a window and 120 pixels down from its top. Figure 4-2 illustrates:

```
MoveTo( 60, 120);
DrawString( "\pThis sentence starts at (60, 120)" );
```

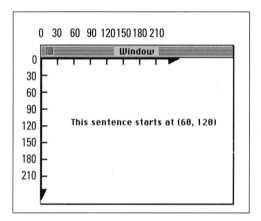

Figure 4-2
Drawn text starts at a particular pixel.

Each window has its own coordinate system, and each system is independent of the window's current location on the screen — the coordinate system floats along with a window as the window moves. That is, point (0, 0) will always be the point located at a window's upper left corner, no matter where the window is currently placed on the screen.

THE GRAPHICS PEN

Lines are often, but not always, drawn with a thickness of a single pixel. Shapes are often, but not always, drawn in solid black. When you draw a line or shape, you have the ability to select the line thickness and fill pattern for the line or shape. Drawing is said to be performed with an invisible *graphics pen.* When you make a call to the Toolbox function `MoveTo()`, you're setting the starting placement of a graphics pen. A call to `DrawString()` then uses this imaginary pen to draw text.

Each window has its own graphics pen. A program can easily change one of the settings of a pen by making a Toolbox call. As an example of making a change to a graphics pen setting, consider a program that changes the thickness at which the graphics pen will draw. When a new window is created, its graphics pen has a line thickness setting of a single pixel. A change to this default value is made by calling `PenSize()`. The first parameter to `PenSize()` is the new pixel width in which lines will be drawn, while the second parameter is the new pixel height in which lines will be drawn. The following snippet sets the graphics pen's line height to 10 pixels, while leaving its width at 1 pixel:

```
PenSize( 1, 10 );
```

Changes to a graphics pen affect all subsequent drawing that takes place in the window to which the pen is associated. Consider the following snippet:

```
PenSize( 1, 10 );
MoveTo( 30, 50 );
Line( 200, 0 );
```

The above code begins by changing the size of a graphics pen. It then calls `MoveTo()` to move the same graphics pen to a point 30 pixels from the left edge of a window and 50 pixels down from the window's top. A horizontal line 200 pixels in length is then drawn using the Toolbox function `Line()`. The first parameter to `Line()` is the horizontal pixel length of the line, while the second parameter is the vertical pixel length. Line drawing is done with the window's graphics pen and begins at the current position of that pen. In this example the position point is (30, 50). Because `PenSize()` was called previous to the drawing of the line, the line will have a height of 10 pixels, as shown in Figure 4-3.

Line thickness is one property of a graphics pen. A second is fill pattern. When a new window opens, its pen's default fill pattern is black — lines and shapes all get drawn in solid black. Your program can call the Toolbox function `PenPat()` to change this pattern. Here is an example that changes the fill pattern to a light gray pattern:

```
PenPat( &qd.ltGray );
```

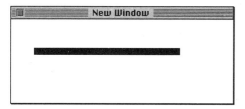

Figure 4-3
The thickness of a line can be changed by setting the line thickness of the graphics pen.

The parameter to PenPat() is a pointer to the pattern that is to be used by the pen. QuickDraw has five predefined patterns available for your use: white, light gray, gray, dark gray, and black. Each of these patterns is represented by an Apple-defined constant: white, ltGray, gray, dkGray, and black. These five constants are defined as part of a global structure named qd. Because your development environment defines this global qd structure, you don't have to declare it in your programs. Instead, to access one of the patterns, simply use the dot operator, as in qd.gray to specify a gray pattern. Because PenPat() requires a pointer to a pattern, you will need to preface the pattern with the & operator.

EXAMPLE PROGRAM: GRAPHICSPEN

The GraphicsPen program opens a window and calls Line() three times to draw three lines. The window is shown in Figure 4-4. You can quit the program by simply clicking the mouse button.

The top line of the three lines uses the default graphics pen settings to draw a line 300 pixels in length:

```
MoveTo( 20, 30 );
Line( 300, 0 );
```

The middle line is drawn with a pen width and height of 10 pixels:

```
PenSize( 10, 10 );
MoveTo( 20, 50 );
Line( 300, 0 );
```

As shown in Figure 4-4, the second line is slightly longer than the first, even though both lines result from identical calls to Line(). This is because the drawing of the middle line takes place after a call to PenSize() changes the pen's size. Because the pen's width is 10 pixels at the time of the drawing of the middle line, the line extends 10 pixels beyond the 300-pixel length specified in the call to Line(). Figure 4-5 adds the pixel coordinates of the starting point and ending point of each of the three lines.

The bottom line is drawn after a call to PenPat() changes the graphics pen's pattern to gray. The result is a gray line, as shown in Figure 4-4. You can experiment by changing the PenPat() parameter to any of the other four predefined patterns and recompiling and rerunning the GraphicsPen program:

```
PenPat( &qd.gray );
MoveTo( 20, 90 );
Line( 300, 0 );
```

Like the middle line, the bottom line has a height of 10 pixels. Keep in mind that a change to a characteristic of a graphics pen stays in effect until the characteristic is again changed. Thus the program's call to PenSize() changes the pen's size for all of the drawing that follows.

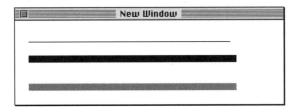

Figure 4-4
The window that results from running the GraphicsPen program.

New Window	
(20, 30)	(321, 30)
(20, 50)	(330, 50)
(20, 90)	(330, 90)

Figure 4-5
The GraphicsPen window, with pixel coordinates added for reference.

```
//_____

#define        rDisplayWindow        128


//_____

void  main( void )
{
    WindowPtr  theWindow;
    Rect       theRect;

    InitializeToolbox();

    theWindow = GetNewWindow( rDisplayWindow, nil, (WindowPtr)-1L );
    SetPort( theWindow );
    MoveTo( 20, 30 );
    Line( 300, 0 );
    PenSize( 10, 10 );
    MoveTo( 20, 50 );
    Line( 300, 0 );

    PenPat( &qd.gray );
    MoveTo( 20, 90 );
    Line( 300, 0 );

    while ( !Button() );
        ;
}
//_____
```

A WINDOW'S GRAPHICS PORT

In Chapter 2 you saw that when a program calls GetNewWindow(), the data from a WIND resource gets loaded into memory. When GetNewWindow() is called, the system reserves a block of memory the size of a WindowRecord data structure. This structure, covered in detail in Chapter 7, holds the information that describes a window. The WIND resource data fills in several of the fields of a WindowRecord and thus becomes a part of the information used to describe a window. The rest of the window's description is held in other fields of the WindowRecord. Of these other fields, the most important to the programmer is the port field, which is of the data type GrafPort. As Figure 4-6 shows, the GrafPort is the first — and largest — member in a WindowRecord.

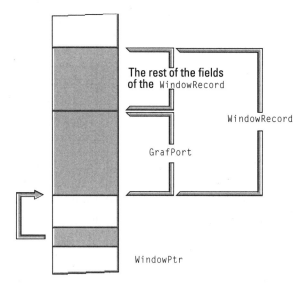

Figure 4-6
The GrafPort *is the first field in a* WindowRecord *data structure.*

A field, or member, of a structure can itself be a structure. The port is such a field. As you will see later in this chapter, and again in Chapter 10, the GrafPort data structure consists of more than two dozen fields. Each of the GrafPort fields describes some part of the *drawing environment* of a window. From your experience as a user of Macintosh programs, you know that the contents of a program's windows can differ. A program that has two open windows may display the text in one window in, say, the Chicago font, and at the same time display the text in the second window in the New York font. The fact that each window has its own drawing environment, or its own set of drawing characteristics, is what makes this possible.

A WindowRecord is the data type that defines a window. And while a call to GetNewWindow() creates a new WindowRecord data structure in memory, a programmer usually simply says that a call to GetNewWindow() creates a new window. In the same vein, unless a programmer is referring to a specific field of a GrafPort, he or she will usually talk about a window's *graphics port* rather than its GrafPort data structure.

THE GRAPHICS PEN AND THE GRAPHICS PORT

Just as the graphics port provides a way for the programmer to conceptually group together the many things that affect a window's drawing environment, so too does the graphics pen. You've just seen that the idea of a graphics port is represented in a program by a data structure (the GrafPort). The graphics pen has no single corresponding data type representation. Instead, changes to the fields of a GrafPort affect what's referred to as the graphics pen.

As an example of making a change to a graphics pen setting, and thus a change to a field of a GrafPort structure, consider a program that changes the line thickness of a graphics pen. As discussed earlier, when a new window is created, its graphics pen has a line thickness setting of a single pixel. A change to this default value is made by calling PenSize().

Toolbox functions that alter a setting of a window's graphics pen actually alter one of the many fields of the window's GrafPort structure. In the case of PenSize(), the GrafPort field that's being changed is the pnSize field. While Chapter 10 supplies the details of many of the GrafPort fields, it may be a good idea to glance at the definition of the GrafPort data structure now:

```
struct GrafPort
{
    short       device;
    BitMap      portBits;
    Rect        portRect;
    RgnHandle   visRgn;
    RgnHandle   clipRgn;
    Pattern     bkPat;
    Pattern     fillPat;
    Point       pnLoc;
    Point       pnSize;
    short       pnMode;
    Pattern     pnPat;
    short       pnVis;
    short       txFont;
    Style       txFace;
    SInt8       filler;
    short       txMode;
    short       txSize;
    Fixed       spExtra;
    long        fgColor;
```

```
long        bkColor;
short       colrBit;
short       patStretch;
Handle      picSave;
Handle      rgnSave;
Handle      polySave;
QDProcsPtr  grafProcs;
};
```

In short, the graphics pen exists as another device for making a programmer's life easier. If you'd like to communicate the idea that the pnSize field of a GrafPort is to be changed, you'd just say that the pen size needs to be changed. You, and whoever you're working with, wouldn't have to know exactly which GrafPort field needs changing. In fact, by working with drawing characteristics in this way, a programmer really need not even be familiar with the notion that there is such a field as the pnSize field.

SETTING THE GRAPHICS PORT

Most of the example programs that you've seen up to this point have made a call to the Toolbox routine SetPort(). This function tells QuickDraw where subsequent drawing commands should be directed. The one parameter to SetPort() is of type GrafPtr, a pointer to a graphics port. Once this call is made, QuickDraw knows which graphics port is to be the recipient of future calls to QuickDraw routines. Here's an example of a call to SetPort():

```
WindowPtr  theWindow;

theWindow = GetNewWindow( rDisplayWindow, nil, (WindowPtr)-1L );
SetPort( theWindow );
```

If you've been paying attention, you may have noticed that the above snippet doesn't quite follow the discussion that immediately precedes it. In particular, it was stated that the parameter to SetPort() should be a GrafPtr, whereas the above snippet uses a WindowPtr. This sleight of hand is made possible by the definitions of a GrafPtr and a WindowPtr:

```
typedef  GrafPort  *GrafPtr;
typedef  GrafPtr    WindowPtr;
```

The first of the two definitions states that a GrafPtr is a pointer to a GrafPort. The second then defines a WindowPtr to be the same as a GrafPtr. A WindowPtr and a GrafPtr, it turns out, both point to the same thing — a GrafPort. Figure 4-7 illustrates this. Because the WindowPtr and GrafPtr both point to a graphics port, a variable of either type can be used as the parameter to SetPort().

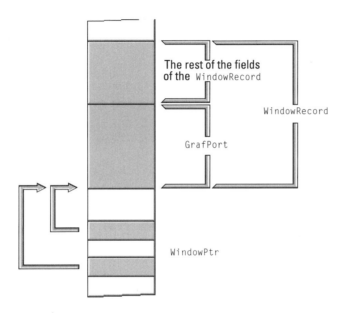

The rest of the fields
of the WindowRecord

WindowRecord

GrafPort

WindowPtr

Figure 4-7

A WindowPtr variable and a GrafPtr variable each point to the same part of a WindowRecord.

When a program has only one window open, the program *may* work properly without this call. Calls to QuickDraw routines such as Line() will usually be directed to the one open window. When a program has more than one window open, problems are *sure* to arise if this call is omitted.

If only one window is open, where else could QuickDraw calls draw to? To the screen itself. The screen itself is a graphics port. While your programs won't need to draw to the screen, the system does — it needs to draw the desktop and menu bar. If your program opens only one window, and it doesn't call SetPort(), there's a chance that graphics could be drawn over the desktop and menu bar.

In the following snippet GetNewWindow() is called twice in order to open two windows, one based on a WIND resource with an ID of 128 and the other on a WIND resource with an ID of 129. After that, a call to SetPort() tells QuickDraw that it should draw to the larger window:

```
#define    rSmallWindow    128
#define    rBigWindow      129

WindowPtr  theWindowSmall;
WindowPtr  theWindowBig;

theWindowBig   = GetNewWindow( rBigWindow, nil, (WindowPtr)-1L );
theWindowSmall = GetNewWindow( rSmallWindow, nil, (WindowPtr)-1L );
SetPort( theWindowBig );
// all QuickDraw calls will result in
// drawing taking place in the big window
```

What happens when a program needs to draw first to one window and then to another? Again, SetPort() is relied upon. To tell QuickDraw to start drawing to a different window, call SetPort() a second time. For this second call, pass a WindowPtr to the new window to draw to. The following example program provides an example of this situation.

EXAMPLE PROGRAM: SETTINGPORTS

The SettingPorts program opens two windows and draws text to each, as shown in Figure 4-8. A click of the mouse button ends the program.

The SettingPorts project requires two resources, both of them WIND resources. Figure 4-9 shows one of the resources, the WIND with an ID of 128. The other WIND resource defines the larger window shown back in Figure 4-8.

The SettingPorts program relies on the SetPort() function to properly perform its drawing. As you look over the source code listing, notice that SetPort() is called three times. It's important to always keep in mind that SetPort() needs to be called each time drawing is to take place in a window other than the one currently being drawn to.

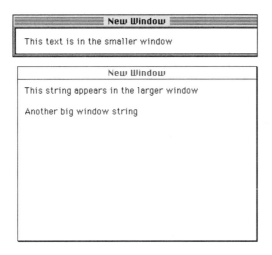

Figure 4-8

The windows that result from running the SettingPorts program.

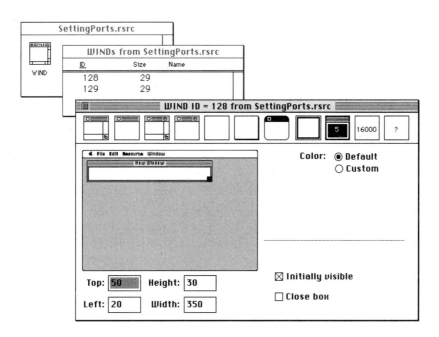

Figure 4-9

One of the two WIND resources used in the SettingPorts project.

```
//_____
#define      rSmallWindow      128
#define      rBigWindow        129
//_____
void  main( void )
{
    WindowPtr  theWindowSmall;
    WindowPtr  theWindowBig;

    InitializeToolbox();

    theWindowBig   = GetNewWindow( rBigWindow, nil, (WindowPtr)-1L );
    theWindowSmall = GetNewWindow( rSmallWindow, nil, (WindowPtr)-1L );

    SetPort( theWindowBig );
    MoveTo( 10, 20 );
    DrawString( "\pThis string appears in the larger window" );

    SetPort( theWindowSmall );
    MoveTo( 10, 20 );
    DrawString( "\pThis text is in the smaller window" );

    SetPort( theWindowBig );
    MoveTo( 10, 50 );
    DrawString( "\pAnother big window string" );

    while ( !Button() );
        :
}
```

Drawing Shapes

Lines, rectangles, ovals, and round rectangles are the most common shapes that a Mac programmer works with. Each of these objects is covered in this section.

LINES

You've already seen one way to draw lines — the Line() function. The Toolbox provides a companion line-drawing routine named LineTo(). The parameters to Line() specify the length of the line to draw. The parameters to LineTo() specify the ending pixel point to draw to. While two identical calls to Line() will always produce two lines of the same length, two identical calls to LineTo() might not. Figure 4-10 shows that the length of a line drawn with LineTo() depends on the location of the graphics pen before the line is drawn. In Figure 4-10, make sure to take note of the fact that both calls to LineTo() have the same parameter values.

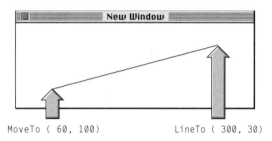

MoveTo (60, 100)   LineTo (300, 30)

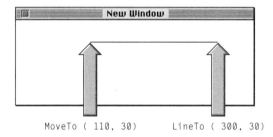

MoveTo (110, 30)   LineTo (300, 30)

Figure 4-10
The length of a line drawn by LineTo() *is dependent on the line's starting point.*

RECTANGLES

A rectangle is created by first setting the boundaries, or coordinates, of the rectangle and then drawing the rectangle. A rectangle's boundaries are held in a variable of type Rect. The Rect data structure consists of four members, each of type short. Each field holds one of the four boundaries that define a rectangle's size and placement in a window. Here is the Rect structure definition:

```
struct  Rect
{
   short  top;
   short  left;
```

```
      short   bottom;
      short   right;
   };
```

To set up a rectangle, call the Toolbox function SetRect(), as shown in this snippet:

```
Rect  theRect;

SetRect( &theRect, 60, 80, 250, 150 );
```

The first parameter to SetRect() is a pointer to a variable of type Rect. After the call to SetRect() is complete, this variable will hold the values that are passed as the remaining parameters to SetRect(). The second parameter specifies the pixel coordinate of the left side of the rectangle, and the third parameter specifies the top of the rectangle. The fourth and fifth parameters define the right and bottom pixel values of the rectangle, respectively. Figure 4-11 shows the rectangle established by the above snippet. To keep the order straight you might want to define appropriately named variables and pass these variables to SetRect(). The following snippet results in a rectangle identical to the one defined above:

```
Rect    theRect;
short   left   =  60;
short   top    =  80;
short   right  = 250;
short   bottom = 150;

SetRect( &theRect, left, top, right, bottom );
```

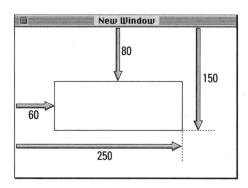

Figure 4-11

SetRect() *establishes the boundaries for a rectangle.*

Figure 4-11 exists to provide you with a reference as to how the parameters to SetRect() are used by the function to establish a rectangle. As such, there are a number of things in the figure that wouldn't actually appear in a window. The four arrows and the numbers beside the arrows wouldn't be drawn to the window, of course. Perhaps not as obvious is that the rectangle itself wouldn't be drawn! SetRect() only sets up the coordinates of a rectangle. To draw the rectangle, your program will call any one of three QuickDraw rectangle-drawing functions. Here's a description of each:

- FrameRect(): Draws a frame around the specified rectangle.
- PaintRect(): Draws the specified rectangle and fills it with the current pen pattern.
- FillRect(): Draws the specified rectangle and fills it with the specified pen pattern.

The first routine, FrameRect(), will draw a hollow rectangle; only the rectangle's frame will be drawn. The second function, PaintRect() will draw a rectangle that is filled in with whatever pattern the graphics pen is set to. The last routine, FillRect(), also draws a filled-in rectangle. The difference between PaintRect() and FillRect() is that PaintRect() uses the current pen pattern, while FillRect() ignores the current pen pattern and instead uses the pattern specified in the second parameter. The following snippet provides an example of a call to each routine:

```
Rect   theRect;

SetRect( &theRect, 60, 80, 250, 150 );
PenPat( &qd.black );
PaintRect( &theRect );

SetRect( &theRect, 55, 75, 245, 145 );
FillRect( &theRect, &qd.gray );
FrameRect( &theRect );
```

Figure 4-12 shows the result of executing the above code Take a look at it before reading the following explanation. In the above snippet a rectangle is first established through a call to SetRect(). Then PenPat() is invoked to set the current pen pattern to black. A call to PaintRect() is then made to draw a solid black rectangle. The rectangle is filled in with a black pattern because that is the current pen pattern. Next, SetRect() is again called. This time the rectangle variable theRect is given coordinates that create a rectangle the same size as the first rectangle, but at a window location 5 pixels to the left and 5 pixels up from the first rectangle. A call to FillRect() draws a rectangle filled with a gray pattern. Finally, this gray rectangle is given a black frame through a call to FrameRect(). The frame is black because like PaintRect(), FrameRect() uses the current pattern when drawing a rectangle. The current pattern is still black (from the call to PenPat()) — the call to FillRect() only changed the pattern for the duration of that one call.

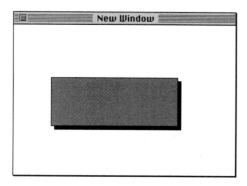

Figure 4-12
The result of calls to three rectangle-drawing functions.

In the above snippet, the same effect could be achieved by replacing the second call to SetRect() with a call to a different Toolbox function — one with a name that would more accurately describe what is taking place. Give up? The function is OffsetRect(), and it's described in Chapter 2. To offset the rectangle theRect 5 pixels to the left and 5 pixels upward, as is being done in the above snippet, replace the second call to SetRect() with this call:

```
OffsetRect( &theRect, -5, -5 );
```

OVALS

If you want to know how to draw an oval, you must first know how to create a rectangle. To set the boundaries for an oval, call SetRect(). To draw the oval, call one of three oval-drawing QuickDraw routines: FrameOval(), PaintOval(), or FillOval(). Each of these functions will draw an oval inscribed within the rectangle defined by the previous call to SetRect(). The following snippet provides an example. Figure 4-13 shows how this oval would look. The dashed lines that make up the bounding rectangle in the figure are just for your reference; only the oval would appear in the window of your program:

```
Rect   theRect;

SetRect( &theRect, 50, 50, 200, 150 );
FrameOval( &theRect );
```

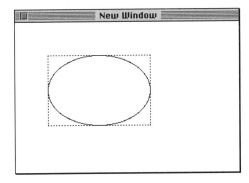

Figure 4-13
An oval's boundaries are established by a call to SetRect().

The routines used to draw solid ovals, PaintOval() and FillOval(), are analogous to the routines used to draw solid rectangles, PaintRect() and FillRect(). The following snippet provides an example:

```
Rect   theRect;

SetRect( &theRect, 30, 20, 90, 100 );
PenPat( &qd.dkGray );
PaintOval( &theRect );

SetRect( &theRect, 100, 120, 200, 200 );
FillOval( &theRect, &qd.ltGray );
```

ROUND RECTANGLES

QuickDraw provides an easy way to draw a rectangle that has rounded edges, like the rectangle that forms the outline of a button in a dialog box. Once again, it's a call to SetRect() that establishes the shape's boundaries. After that, a call to FrameRoundRect(), PaintRoundRect(), or FillRoundRect() draws the round rectangle:

```
Rect  theRect;

SetRect( &theRect, 100, 70, 250, 130 );
FrameRoundRect( &theRect, 40, 30 );
```

The first parameter to FrameRoundRect() is a pointer to the rectangle that holds the boundaries of the round rectangle to draw. The second and third parameters hold the width and height of an oval that is used to determine the amount of rounding that will be given to the corners of the round rectangle. The second parameter holds the width of this oval, while the third parameter holds the height.

Figure 4-14 shows the drawing of a round rectangle in steps. In this figure the first step, shown in the top rectangle, is the setting of the rectangle's boundaries. A call to SetRect() takes care of this. The second through fourth steps all occur with the call to FrameRoundRect(). The rectangle that is shown second from the top has an oval with a width of 40 pixels and a height of 30 pixels set into each corner. The dimensions of this oval come from the second and third parameters in the call to FrameRoundRect(). The next rectangle shows how the rectangle looks after rounding has been applied to its corners. The last rectangle shows how the round rectangle would appear in a window.

The following snippet shows how calls to PaintRoundRect() and FillRoundRect() are made. As they were for FrameRoundRect(), the second and third parameters to these two routines define the amount of rounding that will be applied to the rectangle:

```
Rect  theRect;

SetRect( &theRect, 70, 20, 210, 140 );
PenPat( &qd.ltGray );
PaintRoundRect( &theRect, 20, 20 );

SetRect( &theRect, 90, 130, 200, 220 );
FillRoundRect( &theRect, 40, 50, &qd.black );
```

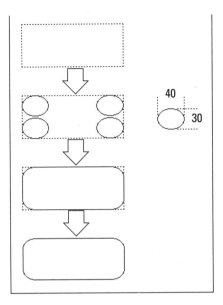

Figure 4-14
The degree of rounding applied to the corners of a round rectangle is based on an oval.

EXAMPLE PROGRAM: SHAPES

The Shapes program opens a single window and draws in it one instance of each of the four types of shapes described in this chapter: a line, a rectangle, an oval, and a round rectangle. Figure 4-15 shows what the window looks like. As usual, click the mouse button to end the program.

Figure 4-16 shows the program's window with the starting and ending coordinates of the line, along with the coordinates for the top left and bottom right corners of the rectangle, oval, and round rectangle. The figure also shows the rectangles used to set the boundaries for the oval and round rectangle. These values should give you a good understanding of how the values used in the Shapes source code relate to the placement of the shapes in a window.

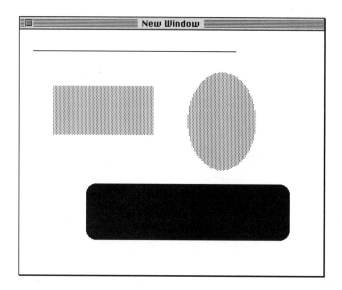

Figure 4-15

The window that results from running the Shapes program.

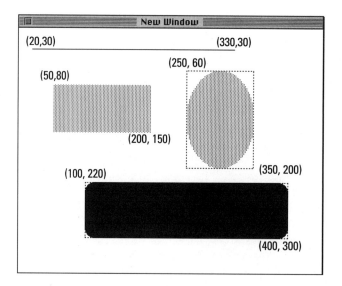

Figure 4-16

The Shapes window with coordinates added for reference.

```
//_____
#define        rDisplayWindow        128
//_____
void main( void )
{
   WindowPtr   theWindow;
   Rect        theRect;

   InitializeToolbox();

   theWindow = GetNewWindow( rDisplayWindow, nil, (WindowPtr)-1L );

   SetPort( theWindow );

   MoveTo( 20, 30 );
   Line( 300, 0 );

   SetRect( &theRect, 50, 80, 200, 150 );
   PenPat( &qd.ltGray );
   PaintRect( &theRect );

   SetRect( &theRect, 100, 220, 400, 300 );
   FillRoundRect( &theRect, 30, 30, &qd.black );

   SetRect( &theRect, 250, 60, 350, 200 );
   PaintOval( &theRect );

   while ( !Button() );
      ;
}
```

Drawing Reference

This section provides a summary of a few of the hundreds of QuickDraw functions used to draw shapes. Refer to Chapter 10's reference section for more function descriptions.

THE GRAPHICS PEN

Setting the starting point for text or line drawing is done by moving an imaginary graphics pen. This same pen also defines drawing characteristics such as the size of lines and the pattern with which shapes are filled.

Pen pattern constants

Apple defined five constants that can be used when working with fill patterns:

- white

- ltGray

- gray

- dkGray

- black

A Toolbox routine that accepts one of these constants as a parameter will expect it to be a part of the qd global variable and will expect a pointer to the pattern. The following example shows how the dark gray constant would be used as a parameter:

```
PenPat( &qd.dkGray );
```

MoveTo()

You move the graphics pen using the MoveTo() and Move() Toolbox functions. MoveTo() moves the pen to a specific pixel point in a window:

```
short  theHorizPixelStart = 10;
short  theVertPixelStart  = 50;

MoveTo( theHorizPixelStart, theVertPixelStart );
```

The first parameter to MoveTo() is the horizontal starting point at which to set the pen. This value is the pixel distance from the left edge of the window. The second parameter is the vertical starting point. This value is the pixel distance from the top of the window's content area — the area excluding the window's title bar. MoveTo() moves the graphics pen but causes no drawing to take place.

Move()

Move() moves the pen a specified number of pixels from its current location:

```
short  theHorizPixelMovement = 30;
short  theVertPixelMovement  = 200;
```

```
MoveTo( theHorizPixelMovement, theVertPixelMovement );
```

The first parameter to Move() is the number of pixels that the graphics pen should be moved in the horizontal direction. This value is in reference to the current location of the graphics pen, not to the left edge of the window. The second parameter is the number of pixels to move in the vertical direction. This value also is in reference to the current pen location. A call to Move() doesn't cause any drawing to take place.

PenSize()

The width and height in which lines are drawn can be set using the PenSize() function. After a call to PenSize(), all lines are drawn using the new graphics pen size.

```
short   thePenWidth = 2;
short   thePenHeight = 5;

PenSize( thePenWidth, thePenHeight );
```

The first parameter to PenSize() is the new pixel width at which the graphics pen is to be set to. The second parameter is the new pixel height.

PenPat()

The pattern that shapes will be filled with can be set using the PenPat() function. After a call to PenPat(), all shape-filling function calls of the form PaintXxxx() will use the new pattern. You use one of the five Apple-defined pen pattern constants that are listed at the start of this reference section:

```
Pattern  thePat = qd.dkGray;

PenPat( &thePat );
```

The parameter to PenPat() is a pointer to the new pattern in which shapes will be filled. Chapter 10 describes how you select other patterns.

GRAPHICS PORTS

Each window has its own drawing environment — its own graphics port.

SetPort()

Before drawing to a window for the first time, and when about to draw to a window other than the one that received the last QuickDraw command, call SetPort(). This function tells QuickDraw which window subsequent drawing should take place in:

```
WindowPtr   theWindow;

SetPort( theWindow );
```

The parameter to SetPort() is defined to be a GrafPtr. Because a window pointer and a graphics port pointer point to the same type of data structure, a graphics port, the parameter to SetPort() can be either a GrafPtr or a WindowPtr variable.

DRAWING SHAPES

QuickDraw provides hundreds of routines that work with shapes. The following are the most commonly called shape drawing functions.

Line()

To draw a line of a specified length, call Line():

```
short   theHorizPixelDistance = 100;
short   theVertPixelDistance  =   0;

Line( theHorizPixelDistance, theVertPixelDistance );
```

The first parameter to Line() is the number of pixels that a line should be drawn in the horizontal direction. The second parameter is the number of pixels in the vertical direction. A first parameter value of 0 draws a vertical line; a second parameter value of 0 draws a horizontal line.

LineTo()

To draw a line that ends at a specific pixel coordinate, call LineTo():

```
short   theHorizPixelEnd = 240;
short   theVertPixelEnd  =  94;

LineTo( theHorizPixelEnd, theVertPixelEnd );
```

The first parameter to LineTo( ) is the horizontal pixel that a line should be drawn to. The second parameter is the vertical pixel coordinate. Line drawing always starts at the current location of the graphics pen.

SetRect( )

The boundaries of a rectangle can be established using a call to SetRect( ):

```
short   left   =  10;
short   top    =  30;
short   right  =  85;
short   bottom = 300;
Rect    theRect;

SetRect( &theRect, left, top, right, bottom );
```

The first parameter to SetRect( ) is a pointer to the rectangle variable that is to have its boundaries set. The remaining parameters hold the pixel coordinates for the rectangle. The left and right parameters use the left edge of the window as a reference; the top and bottom parameter values use the top of the window as a reference.

The individual coordinates of a rectangle can be accessed by using the dot operator with the Rect variable. For example, to store the left boundary of a rectangle in a variable, use the following code:

```
Rect    theRect;
short   theLeftSide;

theLeftSide = theRect.left;
```

FrameRect( )

To draw the frame of a rectangle, with no fill pattern in the rectangle's interior, call FrameRect( ):

```
Rect   theRect;

FrameRect( &theRect );
```

The parameter to FrameRect( ) is a pointer to a Rect variable that holds the boundaries of the rectangle to frame. The coordinates of the rectangle should have previously been established by a call to SetRect( ):

PaintRect()

To paint a rectangle with whatever pattern is current, call `PaintRect()`:

```
Rect  theRect;

PaintRect( &theRect );
```

The parameter to `PaintRect()` is a pointer to a `Rect` variable that holds the boundaries of the rectangle to paint. The coordinates of the rectangle should have previously been established by a call to `SetRect()`.

FillRect()

To fill a rectangle with a pattern of your choosing, call `FillRect()`:

```
Rect     theRect;
Pattern  thePattern = qd.black;

FillRect( &theRect, thePattern );
```

The first parameter to `FillRect()` is a pointer to a `Rect` variable that holds the boundaries of the rectangle to fill. The coordinates of the rectangle should have previously been established by a call to `SetRect()`. The second parameter is the pattern with which to fill the rectangle. A call to `FillRect()` has no lasting effect on the current pen fill pattern.

FrameOval()

To draw the frame of an oval with no fill pattern in the oval's interior, call `FrameOval()`:

```
Rect  theRect;

FrameOval( &theRect );
```

The parameter to `FrameOval()` is a pointer to a `Rect` variable that holds the boundaries into which an oval will be inscribed. The rectangle is used only as an invisible guide for QuickDraw; the rectangle itself will not be drawn to the window.

PaintOval( )

To paint an oval with whatever pattern is current, call PaintOval():

```
Rect  theRect;

PaintOval( &theRect );
```

The parameter to PaintOval() is a pointer to a Rect variable that holds the boundaries of the oval to paint. The coordinates of the rectangle should have previously been established by a call to SetRect(). The rectangle serves as a guide for QuickDraw and will not be drawn in the window.

FillOval( )

To fill an oval with a pattern of your choosing, call FillOval():

```
Rect     theRect;
Pattern  thePattern = qd.gray;

FillOval( &theRect, thePattern );
```

The first parameter to FillOval() is a pointer to a Rect variable that holds the boundaries of the oval to fill. The coordinates of the rectangle should have previously been established by a call to SetRect(). The second parameter is the pattern with which to fill the oval. A call to FillOval() has no lasting effect on the current pen fill pattern. After the call to FillOval(), the graphics pen pattern will be the same as it was before the call.

FrameRoundRect( )

To draw the frame of a rectangle that has rounded corners with no fill pattern in the rectangle's interior, call FrameRoundRect():

```
Rect   theRect;
short  theHorizRound = 40;
short  theVertRound  = 40;

FrameRoundRect( &theRect, theHorizRound, theVertRound );
```

The first parameter to FrameRoundRect() is a pointer to a Rect variable that holds the boundaries of the rectangle to frame. The coordinates of the rectangle should have previously been established by a call to SetRect().

The remaining parameters specify the degree of rounding that QuickDraw should apply to the corners of the rectangle. The second parameter is the pixel width of an oval that will be used as a guide for corner rounding. The third parameter is the pixel height of this oval.

PaintRoundRect( )

To paint a round rectangle with whatever pattern is current, call `PaintRoundRect( )`:

```
Rect    theRect;
short   theHorizRound = 50;
short   theVertRound  = 30;

PaintRoundRect( &theRect, theHorizRound, theVertRound );
```

The first parameter to `PaintRoundRect()` is a pointer to a `Rect` variable that holds the boundaries of the rectangle to paint. The coordinates of the rectangle should have previously been established by a call to `SetRect()`. The second parameter is the pixel width of an oval that will be used as a guide for corner rounding. The third parameter is the pixel height of this oval.

FillRoundRect( )

To fill a round rectangle with a pattern of your choosing, call `FillRoundRect( )`:

```
Rect    theRect;
short   theHorizRound = 50;
short   theVertRound  = 50;
Pattern thePattern = qd.white;

FillRoundRect( &theRect, theHorizRound, theVertRound, thePattern );
```

The first parameter to `FillRoundRect()` is a pointer to a `Rect` variable that holds the boundaries of the rectangle to fill. The coordinates of the rectangle should have previously been established by a call to `SetRect()`. The second parameter is the pixel width of an oval that will be used as a guide for corner rounding. The third parameter is the pixel height of this oval. The last parameter is the pattern that is to be used to fill the round rectangle. A call to `FillRoundRect()` has no lasting effect on the current pen fill pattern.

DRAWING TEXT

Text is drawn to a window much as a line is: The graphics pen is positioned at a starting location, and then a QuickDraw function is called to do the drawing.

DrawString( )

To draw one or more characters of text to a window, call `DrawString()`:

```
Str255 theString = "\pI'm no dummy!";

DrawString( theString );
```

The parameter to `DrawString()` is a string of up to 255 characters. This string should be prefaced with \p and then enclosed in quotations.

5 Events

W hen the user performs an action, such as pressing a key on the keyboard, the Macintosh system notes this action. It also keeps track of auxiliary event information: the circumstances at the time of this action, such as the state of the mouse button; the time the event occurred; the location of the cursor at the moment the action took place; and so on. In Macintosh programming, an action such as a keystroke is referred to as an *event*. Because Macintosh programs wait for events to occur and then react, Mac applications are said to be event-driven.

This chapter describes the details of events and the auxiliary information that accompanies each event. It also shows you how to process events — how to respond to events of different types. If you write programs that watch for, and appropriately handle, different types of events, your applications become event-driven.

The Event Record

In Chapter 1 you were introduced to events, actions to which a Macintosh program responds. The click of the mouse button and the press of a key are examples of events.

EVENTS AND THE QUEUE

When an event occurs, a Macintosh program captures it and saves information about the event in an *event record*. That event record is then stored in an *event queue*. By storing information about an event in a queue, a program is able to take note of, and respond to, more than one event. The importance of the event queue is most noticeable when a program needs to respond to multiple mouse-button presses. When the user double-clicks the mouse button, two mouse-down events occur sequentially.

THE EVENTRECORD DATA TYPE

To store information about a single event, Apple defines the EventRecord data structure:

```
struct EventRecord
{
    MacOSEventKind        what;
    UInt32                message;
    UInt32                when;
    Point                 where;
    MacOSEventModifiers   modifiers;
};
```

Your program can declare an EventRecord variable to hold information about one event:

```
EventRecord    theEvent;
```

After filling this variable with information about an event, any of the EventRecord members can be accessed using the dot operator:

```
Point   thePoint;
thePoint = theEvent.where;
```

Chapter 1 introduced the mechanism for filling an event record, the Toolbox routine WaitNextEvent(). You'll see that routine later in this chapter.

The what field

The first field of the EventRecord, the what field, describes the type of the event. Events are often triggered by user actions, such as the user clicking the mouse button. Events can also occur as the byproduct of user actions. For example, if the user clicks the mouse on an inactive window (a window that lies behind another window), several events occur. The obvious type of event that results from this action is a mouse-down event, the direct result of the user's click of the mouse button. Less obvious may be the other two events that occur: an activate event and an update event. When the hidden window gets clicked, it is activated: Its highlighting changes to show that it is now the frontmost window. Additionally, the window needs to be updated; its contents need to be redrawn.

The what field is defined to be of the MacOSEventKind data type. Looking at the definitions provided below you can see that this data type translates to an unsigned short, a 2-byte type with a range of 0 to 65,535:

```
typedef  UInt16  MacOSEventKind;
typedef  unsigned  short  UInt16;
```

If the MacOSEventKind data type is identical to the unsigned short type, then why bother to define it? Why not declare the what field of the EventRecord to be an unsigned short? Because that would be too easy! Seriously, the additional, apparently unnecessary data types that you'll encounter in your studies of Macintosh programming do have a purpose. They exist to make more obvious the purpose of certain variables and structure fields. For example, if the what field of the EventRecord was defined to be an unsigned short, little information about its purpose would be conveyed to you. On the other hand, by calling this field a MacOSEventKind, the purpose of the what field becomes readily apparent. As you read through this book, and as you study the universal header files that came with your development environment, you'll encounter many more such self-explanatory data types.

While the definition of the what field as a MacOSEventKind type makes it possible for there to be over 65,000 event types, Apple has thankfully defined only a handful:

```
nullEvent     =  0    // no other event occurred
mouseDown     =  1    // mouse button clicked
mouseUp       =  2    // mouse button released
keyDown       =  3    // key pressed
keyUp         =  4    // key released
autoKey       =  5    // key pressed and held down
updateEvt     =  6    // contents of a window need to be redrawn
diskEvt       =  7    // floppy disk has been inserted
activateEvt   =  8    // window has been activated or deactivated
osEvt         = 15    // operating system related event
```

The following snippet hints at how the what field can be used by a program as it determines what action should be taken:

```
EventRecord theEvent;
if ( theEvent.what == mouseDown )
    // handle a click of the mouse
```

In this chapter you will see how a program can watch for, and react to, the mouseDown and keyDown event types. Subsequent chapters will demonstrate how programs can work with some of the other types.

The message field

The what field of an EventRecord gives your program the overall view of what just took place in the program, but it provides no specifics. For instance, if the what field has a value of keyDown, your program knows that the user just pressed a key on the keyboard. But the what field doesn't tell your program which key was pressed. For that information, your program will look to the message field of the same EventRecord.

As you've just read, the keyDown event uses the message field to hold information about which key was pressed. Different event types use the message field to hold different supplemental information. The updateEvt uses this field to hold a pointer to the window that needs updating. The activateEvt uses the message field to hold a pointer to the window that needs activating or deactivating. Some event types, such as the mouseDown event, don't use the message field.

Chapter 6 describes the particulars of how the message field can be used to find out which key was pressed. Chapter 7 discusses the message field as it relates to update events and activate events.

The message field is declared to be of the UInt32 type. This data type is identical to the unsigned long type. As such, it can hold a value greater than 4 billion. More important than this, though, is the fact that this data type occupies 4 bytes. In Macintosh programming, a pointer always occupies 4 bytes. Because the message field at times holds a pointer, the UInt32 data type is the appropriate choice:

```
typedef unsigned long UInt32;
```

The when field

The when field holds the time at which an event occurred. This time is given in the number of ticks, or 60th seconds, since system startup. For example, a when value of 36000 would mean the event occurred 10 minutes after the user started his or her Mac (60 ticks in 1 second, 600 ticks in 10 seconds, 3,600 ticks in 1 minute, 36,000 ticks in 10 minutes). While this information on its own may be of little use to your program, the time between the occurrence of events may be. If your program needs to know the time between mouse-clicks, for instance, it would save the what value at each click of the mouse and then compare that value to the time at which the previous mouse-click occurred. The following snippet could be used in a program that watches for mouse-clicks that occur more than 2 seconds apart:

```
#define      kTooLongTimeTicks     120      // 2 seconds
EventRecord  theEvent;
UInt32       oldTime;
UInt32       currentTime;
if ( theEvent.what == mouseDown )
{
   oldTime = currentTime;
   currentTime = theEvent.what;
   if ( ( currentTime - oldTime ) > kTooLongTimeTicks )
      // handle case of too much time between mouse clicks
}
```

The where field

The where field of an EventRecord holds the pixel location of the cursor at the time an event occurs. Like most EventRecord fields, the where field has greater significance for some event types than for others. For example, the value of the where field is important if the event is a mouseDown event; the location of the cursor indicates which menu was clicked on if the user is making a menu selection, for example.

The where field is of type Point. A Point is a structure with two members, the vertical screen coordinate of the cursor at the time of the event and the horizontal screen coordinate at that time:

```
struct  Point
{
   short  v;
   short  h;
};
```

It's important to realize that the `where` field holds the *global* cursor coordinate, not the *local* coordinate. This means that if the cursor is over a window when the event occurs, the coordinates will be specified relative to the user's screen, not to the window. This chapter's EventBranch example program provides the details of converting the coordinates of a pixel from values global to the screen to values local to a window.

The modifiers field

The `modifiers` field of an `EventRecord` lets your program know which modifier keys were pressed at the time of the event. It also holds the state of the mouse button when the event occurred. A *modifier key* is one that changes, or modifies, the character that is typed when a key is pressed. The Command, Shift, Caps Lock, Option, and Control keys are all modifier keys.

The `modifiers` field is of type `MacOSEventModifiers`. As shown below, this data type is defined to be the same as an `unsigned short`:

```
typedef  UInt16  MacOSEventModifiers;
typedef  unsigned  short  UInt16;
```

More important than the range of values that `modifiers` can hold is its size, 2 bytes. The system uses individual bits in these 2 bytes to hold *flags*, two-state values that are toggled on or off. Six of these 16 bits are unused, while each of the other 10 has an Apple-defined constant that indicates what the bit is used to keep track of:

```
activeFlag      = 0x0001     // bit 0 of low byte
btnState        = 0x0080     // bit 7 of low byte
cmdKey          = 0x0100     // bit 0 of high byte
shiftKey        = 0x0200     // bit 1 of high byte
alphaLock       = 0x0400     // bit 2 of high byte
optionKey       = 0x0800     // bit 3 of high byte
controlKey      = 0x1000     // bit 4 of high byte
rightShiftKey   = 0x2000     // bit 5 of high byte
rightOptionKey  = 0x4000     // bit 6 of high byte
rightControlKey = 0x8000     // bit 7 of high byte
```

To determine if a modifier key was pressed at the time of the event or to see if the mouse button was up or down at that time, you can use one of the above Apple-defined constants as a *mask*. A mask is used to ignore all bit values except the one in question. In the following snippet the `cmdKey` constant is used as a mask to check to see if the `modifiers` field indicates that the Command key was pressed at the time of the event:

```
if ( theEvent.modifiers & cmdKey )
   // handle case of command key being pressed at time of event
```

The above snippet performs an AND operation using the value of `modifiers` and the value of `cmdKey`. If the bit indicated by the `cmdKey` constant is turned on in modifiers, the result of the `if` statement will be `true` and the code beneath it will execute. Chapter 6 gives an example of the use of the `modifiers` field when determining if the user made a menu selection using the Command key rather than the mouse.

Capturing Events

In order to be aware of user actions, a Macintosh program must constantly be on the lookout for the occurrence of an event. When an event does occur, the program must capture it. That is, it needs to store the infor-mation about the event and then continue with its watch for other events.

THE WAITNEXTEVENT() FUNCTION

The system is always aware of any event that occurs. When an event takes place, the system stores information about it in an event queue. By calling the Toolbox routine `WaitNextEvent()` your program can make a request to the system for that information:

```
EventRecord  theEvent;
WaitNextEvent( everyEvent, &theEvent, 15L, nil );
```

The first parameter to `WaitNextEvent()` is a mask that tells the system which types of events your program is interested in. Typically, the Apple-defined constant `everyEvent` is used here to tell the system to return information about any event that occurred. After that, the program will determine which events to handle and which should be ignored. While your programs will normally use `everyEvent`, other Apple-defined constants are available:

```
mDownMask          = 0x0002    // mouse button pressed
mUpMask            = 0x0004    // mouse button released
keyDownMask        = 0x0008    // key pressed
keyUpMask          = 0x0010    // key released
autoKeyMask        = 0x0020    // key repeatedly held down
updateMask         = 0x0040    // window needs updating
diskMask           = 0x0080    // disk inserted
activMask          = 0x0100    // activate/deactivate window
highLevelEventMask = 0x0400    // AppleEvents
osMask             = 0x8000    // operating system events
everyEvent         = 0xFFFF    // all of the above
```

If your program was only interested in mouse-down events (events of type `mouseDown`), then it could pass the `mDownMask` to `WaitNextEvent()`:

```
WaitNextEvent( mDownMask, &theEvent, 15L, nil );
```

The second parameter to `WaitNextEvent()` is a pointer to an `EventRecord`. When the execution of `WaitNextEvent()` is complete, the system will have filled in this `EventRecord` with information about the next event that was in the event queue.

A well-behaved Macintosh program should consider that the user may be running other applications at the same time. When these other programs are running in the background, they should be given the opportunity to carry out any processing tasks when your program is idle. For example, consider a graphics program that is performing complex calculations in order to render a three-dimensional object. If the user clicks on a window in your program to bring your application to the front, and to send the graphics program to the background, your application should allow the graphics program to continue its processing. The third parameter to `WaitNextEvent()` lets your program do just that.

The third parameter to `WaitNextEvent()` is called a *sleep value*. The sleep value specifies how much processing time your program is willing to give up to other applications. If your application specifies a nonzero sleep time and there are no events to process, the system will execute other running applications. When the sleep time has been reached, the system will return to the processing of your application. If your program receives an event (such as a click on one of its windows or a press of a key) while the system is processing a different application, that processing will be interrupted and the system will return to your application. In this way the system can update all running applications while still giving your program a priority status. The sleep value is given in ticks, or 60th seconds. Because this parameter is of type long, you'll append an uppercase *L* to the sleep value to force it to occupy the 4 bytes of the long data type.

The final parameter to `WaitNextEvent()` specifies a region of the screen and is used only by applications that change the look of the cursor as it moves to different areas of the screen. By passing a value of `nil` for this parameter you'll tell `WaitNextEvent()` to leave the cursor in its present state, no matter where it is moved on the screen.

PROCESSING EVENTS USING WAITNEXTEVENT()

A program cannot, of course, foresee when an event will occur. So rather than attempting to time the calling of `WaitNextEvent()` to the occurrence of an event, a program instead continuously calls the function. The call to `WaitNextEvent()` is placed inside a loop, so the function will be executed thousands and thousands of times during the running of a program. Because events happen only occasionally, most of these calls to `WaitNextEvent()` will result in an `EventRecord` that has a `what` field value of 0, or `nullEvent`. When an event of a type that your program is interested in handling finally does occur, your application can handle it from within a `switch` statement, as in this snippet:

```
for (;;)
{
   WaitNextEvent( everyEvent, &theEvent, 15L, nil );
   switch ( theEvent.what )
   {
      case mouseDown:
         ExitToShell();
         break;
   }
}
```

The above snippet is from the IntroProgram example found in Chapter 1. The above event loop uses a `for` statement with no conditions — a `for` loop that will run infinitely unless some action within the loop body terminates it. In this example, that action is a call to the Toolbox function `ExitToShell()`.

When the user clicks the mouse button, the system will recognize the action as an event. The next time WaitNextEvent() is called, an event record with the information about the mouse-down event will be waiting in the event queue. That information will be placed in the EventRecord variable theEvent and returned to the program. The first thing the program should do with this information is examine the what field to determine the type of the event. The switch statement in the above example does this.

The event loop's switch statement can handle any number of event types — the process of handling events is based on the requirements of the program. The following snippet outlines how an event loop would process each event type. The snippet also replaces the loop's for statement with a while statement and adds a global Boolean variable named gDone. Somewhere in the program's code, gDone will be set to true. When that happens, the last pass through the event loop will have been made — the next time the while statement is encountered, the comparison of gDone to false will fail, and the loop, and program, will end. As demonstrated in Chapter 6, it is usually in response to a user's selection of the Quit menu item from the File menu that gDone gets set to true:

```
Boolean  gDone = false;
...
...
while ( gDone == false )
{
    WaitNextEvent( everyEvent, &theEvent, 15L, nil );

    switch ( theEvent.what )
    {
        case mouseDown:
            // handle a click of the mouse button
        case mouseUp:
            // handle a release of the mouse button
        case keyDown:
            // handle a press of a keyboard key
        case keyUp:
            // handle a release of a keyboard key
        case autoKey:
            // handle a keyboard key that is held down
        case updateEvt:
            // handle the redrawing of a window's contents
        case diskEvt:
            // handle a disk inserted into a drive
```

```
        case activateEvt:
            // handle the activation or deactivation of a window
        case osEvt:
            // handle an operating system event
    }
}
```

EXAMPLE PROGRAM: EVENTSINTRO

The EventsIntro program displays a small window like the one pictured in
Figure 5-1. If you press any key, the words "Key pressed" will appear within
the framed rectangle. After a fraction of a second, the words will disappear.
To quit the program, click the mouse button.

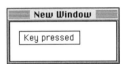

Figure 5-1

The result of running the EventsIntro program.

EventsIntro uses a call to `WaitNextEvent()` in its event loop. If the
returned event is of type `mouseDown` or `keyDown`, the program handles it.
Any other event type will be ignored:

```
//_____
#define      rDisplayWindow      128
//_____
Boolean  gDone = false;
Rect     gEraseRect;
//_____
void  main( void )
{
    WindowPtr    theWindow;
    EventRecord  theEvent;
    long         theLong;
    InitializeToolbox();

    theWindow = GetNewWindow( rDisplayWindow, nil, (WindowPtr)-1L );
    SetPort( theWindow );
    SetRect( &gEraseRect, 10, 10, 100, 30 );
```

```
       FrameRect( &gEraseRect );
       InsetRect( &gEraseRect, 1, 1 );
       while ( gDone == false )
       {
          WaitNextEvent( everyEvent, &theEvent, 15L, nil );

          switch ( theEvent.what )
          {
       case mouseDown:
                 gDone = true;
                 break;

            case keyDown:
                MoveTo( gEraseRect.left + 6, gEraseRect.bottom - 5 );
                DrawString( "\pKey pressed" );
                Delay( 60, &theLong );
                FillRect( &gEraseRect, &qd.white );
                break;
          }
       }
   }
```

As you read through this book you'll notice that most of the example programs *don't* include an event loop. Keep in mind that each example is written with the purpose of demonstrating a single topic. To keep each example short and to the point (and to eliminate source code that doesn't deal with the topic at hand), features that are standard to any complete Macintosh application have been omitted.

THE EVENT LOOP AND FUNCTIONS

You'll find that most Macintosh programs use the event loop's `switch` statement as a "branching station." Rather than include within the `case` labels all of the code that handles an event, calls to application-defined functions are made. These application-defined functions then hold the code used to handle each type of event. For the EventsIntro program, which handles `mouseDown` and `keyDown` events, the `switch` body would look like the one shown in this snippet:

```
switch ( theEvent.what )
{
   case mouseDown:
      HandleMouseDown( theEvent );
      break;
```

```
        case keyDown:
           HandleKeyDown( theEvent );
           break;
     }
```

Most programs also make the event loop itself an application-defined routine. This routine is then called once from main(). You can see from the following example that this approach makes the event loop function one that can be copied and pasted between applications, with little or no modification necessary. Figure 5-2 shows the program's flow of control when this technique is used:

```
void  EventLoop( void )
{
   EventRecord   theEvent;

   while ( gDone == false )
   {
      WaitNextEvent( everyEvent, &theEvent, 15L, nil );

      switch ( theEvent.what )
      {
         case mouseDown:
            HandleMouseDown( theEvent );
            break;
         case keyDown:
            HandleKeyDown( theEvent );
            break;
      }
   }
}
```

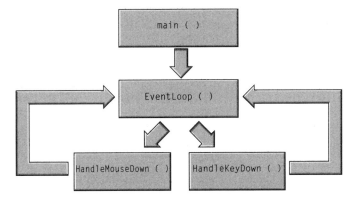

Figure 5-2
The flow of control for a program that handles mouseDown *and* keyDown *events.*

EXAMPLE PROGRAM: EVENTBRANCH

When executed, the EventBranch program looks just like the EventsIntro application, as evidenced in Figure 5-3. The difference lies in the layout of the code and the handling of the `mouseDown` event type. When the user clicks the mouse button outside the framed rectangle in the window, those clicks will be ignored. Only when the cursor is over the "Key pressed" rectangle when the mouse is clicked will the program quit.

Figure 5-3
The result of running the EventBranch program.

The EventBranch resource

Figure 5-4 shows the `WIND` resource used in the EventBranch project. This resource (and resource file) is identical to the one used for this chapter's EventsIntro project. As you look at the figure, take note of the values in the Top and Left edit boxes — they'll be discussed next.

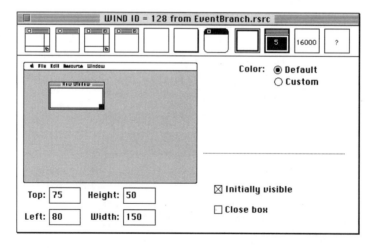

Figure 5-4
The `WIND` resource used by the EventBranch project.

Global coordinates, local coordinates, and EventBranch

Earlier in this chapter it was mentioned that the where field of an EventRecord holds the global cursor location at the time of the event. The global location is the pixel point in terms of where on the screen the cursor is located. This is opposed to the local location, which is the point in terms of a window's coordinate system. Figure 5-5 shows that the top left of the screen has a coordinate of (0, 0), as does the top left of a window, regardless of where the window is located on the screen.

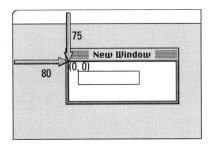

Figure 5-5
Both the screen and a window have their own coordinate systems.

The EventBranch program responds to a mouse-click only if it occurs in the framed rectangle in the program's window. For the program to determine if a mouse-click occurs in this area, it must know the cursor location at the time of the click. This needs to be known in terms of the window's coordinate system. The starting place for finding this information is the where field of the EventRecord. Consider a mouse-click that occurs near the center of the window's rectangle, as shown in the top screen of Figure 5-6. This figure shows the horizontal and vertical pixel values that would be returned in the EventRecord where field, the where.h and where.v values, given that the location of the window is as shown back in Figure 5-5.

To convert a global point to a point local to a window, call the Toolbox function GlobalToLocal(). This routine accepts a pointer to a variable of type Point. When the function has completed, the parameter will have been converted to coordinates local to the current window (the window named in the most recent call to SetPort()):

```
GlobalToLocal( &(theEvent.where) );
```

The bottom screen shown in Figure 5-6 illustrates that after a call to GlobalToLocal(), the cursor point coordinates will have changed from (140, 100) to (60, 25).

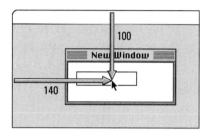

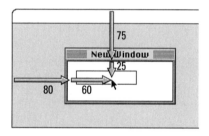

Figure 5-6
A point in global coordinates and that same point in local coordinates.

Once a point has been converted to local coordinates, it can be used in Toolbox routines that expect a point to be in this coordinate system. An example is the function PtInRect(), which is used in the EventBranch program:

```
if ( PtInRect( theEvent.where, &gEraseRect ) )
```

In the above line of code PtInRect() is called within an if statement. PtInRect() returns a value of true if the point named in the first parameter lies in the rectangle named in the second parameter and false if it isn't. If the mouse-click occurred while the cursor was over the framed rectangle, PtInRect() will return true, and the body of the if statement will execute.

In EventBranch, the body of the `if` simply sets the global `Boolean` variable `gDone` to `true` to signal the end of the event loop and the end of the program:

```
if ( PtInRect( theEvent.where, &gEraseRect ) )
    gDone = true;
```

A look at the fields of an EventRecord

Figure 5-7 is a screen dump of the Metrowerks debugger. The screen snapshot was taken after the mouse button was clicked in the window of the EventBranch program. If you use a Symantec compiler, you can run EventBranch with the Symantec debugger on, set a breakpoint near the `mouseDown` case label, and generate a window that holds similar information.

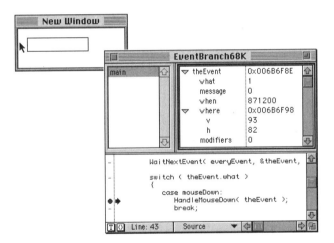

Figure 5-7
The fields of an `EventRecord` as displayed in the Metrowerks debugger.

Figure 5-7 gives you an idea of the values you might find in an `EventRecord` structure when an event occurs. Starting at the top of the debugger window you can see that the value of the `theEvent` is an address. Variable `theEvent` is a structure and as such has no value other than its address, which is provided by the debugger. The individual members of a structure have values, and they are listed underneath `theEvent`.

The first `EventRecord` member, the `what` field, has a value of 1. Referring back to the list of Apple-defined constants used to denote event types, you'll see that the `mouseDown` event type is defined to have a value of 1, as expected.

The next `EventRecord` member, the `message` field, is undefined for a `mouseDown` event — the system adds no supplemental information to the `message` field when the user clicks the mouse button.

The `when` field of the `EventRecord` has a value of 871,200 ticks. Because there are always 60 ticks to 1 second, this value is equivalent to 4 hours and 2 minutes (that's the number of ticks divided by 60 ticks per second, divided by 60 seconds per minute, divided by 60 minutes per hour). That's the amount of time that elapsed since this Macintosh was started and this `mouseDown` event occurred. The EventBranch program doesn't make use of the information found in the `when` field.

The `where` field is of type `Point`, a structure with two members. The value of the `v` member, 93, is the vertical pixel coordinate at which the cursor was when the event occurred. Looking at Figure 5-7 you can see that it looks as if the arrow cursor is perhaps about 15 pixels from the top of the content area of the window. In fact, it is exactly 18 pixels from the top. The reason the `where.v` value is 93 is that this where member returns the pixel coordinates in global values, as discussed earlier. Because the `WIND` resource defines the top of the window to be 75 pixels from the top of the screen, the global vertical pixel value is 93. The same explanation applies to the `where.h` value. The window content area starts 80 pixels from the left edge of the screen. The cursor was just a couple of pixels in from the left edge of the window, so its horizontal coordinate is 82. When these two global coordinate values are converted to local coordinates, they'll represent the pixel (2, 18).

The last `EventRecord` member, the `modifiers` field, holds information about the mouse and modifier keys at the time of the event. Because no modifier keys were down at the time of the event and because the mouse button *was* down, the `modifiers` field has a value of 0. If this had been a `mouseUp` event, the `modifiers` field would have the value of the Apple-defined constant `btnState`, or 128. As described earlier in this chapter, `btnState` has a hexadecimal value of 0x0080, which is decimal 128.

The EventBranch source code listing

The following is the listing for the EventBranch example. You'll find that it follows the style discussed earlier; it has an application-defined event loop function and application-defined routines that each handle one type of event:

```
//_____
#define       rDisplayWindow       128
//_____
Boolean  gDone = false;
Rect      gEraseRect;
//_____
void  main( void )
{
   WindowPtr    theWindow;

   InitializeToolbox();

   theWindow = GetNewWindow( rDisplayWindow, nil, (WindowPtr)-1L );
   SetPort( theWindow );
   SetRect( &gEraseRect, 10, 10, 100, 30 );
   FrameRect( &gEraseRect );
   InsetRect( &gEraseRect, 1, 1 );

   EventLoop();
}
//_____
void  EventLoop( void )
{
   EventRecord  theEvent;

   while ( gDone == false )
   {
      WaitNextEvent( everyEvent, &theEvent, 15L, nil );

      switch ( theEvent.what )
      {
         case mouseDown:
            HandleMouseDown( theEvent );
            break;
         case keyDown:
            HandleKeyDown();
            break;
      }
   }
}
//_____
void  HandleMouseDown( EventRecord theEvent )
```

```
{
    GlobalToLocal( &(theEvent.where) );

    if ( PtInRect( theEvent.where, &gEraseRect ) )
        gDone = true;
}
//_____
void  HandleKeyDown( void )
{
    long  theLong;
    MoveTo( gEraseRect.left + 6, gEraseRect.bottom - 5 );
    DrawString( "\pKey pressed" );
    Delay( 60, &theLong );
    FillRect( &gEraseRect, &qd.white );
}
```

Event Reference

This section summarizes the Toolbox functions used when working with events.

THE EVENT RECORD DATA TYPE

Information about an event is held in an event record, the format of which is defined by the EventRecord data type.

EventRecord

The EventRecord is the data structure used to hold the data for a single event:

```
struct EventRecord
{
    MacOSEventKind       what;
    UInt32               message;
    UInt32               when;
    Point                where;
    MacOSEventModifiers  modifiers;
};
```

The what field is of the MacOSEventKind data type, a 2-byte data type. It is used to hold a number that corresponds to an event type. The message field is of the type UInt32, a 4-byte data type. The message field holds supplemental information particular to the event type. The when field is a 4-byte field that tells when the event occurred. The where member holds the horizontal and vertical pixel coordinates for the cursor at the time the event occurred. The modifiers field is of type MacOSEventModifiers, a 2-byte data type. This field is used to hold information about the state of the mouse button (up or down) and information about any modifier keys (Command, Shift, and so on) that were pressed at the time of the event.

RECEIVING EVENT INFORMATION

The system holds events in an event queue. Your program needs to retrieve event information from this queue in order to determine what actions have taken place.

WaitNextEvent( )

To get information about the most recent event, call WaitNextEvent( ):

```
#define         rMyWindow    128
MacOSEventMask  theMask   = everyEvent;
EventRecord     theEvent;
UInt32          theSleep  = 15L;
RgnHandle       theRegion = nil;
WaitNextEvent( theMask, &theEvent, theSleep, theRegion );
```

The first parameter to WaitNextEvent( ) is an event mask that tells the function which types of events should be retrieved. In most programs you'll use the Apple-defined constant everyEvent and then let your program handle only those types that make sense to your application. The second parameter is an EventRecord that will hold the event information returned by WaitNextEvent( ). The third parameter is a sleep value — the amount of time (in ticks, or 60th seconds) that your program is willing to relinquish to other applications. The final parameter is used when setting up screen regions in which the cursor will change its look.

GlobalToLocal( )

The `GlobalToLocal()` function has been used in this chapter, though it isn't specifically an event-related routine.

To transform a point from global screen coordinates to coordinates local to the current window, call `GlobalToLocal()`. The one parameter to `GlobalToLocal()` is the `Point` to translate:

```
Point  thePoint;
thePoint.h = 100;
thePoint.v = 140;
GlobalToLocal( &thePoint );
```

6

Menus

*S*ince its appearance more than a decade ago, the Macintosh
graphical user interface has served as the model of user-friendly
computing. Menus may be the single most important element of the
Mac's easy-to-use interface. Menus eliminate the need to memorize
numerous commands and provide uniformity among all Macintosh
programs. All but the simplest test applications should allow access to
menus from the menu bar that appears at the top of the screen.

In this chapter, you will learn how to use a resource editor to
define the menu items, or commands, that you want to have appear in
each menu of a program. As you create each new menu item, you'll
be able to assign a ⌘-key equivalent to it. That is, you can designate a
key that, when pressed in conjunction with the ⌘ key, executes the
menu item as if it had been selected from the menu using the mouse.
A resource editor is also used to list the order in which menus will be
displayed in an application's menu bar.

After reading how to set up your program's menus and menu bar
in a resource editor, you'll discover how your program can watch for a
mouse-click and then determine if that click involves the menu bar or
a menu in it. If an event is menu-related, the material in this chapter
will show you how to handle the tasks necessary to properly respond
to a menu selection.

Menu Resources

Menus, and the menu bar that holds menus, are defined using a
resource editor. Creating menus in this graphical way makes for the
easy addition of a new menu or editing of an existing menu.

THE MENU RESOURCE

The menu items, or commands, that appear in a menu are listed in a resource of type MENU. Each menu in your program's menu bar will be defined by a MENU resource. Thus, a program that has only three menus (the Apple, File, and Edit menus, for example) in its menu bar will have three MENU resources.

Both ResEdit and Resorcerer make it easy for you to create MENU resources in your project's resource file. If you use ResEdit, the MENU-creating steps are listed just ahead. If Resorcerer is your resource editor, follow these steps:

STEPS: USING RESORCERER

Step 1. Click the New button in the File Window (the main window that lists the resource types).

Step 2. Scroll to the MENU type in the list and double-click it, or type **MENU** (in uppercase) in the edit box and click the Create button.

Step 3. Type the menu name in the top edit box, or click the button if the menu is to serve as the Apple menu.

Step 4. Select New Item from the Menu menu.

Step 5. Type in the item name, or click the Divider button if the item is to serve as a dashed line.

Step 6. Repeat steps 4 and 5 for each menu item.

Figure 6-1 shows a MENU resource that is being worked on in the Menu Editor of Resorcerer. In this figure you can see that the MENU resource will be used to define the File menu and also that the name of the Quit menu item is being typed in.

Apple refers to the Apple, File, and Edit menus as the three standard menus. They're considered standard because every Macintosh program is expected to include them. The Apple menu allows access to the items in the user's Apple Menu Items folder. The File menu lets the user quit the application (it should minimally contain the Quit command). The Edit menu allows editing. Even if your program doesn't support editing, it should still include the Edit menu — the user expects to see it in a Mac application.

You'll notice that the example programs in other chapters don't include these three menus — or, more likely, any menus at all! Keep in mind that the examples aren't meant to be full-featured Mac programs. Instead, they exist to provide a working example of a single topic.

If you come across a resource file that was created by a resource editor that you don't have, don't be alarmed. Resorcerer can open and work with ResEdit files, and ResEdit can open and work with Resorcerer files. Launch your resource editor, and then use the Open command from the File menu to open the file.

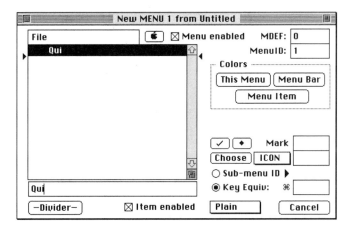

Figure 6-1
Using Resorcerer to create a MENU resource.

If you use ResEdit rather than Resorcerer, follow these steps to create a new MENU resource:

STEPS: USING RESEDIT

Step 1. Select Create New Resource from the Resource menu.

Step 2. Scroll to the MENU type in the list and double-click it, or type **MENU** (in uppercase) in the edit box and click the OK button.

Step 3. Type the menu name in the edit box, or click the ⬛ (Apple menu) radio button if the menu is to serve as the Apple menu.

Step 4. Select Create New Item from the Resource menu.

Step 5. Type in the item name, or click the separator line radio button if the item is to serve as a dashed line.

Step 6. Repeat steps 4 and 5 for each menu item.

Figure 6-2 shows a MENU resource that is being worked on in the Menu Editor of ResEdit. In this figure you can see that the MENU resource will be used to define the File menu. Figure 6-3 shows the same resource as an item is being added to it; you can see that the name of the Quit menu item is being typed in.

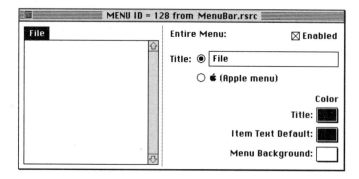

Figure 6-2
Using ResEdit to create a MENU resource.

Creating a MENU for the Apple menu

A MENU resource lists all the items that will appear in a menu. That's true for all application menus — except the Apple menu. The menu items that appear in an application's Apple menu vary from computer to computer. That's because this special menu holds the names of all the items in the user's Apple Menu Items folder.

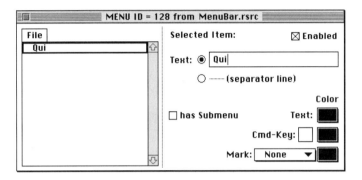

Figure 6-3
Using ResEdit to add a menu item to a MENU reso urce.

If you haven't already done so, launch ResEdit. Select New from the File menu to create a new resource file. Because the majority of programmers use ResEdit, and because ResEdit is often distributed without any documentation, the remaining figures will show the MENU resource as viewed in ResEdit. If you use Resorcerer, refer to the extensive MENU resource information listed in that product's documentation.

If you name the new resource file MenuBar.rsrc, your resource editor windows will match the ones shown in the following figures. Not only that, but you'll be creating the resource file used in this chapter's first example!

To create the Apple menu's MENU resource, begin by selecting Create New Resource from the Resource menu of ResEdit. Type in **MENU** and then click the OK button. When the ResEdit Menu Editor opens, click the radio button in the MENU resource, as shown in Figure 6-4. That designates that the menu's title be the symbol.

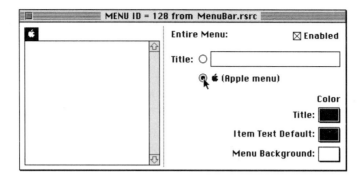

Figure 6-4
Using ResEdit to create a MENU resource to be used for the Apple menu.

The Apple menu can have any number of menu items preceding the names of the items that are in the user's Apple Menu Items folder. Typically an application will have just two items, an About item and a dashed line. Select Create New Item from the Resource menu to add the first item. Then type **About...** in the Menu Editor edit box (see Figure 6-5).

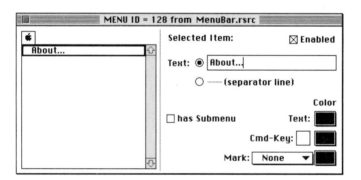

Figure 6-5
Using ResEdit to add a menu item to the Apple MENU resource.

Again select Create New Item from the Resource menu to add a second item to the Apple menu. After you do that, click the separator line radio button, as shown in Figure 6-6. Any menu item in any menu can be turned into a dashed line by clicking this radio button in the Menu Editor.

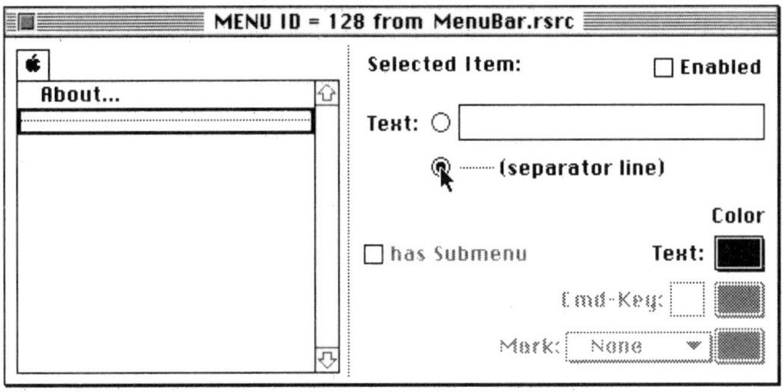

Figure 6-6
Using ResEdit to add a dashed line menu item to the Apple MENU *resource.*

Because there is no way of knowing what programs, folders, and control panels users will have in their Apple Menu Items folder, there's no way these menu items can be listed in a MENU resource. Instead, they'll be added from within the source code, as you'll see later in this chapter. That means that the Apple menu MENU resource is now complete. If you look at the end of the ResEdit menu bar at the top of the screen, you'll see that ResEdit has added your new menu. ResEdit does this so you can see how your new menu will look in an application. While it won't be a functional version of the menu, it will give you a chance to see if it provides the look you want. After looking at the demo menu, click the close box in the title bar of the Menu Editor. When you do, you'll see the new menu in a window that displays all of the MENU resources in your resource file. As shown in Figure 6-7, at this point you'll have just a single MENU resource.

Creating a MENU for the File menu

The preceding section demonstrated how to create the MENU resource used for the Apple menu, the one menu that has a format different from all other menus in a program. In this section you'll create a MENU resource for a File menu. Once you know how to create and edit this MENU resource, you will know the technique for creating a MENU resource for any menu your program might employ.

To begin, select Create New Resource from the Resource menu of ResEdit. Then type in the title for the menu (type **File** if you want to match the book's example). Next, select Create New Item from the Resource menu to add the first item. You can type in any name for this first menu item. If you want your resource to match the one pictured in Figure 6-8, type **Play System Alert.**

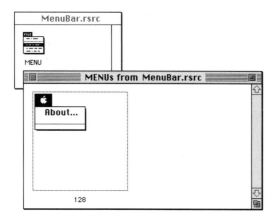

Figure 6-7
The completed Apple MENU resource, as viewed in ResEdit.

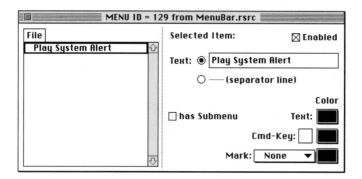

Figure 6-8
Using ResEdit to add a menu item to the File MENU resource.

Select Create New Item from the Resource menu for each additional item you want to have in the menu. In Figure 6-9, a dashed separator line has been added as the second menu item in the File menu. To complete this MENU resource, add a third item and name it Quit.

When you're through with the MENU resource, click the Menu Editor's close box. In Figure 6-10 you can see that the Apple MENU resource has two items and the File MENU resource has three items.

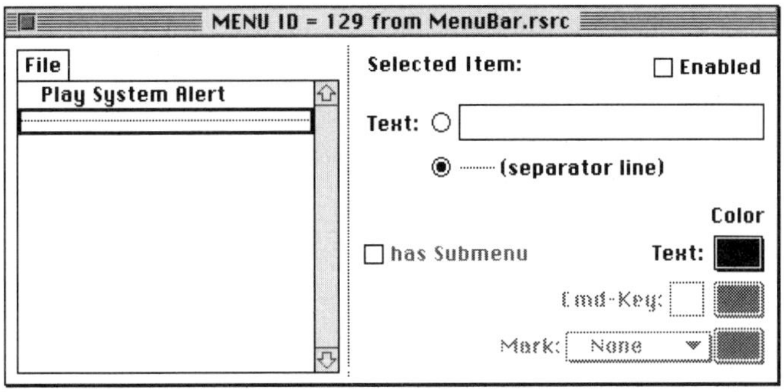

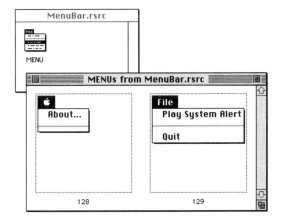

Figure 6-9
Using ResEdit to add a dashed line menu item to the File MENU *resource.*

Figure 6-10
The completed Apple and File MENU *resources, as viewed in ResEdit.*

MENU IDs and item numbers

When you select Create New Resource from the Resource menu and then create the first MENU resource, ResEdit gives it an ID of 128. Each MENU resource you create after that will be numbered consecutively from that starting value, as you can see by looking back at the IDs of the two MENU resources in Figure 6-10. While a resource editor allows you to change the ID of a MENU resource, it is common practice to use this default numbering system when creating the MENU resources for a project. You'll find that most programs have an Apple MENU resource with an ID of 128, a File MENU resource with an ID of 129, and an Edit MENU resource with an ID of 130. The IDs of MENU resources for a program's application-defined menus (any menu other than the three standard menus just mentioned) then begin at 131.

If you do decide to use a numbering system other than the one used by ResEdit, follow these steps to change the ID of a MENU resource:

STEPS: CHANGING THE ID OF A MENU RESOURCE

Step 1. Select Get Resource Info from the Resource menu.

Step 2. Type in the new MENU resource ID, and then click the close box in the title bar of the dialog box.

Step 3. Select Edit Menu & MDEF ID from the MENU menu.

Step 4. Type in the new MENU resource ID in the Menu ID edit box, and then click the OK button.

As listed in the above steps, when changing a MENU resource ID, you need to enter the new ID in two places. You *must* make both of these changes or your program won't recognize the MENU resource and won't place it in the program's menu bar.

Regardless of the numbering system you use, when you're through creating MENU resources, take note of the ID of each MENU resource. Your application will use the MENU resource IDs when identifying which menu a user clicks on. Your program will also use the numbers of the items in each MENU resource to identify which menu item a user selects. In any MENU resource, the first item is item number 1, the second item is item number 2, and so forth.

As you'll see a little later in this chapter, your source code will define a constant for each MENU resource ID and for each item except dashed separator lines. For the two MENU resources described in this section, those definitions should look something like this:

```
#define    mApple      128
#define    iAbout      1
#define    mFile       129
#define    iPlayAlert  1
#define    iQuit       3
```

The above snippet uses the naming convention of prefacing a MENU constant name with a lowercase *m*. Each MENU item constant name is prefaced with a lowercase *i*. Because clicking a dashed separator line in the menu of an application produces no effect, your project won't define a constant for a separator line MENU item. That explains why there is no #define with a value of 2 under the File menu constants in the above snippet.

THE **MBAR** RESOURCE

A resource file can contain any number of MENU resources, and these resources can be given IDs in no particular sequence. Because of this, a project's resource file should also contain an MBAR resource. The MBAR resource defines which MENU resources will appear in an application's menu bar and in what order.

If you use Resorcerer, follow these steps to create a new MBAR resource and to add the menus that will appear in the menu bar:

STEPS: USING RESORCERER TO CREATE A NEW MBAR RESOURCE

Step 1. Click the New button in the File Window (the main window that lists the resource types).

Step 2. Scroll to the MBAR type in the list and double-click it, or type **MBAR** (in uppercase) in the edit box and click the Create button.

Step 3. Click the New button in the Menu Bar Editor to add a menu to the menu bar.

Step 4. Click the Edit button in the Menu Bar Editor.

Step 5. Type in the ID of the MENU resource that represents the menu to add, and then click the OK button.

Step 6. Repeat steps 4 and 5 for each menu that is to be added to the menu bar.

Figure 6-11 shows the Menu Bar Editor for a menu bar that will hold the two MENU resources created earlier in this chapter. The figure also shows that the resource file for this chapter's first example will hold two resource types: MBAR and MENU.

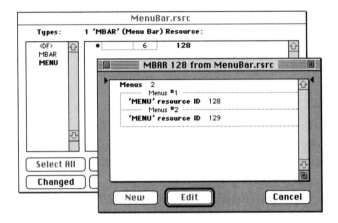

Figure 6-11
Using Resorcerer to create an MBAR resource.

If you use ResEdit, follow the steps listed in the following list to create an MBAR resource and to add menus to it:

STEPS: USING RESEDIT TO CREATE A NEW MBAR RESOURCE

Step 1. Select Create New Resource from the Resource menu.

Step 2. Scroll to the MBAR type in the list and double-click it, or type **MBAR** (in uppercase) in the edit box and click the OK button.

Step 3. Click the row of asterisks in the Menu Bar Editor.

Step 4. Select Insert New Field(s) from the Resource menu.

Step 5. Press the Tab key, and then type in the ID of the MENU resource that should be used for the first menu in the program's menu bar.

Step 6. Repeat steps 4 and 5 for each menu that will appear in the menu bar.

Figure 6-12 shows how the MBAR resource would look for the MENU resources discussed earlier in this chapter. The figure also shows that this chapter's MenuBar example project will use a resource file that holds resources of type MBAR and MENU.

Recall that the Apple MENU resource has an ID of 128, while the File MENU resource has an ID of 129. Placing the number 128 in the first field of the MBAR resource tells the application that uses the resources in this file that the Apple menu should be the first menu (the leftmost menu) in the menu bar. Placing the number 129 in the second field of the MBAR resource tells the application that MENU 129 (the File menu) should be the second menu in the application's menu bar. Both Figures 6-11 and 6-12 show this.

Menu-Handling Source Code

Creating the proper menu-related resources in a project's resource file is the first step of adding menus to your application. Adding menu-handling code to your project's source code is the second and last step.

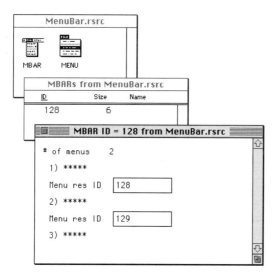

Figure 6-12
Using ResEdit to create a MENU resource.

SETTING UP THE MENU BAR

After your program performs its standard Toolbox initializations, it should set up its menu bar. Here are the steps your program should take to handle this task:

STEPS: SETTING UP A MENU BAR

Step 1. Load the MBAR and MENU resource data into memory and receive a handle to a list of menu information.

Step 2. Specify which MBAR is to be used as the current menu bar.

Step 3. Free the memory referenced by the menu bar list.

Step 4. Get a handle to the MENU resource data for the Apple menu.

Step 5. Append the user's Apple Menu Item folder items to the Apple menu.

Step 6. Draw the menu bar at the top of the screen.

In completing this programming chore, the Toolbox does most of the work. In fact, each of the above six steps is accomplished through a call to a Toolbox function. To begin, the MBAR resource and each of the MENU resources used by the menu bar get loaded by calling the Toolbox function GetNewMBar().

```
#define    mMenuBar    128
Handle     theMenuBar;

theMenuBar = GetNewMBar( rMenuBar );
```

GetNewMBar() expects the resource ID of an MBAR resource as its one parameter. GetNewMBar() loads the data from that resource and from each of the MENU resources named in the MBAR resource. The function then creates a menu list and returns a handle to that list. The menu list holds handles to the data that makes up each menu in the menu bar. After calling GetNewMBar(), specify that the menu list returned by this function be considered the current menu bar.

```
SetMenuBar( theMenuBar );
```

While most programs have only one menu bar, it is possible to write one that is capable of switching from one menu bar to another. A program like that would have more than one MBAR resource. Even if your program has just one menu bar, you'll need to call SetMenuBar(). Pass SetMenuBar() a handle to a menu list and this Toolbox function will mark it as the current menu bar. After this function completes, your program won't have any need for the menu list, so dispose of it by making a call to DisposeHandle(). This function disposes of the memory occupied by the menu list but not the memory occupied by the data loaded from each MENU resource.

```
DisposeHandle( theMenuBar );
```

To work with a specific menu in a menu bar, call the Toolbox function GetMHandle(). This routine returns a handle of type MenuHandle to your program. This handle references the MENU data specified in the function's parameter. The following snippet returns a handle to the Apple menu:

```
#define    mApple    128
MenuHandle theAppleMenu;
theAppleMenu = GetMenuHandle( mApple );
```

Once your program has a handle to a menu, it can make changes to that menu. Later in this chapter you'll see how this handle is used in Toolbox calls that enable or disable a menu item or place a checkmark by a menu item. Here the menu handle is used to add the user's Apple Menu Items folder contents to the Apple menu.

```
MenuHandle theAppleMenu;
AppendResMenu( theAppleMenu, 'DRVR' );
```

The first parameter to the Toolbox function AppendResMenu() is a handle to a menu. The second parameter specifies the type of resources that should be added. For example, a second parameter value of 'FONT' tells AppendResMenu() to add fonts to the menu. In older system versions, desk accessories (driver resources of type 'DRVR') were appended to the Apple menu. More recently, the idea of desk accessories has lost importance. In fact, with the arrival of Copland (System 8), desk accessories will be eliminated altogether. Now, any *desktop object* — that is, any item found in the Apple Menu Items folder — can be added to the Apple menu. For this reason a second parameter value of 'DRVR' is now used to tell AppendResMenu() to search the Apple Menu Items folder and add its contents to the Apple menu.

After all the preceding steps have been taken, it's time to draw the new menu bar to the screen. A call to the Toolbox function DrawMenuBar() takes care of this.

```
DrawMenuBar();
```

DrawMenuBar() uses the information found in the current menu list to draw the menu bar. While your program did make an earlier call to DisposeHandle() to dispose of the handle to this list, the list itself wasn't released from memory.

A Mac program typically takes care of all the menu bar setup tasks in a single function near the start of the program's execution. Such a function is shown here:

```
void SetUpMenuBar( void )
{
   Handle     theMenuBar;
   MenuHandle theAppleMenu;

   theMenuBar = GetNewMBar( rMenuBar );
   SetMenuBar( theMenuBar );
   DisposeHandle( theMenuBar );

   theAppleMenu = GetMenuHandle( mApple );
   AppendResMenu( theAppleMenu, 'DRVR' );
   DrawMenuBar();
}
```

HANDLING A MOUSE-CLICK IN THE MENU BAR

Chapter 5 described how a program watches for, and responds to, events. One of the event types discussed in that chapter is the mouse down event. When WaitNextEvent() encounters a mouse down event in the event queue, the function places the Apple-defined constant mouseDown in the what field of the returned event record. From that chapter's EventBranch program comes an example of an event loop that handles mouseDown events.

```
void EventLoop( void )
{
  EventRecord theEvent;

  while ( gDone == false )
  {
   WaitNextEvent( everyEvent, &theEvent, 15L, nil );

   switch ( theEvent.what )
   {
     case mouseDown:
      HandleMouseDown( theEvent );
      break;
     case keyDown:
      HandleKeyDown( theEvent );
      break;
   }
  }
}
```

Recall that the EventBranch program handled a click of the mouse button by checking to see if the cursor was over a rectangle in the program's window. If it was, the program terminated.

```
void HandleMouseDown( EventRecord theEvent )
{
  GlobalToLocal( &(theEvent.where) );

  if ( PtInRect( theEvent.where, &gEraseRect ) )
   gDone = true;
}
```

The EventBranch version of HandleMouseDown() has the advantage of being a very short function — it's written to show a simplified means of how a mouseDown event could be handled. It has the disadvantage, though, of being able to handle a click of the mouse button in only one way. Now that you're familiar with menus, HandleMouseDown() can be turned into a function that is both less specific and more practical.

```
void HandleMouseDown( EventRecord theEvent )
{
  WindowPtr theWindow;
  short    thePart;
  long     theChoice;

  thePart = FindWindow( theEvent.where, &theWindow );
  switch ( thePart )
  {
```

```
  case inMenuBar:
    theChoice = MenuSelect( theEvent.where );
    break;
  // handle mouse clicks in other locations
  }
}
```

This new version of HandleMouseDown() uses a call to the Toolbox function FindWindow() to determine in what part of the monitor or window the mouse-click occurred. When an event is of type mouseDown, the where field of that event holds the pixel coordinates of the cursor at the time the mouse button was clicked. The FindWindow() function uses this pixel coordinate to determine what general area, or part, of the screen or window the cursor was in at the time of the event. Figure 6-13 shows many of the Apple-defined constants that can be used when referring to the different screen and window parts. In this chapter, only the menu bar part, represented by the inMenuBar constant, will be discussed. The other parts shown in the figure pertain to windows and are discussed in Chapter 7.

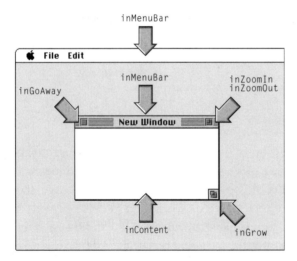

Figure 6-13
Screen and window parts and their Apple-defined part code constants.

The FindWindow() function accepts a Point variable (usually the where field of an EventRecord) and a pointer to a WindowPtr variable as its two parameters. If the coordinates of the Point variable fall anywhere on an open window, FindWindow() fills in the second parameter with a pointer to that window. That lets your program know which window is affected by a click of the mouse button. If no window was involved in the mouse-click, FindWindow() fills in this second parameter with a value of nil. In all cases, FindWindow() returns a part code that tells your program what part of the screen or window the cursor was in when the event took place.

After receiving a part code from FindWindow(), your mouseDown event-handling routine should use a switch statement to compare the part code to the different parts that your program handles. If your program responds to mouse-clicks in the menu bar and, say, in the drag bar, or title bar, of a window, your switch statement would look like this:

```
switch ( thePart )
{
  case inMenuBar:
   theChoice = MenuSelect( theEvent.where );
   break;
  case inDrag:
   // drag (move) the window about the screen
   break;
}
```

The above snippet is intentionally vague concerning the handling of an inDrag mouseDown event. Again, the details of handling window-related part codes are provided in Chapter 7. If the part code is of type inMenuBar, your program should track the cursor as the user moves it about the program's menu bar. The Toolbox function MenuSelect() does just this. Unlike most Toolbox functions, MenuSelect() doesn't quickly perform a task and then return control to your program. Once called, MenuSelect() retains control of your program until the user releases the mouse button. As long as the user holds the mouse button down, MenuSelect() will track the cursor — even if the user moves the cursor off the menu bar and then back onto it again. If the user moves the cursor over a menu name in the menu bar, MenuSelect() handles the dropping of that menu to reveal the menu's items.

The one parameter used by MenuSelect() is of type Point. Your program should pass the where field of the current event to tell MenuSelect() where the cursor was originally located when the event occurred. From then on, MenuSelect() takes care of tracking the cursor without any further input from the program.

MenuSelect() is a very powerful Toolbox routine. But as you'll see in the MenuBar example, it doesn't handle all menu-related tasks. Later in this chapter you'll see some additions to the handling of an inMenuBar part code.

EXAMPLE PROGRAM: MENUBAR

This chapter's first example is a program that displays a menu bar with two
menus in it. Figure 6-14 shows the two menus. When you run the MenuBar
program, you'll see the same items pictured in the File menu of this figure.
Your Apple menu, however, will have different items in it. The items
following the dashed line will be the items found in the Apple Menu Items
folder in the System Folder of your Mac.

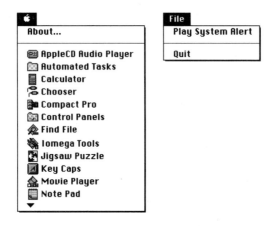

Figure 6-14
The two menus found in the MenuBar program.

As you hold the mouse button and drag the cursor across the menu bar,
a menu will drop down as the cursor moves over its name. If you move the
cursor down the list of menu items, each item in turn will become highlighted. All this is as expected, of course — a call to the Toolbox function
MenuSelect() takes care of all this very standard Macintosh menu-handing.
When you attempt to make a menu selection, however, nothing happens.
That's not what one would expect from a Macintosh program. No program
is perfect, but this is quite a shortcoming! Not to worry — this deficiency
will be quickly remedied in the following pages and in the next example
program. Because the menu items aren't functional, the Quit command in
the File menu doesn't work. Pressing any key will terminate the program.

```
//_____
#define   rMenuBar     128
#define   mApple       128
#define   iAbout       1
#define   mFile        129
#define   iPlayAlert   1
#define   iQuit        3
//_____
Boolean gDone = false;
//_____
void main( void )
{
  InitializeToolbox();
  SetUpMenuBar();

  EventLoop();
}
//_____
void SetUpMenuBar( void )
{
  Handle    theMenuBar;
  MenuHandle theAppleMenu;

  theMenuBar = GetNewMBar( rMenuBar );
  SetMenuBar( theMenuBar );
  DisposeHandle( theMenuBar );

  theAppleMenu = GetMenuHandle( mApple );
  AppendResMenu( theAppleMenu, 'DRVR' );
  DrawMenuBar();
}
//_____
void EventLoop( void )
{
  EventRecord theEvent;

  while ( gDone == false )
  {
   WaitNextEvent( everyEvent, &theEvent, 15L, nil );

   switch ( theEvent.what )
   {
     case mouseDown:
      HandleMouseDown( theEvent );
      break;
     case keyDown:
      gDone = true;
      break;
   }
  }
}
//_____
void HandleMouseDown( EventRecord theEvent )
{
```

```
WindowPtr theWindow;
short    thePart;
long     theChoice;

thePart = FindWindow( theEvent.where, &theWindow );
switch ( thePart )
{
 case inMenuBar:
   theChoice = MenuSelect( theEvent.where );
   break;
}
}
```

Remember, the menu items don't function. That includes the Quit item found in the File menu. You'll need to press any key to quit the program.

HANDLING A MOUSE-CLICK IN A MENU

When the user clicks the mouse button in the menu bar, MenuSelect() is called. This function maintains control until the user releases the mouse button. When that happens, MenuSelect() returns a long value that indicates which menu item was selected. If the user released the button while the cursor wasn't over a menu item, MenuSelect() returns a value of 0.

In the previous version of HandleMouseDown(), the value returned by MenuSelect() wasn't examined — that's why the MenuBar program couldn't react to menu selections. The new version of HandleMouseDown(), shown below, does check the returned value:

```
void HandleMouseDown( EventRecord theEvent )
{
  WindowPtr theWindow;
  short      thePart;
  long       theChoice;

  thePart = FindWindow( theEvent.where, &theWindow );
  switch ( thePart )
  {
   case inMenuBar:
     theChoice = MenuSelect( theEvent.where );
     if ( theChoice != 0 )
      HandleMenuChoice( theChoice );
     break;
  }
}
```

If no menu item is selected by the user, theChoice will be 0. In that
case, the mouseDown event can be considered handled. If a menu item was
selected, further processing of the event is necessary. An application-defined
function named HandleMenuChoice() will take care of that.

```
#define    mApple   128
#define    mFile    129
void HandleMenuChoice( long theChoice )
{
   short theMenu;
   short theMenuItem;

   theMenu = HiWord( theChoice );
   theMenuItem = LoWord( theChoice );
   switch ( theMenu )
   {
    case mApple:
      HandleAppleChoice( theMenuItem );
      break;

    case mFile:
      HandleFileChoice( theMenuItem );
      break;
   }
   HiliteMenu( 0 );
}
```

When a menu item is selected by the user, MenuSelect() stores two
numbers within the one long value. The long data type is a 4-byte, or 2-
word, data type. Half of the long — the upper, or high, word — holds the
ID of the menu. The other half of the long — the lower word — holds the
item number of the menu command. HandleMenuChoice() begins by
calling the Toolbox functions HiWord() and LoWord(). These two functions
serve to extract both the menu and the menu item from the single long
value that was returned by MenuSelect(). A call to HiWord() returns the ID
of the selected menu. A call to LoWord() returns the number of the selected
menu item.

After both the menu and menu item are known, a switch statement is
used to further determine how the selected menu item should be handled.
The body of the switch should hold one case section for each menu. Each
case label should be the ID of a menu. While the code to handle a menu
could be contained under the menu's case label, programs generally keep
this code in an application-defined function. Passing the number of the
selected menu item to the application-defined function lets that function
handle the proper menu item.

The above version of HandleMenuChoice() is written for an application that has only an Apple menu and a File menu. It would be easy to expand this function to handle a third menu by simply adding one more case label and a call to another application-defined function. The project's resource file would also need a couple of changes, too: A new MENU resource would need to be added, and the existing MBAR resource would need to list the ID of the new MENU.

When the user makes a menu selection, a program highlights the menu's name in the menu bar. After the menu command has been handled, the program unhighlights the menu name. The highlighting of the menu name is taken care of by MenuSelect(). The unhighlighting of the name is handled by the Toolbox function HiliteMenu(). Passing this function a value of 0 serves to unhighlight whichever menu is currently highlighted.

Figure 6-15 illustrates a program's flow of control. The figure assumes that a program is using the application-defined functions described in this chapter and shows the functions that get called when a user makes a selection from a program's File menu.

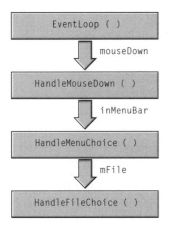

Figure 6-15
The flow of control when a selection is made from the File menu.

A program should be able to handle events of different types and events occurring in different screen or window parts. If an event is menu-related, the program should be able to handle a selection from any of a number of menus. Figure 6-16 expands on the specific case (a mouseDown event in an application's File menu) covered by Figure 6-15. Figure 6-16 shows that the

EventLoop( ), HandleMouseDown( ), and HandleMenuChoice( ) functions all
serve as branching points through which further event-processing takes
place. In Figure 6-16, assume that each arrow leads to an application-
defined function. For example, EventLoop( ) might make calls to functions
named HandleKeyDown( ), HandleMouseDown( ), and, if the other event type
handled by the program was an update event, a function named
HandleUpdateEvent( ).

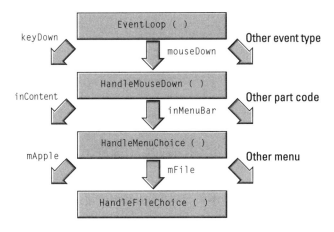

Figure 6-16
An event is handled by a series of branches.

HANDLING AN APPLE MENU ITEM SELECTION

When the user makes a selection from the Apple menu, your program should
call a routine similar to the HandleAppleChoice( ) function shown here:

```
#define    mApple       128
#define    iAbout       1
#define    rAboutAlert  128
void HandleAppleChoice( short theMenuItem )
{
   Str255    theItemName;
   short     theItemNumber;
   MenuHandle theAppleMenu;

   switch ( theMenuItem )
   {
```

```
    case iAbout:
      Alert( rAboutAlert, nil );
      break;

    default:
      theAppleMenu = GetMenuHandle( mApple );
      GetMenuItemText( theAppleMenu, theMenuItem, theItemName );
      theItemNumber = OpenDeskAcc( theItemName );
      break;
  }
}
```

Pass HandleAppleChoice() the number of the selected menu item, and the function will use a switch statement to properly carry out the menu command. If the first menu item is an About item, as is typically the case for a Macintosh program, call the Toolbox function Alert() to display an alert box that holds information about the program. The details of the resources necessary to display an alert, the ALRT and DITL resource types, are topics covered in Chapter 8. If you'd like to verify that an About menu selection is recognized by your program and you don't want to look ahead to Chapter 8, replace the above iAbout code with the following:

```
case iAbout:
  SysBeep( 1 );
  break;
```

The above snippet uses the Toolbox function SysBeep() to play the user's system alert sound. Each time the About menu item is selected, the sound will play. This is the technique used by the next example program, MenuIntro, to test that the About menu item is handled properly.

All of the remaining items in the Apple menu — the names of the desktop objects — are handled by the same small block of code (excluding the dashed line, a selection of which is of course ignored). Here's the code that opens whatever item is selected from the Apple menu:

```
Str255      theItemName;
short       theItemNumber;
MenuHandle  theAppleMenu;

default:
  theAppleMenu = GetMenuHandle( mApple );
  GetMenuItemText( theAppleMenu, theMenuItem, theItemName );
  theItemNumber = OpenDeskAcc( theItemName );
  break;
```

The call to GetMenuHandle() is used to obtain a handle to the Apple menu. This handle is needed as a parameter to the next Toolbox function, called GetMenuItemText(). When passed a menu handle, the number of an item in the menu referenced by the handle, and a Str255 variable, GetMenuItemText() returns the name of the selected item. Unlike with the other menus in a program, your program won't know the names of each of the items in the Apple menu until the program executes. The name returned by GetMenuItemText() is then passed to the Toolbox function OpenDeskAcc() to open the selected desktop object.

The OpenDeskAcc() function takes care of the tasks involved in the opening of a desktop object. Whether the object is a folder, a document, an application, or a control panel, OpenDeskAcc() can open it. After the object is opened, OpenDeskAcc() returns a negative number that can be used as a reference to the opened object. Your programs will generally ignore this value.

HANDLING A FILE MENU ITEM SELECTION

Unlike the handling of commands in the Apple menu, the handling of each menu item in the File menu depends on what items a particular program includes in this menu. The following HandleFileChoice() shows how the items in the File menu of the MenuBar program could be handled. That menu is pictured back in Figure 6-14.

```
#define    iPlayAlert    1
#define    iQuit         3
void HandleFileChoice( short theItem )
{
  switch ( theItem )
  {
   case iPlayAlert:
     SysBeep( 1 );
     break;
   case iQuit:
     gDone = true;
     break;
  }
}
```

If the user selects the first item from the File menu, the Play System Alert item, theItem, will have a value of 1 and the code under the iPlayAlert case will execute. This code simply plays the system alert sound. If the user selects the third item from the File menu (don't forget, the second item is the dashed line), the global `Boolean` variable `gDone` will be set to `true`. When the program next prepares to pass through the event loop, the comparison of `gDone` to `false` will fail and the loop — and program — will end.

 Of what purpose is a Play System Alert menu item? And why is it in the File menu? The answers to these questions are "probably none" and "to provide a simple example of menu item handling."

EXAMPLE PROGRAM: MENUINTRO

Both the MenuIntro program and the previous example program, MenuBar, use the same resources to display the same menus and menu items. The MenuIntro program, however, adds functionality to the menu items. All of the routines that make up the MenuIntro source code listing have been discussed in this chapter, so a walk-through of the listing isn't necessary.

```
//_____
#define    rMenuBar      128
#define    mApple        128
#define    iAbout          1
#define    mFile         129
#define    iPlayAlert      1
#define    iQuit           3
//_____
Boolean gDone = false;
//_____
void main( void )
{
   InitializeToolbox();
   SetUpMenuBar();
   EventLoop();
}
//_____
void SetUpMenuBar( void )
{
   Handle     theMenuBar;
   MenuHandle theAppleMenu;

   theMenuBar = GetNewMBar( rMenuBar );
   SetMenuBar( theMenuBar );
   DisposeHandle( theMenuBar );

   theAppleMenu = GetMenuHandle( mApple );
   AppendResMenu( theAppleMenu, 'DRVR' );
   DrawMenuBar();
```

```
}
//_____
void EventLoop( void )
{
  EventRecord theEvent;

  while ( gDone == false )
  {
   WaitNextEvent( everyEvent, &theEvent, 15L, nil );

   switch ( theEvent.what )
   {
     case mouseDown:
      HandleMouseDown( theEvent );
      break;
   }
  }
}
//_____
void HandleMouseDown( EventRecord theEvent )
{
  WindowPtr theWindow;
  short     thePart;
  long      theChoice;

  thePart = FindWindow( theEvent.where, &theWindow );
  switch ( thePart )
  {
   case inMenuBar:
     theChoice = MenuSelect( theEvent.where );
     if ( theChoice != 0 )
      HandleMenuChoice( theChoice );
     break;
  }
}
//_____
void HandleMenuChoice( long theChoice )
{
  short theMenu;
  short theMenuItem;

  theMenu = HiWord( theChoice );
  theMenuItem = LoWord( theChoice );
  switch ( theMenu )
  {
   case mApple:
     HandleAppleChoice( theMenuItem );
     break;

   case mFile:
     HandleFileChoice( theMenuItem );
     break;
```

```
  }
  HiliteMenu( 0 );
}
//_____
void HandleAppleChoice( short theMenuItem )
{
  Str255     theItemName;
  short      theItemNumber;
  MenuHandle theAppleMenu;

  switch ( theMenuItem )
  {
   case iAbout:
     SysBeep( 1 );
     break;

   default:
     theAppleMenu = GetMenuHandle( mApple );
     GetMenuItemText( theAppleMenu, theMenuItem, theItemName );
     theItemNumber = OpenDeskAcc( theItemName );
     break;
  }
}
//_____
void HandleFileChoice( short theItem )
{
  switch ( theItem )
  {
   case iPlayAlert:
     SysBeep( 1 );
     break;
   case iQuit:
     gDone = true;
     break;
  }
}
```

⌘-KEY EQUIVALENTS

A menu command that is common to most Mac programs, such as the Quit command, is usually assigned a *⌘-key equivalent.* (This also applies to commands that are unique to an application, which the user will use frequently.) A ⌘-key equivalent lets the user press the ⌘ key along with another key to access a menu item, just as if he or she had selected it from the menu.

You'll use your resource editor to mark a menu item as having a ⌘-key equivalent. Open the MENU resource that holds the item to mark and click once on the menu item. Whether you use ResEdit or Resorcerer, you'll then find a text edit box in the lower right corner of the editor's Menu Editor. Click in this edit box, and then hold down the Shift key as you type in the character that is to be used as the ⌘-key equivalent. Figure 6-17 shows that a Q has been entered in the ⌘-Key text edit box of a MENU resource item using ResEdit. Figure 6-18 shows how the ⌘-key equivalent looks in Resorcerer.

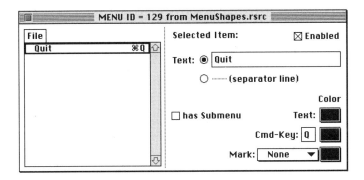

Figure 6-17
Using ResEdit to add a ⌘-key equivalent to a menu item.

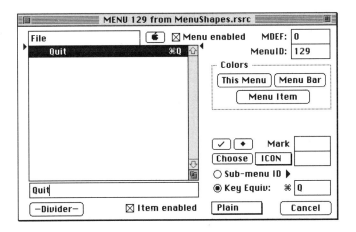

Figure 6-18
Using Resorcerer to add a ⌘-key equivalent to a menu item.

After marking a menu item as having a ⌘-key equivalent, you'll need to add a little code to your program's listing. First, you'll need to make sure your program responds to keyDown events. The following snippet is from the EventLoop() function. Here a keyDown event is handled by calling an application-defined function named HandleKeyDown().

```
switch ( theEvent.what )
{
  case mouseDown:
   HandleMouseDown( theEvent );
   break;
  case keyDown:
   HandleKeyDown( theEvent );
   break;
}
```

The HandleKeyDown() function gets called every time the user presses a key. Its purpose is to determine if the ⌘ key was down at the time that the user pressed a key. If it was, the function determines if the combination of the ⌘ key and the typed key is equivalent to a menu selection. Any such ⌘-key equivalent is then handled by the program's menu-handling routine HandleMenuChoice(), just as if the menu item had been selected from the menu.

```
void HandleKeyDown( EventRecord theEvent )
{
  short theChar;
  long  theChoice;

  theChar = theEvent.message & charCodeMask;

  if ( ( theEvent.modifiers & cmdKey ) != 0 )
  {
   if ( theEvent.what != autoKey )
   {
     theChoice = MenuKey( theChar );
     HandleMenuChoice( theChoice );
   }
  }
}
```

The first thing HandleKeyDown() does is determine which character was typed.

```
short theChar;

theChar = theEvent.message & charCodeMask;
```

When a keyDown event occurs, the 4 bytes of the message field of the event's EventRecord are filled with different pieces of information. One of these bytes holds the character that was typed. As shown in the above snippet, you can use the Apple-defined constant charCodeMask in an AND operation with the message field to extract the character and store its ASCII value in a variable of type short.

After saving the typed character in variable theChar, HandleKeyDown() performs a second AND operation. This time the modifiers field of the event record is AND-ed with the Apple-defined constant cmdKey. If the ⌘ key was down at the time of the keyDown event, the result of this AND operation will be nonzero. If that's the case, HandleKeyDown() makes sure that the event isn't of type autoKey. If it is, the user is holding down a key to type it repeatedly. That doesn't constitute a ⌘-key-equivalent menu selection, so the function ends. If the event isn't an autoKey event, HandleKeyDown() calls the Toolbox function MenuKey().

```
long  theChoice;
theChoice = MenuKey( theChar );
```

MenuKey() returns the same type of information that MenuSelect() returns: a long value that holds both the menu and menu item number of the selected command. Pass MenuKey the typed character, and the function will determine if this character matches the ⌘-key equivalent of any of the application's menu items.

To carry out the menu command, HandleKeyDown() calls the application-defined function HandleMenuChoice(). This is the same function called by HandleMouseDown() when a mouseDown event in the inMenuBar part is being handled.

To see a program that uses the HandleKeyDown() function, run the MenuShapes example found on the CD. A description of that program appears next.

ADDING MENUS TO A MENULESS PROGRAM

You've seen that adding menu-handling capabilities to a program requires, of course, the addition of source code. Most of the example programs in this book don't include menus simply for that reason. Each program is meant to be a short, concise example of the topic that was discussed preceding the program. Including menus in an example program adds to a couple of pages to the program's source code listing and makes it harder to see exactly how the topic the example is meant to demonstrate is implemented.

If you'd like to turn one of the short example programs into a more Mac-like application, feel free to add menus to it. After reading this chapter, you have the knowledge to do just that. As an example of how this can be done, refer to the MenuShapes project on this book's CD. This program adds menus to the Chapter 4 Shapes example.

Figure 6-19 shows the four MENU resources used by the MenuShapes project. Figure 6-20 shows the one MBAR resource used to define the ordering of the four menus in the program's menu bar.

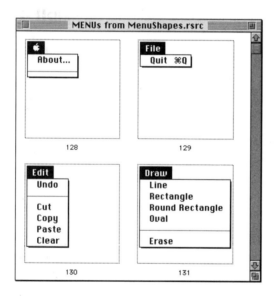

Figure 6-19

The four MENU res ources used by the MenuShapes project.

Menu Reference

This section describes the Toolbox routines that are used to load menu-related resource data into memory, display a menu bar, and respond to a user's selection of a menu item.

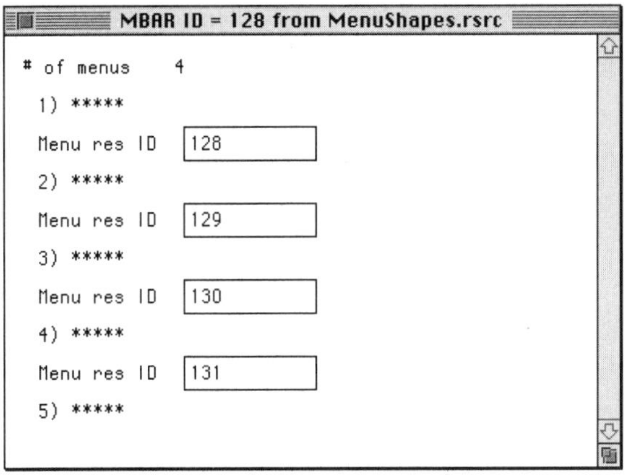

```
╔══════════════════════════════════════════╗
║ ▤▤  MBAR ID = 128 from MenuShapes.rsrc ▤▤ ║ ⬆
╠══════════════════════════════════════════╣
║  # of menus    4                          ║
║   1) *****                                ║
║    Menu res ID   ┌──────────┐             ║
║                  │ 128      │             ║
║                  └──────────┘             ║
║   2) *****                                ║
║    Menu res ID   ┌──────────┐             ║
║                  │ 129      │             ║
║                  └──────────┘             ║
║   3) *****                                ║
║    Menu res ID   ┌──────────┐             ║
║                  │ 130      │             ║
║                  └──────────┘             ║
║   4) *****                                ║
║    Menu res ID   ┌──────────┐             ║
║                  │ 131      │             ║
║                  └──────────┘             ║
║   5) *****                                ║ ⬇
╚══════════════════════════════════════════╝
```

Figure 6-20
The one MBAR resource used by the MenuShapes project.

SETTING UP THE MENU BAR

After creating a MENU resource for each menu and a single MBAR resource for the menu bar, use the routines in this section to turn the resource data into a menu bar with menus.

GetNewMBar( )

Load all of a program's menu-related resource data using a call to this function.

```
#define    rMenuBar    128
Handle     theMenuBar;

theMenuBar = GetNewMBar( rMenuBar );
```

Pass GetNewMBar( ) the ID of an MBAR resource, and the function will return a handle to a menu list, which is a list of handles to the data for each menu.

SetMenuBar( )

After calling GetNewMBar( ) to load MENU and MBAR data, call SetMenuBar( ) to make the menu list returned by GetNewMBar( ) the current menu list.

```
Handle theMenuBar;
SetMenuBar( theMenuBar );
```

Pass `SetMenuBar()` a handle to a menu list, and this function will make that list the current one. While most programs will have only one menu bar in memory, and thus only one menu list, a call to this routine is still necessary.

GetMenuHandle( )

Some Toolbox functions that operate on a menu require a handle to that menu's data. The `GetMenuHandle()` function returns such a handle.

```
#define    mPlayMovie    132
MenuHandle theMenu;
theMenu = GetMenuHandle( mPlayMovie );
```

Pass `GetMenuHandle()` the ID of a `MENU`, and this function will return a handle to the menu's data. The above snippet returns a handle to a menu used for playing movies. The `GetMenuHandle()` routine can be used to obtain a handle to the Apple menu as well. A handle to the Apple menu is needed for adding desktop objects to the Apple menu.

AppendResMenu( )

The Apple menu should hold a menu item for each of the user's desktop objects — each item the user has in the Apple Menu Items folder. A single call to `AppendResMenu()` does this.

```
MenuHandle theAppleMenu;
AppendResMenu( theAppleMenu, 'DRVR' );
```

The first parameter to `AppendResMenu()` should be a handle to the Apple menu. Obtain this handle from a call to `GetMenuHandle()`. The second parameter holds the four-character resource type of the items that should be added to the Apple menu. You can pass a value of `'DRVR'` to tell the function to add all items in the user's Apple Menu Items folder, regardless of their type.

DrawMenuBar( )

To display the menu bar referenced by the current menu list, call
DrawMenuBar( ). If there is more than one menu bar in memory, a prior call
to SetMenuBar( ) establishes which one will be drawn by DrawMenuBar( ).

```
DrawMenuBar();
```

MENUS AND A MOUSE-CLICK

A mouseDown event in the menu bar or a keyDown event that involves the ⌘
key can lead to a menu selection.

FindWindow( )

When a mouseDown event occurs, call FindWindow( ) to determine what part
of the screen or what part of a window the cursor was in when the event
occurred.

```
Point      thePoint = theEvent.where;
WindowPtr  theWindow;
short      thePart;
thePart = FindWindow( thePoint, &theWindow );
```

Pass the point at which the cursor was when a mouseDown event
occurred as the first parameter to FindWindow( ). FindWindow( ) will return
a part code that specifies in what general area the cursor was at the time of
the event. If the cursor was located at any point over a window, a pointer to
that window will be returned in the second parameter to FindWindow( ).

MenuSelect( )

When a mouseDown event occurs in the menu bar, call MenuSelect( ) to
track the cursor as the user moves the mouse.

```
EventRecord theEvent;
long        theChoice;
Point       thePoint = theEvent.where;
theChoice = MenuSelect( thePoint );
```

Pass MenuSelect( ) the cursor location at which a mouseDown event
occurred, and this function will start tracking the movement of the cursor.
MenuSelect( ) remains in control until the user releases the mouse button.

When that happens, the function returns a single long value that represents two things: the menu item that was selected and the menu that holds that item. If no item was selected, the returned value will be 0. Use the Toolbox routines HiWord() and LoWord() to extract the two pieces of information from this one value.

MenuKey( )

If any of the menu items in any of your program's menus has a ⌘-key equivalent, your program should handle keyDown events. When a keyDown event occurs, determine which key was pressed and whether the ⌘ key was down at the time of the event. Then call MenuKey() to determine which menu item should be considered selected.

```
short theChar;
long  theChoice;
theChoice = MenuKey( theChar );
```

Pass MenuKey() the character that was typed, and this function will return the same long value that would be returned by MenuSelect() if the user had made a menu selection with the mouse. Pass the returned long value to the same menu-handling routine that your program calls after MenuSelect() is called.

HiWord( )

To extract the ID of the menu from which a selection was made, call HiWord().

```
long  theChoice;
short theMenu;

theMenu = HiWord( theChoice );
```

Pass HiWord() the long value returned by MenuSelect(). HiWord() will look at only the upper 2 bytes of the 4-byte long and return this value as the menu ID.

LoWord( )

To extract the menu number of the menu item that was selected, call LoWord().

```
long  theChoice;
short theMenuItem;

theMenuItem = LoWord( theChoice );
```

Pass LoWord( ) the long value returned by MenuSelect( ). LoWord( ) will look at only the lower 2 bytes of the 4-byte long and return this value as the number of the selected menu command.

HiliteMenu( )

When a menu selection is made, the name of the menu that holds the selected item will be highlighted in the menu bar. The call to MenuSelect( ) does that. After the menu command has been handled by your program, call HiliteMenu( ) to unhighlight the menu name.

```
HiliteMenu( 0 );
```

If the ID of a menu is passed to HiliteMenu( ), this function will highlight that menu's name in the menu bar. If a value of 0 is passed instead, HiliteMenu( ) will unhighlight whichever menu name is currently highlighted.

HANDLING AN APPLE MENU SELECTION

Because the Apple menu holds items that differ from computer to computer, some special considerations need to be made in handling this menu.

GetMenuItemText( )

In response to the selection of a desktop object from the Apple menu, first call GetMenuItemText( ) to get the name of the menu item.

```
Str255     theItemName;
short      theItemNumber;
MenuHandle theAppleMenu;
GetMenuItemText( theAppleMenu, theMenuItem, theItemName );
```

The first parameter to GetMenuItemText() is a handle to the Apple menu. Call GetMenuHandle() to obtain this MenuHandle. The second parameter is the menu item number of the selected item. This value can be obtained from the lower word of the long value returned by MenuSelect(). The third parameter is a Str255 variable that will be filled in with the name of the menu item when the execution of GetMenuItemText() completes. After the name of the desktop object has been determined, call OpenDeskAcc() to open the object.

OpenDeskAcc( )

You can open, or launch, a desktop object that was selected from the Apple menu by calling OpenDeskAcc().

```
Str255  theItemName;
short   theItemNumber;
theItemNumber = OpenDeskAcc( theItemName );
```

Pass OpenDeskAcc() the name of a desktop object, and this function will open that object and return a reference number to the object. The object's name can be obtained from a call to GetMenuItemText(). The returned reference number can usually be ignored.

7

Windows

*T*he introduction to Chapter 6 stated that menus may be the single most important element of the Mac's easy-to-use interface. If menus do indeed take first place, windows come in second — a very close second. As proof of the significance of windows to a graphical user interface, consider the fact that another (and of course, lesser) operating system is named after them!

In this chapter you'll see how the WIND resource provides the definition of what a window will look like. You'll read of how the WIND resource and a data structure work together to create a window in memory.

As previous chapters have illustrated, loading window data into memory lets your program display a window that is frozen on the screen. While that limited use of a window provides the basis for several short, helpful example programs, it doesn't mimic what a true Macintosh application does with a window. A Mac program isn't supposed to leave windows frozen on the screen — it should let the user drag, resize, zoom, and close them. And when a window gets covered and then uncovered, a program should redraw whatever was in that window prior to its covering. In this chapter you'll read about the programming techniques that enable you to add all these window-related features to your programs.

Window Basics

By this point in your reading you should be comfortable with how a window is defined and how a window is brought to the screen. Chapter 1 introduced you to windows, Chapter 2 described the WIND resource, and

Chapter 4 discussed the WindowRecord data structure. This section, then, serves as a summary of the basics of how a window comes to existence on the user's monitor.

THE WindowRecord DATA TYPE

As you saw in Chapter 4, a WindowRecord data structure in memory provides the representation of a window. Of the many fields of a WindowRecord, the first field, the port member, is the most important to the programmer. The port field is of type GrafPort. That makes it a graphics port, or graphical drawing environment. Figure 7-1 shows that a variable of type WindowPtr points to this first field of a WindowRecord.

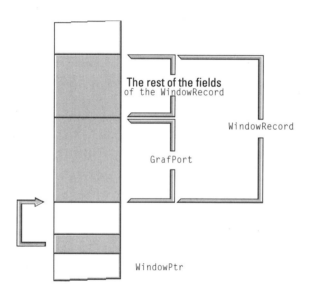

Figure 7-1
A member of type GrafPort is the first field in a WindowRecord data structure.

While the port field is the most important member of the
WindowRecord, in this chapter you will see mention of a few of the other
fields of this data structure. The following is the complete definition of the
WindowRecord data structure:

```
struct WindowRecord
{
    GrafPort      port;
    short         windowKind;
    Boolean       visible;
    Boolean       hilited;
    Boolean       goAwayFlag;
    Boolean       spareFlag;
    RgnHandle     strucRgn;
    RgnHandle     contRgn;
    RgnHandle     updateRgn;
    Handle        windowDefProc;
    Handle        dataHandle;
    StringHandle  titleHandle;
    short         titleWidth;
    ControlRef    controlList;
    WindowPeek    nextWindow;
    PicHandle     windowPic;
    long          refCon;
};
```

DEFINING A WINDOW WITH A WIND RESOURCE

In Chapter 2 you saw that when GetNewWindow() is called to create a
window, data from a WIND resource gets loaded into a WindowRecord
data structure in memory. Although you have used the Window Editor of
ResEdit or Resorcerer to graphically define the look of a window, the
information you specified ends up as numbers that make their way into the
fields of a WindowRecord data structure. Figure 7-2 shows a few of the
ResEdit Window Editor settings and the WindowRecord fields that get filled
by the settings.

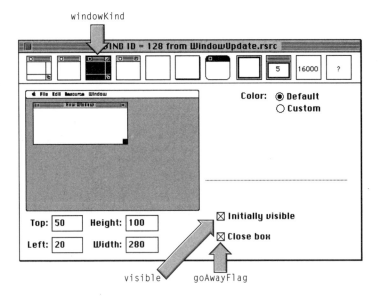

Figure 7-2
Settings in a `WIND` *resource will be copied into a* `WindowRecord` *when a program opens a window.*

Window Updating

When a portion of a window that is obscured comes back into view, its contents need to be redrawn, or updated. While it would be very beneficial to the programmer if the system kept track of all the graphics in a window and faithfully redrew them as needed, this is not the way the Macintosh works. Instead, each time a partially or fully obscured window returns to the forefront, your program needs to call the function or functions that drew the window's contents in the first place.

THE UPDATEEVT EVENT

If a part of a window is off-screen and the user drags that area back on-screen, an update event will occur. If a window is partially or fully concealed by a second window and the user brings the first window to the forefront, an update event will occur. If a dialog box is covering part or all of a window and the user dismisses the dialog box, again an updated event occurs; the same applies when an alert obscures a window. Anytime an obscured part of a window again becomes visible, an update event, an event of type updateEvt, occurs.

Like other event types, the system is responsible for determining when any of the above situations occur and for generating the update event. Your program, through its call to WaitNextEvent(), is responsible for getting this update event information from the event queue and responding to it. In Chapter 5 you saw that the code to handle a mouseDown event is often relegated to an application-defined routine. The same is true of an updateEvt event. The following snippet from an event loop routine shows the switch statement for a program that handles mouse-down and update events:

```
switch ( theEvent.what )
{
  case mouseDown:
   HandleMouseDown( theEvent );
   break;
  case updateEvt:
   HandleUpdate( theEvent );
   break;
}
```

A typical update-handling routine determines which window needs updating, ensures that this window's graphics port is the current port, and draws the window's contents. The following HandleUpdate() routine performs each of these tasks:

```
void HandleUpdate( EventRecord theEvent )
{
  WindowPtr theWindow;

  theWindow = (WindowPtr)theEvent.message;
  SetPort( theWindow );

  BeginUpdate( theWindow );
   DrawWindowContents();
  EndUpdate( theWindow );
}
```

When an update event occurs, the system places a pointer to the affected window in the message field of the event's EventRecord. Casting this pointer to a `WindowPtr` type provides the update function with a window pointer that can be used in subsequent Toolbox calls. One such call, `SetPort()`, appears on the next line in the above snippet.

`HandleUpdate()` relies on an application-defined function named `DrawWindowContents()` to redraw the contents of the window. This function will need to hold all of the code for drawing the entire contents of the window in order to update it. If the window holds just a single line of text, this function might consist of a call to `MoveTo()` and a call to `DrawString()`. On the other hand, if the window holds complex graphics, this function might consist of dozens of calls to QuickDraw routines and to other application-defined drawing routines.

In the above snippet, notice that the call to the window-drawing routine is nested between calls to two Toolbox functions: `BeginUpdate()` and `EndUpdate()`. This serves two purposes: The update region gets cleared, and the amount of drawing necessary to update the window is reduced.

A window's update region is the region that needs to be redrawn when an update event occurs. Figure 7-3 provides an example. The left of the figure shows a window partially obscured by an alert. The right of the figure shows the same window just after the alert has been dismissed. The white area in the window defines the window's update region. Why is it necessary to clear this region? As long as the update region includes any area at all, the system generates an `updateEvt` event. If the update region isn't cleared, the system will continuously and endlessly generate update events. It is the call to `BeginUpdate()` that clears the update region.

Figure 7-3
When a covered part of a window becomes uncovered, the newly exposed area is the window's update region.

If BeginUpdate() clears the update region, how does the system keep track of the area of a window that needs updating? Before it clears the update region, BeginUpdate() temporarily alters a window's *visible region,* which is stored in the visRgn field of a window's GrafPort. This region defines the viewable area of a window — the area that isn't obscured by other windows and is thus visible to the user.

The temporary change that is made to the visible region is shown in Figure 7-4. This figure again uses the situation illustrated in Figure 7-3. Figure 7-3 uses shaded areas to illustrate which part of a window is the visible region. When the alert is on the screen, the entire viewable area of the window is considered the visible region, as shown on the left of the figure. When the alert is dismissed, an update event occurs and the program enters its application-defined update routine. When this routine calls BeginUpdate(), BeginUpdate() temporarily changes the visible region to the update region, as shown on the right of Figure 7-3. BeginUpdate() then clears the update region so that another update event doesn't immediately occur.

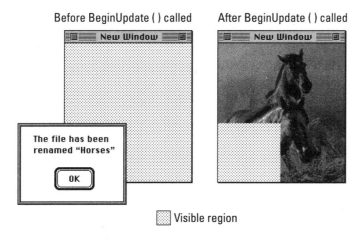

Before BeginUpdate ( ) called   After BeginUpdate ( ) called

New Window   New Window

The file has been renamed "Horses"

OK

Visible region

Figure 7-4
BeginUpdate() temporarily changes a window's visible region to its update region.

More accurately, BeginUpdate() sets the visible region to the intersection of the window's update region and its visible region. This intersection is generally the same as the update region, as shown in Figure 7-4.

After the call to BeginUpdate(), the application-defined window-drawing routine draws the contents of the window. When QuickDraw draws to a window, it draws to the window's visible region. What does that fact mean to the window that is getting updated? That QuickDraw will only draw to the area that was formerly the update region — the area that is now the temporary visible region. So while the application-defined drawing routine holds the QuickDraw commands that draw to the entire window, QuickDraw will draw only to the temporary visible region. That means QuickDraw does less work and updates a window more quickly than it could if it had to draw the contents of the entire window.

Determining just what area of a window needs to be redrawn is done by the call to BeginUpdate() and by QuickDraw. Your application-defined window-drawing function should draw the entire contents of the window. Leave it to the system to determine how much of that routine is actually used!

After drawing has completed, EndUpdate() must be called. This function restores the window's visible region to the actual viewable area of the window. The temporary visible region is used only for the updating of the window. After that the system needs to know the true exposed area of the window.

You must nest the window-drawing routine between calls to BeginUpdate() and EndUpdate(), or update events will be endlessly generated and your program will enter an infinite loop.

EXAMPLE PROGRAM: WINDOWUPDATE

When you run the WindowUpdate program, you'll see a window like the one pictured in Figure 7-5. The window will be fixed on the screen; it can't be moved and it can't be resized.

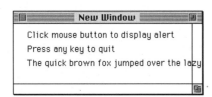

Figure 7-5
The window that appears when WindowUpdate executes.

Yes, the text in the window does indeed spill over to the area normally reserved for a scroll bar. That's an undesirable effect that will be remedied later in this chapter when *clipping* is discussed.

Clicking the mouse button posts the alert shown in Figure 7-6. A click on the OK button dismisses the alert. Another click of the mouse button will again display the same alert. Pressing any key ends the program.

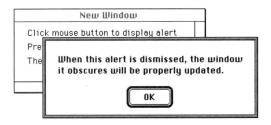

Figure 7-6
To force an update event to occur, the WindowUpdate program displays an alert that covers part of the program's window.

The use of the alert in the WindowUpdate program serves one simple purpose: to trigger an update event. When the alert disappears, the system recognizes that a part of the program's window that was obscured should now be visible. In response to this, the system will draw the frame of the window and add an update event to the event queue. The WindowUpdate program will call `WaitNextEvent()` to retrieve the event information. After the event is determined to be of type `updateEvt`, it will be handled by redrawing the obscured contents of the window.

 Wait a minute — alerts and the resources used to create them haven't been covered in any detail yet! True enough — those are topics described in the next chapter. The posting of an alert over a window makes for such a simple example of how an update event gets generated, however, that a quick look at the creation of an alert makes sense.

Figure 7-7 shows the three resource types used by the WindowUpdate project. The figure also shows the project's one `WIND` resource.

Figure 7-8 and Figure 7-9 show the two resources necessary to produce one alert. The `ALRT` resource looks much like a `WIND` resource. It specifies the size and screen placement that the alert should have when the WindowUpdate program brings the alert to the screen. The `ALRT` resource

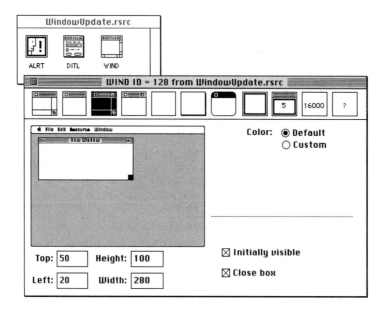

Figure 7-7

The resources used by the WindowUpdate project.

also holds the resource ID of the DITL resource that is to be used in conjunction with this ALRT resource. The DITL resource specifies the items that will appear in the alert. Figure 7-9 shows that this alert will have two items: a button labeled OK, and a text item that describes the purpose of the alert.

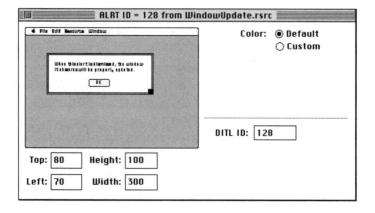

Figure 7-8

The ALRT resource used by the WindowUpdate project.

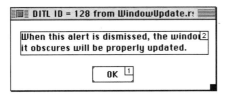

Figure 7-9
The `DITL` resource used by the WindowUpdate project.

As shown in this snippet from the `EventLoop()` function, the
WindowUpdate event loop handles three event types: `mouseDown`, `keyDown`,
and `updateEvt`.

```
#define    rAlert    128
switch ( theEvent.what )
{
  case mouseDown:
   Alert( rAlert, nil );
   break;

  case keyDown:
   gDone = true;
   break;
  case updateEvt:
   HandleUpdate( theEvent );
   break;
}
```

A `mouseDown` event posts the alert on the screen; a call to the Toolbox
function `Alert()` takes care of that. `Alert()` requires two parameters. The
first is the ID of the `ALRT` resource that is to be used to define the alert. The
second is a pointer to an optional event filter function that can be used to
handle events not normally recognized by the `Alert()` function. Passing
`nil` here tells `Alert()` that there is no filter function. As mentioned, alerts
and alert resources are covered in greater depth in Chapter 8.

A `keyDown` event ends the program. Pressing any key results in the
global `Boolean` variable `gDone` being set to `true`. That causes the event
loop to end.

An update event calls the application-defined function `HandleUpdate()`.
The WindowUpdate version of this function is the same as the version
developed earlier in this chapter, but with one addition. Between the calls

to BeginUpdate() and EndUpdate() is a call to the Toolbox function
DrawGrowIcon(). When passed a WindowPtr, this routine draws a size box
in the window's lower-right corner.

```
//_____
#define    rDisplayWindow    128
#define    rAlert            128
#define    kScrollBarSize     16
//_____
Boolean gDone = false;
//_____
void main( void )
{
  WindowPtr theWindow;

  InitializeToolbox();

  theWindow = GetNewWindow( rDisplayWindow, nil, (WindowPtr)-1L );
  ShowWindow( theWindow );
  EventLoop();
}
//_____
void EventLoop( void )
{
  EventRecord theEvent;

  while ( gDone == false )
  {
   WaitNextEvent( everyEvent, &theEvent, 15L, nil );

   switch ( theEvent.what )
   {
     case mouseDown:
      Alert( rAlert, nil );
      break;

     case keyDown:
      gDone = true;
      break;
     case updateEvt:
      HandleUpdate( theEvent );
      break;
   }
  }
}
//_____
void HandleUpdate( EventRecord theEvent )
{
  WindowPtr theWindow;
```

```
    theWindow = (WindowPtr)theEvent.message;
    SetPort( theWindow );

    BeginUpdate( theWindow );
     DrawGrowIcon( theWindow );
     DrawWindowContents();
    EndUpdate( theWindow );
  }
//_____
void DrawWindowContents( void )
{
  MoveTo( 20, 20 );
  DrawString( "\pClick mouse button to display alert" );
  MoveTo( 20, 40 );
  DrawString( "\pPress any key to quit" );
  MoveTo( 20, 60 );
  DrawString( "\pThe quick brown fox jumped over the lazy dog" );
}
```

THE CLIPPING REGION

As you saw in Chapter 4, drawing takes place in a window's graphics port. The area of a window's port is defined by its *port rectangle,* a rectangle that encompasses the entire contents of the window. When a new window is opened, a program can draw anywhere within the port rectangle.

For a window that doesn't have a size box or scroll bars, drawing to the port rectangle works just fine. If a window has either of those, however, drawing must be constrained so that the size box or scroll bars don't get drawn over. A window's *clipping region* is the means of constraining drawing. When a new window opens, its clipping region is the same size as the window's port rectangle. If drawing is to be limited to only a part of the window's port rectangle, the size of the window's clipping region must be changed. Figure 7-10 shows that when a window has a size box and a clipping region the size of the port rectangle, drawing can extend into the areas that are meant for scroll bars.

To prevent drawing from entering the scroll bar areas, the clipping region should be reduced so that these areas are not included in the region. Figure 7-11 shows that when this happens, drawing will not take place in these areas — it will be clipped off at the end of the clipping region.

Clipping region

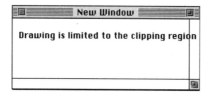

Figure 7-10
If a window's clipping region is the entire window content area, drawing can enter the scroll bar area.

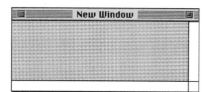
Clipping region

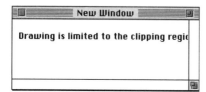

Figure 7-11
If a window's clipping region is changed to exclude the area reserved for scroll bars, drawing will not appear in those excluded areas.

CHANGING THE AREA OF THE CLIPPING REGION

A window's port rectangle is of type Rect, and is in the shape of a rectangle. A window's clipping region is of type Region, and can be any shape.

Unlike the commonly used Rect data type, which can only define a rectangle, the Region data type can define any arbitrary shape. Examples of the use of a Region could include a program that needs to keep track of shapes in the form of a star, a snowman, or a map of North America.

To change a window's clipping region to a region other than a rectangle, you can use QuickDraw region routines discussed in Chapter 10. For instance, to constrain drawing to the shape of a circle you could create a new region defined to be a circle and then set a window's clipping region to the new circle region. More often than not, however, the new clipping region will be in the shape of a window and the shape of the original clipping region — a rectangle.

To redefine a window's clipping region to a nonrectangle shape, use the Toolbox function SetClip(), which is described in this chapter's reference section. To change the clipping area to that of a different rectangle, call the Toolbox routine ClipRect().

```
Rect theRect;
ClipRect( &theRect );
```

Before calling ClipRect() you'll need to define the area of the rectangle that serves as the parameter to ClipRect(). The most common reason to change a window's clipping region is that the window has a size box or scroll bars. To handle that situation, define a rectangle the size of the entire window and then subtract the scroll bar areas from that rectangle. This next snippet adjusts a window's clipping region to account for a window's horizontal and vertical scroll areas.

```
#define    kScrollBarSize    16
Rect       theClipMinusScrollRect;
WindowPtr  theWindow;
SetPort( theWindow );
theClipMinusScrollRect = theWindow->portRect;
theClipMinusScrollRect.right -= kScrollBarSize;
theClipMinusScrollRect.bottom -= kScrollBarSize;

ClipRect( &theClipMinusScrollRect );
// draw to the new clipping region
```

The above code begins by setting the current graphics port to theWindow. You can, of course, assume that this window was previously loaded into memory by a call to GetNewWindow(). Next, a rectangle is set to the size of the window's port rectangle, as defined by the portRect field of the window's GrafPort data structure.

Recall that a variable of type `WindowPtr` points to the first field of a `WindowRecord`, the `GrafPort` field. Chapter 4 discussed the way that many of these fields can be accessed through Toolbox routines rather than directly. When a `GrafPort` member must be accessed directly, use the `->` operator, as in this line from the previous snippet:

```
theClipMinusScrollRect = theWindow->portRect;
```

After that, the right and bottom boundaries of this rectangle are reduced by the width of a scroll bar, which the Toolbox defines to be 16 pixels. Finally, a call to `ClipRect()` sets the current window's clipping region to the size of this rectangle. After the above code executes, any drawing that is performed in the current window will be in the clipping area shown back in Figure 7-11. For instance, if the window is the size of the one pictured in Figure 7-11, the end of the following string would be clipped off as shown in the figure:

```
MoveTo( 10, 30);
DrawString( "\pDrawing is limited to the clipping region" );
```

A program that changes a window's clipping region may not want the change to be permanent. This is especially true of a region that is irregularly shaped. For instance, a program may want to temporarily constrain drawing to, say, a crescent moon shape, and then restore the clipping region to the size of the entire window. It is therefore a good programming practice to save a window's original clipping region before altering it. After changing the region and drawing to the window, the original region can be restored. The following snippet surrounds the previous example with code that does just that:

```
RgnHandle  theOrigClipRgn;
Rect       theClipMinusScrollRect;
WindowPtr  theWindow;
SetPort( theWindow );

theOrigClipRgn = NewRgn();
GetClip( theOrigClipRgn );
theClipMinusScrollRect = theWindow->portRect;
```

```
theClipMinusScrollRect.right -= kScrollBarSize;
theClipMinusScrollRect.bottom -= kScrollBarSize;

ClipRect( &theClipMinusScrollRect );
// draw to the new clipping region
SetClip( theOrigClipRgn );
DisposeRgn( theOrigClipRgn );
```

Before changing the clipping region, the above snippet calls the
Toolbox function NewRgn() to allocate memory for a new region. It then
calls the Toolbox function GetClip() to retrieve the clipping region of the
current window and store it in the new region. After the clipping region is
altered and drawing has taken place, the Toolbox function SetClip() is
called to restore the window's clipping region to its original shape. Finally, a
little housekeeping is performed by calling DisposeRgn() to free the
memory that was allocated in the previous call to NewRgn().

EXAMPLE PROGRAM: CLIPPINGUPDATE

The ClippingUpdate program is very similar to the previous example,
WindowUpdate. Like WindowUpdate, ClippingUpdate displays a window
with text in it and an alert that obscures part of the window, as shown in
Figure 7-12. The difference between the two programs is in the text that is
drawn to the window. Figure 7-13 shows that the text drawn in the
ClippingUpdate window gets clipped at the area of the window that is
designed to hold a vertical scroll bar.

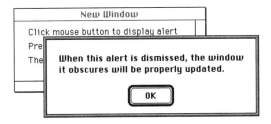

Figure 7-12
*The ClippingUpdate program opens a window and displays an alert that
overlaps that window.*

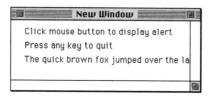

Figure 7-13
When the ClippingUpdate window is updated, the text will be clipped in such a way that the scroll bar areas are not obscured.

The ClippingUpdate project uses the same resources as the WindowUpdate project. Refer back to Figures 7-7, 7-8, and 7-9 if you'd like to take another look at them. The only difference in the source code of the two programs is found in the HandleUpdate() routine. The WindowUpdate program simply called DrawWindowContents() to update the window. The ClippingUpdate program surrounds a call to DrawWindowContents() with the clipping code discussed in this section. The following is the new listing for HandleUpdate(). You can see the complete source code listing by looking back at the WindowUpdate() code or by opening the ClippingUpdate project found on the CD that's included with this book.

```
void HandleUpdate( EventRecord theEvent )
{
    WindowPtr    theWindow;
    RgnHandle    theOrigClipRgn;
    Rect         theClipMinusScrollRect;

  theWindow = (WindowPtr)theEvent.message;
  BeginUpdate( theWindow );
  SetPort( theWindow );

  theOrigClipRgn = NewRgn();
  GetClip( theOrigClipRgn );

  EraseRect( &theWindow->portRect );

  DrawGrowIcon( theWindow );
  theClipMinusScrollRect = theWindow->portRect;
  theClipMinusScrollRect.right -= kScrollBarSize;
  theClipMinusScrollRect.bottom -= kScrollBarSize;

  ClipRect( &theClipMinusScrollRect );

  DrawWindowContents();
```

```
      SetClip( theOrigClipRgn );
      DisposeRgn( theOrigClipRgn );
   EndUpdate( theWindow );
}
```

Windows and mouseDown Events

Proper handling of an updateEvt is important to successfully implementing windows in a Macintosh program. So is the handling of a mouseDown event. In order to move, resize, close, and zoom a window, the user needs to click the window. Fortunately, Chapters 5 and 6 familiarized you with the mouseDown event. That means you can jump right into the handling of such an event when it pertains to a window.

WINDOW-RELATED MOUSEDOWN EVENTS

Chapter 6 introduced you to part codes, Apple-defined constants that are used to represent various areas of a window and the screen. When a mouseDown event occurs, the part of the window or screen in which the cursor was located at the time the mouse was clicked can be determined by calling FindWindow(). This Toolbox function returns a part code. Chapter 6 dealt with menus, so it was the inMenuBar part code that was discussed in that chapter. In this chapter, several window-related part codes will be covered. Figure 7-14 is a repeat of a figure introduced in Chapter 6 and is presented here as a reminder and summary of the different part codes and the areas they represent.

To handle a mouseDown event in the menu bar, Chapter 6 examples added an inMenuBar case label to the application-defined HandleMouseDown() routine. That's the same approach you'll use to handle mouseDown events that occur elsewhere. The following snippet serves as a shell, or skeleton, of a version of HandleMouseDown() that will be able to handle mouse down events in different areas of a window. The remainder of this chapter will be devoted to developing the code that will replace the comment found under each case label.

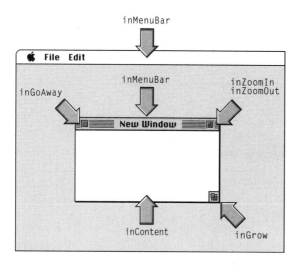

Figure 7-14
The Apple-defined part codes and the areas that they represent.

```
void HandleMouseDown( EventRecord theEvent )
{
  WindowPtr theWindow;
  short     thePart;

  thePart = FindWindow( theEvent.where, &theWindow );

  switch ( thePart )
  {
   case inGoAway:
     // handle mouse button click in window close box
     break;
   case inDrag:
     // handle mouse button click in window drag bar (title bar)
     break;
   case inContent:
     // handle mouse button click in window content
     break;
   case inGrow:
     // handle mouse button click in window size box
     break;
   case inZoomIn:
   case inZoomOut:
     // handle mouse button click in window zoom in/zoom out box
     break;
  }
}
```

THE inGoAway PART CODE: CLOSING A WINDOW

When a mouse-click occurs in the go away box — the close box — of a window, your program should call the Toolbox function TrackGoAway() to determine if the user releases the mouse button while the cursor is still over the close box. TrackGoAway(), like MenuSelect(), is one of a handful of Toolbox routines that take control of a program and stay in control until the user changes his or her action. Once TrackGoAway() is called, this routine maintains control until the user releases the mouse button. As the user drags the cursor in and out of the window's close box, TrackGoAway() highlights and unhighlights the close box.

When the user releases the mouse button, TrackGoAway() returns a value of true if the cursor was over the close box when the mouse button was released, or false if it wasn't. If the returned value is true, close the window by calling the Toolbox function DisposeWindow().

```
WindowPtr    theWindow;
EventRecord theEvent;
if ( TrackGoAway( theWindow, theEvent.where ) == true )
  DisposeWindow( theWindow );
```

The first parameter in TrackGoAway() is a pointer to the window in which the mouseDown event occurred. This pointer is obtained from the call to FindWindow() that is made at the top of HandleMouseDown(). The second parameter is the pixel screen coordinate at which the cursor was located when the event occurred. TrackGoAway() uses this as a reference point for window dragging.

To handle a mouse-click in a window's close box, place the above snippet under the inGoAway label in the HandleMouseDown() routine.

```
case inGoAway:
  if ( TrackGoAway( theWindow, theEvent.where ) == true )
   DisposeWindow( theWindow );
  break;
```

THE inDrag PART CODE: DRAGGING A WINDOW

Dragging a window is accomplished by calling the Toolbox function DragWindow(). When the user clicks the mouse button on the drag bar of a window, a mouseDown event with a part code of inDrag is generated. In response to this situation, a call to DragWindow() should be made. DragWindow() is another of the Toolbox routines that maintains control until the user releases the mouse button. As long as the button is down, DragWindow() will handle the moving of a window as the user drags the cursor about the screen.

```
WindowPtr   theWindow;
EventRecord theEvent;
DragWindow( theWindow, theEvent.where, &qd.screenBits.bounds );
```

The first parameter in DragWindow() is a pointer to the window that received the mouse-click. This pointer comes from the earlier call to FindWindow().

The second parameter is of type Point and specifies the screen location at which the mouseDown event occurred.

The final parameter is a pointer to a Rect. This rectangle tells DragWindow() where on the screen the window is allowed to be dragged. To give the user the freedom to drag the window about the entire screen, use qd.screenBits.bounds. The qd struct variable is a system global variable and as such is available for use by any program. One of the fields of the qd struct is the screenBits field. The screenBits structure is used to keep a map of every bit, or pixel, that makes up the user's screen. The bounds field of the screenBits structure is of type Rect and is used to define the boundaries of the user's screen.

DragWindow() is a powerful function that takes care of all the tasks associated with window dragging. The code under the inDrag case consists of just this function call and a break statement.

```
case inDrag:
   DragWindow( theWindow, theEvent.where, &qd.screenBits.bounds );
   break;
```

THE inContent PART CODE: ACTIVATING A WINDOW

The content area of a window consists of the entire window area that lies beneath the window's title bar, less the size box (if present). A mouse-click in the content of a window generates a mouseDown event with a part code of inContent. A window typically doesn't react in any special way when the user clicks the mouse in it. Instead, if the window is behind any other windows, it should just be brought to the front. A call to the Toolbox function `SelectWindow()` does this. Pass `SelectWindow()` a pointer to the window to be activated, and this routine will change the window's highlighting to activate it. After that, `SelectWindow()` deactivates whichever window was active before the mouse-click. If an already active window is clicked, `SelectWindow()` has no effect.

```
case inContent:
  SelectWindow( theWindow );
  break;
```

THE `inGrow` PART CODE: RESIZING A WINDOW

When the user clicks the mouse button on the size box of a window, call the Toolbox function `GrowWindow()` to shrink or enlarge the window. `GrowWindow()` is another Toolbox function that maintains control of a program until the user releases the mouse. As the user moves the mouse with the button held down, `GrowWindow()` constantly draws an outline of the window as it changes size, as illustrated in Figure 7-15.

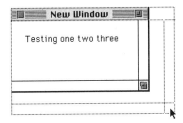

Figure 7-15
The `GrowWindow()` routine displays the outline of the window that is being resized.

Before calling `GrowWindow()`, establish both the minimum and maximum size that a window may have. The minimum size is especially important — your program shouldn't allow a window to shrink to such a small size that it becomes unmanageable. To store the window's minimum and maximum sizes, use a variable of type Rect. Though a Rect variable will be used, your program isn't interested in the rectangle it defines. Instead, a Rect is used simply because it is a convenient means of holding four values. When establishing the window size limits Rect, think of the parameters to SetRect() in the following terms:

```
Rect theGrowLimitsRect;
SetRect( &theGrowLimitsRect, minWidth, minHeight, maxWidth, maxHeight );
```

To define the minimum size of a window to be 50 pixels by 50 pixels and the maximum size to be 10,000 pixels by 10,000 pixels, make the following call to SetRect():

```
Rect theGrowLimitsRect;
SetRect( &theGrowLimitsRect, 50, 50, 10000, 10000 );
```

 If you'd like to let the user expand a window to fill the screen, set the maximum window size to some height and width that is at least as large as the user's screen. The above snippet uses values of 10,000 — your code should use this value or some other ridiculously large number to ensure that a window can fill a user's large monitor.

With the window limits rectangle set, call GrowWindow(). The first parameter in this function is a pointer to the window to resize. As usual, this pointer is obtained from the earlier call to FindWindow(). The second parameter is the pixel coordinate of the cursor at the time the mouseDown event took place. The last parameter to GrowWindow() is a pointer to the rectangle that was set up just prior to the call to GrowWindow().

When the user eventually releases the mouse button, GrowWindow() returns a long value that holds the new size of the window. If the user didn't change the window's size, GrowWindow() returns a value of 0, and no redrawing of the window is necessary. Any other value requires a redrawing of the window.

```
long theNewSize;
theNewSize = GrowWindow( theWindow, theEvent.where,
            &theGrowLimitsRect );
```

The long value returned by GrowWindow() is similar to the value returned by a Toolbox function described in Chapter 6, MenuSelect(). Both routines hold two 2-byte values combined into one 4-byte variable. As was

the case with the value returned by MenuSelect( ), call the Toolbox
functions LoWord( ) and HiWord( ) to extract the two individual values from
the one long variable.

```
short theNewWidth;
short theNewHeight;
theNewWidth = LoWord( theNewSize );
theNewHeight = HiWord( theNewSize );
```

With the window's new size now known, it's time to redraw it. Call
SetPort( ) to make sure the correct window is current. Then call the
Toolbox function EraseRect( ) to erase the old contents of the window.
Pass the portRect field of the window's GrafPort to EraseRect( ) — that
tells the function to erase the entire contents of the window.

```
SetPort( theWindow );
EraseRect( &theWindow->portRect );
```

Erasing the contents of the window is a necessary step when enlarging
the window. If your program doesn't take this step, the old size box will still
be visible when the window is redrawn. Figure 7-16 illustrates this.

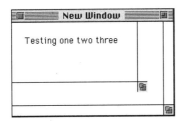

Figure 7-16
Failing to call EraseRect( ) results in the old size box remaining in the window.

After erasing the contents of the window, call the Toolbox routine
SizeWindow( ) to draw the window frame at its new size. Pass
SizeWindow( ) a pointer to the window to be resized, the new window
dimensions, and a Boolean value that indicates whether any new area
added to the content of the window should be included in the next window
update:

```
SizeWindow( theWindow, theNewWidth, theNewHeight, true );
```

Finally, invalidate the content area of the window by making a call to the Toolbox routine `InvalRect()`. Invalidating an area of a window includes that area in the next window update.

```
InvalRect( &theWindow->portRect );
```

The following snippet lists the code that can be used to handle a `mouseDown` event that occurs in the size box of a window:

```
#define    kMinWindSize      50
#define    kMaxWindSize    10000
Rect  theGrowLimitsRect;
long  theNewSize;
short theNewWidth;
short theNewHeight;
case inGrow:
  SetRect( &theGrowLimitsRect, kMinWindSize, kMinWindSize,
      kMaxWindSize, kMaxWindSize );
  theNewSize = GrowWindow( theWindow, theEvent.where,
            &theGrowLimitsRect );
  if ( theNewSize != 0 )
  {
   theNewWidth = LoWord( theNewSize );
   theNewHeight = HiWord( theNewSize );
   SetPort( theWindow );
   EraseRect( &theWindow->portRect );
   SizeWindow( theWindow, theNewWidth, theNewHeight, true );
   InvalRect( &theWindow->portRect );
  }
  break;
```

THE `inZoomIn` AND `inZoomOut` PART CODES: ZOOMING A WINDOW

When a `mouseDown` event occurs in a window's zoom box, call the Toolbox function `TrackBox()`. `TrackBox()` is analogous to the routine that is used to track the movement of the cursor when the user clicks in a window's close box, `TrackGoAway()`. As the user moves the cursor in and out of a zoom box, `TrackBox()` highlights and unhighlights the box. If the cursor is in the zoom box when the mouse button is released, `TrackBox()` returns a value of `true`; if not, it returns `false`.

```
if ( TrackBox( theWindow, theEvent.where, thePart ) == true )
  // zoom the window in or out, as appropriate
```

To zoom a window, begin by calling `SetPort()`. Because of a system bug, this call needs to be made — even if you're sure that the proper window is already the current window. Next, erase the contents of the window by calling the Toolbox routine `EraseRect()`. This step is necessary in order to erase the old size box, as described in the discussion of handling a click in a window's `inGrow` part. After setting the port and erasing the window contents, call the Toolbox function `ZoomWindow()`.

```
SetPort( theWindow );
EraseRect( &theWindow->portRect );
ZoomWindow( theWindow, thePart, false );
```

The first parameter in `ZoomWindow()` is a pointer to the window to shrink or enlarge. The second parameter is the part code returned by the `HandleMouseDown()` call to `FindWindow()`. If the value of the part is `inZoomIn`, `ZoomWindow()` will shrink the window to whatever size the window had before the last zoom out. If the part is `inZoomOut`, the `ZoomWindow()` function will enlarge the window to fill the screen. The final parameter to `ZoomWindow()` is a `Boolean` value that specifies whether the window should be brought to the front (`true`) or left in its current position among other windows (`false`).

After zooming the window, call `InvalRect()` to invalidate the window's content area, thereby forcing an update of the entire window.

```
case inZoomIn:
case inZoomOut:
  if ( TrackBox( theWindow, theEvent.where, thePart ) == true )
  {
    SetPort( theWindow );
    EraseRect( &theWindow->portRect );
    ZoomWindow( theWindow, thePart, false );
    InvalRect( &theWindow->portRect );
  }
  break;
```

Call `SetPort()` before calling `ZoomWindow()`, or your program will more than likely freeze the user's Mac!

EXAMPLE PROGRAM: WINDOWPARTS

When you run WindowParts, a window like the one shown in Figure 7-17 will appear on the screen. The WindowParts program handles mouse down events that occur in any of the parts discussed in this chapter. The window can be dragged, zoomed in or out, closed, or resized. If the window is resized, clipping is properly handled so that drawing doesn't extend into either of the window areas reserved for scroll bars, as shown in Figure 7-18.

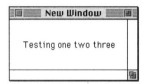

Figure 7-17
The window displayed by the WindowParts program.

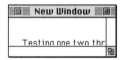

Figure 7-18
When the window is resized, the text that is drawn in the WindowParts window will be clipped.

All of the code in the `HandleMouseDown()` function has been described in this section; the WindowParts version just groups all of the code into one routine. The `HandleUpdate()` function is identical to the version used in this chapter's ClippingUpdate program. The following is the complete listing for WindowParts:

```
//_____
#define    rDisplayWindow    128
#define    kMinWindSize        50
#define    kMaxWindSize     10000
#define    kScrollBarSize      16
//_____
Boolean gDone = false;
```

```
//_____
void main( void )
{
  WindowPtr theWindow;

  InitializeToolbox();

  theWindow = GetNewWindow( rDisplayWindow, nil, (WindowPtr)-1L );
  ShowWindow( theWindow );
  EventLoop();
}
//_____
void EventLoop( void )
{
  EventRecord theEvent;

  while ( gDone == false )
  {
   WaitNextEvent( everyEvent, &theEvent, 15L, nil );

   switch ( theEvent.what )
   {
     case mouseDown:
      HandleMouseDown( theEvent );
      break;
     case keyDown:
      gDone = true;
      break;
     case updateEvt:
      HandleUpdate( theEvent );
      break;
   }
  }
}
//_____
void HandleUpdate( EventRecord theEvent )
{
  WindowPtr theWindow;
  RgnHandle theOrigClipRgn;
  Rect      theClipMinusScrollRect;

  theWindow = (WindowPtr)theEvent.message;
  BeginUpdate( theWindow );
   SetPort( theWindow );

   theOrigClipRgn = NewRgn();
   GetClip( theOrigClipRgn );

   EraseRect( &theWindow->portRect );

   DrawGrowIcon( theWindow );
   theClipMinusScrollRect = theWindow->portRect;
   theClipMinusScrollRect.right -= kScrollBarSize;
   theClipMinusScrollRect.bottom -= kScrollBarSize;
```

```
      ClipRect( &theClipMinusScrollRect );

      DrawWindowContents();

      SetClip( theOrigClipRgn );
      DisposeRgn( theOrigClipRgn );
    EndUpdate( theWindow );
}
//_____
void DrawWindowContents( void )
{
  MoveTo( 20, 40 );
  DrawString( "\pTesting one two three" );
}
//_____
void HandleMouseDown( EventRecord theEvent )
{
  WindowPtr theWindow;
  short     thePart;
  Rect      theGrowLimitsRect;
  long      theNewSize;
  short     theNewWidth;
  short     theNewHeight;

  thePart = FindWindow( theEvent.where, &theWindow );

  switch ( thePart )
  {
   case inGoAway:
     if ( TrackGoAway( theWindow, theEvent.where ) == true )
     {
      DisposeWindow( theWindow );
      gDone = true;
     }
     break;
   case inDrag:
     DragWindow( theWindow, theEvent.where, &qd.screenBits.bounds );
     break;
   case inContent:
     SelectWindow( theWindow );
     break;
   case inGrow:
     SetRect( &theGrowLimitsRect, kMinWindSize, kMinWindSize, kMaxWindSize,
              kMaxWindSize );
     theNewSize = GrowWindow( theWindow, theEvent.where, &theGrowLimitsRect );
     if ( theNewSize != 0 )
     {
      theNewWidth = LoWord( theNewSize );
      theNewHeight = HiWord( theNewSize );
      SetPort( theWindow );
      EraseRect( &theWindow->portRect );
      SizeWindow( theWindow, theNewWidth, theNewHeight, true );
      InvalRect( &theWindow->portRect );
```

```
      }
    break;

  case inZoomIn:
  case inZoomOut:
    if ( TrackBox( theWindow, theEvent.where, thePart ) == true )
    {
      SetPort( theWindow );
      EraseRect( &theWindow->portRect );
      ZoomWindow( theWindow, thePart, false );
      InvalRect( &theWindow->portRect );
    }
    break;
  }
}
```

Windows Reference

This section describes the Toolbox routines that can be used to load and open a window, update a window, and respond to mouse-clicks in a window.

WINDOW DATA TYPES

Each window has a WindowRecord data structure in memory that defines characteristics of the window.

WindowRecord

A window's WindowRecord data structure gets created and allocated in memory when the window is created by a call to GetNewWindow(). Of the many fields of a WindowRecord, the first field — the port member — is the most important to a programmer. The definition of the GrafPort data structure can be found in Chapter 4.

```
struct WindowRecord
{
  GrafPort    port;
  short       windowKind;
  Boolean     visible;
  Boolean     hilited;
  Boolean     goAwayFlag;
```

```
    Boolean      spareFlag;
    RgnHandle    strucRgn;
    RgnHandle    contRgn;
    RgnHandle    updateRgn;
    Handle       windowDefProc;
    Handle       dataHandle;
    StringHandle titleHandle;
    short        titleWidth;
    ControlRef   controlList;
    WindowPeek   nextWindow;
    PicHandle    windowPic;
    long         refCon;
};
```

Window Part Codes

A call to the Toolbox function FindWindow() returns a short value that can
be compared to any of several Apple-defined part code constants. Each part
code is used to represent a particular area on the screen or in a window.

```
inGrow
inZoomIn
inZoomOut
inDrag
inGoAway
inContent
```

LOADING A WINDOW

Before working with a window, you need to load its data into memory.
After that, a WindowPtr variable can be used to access the data that
represents the window.

GetNewWindow( )

You should use a WIND resource and a call to the Toolbox routine
GetNewWindow() to create a window.

```
#define   rDisplayWindow  128
WindowPtr theWindow;
Ptr       windStorage = nil;
theWindow = GetNewWindow( rDisplayWindow, windStorage, (WindowPtr)-1L );
```

Pass `GetNewWindow()` the ID of the `WIND` resource that holds the window information. Pass a `nil` pointer to let the Toolbox allocate memory for the window (as opposed to your supplying a pointer to a memory block). Type cast `-1L` to a `WindowPtr` as the last parameter to tell the Toolbox to place the window in front of all others.

WINDOW UPDATING

When a previously covered window becomes exposed, the system generates an update event — an event of type `updateEvt`. Your program should respond to such an event by updating (that is, redrawing) the affected window's contents.

BeginUpdate( )

Updating a window means redrawing the graphics that make up the contents of the window. Before drawing, call `BeginUpdate()` to temporarily set the window's visible region to the update region and to then clear the update region. If the update region isn't cleared in this manner, the system will not know that the update event has been handled.

```
WindowPtr theWindow;
BeginUpdate( theWindow );
   // redraw window contents
EndUpdate( theWindow );
```

The parameter in `BeginUpdate()` is a pointer to the window that is being updated. This `WindowPtr` can be obtained from the `message` field of the `EventRecord`. After redrawing the window's contents, your program must call `EndUpdate()`.

EndUpdate( )

After redrawing the content area of a window in response to an update event, call `EndUpdate()` to restore the window's visible region to its true viewable area. This region will have been temporarily set to the window update region by the call to `BeginUpdate()` that preceded window-drawing.

```
WindowPtr theWindow;
BeginUpdate( theWindow );
  // redraw window contents
EndUpdate( theWindow );
```

The parameter in EndUpdate() is a pointer to the window that has just been updated. This WindowPtr is obtained from the message field of the EventRecord. Before EndUpdate() was called, its companion function BeginUpdate() should have been called.

ClipRect( )

A window's clipping region can be changed to a rectangle the size of which is specified by the parameter of ClipRect(). This is most often done to limit drawing to an area of a window that excludes the window's scroll bars.

```
Rect theRect;
ClipRect( &theRect );
```

GetClip( )

Before changing a window's clipping region, call GetClip() to preserve the existing clipping region. That allows the region to be restored to its original area by calling SetClip().

```
RgnHandle theOrigClipRgn;
GetClip( theOrigClipRgn );
```

The parameter in GetClip() is a handle to an empty region that will be filled in by GetClip(). Before calling GetClip(), call NewRgn() to allocate memory for the new empty region.

SetClip( )

To restore a window's clipping region to its original region area, call GetClip() before changing the region, then call SetClip() afterwards.

```
RgnHandle theRegion;
SetClip( theRegion );
```

Pass `SetClip()` a handle to a region, and this function will set the current window's clipping region to the area occupied by the region the handle references. The region handle can be obtained by calling `GetClip()`.

NewRgn( )

To allocate memory for a new empty region, call `NewRgn()`. After the allocation, this function will return a handle to the memory. A region can be stored in this memory by calling `GetClip()`.

```
RgnHandle theOrigClipRgn;
theOrigClipRgn = NewRgn();
```

DisposeRgn( )

When through with a temporary region, free the memory it occupies by calling `DisposeRgn()`.

```
RgnHandle theOrigClipRgn;
DisposeRgn( theOrigClipRgn );
```

Pass `DisposeRgn()` a handle to the region to dispose of. If `DisposeRgn()` is used as a part of updating a window, then the region handle to pass will be the one obtained from a call to `NewRgn()`.

DrawGrowIcon( )

When updating a window that has a size box, call `DrawGrowIcon()` to redraw the size box.

```
WindowPtr theWindow;
DrawGrowIcon( theWindow );
```

Pass `DrawGrowIcon()` a pointer to the window that holds the size box. This `WindowPtr` can be obtained from the `message` field of the `EventRecord`. Include the call to `DrawGrowIcon()` as a part of your window-updating routine. That is, nest the call between calls to `BeginUpdate()` and `EndUpdate()`.

WINDOWS AND EVENTS

When the user clicks the mouse button while the cursor is over a window, your program should respond by determining what part of the window the cursor was over. It should then take the appropriate action based on the clicked part.

SetPort( )

Ensure that the proper window will receive whatever actions your program is taking by calling `SetPort()`.

```
GrafPtr thePort;
SetPort( thePort );
```

Pass `SetPort()` a pointer to the graphics port that is to be made the current port. Because a `WindowPtr` is defined to be the same as a `GrafPtr`, your application can pass either a `GrafPtr` or a `WindowPtr` variable in this parameter.

FindWindow( )

When a `mouseDown` event occurs, call `FindWindow()` to determine what part of the screen or window the cursor was in at the time of the event.

```
Point     thePoint = theEvent.where;
WindowPtr theWindow;
short     thePart;

thePart = FindWindow( thePoint, &theWindow );
```

Pass `FindWindow()` the screen coordinates of the cursor at the time of the event. This Point can be found in the `where` field of the `EventRecord`. As the second parameter, pass a pointer to a `WindowPtr` variable. If the event was window-related, `FindWindow()` will return a pointer to the affected window in this variable. When `FindWindow()` completes, it will return a short value that will match one of the Apple-defined part code constants listed near the start of this reference section.

TrackGoAway( )

If `FindWindow()` returns an `inGoAway` part code, call `TrackGoAway()` to track the user's mouse movements.

```
WindowPtr theWindow;
Point      thePoint = theEvent.where;
if ( TrackGoAway( theWindow, thePoint ) == true )
  DisposeWindow( theWindow );
```

Pass TrackGoAway() a pointer to the window that received the mouse-click. This pointer comes from the earlier call to FindWindow(). As the second parameter, pass the Point at which the mouse-click took place. If the user releases the mouse button while the cursor is over the window's close box, TrackGoAway() returns a value of true. In that event, call DisposeWindow() to close the window. A returned value of false should be ignored.

DisposeWindow( )

To free the memory that holds a window structure, call DisposeWindow(). If FindWindow() returns an inGoAway part code and TrackGoAway() then returns a value of true, call DisposeWindow() to close the window.

```
WindowPtr theWindow;
DisposeWindow( theWindow );
```

The parameter in DisposeWindow() is the pointer returned by the call to FindWindow().

DragWindow( )

If FindWindow() returns an inGoAway part code of inDrag, call DragWindow() to drag the window in response to the user's mouse movements.

```
WindowPtr theWindow;
Point      thePoint = theEvent.where;
Rect       theRect = qd.screenBits.bounds;
DragWindow( theWindow, thePoint, &theRect );
```

Pass DragWindow() a pointer to the window to drag. This pointer comes from the earlier call to FindWindow(). The second parameter is the Point at which the event occurred. The final parameter is a pointer to the rectangle that defines the screen boundaries of where the window can be moved to. To allow the window to be dragged anywhere on the user's screen, pass a pointer to qd.screenBits.bounds as this parameter.

SelectWindow( )

If `FindWindow()` returns an `inContent` part code, call `SelectWindow()` to activate the affected window.

```
WindowPtr theWindow;
SelectWindow( theWindow );
```

Pass `SelectWindow()` a pointer to the window to activate. This `WindowPtr` comes from a call to `FindWindow()`.

GrowWindow( )

If `FindWindow()` returns an `inGrow` part code, call `GrowWindow()` to resize the affected window.

```
long  theNewSize;
Rect  theGrowLimitsRect;
Point thePoint = theEvent.where;
theNewSize = GrowWindow( theWindow, thePoint, &theGrowLimitsRect );
```

The first parameter in `GrowWindow()` is a pointer to the window to resize. This pointer comes from a call to `FindWindow()`. The second parameter is the Point at which the cursor was when the event occurred. The final parameter is a pointer to a variable of type `Rect`. This rectangle holds the minimum and maximum pixel dimensions that the window can shrink or grow to. The `left` field of the `Rect` holds the minimum window width, the `top` field holds the minimum window height, the `right` member holds the maximum width of the window, and the `bottom` field holds the maximum height of the window.

InvalRect( )

To add a rectangular area of a window to the window's update region, call `InvalRect()`.

```
Rect theRect = theWindow->portRect;
InvalRect( &theRect );
```

Pass `InvalRect()` a pointer to a rectangle, and the area within that rectangle will be added to the window's update region. If the `portRect` field of the `WindowPtr` is passed, the entire content area of the window will be updated.

SizeWindow( )

Call the Toolbox function `SizeWindow()` to change the size of an open window.

```
WindowPtr  theWindow;
short      theWidth;
short      theHeight;
Boolean    updateFlag = true;
SizeWindow( theWindow, theWidth, theHeight, updateFlag );
```

The `WindowPtr` variable can be obtained from a call to Toolbox function `GetNewWindow()`. The second parameter specifies the new width the window should be sized to, while the third parameter indicates the new height for the window. The last parameter to `SizeWindow()` indicates whether any new area that was added to the window (if `SizeWindow()` enlarges the window) should be updated. Typically this should be set to `true`.

ShowWindow( )

Make an invisible window visible by calling the Toolbox function `ShowWindow()`.

```
WindowPtr  theWindow;
ShowWindow( theWindow )
```

Pass `ShowWindow()` a pointer to the window to make visible. If a window doesn't appear on-screen after calling `GetNewWindow()`, then the visible field of the window's `WindowRecord` structure has not been set to `true`. This can be done from within a resource editor or by calling `ShowWindow()`.

TrackBox( )

If `FindWindow()` returns an `inZoomIn` or `inZoomOut` part code, call `TrackBox()` to track the user's mouse movements.

```
WindowPtr  theWindow;
Point      thePoint = theEvent.where;
short      thePart;
if ( TrackBox( theWindow, thePoint, thePart ) == true )
  // zoom the window in or out, as appropriate
```

Pass TrackGoAway() a pointer to the window that received the mouse-click. This pointer comes from the earlier call to FindWindow(). As the second parameter, pass the Point at which the mouse-click took place. If the user releases the mouse button while the cursor is over the window's zoom box, TrackBox() returns a value of true. In that event, call ZoomWindow() to zoom the window.

ZoomWindow( )

If FindWindow() returns an inZoomIn or inZoomOut part code and TrackBox() returns true, call ZoomWindow() to enlarge or shrink the affected window.

```
WindowPtr  theWindow;
short      thePart;
Boolean    moveToFront;

ZoomWindow( theWindow, thePart, moveToFront );
```

The first parameter to ZoomWindow() is a pointer to the window to zoom. This pointer comes from the earlier call to FindWindow(). The second parameter is the part code returned by FindWindow(). If true is passed as the final parameter, the window will be brought to the front. If false is passed, the window will be left in its current plane among other open windows.

8

Dialogs

A window lets a program communicate with the user — it displays information in the form of text and graphics. A dialog box lets the user communicate with the program by enabling the user to enter a wide variety of information to be used by the program. A dialog box can enable a user to enter text and numbers in editable text boxes for future use by a program, can use a bank of radio buttons to let the user choose one option from several, and can include a checkbox that lets the user toggle an option on and off.

As you'll see in this chapter, a dialog box is a window with a few extras. Those extras are defined in a resource of type DITL. The look of the dialog box itself is provided in a resource of type DLOG. In this chapter you'll see how to create resources of these two types and then how to load these resources into memory for use in a dialog box.

You'll also read up on how a dialog box can be *modal* or *modeless*. A modal dialog box is fixed on the screen, controls the monitor, and ignores mouse-clicks outside the dialog box. On the other hand, a modeless dialog box works like a window: It can be dragged about the screen; it can be sent behind any windows that are on the screen and it can be clicked on to be brought again to the forefront.

About Dialog Boxes

Your knowledge of windows will pay off as you read about dialog boxes. That's because a dialog box is so similar to a window. In this section you'll see the ways in which a dialog box is like a window — and the ways in which it isn't.

THE ALERT, THE MODAL DIALOG BOX, AND THE MODELESS DIALOG BOX

An alert box, generally referred to as simply an alert, is a window that serves to inform or warn the user that a problem has occurred or may occur. An alert usually consists of an eye-catching warning icon, some descriptive text, and one or two buttons. An alert window is immovable and "owns" the screen; that is, when an alert is posted, no action can take place outside of the alert. The alert relinquishes control only after the user dismisses it by clicking on one of its buttons.

Where alerts give information to the user, dialog boxes usually get user input. Dialog boxes come in two states: modal and modeless. A modal dialog box is similar to an alert in that it is fixed on the screen; its name comes from the fact that the user is forced into the mode of working with only the dialog box. Unlike an alert, a modal dialog box can consist of any number of dialog box items — buttons, checkboxes, icons, pictures, and so forth.

A dialog box that is modeless can be freely moved about the screen. Unlike a modal dialog box, a modeless dialog box doesn't control the screen — the user is free to make menu selections or click on a window to make the dialog box inactive. A modeless dialog box doesn't force the user into one mode of action.

Because a modeless dialog box doesn't confine the user's activities, it is more user-friendly and is the preferred type dialog box type. But because a modal dialog box is easier to implement than a modeless one, this chapter discusses the implementation of modal dialog boxes first.

ALERT AND DIALOG RESOURCES

Because alerts and dialog boxes are just fancy windows, you shouldn't be surprised to find out that each is defined by information stored in resources. But while a window needs only one resource (a WIND), an alert or a dialog box needs two.

The size and screen placement of a dialog box are defined by a resource of type DLOG. As you'll see a little later in this chapter, the DLOG resource is very similar to a WIND resource. In fact, there's only one difference between the two: The DLOG resource requires the ID of a DITL resource. Because a dialog box holds items such as buttons and a window doesn't, the definition of a dialog box requires this second resource. The DITL resource is used to define what items will appear in a dialog box.

The ALRT resource is used to define the size and screen placement of an alert. That makes the ALRT resource similar to both the WIND and DLOG resource types. Because the ALRT resource doesn't allow you the freedom to select from a variety of window types to define the look of the alert, as can be done in the WIND and DLOG resources for windows and dialog boxes, the ALRT resource is simpler than both the WIND and DLOG resources.

THE DIALOGRECORD DATA TYPE

Chapter 2 described how a call to GetNewWindow() loads the information stored in a WIND resource into a WindowRecord data structure in memory. After that, the information can be accessed by a WindowPtr variable. If you're comfortable with that concept, you'll appreciate how a program works with a dialog box. A call to the Toolbox function GetNewDialog() loads the information from a DLOG resource and a DITL resource into a DialogRecord data structure in memory. From that point, the information is accessed by a DialogPtr variable. Figure 8-1 illustrates the loading of dialog box resource data.

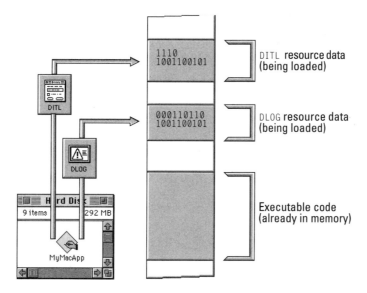

Figure 8-1
A dialog box requires DLOG and DITL resource data that gets loaded into memory.

Figure 8-1 shows that the DLOG and DITL information may get loaded to separate areas of memory. The association between these two blocks of memory is made by the second field of the DialogRecord data structure, the items field. Here's the definition of the DialogRecord data type:

```
struct DialogRecord
{
  WindowRecord window;
  Handle     items;
  TEHandle   textH;
  short      editField;
  short      editOpen;
  short      aDefItem;
};
```

The first field of a DialogRecord structure is a WindowRecord. The second field is a handle that leads to the items that will appear in the dialog box. These first two fields seem to imply that a dialog box is a window with a few extras. That is exactly the case. As you work with dialog boxes in your programs, you'll notice that in most ways they can be treated just like windows. Your program will be able to call window-related Toolbox functions to handle tasks that were covered in Chapter 7. Here are a few examples of the calls that can be made:

- SetPort() to make the dialog box the active port.
- DragWindow() to drag the dialog box.
- SelectWindow() to activate the dialog box.

Dialog Resources

A DLOG resource and a DITL resource are the two dialog-related resources you'll create in order to define one dialog box.

THE DLOG RESOURCE

The DLOG resource defines the look, size, and location of a dialog box, just as a WIND resource does for a window. The DLOG also holds the ID of the DITL resource that lists the dialog items that are to appear in the dialog box the DLOG defines. If you use ResEdit, follow these steps:

STEPS: CREATING A DLOG RESOURCE IN RESEDIT

Step 1. Select Create New Resource from the Resource menu.
Step 2. Scroll to the DLOG type in the list and double-click on it, or type
DLOG (in uppercase) in the editable text box and click on OK.

After you perform the second step, ResEdit will open a new DLOG resource. Figure 8-2 shows what you'll see. You can click on any of the icons along the top of the DLOG to set the look of the dialog box, just as you did with a WIND resource. A modal, or nonmovable dialog box, typically has no title bar. In ResEdit you can achieve this look by clicking on the window icon that's fourth from the right. You establish the size of the dialog box by typing values in the four editable text boxes that lie at the bottom left of the DLOG.

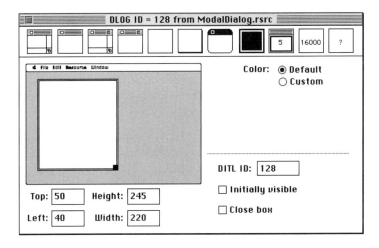

Figure 8-2
A DLOG resource being edited in ResEdit.

You can set the ID of the DITL resource that will be used by this DLOG by typing the ID in the DITL ID editable text box. While the DITL used by a DLOG doesn't have to share the same ID as the DLOG, programmers usually pair a DLOG and DITL this way. The DITL resource is discussed a few pages ahead.

If you use Resorcerer rather than ResEdit, follow these steps to create a new DLOG resource:

STEPS: CREATING A DLOG RESOURCE IN RESORCERER

Step 1. Click on the New button in the File Window (the main window that lists the resource types).

Step 2. Scroll to the DLOG type in the list and double-click on it, or type DLOG (in uppercase) in the editable box and click on the Create button.

After Step 2, Resorcerer will open an empty DLOG like the one pictured in Figure 8-3. Where the DLOG Editor in ResEdit displays a miniview of the dialog box that will result from the DLOG, the Resorcerer Dialog Editor displays the DLOG just as the dialog box will appear in a program. You can change the size, initial screen placement, and look of the dialog box by selecting Set Dialog Info from the Dialog menu. When choosing a look for a dialog box, consider that a modal (immovable) dialog box typically has the look shown in Figure 8-3.

Figure 8-3
A DLOG resource being edited in Resorcerer.

You can set the ID of the DITL resource that will be used by this DLOG in the Set Dialog Info window. Programmers generally give the DITL the same ID as the DLOG, although that's not a requirement. The DITL resource is discussed next.

THE **DITL** RESOURCE

The DITL (Dialog ITem List) resource lists the dialog items that will appear in a dialog box. The look of the dialog box is established by a DLOG resource, while the items in that dialog box are established by a DITL resource.

To create a DITL resource in ResEdit, begin by opening the previously created DLOG resource. Double-click on the miniature dialog box that appears in the small desktop on the left side of the DLOG Editor. When you do that, ResEdit creates and opens a new, empty DITL resource, as shown in Figure 8-4. This DITL will be the size of the DLOG, as specified in the DLOG Editor.

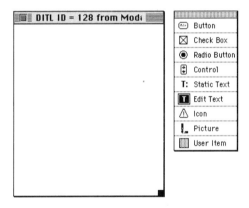

Figure 8-4
A DITL resource being edited in ResEdit.

When ResEdit opens a DITL resource, it also opens a palette of dialog items. To add an item to a DITL, click on the item in the palette. With the mouse button held down, drag the item to the DITL, and then release the button. You can change the location of the item at any time by clicking on it and dragging it. You can change the item's size by clicking on the lower right corner of the item and dragging. You can also change these item characteristics by double-clicking on an item and entering new values in the window that opens. Figure 8-5 shows the result of double-clicking on a button.

Resorcerer uses a DITL-editing approach that differs from the one used by ResEdit. Where ResEdit uses separate DLOG and DITL editors, Resorcerer uses a single Dialog Editor. When you create a new DLOG resource in Resorcerer, a new DITL resource is created as well. Both the DLOG and DITL are displayed together just as you'd see them in a program: as a single

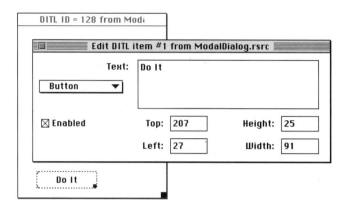

Figure 8-5
Double-clicking on a DITL item in ResEdit brings up a window that allows editing of that item.

dialog box. To add an item to a DITL, first create a DLOG. Then choose New Item from the Item menu, and select an item from the hierarchical menu that is displayed. Figure 8-6 shows a new button being added to a DITL.

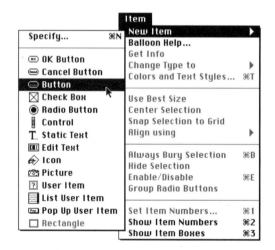

Figure 8-6
Adding an item to a DITL resource in Resorcerer.

Once an item has been added, you can change its size by clicking on the item's lower right corner and dragging. You can move the item in the dialog box by clicking on the item and dragging. You can also change these characteristics by double-clicking on the item and entering new values in the window that opens, as shown in Figure 8-7.

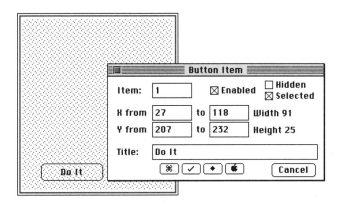

Figure 8-7
Double-clicking on a DITL item in Resorcerer brings up a window that allows editing of that item.

When you add an item to a DITL resource, your resource editor gives that item a number. If you use ResEdit, you can have the editor display the item numbers by selecting Show Item Numbers from the DITL menu. If you use Resorcerer, select Show Item Numbers from the Item menu. Figure 8-8 shows how ResEdit displays the item numbers for a DITL that holds four items. Resorcerer also places a small number by each item.

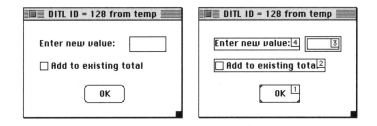

Figure 8-8
ResEdit allows for the display of item numbers in a DITL resource.

Working With a Modal Dialog Box

A modal dialog box is a dialog box that is fixed on the screen. When a modal dialog box is open, mouse-clicks outside the dialog box are ignored; the modal dialog box "owns" the screen.

OPENING AND DISPLAYING THE DIALOG BOX

To display a dialog box, you first load a `DLOG` resource and its `DITL` resource into memory. To take care of this task, call the Toolbox function `GetNewDialog()`.

```
#define   rDisplayDialog   128
DialogPtr theDialog;
theDialog = GetNewDialog( rDisplayDialog, nil, (WindowPtr)-1L );
```

The first parameter is the resource ID of a `DLOG` resource. Because the `DLOG` specifies which `DITL` resource is to be used with the `DLOG`, `GetNewDialog()` doesn't require that the ID of the `DITL` be passed to it. The second and third parameters in `GetNewDialog()` serve similar purposes to the second and third parameters in `GetNewWindow()`. The second parameter is used to specify the memory location where the dialog data should be stored, while the third parameter tells whether the dialog box should appear in front of all other windows.

If the `DLOG` resource specifies that the dialog box be visible, the dialog box will appear on the screen right after the call to `GetNewDialog()`. A call to `ShowWindow()` can also be used to display the dialog box:

```
DialogPtr theDialog;
ShowWindow( theDialog );
```

Recall that Toolbox routines that are used for windows can be used for dialog boxes as well. This is possible because both a `WindowPtr` and a `DialogPtr` point to the same thing: a `WindowRecord`. While a `DialogPtr` actually points to a `DialogRecord`, the first member of the `DialogRecord` is a `WindowRecord`.

MAINTAINING THE DIALOG BOX

Once a modal dialog box is posted to the screen, your program should enter a loop. At each pass through the loop, the Toolbox function ModalDialog() is called. The first parameter to ModalDialog() is a pointer to an optional filter function. The second parameter is a pointer to a dialog box item number.

```
short    theItem;
Boolean  doneWithDialog = false;

while ( doneWithDialog == false )
{
  ModalDialog( nil, &theItem );

  switch ( theItem )
  {
   // handle mouse clicks on dialog items
  }
}
```

ModalDialog() watches for a mouse-click on an item in the dialog box. If the user does click on an item, ModalDialog() returns the item number of that item. Recall that when you create a DITL resource and add items to it, your resource editor assigns a number to each item. That number enables you to identify each item from within your source code.

Figure 8-9 shows a modal dialog box with four items. At the bottom of the figure is the DITL resource that defines those items. In the DITL you can see that the OK button is item number 1, the checkbox is item number 2, the editable text box is item number 3, and the static text item is item number 4.

Your source code should define a constant for each enabled item in a dialog box. The enabled items are the items that will respond in some way to a mouse-click. In Figure 8-9, items 1 through 3 would be enabled items. A program typically ignores a mouse-click on a static text item, so a constant needn't be defined for the fourth DITL item. Here are the #define directives that could be used for the dialog box pictured in Figure 8-9:

```
#define    kOKButton       1
#define    kAddCheckbox    2
#define    kNewValueEdit   3
```

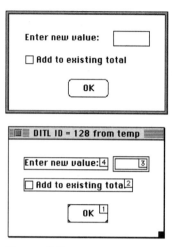

Figure 8-9

Use your resource editor's item number display option to get the item numbers of DITL *items.*

Using the above #define directives, the dialog box loop that was presented earlier can now be expanded upon:

```
while ( doneWithDialog == false )
{
   ModalDialog( nil, &theItem );

   switch ( theItem )
   {
    case kAddCheckbox:
      // handle mouse click in checkbox
      break;
    case kOKButton:
      // handle mouse click on the OK button
      break;
   }
}
```

Each button or checkbox in a dialog box should get a case label. The code under a case label performs the task or tasks appropriate for a mouse-click on that button or checkbox. The simplest item to implement is an OK (or Cancel, or Done) button. Toggling the value of the Boolean variable doneWithDialog from false to true ends the while loop.

```
case kOKButton:
   doneWithDialog = true;
   break;
```

You've probably noticed that there is no case label for the editable text item in the `while` loop snippet. The `ModalDialog()` function takes care of the handling of any typing that takes place in any editable text boxes; your code won't have to watch for or support keystrokes when a modal dialog box is on the screen.

THE EFFECT OF A MOUSE-CLICK ON A DIALOG ITEM

When a user clicks on a button, radio button, or checkbox, `ModalDialog()` will report the item number of the item. It's up to your application to then take the appropriate action. When a dialog item is clicked on, the action that follows is expected to be the same from program to program. Here are the item actions that are universal to Mac dialog boxes:

- A click on a radio button should turn that button on and turn the previously on button to off.
- A click on a checkbox should toggle the state of that checkbox. That is, if the checkbox was on before the click, it should turn off. If it was off, it should turn on.
- A click on a button should highlight that button while the cursor is over the button and the mouse button is held down.

The above list describes the actions that are the same for all programs. There are also application-specific actions that go along with a mouse-click on an item. For a click on a radio button or a checkbox, these actions usually go on out of the user's sight. The effects of the actions usually are not noticeable until a later point in the program. For example, a click on a checkbox titled "Add to existing total" may result in a global flag being set in the program. Anytime during the execution of the program, this flag could be examined to see if a user-entered bonus point value should be added if a game player scores, say, a bullseye in an archery game.

While radio button and checkbox application-specific actions take place behind the scene and are noticeable at a later time, button application-specific actions usually take place immediately after the button is clicked. The OK button and Cancel buttons found in most dialog boxes are two examples. Clicking on either of these immediately dismisses the dialog box. The ModalDialog example program in this chapter provides an example of the effects of each of the primary dialog items discussed here.

ACCESSING A DIALOG ITEM

A program that posts a dialog box needs to be able to access the items in that dialog box. Here's why:

- If the user clicks on a checkbox, a program needs to access the checkbox item to get the current state of the checkbox (checked or unchecked), so it can toggle the checkbox to the opposite state.

- If the user clicks on a radio button, a program must access both the "old" radio button (the one that was on before the mouse-click) and the "new" radio button (the one that was just clicked on) so that one can be turned off and the other turned on.

- Once the user clicks on an OK button (or some similarly named button), a program needs to access an editable text box in order to get the user-entered string from that box.

Accessing an item starts with obtaining a handle to the item. To be able to work with each enabled item in a dialog box, your program should be aware of the item numbers of enabled items. The same application-defined constants that were used in the dialog box `while` loop can be used here. The #define directives used for the dialog box pictured back in Figure 8-9 are repeated below:

```
#define    kOKButton        1
#define    kAddCheckbox     2
#define    kNewValueEdit    3
```

The Toolbox function `GetDialogItem()` is used to get a handle to an item. When passed a dialog pointer and an item number in the first two parameters, `GetDialogItem()` returns a handle to the item in the fourth parameter. `GetDialogItem()` also returns the item's type in the third parameter and the coordinates of the rectangle that surrounds the item in the fifth parameter. These two values are usually ignored by the program.

```
DialogPtr  theDialog;
short      theType;
Handle     theHandle;
Rect       theRect;
Str255     theText;
GetDialogItem( theDialog, theItem, &theType, &theHandle, &theRect);
```

As you're about to see, what a program does with the item's handle depends upon what type of item is being worked with.

The checkbox item

When a mouse-click occurs on a checkbox item, first call GetDialogItem() to obtain a handle to the checkbox. Then pass this handle to the Toolbox function GetControlValue(). GetControlValue() accepts only a particular type of handle — a ControlHandle — so you'll need to typecast the generic handle that was returned by GetDialogItem().

```
Handle theHandle;
short  theOldSetting;

theOldSetting = GetControlValue( ( ControlHandle )theHandle );
```

GetControlValue() returns a short with a value of either 0 or 1. A value of 0 is interpreted as a checkbox that is off, or unchecked. A value of 1 means the checkbox is currently on, or checked. Your program should then call the Toolbox routine SetControlValue() to toggle the checkbox to its opposite state.

```
if ( theOldSetting == 1 )
  SetControlValue( ( ControlHandle )theHandle, 0);
else
  SetControlValue( ( ControlHandle )theHandle, 1 );
```

Like GetControlValue(), the SetControlValue() function requires that the handle passed to it be of type ControlHandle. The second parameter to SetControlValue() is the value that the control should be set to.

If you like to use constants to add clarity to your source code, define a constant that makes it readily apparent that a value of 1 turns a control on and a value of 0 turns a control off.

```
#define   kControlOn    1
#define   kControlOff   0
```

Using the above constants turns the control-setting code into a snippet that looks like this:

```
if ( theOldSetting == kControlOn )
  SetControlValue( ( ControlHandle )theHandle, kControlOff);
else
  SetControlValue( ( ControlHandle )theHandle, kControlOn );
```

The toggling of a checkbox is a task so common to Macintosh programming that you'll want to write a simple utility routine that can be included in any of your programs. The SetCheckBox() function shown below can be incorporated unchanged into your latest project:

```
Boolean SetCheckBox( DialogPtr theDialog, short theItem )
{
    short    theType;
    Handle   theHandle;
    Rect     theRect;
    short    theOldSetting;
    Boolean  checkBoxOn;

    GetDialogItem( theDialog, theItem, &theType, &theHandle, &theRect );

    theOldSetting = GetControlValue( ( ControlHandle )theHandle );

    if ( theOldSetting == kControlOn )
    {
     SetControlValue( ( ControlHandle )theHandle, kControlOff);
     checkBoxOn = false;
    }
    else
    {
     SetControlValue( ( ControlHandle )theHandle, kControlOn );
     checkBoxOn = true;
    }
    return ( checkBoxOn );
}
```

Pass SetCheckBox() a pointer to a dialog box and the item number of the checkbox to toggle. SetCheckBox() will check or uncheck the checkbox as appropriate and then return a Boolean value that tells whether the checkbox has just been turned on (true) or off (false). Here is a snippet that calls SetCheckBox():

```
#define  kAddCheckbox   2
Boolean  gAddBonusToTotal;
DialogPtr theDialog;
gAddBonusToTotal = SetCheckBox( theDialog, kAddCheckbox   );
```

The above call to SetCheckBox() would be made when
ModalDialog() returns a clicked-on item value of kAddCheckBox.
SetCheckBox() then toggles the checkbox and returns a Boolean value that
lets the program know if the checkbox is now on or off. The Boolean
variable is declared at the global level so that it can be used at any point
during the execution of the program — even after the dialog box has long
since been dismissed.

The radio button item

The setting of radio buttons works in a manner similar, but not identical, to
the setting of a checkbox. The similarity is that GetDialogItem() is again
called to get a handle to the item and SetControlValue() is again used to
set the value of the item. The difference is that a click on a radio button
requires two items to change values, while a click on a checkbox requires
that only the value of the one checkbox item be changed. Unlike a
checkbox, which can appear in a dialog box without other checkboxes,
radio buttons always exist in groups of at least two. A checkbox is used in a
simple yes/no or true/false situation, whereas radio buttons are used when
multiple options are available.

When ModalDialog() returns the item number of a radio button, your
program should call GetDialogItem() and SetControlValue() to first turn
off whatever radio button is currently on. To keep track of the radio button
currently on, store the button's item number in a global variable:

```
short gOldRadio;
```

Before turning the newly clicked button on, get a handle to the button
that is currently on. Turn that button off by passing 0 (kControlOff) to
SetControlValue().

```
DialogPtr  theDialog;
short      theType;
Handle     theHandle;
Rect       theRect;
GetDialogItem( theDialog, gOldRadio, &theType, &theHandle, &theRect );
SetControlValue( ( ControlHandle )theHandle, kControlOff );
```

The above snippet refers to the radio button that is currently on as the old
radio button. Whichever radio button was just clicked on is considered the
new radio button. Again call GetDialogItem() and SetControlValue() to

turn the newly clicked button on. This time pass SetControlValue() a value of 1 (kControlOn). The following snippet turns on a radio button with an item number of 5:

```
#define    k25PointBonus    5
GetDialogItem( theDialog, k25PointBonus, &theType, &theHandle, &theRect );
SetControlValue( ( ControlHandle )theHandle, kControlOn );
```

One last step needs to be taken care of before the handling of a click on a radio button can be considered complete. In preparation for the next click on a radio button, the newly clicked button is now considered the old radio button. The global variable is now set to the item number of this button. Note that in order for the setting of the buttons to work properly this step must be performed after one button has been turned off and another one turned on:

```
gOldRadio = k25PointBonus;
```

Like a mouse-click on a checkbox, a click on a radio button is a task that most programs will need to be able to handle. You can paste the SetRadioButtons() function listed below into your source code file to add radio button handling to your project:

```
void SetRadioButtons( DialogPtr theDialog, short theNewRadio )
{
   short    theType;
   Handle   theHandle;
   Rect     theRect;
   GetDialogItem( theDialog, gOldRadio, &theType, &theHandle, &theRect );
   SetControlValue( ( ControlHandle )theHandle, kControlOff );
   GetDialogItem( theDialog, theNewRadio, &theType, &theHandle, &theRect );
   SetControlValue( ( ControlHandle )theHandle, kControlOn );
   gOldRadio = theNewRadio ;
}
```

Pass SetRadioButtons() a pointer to a dialog box and the item number of the clicked-on radio button, and SetRadioButtons() will turn the old button off and the new button on.

```
void SetRadioButtons( DialogPtr theDialog, short theNewRadio )
{
   short    theType;
   Handle   theHandle;
   Rect     theRect;
   GetDialogItem( theDialog, gOldRadio, &theType, &theHandle, &theRect );
   SetControlValue( ( ControlHandle )theHandle, kControlOff );
```

```
    GetDialogItem( theDialog, theNewRadio, &theType, &theHandle, &theRect );
    SetControlValue( ( ControlHandle )theHandle, kControlOn );

    gOldRadio = theNewRadio ;
}
```

The editable text box item

When a user types in an editable text box item, your program doesn't need to respond in any way. Once the user moves the cursor into the editable text box and clicks the mouse button, all characters that are typed will appear in the box. It isn't until the user clicks on a button such as an OK or Done button that your program needs to be concerned with the contents of an editable text box.

When the user signals that typing is complete (usually by dismissing the dialog box), your program should call the now-familiar GetDialogItem() routine to get a handle to an editable text box item. Follow that call with a call to the Toolbox function GetDialogItemText() to get the string from the item.

```
DialogPtr theDialog;
short     theType;
Handle    theHandle;
Rect      theRect;
Str255    theText;
GetDialogItem( theDialog, theItem, &theType, &theHandle, &theRect );
GetDialogItemText( theHandle, theText );
```

The first parameter to GetDialogItemText() is a handle to the editable text box item. Note that the generic handle returned by GetDialogItem() can be used as is; no typecasting is necessary. The second parameter to GetDialogItemText() is a Str255 string variable that will be filled with the contents of the editable text box when GetDialogItemText() completes execution.

An application-defined routine that pulls a string from an editable text box can be written using the two Toolbox routines just discussed. When passed a dialog pointer, the item number of an editable text box, and a string variable, the GetStringFromEditBox() routine fills the passed string variable with the contents of the edit box specified by the second parameter.

```
void GetStringFromEditBox( DialogPtr theDialog,
                           short      theItem,
                           Str255     theText )
{
  short  theType;
  Handle theHandle;
  Rect   theRect;
  GetDialogItem( theDialog, theItem, &theType, &theHandle, &theRect );
  GetDialogItemText( theHandle, theText );
}
```

A program that needs to get the string from an editable text box item with an item number of 3 and is then to write the string to the dialog box should call `GetStringFromEditBox()` as follows:

```
#define    kNewValueEdit    3
DialogPtr theDialog;
Str255    theString;
GetStringFromEditBox( theDialog, kNewValueEdit, theString );
SetPort( theDialog );
MoveTo( 20, 50 );
DrawString( theString );
```

Notice in the above snippet that drawing to a dialog box is preceded by a call to `SetPort()`, to make sure that drawing takes place in the dialog box. As mentioned earlier in this chapter and as demonstrated in the above snippet, Toolbox routines that work with windows accept a `DialogPtr` variable in place of a `WindowPtr` variable.

EXAMPLE PROGRAM: MODALDIALOG

The ModalDialog program displays a modal dialog like the one shown in Figure 8-10. The ModalDialog program demonstrates the handling of the four primary item types: the editable text box, the radio button, the checkbox, and the button.

After typing some characters in the editable text box, click on one of the two radio buttons to indicate whether the entered text should be converted to uppercase or lowercase characters. When the Do It button is clicked, the text in the editable text box will be converted and the altered string will be written back to the editable text box, replacing the original string. To also have the converted text echoed to the dialog box, check the Print text

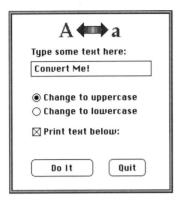

Figure 8-10
The modal dialog box displayed in the ModalDialog program.

below checkbox. Figure 8-11 shows the result of clicking on the Do It button when the dialog box items are set as shown in Figure 8-10. To end the program, press the Quit button.

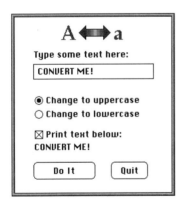

Figure 8-11
After you click on the Do It button, the case of the string in the editable text box is changed.

ModalDialog resources

The ModalDialog project requires three resources: a DLOG, a DITL, and a PICT. Figure 8-12 shows these resource types and the DLOG resource as viewed from ResEdit.

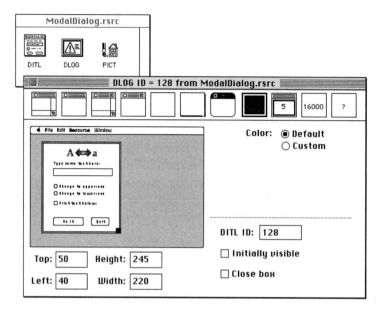

Figure 8-12

The DLOG used in the ModalDialog project.

Earlier you read that to create a DITL resource in ResEdit you can double-click on the empty, miniature dialog box that's displayed on the left side of the DLOG resource. In Figure 8-12 you can see that after you add items to the DITL, and then return to the DLOG, the DLOG now displays the items in the miniature dialog box.

Figure 8-13 provides a ResEdit look at the one DITL resource used by the ModalDialog project. The left of the figure shows the DITL as you'd normally view it in ResEdit. The right side of the figure shows the same DITL after Show Item Numbers has been chosen from the DITL menu. Resorcerer provides a similar menu item in its Item menu.

The source code listing for ModalDialog defines six constants that pertain to the project's DITL resource. You can compare these constants to the dialog item numbers shown in Figure 8-13:

```
#define    kDoItButton          1
#define    kTextToChangeEdit     2
#define    kUppercaseRadio       3
#define    kLowercaseRadio       4
#define    kEchoToDialogCheck    5
#define    kQuitButton           6
```

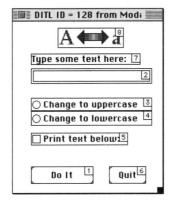

Figure 8-13
The `DITL` *used in the ModalDialog project: with and without the item numbers shown.*

The above constants are used throughout the ModalDialog source code listing when referring to particular items. In particular, the constants are used in calls to `GetDialogItem()`.

You will notice that two of the eight items pictured in Figure 8-13 aren't represented by constants. As mentioned, items that don't respond to mouse-clicks don't need to be recognized by a program. For the ModalDialog program, these items include one static text item (the label above the editable text box item) and one picture item (the logo at the top of the dialog box).

Displaying the dialog box

The ModalDialog program works by first initializing the Toolbox, then posting the modal dialog box.

```
void main( void )
{
  InitializeToolbox();
  OpenChangeTextDialog();
}
```

The `OpenChangeTextDialog()` begins by calling `GetNewDialog()` to load the dialog box data to memory. Before working with the dialog box, the returned dialog pointer is checked to ensure that the loading of the data was successful. Because a dialog box might have numerous dialog items,

Adding a picture to a dialog box is easy. Whether you use existing clip art or draw your own picture in a graphics program, copy the picture to the clipboard. Open your project's resource file and paste the picture into it. Both ResEdit and Resorcerer will convert the picture to a resource of type PICT. Next, open the DITL resource that will be used for the dialog box. Add a Picture item to the DITL. If you use ResEdit, click on the Picture item in the DITL palette, drag the Picture item to the DITL, and release the mouse button. If you use Resorcerer, select Picture from the hierarchical menu that appears when you select New Item in the Item menu.

Whichever resource editor you use, double-click on the newly added Picture item in the DITL resource editor. A window that lets you select the picture to use and resize the picture item will open. Make sure the Picture item's ID matches the ID that your resource editor gave the PICT when it was pasted into the resource file. Notice that your resource editor will force the PICT resource to whatever size you give the Picture item. To obtain the exact pixel size of the PICT resource, paste it into the Scrapbook. If you're using System 7.5 or later, the Scrapbook lists the picture's dimensions. Type those numbers into the window that appears when you double-click on the Picture item.

including any number of memory-consuming picture items, this check is a good precaution. If any value other than nil is returned, your program should assume that all is okay and proceed.

```
theDialog = GetNewDialog( rDisplayDialog, nil, (WindowPtr)-1L );
if ( theDialog == nil )
  ExitToShell();
```

Next, dialog items that require an initial setting need to be handled. First, one of the two radio buttons is set by calling SetRadioButtons(). Whatever item the global variable gOldRadio is set to will be turned on by this call. The checkbox is then given an initial value by calling SetCheckBox().

```
SetRadioButtons( theDialog, gOldRadio );
if ( gEchoTextToDialog == true )
  gEchoTextToDialog = SetCheckBox( theDialog, kEchoToDialogCheck );
```

After the items are set in the dialog box, a call to ShowWindow() displays the dialog box. If you look way back to Figure 8-12, you'll see that the DLOG resource that defines the look of the dialog box leaves the initially visible checkbox unchecked. While not required, it's a good idea to leave a dialog box hidden while its items are being set. That way, when

BY THE WAY

The ModalDialog program is written in such a way that the values of its dialog box items will be remembered even after the dialog box is dismissed. You can verify this by adding a second call to `OpenChangeTextDialog()` in main().

```
void main( void )
{
    InitializeToolbox();
    OpenChangeTextDialog();
    OpenChangeTextDialog();
}
```

When the modal dialog box opens, click on the radio buttons and checkbox to give the items any settings you want. Before clicking on the Quit button, take note of the state of the radio buttons and the checkbox. After you dismiss the dialog box, it will again open — thanks to the addition of the second call to `OpenChangeTextDialog()`. Notice that the radio buttons and the checkbox are set to whatever state they were left in. The use of the global variables `gOldRadio` and `gEchoTextToDialog` ensure that this will happen.

the dialog box is displayed, it will appear with all its items already set to their initial values. While it only takes a moment to calculate the settings for the ModalDialog dialog box, a program with several items will take a little longer.

Handling a mouse-click on a radio button

After the dialog box is posted, `OpenChangeTextDialog()` enters the loop that holds the call to the Toolbox function `ModalDialog()` and the code that handles mouse-clicks on enabled items. To respond to user mouse-clicks in the modal dialog, the program uses the same `SetCheckBox()` and `SetRadioButtons()` functions developed in this chapter. Here's how a click on the Change to uppercase radio button is handled:

```
case kUppercaseRadio:
    SetRadioButtons( theDialog, kUppercaseRadio );
    gConvertToUpper = true;
    break;
```

After `SetRadioButtons()` turns the radio button on, the global variable `gConvertToUpper` is set to true. If the user instead clicks on the Change to lowercase radio button, `gConvertToUpper` will be set to false.

Handling a mouse-click on the Do It button

In the above snippet, notice that the text in the editable text box isn't converted at the time of the mouse-click on the radio button. A click on a radio button can change a program setting, but it shouldn't perform the intended action immediately. Instead, the action should take place after the user is allowed to finalize his or her decision. A click on the Do It button is taken to be this approval.

```
case kDoItButton:
  ConvertText( theDialog, kTextToChangeEdit );
  EchoConvertedTextToDialog( theDialog, kTextToChangeEdit );
  break;
```

A click on the Do It button causes the application-defined ConvertText() function to execute. This routine calls GetDialogItem() and GetDialogItemText() to get a copy of the string that the user typed in the editable text box.

```
GetDialogItem( theDialog, theItem, &theType, &theHandle, &theRect);
GetDialogItemText( theHandle, theText );
```

Next, the UppercaseText() or LowercaseText() Toolbox routine is called to convert the string to either uppercase or lowercase. To make this decision, the global variable gConvertToUpper is examined.

```
Str255 theText;
if ( gConvertToUpper == true )
  UppercaseText( (Ptr)theText, theText[0] + 1, smSystemScript );
else
  LowercaseText( (Ptr)theText, theText[0] + 1, smSystemScript );
```

The UppercaseText() and LowercaseText() routines use the same three parameters. The first parameter is a pointer to the string to alter. Because these functions are expecting a generic pointer, typecast the Str255 variable to a Ptr. The second parameter specifies the number of characters that are to be converted. The last parameter is a script code that tells the Toolbox function how to go about converting the characters. The Apple-defined constant smSystemScript should be used here.

BY THE WAY

The Str255 data type is an array of characters, with the length of the string held in the first element of the array. Consider the following Str255 variable declaration and initialization:

```
Str255 theText = "\pDog";
```

For the above string, the array element values would look like this:

```
theText[0]   3™
theText[1]   D
```

```
theText[2]   o
theText[3]   g
```

The second parameter in UppercaseText() is the number of characters to be converted. This number should include the length character, the [0] element. In the example shown in this sidebar, a value of 4 should be passed: the length of the string, or 3, plus the element that holds the length value. That explains why the second parameter to UppercaseText() is theText[0] + 1.

After the text from the editable text box is converted to either uppercase or lowercase, the altered string is displayed back in the editable text box, replacing the text the user entered. A call to the Toolbox function SetDialogItemText() takes care of this task.

```
SetDialogItemText( theHandle, theText );
```

After the user-entered string is converted and redisplayed in the editable text box, an application-defined function named EchoConvertedTextToDialog() is called. This routine begins by filling a rectangle with a white pattern to erase any text that lies beneath the dialog box checkbox.

```
SetRect( &theRect, 25, 180, 230, 200 );
FillRect( &theRect, &qd.white );
```

If the dialog box checkbox is checked at the time that the Do It button is clicked, the global variable gEchoTextToDialog will have a value of true and the string that was obtained from the editable text box and converted will be drawn below the checkbox, as shown back in Figure 8-11. The purpose of this feature is to show that drawing to a dialog box is just the same, and just as simple, as drawing to a window. In the following snippet, MoveTo() is called to move the graphics pen, while DrawString() is called to write the string to the current port. Recall that the dialog box was made the current port by an earlier call to SetPort().

```
short   theType;
Handle  theHandle;
Rect    theRect;
Str255  theText;
if ( gEchoTextToDialog == true )
{
  GetDialogItem( theDialog, theItem, &theType, &theHandle, &theRect);
  GetDialogItemText( theHandle, theText );
  MoveTo( 30, 190 );
  DrawString( theText );
}
```

Disposing of the dialog box

When the program is through with the dialog box, the Toolbox function DisposeDialog() is called to free the memory occupied by the dialog box resources.

```
DisposeDialog( theDialog );
```

DisposeDialog() is called after the while loop code in OpenChangeTextDialog(). When the user clicks on the Quit button, the Boolean variable doneWithDialog gets set to true and the while loop ends. When that happens, it's time to dismiss the dialog box — DisposeDialog() takes care of that. The following snippet summarizes how OpenChangeTextDialog() works and shows the placement of the call to DisposeDialog():

```
void OpenChangeTextDialog( void )
{
  // variable declarations
  // open and display the dialog box
  // initialize buttons and checkbox

  while ( doneWithDialog == false )
  {
   ModalDialog( nil, &theItem );

   switch ( theItem )
   {
     // handle mouse button clicks on items
   }
  }
  DisposeDialog( theDialog );
}
```

The ModalDialog example source code listing

The following is the complete source code listing for the ModalDialog example program. As you look through the listing, take note of how the initial values of the global variables affect what's seen in the dialog box when it gets displayed.

```
//_____
#define    rDisplayDialog      128
#define    kDoItButton          1
#define    kTextToChangeEdit    2
#define    kUppercaseRadio      3
#define    kLowercaseRadio      4
#define    kEchoToDialogCheck   5
#define    kQuitButton          6
#define    kControlOn           1
#define    kControlOff          0
//_____
Boolean gDone = false;
short   gOldRadio = kUppercaseRadio;
Boolean gConvertToUpper = true;
Boolean gEchoTextToDialog = false;
//_____
void main( void )
{
  InitializeToolbox();
  OpenChangeTextDialog();
}
//_____
void OpenChangeTextDialog( void )
{
  DialogPtr theDialog;
  short    theItem;
  Boolean  doneWithDialog = false;
  theDialog = GetNewDialog( rDisplayDialog, nil, (WindowPtr)-1L );
  if ( theDialog == nil )
   ExitToShell();
  SetRadioButtons( theDialog, gOldRadio );
  if ( gEchoTextToDialog == true )
   gEchoTextToDialog = SetCheckBox( theDialog, kEchoToDialogCheck );
  ShowWindow( theDialog );
  SetPort( theDialog );

  while ( doneWithDialog == false )
  {
   ModalDialog( nil, &theItem );

   switch ( theItem )
   {
     case kUppercaseRadio:
       SetRadioButtons( theDialog, kUppercaseRadio );
       gConvertToUpper = true;
```

```
      break;
    case kLowercaseRadio:
     SetRadioButtons( theDialog, kLowercaseRadio );
     gConvertToUpper = false;
     break;
    case kEchoToDialogCheck:
     gEchoTextToDialog = SetCheckBox( theDialog, kEchoToDialogCheck );
     break;
    case kQuitButton:
     doneWithDialog = true;
     break;
    case kDoItButton:
     ConvertText( theDialog, kTextToChangeEdit );
     EchoConvertedTextToDialog( theDialog, kTextToChangeEdit );
     break;
   }
  }
  DisposeDialog( theDialog );
}
//_____
void ConvertText( DialogPtr theDialog, short theItem )
{
  short  theType;
  Handle theHandle;
  Rect   theRect;
  Str255 theText;
  GetDialogItem( theDialog, theItem, &theType, &theHandle, &theRect);
  GetDialogItemText( theHandle, theText );

  if ( gConvertToUpper == true )
   UppercaseText( (Ptr)theText, theText[0] + 1, smSystemScript );
  else
   LowercaseText( (Ptr)theText, theText[0] + 1, smSystemScript );

  SetDialogItemText( theHandle, theText );
}
//_____
void EchoConvertedTextToDialog( DialogPtr theDialog, short theItem )
{
  short  theType;
  Handle theHandle;
  Rect   theRect;
  Str255 theText;
  SetRect( &theRect, 25, 180, 230, 200 );
  FillRect( &theRect, &qd.white );
  if ( gEchoTextToDialog == true )
  {
   GetDialogItem( theDialog, theItem, &theType, &theHandle, &theRect);
   GetDialogItemText( theHandle, theText );
   MoveTo( 30, 190 );
   DrawString( theText );
  }
}
```

```
//_____
Boolean SetCheckBox( DialogPtr theDialog, short theItem )
{
    short    theType;
    Handle   theHandle;
    Rect     theRect;
    short    theOldSetting;
  Boolean checkBoxOn;

  GetDialogItem( theDialog, theItem, &theType, &theHandle, &theRect );

  theOldSetting = GetControlValue( ( ControlHandle )theHandle );

  if ( theOldSetting == kControlOn )
  {
   SetControlValue( ( ControlHandle )theHandle, kControlOff);
   checkBoxOn = false;
  }
  else
  {
   SetControlValue( ( ControlHandle )theHandle, kControlOn );
   checkBoxOn = true;
  }
  return ( checkBoxOn );
}
//_____
void SetRadioButtons( DialogPtr theDialog, short theNewRadio )
{
  short  theType;
  Handle theHandle;
  Rect   theRect;
  GetDialogItem( theDialog, gOldRadio, &theType, &theHandle, &theRect );
  SetControlValue( ( ControlHandle )theHandle, kControlOff );

  GetDialogItem( theDialog, theNewRadio, &theType, &theHandle, &theRect );
  SetControlValue( ( ControlHandle )theHandle, kControlOn );

  gOldRadio = theNewRadio ;
}
```

Working with a Modeless Dialog Box

A modal dialog box is easy to work with: A call to GetNewDialog() displays
the dialog box, and repeated calls to ModalDialog() inform your program
of user actions in the dialog box. Supporting a modeless dialog box, on the
other hand, requires a little extra programming effort — so why not just
stick to modal dialog boxes in your program? Because you're a programmer

and you enjoy a challenge? Perhaps, but the main reason is because Macintosh users expect to control a program — they don't want the program to control them. When a modal dialog box is on the screen, no other action can take place. A modeless dialog box lets the user select other windows or make menu choices.

OPENING AND DISPLAYING THE DIALOG BOX

To display a modeless dialog box, call to `GetNewDialog()` to load a `DLOG` resource and its `DITL` resource into memory, just as was done for the display of a modal dialog box.

```
#define    rDisplayDialog    128
DialogPtr theDialog;
theDialog = GetNewDialog( rDisplayDialog, nil, (WindowPtr)-1L );
```

The `DITL` resource for a modeless dialog box can contain the same items as a `DITL` resource used by a modal dialog. The `DLOG` will be slightly different, though. While a modal dialog usually uses a picture-frame look for the border of the immovable modal dialog box, a modeless dialog box should have a title bar — just as a window does. Figure 8-14 shows a `DLOG` resource used for a modeless dialog box. This ResEdit view of the resource shows that the dialog box will include a title, or drag, bar at its top.

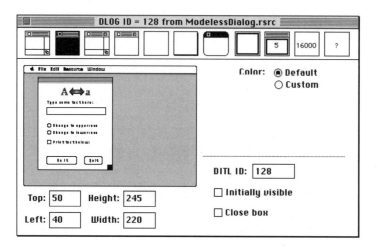

Figure 8-14
The `DLOG` used for a modeless dialog box includes a title bar.

Look familiar? A DLOG displayed in ResEdit shows a small view of the DITL items that will appear in the dialog box based on that DLOG. The items shown in the dialog box pictured in Figure 8-14 are identical to the ones used in this chapter's ModalDialog example program. The ModelessDialog example program, presented later in this chapter, is based on the ModalDialog program. Each program displays a dialog box with the same items. The only difference is that the ModalDialog program displays the dialog items in a modal dialog box while the ModelessDialog program uses — you guessed it — a modeless dialog box.

After the dialog box resource data is loaded into memory, set any checkboxes or radio buttons to their initial values. Again, this is the same procedure used when opening a modal dialog box: Call application-defined routines such as SetRadioButtons() and SetCheckBox() to turn on a radio button and check a checkbox. After the dialog box is open, however, the handling of it differs from the handling of a modal dialog box.

THE EVENT LOOP AND DIALOG-RELATED EVENTS

Because a modeless dialog box doesn't take control of a program, your code shouldn't go into a dialog box–controlled loop as it would for a modal dialog box. Instead, your program should call an application-defined dialog-handling routine from within the program's event loop. By letting the event loop take care of events involving the dialog box, your program also allows for the handling of any event *not* related to the dialog box. When a modal dialog box is on the screen, events such as mouse-clicks in the menu bar are ignored. When a modeless dialog box is on the screen, the program will take care of this type of event. Here is an outline of how an event loop looks for a program that makes use of a modeless dialog box:

```
void EventLoop ( void )
{
  EventRecord  theEvent;
  Boolean    is DialogEvent;

  while ( gDone == false )
  {
  WaitNextEvent( everyEvent, &theEvent, 15L, nil );
  if ( FrontWindow() != nil )
    isDialogEvent = HandleDialogEvent( theEvent );
```

```
      if ( isDialogEvent == false )
      {
        switch ( theEvent.what )
        {
         // handle events of type mouseDown, keyDown, etc.
        }
      }
    }
  }
```

Looking at the above snippet you'll notice that there aren't too many differences between this new version of EventLoop() and previous versions. WaitNextEvent() is still called to obtain information about the next event in the event queue, and a switch statement is still used to branch to other parts of the program to handle the event. What's different is that EventLoop() now first checks to see if an event is dialog-related before handling the event from within the switch statement.

The new version of EventLoop() calls FrontWindow() to see if a window or dialog box is open. If at least one window or dialog box is open, the Toolbox function FrontWindow() returns a pointer to whichever is frontmost. If there are no windows or dialogs on the screen, FrontWindow() returns a nil pointer. If the pointer is nil, EventLoop() knows the event isn't dialog-related. If the pointer isn't nil, EventLoop() assumes that a dialog box might be involved. In that case, the application-defined function HandleDialogEvent() is called to check to see if the event involves a mouse-click in the content area of a modeless dialog box. If it does, HandleDialogEvent() does what its name suggests: It handles the event. It also returns a value of true to EventLoop().

Before processing an event in its switch statement, EventLoop() checks the Boolean value returned by HandleDialogEvent(). Did HandleDialogEvent() already handle the event? If so, everything is taken care of and EventLoop() doesn't need to work with the event — the switch statement body can be skipped. On the other hand, if HandleDialogEvent() didn't handle the event, EventLoop() needs to. If that's the case, EventLoop() will execute the switch statement code that handles events in the same way they've been handled in the past.

EVENTS AND THE MODELESS DIALOG BOX

The decision as to whether or not EventLoop() handles an event is based on the result returned by the application-defined HandleDialogEvent() function. Before looking at the code that makes up this function, study the following summary of what the function does:

```
Boolean HandleDialogEvent( EventRecord theEvent )
{
  if the event isn't dialog-related
     return false
  if the event is an update or activate of a dialog box
     let the Toolbox handle it
     return true
  if the event is a mouse click on a dialog box item
     handle the event
     return true
}
```

Near the start of HandleDialogEvent() the function declares a Boolean variable and initializes it to false.

```
Boolean eventHandled = false;
```

If HandleDialogEvent() doesn't handle the event, the value of eventHandled will be returned, unchanged, to EventLoop(). That will let EventLoop() know that it must handle the event. After initializing eventHandled, HandleDialogEvent() checks to see if the event involves a dialog box. A call to the Toolbox function IsDialogEvent() returns a value of true if the event is dialog-related or false if it is not:

```
if ( IsDialogEvent( &theEvent ) == true )
  // handle the event
```

If IsDialogEvent() returns a value of false, the rest of the code in the HandleDialogEvent() routine gets skipped. The event isn't dialog-related, so it's back to EventLoop() for the handling of the event. If IsDialogEvent() returns a value of true, HandleDialogEvent() proceeds to the next Toolbox function call.

```
if ( DialogSelect( &theEvent, &theDialog, &theItem ) == true )
```

The DialogSelect() function is similar to the ModalDialog() function in that it returns the item number of a clicked-on item. DialogSelect() is more powerful by virtue of its ability to also respond to update events and activate events. If a dialog box needs updating or activating, DialogSelect() will take care of things and then return a value of false. That tells HandleDialogEvent() that the event has been taken care of. If the event involves a mouse-click on an enabled item, DialogSelect() will return the item number of the clicked-on item and a value of true. That tells HandleDialogEvent() that it must perform further processing: It must handle the mouse-click in a way appropriate to the item that was clicked on. The means of doing that is a switch statement.

```
switch ( theItem )
{
   // handle a mouse button click on a dialog box item
}
```

The code that appears within the body of the HandleDialogEvent() switch statement may be identical to the code that appears in the switch statement of the loop that controls a modal dialog box. The following snippet is an example of what HandleDialogEvent() looks like. To demonstrate the format of this function while still keeping things simple, this version of HandleDialogEvent() is useful for a modeless dialog box like the one pictured in Figure 8-15. That dialog box has only a single enabled item, a Quit button. The ModelessDialog example program that follows provides a look at a more practical version of the HandleDialogEvent() function:

```
Boolean HandleDialogEvent( EventRecord theEvent )
{
   DialogPtr  theDialog;
   short      theItem;
   Boolean    eventHandled = false;

   if ( IsDialogEvent( &theEvent ) == true )
   {
    if ( DialogSelect( &theEvent, &theDialog, &theItem ) == true )
    {
      switch ( theItem )
      {
        case kQuitButton:
          gDone = true;
          break;
```

```
      }
    }
    eventHandled = true;
  }
  return ( eventHandled );
}
```

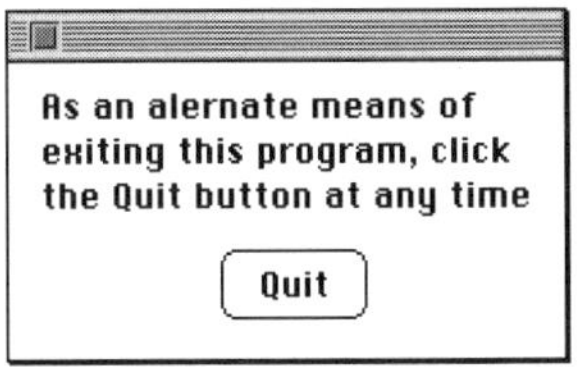

Figure 8-15
An example of a simple modeless dialog box.

EXAMPLE PROGRAM: MODELESSDIALOG

Some example programs require a lengthy walk-through to make it clear
what's happening in the source code. The ModelessDialog example isn't
one of these; if you are familiar with this chapter's ModalDialog example
program, you're most of the way to understanding the ModelessDialog
source code listing. That's because ModelessDialog does exactly what
ModalDialog does: It converts a user-entered string to either uppercase or
lowercase. The two programs are so similar, in fact, that they use the same
DITL resource. The only difference is that ModelessDialog uses a modeless
dialog box in place of the modal dialog box used by the ModalDialog
program. Figure 8-16 shows that the items in the ModelessDialog dialog box
are identical to those found in the ModalDialog dialog box. The difference
in looks between the dialog boxes can be found in the title bar — the
modeless dialog box has one, and the modal dialog box used in the
previous example doesn't.

Handling other events
ModelessDialog includes a HandleMouseDown() routine to take care of
events that don't involve a dialog box update or activate or a mouse-click in
the content of the dialog box. What types of events are left? In this program,
mouse-clicks in the window's drag bar.

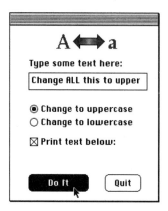

Figure 8-16
The modeless dialog box displayed by the ModelessDialog program.

```
void HandleMouseDown( EventRecord theEvent )
{
  WindowPtr  theWindow;
  short      thePart;
  thePart = FindWindow( theEvent.where, &theWindow );

  switch ( thePart )
  {
   case inDrag:
     DragWindow( theWindow, theEvent.where, &qd.screenBits.bounds );
     break;
  }
}
```

Notice that the code that handles a mouseDown event in the title bar of a modeless dialog box is no different from the code that handles the same event in the title bar of a window. The same would hold true if the ModelessDialog program supported mouse-clicks in other areas of the dialog box, such as a close box. For more information on handling mouse down events, refer back to Chapter 7. There you'll see a HandleMouseDown() routine very similar to the one listed above.

The ModelessDialog source code listing

```
//_____
#define    rDisplayDialog      128
#define    kDoItButton           1
#define    kTextToChangeEdit     2
#define    kUppercaseRadio       3
```

```
#define    kLowercaseRadio      4
#define    kEchoToDialogCheck   5
#define    kQuitButton          6
#define    kControlOn           1
#define    kControlOff          0
//_____
Boolean gDone = false;
short   gOldRadio = kUppercaseRadio;
Boolean gConvertToUpper = true;
Boolean gEchoTextToDialog = false;
//_____
void main( void )
{
  InitializeToolbox();
  OpenChangeTextDialog();

  EventLoop();
}
//_____
void OpenChangeTextDialog( void )
{
  DialogPtr theDialog;
  theDialog = GetNewDialog( rDisplayDialog, nil, (WindowPtr)-1L );
  if ( theDialog == nil )
   ExitToShell();
  SetRadioButtons( theDialog, gOldRadio );
  if ( gEchoTextToDialog == true )
   gEchoTextToDialog = SetCheckBox( theDialog, kEchoToDialogCheck );
  ShowWindow( theDialog );
  SetPort( theDialog );
}
//_____
void EventLoop( void )
{
  EventRecord   theEvent;
  Boolean   is  DialogEvent;

  while ( gDone == false )
  {
   WaitNextEvent( everyEvent, &theEvent, 15L, nil );
   if ( FrontWindow() != nil )
     isDialogEvent = HandleDialogEvent( theEvent );

   if ( isDialogEvent == false )
   {
     switch ( theEvent.what )
     {
      case mouseDown:
        HandleMouseDown( theEvent );
        break;
     }
   }
  }
}
```

```
//_____
Boolean HandleDialogEvent( EventRecord theEvent )
{
  DialogPtr theDialog;
  short     theItem;
  Boolean   eventHandled = false;

  if ( IsDialogEvent( &theEvent ) == true )
  {
   if ( DialogSelect( &theEvent, &theDialog, &theItem ) == true )
   {
     switch ( theItem )
      {
       case kUppercaseRadio:
         SetRadioButtons( theDialog, kUppercaseRadio );
         gConvertToUpper = true;
         break;
       case kLowercaseRadio:
         SetRadioButtons( theDialog, kLowercaseRadio );
         gConvertToUpper = false;
         break;
       case kEchoToDialogCheck:
         gEchoTextToDialog = SetCheckBox( theDialog, kEchoToDialogCheck );
         break;

       case kQuitButton:
         gDone = true;
         break;
       case kDoItButton:
         ConvertText( theDialog, kTextToChangeEdit );
         EchoConvertedTextToDialog( theDialog, kTextToChangeEdit );
         break;
      }
   }
   eventHandled = true;
  }
  return ( eventHandled );
}
//_____
void ConvertText( DialogPtr theDialog, short theItem )
{
  short  theType;
  Handle theHandle;
  Rect   theRect;
  Str255 theText;
  GetDialogItem( theDialog, theItem, &theType, &theHandle, &theRect);
  GetDialogItemText( theHandle, theText );

  if ( gConvertToUpper == true )
   UppercaseText( (Ptr)theText, theText[0] + 1, smSystemScript );
  else
   LowercaseText( (Ptr)theText, theText[0] + 1, smSystemScript );
```

```
   SetDialogItemText( theHandle, theText );
}
//_____
void EchoConvertedTextToDialog( DialogPtr theDialog, short theItem )
{
  short   theType;
  Handle theHandle;
  Rect    theRect;
  Str255 theText;
  SetRect( &theRect, 25, 180, 230, 200 );
  FillRect( &theRect, &qd.white );
  if ( gEchoTextToDialog == true )
  {
   GetDialogItem( theDialog, theItem, &theType, &theHandle, &theRect);
   GetDialogItemText( theHandle, theText );
   MoveTo( 30, 190 );
   DrawString( theText );
  }
}
//_____
void HandleMouseDown( EventRecord theEvent )
{
  WindowPtr theWindow;
  short     thePart;
  thePart = FindWindow( theEvent.where, &theWindow );

  switch ( thePart )
  {
   case inDrag:
     DragWindow( theWindow, theEvent.where, &qd.screenBits.bounds );
     break;
  }
}
//_____
Boolean SetCheckBox( DialogPtr theDialog, short theItem )
{
  short   theType;
  Handle theHandle;
  Rect    theRect;
  short   theOldSetting;
  Boolean checkBoxOn;

  GetDialogItem( theDialog, theItem, &theType, &theHandle, &theRect );

  theOldSetting = GetControlValue( ( ControlHandle )theHandle );

  if ( theOldSetting == kControlOn )
  {
   SetControlValue( ( ControlHandle )theHandle, kControlOff);
   checkBoxOn = false;
  }
  else
  {
```

```
        SetControlValue( ( ControlHandle )theHandle, kControlOn );
        checkBoxOn = true;
    }
    return ( checkBoxOn );
}
//_____
void SetRadioButtons( DialogPtr theDialog, short theNewRadio )
{
    short   theType;
    Handle  theHandle;
    Rect    theRect;
    GetDialogItem( theDialog, gOldRadio, &theType, &theHandle, &theRect );
    SetControlValue( ( ControlHandle )theHandle, kControlOff );

    GetDialogItem( theDialog, theNewRadio, &theType, &theHandle, &theRect );
    SetControlValue( ( ControlHandle )theHandle, kControlOn );

    gOldRadio = theNewRadio ;
}
```

Alerts

When the user needs to be warned about, or prevented from, taking a particular action, a program should post an alert. An alert looks like a simple dialog box. It usually consists of a sentence or two of text, an OK button, and possibly a Cancel button. An alert behaves as a modal dialog box does — action can't take place elsewhere until the alert is dismissed.

Now that you know about dialog boxes and the DLOG and DITL resources, your study of the use of alerts can be short and to the point. That's because an alert is nothing more than a stripped-down modal dialog box. In fact, an alert could be implemented using a modal dialog box that had a DITL with just one or two buttons. So why not just use a simple modal dialog box in place of an alert? Because the Toolbox offers more support for the alert than it does for a modal dialog box. As you'll see in this section, your code only needs to make a single Toolbox call to display and handle an alert.

THE ALERT RESOURCES

An alert requires two resources: an ALRT and a DITL. The ALRT resource defines the size and placement of the alert. The DITL defines the items that will appear in the alert — just as it defines the items that will appear in a dialog box. To create an ALRT resource in ResEdit, follow these two simple steps:

STEPS: CREATING AN ALRT RESOURCE IN RESEDIT

Step 1. Select Create New Resource from the Resource menu.
Step 2. Scroll to the ALRT type in the list and double-click on it, or type ALRT (in uppercase) in the editable text box and click on the OK button.

ResEdit opens an Alert editor like the one shown in Figure 8-17. As you can see in this figure, the ALRT is similar to the DITL. The difference is that an alert comes in only one flavor — you can't change the overall look of the alert window.

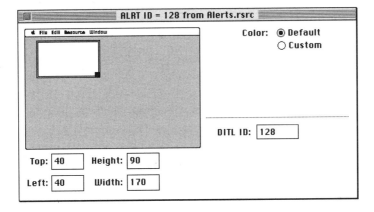

Figure 8-17
An ALRT resource as viewed in ResEdit.

To create a DITL that will be used with this ALRT, double-click on the small alert that's on the left side of the ALRT resource. This is the same technique used to create a new DITL for a DLOG resource. For additional information on working with dialog items, refer back to this chapter's discussion of the DITL resource.

If you use Resorcerer rather than ResEdit, follow these steps to create a new ALRT resource:

STEPS: CREATING AN ALRT RESOURCE IN RESORCERER

Step 1. Click on the New button in the File window (the main window that lists the resource types).

Step 2. Scroll to the ALRT type in the list and double-click on it, or type **ALRT** (in uppercase) in the editable box and click on the Create button.

After Step 2, Resorcerer will open an empty ALRT resource. Working with an ALRT in Resorcerer is just like working with a DLOG resource. Select Set Alert Info from the Alert menu to change the size and initial screen placement of the alert. To add an item to the ALRT, select an item from the hierarchical menu that gets displayed when you select New Item from the Item menu, just as you would do to add an item to a DLOG resource. For more information on this process, refer back to this chapter's discussion of the DITL resource.

THE ALERT-HANDLING SOURCE CODE

An alert consists of one or two buttons, some informative (or warning) text, and perhaps an icon in the upper left corner of the alert. The Toolbox routine Alert() posts an alert that controls the screen until the user dismisses it. The Alert() routine has three companion functions — NoteAlert(), CautionAlert(), and StopAlert() — that all work in the same way as the Alert() function. The only difference among these three functions is the icon that each displays in the upper left corner of the alert. Figure 8-18 shows the icon that each function substitutes in place of the dashed rectangle shown in the figure.

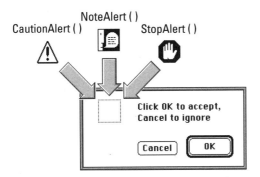

Figure 8-18
An alert can display no icon, or any one of three system icons.

All four of the alert functions will automatically highlight the button that has an item number of 1. That means you should make the alert's default button the first item in the alert's DITL resource.

To display an alert that has no icon, call Alert(). Pass the ID of an ALRT resource as the first parameter and a nil pointer as the second parameter. The second parameter is useful only when an optional filter function is used to provide additional event-handling:

```
#define     rMessageAlert    128
Alert( rMessageAlert, nil );
```

The above snippet works best for an alert that has a single button. An example might be an alert that is used to simply provide the user with some information. Because the user isn't expected to make a decision, only an OK button would be provided in this type of alert.

If an alert requires the user to make a decision, the short value returned by the Alert() function should be examined. This returned value holds the item number of the button that the user clicked on. The following snippet shows how to handle an alert that displays an OK button and a Cancel button:

```
#define     rMessageAlert    128
#define     kOKButton          1
#define     kCancelButton      2
short theItem;
```

```
theItem = Alert( rMessageAlert, nil );

if ( theItem == kOKButton )
  // take action appropriate for OK button selection
else
  // take action appropriate for Cancel button selection
```

EXAMPLE PROGRAM: ALERTS

The Alerts program displays either one alert or four alerts. The number depends on the action taken when the first alert is posted. This first alert is shown on the left side of Figure 8-19. If the user clicks on the OK button, the three alerts on the right side of the figure appear, one after the other. If the user clicks on the Cancel button, the program exits without displaying any of the three other alerts.

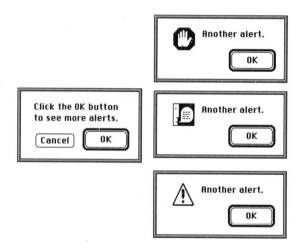

Figure 8-19
The Alerts program displays up to four alerts.

The resource file for the Alerts project consists of two ALRT resources and two DITL resources. One ALRT (with an ID of 128) defines the slightly larger alert shown on the left of Figure 8-19. One DITL (with an ID of 128) defines the two buttons and one static text item that appear in that alert. The other ALRT and DITL (each with an ID of 129) are used for all three of the alerts shown on the right side of Figure 8-19. The different icon that appears in each of these three alerts is the result of the different Toolbox routines used to display the alerts:

```
//_____
#define      rTwoButtonAlert      128
#define      rOneButtonAlert      129
#define      kOKButton              1
#define      kCancelButton          2
//_____
void main( void )
{
  short theItem;

  InitializeToolbox();
  theItem = Alert( rTwoButtonAlert, nil );

  if ( theItem == kOKButton )
  {
   NoteAlert( rOneButtonAlert, nil );
   CautionAlert( rOneButtonAlert, nil );
   StopAlert( rOneButtonAlert, nil );
  }
}
```

Dialog Reference

This section describes the Toolbox routines that are used to work with modal dialog boxes, modeless dialog boxes, and alerts.

OPENING AND CLOSING A DIALOG BOX

The technique used to open a dialog box is similar to that used to open a window. First, resource data needs to be loaded into memory. After that, the dialog box needs to be displayed.

GetNewDialog( )

To load the data from a DLOG and DITL resource, call GetNewDialog( ).

```
#define   rDisplayDialog   128
DialogPtr theDialog;
theDialog = GetNewDialog( rDisplayDialog, nil, (WindowPtr)-1L );
```

The first parameter to GetNewDialog() is the resource ID of a DLOG resource. The second parameter is used to specify the memory location where the dialog data should be stored, while the third parameter tells whether the dialog box should appear in front of all other windows.

ShowWindow( )

Make an invisible dialog box visible by calling the Toolbox function ShowWindow():

```
DialogPtr theDialog;
ShowWindow( theDialog);
```

Pass ShowWindow() a pointer to the dialog box to make visible. If a dialog box doesn't appear on screen after calling GetNewDialog(), then the visible field of the WindowRecord structure that is a part of the DialogRecord has not been set to true. This can be done from within a resource editor or by calling ShowWindow().

DisposeDialog( )

To close a dialog box and free the memory associated with it, pass a pointer to the dialog box to the Toolbox function DisposeDialog().

```
DialogPtr theDialog;
DisposeDialog( theDialog );
```

USING A MODAL DIALOG BOX

A modal dialog box controls the screen; mouse-clicks outside the dialog box are ignored. Displaying a modal dialog on the screen is achieved through a call to GetNewDialog().

ModalDialog( )

Once a dialog box is displayed, it can be either a modal or modeless dialog box. If the dialog box is controlled by repeatedly calling the Toolbox function ModalDialog(), the dialog box is considered a modal dialog box.

```
short theItem;

ModalDialog( nil, &theItem );
```

The first parameter in ModalDialog() is a pointer to an optional filter function. Pass a value of nil here to let ModalDialog() do all of the work. The second parameter is a pointer to a variable of type short. When the user clicks the mouse button on an enabled item in the dialog box, ModalDialog() will return the item's number in this parameter.

USING A MODELESS DIALOG BOX

A modeless dialog box is more user-friendly than a modal dialog box. A modeless dialog box allows the user to work outside the dialog box; mouse-clicks outside the dialog box are not ignored. Displaying a modeless dialog on the screen is achieved through a call to GetNewDialog().

IsDialogEvent( )

To determine if an event is dialog-related, call IsDialogEvent().

```
EventRecord theEvent;
if ( IsDialogEvent( &theEvent ) == true )
   // handle the event
```

The parameter in IsDialogEvent() is the EventRecord of the event to test. A call to the Toolbox function IsDialogEvent() returns a value of true if the event is dialog-related or false if it is not.

DialogSelect( )

Once an event is known to be dialog-related, pass it to DialogSelect() for further processing.

```
EventRecord  theEvent;
DialogPtr    theDialog;
short        theItem;
if ( DialogSelect( &theEvent, &theDialog, &theItem ) == true )
```

The first parameter in DialogSelect() is the EventRecord of the event to process. The second parameter is a pointer to the dialog box in which the event occurred. If an update event or activate event that involves a dialog box occurs, DialogSelect() will handle it. If the event is a mouseDown event, DialogSelect() will use the third parameter to return the item number of the clicked-on item.

WORKING WITH DIALOG BOX ITEMS

When the user clicks on an item in a dialog box, your program should get a handle to that item. Once your program has a handle, the value of the item can be obtained or changed.

GetDialogItem( )

To get a handle to a dialog box item, call `GetDialogItem()`. This function can be used to obtain a handle to any item, not just to an item that has received a mouse-click.

```
DialogPtr  theDialog;
short      theType;
Handle     theHandle;
Rect       theRect;
Str255     theText;
GetDialogItem( theDialog, theItem, &theType, &theHandle, &theRect);
```

Pass `GetDialogItem()` a pointer to the dialog box that holds the item in question and the item number of the item. In return, `GetDialogItem()` will fill its third, fourth, and fifth parameters with information about the item. The third parameter will hold the type of the item; the fourth parameter will hold a handle to the item; and in the fifth parameter the coordinates of the rectangle that surrounds the item will be stored. Your program will usually be interested in the fourth parameter, the handle to the item.

GetControlValue( )

After calling `GetDialogItem()` to obtain a handle to an item, call `GetControlValue()` to get the value of the item.

```
Handle theHandle;
short  theValue;

theValue = GetControlValue( ( ControlHandle )theHandle );
```

Pass `GetControlValue()` a handle to the item whose value needs to be found. Typecast the handle to a `ControlHandle`. In exchange, `GetControlValue()` will place the current value of the control item in the returned short variable. Call `SetControlValue()` to change the value of the control.

SetControlValue( )

After calling GetDialogItem( ) to receive a handle to an item, call
SetControlValue( ) to give the item a new value.

```
Handle  theHandle;
short   theNewValue = 1;
SetControlValue( ( ControlHandle )theHandle, theNewValue );
```

Pass SetControlValue( ) a handle to the item whose value needs to be
found. Typecast the handle to a ControlHandle. The second parameter
holds the new value for the control. A value of 1 turns the control on, and a
value of 0 turns it off. Call GetControlValue( ) if you need to check the
current control value before setting it to a new value.

GetDialogItemText( )

After calling GetDialogItem( ) to obtain a handle to an editable text item,
call GetDialogItemText( ) to get the text that is currently in the item.

```
Handle  theHandle;
Str255  theText;
GetDialogItemText( theHandle, theText );
```

Pass GetDialogItemText( ) a handle to the editable text item. Note that
this handle should not be typecast to a ControlHandle.
GetDialogItemText( ) will fill the second parameter with the text that is in
the item. Call SetDialogItemText( ) if you want to place a new string in
this editable text item.

SetDialogItemText( )

After calling GetDialogItem( ) to get a handle to an editable text item, call
SetDialogItemText( ) to place a new string in the item:

```
Handle  theHandle;
Str255  theText;
SetDialogItemText( theHandle, theText );
```

Pass SetDialogItemText( ) a handle to the editable text item. This
handle should not be typecast to a ControlHandle. SetDialogItemText( )
will place the text from the Str255 parameter into the editable text item.
Call GetDialogItemText( ) if you want to get the current text from the item.

ALERTS

To implement an alert, use one of the four Toolbox functions described below. Each routine is capable of supporting an alert without any other code or Toolbox calls.

Alert( )

To display an alert that has no icon in its upper left corner, call `Alert()`.

```
#define     rTheAlert    128
short       theItem;

theItem = Alert( rTheAlert, nil );
```

The first parameter to `Alert()` is the ID of the `ALRT` resource that defines the alert to be displayed. The second parameter is a pointer to an optional filter function that can be used for additional event processing. Pass a value of `nil` here to let `Alert()` do all of the work. When the user dismisses the alert, the `Alert()` function will return the item number of the clicked-on button.

NoteAlert( )

To display an alert that has a message icon in its upper left corner, call `NoteAlert()`. `NoteAlert()` works just like `Alert`; see the description of that routine for more information.

```
#define     rMessageAlert   128
short       theItem;

theItem = NoteAlert( rMessageAlert, nil );
```

CautionAlert( )

To display an alert that has a warning icon in its upper left corner, call `CautionAlert()`. `CautionAlert()` works just like `Alert()`; see the description of that routine for more information.

```
#define     rWarnAlert   128
short       theItem;

theItem = CautionAlert( rWarnAlert, nil );
```

StopAlert( )

To display an alert that has a stop sign icon in its upper left corner, call
StopAlert(). StopAlert() works just like Alert(); see the description of
that routine for more information.

```
#define    rDangerAlert   128
short      theItem;

theItem = StopAlert( rDangerAlert, nil );
```

9

Text

*T*he MoveTo() and DrawString() functions that are a part of QuickDraw provide an easy way for your application to draw text to a window or dialog box. But this method of placing text on the screen has a few drawbacks. First, using DrawString() to write large amounts of user-entered text is an awkward process. Second, the text drawn by DrawString() is not editable. To overcome these obstacles, the Macintosh Toolbox has a second means of working with text — TextEdit.

TextEdit is a set of data structures and Toolbox routines that make it easy for your program to display user-entered text and to let the user edit that text. As you'll learn in this chapter, your program can define a text area of any size in a window. This area is then used to display the text that the user types. In this chapter you'll learn how to create such a text area and how to manage the text that appears in this area. You'll see how your program can use TextEdit to support scrolling, text selection, and text-editing operations such as cut, copy, and paste.

TextEdit and Static Text

TextEdit is usually used for displaying editable text. But TextEdit also provides a simple means to display a static, or noneditable, string within a window or dialog box.

THE TEXT BOX

You've seen that QuickDraw lets you draw a line of text anywhere within a window by using the Toolbox routine `Move()` or `MoveTo()` to position the graphics pen and then calling the Toolbox function `DrawString()` to draw a string. TextEdit lets you perform a similar task using the `TETextBox()` function.

The difference between the text that results from a call to `DrawString()` and a call to `TETextBox()` is in *word-wrapping*. When you call `DrawString()`, the text that is drawn always appears on a single line. If the end of the graphics port that the text is being drawn to is reached before the end of the text string, the remainder of the string is truncated and lost. The string drawn with `TETextBox()`, on the other hand, can appear on more than one line. Your program doesn't have to specify how many lines. Instead, your program specifies an area in which the text should be drawn. TextEdit will determine from the length of the string and the area provided how many lines to break the string into.

Besides wrapping text to a given area, `TETextBox()` will justify the text in one of three ways. By using one of three Apple-defined constants in the call to `TETextBox()`, the text can be positioned within the box in the three ways shown in Figure 9-1.

Figure 9-1
Apple-defined constants and the text justification that they produce.

The following snippet shows how a call to `TETextBox()` can be used to draw a string to a box in a window or dialog box:

```
Rect    theTextRect;
short   theJust;
Str255  theString = "\pThese words appear in the text box";
long    theLength;
theLength = theString[0];
SetRect( &theTextRect, 20, 20, 120, 80 );
theJust = teFlushLeft;
TETextBox( (Ptr)(theString+1), theLength, &theTextRect, theJust );
```

The first parameter in TETextBox() is a pointer to the text to draw. When a variable of type Str255 is passed, two factors must be taken into account. The first thing to consider is that a Str255 variable uses the Macintosh Pascal format of storing the length of the string (that is, the number of characters in the string) in the first byte of the string. When using TETextBox() to draw a string in Str255 format, this first byte should be skipped. The second thing to consider is that a Str255 is an array of characters. In C, the name of an array (and thus the name of a Str255 variable) can be used as a pointer. That means that in the above snippet theString holds the address of the first byte of the string to draw. Considering these two points together means that theString + 1 holds the address of the start of the characters to draw. Finally, TETextBox() expects a generic pointer, so theString + 1 should be typecast.

The second parameter in TETextBox() is the length, in characters, of the string to draw. As you've just read, the length of a string in Str255 format is held in the first byte of the string. The content of the first byte of theString is found in the first element of the string: theString[0].

The third parameter in TETextBox() is a pointer to the rectangle to which the text should be drawn. The final parameter is one of the Apple-defined constants (teFlushLeft, teFlushRight, teCenter) that specify how the text should be justified.

The above snippet will result in a text box like the one shown on the left of Figure 9-1. Almost. The TETextBox() function doesn't draw a frame around the text. The rectangle that is passed as the third parameter to TETextBox() describes the coordinates of the box in which text should be drawn — it isn't used to frame the text. To do that, call the Toolbox function FrameRect(). Base the size of the framing rectangle on the TETextBox() rectangle, but add a buffer of a few pixels so that the text will not brush up against the frame.

```
Rect theTextRect;
Rect theFrameRect;
theFrameRect = theTextRect;
InsetRect( &theFrameRect, -5, -5 );
FrameRect( &theFrameRect );
```

In the above snippet, the Toolbox function InsetRect() is used to define a rectangle that is 10 pixels wider and 10 pixels higher than the text box rectangle. The first parameter in InsetRect() is a rectangle whose size is to be altered. The second and third parameters specify how much the first-parameter rectangle should be grown or shrunk. Because the routine is typically used to shrink a rectangle, positive values specify how many pixels the rectangle should be shrunk by. Negative values then specify how many pixels the rectangle should grow by. A second parameter value of -5 tells InsetRect() to expand both the left and right side of theFrameRect by five pixels. A third parameter value of -5 tells InsetRect() to expand both the top and bottom of theFrameRect by five pixels. The result is a framed rectangle that provides a five-pixel empty zone along each edge of the text box.

EXAMPLE PROGRAM: TEXTBOX

The TextBox program opens a window with a small text box in it. A single string is drawn left-justified within the box, as shown in Figure 9-2. As is the case with any text drawn with a call to TETextBox(), the text that appears in the window cannot be selected or edited. To quit the TextBox program, click the mouse button.

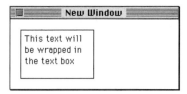

Figure 9-2
The TextBox program displays a window with a box of noneditable text.

```
//_____
#define    rTextWindow      128
#define    kTextRectLeft     20
#define    kTextRectRight   120
#define    kTextRectTop      20
#define    kTextRectBottom   80
//_____
void main( void )
{
   WindowPtr theWindow;
   Rect      theTextRect;
   Rect      theFrameRect;
   short     theJust;
   Str255    theString = "\pThis text will be wrapped in the text box";
```

```
InitializeToolbox();
theWindow = GetNewWindow( rTextWindow, nil, (WindowPtr)-1L );
SetPort( theWindow );
ShowWindow( theWindow );
theJust = teFlushLeft;
SetRect( &theTextRect, kTextRectLeft, kTextRectTop,
    kTextRectRight, kTextRectBottom );
theFrameRect = theTextRect;
InsetRect( &theFrameRect, -5, -5 );
FrameRect( &theFrameRect );
TETextBox( (Ptr)(theString+1), theString[0], &theTextRect, theJust );
while ( !Button() )
  ;
}
```

TextEdit

The TETextBox() routine and the text box that it creates don't do justice to
the power of TextEdit. As you're about to learn, TextEdit enables a programmer to add editable text to any area of a window or dialog box through the
use of just a few Toolbox routines.

THE TEXT EDIT RECORD

To display editable text in a window, your program will create a *text edit
record* — usually referred to as an edit record. An edit record holds up to
32,768 characters, or 32 MB of text. But an edit record contains more than
just text. It also holds the *editing environment* for a block of text, much as a
graphics port holds the drawing environment for a window. An edit record
keeps track of such things as where the text is displayed in a window and
the font the text is to appear in. The information in an edit record is stored
in a TERec data structure, the definition of which is shown here:

```
struct TERec
{
  Rect      destRect;
  Rect      viewRect;
  Rect      selRect;
  short     lineHeight;
  short     fontAscent;
```

```
    Point            selPoint;
    short            selStart;
    short            selEnd;
    short            active;
    WordBreakUPP     wordBreak;
    TEClickLoopUPP   clickLoop;
    long             clickTime;
    short            clickLoc;
    long             caretTime;
    short            caretState;
    short            just;
    short            teLength;
    Handle           hText;
    long             hDispatchRec;
    short            clikStuff;
    short            crOnly;
    short            txFont;
    Style            txFace;
    SInt8            filler;
    short            txMode;
    short            txSize;
    GrafPtr          inPort;
    HighHookUPPPhigh Hook;
    CaretHookUPP     caretHook;
    short            nLines;
    short            lineStarts[16001];
};
```

The fields of the TERec structure aren't accessed directly. Instead, Toolbox routines shield you from the need to become familiar with the type and purpose of each field. For example, the Toolbox function TEActivate() is used to set the active field of a TERec, thus making your program aware of which one of possibly several edit records is to be the recipient of typed characters. This method of indirect access is similar to the way in which the fields of a GrafPort structure are accessed. Recall that a GrafPort — used to hold drawing environment information — is also accessed through Toolbox functions. An example is a call to the Toolbox function that changes the pattern in which shapes are filled. The PenPat() function changes the value of the fillPat field of a GrafPort.

THE DESTINATION AND VIEW RECTANGLES

Each edit record has two rectangles that are used in conjunction with each other to display the text held in the edit record. The *destination rectangle* specifies the area that is to hold the text. The *view rectangle* specifies the area that is viewable by the user. The coordinates of these two rectangles are often the same, but it's possible to make them different. Figure 9-3 illustrates an example where the view rectangle is smaller than the destination rectangle, thus cutting off some of the text from the sight of the user. Figure 9-4 shows what the user would see given the destination and view rectangles used in Figure 9-3.

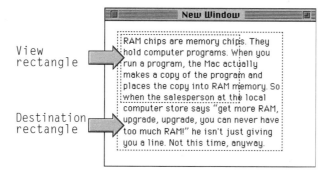

Figure 9-3
An edit record's view rectangle and destination rectangle can differ in size.

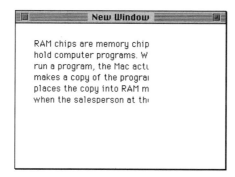

Figure 9-4
The text that is displayed as a result of the view and destination rectangles used in Figure 9-3.

CREATING AND DISPOSING OF A TEXT EDIT RECORD

Before creating a new text edit record, establish the coordinates of the destination and view rectangles that will be used by the edit record. The following snippet defines a destination rectangle 200 pixels across by 100 pixels in height and then sets the view rectangle to those same coordinates.

```
Rect theDestRect;
Rect theViewRect;
SetRect( &theDestRect, 10, 10, 210, 110 );
theViewRect = theDestRect;
```

To create a new edit record, call TENew(). This Toolbox function allocates memory for a new TERec data structure and returns a handle to that memory to your program. The following snippet shows why the destination rectangle and view rectangle were defined before creating the new edit record — pointers to these rectangles serve as the two parameters to TENew():

```
TEHandle theTErecord;
Rect     theDestRect;
Rect     theViewRect;
SetRect( &theDestRect, 10, 10, 200, 100 );
theViewRect = theDestRect;
theTErecord = TENew( &theDestRect, &theViewRect );
```

The text that will appear in the new text edit record will have whatever text characteristics are being used in the current window. For example, if the following snippet appeared *before* the above code was executed, the text in the edit record created by TENew() would appear in 14-point Times:

```
SetPort( theWindow );
TextFont( times );
TextSize( 14 );
// set rectangles and create new edit record
```

Make sure a call to GetNewWindow() precedes the call to TENew(); TENew() uses information from the current port. A window needn't be visible at the time TENew() is called, but one must be open. Don't call TENew() too early in your program just to get the task of creating an edit record out of the way.

Call the Toolbox function TEDispose() when your program is through with an edit record. TEDispose() deallocates all of the memory associated with the edit record referenced by the handle passed to the function.

```
TEHandle theTErecord;
TEDispose( theTErecord );
```

USER INPUT AND THE TEXT EDIT RECORD

The hText field of a TERec data structure is a handle to an area of memory that is to hold the text of the edit record. When a new edit record is created by a call to TENew(), the memory referenced by the hText handle is empty. As the user types, the typed characters are added to the memory referenced by hText.

If the characters resulting from the user's keystrokes are to be entered into the edit record, the Toolbox function TEKey() should be used. The following snippet adds an uppercase letter *A* to the edit record:

```
TEHandle theTErecord;
TEKey( 'A', theTErecord );
```

TEKey() adds the character named in the first parameter to the edit record referenced by the handle in the second parameter. TEKey() adds the character, but doesn't display it. To do that, call TEUpdate().

```
TEUpdate( &theWindow->portRect, theTErecord );
```

The first parameter in TEUpdate() is a pointer to a rectangle that needs updating. Passing the portRect field of the GrafPort that theWindow points to means that the entire window will be updated. The second parameter is a handle to the edit record that holds the newly added text.

If you think using TEKey() to add a particular character to an edit record seems a bit like simulating user input, you're absolutely correct. After the introductory example to TextEdit — the TEIntro program described next — you'll see how TEKey() can be used to really accept user-typed characters.

EXAMPLE PROGRAM: TEINTRO

When you run TEIntro, you'll see a window like the one shown in Figure 9-5. The window holds a framed box with the characters "Text!" in it.

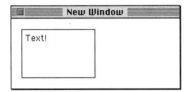

Figure 9-5
The TEIntro program displays a window with a text area with five characters in it.

TENew() uses the coordinates of the two passed-in rectangles to establish the edit record's destination and view rectangles, but it doesn't draw a frame around the view rectangle. Your program will need to do that. TEIntro does that in the same way this chapter's TextBox program does: A rectangle the size of the view rectangle is enlarged slightly, and then FrameRect() is called to draw the frame.

To add the five characters to the edit record, TEKey() is invoked five times. After the fifth call, TEUpdate() is called to update the window (which of course includes the destination and view rectangles).

TEIntro declares both the text edit record handle and frame rectangle variables at the global level. While this is not necessary in such a very short program, it was done to provide consistency with the next two example programs presented in this chapter. In those examples, providing these variables global scope will be important.

```
//_____
#define    rTextWindow      128
#define    kTextRectLeft     20
#define    kTextRectRight   120
#define    kTextRectTop      20
#define    kTextRectBottom   80
//_____
TEHandle gTErecord;
Rect   gFrameRect;
//_____
void main( void )
{
```

```
        WindowPtr theWindow;
        Rect     theDestRect;
        Rect     theViewRect;
        InitializeToolbox();
        theWindow = GetNewWindow( rTextWindow, nil, (WindowPtr)-1L );
        SetPort( theWindow );
        ShowWindow( theWindow );

        SetRect( &theDestRect, kTextRectLeft, kTextRectTop,
            kTextRectRight, kTextRectBottom );
        theViewRect = theDestRect;

        gTErecord = TENew( &theDestRect, &theViewRect );
        TEKey( 'T', gTErecord );
        TEKey( 'e', gTErecord );
        TEKey( 'x', gTErecord );
        TEKey( 't', gTErecord );
        TEKey( '!', gTErecord );

        TEUpdate( &theWindow->portRect, gTErecord );
        gFrameRect = theDestRect;
        InsetRect( &gFrameRect, -5, -5 );
        FrameRect( &gFrameRect );
        while ( !Button() )
          ;
        TEDispose( gTErecord );
    }
```

TextEdit and Events

If your event-handling program includes a window that uses TextEdit, you'll
need to make a few additions to your program's event loop. Besides
handling the updateEvt, mouseDown, and keyDown events that you are used
to working with, such programs usually also respond to two event types
you may not be familiar with: null events and activate events. The following
version of EventLoop() looks for an event of any of these five types. When
WaitNextEvent() reports that one of these events has occurred,
EventLoop() then calls an application-defined routine to do the actual work
of handling that event. Each application-defined routine is described in the
text that follows the EventLoop() listing.

```
    void EventLoop( void )
    {
      EventRecord theEvent;
```

```
      while ( gDone == false )
      {
       WaitNextEvent( everyEvent, &theEvent, 15L, nil );

       switch ( theEvent.what )
       {
         case nullEvent:
          HandleNull();
          break;
         case activateEvt:
          HandleActivate( theEvent );
          break;
         case updateEvt:
          HandleUpdate( theEvent );
          break;

         case keyDown:
          HandleKeyDown( theEvent );
          break;
       }
      }
   }
```

The null event

When the event queue is empty, `WaitNextEvent()` returns an event of type
`nullEvent`. This null event lets your program know that none of the events
it typically handles, such as a window update or a mouse-click, are waiting
to be taken care of. Since there's nothing to be done, many programs
choose to simply ignore events of type `nullEvent`. All the example
programs you've seen up to this point haven't included any code to handle
a null event. If your program uses TextEdit, however, it should watch for
and respond to null events.

When your program receives a null event, it can perform idle processing — taking care of simple, low-priority chores that can be handled in
between the processing of higher-priority tasks. The most common example
of an idle processing task is the blinking of the caret. The caret is the short
vertical line that appears in a block of text and marks the current insertion
point for typed characters. A program that includes editable text should also
include a blinking caret. The Toolbox function `TEIdle()` is responsible for
blinking the caret in the edit record whose handle is passed to it.

```
   TEIdle( gTErecord );
```

To consistently blink the caret, TEIdle() must be called frequently. Because null events occur *very* frequently (when no other events occur, every pass through the event loop generates one), TEIdle() should be called in response to such an event.

```
TEHandle   gTErecord;
case null Event:
  TEIdle( gTErecord );
  break;
```

If your program includes an application-defined function for the handling of each event type, then the case nullEvent code might instead look like this:

```
case nullEvent:
  HandleNull();
  break;
```

While this example produces a HandleNull() function that is quite trivial, you may still want to make use of such a routine to provide consistency in your program. If you look back at the above version of EventLoop() you'll see that the occurrence of an event of any type results in a call to an application-defined routine to handle that event.

```
void HandleNull( void )
{
   TEIdle( gTErecord );
}
```

The activate event

When a window other than the frontmost window gets clicked on, two activate events are generated. The fact that both events are of type activateEvt can be misleading; the first event specifies which window needs to be *deactivated,* while the second specifies which window needs to be *activated.* As with null events, some programs don't handle events involving window activation. That's because the system takes care of the work of properly highlighting and unhighlighting windows as they become active and inactive. A program that uses TextEdit should, however, watch for activation events.

When an event is of type `activateEvt`, the event record's `modifiers` field holds the information that tells whether the event involves window activation or deactivation. Your program can perform an AND operation on the `modifiers` field and the Apple-defined constant `activeFlag` to determine the nature of the event. If the result of the following operation is anything but 0, the event involves window activation; if the result is 0, the event involves window deactivation:

```
if ( ( theEvent.modifiers & activeFlag ) != 0 )
  // result isn't 0, handle window activation
else
  // result is 0, handle window deactivation
```

An application can have more than one open window, each containing an edit record. However, only one of these records can be active at any given time. The active record should be the edit record in the frontmost window. If a window has an edit record, that record needs to be made active when the window is clicked on. If the frontmost window has an edit record and a different window is clicked on, the edit record in the frontmost window needs to be deactivated.

In response to a deactivate event, call `TEDeactivate()` to deactivate the currently active edit record. In response to an activate event, call `TEActivate()` to activate the edit record. When the user begins to type, characters will be assigned to the correct edit record.

```
if ( ( theEvent.modifiers & activeFlag ) != 0 )
  TEActivate( gTErecord );
else
  TEDeactivate( gTErecord );
```

As with the handling of a null event, you can incorporate the code to handle an activate event in an application-defined activate-handling routine.

```
TEHandle gTErecord;
void HandleActivate( EventRecord theEvent )
{
  if ( ( theEvent.modifiers & activeFlag ) != 0 )
    TEActivate( gTErecord );
  else
    TEDeactivate( gTErecord );
}
```

The key down event

In the TEIntro example, `TEKey()` was called five times to deposit five characters in the edit record. When characters are instead being entered one at a time from the keyboard, you'll call `TEKey()` at each `keyDown` event.

To determine which character to enter into the edit record, perform an AND operation on the `message` field of the event record and the Apple-defined constant `charCodeMask`.

```
short theChar;
theChar = theEvent.message & charCodeMask;
```

As described in Chapter 6, when a `keyDown` event occurs, the `message` field of the event record gets filled with more than one piece of information. The above operation extracts just the typed character information from the `message` field.

Once the typed character is known, pass it to `TEKey()`. This function will add the character to the edit record referenced by the handle that is passed as the second parameter to `TEKey()`:

```
TEKey( theChar, gTErecord );
Here's the function that can be used when WaitNextEvent() returns an event
    of type keyDown:
void HandleKeyDown( EventRecord theEvent )
{
  short theChar;

  theChar = theEvent.message & charCodeMask;
  TEKey( theChar, gTErecord );
}
```

The update event

As you saw in this chapter's TEIntro example, anytime text is added to an edit record, that record needs to be updated.

```
TEUpdate( &theWindow->portRect, gTErecord );
```

In the TEIntro example, `TEUpdate()` was called a single time — after `TEKey()` was called five times. The result was that the five characters were added to the edit record and then displayed all at once. More typically, your program will instead call `TEKey()` at each keystroke, and your program will want to display each character as it is typed. To do that, call `TEUpdate()`

after every keystroke. The best way to accomplish that task is to call TEUpdate() in response to an update event. Each time a keyDown event occurs and TEKey() is called, an update event will be generated. Your program can respond to that event as follows:

```
BeginUpdate( theWindow );
  SetPort( theWindow );
  EraseRect( &theWindow->portRect );
  TEUpdate( &theWindow->portRect, gTErecord );
EndUpdate( theWindow );
```

Before calling TEUpdate(), call EraseRect() to make sure that the caret gets erased if the window gets deactivated. The following routine can be called in response to an update event. This function adds a call to the Toolbox function FrameRect() to make sure the edit box border gets redrawn.

```
void HandleUpdate( EventRecord theEvent )
{
  WindowPtr theWindow;

  theWindow = (WindowPtr)theEvent.message;
  BeginUpdate( theWindow );
   SetPort( theWindow );
   EraseRect( &theWindow->portRect );
   FrameRect( &gFrameRect );
   TEUpdate( &theWindow->portRect, gTErecord );
  EndUpdate( theWindow );
}
```

EXAMPLE PROGRAM: TEINPUT

The TEInput program opens a window that holds a text box like the one shown in Figure 9-6. Without clicking the mouse button, begin typing. When you do, the characters you type will appear in the edit box. When the characters reach the right side of the box, they'll word-wrap to the next line. If you type enough characters, they will continue to be entered into the edit record, but they won't appear in the view rectangle. You also won't be able to scroll down to see them. The next program in this chapter, TEScrollText, remedies this shortcoming. When you're done typing, click the mouse button to end the program.

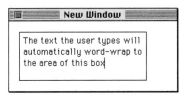

Figure 9-6
The TEInput program displays a window with an area that holds user-entered text.

TEInput uses the application-defined routines discussed in this chapter to handle null, active, key down, and update events. A mouse down event is handled by simply setting the global `Boolean` variable `gDone` to `true`. In the next example, TEScrollEdit, the `mouseDown` events will be handled in a more thorough manner.

```
//_____
#define     rTextWindow        128
#define     kTextRectLeft       20
#define     kTextRectRight     200
#define     kTextRectTop        20
#define     kTextRectBottom     80
//_____
Boolean   gDone = false;
TEHandle  gTErecord;
Rect      gFrameRect;
//_____
void main( void )
{
  WindowPtr theWindow;
  InitializeToolbox();
  theWindow = GetNewWindow( rTextWindow, nil, (WindowPtr)-1L );
  SetPort( theWindow );
  ShowWindow( theWindow );
  SetUpTextEdit();
  EventLoop();
  TEDispose( gTErecord );
}
//_____
void SetUpTextEdit( void )
{
  Rect theDestRect;
  Rect theViewRect;
  SetRect( &theDestRect, kTextRectLeft, kTextRectTop,
      kTextRectRight, kTextRectBottom );
  theViewRect = theDestRect;
  gTErecord = TENew( &theDestRect, &theViewRect );
  gFrameRect = theDestRect;
  InsetRect( &gFrameRect, -5, -5 );
```

```
   }
//_____
void EventLoop( void )
{
  EventRecord theEvent;

  while ( gDone == false )
  {
   WaitNextEvent( everyEvent, &theEvent, 15L, nil );

   switch ( theEvent.what )
   {
     case nullEvent:
      HandleNull();
      break;
     case activateEvt:
      HandleActivate( theEvent );
      break;
     case updateEvt:
      HandleUpdate( theEvent );
      break;

     case keyDown:
      HandleKeyDown( theEvent );
      break;
     case mouseDown:
      HandleMouseDown();
      break;
   }
  }
}
//_____
void HandleNull( void )
{
  TEIdle( gTErecord );
}
//_____
void HandleActivate( EventRecord theEvent )
{
  if ( ( theEvent.modifiers & activeFlag ) != 0 )
   TEActivate( gTErecord );
  else
   TEDeactivate( gTErecord );
}
//_____
void HandleKeyDown( EventRecord theEvent )
{
  short theChar;

  theChar = theEvent.message & charCodeMask;
  TEKey( theChar, gTErecord );
```

```
}
//_____
void HandleUpdate( EventRecord theEvent )
{
  WindowPtr theWindow;

  theWindow = (WindowPtr)theEvent.message;
  BeginUpdate( theWindow );
   SetPort( theWindow );
   EraseRect( &theWindow->portRect );
   FrameRect( &gFrameRect );
   TEUpdate( &theWindow->portRect, gTErecord );
  EndUpdate( theWindow );
}
//_____
void HandleMouseDown( void )
{
  gDone = true;
}
```

TextEdit and Editable Text

TextEdit allows your programs to easily support user-entered text in one or more text areas in a window. TextEdit also makes it easy for your program to support the editing of that text. With the use of just a few Toolbox commands, your program will enable the user to cut, copy, and paste text from or to the view rectangle of an edit record.

SCROLLING TEXT

The view rectangle in which text is displayed doesn't have to be large enough to display all of the text the user enters. On the contrary, because an edit record is capable of holding over 32,000 characters, there's a good chance that in many cases only a subset of the user-entered text will be shown. So users can view portions of the text that aren't currently displayed, TextEdit provides an autoscroll feature.

To scroll through a section of text, the user begins by positioning the cursor over the text in a view rectangle and then clicking the mouse button. With the mouse button still pressed, the user can drag the cursor down to scroll to text farther down in the edit record. Dragging the cursor up scrolls text that is farther up into view. Only a single Toolbox function is needed to add this autoscroll feature to an edit record — the TEAutoView() routine. A call to TEAutoView() should be made soon after the edit record is created, as shown here:

```
TEHandle gTErecord;
gTErecord = TENew( &theDestRect, &theViewRect );
TEAutoView( true, gTErecord );
```

The first parameter in TEAutoView() is a Boolean value that either turns autoscrolling on (true) or off (false). Calling TEAutoView() with a first parameter value of true doesn't perform any scrolling — it enables automatic scrolling. Once TEAutoView() has been called, anytime the user clicks on text and drags the cursor, the text in the edit record will scroll.

MOUSE DOWN EVENTS IN A TEXT AREA

When a window holds an edit record, events of type mouseDown should be examined to see if the user clicked the mouse button while the cursor was over the edit record's text area. To do this, use the GlobalToLocal() and PtInRect() Toolbox functions, with which you're already familiar; you've seen them in Chapter 5. As in that chapter, here you'll use this pair of functions to convert the cursor's location at the time of the mouse-click from global screen coordinates to coordinates local to a window.

```
Rect gFrameRect;
GlobalToLocal( &(theEvent.where) );

if ( PtInRect( theEvent.where, &gFrameRect ) )
   // handle mouse button click in text area
```

When an event is a mouseDown event, the where field holds the global pixel coordinates of the cursor at the time of the mouse-click. GlobalToLocal() converts these coordinates to ones that apply to the current window's coordinate system. The PtInRect() function then tests this converted point to see if it falls within the rectangle specified in the second parameter to PtInRect(). In the above snippet, the mouse-click is tested to see if the cursor was at any point over the rectangle that frames the text area.

If it turns out that the cursor was over the text area (PtInRect() returns true) at the time of the mouse-click, the Toolbox function TEClick() should be called. TEClick() is another of the Toolbox routines that takes control for as long as the user holds the mouse button down. As the user drags the cursor, TEClick() will highlight any text the user drags over. In other words, TEClick() is responsible for setting the text *selection range*.

```
Boolean shiftKeyDown;

TEClick( theEvent.where, shiftKeyDown, gTErecord );
```

The first parameter in TEClick() is the cursor's pixel location at the time the mouseDown event occurred. The second parameter is a Boolean value that tells whether or not the Shift key was down at the time of the mouse-click. If it was, TEClick() highlights all of the text from the old insertion point up to the point of the mouse-click. The last parameter in TEClick() is a handle to the affected edit record.

When a mouseDown event occurs, the system sets a flag for each modifier key that is being held down at the time of the mouse-click. Recall that modifier keys are keys such as the ⌘, Shift, and Option keys. These flags are all kept in the modifiers field of the event record. To determine whether the Shift key was one of the modifier keys that was pressed, perform an AND operation on the modifiers field and the Apple-defined constant shiftKey. If the result of the following operation is anything but 0, the Shift key was down. If the result is 0, the Shift key was up. Assign the result of this operation to the Boolean variable shiftKeyDown.

```
shiftKeyDown = ( ( theEvent.modifiers & shiftKey ) != 0 );
```

The following version of HandleMouseDown() can be used in an application that has a window with an edit record:

```
void HandleMouseDown( EventRecord theEvent )
{
   Boolean shiftKeyDown;

   GlobalToLocal( &(theEvent.where) );

   if ( PtInRect( theEvent.where, &gFrameRect ) )
   {
    shiftKeyDown = ( ( theEvent.modifiers & shiftKey ) != 0 );
    TEClick( theEvent.where, shiftKeyDown, gTErecord );
   }
}
```

EDITING TEXT IN A TEXT AREA

A program that uses TEClick() to highlight a section of edit record text is capable of giving the user the power to copy or cut that text. The Toolbox functions TECut() and TECopy() make this possible. Both routines require a single parameter, a handle to the edit record from which to cut or copy the selected text. Here's a call to TECut():

```
TEHandle gTErecord;
TECut( gTErecord );
```

Calling TECut() or TECopy() will place the selected text in a *local scrap*, a private scrap recognized only by your application. If the user launches another application (or clicks on a window of another already-running application), the cut or copied text will not be transferred to the *desk scrap,* the scrap common to all applications. To make sure the text does get transferred, call TEToScrap() after cutting or copying text. Before the text is transferred to the desk scrap, call ZeroScrap() to clear the desk scrap of its current contents.

```
TECut( gTErecord );
ZeroScrap();
TEToScrap();
```

Pasting text from the scrap to an edit record is accomplished using the Toolbox function TEPaste(). The one value passed to this function is the handle to the edit record that is to receive the pasted text.

```
TEPaste( gTErecord );
```

The TEToScrap() function takes care of transferring cut or copied text to the desk scrap. To move text in the other direction — that is, to copy the contents of the desk scrap to your application's private scrap — call TEFromScrap() before calling TEPaste().

```
TEFromScrap();
TEPaste( gTErecord );
```

If the user copies text in a different application and then switches to your application, the call to TEFromScrap() ensures that the user has access to the text in the desk scrap.

Your application can use the abovementioned functions to implement the Cut, Copy, and Paste items found in a program's Edit menu. Chapter 6 discusses how an application-defined `HandleMenuChoice()` function is used as a branching point from which other application-defined routines are called to handle each particular menu. One such routine could be the `HandleEditChoice()` function shown here:

```
void HandleEditChoice( short theItem )
{
  switch ( theItem )
  {
   case iCut:
     TECut( gTErecord );
     ZeroScrap();
     TEToScrap();
     break;

   case iCopy:
     TECopy( gTErecord );
     ZeroScrap();
     TEToScrap();
     break;

   case iPaste:
     TEFromScrap();
     TEPaste( gTErecord );
     break;
  }
}
```

EXAMPLE PROGRAM: TESCROLLEDIT

TEScrollEdit is an adaptation of the previous example, TEInput. When you run TEScrollEdit, you'll see the familiar window with the framed text area, as shown in Figure 9-7. Unlike the TEInput program, though, TEScrollEdit allows you to click and drag in the text area to scroll through the text and to make a selection. The addition of a single call to `TEAutoView()` in the application-defined `SetUpTextEdit()` function enables automatic scrolling.

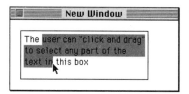

Figure 9-7
The TEScrollEdit program displays a window with an area that holds editable text.

For simplicity, TEScrollEdit doesn't include an Edit menu, but the program still lets you edit the text in the text area. After making a selection, type ⌘-X to cut the selected text or ⌘-C to copy it. Click elsewhere in the text area, and then type ⌘-V to paste the text back into the text area. To handle keyboard editing, the application-defined `HandleKeyDown()` function described in the TEInput example has been altered. Before calling `TEKey()` to accept input from the keyboard, this new version of `HandleKeyDoen()` first checks to see if the ⌘ key was pressed at the time of the keyDown event. If it was and the other key pressed was the X, C, or V key, the keystrokes are treated as if an Edit menu Cut, Copy, or Paste menu command was made. The test for the press of the ⌘ key is similar to the test for the press of the Shift key, which was described a few pages back in the section on handling a mouse down event.

```
if ( ( theEvent.modifiers & cmdKey ) != 0 )
```

The following snippet provides an overview of how `HandleKeyDown()` works in the TEScrollEdit program:

```
void HandleKeyDown( EventRecord theEvenL )
{
  short theChar;

  theChar = theEvent.message & charCodeMask;
  if ( ( theEvent.modifiers & cmdKey ) != 0 )
  {
   switch ( theChar )
   {
     // handle cut, copy, and paste commands
   }
  }
}
```

```
   else
   {
    TEKey( theChar, gTErecord );
   }
 }
```

Except for HandleMouseDown(), which now calls TEClick() to handle a mouse-click in the text area, the rest of the TEScrollEdit listing is very similar to the TEInput listing.

```
//_____
#define    rTextWindow       128
#define    kTextRectLeft      20
#define    kTextRectRight    200
#define    kTextRectTop       20
#define    kTextRectBottom    80
//_____
Boolean  gDone = false;
TEHandle gTErecord;
Rect   gFrameRect;
//_____
void main( void )
{
  WindowPtr theWindow;
  InitializeToolbox();
  theWindow = GetNewWindow( rTextWindow, nil, (WindowPtr)-1L );
  SetPort( theWindow );
  ShowWindow( theWindow );
  SetUpTextEdit();
  EventLoop();
  TEDispose( gTErecord );
}
//_____
void SetUpTextEdit( void )
{
  Rect theDestRect;
  Rect theViewRect;
  SetRect( &theDestRect, kTextRectLeft, kTextRectTop,
      kTextRectRight, kTextRectBottom );
  theViewRect = theDestRect;
  gTErecord = TENew( &theDestRect, &theViewRect );
  TEAutoView( true, gTErecord );

  gFrameRect = theDestRect;
  InsetRect( &gFrameRect, -5, -5 );
}
//_____
void EventLoop( void )
```

```
    {
      EventRecord theEvent;

      while ( gDone == false )
      {
       WaitNextEvent( everyEvent, &theEvent, 15L, nil );

       switch ( theEvent.what )
       {
         case nullEvent:
          HandleNull();
          break;
         case activateEvt:
          HandleActivate( theEvent );
          break;
         case updateEvt:
          HandleUpdate( theEvent );
          break;

         case keyDown:
          HandleKeyDown( theEvent );
          break;
         case mouseDown:
          HandleMouseDown( theEvent );
          break;
       }
      }
    }
//_____
void HandleNull( void )
{
    TEIdle( gTErecord );
}
//_____
void HandleActivate( EventRecord theEvent )
{
    if ( ( theEvent.modifiers & activeFlag ) != 0 )
     TEActivate( gTErecord );
    else
     TEDeactivate( gTErecord );
}
//_____
void HandleUpdate( EventRecord theEvent )
{
    WindowPtr theWindow;

    theWindow = (WindowPtr)theEvent.message;
    BeginUpdate( theWindow );
     SetPort( theWindow );
     EraseRect( &theWindow->portRect );
     FrameRect( &gFrameRect );
     TEUpdate( &theWindow->portRect, gTErecord );
```

```
  EndUpdate( theWindow );
}
//_____
void HandleMouseDown( EventRecord theEvent )
{
  Boolean shiftKeyDown;

  GlobalToLocal( &(theEvent.where) );

  if ( PtInRect( theEvent.where, &gFrameRect ) )
  {
   shiftKeyDown = ( ( theEvent.modifiers & shiftKey ) != 0 );
   TEClick( theEvent.where, shiftKeyDown, gTErecord );
  }
  else
  {
   gDone = true;
  }
}
//_____
void HandleKeyDown( EventRecord theEvent )
{
  short theChar;

  theChar = theEvent.message & charCodeMask;
  if ( ( theEvent.modifiers & cmdKey ) != 0 )
  {
   switch ( theChar )
   {
     case 'x':
      TECut( gTErecord );
      ZeroScrap();
      TEToScrap();
      break;

     case 'c':
      TECopy( gTErecord );
      ZeroScrap();
      TEToScrap();
      break;

     case 'v':
      TEFromScrap();
      TEPaste( gTErecord );
      break;
   }
  }
  else
  {
   TEKey( theChar, gTErecord );
  }
}
```

EXAMPLE PROGRAM: TEMULTIPLEEDIT

All of the example programs in this chapter have displayed a single window with a single edit record. To get an idea of how multiple edit records are handled, run the TEMultipleEdit program. When you do, you'll see two windows: a small one in the background, and a larger one in the fore-ground. As shown in Figure 9-8, each has an edit record associated with it.

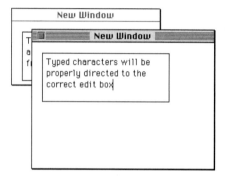

Figure 9-8
The TEMultipleEdit program displays two windows, each with an edit record.

Clicking on either window brings that window to the front and directs typed characters to the text area of that window. While TEMultipleEdit supports the activating and deactivating of each window, it doesn't support other mouseDown events such as dragging or window closing. To add those features, refer to Chapter 7. To quit the program, move the cursor over the empty menu bar and click the mouse button.

After typing characters into a text area, you can click the mouse button over the text area and drag the mouse to scroll through the text. Text that is cut or copied from a text area in one window can be pasted into that same area. You can also copy text from one window and then click on the inactive window and paste the text into the text area of that window. To keep track of the program's two windows, two global variables are declared.

```
WindowPtr gSmallWindow;
WindowPtr gLargeWindow;
```

TEMultipleEdit declares three global TEHandle variables. Each of the first two variables will be assigned values when TENew() is called twice to create two edit records, one for each window. The third TEHandle variable, gCurrentTErecord, will change values during the running of the program.

```
TEHandle gLargeWindTErecord;
TEHandle gSmallWindTErecord;
TEHandle gCurrentTErecord;
```

After initializing the Toolbox, the program opens the first window and then calls the application-defined SetUpTextEdit() function to create a TERec for that window. This process is repeated for the second window. The program then enters the event loop to handle the user's actions. Here's a look at the main() function of TEMultipleEdit:

```
void main( void )
{
   InitializeToolbox();
   gSmallWindow = GetNewWindow( rSmallTextWindow, nil, (WindowPtr)-1L );
   SetPort( gSmallWindow );
   ShowWindow( gSmallWindow );
   SetUpTextEdit( rSmallTextWindow );
   gLargeWindow = GetNewWindow( rLargeTextWindow, nil, (WindowPtr)-1L );
   SetPort( gLargeWindow );
   ShowWindow( gLargeWindow );
   SetUpTextEdit( rLargeTextWindow );
   EventLoop();
   if ( gSmallWindTErecord != nil )
   {
    TEDispose( gSmallWindTErecord );
    gSmallWindTErecord = nil;
   }
   if ( gLargeWindTErecord != nil )
   {
    TEDispose( gLargeWindTErecord );
    gLargeWindTErecord = nil;
   }
}
```

The version of SetUpTextEdit() used in this program accepts a parameter that specifies which of the two edit records should be created: the one for the smaller window or the one for the larger window. This parameter is used to determine which edit record to create, to set automatic scrolling for that edit record, and to make that record the current record.

```
void SetUpTextEdit( short theWindSize )
{
  Rect theDestRect;
  Rect theViewRect;
  SetRect( &theDestRect, kTextRectLeft, kTextRectTop,
      kTextRectRight, kTextRectBottom );
  theViewRect = theDestRect;
  if ( theWindSize == rSmallTextWindow )
  {
   gSmallWindTErecord = TENew( &theDestRect, &theViewRect );
   TEAutoView( true, gSmallWindTErecord );
   gCurrentTErecord = gSmallWindTErecord;
  }
  else
  {
   gLargeWindTErecord = TENew( &theDestRect, &theViewRect );
   TEAutoView( true, gLargeWindTErecord );
   gCurrentTErecord = gLargeWindTErecord;
  }

  gFrameRect = theDestRect;
  InsetRect( &gFrameRect, -5, -5 );
}
```

The two windows in TEMultipleEdit each use an edit record with a text area that is the same size and in the same window location. That's why the program can get away with keeping track of only one framing rectangle. If the windows had text areas that differed, it would make sense to have to set up routines (such as SetUpSmallTextEdit() and SetUpLargeTextEdit()) rather than litter the one routine with several if-else statements.

The key to determining which edit record should be the recipient of mouse-clicks, character input, and editing is in the program's handling of window activation. When a window gets clicked on, a mouseDown event is generated. If the mouse-click takes place on a window's drag bar or in a window's content area, the mouseDown event is handled by calling SelectWindow() to make that window the current window. This action in turn generates an activate event. The following application-defined routine is used to handle an event of type activateEvt:

```
void HandleActivate( EventRecord theEvent )
{
  WindowPtr theWindow;

  theWindow = (WindowPtr)theEvent.message;
```

```
 if ( theWindow == gSmallWindow )
  gCurrentTErecord = gSmallWindTErecord;
 else
  gCurrentTErecord = gLargeWindTErecord;

 if ( ( theEvent.modifiers & activeFlag ) != 0 )
  TEActivate( gCurrentTErecord );
 else
  TEDeactivate( gCurrentTErecord );
}
```

When an activate event occurs, the message field of the event record holds a pointer to the affected window. HandleActivate() compares that WindowPtr with the WindowPtr variable used to keep track of the smaller of the two windows. If the pointers match, it is the smaller window that is the recipient of the activate event. HandleActivate() then sets the value of the global variable that is used to keep track of the current edit record to the value of the handle that corresponds to the affected window. The routine then goes on to either activate or deactivate that edit record, depending on the type of the activate event.

After a window is activated, gCurrentTErecord holds a handle to the edit record of the active window. The value of gCurrentTErecord remains the same until the other window gets activated. That means that gCurrentTErecord always holds a handle to the proper edit record, the edit record associated with the active window. Anytime a TextEdit function is called, gCurrentTErecord is the TEHandle that should be passed to the function. For example, when the user presses a key on the keyboard, TEKey() will place the typed character in the proper edit record — the active record referenced by gCurrentTErecord.

```
TEKey( theChar, gCurrentTErecord );
```

TEMultipleEdit uses much of the source code found in the previous example, TEScrollEdit. If you'd like to see the complete source code listing, refer to the TEMultipleEdit.c source code file on the book's CD.

If one or more windows or dialog boxes *won't* use an edit record, you'll want to incorporate edit record tests in your code. When a window or dialog box doesn't have an edit record, set the global variable gCurrentTErecord to nil when that window or dialog box becomes active. Then, before calling a TextEdit Toolbox routine, verify that an edit record is active. For instance, before calling TEIdle() make sure that a text edit record is active. Here's how HandleNull() would look in a program that is capable of displaying windows or dialogs without edit records:

```
void HandleNull( void )
{
  if ( gCurrentTErecord != nil )
    TEIdle( gCurrentTErecord );
}
```

Text Reference

This section describes the Toolbox routines used by TextEdit to create and maintain text edit records.

TEXT BOXES

TextEdit provides a quick-and-dirty means of placing a noneditable string within a box in a window or dialog box. The text that is placed in this box can be justified in a number of ways and will be word-wrapped to the size of the box.

TETextBox( )

To place a text box that will hold noneditable text in a window, call TETextBox().

```
Str255  theStr = "\pThe text";
Rect    theRect;
short   theJust = teFlushRight;
TETextBox( (Ptr)(theStr+1), theStr[0], &theRect, theJust );
```

The first parameter in TETextBox() is a pointer to the text to draw. If a Str255 variable is passed, increment the string name by 1. This has the effect of pointing to the second character in the string. The first character holds the string length and should be skipped. Typecast the resulting string to a generic pointer. The second parameter is the length of the string. Use the first character of a `Str255` variable as this parameter. The third parameter is a pointer to the rectangle to which the text should be drawn. The final parameter is one of the Apple-defined constants (`teFlushLeft`, `teFlushRight`, `teCenter`) that specify the justification of the text.

CREATING AND DISPOSING OF A TEXT EDIT RECORD

A text edit record is associated with a window. Before creating a new edit record, make sure a window has been opened using a call to `GetNewWindow()`.

TENew( )

To create a new text edit record, a data structure of type `TERec`, call `TENew()`.

```
TEHandle theTErecord;
Rect     theDestRect;
Rect     theViewRect;
theTErecord = TENew( &theDestRect, &theViewRect );
```

The first parameter in `TENew()` is a pointer to a rectangle that will serve as the destination rectangle for the text. The second parameter is a pointer to a view rectangle. Any text entered into the record will be justified and word-wrapped according to the boundaries of the destination rectangle — but only the text that falls within the boundaries of the view rectangle will be displayed. After executing, `TENew()` returns a handle to the area of memory that holds the newly allocated `TERec` data structure.

TEDispose( )

When your program is finished with an edit record, call the Toolbox function `TEDispose()`. This routine releases all of the memory associated with the edit record referenced by the passed handle.

```
TEHandle theTErecord;
TEDispose( theTErecord );
```

USER-ENTERED TEXT

A text edit record supports user-entered, editable text. The TEKey() function is your means of adding a single character to an existing edit record.

TEKey( )

To add a character to the text of an edit record, call TEKey(). TEKey() adds a character but doesn't display it. To do that, call TEUpdate().

```
short    theChar;
TEHandle theTErecord;

theChar = theEvent.message & charCodeMask;
TEKey( theChar, theTErecord );
```

Pass TEKey() a short that represents the character to add to the edit record. The typed character can be extracted from the message field of the event record as shown above. The second parameter is a handle to the edit record that is to receive the character.

UPDATING AN EDIT RECORD

When a text area in a window becomes obscured and then visible, the text area needs to be updated. When TEKey() is called to accept the input of a single character, the text area needs to be updated in order to display that character. The time to perform these updates is when an event of updateEvt occurs.

TEUpdate( )

To update the text that's displayed in an edit record text area, call TEUpdate(). Calling this function in response to an event of type updateEvt will ensure that each typed character is displayed immediately after it is typed.

```
WindowPtr theWindow;
TEHandle  theTErecord;
BeginUpdate( theWindow );
  SetPort( theWindow );
  EraseRect( &theWindow->portRect );
  // draw window contents
  TEUpdate( &theWindow->portRect, theTErecord );
EndUpdate( theWindow );
```

The first parameter in `TEUpdate()` is a pointer to a rectangle to update. The `portRect` field of a window encompasses the entire window, so passing a pointer to this rectangle guarantees that the edit record's view rectangle will be included in the update. The second parameter is a handle to the edit record that holds the text to update. As shown above, call `TEUpdate()` between calls to `BeginUpdate()` and `EndUpdate()`; see Chapter 7 for information on those two Toolbox functions. Besides updating the edit record, update the rest of the window's contents as described in Chapter 7.

TEIdle( )

To blink the caret in a text area, call `TEIdle()`. To blink the caret consistently, call `TEIdle()` at every occurrence of an event of type `nullEvent`. Pass `TEIdle()` a handle to the active edit record.

```
TEHandle theTErecord;
TEIdle( theTErecord );
```

TEActivate( )

When an event of type `activateEvt` occurs and the event record's `modifiers` field indicates that the event is an activate event (as opposed to a deactivate event), call `TEActivate()` to activate the edit record for the window that was clicked on. Pass `TEActivate()` a handle to the edit record that is to be activated.

```
EventRecord theEvent;
TEHandle    theTErecord;
if ( ( theEvent.modifiers & activeFlag ) != 0 )
  TEActivate( theTErecord );
else
  // call TEDeactivate() to deactivate the edit record
```

TEDeactivate( )

When an `activateEvt` event occurs and the `modifiers` field of the event record indicates that the event is a deactivate event (as opposed to an activate event), call `TEDeactivate()` to deactivate the edit record for the window that is becoming inactive. Pass `TEDeactivate()` a handle to the edit record that is to be deactivated.

```
EventRecord theEvent;
TEHandle    theTErecord;
if ( ( theEvent.modifiers & activeFlag ) != 0 )
  // call TEActivate() to activate the edit record
else
  TEDeactivate( theTErecord );
```

EDITING TEXT EDIT RECORD TEXT

TextEdit exists to enable you to easily add text-editing capabilities to your applications. A handful of Toolbox routines make this possible.

TEAutoView( )

To let the user select any portion of the text in an edit record, enable automatic scrolling by calling TEAutoView() soon after the edit record is created:

```
TEHandle theTErecord;
Boolean  autoEnabled = true;
TEAutoView( autoEnabled , theTErecord );
```

The first parameter in TEAutoView() is a Boolean value that indicates whether autoscrolling should be enabled (true) or disabled (false). The second parameter is a handle to the affected edit record.

TEClick( )

To track the cursor as the user holds the mouse button down and drags over the text of an edit record, call TEClick(). This routine will highlight any text that the cursor traverses. When the user releases the mouse button, the highlighted text becomes the selected text for editing.

```
EventRecord theEvent;
Rect        theRect;
TEHandle    theTErecord;
Boolean     shiftKeyDown;

GlobalToLocal( &(theEvent.where) );
```

```
if ( PtInRect( theEvent.where, &theRect ) )
{
  shiftKeyDown = ( ( theEvent.modifiers & shiftKey ) != 0 );
  TEClick( theEvent.where, shiftKeyDown, theTErecord );
}
```

The first parameter in `TEClick()` is the coordinates at which the cursor was located at the time of the mouse-click. Before calling `TEClick()`, call `GlobalToLocal()` to convert the where field of the event record to coordinates local to the window that holds the edit record. Then call `PtInRect()` to determine if the cursor was over the text area at the time of the mouse-click. The second parameter is a `Boolean` value that indicates whether the Shift key was down at the time of the mouse-click. You can get this information as shown above. The third parameter is a handle to the affected edit record.

TECut( )

To cut selected text from an edit record, call `TECut()`. The one parameter passed to `TECut()` is a handle to the edit record to cut the text from. The `TECut()` routine cuts the selected text and places it in a private scrap (an area accessible only by your application). To copy the cut text to the desk scrap (which is accessible by other applications), call `ZeroScrap()` and `TEToScrap()` after cutting the text.

```
TEHandle theTErecord;
TECut( theTErecord );
ZeroScrap();
TEToScrap();
```

TECopy( )

To copy selected text from an edit record, call `TECopy()`. The one parameter passed to `TECopy()` is a handle to the edit record to copy the text from. To copy the text to the desk scrap, call `ZeroScrap()` and `TEToScrap()`, as discussed in the `TECut()` section of this chapter's reference:

```
TEHandle theTErecord;
TECopy( theTErecord );
ZeroScrap();
TEToScrap();
```

TEPaste( )

To paste text from the private scrap, call `TEPaste()`. The one parameter passed to `TEPaste()` is a handle to the edit record to paste the text to. If your program follows calls to `TECut()` and `TECopy()` with a call to `TEToScrap()`, then it should precede the call to `TEPaste()` with a call to `TEFromScrap()`.

```
TEHandle theTErecord;
TEFromScrap();
TEPaste( theTErecord );
```

TEFromScrap( )

To copy text from the desk scrap to the local, private application scrap, call `TEFromScrap()`.

```
TEFromScrap();
```

TEToScrap( )

To copy text from the local, private application scrap to the desk scrap, call `TEToScrap()`.

```
TEToScrap();
```

ZeroScrap( )

To empty the current contents of the desk scrap, call `ZeroScrap()`.

```
ZeroScrap();
```

Multimedia: Graphics, Sound, and Movies

*T*he topics covered in Part I and Part II provide an important base for writing a Macintosh application — each topic is essential to writing a program that looks and behaves as expected of a Mac program. Now it's time for the *fun* stuff!

10 QuickDraw Graphics

*C*hapter 4 described the basic QuickDraw shapes: the line, rectangle, oval, and round rectangle. In this chapter you'll learn how to draw more-complex shapes: polygons and regions. Knowledge of these two types of shapes let you move beyond the simplistic graphics covered earlier in this book.

Programs that rely on user interaction often require that the user click the mouse button while the cursor is over a certain part of a window. Often this area is a rectangle that acts as a button. Regions allow you to expand on this idea by allowing this clickable area to be any size and shape. This chapter shows you how to implement such a feature in your own program.

In Chapter 4 you learned about five patterns that can be used to easily add a fill to any QuickDraw shape. In this chapter you'll learn a lot more about patterns. You'll find out about the more than three dozen additional patterns that are predefined for your use. You'll also learn how to create your own individual patterns, as well as lists that hold several patterns. Once you know all about patterns, you'll be able to use them when working with any QuickDraw shape, including the polygon and region shapes you read about in this chapter.

Polygons and Regions

The QuickDraw shapes discussed in Chapter 4 will serve most of your drawing needs. But there will be occasional situations where a program of yours must draw a shape that is more complicated than the basic shapes described in Chapter 4. The polygon and region shapes fit this bill.

POLYGONS

A polygon can be defined as a shape that consists of a series of connected straight lines, where the end of the last line meets that start of the first line. Using this definition, a rectangle could be considered a polygon. Because QuickDraw specifically defines the rectangle shape and provides Toolbox functions to work with it, there's no need for a developer to attempt to redefine the rectangle. Other, less symmetrical shapes are better candidates for creation as polygons. Figure 10-1 shows a window that holds three polygons.

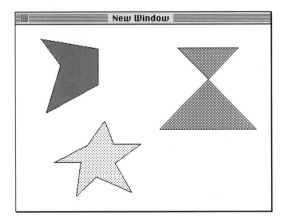

Figure 10-1
A window with three polygons drawn in it.

Drawing a Polygon

You can draw a polygon using a series of calls to `Move()`, `MoveTo()`, `Line()`, and `LineTo()`. Consider the following three QuickDraw calls used to draw the V shape shown in Figure 10-2:

```
MoveTo( 50, 50 );
LineTo( 125, 200 );
LineTo( 200, 50 );
```

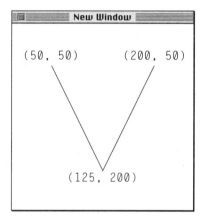

Figure 10-2
The result of calling MoveTo() *and* LineTo().

The two lines drawn that make up the V in Figure 10-2 don't qualify as a polygon — the end of the last line doesn't meet the start of the first line. To make the shape a little more interesting and to turn it into a polygon, the following series of QuickDraw calls would work. The result is shown in Figure 10-3.

```
MoveTo( 50, 50 );
LineTo( 125, 200 );
LineTo( 200, 50 );
LineTo( 170, 50 );
LineTo( 125, 140 );
LineTo( 80, 50 );
LineTo( 50, 50 );
```

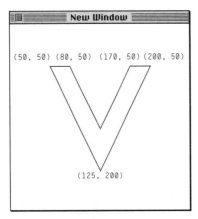

Figure 10-3
The result of calling `LineTo( )` *several times.*

The Polygon data type

The shape shown in Figure 10–3 is a polygon. But a program won't recognize it as such. Because the shape is really nothing more than lines drawn with `LineTo( )` commands, a program views the shape as nothing more than several unrelated lines. To force a program to group the series of lines together into something it considers a single shape, surround the QuickDraw calls with calls to the Toolbox functions `OpenPoly( )` and `ClosePoly( )`.

```
PolyHandle thePolygon;
thePolygon = OpenPoly();
   MoveTo( 50, 50 );
   LineTo( 125, 200 );
   LineTo( 200, 50 );
   LineTo( 170, 50 );
   LineTo( 125, 140 );
   LineTo( 80, 50 );
   LineTo( 50, 50 );
ClosePoly();
```

A call to `OpenPoly( )` allocates memory for a data structure of type `Polygon` and returns a handle to the memory. It also directs all subsequent QuickDraw calls to be made to the `Polygon` data structure, not to the current window. When you are satisfied that you've created the desired polygon, call `ClosePoly()`. That tells your program that the creation of the polygon is complete and that any QuickDraw calls that follow should again be sent to the current window.

Creating a polygon doesn't draw that polygon to the screen. Instead, it stores the definition of the polygon in memory. Once a polygon is defined, use its handle to work with it. There are several QuickDraw functions that accept a handle to a polygon. The `FramePoly()` routine is one example.

```
FramePoly( thePolygon );
```

To paint a polygon with the current pen pattern, call `PaintPoly()`. To erase a polygon from a window, call `ErasePoly()`. Each of these routines requires a single parameter: a `PolyHandle`. To fill a polygon with a pattern other than the current pen pattern, call `FillPoly()`. `FillPoly()` requires a `PolyHandle` as its first parameter and a pointer to a pattern as its second parameter. The following snippet shows a call to each of these routines:

```
PolyHandle  thePolygon;
FillPoly(  thePolygon, &qd.black );
FramePoly(  thePolygon );
ErasePoly(  thePolygon );
PaintPoly(  thePolygon );
```

When finished with a polygon, call `KillPoly()` to free the memory associated with the polygon — the memory referenced by the `PolyHandle`.

```
KillPoly( thePolygon );
```

EXAMPLE PROGRAM: POLYGONLETTER

The PolygonLetter example creates the same polygon described in the preceding text, a polygon in the shape of the letter V. The program then fills the polygon with a light gray pattern. Figure 10–4 shows the window displayed by PolygonLetter. To end the program, just click the mouse button.

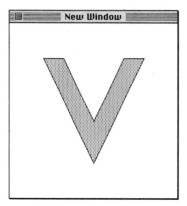

Figure 10-4

The window displayed by the PolygonLetter program.

```
//_____
#define    rDisplayWindow        128

//_____
void main( void )
{
  WindowPtr  theWindow;
  PolyHandle thePolygon;

  InitializeToolbox();

  theWindow = GetNewWindow( rDisplayWindow, nil, (WindowPtr)-1L );
  SetPort( theWindow );

  thePolygon = OpenPoly();
   MoveTo( 50, 50 );
   LineTo( 125, 200 );
   LincTo( 200, 50 );
   LineTo( 170, 50 );
   LineTo( 125, 140 );
   LineTo( 80, 50 );
   LineTo( 50, 50 );
  ClosePoly();

  FillPoly( thePolygon, &qd.ltGray );
  FramePoly( thePolygon );

  KillPoly( thePolygon );

  while ( !Button() )
    ;
}
```

REGIONS

The polygon enables you to create shapes more complex than the primitive shapes discussed in Chapter 4. The region enables you to create shapes that are more sophisticated than polygons. A region is established by combining shapes into a single, new shape. The combined shapes can include any combination of lines, rectangles, ovals, round rectangles, polygons, and other regions. Figure 10-5 shows a window that holds three regions.

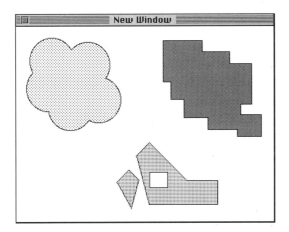

Figure 10-5
A window displaying three regions.

 As you can see in Figure 10–5, a region can include more than one object, and it can also include objects that have holes in them. The region at the bottom of the window in Figure 10–5 provides an example of both of these region properties.

Drawing a region

Like a polygon, a region can be drawn using a series of calls to `Move()`, `MoveTo()`, `Line()`, and `LineTo()`. But a region can also include calls to such shape-drawing QuickDraw functions as `FrameRect()`, `FrameOval()`, and `FrameRoundRect()`. Consider the QuickDraw calls used to draw the oval and rectangle shown in Figure 10-6. In the next section you'll see how these same Toolbox calls can be used to create a single region.

```
SetRect( &theRect, 50, 50, 150, 150 );
FrameOval( &theRect );
SetRect( &theRect, 100, 100, 200, 200 );
FrameRect( &theRect );
```

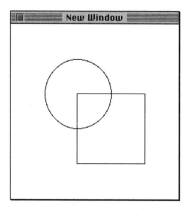

Figure 10-6
An oval and rectangle drawn in a window.

The Region data type

Just as a program needs to call OpenPoly() and ClosePoly() to designate which QuickDraw commands are to define a polygon, a program needs to call OpenRgn() and CloseRgn() to define a region.

```
RgnHandle theRegion;

theRegion = NewRgn();
OpenRgn();
  SetRect( &theRect, 50, 50, 150, 150 );
  FrameOval( &theRect );
  SetRect( &theRect, 100, 100, 200, 200 );
  FrameRect( &theRect );
CloseRgn( theRegion );
```

To create a polygon, you call OpenPoly() to allocate memory for a new Polygon data structure. Creating a new Region data structure works a little differently. OpenRgn() doesn't allocate memory for you — you need to do that prior to the call to OpenRgn(). The Toolbox function NewRgn() allocates memory for an empty region and returns a handle to that memory.

`OpenRgn()` then begins defining a region, storing the definition in temporary memory. A call to `CloseRgn()` ends the region definition and stores the region data that had been saved in temporary memory to the memory referenced by `theRegion`.

Don't use fill or paint routines like `FillRect()` or `PaintOval()` when defining a region. Use only frame routines like `FrameRect()` or `FrameOval()`. When calls to fill and paint functions are placed between calls to `OpenRgn()` and `CloseRgn()`, the areas that those calls should define will not become part of the region. Instead, define the region with frame routines, and then use one of the region-drawing functions like `FillRgn()` or `PaintRgn()` to add a pattern to the entire region.

Once a region has been defined, use any of several Toolbox functions to draw the region. A call to `FrameRgn()` frames the region. A call to `PaintRgn()` paints the region using the current pen pattern. `EraseRgn()` erases the region. Each of these three routines accepts a `RgnHandle` as its single parameter. To fill a region with a pattern other than the current pen pattern, call `FillRgn()`. Pass `FillRgn()` a `RgnHandle` and a pointer to a pattern. The following snippet fills the region defined in the previous snippet with a light gray pattern and then frames the region. Figure 10-7 shows the result.

```
FillRgn( theRegion, &qd.ltGray );
FrameRgn( theRegion );
```

The region shown in Figure 10-7 may not be what you were expecting to see. When a single region is formed from calls to QuickDraw shape-drawing routines, an intersecting area like the one in Figure 10–7 becomes a hole in the region. You can omit a hole and instead define a solid region by first defining two separate regions then combining them into a single region. Here is how an oval region and a rectangle region could be created:

```
RgnHandle   theOvalRegion;
RgnHandle   theRectRegion;

theOvalRegion = NewRgn();
theRectRegion = NewRgn();
```

```
OpenRgn();
   SetRect( &theRect, 50, 50, 150, 150 );
   FrameOval( &theRect );
CloseRgn( theOvalRegion );
OpenRgn();
   SetRect( &theRect, 100, 100, 200, 200 );
   FrameRect( &theRect );
CloseRgn( theRectRegion );
```

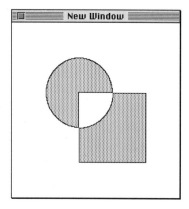

Figure 10-7
A region that has been filled and framed.

The Toolbox function UnionRgn() can be used for the task of combining two regions. Pass the RgnHandle for each of the two regions to join. Pass a RgnHandle to the region that will result from this combination:

```
RgnHandle   theRegion;
theRegion = NewRgn();
UnionRgn( theOvalRegion, theRectRegion, theRegion );
```

Region-drawing routines that operate on the resulting combined region will now affect the area that represents the combined area of the two regions. Figure 10–8 illustrates how FillRgn() and FrameRgn() affect the region that was created from the previous call to UnionRgn():

```
FillRgn( theRegion, &qd.ltGray );
FrameRgn( theRegion );
```

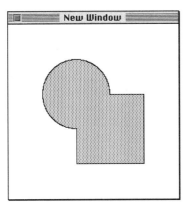

Figure 10-8
A solid region that has been filled and framed.

When finished with a region, call DisposeRgn() to free the memory associated with the region — the memory referenced by the RgnHandle.

```
KillPoly( thePolygon );
```

EXAMPLE PROGRAM: REGIONCLICK

The RegionClick program creates and draws the region shown in Figure 10–8. Clicking the mouse button while the cursor is over any part of the shaded region will end the program.

Making your program aware of mouse-clicks in a rectangle is easy: Define and draw a rectangle using SetRect() and FrameRect(), and then use the Toolbox function PtInRect() to determine if the point of a mouse-click falls within the boundaries of this rectangle. The Chapter 5 example program EventBranch does exactly that. You can make your program far more interesting, though, if you give it the ability to recognize mouse-clicks in irregularly shaped objects. For example, your program might display a map of the United States. When the user clicks on a state — anywhere on a state — your program might open a window that displays information about that state.

The Toolbox function PtInRgn() makes it possible to test a mouseDown event to see if the cursor was over a region at the time of the event. Before calling `PtInRgn()`, call `GlobalToLocal()` to convert the pixel location of the cursor from coordinates global to the screen to ones that are local to the current window. The following snippet shows the code pertinent to this test:

```
EventRecord theEvent;
RgnHandle   gClickableRegion;
GlobalToLocal( &(theEvent.where) );
if ( PtInRgn( theEvent.where, gClickableRegion ) )
  gDone = true;

//_____
#define    rDisplayWindow    128

//_____
Boolean  gDone = false;
RgnHandle gClickableRegion;

//_____
void main( void )
{
  WindowPtr  theWindow;
  Rect     theRect;
  RgnHandle  theOvalRegion;
  RgnHandle  theRectRegion;

  InitializeToolbox();

  theWindow = GetNewWindow( rDisplayWindow, nil, (WindowPtr)-1L );
  SetPort( theWindow );

  theOvalRegion = NewRgn();
  theRectRegion = NewRgn();
  gClickableRegion = NewRgn();

  OpenRgn();
   SetRect( &theRect, 50, 50, 150, 150 );
   FrameOval( &theRect );
  CloseRgn( theOvalRegion );
  OpenRgn();
   SetRect( &theRect, 100, 100, 200, 200 );
   FrameRect( &theRect );
  CloseRgn( theRectRegion );
  UnionRgn( theOvalRegion, theRectRegion, gClickableRegion );
  DisposeRgn( theOvalRegion );
  DisposeRgn( theRectRegion );

  FillRgn( gClickableRegion, &qd.ltGray );
  FrameRgn( gClickableRegion);

  EventLoop();

  DisposeRgn( gClickableRegion );
}
```

```
//_____
void EventLoop( void )
{
  EventRecord theEvent;

  while ( gDone == false )
  {
  WaitNextEvent( everyEvent, &theEvent, 15L, nil );

   switch ( theEvent.what )
   {
     case mouseDown:
      GlobalToLocal( &(theEvent.where) );
      if ( PtInRgn( theEvent.where, gClickableRegion ) )
        gDone = true;
      break;
   }
  }
}
```

Patterns

Chapter 4 introduced you to patterns. There you experimented with the five different patterns that are predefined for you and easily available for your use in any program. With the Mac's superior graphics capabilities, it certainly should come as no surprise that there are several more predefined patterns available and a countless number of patterns you can define yourself.

In Chapter 4 you used the five predefined patterns when setting the graphics pen pattern and in QuickDraw fill routines. Recall that each of those five patterns is represented by a field in the global variable qd. The qd variable is of the QuickDraw data structure type QDGlobals. As shown in the definition of the QDGlobals data structure, each of the five fields used to hold a pattern is of type Pattern.

```
struct QDGlobals
{
  char    privates[76];
  long    randSeed;
  BitMap  screenBits;
  Cursor  arrow;
  Pattern dkGray;
  Pattern ltGray;
```

```
        Pattern gray;
        Pattern black;
        Pattern white;
        GrafPtr       thePort;
    };
    extern QDGlobals qd;
```

NOTE Which is it, pattern or `Pattern`? It's both. When discussing a pattern in general, it's a lowercase *p*. When specifically referring to the Macintosh `Pattern` data type, it's an uppercase *P*.

From Chapter 4 you know that to use one of the five predefined patterns, you just access the appropriate field of the `qd` variable. If the pattern is to be used as a parameter to a Toolbox function that requires a pointer to variable of type `Pattern`, preface the `qd` variable with the `&` operator. Here is an example that fills an oval with a light gray pattern:

```
    Rect theRect;
    SetRect( &theRect, 35, 50, 300, 100 );
    FillOval( &theRect, &qd.ltGray );
```

THE SYSTEM PATTERNS

While it's handy to have a few patterns that are so readily available, the five predefined ones are of limited usefulness. Fortunately, Apple has seen to it that programmers have easy access to more than just the five patterns that are a part of the `QDGlobals` data structure.

The System pattern list

In the System file of every Mac, 38 more patterns reside. Each of these standard patterns is a pattern resource of type `PAT`, and all 38 of these individual resources are grouped together in a single pattern list resource of type `PAT#`.

Later in this chapter you'll learn more about these two resource types, including how to create your own `PAT` resources. For now it is adequate to know that individual patterns in a pattern list are accessed by an index. Index values start at 1 and increment by 1 up to the last pattern in the pattern list. For the System pattern list with 38 patterns, the individual patterns are thus referred to by the numbers 1 through 38. Figure 10-9 shows the 38 patterns stored in the System file and the index value of each.

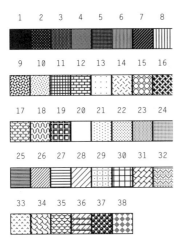

Figure 10–9
The 38 standard patterns found in the System file.

Accessing a pattern from the System pattern list

To access one of the 38 patterns in the System pattern list, call the Toolbox function GetIndPattern().

```
Pattern thePattern;
short    thePatternListID = sysPatListID;
short    thePatternIndex = 19;
GetIndPattern( &thePattern, thePatternListID, thePatternIndex );
```

The first parameter in GetIndPattern() is a pointer to a variable of type Pattern. When the call to GetIndPattern() has completed, the variable named in this parameter will hold a single pattern from a pattern list. The second and third parameters are used to specify which pattern ends up in the first parameter.

The second parameter in GetIndPattern() holds the resource ID of the pattern list that is to be accessed. Although the System file holds only a single pattern list resource, it is still necessary to specify which list is to be accessed. That's because GetIndPattern() can also be used with pattern list resources you create. To use the System list, pass the Apple-defined constant sysPatListID in this second parameter.

After specifying which pattern list to use, identify which pattern to access from that list. The third parameter to GetIndPattern() is used for this purpose. When using the System pattern list, this parameter can have a value in the range of 1 to 38.

After GetIndPattern() executes, your program can use the Pattern variable thePattern just as it would use any of the five predefined QDGlobals patterns. The following snippet passes a pointer to thePattern to FillRect(). The result of running the following code would be a rectangle 100 pixels in width and 200 pixels in height. If the 19th pattern from the system list was accessed, as was done in the above snippet, this rectangle would be filled with the waffle pattern shown under the number 19 back in Figure 10-9.

```
Rect theRect;
SetRect( &theRect, 50, 20, 150, 220 );
FillRect( &theRect, &thePattern );
```

EXAMPLE PROGRAM: SYSPATTERNS

The SysPatterns program displays a window that holds 38 small rectangles, as shown in Figure 10-10. Each of the rectangles is filled with one of the 38 patterns found in the system pattern list. After viewing the SysPatterns window, click the mouse button to end the program.

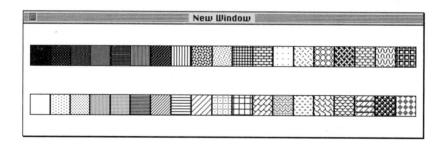

Figure 10-10
The result of running the SysPatterns program.

The SysPatterns program uses a loop to call `GetIndPattern()` 38 times. At each pass through the loop, the index that is used as the final parameter to `GetIndPattern()` is incremented. This index is checked to see when half of the patterns have been drawn. After 19 patterns have been drawn, the program starts a second row of rectangles.

The SysPatterns program defines several constants. The majority of these definitions exist for the purpose of setting the initial placement of the rectangle that gets filled with a pattern.

```
//_____
#define    rDisplayWindow       128
#define    kFirstPatternIndex     1
#define    kLastPatternIndex      38
#define    kRectWidth             30
#define    kRectHeight            30
#define    kRectLeft              10
#define    kRectRight      kRectLeft + kRectWidth
#define    kRectTopRow1           30
#define    kRectBottomRow1    kRectTopRow1 + kRectHeight
#define    kRectTopRow2          100
#define    kRectBottomRow2    kRectTopRow2 + kRectHeight


//_____
void main( void )
{
  WindowPtr theWindow;
  Rect      theRect;
  Pattern   thePattern;
  short     thePatternListID = sysPatListID;
  short     thePatternIndex;
  int       i;

  InitializeToolbox();

  theWindow = GetNewWindow( rDisplayWindow, nil, (WindowPtr)-1L );
  SetPort( theWindow );
  SetRect( &theRect, kRectLeft, kRectTopRow1, kRectRight, kRectBottomRow1 );
  for ( i = kFirstPatternIndex; i <= kLastPatternIndex; i++ )
  {
   thePatternIndex = i;
   GetIndPattern( &thePattern, thePatternListID, thePatternIndex );
   FillRect( &theRect, &thePattern );
   FrameRect( &theRect );
   if ( i == ( kLastPatternIndex / 2 ) )
     SetRect( &theRect, kRectLeft, kRectTopRow2, kRectRight, kRectBottomRow2
     );
   else
         OffsetRect( &theRect, kRectWidth, 0 );
  }
  while ( !Button() )
   ;
}
```

THE PAT# RESOURCE

You've seen that the System patterns are held in a single pattern list resource of type PAT#. Your program can make use of other pattern lists as well — PAT# resources that you create in a resource editor.

Creating a PAT# resource in ResEdit

To create a pattern list resource in ResEdit, select Create New Resource from the Resource menu. Type PAT# in the editable text box, and then click on the OK button. In response ResEdit will open a PAT# editor like the one shown in Figure 10-11. Use any of the tools in the editor's tool palette to edit a single pattern. When satisfied with the results, choose Insert New Pattern from the Resource menu. ResEdit adds a second, empty pattern to the PAT# resource. Continue adding and editing as many patterns as you want. When you close the PAT# editor, ResEdit will display a small view of all of the patterns you have created for this one pattern list. See Figure 10-12 for an example.

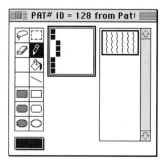

Figure 10-11
Using ResEdit to edit a pattern in a pattern list.

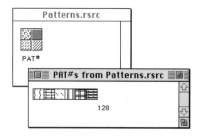

Figure 10-12
A list of patterns, as viewed in ResEdit.

Creating a PAT# resource in Resorcerer

To create a pattern list resource in Resorcerer, click on the New button in the main Resorcerer window. Type PAT# in the editable text box, and then click on the Create button. When you do that, Resorcerer will open an empty list that will be used to display any patterns you create for this resource, as shown in Figure 10-13.

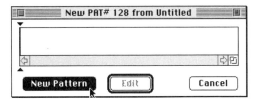

Figure 10-13
Using Resorcerer to create a new pattern in a pattern list.

Click on the New Pattern button to create the first pattern. Move the cursor over the left rectangle and click the mouse button to turn on a pixel in the pattern. When you do that, the rectangle on the right side of the pattern list editor will show how your new pattern will look. Figure 10-14 provides an example.

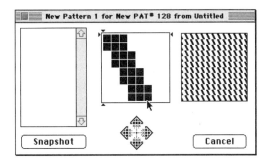

Figure 10-14
Using Resorcerer to edit a pattern in a pattern list.

When satisfied that the pattern is complete, close the editor. Your new pattern will then show up in the formerly empty list of patterns. To add a second pattern, again click on the New Pattern button. Repeat this process for each pattern. Figure 10-15 shows a pattern list with four patterns in it.

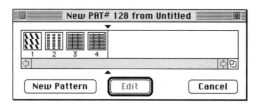

Figure 10-15

A list of patterns, as viewed in Resorcerer.

Using a PAT# resource

Your program can access a pattern from your own pattern list in the same way that it accesses a pattern from the System pattern list — by making a call to GetIndPattern(). Instead of passing the Apple-defined constant sysPatListID (which has the value of the PAT# resource in the System file), pass the resource ID of your own PAT# resource. The following snippet returns the third pattern from a PAT# resource with an ID of 128, like the PAT# resource created in ResEdit or Resorcerer in the previous sections:

```
#define    rMyPatternList    128
Pattern    thePattern;
short      thePatternListID = sysPatListID;
short      thePatternIndex = 3;
GetIndPattern( &thePattern, thePatternListID, thePatternIndex );
```

The returned pattern can be used in any routine that requires a Pattern (or a pointer to a Pattern) as a parameter. Here a rectangle is being filled with the first pattern from a pattern list with an ID of 128:

```
#define    rMyPatternList    128
Rect       theRect;
Pattern    thePattern;
short      thePatternListID = sysPatListID;
short      thePatternIndex = 1;
GetIndPattern( &thePattern, thePatternListID, thePatternIndex );
SetRect( &theRect, 10, 10, 50, 50 );
FillRect( &theRect, &thePattern );
```

THE PAT RESOURCE

If your program will make use of only one or two patterns, you might want to use PAT resources rather than a PAT# resource. Where a PAT# resource holds several patterns in a list, a PAT resource always holds only a single pattern.

NOTE The fourth character in the name of the PAT resource is a space. Remember, resource types always have a four-character name.

Creating a PAT resource in ResEdit

To create a pattern resource in ResEdit, select Create New Resource from the Resource menu. Type PAT in the editable text box, making sure to type a space as the fourth character. Then click on the OK button. ResEdit will open a PAT editor like the one shown in Figure 10-16. This editor is very similar to the PAT# editor shown earlier in this chapter. Use the tools in the tool palette to edit the pattern. When finished, close the PAT editor.

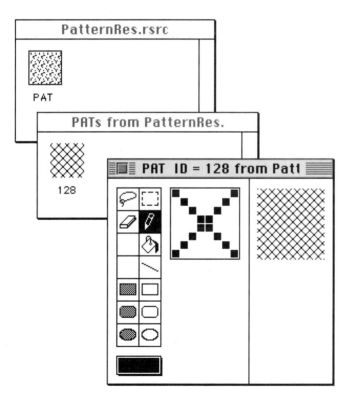

Figure 10-16
Using ResEdit to edit a pattern in a pattern resource.

Creating a PAT resource in Resorcerer

To create a pattern resource in Resorcerer, click on the New button in the main Resorcerer window. Type PAT in the editable text box, making sure to type a space as the fourth character. Then click on the Create button. When you do that, Resorcerer will open the same editor used to create the individual patterns for a PAT# resource. Use this editor to create a pattern, and then close the editor. Figure 10-17 provides an example.

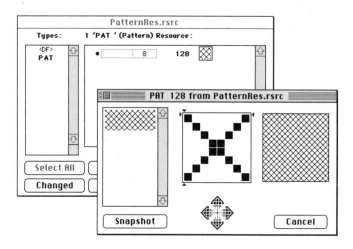

Figure 10-17
Using Resorcerer to edit a pattern in a pattern resource.

Using a PAT resource

To make use of a pattern stored in a PAT resource, first call the Toolbox function GetPattern() to load the pattern into memory and receive a handle to the pattern data in memory. Pass GetPattern() the ID of the PAT resource that holds the pattern you wish to access.

```
#define    rMyPattern    128
PatHandle thePatternHandle;

thePatternHandle = GetPattern( rMyPattern );
```

Once your program has a handle to the PAT resource data, the handle can be dereferenced and used in any Toolbox call that requires a variable of type Pattern as one of its parameters. Consider the Toolbox function FillRect(). In Chapter 4 you used this function as follows:

```
Rect theRect;
SetRect( &theRect, 50, 50, 100, 100 );
FillRect( &theRect, &qd.gray );
```

The FillRect() function prototype lists the second parameter as a pointer to a Pattern. The gray field of the global qd variable is of type Pattern, so &qd.gray is a pointer to a Pattern. To use the PAT data in a call to FillRect(), pass a pointer to the Pattern data by dereferencing the PatHandle variable thePatternHandle one time.

```
FillRect( &theRect, *thePatternHandle );
```

A second function that expects a pointer to a Pattern as a parameter is the Toolbox function that is used to change the graphics pen pattern — PenPat().

```
PenPat( &qd.dkGray );
```

To use your own Pattern, again deference the PatHandle a single time.

```
PenPat( *thePatternHandle );
```

Some Toolbox functions have the potential side effect of moving blocks of memory; PenPat() is one such function. When you call PenPat() with one of the five predefined patterns as a parameter, this trait of PenPat() is not of concern. When you pass a dereferenced handle as a parameter, however, you should play it safe by locking the handle before the call to PenPat() and then unlocking it after the call.

```
HLock( (Handle)thePatternHandle );
  PenPat( *thePatternHandle);
HUnlock( (Handle)thePatternHandle );
```

The snippet that calls `PenPat()` with a parameter of `&qd.gray` doesn't wrap the call to `PenPat()` in calls to `HLock()` and `HUnlock()` as the snippet that uses the dereferenced pattern does. Here's why this is so.

In the first call to `PenPat()` a pointer to a global data structure is being passed. A pointer leads to a block of data that can't be moved by the Memory Manager. In this first example, that block of data happens to hold global data that is fixed in memory.

In the second call to `PenPat()`, a dereferenced handle is being passed. A handle leads to a block of memory that *can* be moved by the Memory Manager. In this second example the block of data is the `PAT` resource data that your program loaded to memory.

What happens if you omit the calls to `HLock()` and `HUnlock()`? The code could very well execute just fine. While a call to `PenPat()` can potentially move memory, it doesn't always do so.

After the pen pattern is changed, subsequent calls to QuickDraw routines will be affected. Consider a call to `Line()`. In the following snippet a horizontal line 15 pixels in height will be drawn. But instead of the line being drawn in black, the line will have the pattern defined in the `PAT` resource.

```
PenSize( 1, 15 );
MoveTo( 20, 50 );
Line( 250, 0 );
```

EXAMPLE PROGRAM: PATTERNRES

The PatternRes program uses the pattern found in a `PAT` resource like the one pictured back in Figures 10-16 and 10-17 to draw the diagonal line and the rectangle shown in Figure 10-18. To quit this simple program, click the mouse button.

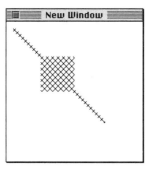

Figure 10-18
The result of running the PatternRes program.

```
//_____
#define    rDisplayWindow       128
#define    rCrosshatchPattern   128

//_____
void main( void )
{
  WindowPtr theWindow;
  Rect      theRect;
  PatHandle thePatternHandle;

  InitializeToolbox();

  theWindow = GetNewWindow( rDisplayWindow, nil, (WindowPtr)-1L );
  SetPort( theWindow );

  thePatternHandle = GetPattern( rCrosshatchPattern );

  SetRect( &theRect, 50, 50, 100, 100 );
  FillRect( &theRect, *thePatternHandle );

  HLock( (Handle)thePatternHandle );
   PenPat( *thePatternHandle);
  HUnlock( (Handle)thePatternHandle );
  PenSize( 5, 5 );
  MoveTo( 10, 10 );
  LineTo( 140, 140 );
  while ( !Button() )
   ;
}
```

QuickDraw Graphics Reference

This section describes the Toolbox routines that can be used to define and then draw polygons and regions. It also describes the Toolbox functions used to access pattern resources.

POLYGONS

To draw a shape other than a line, rectangle, oval, or round rectangle, consider creating the shape as a polygon. A series of lines, with the end of the last line meeting the start of the first line, defines a polygon.

OpenPoly()

To allocate memory for a `Polygon` data structure that will hold the definition of one polygon, call `OpenPoly()`. `OpenPoly()` also directs subsequent QuickDraw commands to this polygon. After completion of the polygon, `ClosePoly()` must be called.

```
PolyHandle thePolygon;
thePolygon = OpenPoly();
  // QuickDraw commands to Move(), MoveTo(), Line(), and LineTo()
ClosePoly();
```

OpenPoly() requires no passed values. `OpenPoly()` returns a handle to the newly allocated `Polygon` data structure. `OpenPoly()` and `ClosePoly()` define a polygon but do not draw it.

ClosePoly()

After defining a polygon by calling `OpenPoly()` and then making a series of QuickDraw calls, call `ClosePoly()` to end the definition.

```
PolyHandle thePolygon;
thePolygon = OpenPoly();
  // QuickDraw commands to Move(), MoveTo(), Line(), and LineTo()
ClosePoly();
```

ClosePoly() has no parameters. `OpenPoly()` and `ClosePoly()` define a polygon but don't draw it.

KillPoly( )

When you're through with a polygon, call `KillPoly()` to release the memory occupied by the polygon's `Polygon` data structure. Pass `KillPoly()` a handle to the polygon to dispose of.

```
PolyHandle thePolygon;
KillPoly( thePolygon );
```

FramePoly( )

After defining a polygon, call `FramePoly()` to draw a frame around it. Pass `FramePoly()` a handle to the polygon to frame.

```
PolyHandle thePolygon;
FramePoly( thePolygon );
```

PaintPoly( )

After a polygon has been defined, call `PaintPoly()` to paint the interior of the polygon with the current pattern of the graphics pen. Pass `PaintPoly()` a handle to the polygon to frame.

```
PolyHandle thePolygon;
PaintPoly( thePolygon );
```

FillPoly( )

After defining a polygon, call `FillPoly()` to fill the interior of the polygon with a pattern of your choosing.

```
PolyHandle thePolygon;
Pattern    thePattern = qd.dkGray;
FillPoly( thePolygon, &thePattern );
```

The first parameter to `FillPoly()` is a handle to the polygon to fill. The second parameter is a pointer to the pattern to use as the fill.

ErasePoly( )

After defining and drawing a polygon, call `ErasePoly()` to erase it. Pass `ErasePoly()` a handle to the polygon to erase.

```
PolyHandle thePolygon;
ErasePoly( thePolygon );
```

InvertPoly( )

After defining a polygon, call `InvertPoly()` to invert each pixel within the content area of the polygon. Any black pixels will become white, while any white pixels will become black. Pass `InvertPoly()` a handle to the polygon to invert:

```
PolyHandle thePolygon;
InvertPoly( thePolygon );
```

REGIONS

To draw a shape that is more complex than a polygon, create the shape as a region. A region results from the combining of any other shapes and lines.

NewRgn( )

Before defining the shape of a region, allocate memory for the region by calling `NewRgn()`:

```
RgnHandle theRegion;

theRegion = NewRgn();
```

OpenRgn( )

`OpenRgn()` directs subsequent QuickDraw commands to temporary memory. The shape that results from the combination of the individual shapes created by the QuickDraw calls is the region. After completion of the region, `CloseRgn()` must be called.

```
RgnHandle theRegion;
```

```
OpenRgn();
 // QuickDraw commands to Line(), FrameRect(), FrameOval(), etc.
CloseRgn( theRegion );
```

CloseRgn()

After defining a region by calling `OpenRgn()` and then making a series of QuickDraw calls, call `CloseRgn()` to end the definition. Pass `CloseRgn()` a handle to the memory that should hold the region definition.

```
RgnHandle theRegion;

OpenRgn();
 // QuickDraw commands to Line(), FrameRect(), FrameOval(), etc.
CloseRgn( theRegion );
```

DisposeRgn()

When through with a region, call `DisposeRgn()` to release the memory occupied by the region's `Region` data structure. Pass `DisposeRgn()` a handle to the region to dispose of.

```
RgnHandle theRegion;
DisposeRgn( theRegion );
```

FrameRgn()

After defining a region, call `FrameRgn()` to draw a frame around it. Pass `FrameRgn()` a handle to the region to frame.

```
RgnHandle theRegion;
FrameRgn( theRegion );
```

PaintRgn()

After a region has been defined, call `PaintRgn()` to paint the interior of the region with the current pattern of the graphics pen. Pass `PaintRgn()` a handle to the region to frame.

```
RgnHandle theRegion;
PaintRgn( theRegion );
```

FillRgn()

After defining a region, call `FillRgn()` to fill the interior of the region with a pattern of your choosing.

```
RgnHandle theRegion;
Pattern   thePattern = qd.black;
FillRgn( theRegion, &thePattern );
```

The first parameter to `FillRgn()` is a handle to the region to fill. The second parameter is a pointer to the pattern to use as the fill.

EraseRgn()

After defining and drawing a region, call `EraseRgn()` to erase it. Pass `EraseRgn()` a handle to the region to erase.

```
RgnHandle theRegion;
EraseRgn( theRegion);
```

InvertRgn()

After defining a region, call `InvertRgn()` to invert each pixel within the content area of the region. Any black pixels will become white, and any white pixels will become black. Pass `InvertRgn()` a handle to the region to invert.

```
RgnHandle theRegion;
InvertRgn( theRegion);
```

UnionRgn()

To combine two regions into one new region, call `UnionRgn()`.

```
RgnHandle theSmallRegion;
RgnHandle theBigRegion;
RgnHandle theCombinedRegion;
UnionRgn( theSmallRegion, theBigRegion, theCombinedRegion );
```

The first and second parameters in `UnionRgn()` are handles to the two regions that are to be combined. The third parameter is a handle to the memory that will hold the new, combined region.

GlobalToLocal( )

If `PtInRgn()` is to be called to test a mouse-click for inclusion in a region, first call `GlobalToLocal()` to convert the coordinates of the cursor from global screen coordinates to coordinates local to the current window.

```
Point thePoint = theEvent.where;
GlobalToLocal( &thePoint );
```

PtInRgn( )

To test a mouse-click for inclusion in a region, call `PtInRgn()`.

```
Point     thePoint;
RgnHandle theRegion;
if ( PtInRgn( thePoint, theRegion ) )
  // handle mouse-click in region
```

The first parameter to `PtInRgn()` is a Point variable that holds the location of the cursor at the time of the mouse-click. Call `GlobalToLocal()` before passing this point to `PtInRgn()`. The second parameter is the region that is being tested. If the point specified in the first parameter is within the boundaries of the region specified in the second parameter, `PtInRgn()` returns a value of `true`. If the point is outside of the region, `PtInRgn()` returns a value of `false`.

PATTERNS

The Macintosh system defines several patterns for use by your programs. Additionally, pattern resources enable you to define and store your own patterns for use in any of your programs.

GetIndPattern( )

To access a single pattern from a pattern list resource (a resource of type PAT#), call `GetIndPattern()`.

```
Pattern thePattern;
short   thePatternListID = sysPatListID;
short   thePatternIndex = 2;
GetIndPattern( &thePattern, thePatternListID, thePatternIndex );
```

The first parameter to GetIndPattern() is a pointer to a variable of type Pattern. After the call to GetIndPattern() completes, this variable will hold a pattern that can be used in any Toolbox function that requires a Pattern as a parameter. The second parameter is the ID of the PAT# resource that holds the pattern to access. To use the System pattern list, which contains 38 patterns, pass the Apple-defined constant sysPatListID. The third parameter is an index into the PAT# resource. Individual patterns within the list are numbered starting at an index value of 1.

GetPattern()

To access the pattern stored in a pattern resource (a resource of type PAT), call GetPattern().

```
#define    rSlashPattern    128
PatHandle thePatternHandle;

thePatternHandle = GetPattern( rSlashPattern );
```

The parameter to GetPattern() is the resource ID of the PAT resource to access. GetPattern() will load the pattern into memory and return a handle to the memory in the thePatternHandle variable.

11 Programming With Color

*F*or the first few years of its existences the Macintosh did not support color. Still, from its inception the Mac has been known as a graphics machine. The power of QuickDraw made it easy for any programmer to turn a text-based program into a more exciting graphics-based application. Once color capabilities were added to the Mac, the power of the new Color QuickDraw routines not only kept it easy for programmers to add graphics to programs, it also made it easy for them to add rich, colorful graphics to all of their applications.

In this chapter you'll learn about the system the Macintosh uses for defining colors. You'll read how to select a color from within your code, and you'll see an almost unbelievably simple means for letting users quickly and easily make color selections of their own choosing. Whether your program or the user specifies a color, you'll be able to easily use that color to fill any shape, or even the background of an entire window. If you were afraid that color programming techniques might be too complex to tackle, this chapter will alleviate those fears.

In Chapter 10 you learned all about black-and-white pattern resources and how to use those patterns in shape drawing. This chapter expands upon those techniques for monochrome pattern drawing. Here you'll learn how to create color patterns and see how to fill any type of shape with one of these patterns.

RGB Colors and the Color Picker

Older Macintosh computers like the Mac Plus came with a built-in monochrome screen. A pixel on such a screen was composed of a single-color dot capable of being set to only two states: black or white. The color monitors that Macs now come with (or that are added as an option) use three dots for each pixel. These red, green, and blue dots, each capable of being illuminated in a large range of intensities, allow a single pixel to have hundreds, thousands, or even millions of different states, or colors.

RGB COLORS

No matter what kind of data a computer works with, to the computer the data is always nothing more than a collection of numbers. You've seen that while a resource editor displays a resource graphically, a look at the same resource in a hex editor reveals the resource to be nothing more than a series of hexadecimal numbers. And while a word displayed in a window looks as if it is composed of alphanumeric characters, it turns out that each character is nothing more than an ASCII number. The representation of colors is no different.

If you pry open your the case of your Macintosh, you of course won't find numbers floating around inside. Numbers are still too abstract a concept for the electronic components that make up a computer. To the Mac's CPU, all that really matters is the level of voltage at any memory location. But a topic like that is best left to computer and electrical engineers!

Computers are capable of using a variety of schemes, or systems, to give each color a different value. The system used by QuickDraw is the RGB color model. RGB stands for the colors of the three dots that make up each pixel: red, green, and blue. In the RGB model, each color is the result of the combination of three values. Each value represents a color level of one of the three colors. A few specific examples using the RGBColor data type should clarify how RGB colors work. First, the definition of the RGBColor data structure:

```
struct RGBColor
{
  unsigned short red;
```

```
  unsigned short green;
  unsigned short blue;
};
```

The unsigned short is a 2-byte data type capable of holding a value in the range of 0 to 65,535. In the RGB color system, an RGBColor field that has a value of 0 means that none of that color is present, while a value of 65,535 means that the color of that field is at its most intense. As an example, consider an RGBColor variable that is set to hold the color red.

```
RGBColor theRedColor;
theRedColor.red   = 65535;
theRedColor.green =     0;
theRedColor.blue  =     0;
```

The color defined in the above snippet has a red component at its maximum, while its green and blue components are at their minimum. This produces a pure red color. To produce a color other than red, green, or blue, you mix levels of the three fields. Because a mix of red and blue produces purple, the following snippet defines a variable that holds a purple color:

```
RGBColor thePurpleColor;
thePurpleColor.red   = 65535;
thePurpleColor.green =     0;
thePurpleColor.blue  = 65535;
```

You don't have to use the maximum and minimum values when assigning a field a color level. Where the field values in the above snippet produce a very light, bright purple, the following snippet produces a rich, dark purple:

```
RGBColor thePurpleColor;
thePurpleColor.red   = 32000;
thePurpleColor.green =     0;
thePurpleColor.blue  = 32000;
```

NOTE You may be familiar with the definition of white as the absence of all color, and the definition of black as the combination of all colors. You'll see that this holds true if you mix a dozen colors of paint together; the resulting color will be much darker than any of the individual paints. With that said, why is it that in the RGB model, lower red, green, and blue values produce darker colors, while higher values produce lighter colors? Why does "mixing" the maximum value of 65,535 for each color produce white and not black? The answer lies in how graphics displays work. Combining three colored lights produces more light than a single colored light, just as three lit light bulbs produce more light than one bulb. So more means brighter. The RGB system simply reflects this fact: Higher RGB values mean brighter colors. When all three RGB values are at their most intense, white light is produced. When all are at their lowest, darkness, or black, is produced.

Determining the field values for a particular color isn't always easily done by using guesswork alone. As you will see later in this chapter, Apple's Color Picker utility can aid you in producing a desired color. The Color Picker also provides an easy means for letting users of your program specify colors of their choosing.

COLORS AND SHAPE DRAWING

Once you've declared and assigned a color to an RGBColor variable, you can use the variable's color when drawing shapes. You can use any of the QuickDraw shape-drawing routines just as they're described in Chapter 4 and Chapter 10. PaintRect(), FillOval(), FramePoly() will all work without modification. The only change you'll need to make involves the foreground color of the window that is to be drawn to. Normally, a window's foreground color is black — that's why by default the graphics pen draws in black. By calling the Toolbox routine RGBForeColor(), you can change a window's foreground color. After you do that, all subsequent drawing takes place in the new foreground color. Here's an example that draws a green oval in the upper left of a window:

```
RGBColor theGreenColor;
theGreenColor.red   =     0;
theGreenColor.green = 50000;
theGreenColor.blue  =     0;
RGBForeColor( &theGreenColor );
SetRect( &theRect, 10, 10, 100, 100 );
PaintOval( &theRect );
```

The RGBForeColor() requires one parameter: a pointer to a variable of type RGBColor. This variable holds the definition of the color that the current window's foreground should be set to.

The RGBForeColor() function has a companion routine that changes the background color of a window. A call to RGBBackColor() changes the background color of the current window. Instead of windows with white backgrounds, your program can easily create windows with backgrounds of any available color. The following snippet changes the background of the current window to a light gray color:

```
RGBColor theGrayColor ;
theGrayColor.red   = 55000;
theGrayColor.green = 55000;
theGrayColor.blue  = 55000;
RGBBackColor( &theGrayColor );
```

 Remember, if all three fields of an RGBColor variable are at their maximum value of 65,535, the result is the color white. If each field color value is lowered by an equal or near equal amount, a shade of gray is produced. The lower the values, the darker the gray. Once each field value is very low (near 0), a very, very dark shade of gray is produced. That shade is black!

COLORS AND COLOR WINDOWS

Up to this point, you have loaded WIND data into memory by calling the Toolbox function GetNewWindow(). The Toolbox provides a companion routine to GetNewWindow() named GetNewCWindow(). If you haven't already guessed it, the *C* in this Toolbox name stands for *color*. Here's a call to GetNewCWindow():

```
#define  rDisplayWindow   128
WindowPtr theWindow;

theWindow = GetNewCWindow( rDisplayWindow, nil, (WindowPtr)-1L );
```

The parameters to GetNewCWindow() are identical to those used in a call to GetNewWindow(). The WIND resource, too, can be identical. So what is different? The data structure that the WIND data gets loaded to. You know that a call to GetNewWindow() loads window data into a WindowRecord. A call to GetNewCWindow() loads window data into a CWindowRecord.

 The above text states that the WIND resource loaded by a call to GetNewCWindow() *can* be identical to a WIND resource loaded by a call to GetNewWindow(). That hints that the WIND resource may not *have* to be the same. Chapter 12 bears this out. A WIND resource used for a color window may optionally include information that is used to add color to various parts of the window, such as the window's frame or the title that appears in the window's drag bar.

A CWindowRecord is the same as a WindowRecord in all respects except one: The first field, the port field, is of type CGrafPort in the CWindowRecord. You will recall from Chapter 7 that the port field of a WindowRecord is of type GrafPort.

Originally the Macintosh had no color, and QuickDraw was for monochrome drawing. So the GrafPort, which defines the drawing environment for black-and-white drawing, was sufficient. When the Mac did come to support color, Apple developed a new QuickDraw, Color QuickDraw. Along with Color QuickDraw came the CGrafPort. The CGrafPort defines the drawing environment for color drawing. Many of the drawing functions that you'll encounter in this chapter are Color QuickDraw functions and, as such, are expecting to draw to a CGrafPort. While they may in fact draw to a GrafPort, the colors you are expecting to see will not appear.

Will any color at all appear in a window created by a call to GetNewWindow()? Yes. While thought of as black-and-white, the original QuickDraw supports color to a very limited extent. Color QuickDraw of course fully supports color.

Once a color window has been created by the call to GetNewCWindow(), the window can be used in the same way as a window created by a call to GetNewWindow(). Actions such as dragging and closing the window are performed exactly as described in Chapter 7.

EXAMPLE PROGRAM: FOREBACKCOLOR

The ForeBackColor program displays a window like the one shown in Figure 11-1. The background of the window is red; the rectangle is blue; the oval is purple; and the text is white. After verifying this on your screen, click the mouse button to end the program.

Figure 11-1
The color window displayed by the ForeBackColor program.

The ForeBackColor program calls RGBBackColor() to set the window's background color. Once RGBBackColor() is called, the window's background color doesn't get changed until the window gets updated. In a program that includes an event loop and basic window-handling code, this would be no problem. The call to RGBBackColor() would cause an update event to occur. As you read in Chapter 7, an event-handling program would then respond by calling BeginUpdate() and EndUpdate(), with window content drawing calls in between. In the ForeBackColor program, though, update events are ignored. To force the program to update the window after the call to RGBBackColor(), BeginUpdate() and EndUpdate() are explicitly called.

```
RGBBackColor( &gRedColor );

BeginUpdate( theWindow );
  EraseRect( &theWindow->portRect );
EndUpdate( theWindow );
```

Your event-driven program won't need to include calls to BeginUpdate() and EndUpdate() after a call to RGBBackColor(); your program's updateEvt-handling code will take care of properly updating the window's background color.

```
//_____
#define    rDisplayWindow    128
#define    kBoxTop           20
#define    kBoxBottom        120
#define    kBoxLeft          30
#define    kBoxRight         260
#define    kOvalTop          kBoxTop + 20
#define    kOvalBottom       kBoxBottom - 20
```

```
#define    kOvalLeft     kBoxLeft + 20
#define    kOvalRight    kBoxRight - 20
//_____
RGBColor gRedColor;
RGBColor gBlueColor;
RGBColor gPurpleColor;
RGBColor gWhiteColor;
//_____
void main( void )
{
  WindowPtr theWindow;
  Rect      theRect;

  InitializeToolbox();
  DefineColors();

  theWindow = GetNewCWindow( rDisplayWindow, nil, (WindowPtr)-1L );
  SetPort( theWindow );
  RGBBackColor( &gRedColor );

  BeginUpdate( theWindow );
   EraseRect( &theWindow->portRect );
  EndUpdate( theWindow );

  RGBForeColor( &gBlueColor );
  SetRect( &theRect, kBoxLeft, kBoxTop, kBoxRight, kBoxBottom );
  PaintRect( &theRect );
  RGBForeColor( &gPurpleColor );
  SetRect( &theRect, kOvalLeft, kOvalTop, kOvalRight, kOvalBottom );
  PaintOval( &theRect );
  RGBForeColor( &gWhiteColor );
  MoveTo( kOvalLeft + 20, kOvalBottom - 25 );
  DrawString( "\pBlue, Red, Purple, White" );

  while ( !Button() )
    ;
}
//_____
void DefineColors( void )
{
  gBlueColor.red     = 0;
  gBlueColor.green   = 0;
  gBlueColor.blue    = 65535;

  gRedColor.red      = 65535;
  gRedColor.green    = 25000;
  gRedColor.blue     = 25000;
  gPurpleColor.red   = 45000;
  gPurpleColor.green = 0;
  gPurpleColor.blue  = 45000;
  gWhiteColor.red    = 65535;
  gWhiteColor.green  = 65535;
  gWhiteColor.blue   = 65535;
}
```

THE COLOR PICKER

Assigning values to the fields of an RGBColor variable to adjust a color setting in your program is something that you, the programmer, are capable of doing. A user of your program, however, shouldn't be expected to know about the RGB color model or the RGBColor data structure. If your program lets the user change colors used by your program, he or she should be provided with an easy mechanism for doing so. Enter the Color Picker.

The Color Picker, shown in Figure 11-2, is an Apple utility that enables a user to change a color setting by adjusting three sliders in a dialog box. Each slider represents one of the three RGB colors. As the user moves the thumb of a slider, the effects of the changing level of intensity for that one color can be seen in the bottom half of the rectangle at the top right of the Color Picker. The top half of the rectangle displays the original color that was in use when the Color Picker was first displayed.

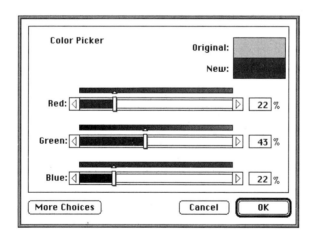

Figure 11-2
The System 7.5 version of the Color Picker.

Users with System 7.5 on their Macs see the Color Picker shown in Figure 11-2. Users with System 7.1 see a version of the Color Picker like the one pictured in Figure 11-3. Rather than use a set of three sliders to control color selection, a user with the Color Picker shown in Figure 11-3 clicks anywhere on the color wheel to select a color. Moving the thumb on the one vertical slider will then increase or decrease the brightness of the selected color.

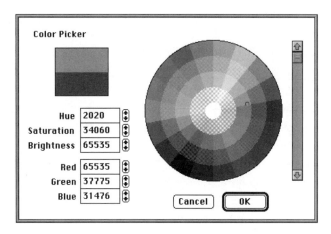

Figure 11-3
The System 7.1 version of the Color Picker.

From a programmer's perspective, the older Color Picker actually has one advantage over the newer Color Picker. The System 7.1 Color Picker displays the RGB values of the color being displayed. If you have a color that you'd like to know the RGB values for, you can click on the color in the color wheel and then look at the values the Color Picker displays in the three edit boxes at the bottom of the dialog box.

Your program can bring up the Color Picker at any time by calling the Toolbox function GetColor().

```
Boolean   colorSelected;
Point     thePoint = { 50, 30 };
Str255    thePrompt = "\pMy Color Picker!";
RGBColor  theStartColor;
RGBColor  theEndColor;
colorSelected = GetColor( thePoint, thePrompt,
          &theStartColor, &theEndColor );
```

The first parameter in GetColor() is a point that is used in the placement of the Color Picker dialog box. This point specifies where the top left corner of the dialog box should appear. The above snippet declares and initializes a Point variable named thePoint. Using thePoint, GetColor() will place the top left corner of the Color Picker 50 pixels from the top of the screen and 30 pixels from the left.

BY THE WAY

Notice that to assign a `Point` a pair of coordinates at the time of initialization you specify first the vertical value and then the horizontal value. These values are placed between a pair of braces.

```
Point thePoint = { 140, 40 };
```

As an aside, a `Rect` variable can be initialized in a similar manner.

```
Rect theRect = { 10, 50, 100, 300 };
```

When initializing a rectangle in this way, the order of the coordinates differs from the order used when calling `SetRect()`. Here's the coordinate order for both the initialization of a `Rect` and the assignment of a `Rect` using `SetRect()`:

```
Rect theRect = { top, left, bottom, right }; // initialize
SetRect( &theRect, left, top, right, bottom ); // assign
```

The second parameter in `GetColor()` is a string that serves as a title for the Color Picker. As shown in Figures 11-2 and 11-3, this string will be placed in the top left corner of the dialog box.

When the Color Picker dialog box opens, it displays a rectangle that displays both the original color (the color before any changes are made) and the new color that the user selects. The third parameter to `GetColor()` is a pointer to an `RGBColor` that represents the original color. You need to pass `GetColor()` this `RGBColor` variable so that the function knows what color your program considers the original color. When the user dismisses the dialog box, `GetColor()` will return the user's color selection in the form of an `RGBColor` in the fourth parameter.

When the user dismisses the Color Picker, `GetColor()` returns a `Boolean` value that specifies whether the user accepted or canceled his or her color change. If a value of `true` is returned, your program should consider the original color — the color used before the Color Picker opened — as the old color. The color selected by the user, the color returned in the fourth parameter of `GetColor()`, should now be considered the new color. Assuming that the old and new colors are being stored in global `RGBColor` variables, a snippet that performs the above task might look like this:

```
if ( colorSelected == true )
{
  gUsersOldColor = theStartColor;
  gUsersNewColor = theEndColor;
}
```

If your program does store colors in global variables, then those colors can always be used in calls to `RGBForeColor()` and `RGBBackColor()` without regard for whether, or when, the user makes color-setting changes. Using the code described in the above snippets, the `gUsersNewColor` variable will always hold the color the user has last selected. The PickColors program provides an example of this.

EXAMPLE PROGRAM: PICKCOLORS

When you launch PickColors, a small window opens. Then the Color Picker dialog box is displayed. Adjust the sliders to a color of your choosing, and then click on the OK button. The Color Picker will be dismissed, and two small rectangles will be drawn in the window. The rectangle on the left will be drawn in the original color, and the rectangle on the right will be drawn in the newly selected color. Figure 11-4 illustrates. The program incorporates a loop so that this process repeats; the Color Picker will again open, and two rectangles will again be drawn when the Color Picker is dismissed. After the third time the Color Picker is dismissed, click the mouse button to end the program.

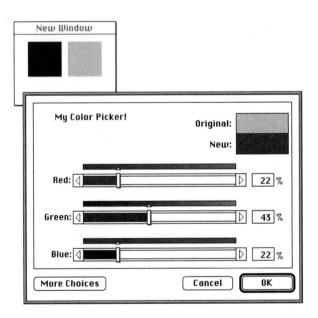

Figure 11-4
The PickColors program displays a window and the Color Picker.

The range of colors displayed in the Color Picker depends upon the number of colors your Macintosh is capable of displaying. The number of colors a Mac can display is dependent on the amount of memory it devotes to video. Choose the Monitors control panel to see the maximum number of colors, and the different color levels, that your particular computer can be set to.

The application-defined function `DisplayColorPicker()` is responsible for posting the Color Picker to the screen. This function begins by setting the value of the local `RGBColor` variable `theStartColor` to the user's current color choice.

```
theStartColor = gUsersNewColor;
```

A pointer to the variable `theStartColor` is then passed as the third parameter to `GetColor()`. The color held in `theStartColor` then serves as the original color that will be displayed in half of the display rectangle in the Color Picker. The color passed in the fourth parameter to `GetColor()` is unimportant — `GetColor()` will fill this variable with an `RGBColor` value after the user makes a color selection and clicks on the dialog box's OK button.

```
colorSelected = GetColor( thePoint, thePrompt,
            &theStartColor, &theEndColor );
```

Here is the listing for the PickColors program. Note that the universal header file ColorPicker.h is included to provide access to the `GetColor()` function.

```
//_____
#include <ColorPicker.h>
//_____
#define     rDisplayWindow     128
#define     kNumColorPicks       3
#define     kBoxTop             10
#define     kBoxBottom          60
#define     kOldBoxLeft         20
#define     kOldBoxRight        70
#define     kNewBoxLeft         80
#define     kNewBoxRight       130
//_____

RGBColor  gUsersNewColor;
RGBColor  gUsersOldColor;
```

```
//_____
void main( void )
{
  WindowPtr theWindow;
  Rect      theRect;
  int       i;

  InitializeToolbox();
  theWindow = GetNewCWindow( rDisplayWindow, nil, (WindowPtr)-1L );
  SetPort( theWindow );
  for ( i = 1; i <= kNumColorPicks; i++ )
  {
    DisplayColorPicker();

    RGBForeColor( &gUsersOldColor );
    SetRect( &theRect, kOldBoxLeft, kBoxTop, kOldBoxRight, kBoxBottom );
    PaintRect( &theRect );
    RGBForeColor( &gUsersNewColor );
    SetRect( &theRect, kNewBoxLeft, kBoxTop, kNewBoxRight, kBoxBottom );
    PaintRect( &theRect );
  }

  while ( !Button() )
    ;
}
//_____
void DisplayColorPicker( void )
{
  Boolean  colorSelected;
  Point    thePoint = { 140, 40 };
  Str255   thePrompt = "\pMy Color Picker!";
  RGBColor theStartColor;
  RGBColor theEndColor;

  theStartColor = gUsersNewColor;

  colorSelected = GetColor( thePoint, thePrompt, &theStartColor, &theEndColor
     );
  if ( colorSelected == true )
  {
    gUsersOldColor = theStartColor;
    gUsersNewColor = theEndColor;
  }
}
```

If an initial color isn't specified, the first time the Color Picker opens the original color will be black. That's what happens in the PickColor program. You can easily modify the program so that it starts with a different color. Define a global `RGBColor` variable and assign its three fields values — the `gRedColor` variable in this chapter's ColorShapes program is an example. Then, near the start of the program, assign the `gUsersNewColor` variable the value of the defined color variable.

THE COLOR PICKER AND MULTIPLE COLOR SETTINGS

The PickColors example program assumes that the user will be allowed to change only one color setting. Your program may have several color settings that you'll want to give the user control of. In that case, you'll want to display the Color Picker more than one time — you'll display it once for each setting the user wants to change.

Consider a program that has separate color settings for the drawing of rectangles and the drawing of ovals. Instead of declaring two global RGBColor variables, as the PickColors program did, this program might declare four:

```
RGBColor gOvalOldColor;
RGBColor gOvalNewColor;
RGBColor gRectOldColor;
RGBColor gRectNewColor;
```

To set the color of one of the settings, such as the color used to draw rectangles, the DisplayColorPicker() routine developed in the PickColors example would be called. Pointers to the two RGBColor variables used to keep track of the rectangle color would be passed to the function:

```
DisplayColorPicker( &gRectOldColor, &gRectNewColor );
```

Of course, the above technique requires a few changes to the application-defined DisplayColorPicker() function. First, the function needs to be defined with two parameters.

```
void DisplayColorPicker( RGBColor *theOldColor,
        RGBColor *theNewColor )
```

Next, the saving of the original color needs to include a dereferencing of the passed-in pointer theNewColor.

```
theStartColor = *theNewColor;
```

Finally, after the Color Picker is dismissed, the assignment of the new and old colors must include a dereferencing of both passed-in pointers.

```
*theOldColor = theStartColor;
*theNewColor = theEndColor;
```

Here's a look at the new version of the `DisplayColorPicker()` function:

```
void DisplayColorPicker( RGBColor *theOldColor,
            RGBColor *theNewColor )
{
  Boolean  colorSelected;
  Point    thePoint = { 140, 40 };
  Str255   thePrompt = "\pMy Color Picker!";
  RGBColor theStartColor;
  RGBColor theEndColor;

  theStartColor = *theNewColor;

  colorSelected = GetColor( thePoint, thePrompt,
             &theStartColor, &theEndColor );
  if ( colorSelected == true )
  {
   *theOldColor = theStartColor;
   *theNewColor = theEndColor;
  }
}
```

To adjust both the rectangle-drawing color and the oval-drawing color, invoke `DisplayColorPicker()` twice.

```
DisplayColorPicker( &gRectOldColor, &gRectNewColor );
DisplayColorPicker( &gOvalOldColor, &gOvalNewColor );
```

After the user has set both color levels, call `RGBForeColor()` before the drawing of any shape.

```
RGBForeColor( gRectNewColor );
// draw rectangle
RGBForeColor( gOvalNewColor );
// draw oval
```

Patterns and Color

Chapter 10 provided you with the details of creating and using pattern resources. But the patterns created in that chapter were all black-and-white. The Mac is just as capable of displaying color patterns. Now that you know you can create color pattern resources and now that you know about using color in your programs, you may wish you had never invested any time in learning about monochrome patterns. Not to worry, though. As you're about to see, the techniques you read about in Chapter 10 apply directly to the topic of color patterns.

THE PPAT RESOURCE

In Chapter 10 you learned that using a black-and-white pattern to fill a shape begins with the creation of a pattern resource — a PAT resource. When working with color, a color pattern resource analogous to the PAT resource is used — the ppat resource. Color patterns are referred to as pixel patterns, so a color pattern resource has the four-character name ppat.

Creating a ppat Resource in ResEdit

To create a color pattern resource in ResEdit, select Create New Resource from the Resource menu. Type ppat in the editable text box, and then click on the OK button. ResEdit will then open a ppat editor like the one shown in Figure 11-5. This editor is very similar to the PAT editor shown in Figure 10-16 in Chapter 10. The ppat editor lets you create two versions of the same resource. Click on the top rectangle on the right side of the editor, and any editing you do in the rectangle on the left of the editor will be in color — and will apply to the color version of the resource. Click on the bottom rectangle of the right side, and editing applies to a black-and-white version of the same resource. The black-and-white version will only be used by your program if a user runs the program on a Macintosh that has its monitor set to display monochrome.

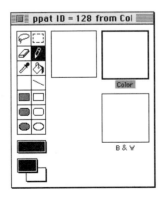

Figure 11-5
The ResEdit color pattern resource editor.

To turn individual pixels on and off in the pattern, use the Pencil tool from the editor's tool palette. You can set the color the pencil uses by clicking on the rectangle at the bottom left of the editor. Figure 116 shows the color palette that gets displayed when this rectangle is clicked on.

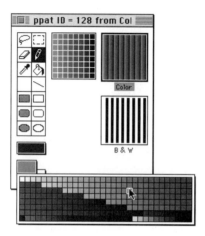

Figure 11-6
Using ResEdit to edit a pattern in a color pattern resource.

While a color pattern is generally 8 pixels by 8 pixels in size, it can be larger. If you select Pattern Size from the ppat menu in ResEdit, you'll see the dialog box shown in Figure 11-7. Click on a new pattern size, and then click on the Resize button. ResEdit will respond by enlarging the ppat editor, displaying an editing grid of the proper size.

Creating a ppat Resource in Resorcerer

To create a color pattern resource in Resorcerer, click on the New button in Resorcerer's main window. Type ppat in the editable text box, and then click on the Create button. Resorcerer will then open a Pattern Editor like the one shown in Figure 11-8. The Pattern Editor lets you create two versions of the same resource. Click on the small rectangle labeled "Color" on the right side of the editor, and any editing you do in the large grid will be in color and will apply to the color version of the resource. Click on the small rectangle labeled "1 bit," and editing will apply to a black-and-white version of the same resource. The black-and-white version only gets used by a program if the user runs the program on a Macintosh that has its monitor set to display monochrome.

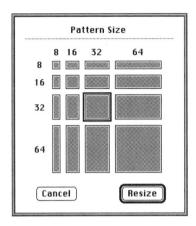

Figure 11-7
Changing the size of a ppat *resource in ResEdit.*

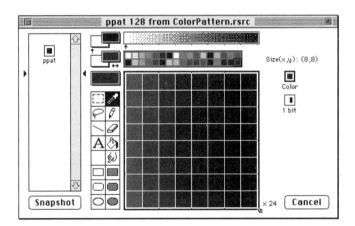

Figure 11-8
The Resorcerer color pattern editor.

To turn an individual pixel in the pattern on or off, use the Pencil tool from the editor's tool palette. To change the color used by the Pencil, click on the rectangle located to the left of the editor's color palette, as is being done in Figure 11-9. Choose any color from the larger palette that appears.

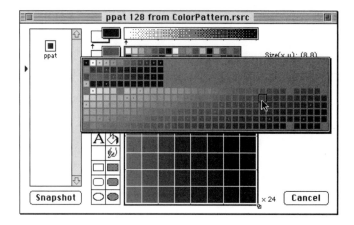

Figure 11-9
Using ResEdit to edit a pattern in a color pattern resource.

Color patterns are usually thought of as 8 pixels by 8 pixels in size, but they don't have to be. If you select Set Size from the PixelPattern menu in Resorcerer, you will see the dialog box shown in Figure 11-10. Click on a new pattern size in this dialog box, and then click on the Resize button. Resorcerer will then change the size of the editing grid in the Pattern Editor.

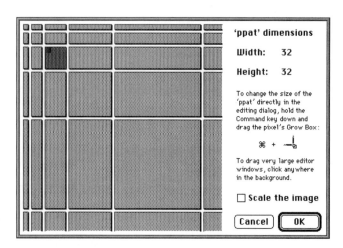

Figure 11-10
Changing the size of a ppat resource in Resorcerer.

Using a ppat resource

At the start of this chapter's introduction to color patterns, it was stated that working with color patterns is very similar to working with black-and-white patterns. Since the black-and-white pattern information from the previous chapter is still fresh in your mind, a direct comparison of the two methods should prove enlightening.

To load a black-and-white PAT pattern into memory, you pass the Toolbox function GetPattern() the ID of the pattern to load.

```
PatHandle thePatternHandle;

thePatternHandle = GetPattern( 128 );
```

To load a color ppat pattern into memory, you pass the Toolbox function GetPixPat() the ID of the pattern to load.

```
PixPatHandle thePixelPattern;
thePixelPattern = GetPixPat( 128 );
```

A monochrome pattern is stored in memory in the format of a Pattern data structure. As shown in the GetPattern() snippet, the GetPattern() function returns a PatHandle to the black-and-white pattern data in memory.

A color pattern is stored in memory in the format of a PixPat data structure. As shown in the GetPixPat() snippet, the GetPixPat() function returns a PixPatHandle to the color pattern data in memory.

The pattern used by the graphics pen can be set to a black-and-white pattern by using a doubly dereferenced PatHandle in a call to PenPat().

```
PatHandle thePatternHandle;

PenPat( **thePatternHandle );
```

The pattern used by the graphics pen can be set to a color pattern by using a PixPatHandle in a call to PenPixPat().

```
PixPatHandle thePixelPattern;
PenPixPat( thePixelPattern );
```

Once the pen pattern has been set, your program can use a paint function (such as `PaintRect()` or `PaintPoly()`) in the same way.

```
PaintOval( &theRect );
```

To use a fill function with a monochrome pattern, pass a singly dereferenced `PatHandle` as the second parameter.

```
PatHandle thePatternHandle;
FillRect( &theRect, *thePatternHandle );
```

To use a fill function with a color pattern, pass a `PixPatHandle` as the second parameter to a color fill routine that is analogous to a black-and-white fill routine. For example, instead of using `FillRect()`, use `FillCRect()`.

```
PixPatHandle thePixelPattern;
FillCRect( &theRect, thePixelPattern );
```

Every fill routine used with monochrome patterns has a color counterpart. The only difference in the routine names is that the color routine has a *C* in its name. For example, use `FillCOval()` and `FillCPoly()` in place of `FillOval()` and `FillPoly()`. The first parameter in either version of the routine is the same. The second parameter in the black-and-white routine is a pointer to a pattern. The second parameter in the color routine is a `PixPatHandle`. The ColorPattern program provides an example of how one of these functions can be used.

EXAMPLE PROGRAM: COLORPATTERN

The ColorPattern program makes use of two `ppat` resources. The program sets the pen pattern to one of the two color patterns and then calls `LineTo()` to draw a diagonal line. ColorPattern then makes a call to `FillCRect()`, passing a `PixPatHandle` to the second color pattern. Figure 11-11 shows the graphics that result from these QuickDraw calls. Clicking the mouse button ends the program.

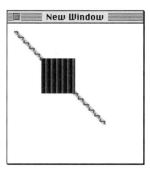

Figure 11-11
The window displayed by the ColorPattern program.

Figures 11-6 and 11-8 show one of the pixel pattern resources in ResEdit and Resorcerer, respectively. This resource is used to fill the rectangle. Figure 11-12 shows the second pixel pattern resource as viewed in ResEdit. This pattern is used when drawing the line.

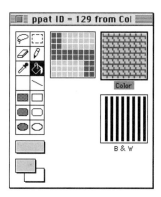

Figure 11-12
A ppat resource used by the ColorPattern program.

```
//_____
#define    rDisplayWindow      128
#define    rRedBlackPattern     128
#define    rPurplePattern       129
//_____
void main( void )
{
```

```
WindowPtr   theWindow;
Rect        theRect;
PixPatHandle thePixelPattern;
InitializeToolbox();
theWindow = GetNewCWindow( rDisplayWindow, nil, (WindowPtr)-1L );
SetPort( theWindow );
thePixelPattern = GetPixPat( rPurplePattern );
PenPixPat( thePixelPattern );

PenSize( 5, 5 );
MoveTo( 10, 10 );
LineTo( 140, 140 );
thePixelPattern = GetPixPat( rRedBlackPattern );
SetRect( &theRect, 50, 50, 100, 100 );
FillCRect( &theRect, thePixelPattern );
while ( !Button() )
   ;
}
```

Color Programming Reference

This section describes the QuickDraw and Color QuickDraw routines that are used for drawing in color and working with color patterns.

COLOR WINDOWS

If a window is to be the recipient of Color QuickDraw drawing, it should be created as a color window. A call to GetNewCWindow() achieves this.

GetNewCWindow( )

To create a window that has a color graphics port, and thus fully supports color drawing, call GetNewCWindow().

```
#define   rColorWindow  128
WindowPtr theWindow;
Ptr       windStorage = nil;
theWindow = GetNewCWindow( rColorWindow, windStorage, (WindowPtr)-1L
);
```

The GetNewCWindow() function uses the exact same parameters as the GetNewWindow() function defined in Chapter 7. Pass GetNewCWindow() the ID of the WIND resource that holds the window information. Pass a nil pointer to let the Toolbox allocate memory for the window (as opposed to your supplying a pointer to a memory block). Type cast -1L to a WindowPtr as the last parameter, to tell the Toolbox to place the window in front of all others.

DEFINING COLORS

The Macintosh uses the RGB color system to define individual colors. For Mac programmers, this system relies on the RGBColor data type.

RGBColor Data Type

A variable of type RGBColor holds the definition of a single color.

```
struct RGBColor
{
  unsigned short red;
  unsigned short green;
  unsigned short blue;
};
```

Any one of millions of colors can be defined by giving each of the three fields of an RGBColor a value in the range of 0 to 65,535. The higher the value of a field, the more intense (or lighter) that color will be. The lower the value of a field, the less intense (or darker) that color will be. When all three fields have a value of 0, the color black is defined. When all three fields have a value of 65,535, the color white is defined. The following example defines a shade of the color green:

```
RGBColor theGreenColor;
theGreenColor.red   =     0;
theGreenColor.green = 65535;
theGreenColor.blue  =     0;
```

DRAWING WITH COLOR

Once an RGB color has been defined, that color can be used in the drawing of any shape.

RGBForeColor( )

To set the foreground color of the current color window, call
RGBForeColor().

```
RGBColor theOrangeColor;
RGBForeColor( &theOrangeColor );
```

Pass this RGBForeColor() a pointer to an RGBColor. The calling of this routine sets the color that will be used in all subsequent calls to QuickDraw paint routines. To draw shapes to a different color, again call RGBForeColor().

RGBBackColor( )

To set the background color of the current color window, call
RGBBackColor().

```
RGBColor thePinkColor;
RGBBackColor( &thePinkColor );
```

Pass this RGBBackColor() a pointer to an RGBColor. By default, a window's background color is white, but it doesn't have to be. A call to RGBBackColor() sets the color that will be used for the background of the current color window. Once the background color is set, the RGBBackColor() routine does not need to be called again. Any time the affected window needs updating, the specified background color will be used in the update.

Shape-drawing routines

All the paint shape-drawing routines described and defined in Chapter 4 can be used when drawing in color. Before using a QuickDraw drawing function, call RGBForeColor() to set the current window's foreground color to the desired drawing color. Then call the drawing routine exactly as done when drawing with a black graphics pen. The following code draws a solid blue rectangle and serves as an example of how any of the QuickDraw functions can be used. Both the RGBForeColor() function and the defining of colors are described elsewhere in this reference section.

```
RGBColor theBlueColor;
RGBForeColor( &theBlueColor );
SetRect( &theRect, 10, 10, 80, 100 );
PaintRect( &theRect );
```

USING THE COLOR PICKER

Apple supplies a color-picking utility that allows all programs to share a common interface for letting the user select a color. The Color Picker is an easy-to-add, easy-to-use utility.

GetColor( )

To display the Color Picker utility, call GetColor(). Be aware that the Color Picker has a different look in System 7.5 than it does in System 7.1.

```
Boolean   colorSelected;
Point     thePoint = { 100, 30 };
Str255    thePrompt = "\pForeground Color Picker";
RGBColor theStartColor;
RGBColor theEndColor;
colorSelected = GetColor( thePoint, thePrompt,
            &theStartColor, &theEndColor );
```

The first parameter in GetColor() is a point that is used in the placement of the Color Picker dialog box. This point specifies where the top left corner of the dialog box should appear. The second parameter is a string that serves as a title for the Color Picker. The third parameter is a pointer to an RGBColor that represents the original color — the color the user last selected. The fourth parameter will hold the color selected by the user from the Color Picker dialog box.

PATTERNS

Opening a color window allows for the use of color patterns. A color pattern is defined in a resource of type ppat and is displayed by a variety of Color QuickDraw routines.

GetPixPat( )

To load the data from a ppat resource to a PixPat data structure in memory, call GetPixPat().

```
PixPatHandle thePixelPattern;
thePixelPattern = GetPixPat( 128 );
```

The parameter in GetPixPat() is the ID of the pixel pattern resource, or ppat resource, that is to be loaded into memory. When the call to GetPixPat() has completed, a handle to the pixel pattern data will be returned to the program.

PenPixPat( )

To set the pattern of the graphics pen to a color pattern, call PenPixPat().

```
PixPatHandle thePixelPattern;
PenPixPat( thePixelPattern );
```

The PixPatHandle that is passed to PenPixPat() is a handle to a color pattern retrieved from a ppat resource by a call to GetPixPat().

Shape-Drawing Routines

A color pattern version exists for each of the fill shape-drawing routines described and defined in Chapter 4 and Chapter 10. Each routine accepts the same first parameter as its black-and-white counterpart. The second parameter is a PixPatHandle variable that is a handle to the color pattern to use as the fill. This handle can be obtained by a call to GetPixPat(). The following example fills a rectangle with a color pixel pattern:

```
PixPatHandle thePixelPattern;
FillCRect( &theRect, thePixelPattern );
```

Other color pattern fill routines include FillCOval(), FillCRoundRect(), FillCPoly(), and FillCRgn().

12 Color and Macintosh Interface

*C*hapter 11 described how you can draw *in* color in a Window. In this chapter you'll learn how to add color *to* a window. Through the use of a window color table resource, you'll be able to add color to a window's frame, title, or content area.

Adding color to a window is just one way to brighten up the interface of a program. The dialog color table resource and the menu color table resource also enable you to add color to a program's dialog boxes and menus.

You've probably noticed that most Mac applications use little or no color in their interface elements. That's to provide consistency from program to program. If you do decide to add color to your program's interface, you'll want to do so judiciously — only add a touch here and a touch there for some special, specific effect.

Color Windows

You can add a little flair to your application's windows by using color in their frames, titles, and content. The wctb resource makes this possible.

WINDOW PARTS

In Chapter 7 you saw that Apple defines several part code constants that are used to describe different areas, or parts, of a window. These part codes (such as inDrag and inGrow) are used when a mouseDown event occurs.

When working with color windows, the term "window parts" arises again. These part names don't match the constants used for handling mouseDown events. Instead, they are part of the terminology used by both programmers and nonprogrammers when describing an area of a window. As you'll see just ahead, resource editors make it easy to add color to certain parts of a window. Figure 12-1 shows the names that are often used when referring to the various window parts that can have color added to them.

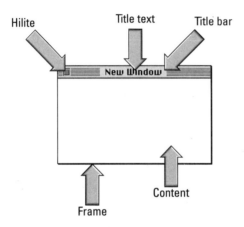

Figure 12-1
Window parts that can have color added to them.

The *content* part of a window includes the entire drawing area of the window. The *frame* part is the 1-pixel and 2-pixel border that surrounds the window. A window's *hilite* parts are the areas in the close box and zoom box. These areas change their look when a mouse-click occurs within their boundaries. A window's *title text* is its title — the window title. The *title bar* part is the area of the window that serves as a background for the window title.

The Color control panel lets the user change the color of the title bar and hilite areas of any window that is displayed on-screen. Figure 12-2 shows the Color control panel as it looks under System 7.5. Because window colors that are set in the Color control panel are a *systemwide feature* (a feature that affects any Macintosh window, not just windows in the Finder), the System will override changes you make to the title bar color and the hilite color of a window used in your application. Your program can, however, still make color changes to the color of the content, the frame, and the title of the windows used by the program.

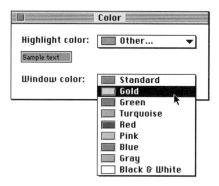

Figure 12-2
The Color control panel allows a user to add color to all windows.

The colors used in the various parts of a window are defined in a resource of type `wctb`. This window color table resource resides in the System file and is used by all windows displayed by any program. This explains why a single change in the Color control panel affects any window that appears on the screen.

When you define a `WIND` resource in a project's resource file and then use that `WIND` in a call to `GetNewWindow()`, the result is a window that may or may not display color in some of its parts. Whether it includes color is up to the user. If the user has decided that windows displayed on his or her machine should include color in their parts, the window created by your program will be displayed in the user's choice of colors. The Color control panel, however, only allows changes to the title bar and highlights parts of a window.

If your program defines windows that include color in any window parts other than the title bar and hilite parts, your program's windows will be displayed using those colors, regardless of the user's color preferences. As you'll see a little later, if your application is using a window that displays color in a window part not controlled by the Color control panel, the Toolbox routine `GetNewCWindow()` should be used instead of `GetNewWindow()`.

Defining the colors of a window's parts can be done in a resource editor. By defining the colors used by a `WIND` resource, all windows that use that `WIND` resource will also include those colors. If you use ResEdit as your resource editor, read the next section. If you use Resorcerer, skip over the next section.

RESEDIT AND WINDOW COLORS

When you create a WIND resource in ResEdit, two Color radio buttons always appear in the upper right corner of the WIND Editor. Normally, the button labeled Default is selected. If you click on the button labeled Custom, five rectangles, each with a window part label beside it, will appear. Figure 12-3 shows these rectangles.

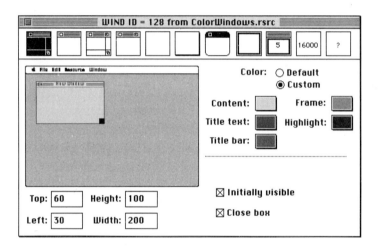

Figure 12-3
The Custom radio button in a WIND resource allows for the addition of color.

Each rectangle shown in Figure 12-3 serves as a pop-up menu. Each pop-up menu displays a palette of colors that lets you change the color for one part of the window that will eventually be created from this WIND resource. You change a part's color by clicking on the rectangle by the part's label and then selecting a color from the palette that appears.

In Figure 12-4, the rectangle labeled Content has been clicked on. The number of colors that appear in the resulting palette is dependent on the *pixel depth* of your monitor. That is, ResEdit will display more color options on monitors that are capable of displaying more colors. In Figure 12-4, the content color that will be used by windows created from this WIND resource is being changed on a computer that has a monitor set to display 256 colors. While the gray-scale figure, of course, can't show the various colors that are available, it does show that there are 8 rows of color choices, with 32 colors in each row.

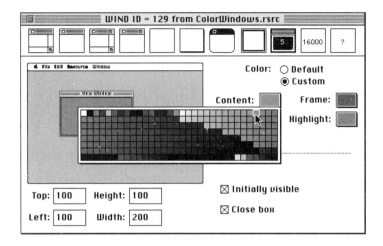

Figure 12-4
Clicking on one of the five rectangles brings up a palette of colors.

When you make a color change to a WIND, ResEdit will reflect that change in the small window that is displayed on the left side of the WIND Editor. For example, in Figure 12-4 you can see that the small window no longer has a white content area, as is normally the case.

Figure 12-5 shows a ResEdit resource file that contains both WIND and wctb resources. The wctb resources were not explicitly created using the Create New Resource command in the Resource menu, as most resources are. Instead, ResEdit created them automatically. The first time you make a selection from one of the pop-up palettes in a WIND resource, ResEdit will display the alert shown in Figure 12-6. As mentioned, the colors of a window's parts are governed by a wctb resource. When you use any of the five color palettes in a ResEdit WIND resource to make a color change to a window part, ResEdit automatically creates a new wctb resource that will be associated with the WIND resource being edited. As described in Figure 12-6, the wctb will be given the same ID as the WIND resource.

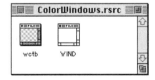

Figure 12-5
A resource file with WIND and wctb resources.

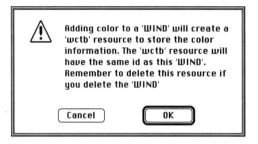

Figure 12-6
Adding color to a WIND *resource causes ResEdit*
to automatically create a wctb *resource.*

    If you double-click on the wctb icon in ResEdit's main window — the wctb icon shown in Figure 12-5 — you'll encounter a list of all wctb resources in the resource file. Because a wctb resource is always paired with a WIND ID, for each wctb resource there should be a WIND resource with the same ID. If you double-click on one of the wctb resources in the list, the WIND editor will open, not a wctb editor. ResEdit opens the WIND that corresponds to the wctb because wctb editing takes place in the WIND, as you've just seen.

Now that you know how to add color to a window from within a WIND resource, skip the next section and read on to see how your source code can take advantage of your color specifications.

RESORCERER AND WINDOW COLORS

When you create a WIND resource in Resorcerer, you use the Set Window Info command from Resorcerer's Window menu to make changes to the WIND settings. Figure 12-7 shows the window that opens when you choose Set Window Info.

At the bottom of the Set Window Info dialog box are five rectangles, each with a window part label beside it. Each of these rectangles lets you change the color of one window part. Resorcerer provides two means of doing this. If you are familiar with the RGB color system (red, green, blue), you can enter three numbers (each in the range of 0 to 65535) to define a color. If you don't know the RGB values for a color you have in mind, instead double-click on one of the part rectangles. When you do, a dialog box that holds Apple's Color Picker will open. As shown in Figure 12-8, the Color Picker enables you to select a color by varying the placement of any or all of the three sliders in the picker.

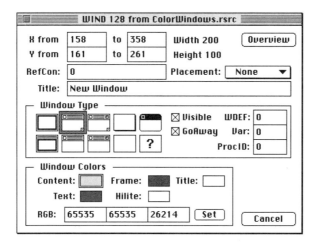

Figure 12-7
Adding color to a window in Resorcerer is accomplished through the Set Window Info window.

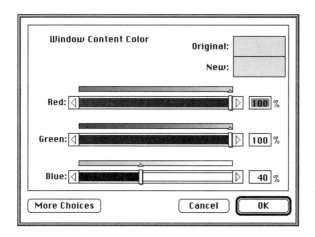

Figure 12-8
Double-clicking on one of the five rectangles in the Set Window Info window brings up the Color Picker.

When satisfied with a color, click on the Color Picker OK button. The color change will be shown in the rectangle in Resorcerer's Show Window Info dialog box.

After changing one or more window part colors, you will notice that Resorcerer has added a new resource type to the resource file you're working with. When window colors are specified in a WIND resource, Resorcerer automatically creates a new wctb resource. Resorcerer gives this new wctb resource an ID that's the same as the ID of the WIND resource you're working on. The matching resource ID is the tie that binds the wctb to the WIND.

Now that you have made color additions to a WIND resource, you need to let your source code in on the changes. That's an easy step to take, as you are about to see.

COLOR WINDOW SOURCE CODE

When a program calls GetNewWindow(), the Window Manager looks for a WIND resource with the ID specified in the first parameter to this Toolbox routine. When a program calls GetNewCWindow(), the Window Manager again looks for the specified WIND resource. But it also looks for a wctb resource with the same ID as the WIND resource. If one exists, the colors specified in that resource will be used with the window that GetNewCWindow() creates.

```
#define   rPinkWindow  129
WindowPtr theWindow;

theWindow = GetNewCWindow( rPinkWindow, nil, (WindowPtr)-1l );
```

As you saw in Chapter 11, the parameters to GetNewCWindow() are the same as they are for GetNewWindow(): the ID of a WIND resource, a pointer to an area in memory in which the window data is to be stored, and a value that indicates if the window should appear in front of all others currently on the screen.

Once a color window has been created by the call to GetNewCWindow(), no special treatment of it is necessary. As demonstrated in the example program that follows, an application works with a color window just as it does with a monochrome window.

EXAMPLE PROGRAM: COLORWINDOWS

The ColorWindows program displays two windows, as shown in Figure 12-9, both of which have color added to their content, frame, and title. The close box and the title bar may also display color; that depends on the setting you have selected from the Color control panel on your Macintosh.

Figure 12-9
The two windows displayed by the ColorWindows program.

The ColorWindows program has a simple event loop like the one described in Chapter 7. The event loop watches for mouseDown and keyDown events. A click of the mouse will send the program to the application-defined HandleMouseDown() function, where the closing, dragging, or selection of a window is handled. A press of a key will be noted as a keyDown event, and the event loop will end the program.

To make changes to the parts of one of the program's windows, open the ColorWindows.rsrc resource file. Open one of the WIND resources and change the color of one or more of the window's parts, as described earlier in this chapter. Save your changes, close the resource file, and use your development environment to build a new application from the ColorWindows project. The resulting program will display a window that uses your new colors.

```
//_____
#define  rGrayWindow  128
#define  rPinkWindow  129
//_____
Boolean gDone = false;
//_____
void main( void )
{
  WindowPtr theWindow;
```

```
  InitializeToolbox();
  theWindow = GetNewCWindow( rGrayWindow, nil, (WindowPtr)-1L );
  theWindow = GetNewCWindow( rPinkWindow, nil, (WindowPtr)-1L );
  EventLoop();
}
//_____
void EventLoop( void )
{
 EventRecord theEvent;

 while ( gDone == false )
 {
  WaitNextEvent( everyEvent, &theEvent, 15L, nil );

  switch ( theEvent.what )
  {
   case mouseDown:
   HandleMouseDown( theEvent );
   break;
   case keyDown:
   gDone = true;
   break;
  }
 }
}
//_____
void HandleMouseDown( EventRecord theEvent )
{
 WindowPtr theWindow;
 short   thePart;

 thePart = FindWindow( theEvent.where, &theWindow );

 switch ( thePart )
 {
  case inGoAway:
   if ( TrackGoAway( theWindow, theEvent.where ) == true )
   DisposeWindow( theWindow );
   break;
  case inDrag:
   DragWindow( theWindow, theEvent.where, &qd.screenBits.bounds );
   break;
  case inContent:
   SelectWindow( theWindow );
   break;
 }
}
```

Color Dialog Boxes

The technique for adding color to dialog box parts is as easy as the technique for adding color to window parts.

DIALOG BOX PARTS

Because a dialog box is essentially a gussied-up window, dialog box parts are the same as window parts. Your resource editor lets you easily set the dialog box title, content, and frame color, just as it does for the analogous window parts.

When a resource editor is used to add color to any part of a dialog box, the resource editor will create a new dctb resource. This dialog color table resource — analogous to the window color table resource, or wctb resource, that is used in conjunction with the WIND resource — has the same ID as the DLOG resource it holds information for.

When you define a DLOG resource in a project's resource file and then use that DLOG in a call to GetNewDialog(), the result is a dialog box that is capable of displaying color in some of its parts. If a dctb resource is present, color will be used. If a dctb resource isn't available, the dialog box will appear in black-and-white.

Because the information in this chapter's Color Windows section directly applies to the adding of color to a dialog box, the following two sections that describe resource editors and the dctb resource will be brief. If you skipped the Color Windows section, go back and read it now. If you use ResEdit as your resource editor, read the next two sections. If you use Resorcerer, skip over the next two sections to get to the Resorcerer information.

RESEDIT AND DIALOG BOX COLORS

In ResEdit, the editor used to edit a DLOG resource is very similar to the editor used to edit a WIND resource. Now that you're familiar with the process of adding color to a window via the WIND editor, you're all set to do the same to a dialog box via the DLOG editor.

Like the WIND editor, the DLOG editor has a Custom radio button that is used to display the color-editing settings in the editor. After clicking on the Custom radio button, click on any of the five rectangles to bring up a color palette like the one shown in Figure 12-10.

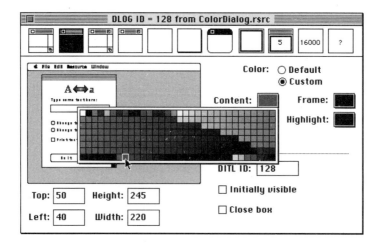

Figure 12-10
The Custom radio button in a DLOG resource allows for the addition of color.

Adding color to any part of a dialog box will result in ResEdit's creating a new dctb resource. It will also result in the display of an alert that informs you that ResEdit is taking the liberty of doing so.

ResEdit and Dialog Box Colors

Now that you have added color to a dialog box, you may also want to add color to the items in that dialog box. Unfortunately, ResEdit provides no easy way of doing this. If you'd like to colorize dialog box items, you'll want to purchase a copy of the "other" resource editor, Resorcerer.

RESORCERER AND DIALOG BOX COLORS

The steps used to add color to a dialog box in Resorcerer are the same as the ones for adding color to a window: A menu selection brings up an Info window, and a double-click on a part rectangle in that window brings up the Color Picker.

When you create a DLOG resource in Resorcerer, you use the Set Dialog Info command from Resorcerer's Dialog menu to make changes to the DLOG settings. Figure 12-11 shows the window that opens when you choose Set Dialog Info. To add color to a dialog box part, double-click on one of the five rectangles at the bottom of the window. The standard Color Picker will then be displayed. Change the slider settings in the Color Picker, and then click on the OK button.

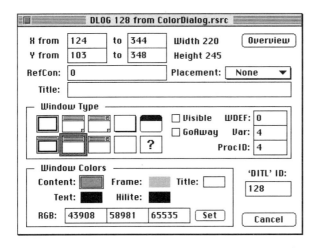

Figure 12-11
Dialog box colors are added from the Set Dialog Info window.

After setting the color of a dialog box part, Resorcerer will add a new dctb resource to the resource file you're working with. This dctb resource will have the same ID as the ID of the DLOG resource you're working on.

RESORCERER AND DIALOG BOX ITEM COLORS

The dctb resource holds information about the colors used for the various parts of a dialog box. But the color settings in that resource have no bearing on the colors of button dialog items in a dialog box. In the dialog box pictured on the left of Figure 12-12 you can see that while color has been added to the content of a dialog box, the button in that dialog box is still white. If color is to be added to a dialog box item — as it is for the button in the dialog box on the right of Figure 12-12 — an ictb, or item color table, resource must be created.

Figure 12-12
An ictb resource is used to add color to dialog box items, as shown in the dialog box on the right.

Figure 12-12 shows that changing the content color of a dialog box is all that's needed in order to also change the background color of a checkbox item. The same is true for a radio button item and a static text item. No ictb resource is necessary for content color to be applied to items of these three types.

A single ictb resource holds color information for all the items in a dialog box. It also can hold font information for static text items and editable text box items. To create an ictb resource in Resorcerer, take the following steps:

STEPS: USING RESORCERER TO CREATE AN ictb RESOURCE

Step 1. Open the DLOG resource that the ictb is to be paired with.
Step 2. Click on the item whose color or text you want to change. To have changes affect more than one item, hold down the Shift key as you click on items.
Step 3. Select Colors and Text Styles from the Items menu.
Step 4. Make the desired color and font changes in the window that opens.

In Figure 12-13, the static text item near the top of the DLOG and the Do It button at the bottom left of the dialog have been selected. That means that the Colors and Text Styles command will be affecting these two items.

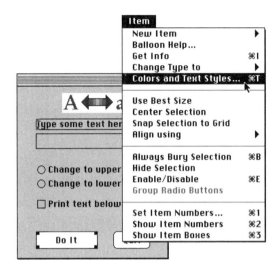

Figure 12-13
The Colors and Text Styles menu in Resorcerer allows for the addition of color to items.

Selecting Colors and Text Styles from the Items menu brings up the window shown in Figure 12-14. As you can see in this figure, the window is divided into three sections. The top two sections, Text Item Style and Text Item Color, affect only static text items and editable text items. The bottom section, Control Item Color, affects only control items such as buttons. If no text items are selected when this window opens, the top two sections in the window will be dim, or disabled. If no control items are selected when the window opens, the bottom section will be dim.

As you can see in Figure 12-14, the ictb resource provides you with an opportunity to change a wide variety of item characteristics. After making the desired changes, click on the OK button. Resorcerer will apply your color and font changes to the DLOG resources so you can see what the resulting dialog box will look like.

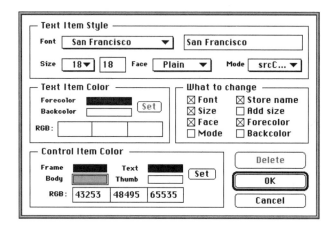

Figure 12-14
The Colors and Text Styles window with font and color changes.

One of the primary uses of the `ictb` resource is to make buttons have the same color as the content of the dialog box, as shown in the dialog box pictured on the right side of Figure 12-12. To do this, take the following steps:

STEPS: USING RESORCERER TO MAKE THE COLOR OF BUTTONS MATCH THE COLOR OF DIALOG BOX CONTENT

Step 1. With a `DLOG` resource open, select Set Dialog Info from the Dialog menu.

Step 2. Double-click on the Content rectangle to bring up the Color Picker.

Step 3. Use the Color Picker to set the dialog box content color, and then click on the OK button.

Step 4. Take note of the three RGB colors that define the content color (see bottom of Figure 12-11).

Step 5. Save the color changes, and close the color settings window.

Step 6. Click on the button that is to have color added to it.

Step 7. Select Colors and Text Styles from the Items menu.

Step 8. Type in the same three RGB colors that were noted in Step 4.

Step 9. Click on the OK button to save the changes.

COLOR DIALOG BOX SOURCE CODE

When creating a color window, your program calls GetNewCWindow() rather than GetNewWindow(). That forces the Window Manager to recognize the wctb resource that is in your application's resource fork. To create a color dialog, there is no special Toolbox call to make. Instead, call GetNewDialog(), just as you have done in the past to display a monochrome dialog box.

When a call to GetNewDialog() is made, the Dialog Manager will always search the application's resource fork for a matching dctb resource. The Dialog Manager will also search for an ictb resource with an ID that corresponds to the ID of the DLOG resource specified in the call to GetNewDialog(). If the dctb resource is found, the dialog box will display color in its parts. If the ictb resource is found, the dialog box will additionally display color in its dialog items.

As is the case for a color window, once a color dialog box has been created, no special treatment of it is necessary. The Dialog Manager will handle color considerations when updating the dialog box.

EXAMPLE PROGRAM: COLORDIALOG

The ColorDialog program is similar to Chapter 8's ModelessDialog application. The only difference is in the display of the program's modeless dialog box. As shown in Figure 12-15, the new program adds color to the content of the dialog box. The program also changes the look of three of the dialog items: The two buttons are in color and the static text item is displayed in the San Francisco font.

If you don't have the San Francisco font in your system, the text of the static text item won't match that shown in Figure 12-15. Keep this fact in mind when changing the font of dialog box text items: In order for a user to view the text item as you intend it to be viewed, the user must have the font you selected in his or her system. For this reason you should stick with common fonts such as the system font (Chicago), Monaco, or Geneva.

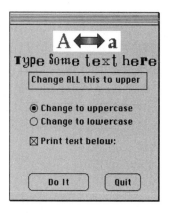

Figure 12-15
The dialog box displayed by the ColorDialog program.

The source code for a program that displays a color dialog box is the same as it is for a similar program that displays a monochrome dialog box. That means the source code for the ColorDialog program should be the same as the source code for the program on which it is based: the Chapter 8 ModelessDialog example. The two listings are, in fact, identical. To see the source code, refer back to Chapter 8 or examine the ColorDialog.c source code file on the included CD.

To make changes to the parts of one of the program's dialog boxes, open the ColorDialog.rsrc resource file. Open the DLOG resource and change the color of one or more of the dialog box parts, as described in the Color Windows section of this chapter. Save your changes, close the resource file, and use your development environment to build a new application from the ColorDialog project. The resulting program will display a dialog box that uses your new colors. To change the color of a dialog box item or to change the text displayed in the static text item, use Resorcerer to edit item colors or text, as described a few pages back.

Color Menus

While some programs do add a little color to windows and dialog boxes, very few make use of color in menus and the menu bar. If you feel you must add color to a program's menus, do so sparingly.

MENU PARTS

To add color to a program's menu bar or its menus, you'll again make use of a color resource: the `mctb`, or menu color table resource. From a single `mctb` resource you can assign color to any or all of the menu parts shown in Figure 12-16.

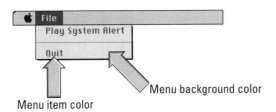

Figure 12-16
The parts of a menu bar and menus that can have color added to them.

Both ResEdit and Resorcerer let you define colors for each MENU resource in a resource file; that enables you to give each menu in a program's menu bar a different color. If you are going to add any color at all to a program's menu bar, you certainly won't want to do so in such a garish manner. Instead, make all the program's menus the same color. To do that, create a single `mctb` resource with an ID of 0. When your program calls `GetNewMBar()` to load the menu bar, it will look for an `mctb` resource that has an ID of 0. If it finds one, it will use the colors specified in that resource for each of the individual menus in the program's menu bar.

If you use ResEdit, read the next section to see how to create the `mctb` resource with an ID of 0. If you're fortunate enough to own Resorcerer, you'll want to be sure to skip to the following section — the steps involved in creating color menus using ResEdit are much more involved than those used with Resorcerer. Resorcerer's MENU Editor, which allows for the editing of `mctb` resources, is *much* easier to use then ResEdit's editor.

If you want to try adding color to an existing program, make a copy of that program's project, source code, and resource files. This chapter's color menu example does that with Chapter 6's MenuIntro program. The three files from that example were copied, renamed, and turned into a program named ColorMenus — the resulting files can be found on the CD that's included with this book.

ResEdit and Menu Colors

To add color to a program's menus, you will create a single mctb resource. Begin by using ResEdit to open a resource file. Then select Create New Resource from the Resource menu. Type mctb in the editable text box, and then click on the OK button. ResEdit will create a new mctb resource. ResEdit generally gives the first resource of any resource type an ID of 128, and the mctb resource is no exception.

An mctb resource that is used to set the colors of an individual menu is edited from within the ResEdit MENU Editor. Because of this, when you create a new mctb resource, ResEdit will automatically open the MENU Editor for you. ResEdit will also assume that the new mctb with an ID of 128 will hold a menu-coloring entry that is to be paired with a MENU resource with an ID of 128. If the resource file you're using has a MENU resource with an ID of 128, ResEdit will open that MENU resource in the MENU Editor.

When you create a new mctb resource and ResEdit opens a MENU resource, the resource editor is trying to do you a service. In this instance, however, ResEdit's efforts are actually a disservice. You want to create an entry in the mctb resource that will be used to set the colors in the entire menu bar, not just in an individual menu. Without doing any editing, click on the close box in the MENU Editor window to close MENU 128. If you started with a copy of the MenuIntro resource file, your screen should look similar to the one shown in Figure 12-17. Depending on the resource file you did start with, the types of resources in your file may differ from those pictured.

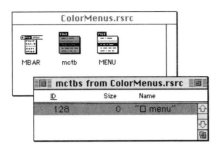

Figure 12-17
After creating a new mctb resource, close the
MENU Editor to display the mctb *list.*

With the new mctb resource highlighted, as shown in Figure 12-17, select Get Resource Info. In the window that opens, change the resource ID to 0. You can also give the resource a descriptive name, as shown in Figure 12-18.

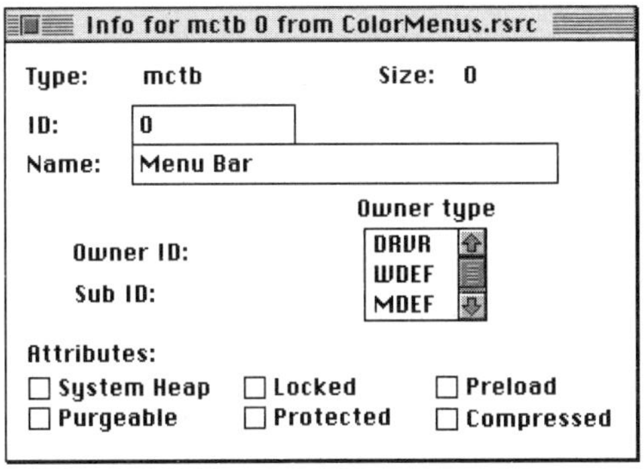

Type: mctb	**Size:** 0	
ID: 0		
Name: Menu Bar		

Figure 12-18
The Get Resource Info window is used to change the ID of a mctb *resource.*

After changing the mctb resource ID to 0, click on the close box of the Info window. Then double-click on the mctb resource to open the mctb Editor. Because the mctb resource ID doesn't match the ID of any MENU resource, the mctb Editor rather than the MENU Editor will open. Your screen will display a window like the one shown in Figure 12-19. Click on the row of asterisks, and then select Insert New Item from the Resource menu.

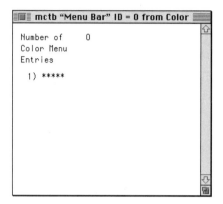

Figure 12-19

An empty mctb resource.

ResEdit will add a number of editable text box items to the mctb Editor window; they're shown in Figure 12-20. To further specify that this mctb be used for the entire menu bar, type a 0 in the first two boxes, the ones labeled Menu ID and Item No. (refer to Figure 12-20). Next, you'll enter RGB color values in all of the remaining editable text boxes, with the exception of the box labeled Reserved. Enter a 0 in that box. Again refer to Figure 12-20.

The mctb resource lets you specify a color for each of the four menu parts shown back in Figure 12-16. Figure 12-20 shows that each menu part requires three RGB color values to define a single color. After determining the three RGB values for each color, enter the values in the appropriate editable text box.

A color that is defined by the RGB format requires three values: a level of red, a level of green, and a level of blue. Each of these values ranges from 0 to 65,535. If you aren't familiar with the RGB color system, experiment by entering different values in the mctb resource and checking the results in the program you build.

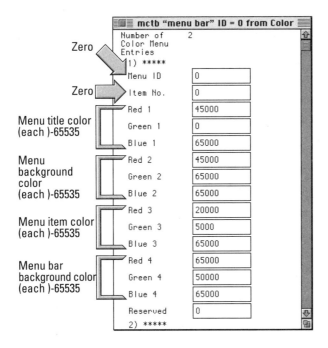

Figure 12-20
A single entry in an mctb *resource contains several editable text boxes.*

After entering all the RGB values, you need to create a second entry in this same mctb resource. This second entry is a dummy item that serves to mark the end of the color table. To create this dummy item, scroll to the bottom of the mctb Editor window. Click on the row of asterisks by the number 2. Then again select Insert New Field from the Resource menu. Another set of editable text boxes will appear. Enter a value of -99 in the first box (the box labeled Menu ID), and a 0 in each of the remaining boxes. Figure 12-21 illustrates. Then save the resource.

Negative
ninety nine

Each value
should be zero

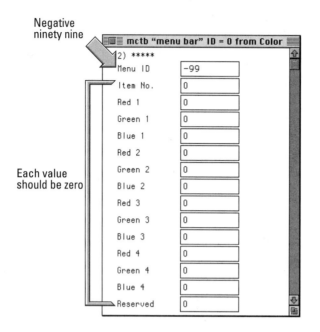

Figure 12-21
A second entry, a dummy item with an ID of -99, must
be added to the mctb *resource.*

You *must* add this second dummy item, and it *must* have a Menu ID value of -99. A program that attempts to use a menu bar mctb resource that doesn't have this second item will crash.

RESORCERER AND MENU COLORS

Resorcerer enables you to easily add color to menus and the menu bar. To begin, open a resource file. Then open *any* MENU resource in that file. Click on the Menu Bar button in the Colors section of the Menu Editor, as in Figure 12-22.

Adding color usually isn't the first task you do in a resource file. First, you'll most likely create the MENU resources and the MBAR resource. This isn't to say you can't create an mctb resource first. To do so, select New Resource from the Resource menu. Type mctb and click on the Create button. Resorcerer will open the Menu Editor for a MENU resource with an ID of 128. You can now create both the Apple MENU resource and the mctb resource at the same time.

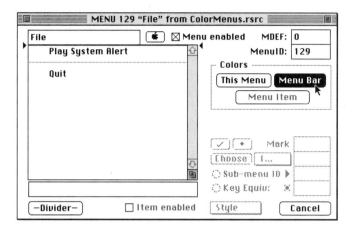

Figure 12-22
An *mctb* resource can be created from within any *MENU* resource.

After clicking on the Menu Bar button, a window like the one shown in Figure 12-23 will appear. This window lets you set the colors of the four menu bar parts shown back in Figure 12-16. Double-click on any one of the four rectangles to bring up the Color Picker, which was described in this chapter's Color Windows section. Make the desired color change, and then dismiss the Color Picker. To edit any other menu parts, double-click on its rectangle as described. When finished, click on the close box of the window shown in Figure 12-23.

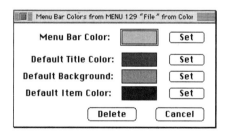

Figure 12-23
The menu parts can be given color from the window that opens when the Menu Bar button is clicked on in the *MENU* resource.

To get an idea of how an `mctb` resource looks, view the completed `mctb` resource in the Menu Editor. First click on the `mctb` type listed on the left side in Resorcerer's main window, as shown in Figure 12-24. Then double-click on the one `mctb` resource shown in the left of the window. Resorcerer will open the Menu Editor and display the `mctb` resource in it.

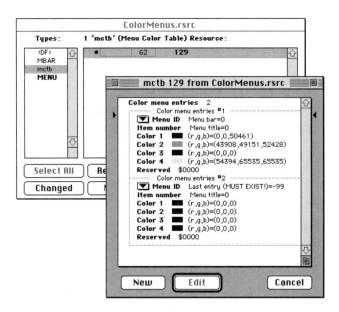

Figure 12-24
An mctb resource can be edited in the Menu Editor of Resorcerer.

The Menu Editor shows that the `mctb` resource with ID 129 holds two entries. The first entry, with a Menu ID of 0, defines the menu bar colors. The second entry is a dummy entry used to signal the end of the resource. An `mctb` resource must end with this dummy entry that has a Menu ID of -99.

A point of confusion may be the fact that there is more than one ID involved here. An `mctb` resource, like any resource, has an ID. The one in the above example has an ID of 129. Within the `mctb` resource can be any number of entries. Each entry has its own ID.

Within that `mctb` resource you can have any number of entries. An entry can define a set of colors that will be used for all menus, or an entry can define the colors that will appear in just one menu. If you give an entry a Menu ID of 0, as with the `mctb` resource created above, the colors defined in that entry will be used for all menus in a menu bar.

Earlier it was stated that the Toolbox function GetNewMBar() searches for an mctb resource with an ID of 0. If it finds this resource, it uses the colors defined within it on the application's menu bar. If there is no mctb with a resource ID of 0, GetNewMBar() then looks at each of any other mctb resources that may be in the resource fork. It will look inside each mctb resource for an entry with a Menu ID of 0. If it finds such an entry, it uses the colors defined there.

EXAMPLE PROGRAM: COLORMENUS

Adding color to a program's menu bar and menus means making additions to a project's resource file, not to its source code file. This chapter's ColorMenus example is simply the Chapter 6 MenuIntro example, renamed. When you run ColorMenus, you will see the menu bar pictured back in Figure 12-16. The menu bar and each menu will be displayed in color. To see the listing for ColorMenus, refer to the MenuIntro example in Chapter 6, or look at the ColorMenus.c source code file on the included CD.

One last reminder: Macintosh programs should use color sparingly in windows, dialog boxes, and menus. True, the Mac is known for exciting, colorful graphics. But when it comes to the interface of a program, Mac users expect consistency. If you do add color, do so sparingly and for good effect — don't shock your users!

Color Interface Reference

Only one new Toolbox function is necessary when adding color to the interface of your applications. To add color to a window, GetNewCWindow() is used. A dialog box that includes color is brought to the screen with the same GetNewDialog() function discussed in Chapter 8. A menu bar that includes color relies on the same GetNewMBar() function described in Chapter 6.

LOADING A COLOR WINDOW

Before working with a window that includes color in any of its parts, you need to load its data into memory. After that, a `WindowPtr` variable can be used to access the data that represents the window.

GetNewWindow( )

You should use a `WIND` resource, a `wctb` resource, and a call to the Toolbox routine `GetNewCWindow()` to create a color window.

```
#define    rColorWindow 128
WindowPtr theWindow;
Ptr        windStorage = nil;
theWindow = GetNewCWindow( rColorWindow, windStorage, (WindowPtr)-1L
);
```

The `GetNewCWindow()` function uses the exact same parameters as the `GetNewWindow()` function does. Pass `GetNewCWindow()` the ID of the `WIND` resource that holds the window information. Pass a `nil` pointer to let the Toolbox allocate memory for the window (as opposed to your supplying a pointer to a memory block). Type cast -1L to a `WindowPtr` as the last parameter to tell the Toolbox to place the window in front of all others. You do not need to specify the `wctb` resource — `GetNewCWindow()` automatically looks for, and loads, information found in a `wctb` resource that has the same ID as the `WIND` resource it uses.

13 Sound

*T*he audio hardware now standard on every Macintosh includes one or more internal speakers for generating sounds. Mac programmers can make use of this capability in conjunction with Sound Manager 3.0 software (which is built into every PowerPC-based Macintosh and is available as a system extension for 68K-based Macs) to easily add sound to any Macintosh application.

In this chapter you'll read about sound file formats, how to convert files from one type to another, and how to use Sound Manager Toolbox routines to play these different types of sound files. You'll also find out how sounds can be stored as sound resources within your application. And of course, you'll see how your application can play these same resources. Finally, you'll read up on how to change the speaker volume so that a user of your sound-playing program is sure to hear every noise your program makes.

Sound Manager 3.0

The Mac has always had sound — but it hasn't always had the Sound Manager. The latest version of the Sound Manager is the most powerful yet.

HISTORY OF THE SOUND MANAGER

Though the Macintosh has always had sound routines as part of the
Toolbox, the Sound Manager wasn't introduced until the release of System
6.0. Version 2.0 of the Sound Manager (referred to at the time of release as
the enhanced Sound Manager) was included as a part of System 6.0.7.
Version 3.0 became a part of System 7.5. A Mac owner who hasn't upgraded
to System 7.5 can still add the capabilities of Sound Manager 3.0 by adding
the Sound Manager system software extension to his or her Extensions
folder in the System Folder.

That last point is worth repeating. If you're using System 7.5, you have
Sound Manager 3.0 — it's part of your system software. If you're using an
earlier version of the Mac system software (such as 7.1), you can get the
Sound Manager 3.0 extension from Apple and add it to your Extensions
folder.

Sound Manager 3.0 improves upon how the Mac works with sound,
and adds new sound-playing capabilities to the Macintosh. Some of the
Toolbox routines discussed in this chapter are available only in version 3.0
(and beyond) of the Sound Manager.

CHECKING FOR THE PRESENCE OF SOUND MANAGER 3.0

Most Mac owners now have Sound Manager 3.0 as a part of their system
software, whether as part of their System 7.5 software or as a software
extension in their Extensions folder. Most, but not all. Before your application jumps right in and starts calling Sound Manager Toolbox routines,
check for the presence of version 3.0 (or later) of the Sound Manager.

One of the data types available to Mac programmers is the NumVersion
type. A few Toolbox routines return a filled data structure of this type so
that your program can determine if certain system software is available on
the user's machine. Here's the definition of the NumVersion data type:

```
struct  NumVersion
{
    UInt8    majorRev;
    UInt8    minorAndBugRev;
    UInt8    stage;
    UInt8    nonRelRev;
};
```

UInt8?

Apple defines the UInt8 type to be the same as the Byte type. The Byte type? That data type is defined to be an unsigned char. That means that a UInt8 has the same range of values as an unsigned char — which is 0 to 255. As a reminder, a signed char has a range of -128 to +127.

So, if a UInt8 is nothing more than an unsigned char, why didn't Apple just define each of the four NumVersion fields as unsigned char types? For clarity. Yes, honestly, for clarity! Though calling each field an unsigned char would have the same effect as calling each a UInt8, it would be misleading in that programmers might be led to believe that the NumVersion fields had something to do with characters.

When a Toolbox routine returns a NumVersion, you can check the majorRev field to see if it meets your program's minimum requirement. In the case of your check for Sound Manager 3.0, you'll call the Toolbox routine SndSoundManagerVersion() and check to see if the majorRev field of the returned NumVersion has a value of at least 3. This snippet does that:

```
NumVersion  theVersion;
theVersion = SndSoundManagerVersion();
if ( theVersion.majorRev < 3 )
    ExitToShell();
```

Add this check to any program that uses the routines discussed in this chapter. You have Sound Manager 3.0, but are you sure every user of your programs will have it too? Sound Manager 3.0 cannot be used on older Macintosh computers. Unfortunately, owners of the Mac Plus, Mac Classic, and Mac SE are out of luck.

Sound Resources

Your program can play a sound that is stored either as a sound resource or as a sound file. This section discusses sound resources, and the next section is about sound files.

ABOUT SOUND RESOURCES

The snd resource type holds the data for a sound. Storing a sound as a resource in your application's resource fork (rather than as a separate sound file) ensures that the sound will always accompany your application and will always be available for your application's use.

Sounds can be obtained from a number of sources, though usually in the form of sound files rather than sound resources. This isn't a problem, since a sound resource can easily be extracted from a sound file, as discussed in this chapter's "Sound Files" section. You'll find sound files available from the following sources:

- From the software libraries of online services such as CompuServe, America Online, and eWorld.

- From commercial sources — for about 25 dollars you can buy a CD containing more than 1,000 sounds.

- By creating them yourself, using your Mac's built-in microphone, or by plugging a sound digitizer into the back of your computer.

This book's CD contains a snd resource; it's in the resource file of this chapter's sndResource example program (see Figure 13-1).

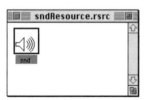

Figure 13-1
A snd resource in a resource file.

PLAYING THE SYSTEM ALERT SOUND

Users can select one of several sounds, which are listed in the Sound control panel, to be the system alert sound — the sound that plays when the user clicks the mouse outside of an alert or dialog box or makes some other "mistake." Figure 13-2 shows a typical Sound control panel.

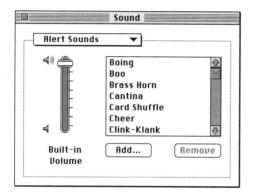

Figure 13-2
The Sound control panel.

Each of the system alert sounds displayed in a user's Sound control panel has a corresponding snd resource in the user's System file. Your program can play this sound by calling the Toolbox routine SysBeep(), as follows:

```
SysBeep( 1 );
```

The parameter to SysBeep() is a remnant from days gone by. Originally, SysBeep() always played a simple beep sound. The parameter specified the duration of this beep, in sixtieths of a second. Now, because there are a variety of system alert sounds — each already having a set duration — there's no need for this parameter. You can pass any integer value and the effect will be the same — the user's current system alert sound will play one time.

You can use a resource editor such as ResEdit or Resorcerer to copy and paste any snd resource from the System file to a resource file. You can also turn any one of these snd resources into a sound file, as described in this chapter's "Sound Files" section.

PLAYING A SOUND RESOURCE

The Toolbox function SysBeep() is a fast and simple way to play a sound resource — but only the user's current system alert sound snd resource. For your program to play one of its own snd resources, you'll rely on the Toolbox function SndPlay().

SndPlay() requires a handle to a snd resource, so you'll need to obtain that before calling this routine. As you saw in Chapter 3, the Toolbox function GetResource() is used to get a handle to a resource. Pass GetResource() the type of resource you're interested in (a snd resource) and the ID of the resource. Assuming your program has a snd resource with an ID of 9000, here's how the call to GetResource() would look:

```
Handle  theHandle;

theHandle = GetResource( 'snd ', 9000 );
```

Make sure to include a space after the *d* in the snd resource type. Resource types are always four characters. The fourth character of the snd resource just happens to be a space.

Once you have a handle to the sound resource, call SndPlay() to play the sound.

```
OSErr  theError;
theHandle = GetResource( 'snd ', 9000 );
HLock( theHandle );
    theError = SndPlay( nil, (SndListHandle)theHandle, false );
HUnlock( theHandle );
```

For snd resources (and snd resources only), Apple reserves all IDs less than 8192 for its own use. Your snd resources should always be given IDs greater than 8191.

The first parameter to SndPlay() is a pointer to a *sound channel*. The Sound Manager always uses a sound channel to store sound-playing information about a sound. If you pass a value of nil as this first parameter — as in the above example — the Sound Manager will take care of the allocation of a sound channel for you.

The second parameter to SndPlay() is a handle to the sound resource to play. The call to GetResource() returned a generic handle, while SndPlay() requires a specific type of handle — a SndListHandle. Simply typecast the generic handle, and SndPlay() will be satisfied.

The final parameter to SndPlay() is a Boolean value that specifies whether the sound should be played asynchronously (true) or synchronously (false). When a sound is played asynchronously, other non-sound-related actions can take place at the same time as the playing of the sound. Conversely, when a sound is played synchronously, no other actions take place until the sound has completed. The above example plays the sound synchronously.

To play a sound asynchronously, you need to allocate your own sound channel. If you let the Sound Manager allocate the sound channel (as happens when you pass nil as the first parameter), the sound will always be played synchronously — regardless of the value passed as the third parameter to SndPlay(). Because asynchronous sound play involves callback procedures — a topic that is beyond the scope of this text — you won't find the subject covered here.

As you can see from the above snippet, a sound handle should be locked for the duration of its playing. Use the Toolbox routines HLock() and HUnlock() to assure that the sound data that has been loaded into memory doesn't move during the time that SndPlay() is executing.

If your program will be playing more than a single sound resource, you'll find it handy to have an application-defined routine in your program to play one sound one time. The PlayOneSoundResource() does just that. When passed the resource ID of a snd resource, PlayOneSoundResource() loads that sound into memory, plays it, and then releases the memory the sound occupies. When complete, the function returns an OSErr so that the calling routine knows whether or not the sound was successfully played.

```
OSErr  PlayOneSoundResource( short sndResourceID )
{
   Handle  theHandle;
   OSErr   theError;

   theHandle = GetResource( 'snd ', sndResourceID );

   if ( theHandle == nil )
   {
      return ( resProblem );
   }
   else
   {
      HLock( theHandle );
         theError = SndPlay( nil, (SndListHandle)theHandle, false );
      HUnlock( theHandle );

      ReleaseResource( theHandle );
      return ( theError );
   }
}
```

If the call to GetResource() fails (perhaps there is no snd resource with an ID of sndResourceID in the resource fork), GetResource() will return a value of nil. Before attempting to play the sound, the PlayOneSoundResource() routine checks the returned handle to make sure a snd resource was in fact returned. If one wasn't, the routine ends by returning the Apple-defined constant resProblem — one of the many constants Apple uses to provide feedback on errors. That way the calling routine knows that the attempt to play the sound failed due to some problem with the sound resource.

If the call to GetResource() is successful, PlayOneSoundResource() goes on to play the sound. The snd resource is then released from memory and the routine returns the OSErr value returned by SndPlay(). If the sound was successfully played, the variable theError will have a value of noErr. The calling routine can check this returned value to make sure the sound was played. Here's an example of how PlayOneSoundResource() is called from main() and how main() checks to ensure that the sound was in fact played:

```
void  main( void )
{
   OSErr  theError;

   InitializeToolbox();
   theError = PlayOneSoundResource( 9000 );

   if ( theError != noErr )
      ExitToShell();
}
```

EXAMPLE PROGRAM: SNDRESOURCE

The sndResource example uses the PlayOneSoundResource() function developed in the preceding section to play a sound resource. In this program and all others that use Sound Manager routines, the Sound.h universal header file is included.

You won't see any menus or windows when you run sndResource. The program simply loads a snd resource, plays it, and then quits. If snd 9000 is not present in the application's resource fork, or if any problem is encountered playing the sound, PlayOneSoundResource() will return an OSErr value other than noErr. If that happens, main() chooses to end the program with a call to ExitToShell(). Hopefully, your program will terminate in a more graceful manner — such as by first displaying an alert that tells the user the type of error that occurred.

```
//_____
#include <Sound.h>
//_____
void    InitializeToolbox( void );
OSErr   PlayOneSoundResource( short );
//_____
#define    rBarkingSound        9000
//_____
void  main( void )
{
   NumVersion   theVersion;
   short        sndResourceID;
   OSErr        theError;

   InitializeToolbox();
   theVersion = SndSoundManagerVersion();

   if ( theVersion.majorRev < 3 )
      ExitToShell();

   sndResourceID = rBarkingSound;
   theError = PlayOneSoundResource( sndResourceID );

   if ( theError != noErr )
      ExitToShell();
}
//_____
OSErr  PlayOneSoundResource( short sndResourceID )
{
   Handle   theHandle;
   OSErr    theError;

   theHandle = GetResource( 'snd ', sndResourceID );

   if ( theHandle == nil )
   {
      return ( resProblem );
   }
   else
   {
      HLock( theHandle );
         theError = SndPlay( nil, (SndListHandle)theHandle, false );
      HUnlock( theHandle );

      ReleaseResource( theHandle );
      return ( theError );
   }
}
```

Sound Files

A sound doesn't have to be stored within the application that uses it — it can instead be saved to its own file and then used by one or more applications.

ABOUT SOUND FILES

Sound resources are convenient to use because the sounds are embedded within an application. There are cases, however, when you'll want to consider storing sounds in files rather than in your program's resource fork. Here are a few situations where storing sounds in files makes sense:

- If you have more than one application that will make use of the same sound.
- If your application will let the user select a sound to play from a list of sounds.
- If you'll be occasionally updating or changing sounds and you'd rather redistribute just the sounds rather than the application.
- If your sounds are large. Apple recommends that a sound resource should be kept to less than half a megabyte in size — sound files don't have this limit.

SOUND FILE FORMATS

Apple has defined two file formats for sound files: the Audio Interchange File Format (AIFF) and the Audio Interchange File Format Extension for Compression (AIFF-C). Like all Macintosh files, sound files have a four-character type associated with them. AIFF sound files have a type of AIFF, while AIFF-C sound files have a type of AIFC.

From Chapter 2 you know that Macintosh files can consist of two parts, or forks. An application file usually has an empty data fork and a nonempty resource fork — the resource fork holds the various resources that make up a program's interface. An AIFF sound file, on the other hand, has an empty resource fork and a nonempty data fork — the data fork holds the data that makes up the sound.

You should refer to Chapter 2 for more information on resource and data forks.

An application generally has all of its executable code and resources in its resource fork. A sound file has the data that makes up a sound stored in its data fork. Figure 13-3 contrasts a 68K application file with an AIFF sound file.

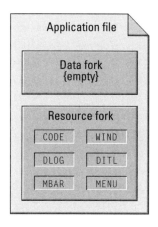

Figure 13-3
The forks of an application file and an AIFF sound file.

On the left of Figure 13-3 is an application file with several common resource types in its resource fork. The CODE resource type holds the application's executable code. On the right of the same figure is an AIFF sound file. The 1s and 0s in the data fork represent the data that makes up the sound held in the file. Later in this chapter you'll see that for an application to play the sound that is held in an AIFF sound file, the application must first open the sound file's data fork.

 The application pictured in Figure 13-3 is a 68K program. An Application built using a PowerPC compiler (a native PowerPC application) will have its code stored in the application data fork rather than in CODE resources. All other resources will appear in the resource fork.

While sound files are usually distributed in either the AIFF or AIFF-C format, there is a sound file type that the average Macintosh user is probably more familiar with — the Finder sound file, or System 7 sound file. While an AIFF or AIFF-C sound file may or may not have a distinctive icon (depending on the application that created the file), the Finder sound file certainly does. Figure 13-4 shows this.

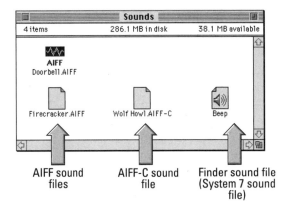

Figure 13-4
Icons for AIFF, AIFF-C, and Finder sound files.

A Finder sound file has a different format from that of an AIFF sound file. In a Finder sound file, the data for a sound is stored in a snd resource in the file's resource fork. The file's data fork goes empty (see Figure 13-5).

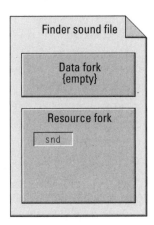

Figure 13-5
A Finder sound file has its sound data stored as a snd resource in its resource fork.

While AIFF and AIFF-C files need an application to play them, a Finder sound file can be played directly from the Finder. The user need only double-click on a sound file's icon to play the sound held within the file. If your program is to play a sound file, it will need to first open the resource fork of the file so that the file's snd resource can be accessed. You'll see how to do that later in this chapter. Because a Finder sound file holds sound data in a `snd` resource, once the file's resource fork is open the sound within it can be played by calling the Toolbox function `SndPlay()`.

OPENING A SOUND FILE

The Toolbox makes playing AIFF and AIFF-C sound files easy. But before the sound within a file can be played, the file must first be opened. Since AIFF and AIFF-C file sound data is held in the data fork of the file, you can use the File Manager routine `FSpOpenDF()` to open a sound file's data fork. Here's a typical call to `FSpOpenDF()`:

```
FSSpec  theFSSpec;
short   sndFileRefNum;
OSErr   theError;
theError = FSpOpenDF( &theFSSpec, fsRdPerm, &sndFileRefNum );
```

`FSpOpenDF()` requires three parameters. The first is a pointer to an `FSSpec`, a file system specification. The `FSSpec` provides information about where the sound file is located on disk. The second parameter is a *permission level.* Passing `FSpOpenDF()` the Apple-defined constant `fsRdPerm` tells the File Manager to open the file with read permission only. That is, the file data can be read, but the application that opens the file cannot write to it. The last parameter to `FSpOpenDF()` is a variable of type `short` that will serve as a file reference number. After opening the file, the File Manager will fill this variable with the reference number.

Only enough information to give you a working knowledge of file handling is provided in this chapter. Chapter 15 describes the `FSSpec`data type in greater detail.

Before calling `FSpOpenDF()`, you'll need to create the `FSSpec` for the sound file that is to be opened. If you know the name of the file and if it will reside in the same directory as your application, then you can call the Toolbox function `FSMakeFSSpec()`, as shown below. This snippet assumes that the program is to create an FSSpec for a file with the name Doorbell.

```
OSErr   theError;
FSSpec  theFSSpec;

theError = FSMakeFSSpec( 0, 0, "\pDoorbell", &theFSSpec );
```

BY THE WAY

If you aren't familiar with file pathnames, the FSSpec data type, and the `FSMakeFSSpec()` routine, refer to Chapter 15. If you just want to know enough to get a file open, continue on with this note.

As its first parameter, `FSMakeFSSpec()` accepts a volume reference number, a number that tells what disk the file is on. The second parameter is the file's parent directory, the folder the file resides in. The third parameter is the file's name, in the form of a `Str255`. The last parameter is the `FSSpec` data structure that `FSMakeFSSpec()` fills with information about the file's path.

By passing a volume reference number of 0 and a parent directory of 0, you tell `FSMakeFSSpec()` that the sound file is on the startup drive and in the same directory, or folder, as the application that is to use the file. Refer to Chapter 15 for a description of how to access a file that is in a directory other than the one the application resides in.

Since any sound file that is to be played needs to first be opened, it is useful to have a routine that, when given a file name, opens the file and returns the file reference number. `OpenSoundFile()` is just such a function.

```
OSErr  OpenSoundFile( Str255 theFileName, short *sndFileRefNum )
{
    FSSpec  theFSSpec;
    OSErr   theError;

    theError = FSMakeFSSpec( 0, 0, theFileName, &theFSSpec );
    if ( theError == noErr )
        theError = FSpOpenDF( &theFSSpec, fsRdPerm, sndFileRefNum );
    return ( theError );
}
```

NOTE

Because the goal of `OpenSoundFile()` is to set the value of the `sndFileRefNum` variable, it needs to receive this variable as a pointer. That way the change in value that is made by the `FSpOpenDF()` routine will "stick" after the `OpenSoundFile()` routine ends.

Assuming that an AIFF or AIFF-C sound file named Doorbell exists in your application's directory, your code could make the following call to `OpenSoundFile()` to open the file:

```
Str255  theFileName = "\pDoorbell";
short   sndFileRefNum;
OSErr   theError;
theError = OpenSoundFile( theFileName, &sndFileRefNum );
```

After `OpenSoundFile()` executes, your program will have a reference number to the open sound file, something you'll make use of when playing the sound that's in that file.

PLAYING A SOUND FILE

Just as the Toolbox provides a single powerful routine for playing sound resources (`SndPlay()`), it also provides one for playing sound files, `SndStartFilePlay()`. Because `SndStartFilePlay()` requires a reference number to an open sound file, your code will need to first call the application-defined `OpenSoundFile()` routine that was just described.

```
Str255   theFileName = "\pDoorbell";
short    sndFileRefNum;
OSErr    theError;
theError = OpenSoundFile( theFileName, &sndFileRefNum );
theError = SndStartFilePlay( nil, sndFileRefNum, 0,
                             51200, nil, nil, nil, false );
```

`SndStartFilePlay()` looks a little imposing in that it requires eight parameters. The good news is that most of these parameters can simply be set to `nil` and the routine will still work just fine.

The first parameter to `SndStartFilePlay()` is a pointer to a sound channel. As with the `SndPlay()` Toolbox routine, you can pass a `nil` pointer to let the Sound Manager allocate the sound channel for you.

The second parameter is a reference number to an open AIFF or AIFF-C file. Though AIFF-C files are compressed, `SndStartFilePlay()` is capable of playing them without any extra programming effort on your part. As discussed, obtain this file reference number from a call to the Toolbox routine `FSpOpenDF()`.

While the `SndStartFilePlay()` routine is generally used to play a sound file, it can also be used to play a sound resource — though Apple recommends you use `SndPlay()` instead. If you follow Apple's advice, you'll pass a 0 as the third parameter to `SndStartFilePlay()` to indicate that a sound file rather than a sound resource is to be played.

The fourth parameter designates the size of a buffer (a block of free bytes of memory) that the Sound Manager can use in the playing of the sound file. This buffer is necessary because the Sound Manager doesn't read in all of the sound data from the sound file at one time. A sound file can be up to several megabytes in size, so reading the entire file at once could have the very undesirable effect of using up more RAM than the user has. Instead, the Sound Manager reads in part of the file, storing the data in this *input buffer*. As the sound is played, more sound data is read into the buffer, overwriting the no-longer-needed data that has already been played. For successful sound play, Apple recommends a buffer size of *at least* 20,480 bytes, or 20K. The above snippet arbitrarily uses a value of 51,200, or 50K.

The fourth parameter to `SndStartFilePlay()` gives the size of the input buffer, but it doesn't actually allocate the buffer. That's the job of the fifth parameter. If you pass a `nil` pointer here, the Sound Manager will handle the buffer allocation for you.

`SndStartFilePlay()` is capable of playing either a part of a sound file's sound or all of the sound. To play the entire sound, pass a `nil` pointer as the sixth parameter.

Asynchronous sound play (performing other actions while a sound plays) requires the use of a completion routine. For synchronous play (playing a sound without other actions, as described in this book), pass a nil pointer as the seventh parameter.

If `SndStartFilePlay()` is to play a sound asynchronously, pass a value of `true` as the last parameter. Otherwise, pass a value of `false`.

EXAMPLE PROGRAM: PLAYSOUNDFILE

Like the sndResource example, PlaySoundFile doesn't have an interface — no menus, no windows. This simple program just plays the sound that is in the AIFF sound file named Doorbell and then quits.

Before playing the sound, PlaySoundFile calls an application-defined routine that was developed a few pages back, `OpenSoundFile()`. Once the file is open and a reference number is obtained, a call to the Toolbox routine `SndStartFilePlay()` plays the entire doorbell sound found in the sound file.

```
//_____
#include <Sound.h>
//_____
void   InitializeToolbox( void );
```

```
OSErr  OpenSoundFile( Str255, short * );
//_____
void  main( void )
{
   NumVersion  theVersion;
   short       sndFileRefNum;
   Str255      theFileName = "\pDoorbell";
   OSErr       theError;

   InitializeToolbox();

   theVersion = SndSoundManagerVersion();

   if ( theVersion.majorRev < 3 )
      ExitToShell();
   theError = OpenSoundFile( theFileName, &sndFileRefNum );
   theError = SndStartFilePlay( nil, sndFileRefNum, 0,
                                  51200, nil, nil, nil, false );
   if ( theError != noErr )
      ExitToShell();
}
//_____
OSErr  OpenSoundFile( Str255 theFileName, short *sndFileRefNum )
{
   FSSpec  theFSSpec;
   OSErr   theError;

   theError = FSMakeFSSpec( 0, 0, theFileName, &theFSSpec );
   if ( theError == noErr )
      theError = FSpOpenDF( &theFSSpec, fsRdPerm, sndFileRefNum );
   return ( theError );
}
```

SELECTING A SOUND FILE TO PLAY

The above example program shows how to play a sound file when the sound file name was known beforehand. A situation like this is common in some applications (such as games, multimedia programs, and educational tutorials), but there are other instances where your program will instead let the user select a sound file to play. For those applications, use the File Manager routine `StandardGetFile()` to display the standard Open dialog box that is shown in Figure 13-6.

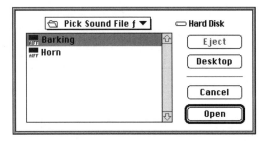

Figure 13-6
The standard Open dialog box displaying two AIFF sound files.

If adding the standard Open dialog box to one of your programs is something you haven't done in the past, try the example given here. If you need more background on the StandardGetFile() function, refer to Chapter 15.

Here's a call to the Toolbox routine StandardGetFile():

```
SFTypeList          typeList = { 'AIFF', 'AIFC', 0, 0 };
StandardFileReply   theReply;
OSErr               theError;

StandardGetFile( nil, 2, typeList, &theReply );
```

In Figure 13-6 you can see that the file list in the standard Open dialog box only displays the names of sound files — all other file types are filtered out. The StandardGetFile() function lets you easily display up to four different file types in the Open dialog box scroll list. Text editors display files of type 'TEXT', while graphics programs often show 'PICT' files. A program that plays sound files should display 'AIFF' and 'AIFC' files.

The first parameter to StandardGetFile() is a pointer to an optional filter function. The filter function is useful only if you intend to tell StandardGetFile() to display only certan files from the type or types listed. Generally, you'll want the standard Open dialog box to display all files of a given type (such as TEXT). If you don't need the filter function, pass a nil pointer.

The second parameter indicates the number of file types that will be displayed. In the above snippet two file types are to be displayed (AIFF and AIFC).

The third parameter to `StandardGetFile()` names the file types that should be displayed in the dialog box list. Only file types mentioned here will be shown in the standard Open dialog box. The `SFTypeList` variable is used to hold up to four 4-character file types.

The fourth parameter to `StandardGetFile()` is a pointer to a variable of type `StandardFileReply`. After the user selects a file from the standard Open dialog box (or clicks the Cancel button), the Toolbox will fill in the fields of this parameter. Of most interest are the `sfGood` and the `sfFile` fields. The `Boolean` `sfGood` field will have a value of `true` if a file was selected and a value of `false` if the Cancel button was clicked. If a file was selected from the list, the `FSSpec` `sfFile` field will be filled with path information about that file.

Earlier in this chapter you saw an application-defined routine named `OpenSoundFile()`. It used a call to `FSMakeFSSpec()` to create an `FSSpec` for a sound file that had its name passed as a parameter. A new version of `OpenSoundFile()` appears below. Rather than pass a file name to the function, this version makes a call to `StandardGetFile()` to allow the user to name the sound file to open.

The call to `StandardGetFile()` displays the standard Open dialog box for the user. If the user double-clicks on a sound file (or clicks the Open button), the program will place a value of true in the `sfGood` field of the StandardFileReply. `FSpOpenDF()` will get called to open the sound file. If the user clicks on the Cancel button instead, `sfGood` will be false and theError will get set to the Apple-defined constant `userCanceledErr`.

```
OSErr  OpenSoundFile( short *sndFileRefNum )
{
    SFTypeList          typeList = { 'AIFF', 'AIFC', 0, 0 };
    StandardFileReply   theReply;
    OSErr               theError;

    StandardGetFile( nil, 2, typeList, &theReply );
    if ( theReply.sfGood == true )
        theError = FSpOpenDF( &theReply.sfFile, fsRdPerm, sndFileRefNum );
    else
        theError = userCanceledErr;
    return ( theError );
}
```

A call to the new version of OpenSoundFile() requires that only a pointer to a short variable be passed. OpenSoundFile() will let the user select a file to open, open that file, and then fill the passed-in variable with a reference number to the opened sound file. Here's how a call to OpenSoundFile() looks:

```
short   sndFileRefNum;
OSErr  theError;
theError = OpenSoundFile( &sndFileRefNum );
if ( theError != noErr )
   ExitToShell();
```

EXAMPLE PROGRAM: PICKSOUNDFILE

The PickSoundFile uses the new version of the OpenSoundFile() routine to display the standard Open dialog box, which lets the user select a sound file to play. After that, the program calls SndStartFilePlay() to play the sound from the open sound file — just as the previous example program (PlaySoundFile) did.

```
//_____
#include <Sound.h>
//_____
void   InitializeToolbox( void );
OSErr  OpenSoundFile( short * );
//_____
void  main( void )
{
   NumVersion  theVersion;
   short       sndFileRefNum;
   OSErr       theError;
   InitializeToolbox();
   theVersion = SndSoundManagerVersion();
   if ( theVersion.majorRev < 3 )
      ExitToShell();
   theError = OpenSoundFile( &sndFileRefNum );
   if ( theError != noErr )
      ExitToShell();
   theError = SndStartFilePlay( nil, sndFileRefNum, 0,
                                51200, nil, nil, nil, false );
   if ( theError != noErr )
      ExitToShell();
}
//_____
OSErr  OpenSoundFile( short *sndFileRefNum )
```

```
{
    SFTypeList         typeList = { 'AIFF', 'AIFC', 0, 0 };
    StandardFileReply  theReply;
    OSErr              theError;

    StandardGetFile( nil, 2, typeList, &theReply );
    if ( theReply.sfGood == true )
        theError = FSpOpenDF( &theReply.sfFile, fsRdPerm, sndFileRefNum );
    else
        theError = userCanceledErr;
    return ( theError );
}
```

PREVIEWING A SOUND FILE BEFORE PLAYING

If your program allows users to open sound files, you might consider letting them do so by using the standard Open preview dialog box rather than the standard Open dialog box. The difference? The standard Open preview dialog box adds a Show Preview checkbox that, when checked, expands the standard Open dialog box. The expanded dialog box displays a speaker icon and a Play Sound button. When the user clicks on the Play Sound button, the sound in the currently highlighted sound file will play. This enables the user to preview sounds before opening any sound file. Figure 13-7 shows the dialog box collapsed, and Figure 13-8 shows the same dialog box expanded.

Figure 13-7
The standard Open preview dialog box, collapsed.

Figure 13-8

The standard Open preview dialog box, expanded.

The standard Open preview dialog box is actually a part of the QuickTime Movie Toolbox — the topic of Chapter 14. In that chapter you'll read a lot more about the standard Open preview dialog box. If you'd like to try it out now, you'll need to make some additions to your source code.

- Add a #include directive for the Movies.h universal header file.
- Add a call to the routine that initializes the Movie Toolbox: EnterMovies().
- Change the existing call from StandardGetFile() to StandardGetFilePreview().

Here's the necessary #include directive to add:

```
#include <Movies.h>
```

A call to EnterMovies() returns an OSErr. Make the call as follows:

```
OSErr  theError;
theError = EnterMovies();
```

Finally, change StandardGetFile() to StandardGetFilePreview(). The four parameters remain the same.

```
SFTypeList          typeList = { 'AIFF', 'AIFC', 0, 0 };
StandardFileReply   theReply;
StandardGetFilePreview( nil, 2, typeList, &theReply );
```

You'll find an example program named PreviewSoundFile on the CD that's included with this book. Except for the #include directive, the call to EnterMovies(), and the change from StandardGetFile() to StandardGetFilePreview(), the source code for PreviewSoundFile is the same as the code for the PickSoundFile example.

Important: In order to run a program that makes use of Movie Toolbox routines such as EnterMovies() and StandardGetFilePreview(), the user must have the QuickTime extension in his or her system. Chapter 14 discusses the QuickTime extension, checking for its presence, and the Movie Toolbox routines that are briefly described here.

PLAYING FINDER FILES

In the Macintosh world, sounds are often distributed as Finder sound files — also referred to as System 7 sound files. As you read earlier in this chapter, the chief difference between AIFF sound files and Finder sound files lies in the location of the sound data. An AIFF file keeps the data in its data fork, while a Finder sound file keeps the data as a snd resource in its resource fork.

You've already seen how to play a snd resource — first call the Toolbox function GetResource() to load the sound resource into memory, and then call the Toolbox function SndPlay() to play the sound. If your program plays Finder files, you'll again follow these steps. You will, however, have to first open the resource fork of the Finder sound file.

A resource in the resource fork of an application is always available to the application; the system opens an application's resource fork when the program is launched. A resource found in the resource fork of an external file is a different story. Your program will have to open the resource fork of that file before its resource can be accessed. A call to the Toolbox routine FSpOpenResFile() will accomplish that. The following snippet uses a call to FSMakeFSSpec() to create an FSSpec for a Finder sound file named Meow. Alternatively, you could let the user select the System 7 sound file to play by using a call to StandardGetFile() or StandardGetFilePreview() in place of the call to FSMakeFSSpec().

```
OSErr   theError;
short   finderFileRefNum;
FSSpec  theFSSpec;
theError = FSMakeFSSpec( 0, 0, "\pMeow", &theFSSpec );
finderFileRefNum = FSpOpenResFile( &theFSSpec, fsRdPerm );
```

Refer to Chapter 2 and Chapter 15 for the details about working with multiple resource files. Those chapters describe resource forks and resource-handling Toolbox routines such as `FSpOpenResFile()`.

A Mac program is capable of having more than one resource file open at any given time. Therefore it is necessary to set, and keep track of, which resource fork is currently in use. As it does for open data forks, the system assigns a reference number to each open resource fork. Before working with a Finder file, your code should perform steps similar to these:

1. Save the reference number of the application's resource fork.

2. Open the resource fork of the Finder sound file.

3. Make the Finder file's resource fork the current resource fork.

4. Load the sound resource.

5. Play the sound.

6. Make the application's resource fork the current resource fork.

Figure 13-9 illustrates how two open resource forks may each hold a `snd` resource. Making the correct resource fork current ensures that the desired sound resource gets loaded into memory.

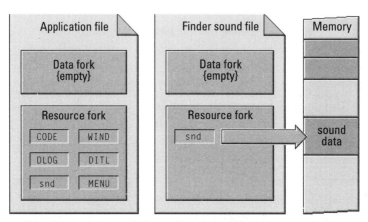

Because two resource forks can be open, and both may contain the same resource types, resource fork reference numbers are used to pick the correct fork to load the `snd` resource from

Figure 13-9

An application can have more than one resource fork open at any time.

To save the reference number of the current resource file (which at the start of the program is the application's resource fork), call the Toolbox routine CurResFile( ):

```
short   appRefNum;
appRefNum = CurResFile( );
```

To open the resource fork of the Finder file, create an FSSpec for the file by calling FSMakeFSSpec( ) or one of the routines that display an Open dialog box. Then call FSpOpenResFile( ).

```
OSErr    theError;
short    finderFileRefNum;
FSSpec  theFSSpec;
theError = FSMakeFSSpec( 0, 0, "\pMeow", &theFSSpec );
finderFileRefNum = FSpOpenResFile( &theFSSpec, fsRdPerm );
```

Call the Toolbox routine UseResFile( ) to use the now-open resource fork of the Finder sound file.

```
UseResFile( finderFileRefNum );
```

Refer to Chapter 2 for an introduction to forks and a discussion of the UseResFile( ) and CurResFile( ) functions.

At this point there are two open resource forks, the application's resource fork and the Finder file's resource fork. It's the file's fork that is now the current resource fork. A call to GetResource( ) will now affect the Finder file's resource fork rather than the application's resource fork. You can use the application-defined routine PlayOneSoundResource( ), developed for this chapter's sndResource example program, to take care of the calls to GetResource( ) and SndPlay( ).

```
short   sndResourceID;
OSErr   theError;
sndResourceID = rMeowSound;
theError = PlayOneSoundResource( sndResourceID );
```

After the sound has played, reestablish the application's resource fork as the current resource fork.

```
UseResFile( appRefNum );
```

EXAMPLE PROGRAM: PLAYFINDERFILE

The PlayFinderFile program opens a Finder sound file (System 7 sound file) named Meow, provided the file is in the same directory as the PlayFinderFile application.

With very little effort you should be able to change the program so that the user gets to select a Finder sound file to play. Refer to this chapter's PickSoundFile and PreviewSoundFile example programs.

Before playing the sound file, the program must open it. The application-defined routine OpenResourceFile() takes care of this. OpenResourceFile() requires two parameters: the name of a Finder sound file, and a pointer to a short variable that will hold the reference number for the resource fork of the sound file. OpenResourceFile() first creates an FSSpec for the file and then opens the file's resource fork with a call to the Toolbox routine FSpOpenResFile(). FSpOpenResFile() returns a reference number for that fork. If for some reason the attempt to open the file fails, the Toolbox will return a value of -1 as the reference number. In that event, call on the Resource Manager to determine what type of error occurred.

```
OSErr  OpenResourceFile( Str255 theFileName, short *resFileRefNum )
{
    FSSpec  theFSSpec;
    OSErr   theError;

    theError = FSMakeFSSpec( 0, 0, theFileName, &theFSSpec );

    if ( theError == noErr )
    {
        *resFileRefNum = FSpOpenResFile( &theFSSpec, fsRdPerm );

        if ( *resFileRefNum == -1 )
            theError = ResError();
    }

    return ( theError );
}
```

BY THE WAY

Note that FSpOpenResFile() returns the reference number as a short — not as a pointer to a short. That's why the pointer variable resFileRefNum has to be dereferenced.

```
*resFileRefNum = FSpOpenResFile( &theFSSpec, fsRdPerm );
```

To play the sound from the Finder sound file, PlayFinderFile relies on the same PlayOneSoundResource() routine that was developed for the first example program in this chapter, sndResource. Refer back to the "Sound Resource" section of this chapter if you have questions about how the application-defined PlayOneSoundResource() function works.

Earlier you read that there are six steps to follow for the proper playing of a Finder sound file — those steps are repeated below. Figure 13-10 shows a snippet of code from the main() function of PlayFinderFile. The code in the snippet has been numbered so that you can easily see the sequence in which the program executes the six steps.

1. Saves the reference number of the application's resource fork.

2. Opens the resource fork of the Finder sound file.

3. Makes the Finder file's resource fork the current resource fork.

4. Loads the sound resource.

5. Plays the sound.

6. Makes the application's resource fork the current resource fork.

```
(1)   appRefNum = CurResFile();

(2)   theError = OpenResourceFile( theFileName, &finderFileRefNum );
      if ( theError != noErr )
         ExitToShell();

(3)   UseResFile( finderFileRefNum );

(4)(5) sndResourceID = MEOW_SOUND_ID;
      theError = PlayOneSoundResource( sndResourceID );
      if ( theError != noErr )
         ExitToShell();

(6)   UseResFile( appRefNum );
```

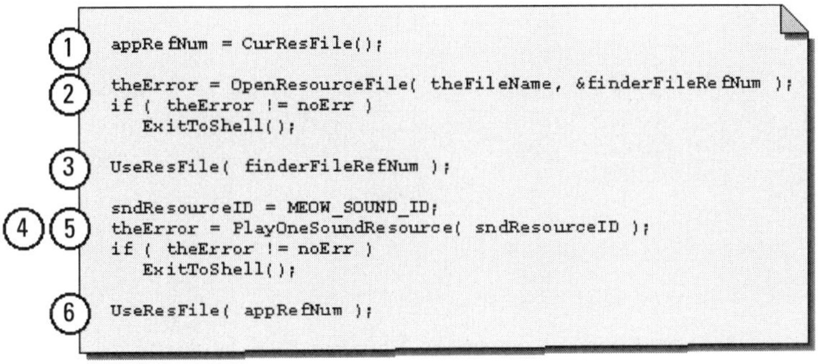

Figure 13-10
The six steps to play a Finder sound file.

Here's the source code listing for the PlayFinderFile program:

```
//_____
#include <Sound.h>
//_____
void   InitializeToolbox( void );
OSErr  PlayOneSoundResource( short );
```

```
OSErr  OpenResourceFile( Str255, short * );
//_____
#define   rMeowSound       9000
//_____
void  main( void )
{
   NumVersion  theVersion;

   OSErr       theError;
   Str255      theFileName = "\pMeow";
   short       appResNum;
   short       finderFileRefNum;

   InitializeToolbox();
   theVersion = SndSoundManagerVersion();
   if ( theVersion.majorRev < 3 )
      ExitToShell();

   appRefNum = CurResFile();
   theError = OpenResourceFile( theFileName, &finderFileRefNum );
   if ( theError != noErr )
      ExitToShell();
   UseResFile( finderFileRefNum );
   theError = PlayOneSoundResource( rMeowSound
   if ( theError != noErr )
      ExitToShell();

   UseResFile( appRefNum );
}
//_____
OSErr  OpenResourceFile( Str255 theFileName, short *resFileRefNum )
{
   FSSpec  theFSSpec;
   OSErr   theError;

   theError = FSMakeFSSpec( 0, 0, theFileName, &theFSSpec );

   if ( theError == noErr )
   {
      *resFileRefNum = FSpOpenResFile( &theFSSpec, fsRdPerm );

      if ( *resFileRefNum == -1 )
         theError = ResError();
   }

   return ( theError );
}
//_____
OSErr  PlayOneSoundResource( short sndResourceID )
```

```
{
   Handle   theHandle;
   OSErr    theError;

   theHandle = GetResource( 'snd ', sndResourceID );

   if ( theHandle == nil )
   {
      return ( resProblem );
   }
   else
   {
      HLock( theHandle );
         theError = SndPlay( nil, (SndListHandle)theHandle, false );
      HUnlock( theHandle );

      ReleaseResource( theHandle );
      return ( theError );
   }
}
```

Converting Sound Files and Sound Resources

As mentioned in this chapter's "Sound Resources" section, sound files are available from a variety of sources including online services and commercial CDs. If you're searching for a particular sound, you may not be able to be selective about the file format you get the sound in. That could present a problem if you're writing your program in such a way that it works with only one file format.

Rather than write a program that works with both AIFF and Finder sound files, you might settle on one format. This is especially true if your program is a multimedia or educational program. Applications like these usually don't give the user the option of selecting sounds but instead play different sounds on their own, often from sound files stored in folders. If you've accumulated the sound files your application needs, you'll want to keep your code as simple as possible by having it only work with one file format. What if your collection of sound files includes files of more than one format? You'll simply perform a one-time conversion of all of the files that are in the undesired format.

SOUND FILE FORMAT DIFFERENCES

You've already seen the difference between AIFF sound files and Finder sound files. An AIFF (and AIFC) sound file keeps its sound data in its data fork, while a Finder sound file keeps its sound data in a snd resource in its resource fork.

THE SOUNDAPP SOUND FILE UTILITY

To convert an AIFF sound file to a Finder sound file, the sound data has to be moved from the file's data fork to its resource fork. The opposite is true for the conversion of a Finder sound file to an AIFF sound file. If you think this sounds like a task that could be tricky, don't be concerned — there are utility programs that exist for just this kind of chore. One such program is SoundApp, a copy of which is included on this book's CD.

Figure 13-11 shows a folder that holds an AIFF file and a Finder sound file. While AIFF files often have a generic document icon, the one in the figure has the distinctive icon given to all AIFF files created by the SoundApp utility. If your sound-playing program plays only AIFF files and you have a sound in Finder sound file format (such as the Meow file in the figure), you can use SoundApp to easily convert that file to AIFF format.

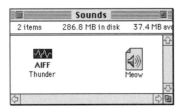

Figure 13-11
A folder with an AIFF sound file and a Finder sound file.

To convert a file, launch the SoundApp application. Select Convert To from the Options menu. Choosing this command displays a hierarchical menu that holds a list of file format types you can use to convert a sound file to AIFF format. Select AIFF from this menu, as shown in Figure 13-12. Then select Convert from the File menu to choose a file to convert. Again refer to Figure 13-12.

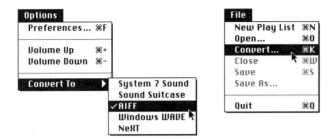

Figure 13-12
The SoundApp menu items used to convert a Finder file to an AIFF file.

Selecting Convert from the File menu displays the standard Open dialog box. Click on a file in the list, and click the Open button, as shown in Figure 13-13.

Figure 13-13
The SoundApp Convert dialog box.

After you click the Open button, SoundApp will display another dialog box. Here you'll be given the opportunity to name a new folder that will hold the converted file. A new folder is needed because SoundApp will create a new file with the same name as the original file. After entering a folder name (or leaving the default name), click the Save button, as shown in Figure 13-14.

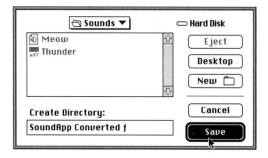

Figure 13-14
The SoundApp Create Directory dialog box.

SoundApp performs the file conversion very quickly. If you're observant, though, you'll see a window appear briefly on your screen. Figure 13-15 shows a typical conversion window.

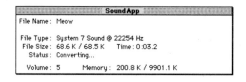

Figure 13-15
SoundApp displays an information window as a file is being converted.

When the conversion is complete, you'll find a new folder with a new file in it. Figure 13-16 shows that SoundApp preserves the original file and places the new file in its own folder.

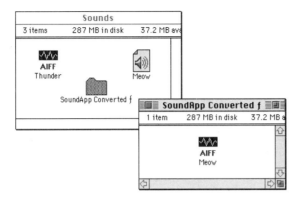

Figure 13-16
After a file is converted, a new folder with a new file is created.

SYSTEM 7 SOUNDS AND THE SYSTEM FOLDER

A few sources for obtaining sound files have been mentioned in this chapter. While online services and mail order houses are convenient, there's one source that is more convenient still — your Macintosh System file.

If you open your System Folder and double-click on the System file, a window opens. Icons appear, which represent various keyboard layouts that your Mac recognizes and icons for the system alert sounds. Each system alert sound is stored as a System 7 sound file. You can leave a sound as part of your system *and* convert it to a usable sound file by holding down the Option key and dragging the System 7 sound file out of the System folder and onto the desktop, as shown in Figure 13-17.

After dragging the file out of the System folder and releasing the mouse button, you'll have a new System 7 sound file. If one of your programs plays Finder sound files, you're all set. If your program instead plays AIFF files, convert the new System 7 sound file to an AIFF file using a utility such as SoundApp.

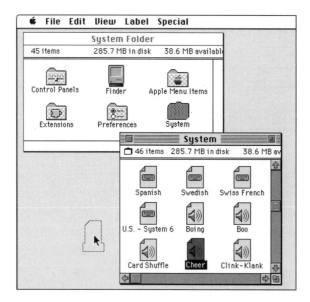

Figure 13-17
Creating a Finder sound file from a system alert sound.

Adjusting the Speaker Volume

Apple makes it easy for a Macintosh user to set the speaker volume of his or her computer — the Sound control panel is always just a mouse-click away. Since users set the speaker volume to the level they desire, why would you want one of your programs to ever go behind their backs and change this hardware setting? Perhaps your program will have a menu item that lets the user change the volume. Maybe your program might have something so important to say that you'll want to make sure that the user has the volume on — even if it's just for a moment while you play a single sound. Whatever the reason, if you need to adjust the speaker volume, you'll find that the Sound Manager makes it easy.

SPEAKER VOLUME SETTINGS AND THE TOOLBOX

Starting with version 3.0 of the Sound Manager, the Toolbox allows you to control the speaker volume level for the system alert independently from the volume for all other sound output. As you'll see, one Toolbox routine sets the volume level for calls to SysBeep(), while a different Toolbox routine sets the volume level for all other sound-playing routines (such as SndPlay() and SndStartFilePlay()). In either case, though, the sound-setting routine accepts a single parameter — the volume level to set the speaker or speakers to.

The parameter that sets the speaker volume level is of type long. The Toolbox looks at this long as two separate values: One value determines the right speaker volume setting, and the other determines the left speaker volume setting. With this in mind you'll pass this long as a hexadecimal value, with the left four hexadecimal digits representing the right speaker and the right four digits representing the left speaker. Table 13-1 shows several 4-digit hexadecimal values and the level of sound each represents.

Table 13-1
Hexadecimal Representation of Sound Levels.

Hex Value	Speaker Volume
0x0100	full volume
0x0200	2 times full volume
0x0400	4 times full volume
0x0600	6 times full volume
0x00A0	2/3 full volume
0x0080	1/2 full volume
0x0050	1/3 full volume
0x0040	1/4 full volume
0x0020	1/8 full volume
0x0000	speaker off

A number is identified as being hexadecimal by the *0x* that precedes its digits. Thus 0x10A4 and 0x00204E05 are both examples of hexadecimal values.

You'll find a more extensive list of speaker volume hex values in the "Sound Reference" section at the end of this chapter.

To create a single value that holds both speaker settings, use two 4-digit hexadecimal numbers together. The following hex number holds a value that would set the right speaker to three times its full volume and would set the left speaker to one-eighth of its full volume:

```
0x03000020
```

For further clarification, Figure 13-18 shows an example that sets the right speaker to two times its full volume and sets the left speaker to one half of its full volume.

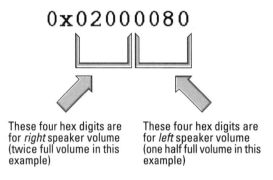

These four hex digits are for *right* speaker volume (twice full volume in this example)

These four hex digits are for *left* speaker volume (one half full volume in this example)

Figure 13-18
The right and left speaker volumes are embedded within a single hexadecimal long.

DEFAULT OUTPUT SOUND VOLUME

You can adjust the volume level at which sound is played by calling the Toolbox routine SetDefaultOutputVolume( ). Pass in the new volume level (using a hex value as described on the preceding pages) as the only parameter. Here's an example that sets the volume level to four times the normal highest level:

```
long  theNewVolume = 0x04000400;
SetDefaultOutputVolume( theNewVolume );
```

After the call to SetDefaultOutputVolume( ), all calls to the Toolbox routines SndPlay( ) and SndStartFilePlay( ) will result in sounds that are played at the new setting.

Executing SetDefaultOutputVolume( ) will actually change the position of the slider in the Sound control panel of the user's Macintosh. Figure 13-19 shows that passing SetDefaultOutputVolume( ) a value of 0x00800080 will result in the slider's being moved to the midpoint of the scale.

If the bottom mark of the Sound control panel scale is thought of as 0 and the top mark 7, then the midpoint would be 3.5. In System 7.5, this is where the slider will end up. In earlier systerm versions, however, the slider always positions itself at one of eight marks on the scale. The above call to SetDefaultOutputVolume() would place the slider at the fourth mark from the bottom — a value of 3, or 3.5 rounded off. The Sound Manager, though, would recognize the new volume as exactly half the full volume level.

Regardless of where the slider starts out...

...after passing the routine SetDefault OutputVoulue() a value of 0x00800080, the slider will move to the halfway point of the scale

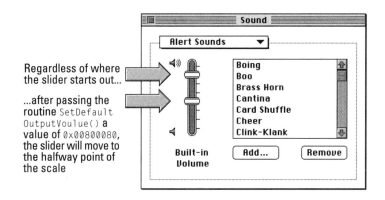

Figure 13-19
SetDefaultOutputVolume() changes the slider setting in the Sound control panel.

Because SetDefaultOutputVolume() actually changes a systemwide feature of the user's computer, you'll want to make sure to return the volume to its original setting once your application has made use of the new setting. Before changing the output volume, use the Toolbox function GetDefaultOutputVolume() to save the output volume level as set by the user. The Sound Manager will fill the passed pointer with the current volume. Then, play your sound or sounds and return the volume to its original setting. Here's a snippet that does just that:

```
long   theOriginalVol;
long   theNewVol;
GetDefaultOutputVolume( &theOriginalVol );  // save original volume
theNewVol = 0x00800080;
SetDefaultOutputVolume( theNewVol );        // set to new volume
// play snd resource or sound file sounds

SetDefaultOutputVolume( theOriginalVol );   // restore original volume
```

A systemwide feature is one that affects the system of a Mac, not just an individual application. Speaker volume is one such feature. The desktop pattern is another.

As mentioned, you can use `SndPlay()` or `SndStartFilePlay()` to play a sound. The following snippet saves the original volume, sets the volume to a new level, calls the previously defined application-specific function `PlayOneSoundResource()` to play a `snd` resource, and then restores the speaker volume to its initial setting;

```
long    theOriginalVol;
long    theNewVol;
short   sndResourceID;
OSErr   theError;
GetDefaultOutputVolume( &theOriginalVol );
theNewVol = 0x00800080;
SetDefaultOutputVolume( theNewVol );
sndResourceID = rBarkingSound
theError = PlayOneSoundResource( sndResourceID );
if ( theError != noErr )
   ExitToShell();

SetDefaultOutputVolume( theOriginalVol );
```

SYSTEM ALERT SOUND VOLUME

Starting with Sound Manager 3.0, you can treat the volume level of the system alert sound as a separate entity from the volume level of all other sounds. Use the Toolbox routine `SetSysBeepVolume()` to change the volume level for subsequent calls to `SysBeep()`. Pass in the new volume level (again using a hex value as described earlier) as the only parameter. Here's an example that sets the system alert volume to two times its highest level:

```
theNewVolume = 0x02000200;
SetSysBeepVolume( theNewVolume );
```

After the call to `SetSysBeepVolume()`, all calls to the Toolbox routine `SysBeep()` will result in the system alert sound being played at the volume level set in `SetSysBeepVolume()`.

It's important to note that only calls to SysBeep() will be affected by this new volume level. Calls to SndPlay() and SndStartFilePlay() will still play at the user's volume setting.

A Macintosh user generally sets the speaker volume to the exact level he or she is most comfortable with. As with the default output volume, if your application changes the system alert volume level, it should also restore it to its original level. That means calling the Toolbox routine GetSysBeepVolume() *before* changing the volume. Pass this routine a pointer to a long variable, and the Sound Manager will return the current volume level. After calling SysBeep(), again call SetSysBeepVolume() to reset the volume.

```
long   theOriginalVol;
long   theNewVol;
GetSysBeepVolume( &theOriginalVol );  // save original volume
theNewVol = 0x02000200;
SetSysBeepVolume( theNewVol );        // set to new volume
SysBeep( 1 );
SetSysBeepVolume( theOriginalVol );   // restore original volume
```

After changing the volume, call SysBeep() to play the system alert sound at the new volume. When it's done, restore the volume to its original setting:

SetSysBeepVolume() doesn't change the slider position in the Sound control panel, as SetDefaultOutputVolume() does.

EXAMPLE PROGRAM: SOUNDVOLUME

The SoundVolume program demonstrates how to save the current default output volume level, change it, play a snd resource, and then restore the volume to its original setting. After that, the program does the same with the system alert sound volume level, except that the system alert sound is played once, rather than a sound resource.

When you run SoundVolume, you'll hear the sound resource played at half the highest volume of your Mac's speakers. The system alert is played at twice the normal highest volume of your computer's speakers.

To play the sound resource, SoundVolume uses the same application-defined routine that you've seen elsewhere in this chapter, PlayOneSoundResource().

```
//_____
#include <Sound.h>
//_____
void   InitializeToolbox( void );
OSErr  PlayOneSoundResource( short );
//_____
#define    rBarkingSound
//_____
void  main( void )
{
   NumVersion  theVersion;
   short       sndResourceID;
   OSErr       theError;
   long        theOriginalVol;
   long        theNewVol;

   InitializeToolbox();

   theVersion = SndSoundManagerVersion();
   if ( theVersion.majorRev < 3 )
      ExitToShell();
   GetDefaultOutputVolume( &theOriginalVol );
   theNewVol = 0x00800080;
   SetDefaultOutputVolume( theNewVol );
   sndResourceID = rBarkingSound
   theError = PlayOneSoundResource( sndResourceID );
   if ( theError != noErr )
      ExitToShell();

   SetDefaultOutputVolume( theOriginalVol );

   GetSysBeepVolume( &theOriginalVol );
   theNewVol = 0x02000200;
   SetSysBeepVolume( theNewVol );
   SysBeep( 1 );
   SetSysBeepVolume( theOriginalVol );
}
//_____
OSErr  PlayOneSoundResource( short sndResourceID )
{
   Handle  theHandle;
   OSErr   theError;

   theHandle = GetResource( 'snd ', sndResourceID );

   if ( theHandle == nil )
   {
      return ( resProblem );
   }
   else
   {
      HLock( theHandle );
```

```
        theError = SndPlay( nil, (SndListHandle)theHandle, false );
    HUnlock( theHandle );

    ReleaseResource( theHandle );
    return ( theError );
  }
}
```

Sound Reference

The following pages summarize the Toolbox functions that enable you to add sound to any of your Mac applications.

SOUND MANAGER VERSION INFORMATION

Don't make the assumption that all users who try your program have version 3.0 of the Sound Manager system software installed on their Macintosh.

SndSoundManagerVersion( )

Before using Sound Manager functions, call the Toolbox function SndSoundManagerVersion(). This routine will return a variable of type NumVersion. Check the majorRev field of the NumVersion data structure to ensure that it has a value of at least 3.

```
#include <Sound.h>
NumVersion  theVersion;
theVersion= SndSoundManagerVersion();
if ( theVersion.majorRev < 3 )
   // display an alert and/or exit
```

PLAYING A SOUND RESOURCE

Sound data can be stored as a sound resource (resource type snd). A resource of this type can be placed in the resource fork of your application or in a Finder sound file (System 7 sound file).

SysBeep( )

The SysBeep() function plays whichever system alert sound is currently selected in the user's Sound control panel. Each system alert sound is stored as a snd resource in the user's System file.

```
short  duration = 1;
SysBeep( duration );
```

The duration parameter to SysBeep() was of use on earlier Macs but is of no consequence now. Passing any short value will have the same result — the user's current system alert will play one time.

GetResource( )

Before playing a sound resource (other than the system alert sound), you'll need to load the resource into memory. Call GetResource() to perform this task.

```
Handle   theHandle;
ResType  theResType = 'snd ';
short    theResID = 9000;

theHandle = GetResource( theResType, theResID );
```

GetResource() isn't just used for loading a snd resource into memory — it works for other resource types as well. Therefore, the first parameter is necessary to tell the Toolbox which type of resource to look for. The ResType parameter should be enclosed in single quotes. Resource types are always four characters — make sure to add the trailing blank space to the snd resource. The second parameter to GetResource() is the resource ID. Note that for sound resources, Apple reserves all IDs less than 8192.

SndPlay( )

Once you've obtained a handle to a sound resource, play the sound data that the handle references by calling SndPlay().

```
Handle         theHandle;
OSErr          theError;
SndChannelPtr  theSndChan = nil;
Boolean        asynch = false;
theHandle = GetResource( 'snd ', 9000 );
theError = SndPlay( theSndChan, (SndListHandle)theHandle, asynch );
```

The first parameter to SndPlay() is a pointer to a sound channel. If you'd like the Sound Manager to take care of the allocation of a sound channel, pass a nil pointer here. Always load a sound resource before attempting to play it. GetResource(), described earlier in this "Sound Reference" section, can be used to load a sound resource and obtain a generic handle to the sound data in memory. When you pass this handle as the second parameter to SndPlay(), you may need to typecast it to the data type expected by SndPlay(), a SndListHandle (the universal header files used by some versions of some compilers don't require this typecast). The third parameter to SndPlay() is a Boolean that tells the Sound Manager whether this sound will be played asynchronously (true, other actions can take place simultaneously) or synchronously (false, no other actions can take place until the sound has completed playing).

When SndPlay() completes, it will return an OSErr. To check to see if the sound resource was played without error, compare this returned value with the Apple-defined constant noErr. If they are equal, the playing of the sound was successful.

CREATING AN FSSPEC FOR A SOUND FILE

Your program must first open a sound file before it attempts to play the sound data that is stored in that file. Before opening a sound file, the program needs a file system specification, or FSSpec, for the file. This section lists three Toolbox routines — FSMakeFSSpec(), StandardGetFile(), and StandardGetFilePreview()— that create an FSSpec for a sound file.

FSMakeFSSpec( )
Some Sound Manager routines need to know where on disk a sound file is located. This path must be provided in the form of an FSSpec variable. To create an FSSpec for a sound file (whether an AIFF, AIFF-C, or Finder sound file) that has both a file name and path that are known in advance, call FSMakeFSSpec().

```
OSErr    theError;
short    volRefNum = 0;
long     dirID = 0;
Str255   soundFileName = "\pCarCrash.AIFF";
```

```
FSSpec  theFSSpec;
theError = FSMakeFSSpec( volRefNum, dirID,
                         soundFileName , &theFSSpec );
```

A volume reference number of 0 tells the Toolbox that the file is on the startup hard drive. A parent directory ID of 0 means that the file is in the same folder as the application. The sound file name, CarCrash.AIFF, is the name of the sound file as it appears on the user's desktop. FSMakeFSSpec() fills in the fields of the last parameter. Use this last parameter in subsequent Sound Manager functions that require an FSSpec.

To create an FSSpec for a sound file that is selected by the user, call either StandardGetFile() or StandardGetFilePreview() rather than FSMakeFSSpec().

StandardGetFile( )

The StandardGetFile() routine displays the standard Open dialog box that lets the user open a movie.

```
SFTypeList         typeList = { 'AIFF', 'AIFC', 0, 0 };
StandardFileReply  theReply;
FileFilterProcPtr  procPtr = nil;
short              numFileTypes = 2;
StandardGetFile( procPtr, numFileTypes, typeList, &theReply );
```

The first parameter is used only if you want to mask out certain files from being displayed in the dialog box list. Typically, you'll use StandardGetFile() to display sound files that are of either the AIFF or AIFF-C format. To display these two file types, pass 2 as the second parameter. The typeList variable defines up to four file types to display. Specify 'AIFF' for AIFF formatted sound files and 'AIFC' for AIFF-C formatted files. The last parameter is filled in by the Toolbox after the user selects a sound file from the standard Open dialog box. The sfFile field of the StandardFileReply variable theReply is of type FSSpec. After the user selects a sound file, the sfFile field will hold the FSSpec of the file. Use theReply.sfFile in subsequent Sound Manager functions that require an FSSpec.

StandardGetFilePreview( )

StandardGetFilePreview() is a part of the Movie Toolbox. Like StandardGetFile(), it displays the standard Open dialog box. The dialog box posted by StandardGetFilePreview(), however, has a checkbox that allows the user to expand the dialog box such that it displays a Play Sound button that enables the user to play a sound without opening it.

```
SFTypeList          typeList = { 'AIFF', 'AIFC', 0, 0 };
StandardFileReply   theReply;
FileFilterProcPtr   procPtr = nil;
short               numFileTypes = 2;
StandardGetFilePreview( procPtr, numFileTypes, typeList, &theReply );
```

The parameters to StandardGetFilePreview() are identical to those used with StandardGetFile(). Refer to that routine description for information about each parameter.

OPENING AN AIFF OR AIFF-C SOUND FILE

After creating an FSSpec for an AIFF or AIFF-C sound file, open the file's data fork in preparation for the playing of the sound data.

FSpOpenDF( )

Before playing an AIFF or AIFF-C sound file, open its data fork by calling FSpOpenDF().

```
FSSpec  theFSSpec;
short   sndFileRefNum;
OSErr   theError;
theError = FSpOpenDF( &theFSSpec, fsRdPerm, &sndFileRefNum );
```

The first parameter to FSpOpenDF() is a pointer to an FSSpec. You can use either FSMakeFSSpec(), StandardGetFile(), or StandardGetFilePreview() to obtain this file system specification. The second parameter is a permission level — use the Apple-defined constant fsRdPerm to indicate that the data fork is to be opened with read permission only. The third parameter is a short variable that will hold a file reference number. After opening the data fork, the File Manager will fill this variable with a reference number that can be used in subsequent Toolbox calls.

PLAYING AN AIFF OR AIFF-C SOUND FILE

After opening the data fork of an AIFF or AIFF-C sound file, play the sound data.

SndStartFilePlay( )

If a sound is stored in an AIFF or AIFF-C sound file, use
SndStartFilePlay() to play it. If the sound is in a Finder sound file, use
SndPlay() instead.

```
short                  sndFileRefNum;
OSErr                  theError;
SndChannelPtr          theSndChan = nil;
short                  theResID = 0;
long                   theBufferSize = 51200;   // 50K buffer
void                   *theBufferPtr = nil;
AudioSelectionPtr      thePartPtr = nil;
FilePlayCompletionUPP  theCompletionPtr
Boolean                asynch = false;
theError = SndStartFilePlay( theSndChan, sndFileRefNum,
                    theResID, theBufferSize,
                    theBufferPtr, thePartPtr,
                    theCompletionPtr, asynch );
```

The first parameter to SndStartFilePlay() is a pointer to a sound
channel. Pass a nil pointer to let the Sound Manager allocate the sound
channel. The second parameter is a reference number to an open AIFF or
AIFF-C file. This reference number is obtained from a call to FSpOpenDF().
If SndStartFilePlay() is to play a snd resource rather than a sound file
(not recommended by Apple), then the third parameter is the resource ID.
Pass a value of 0 when playing a sound file.

The fourth parameter is the size of a buffer that the Sound Manager will
use as it plays the sound. The buffer does not have to be as large as the
sound data, but it should always be at least 20K (20,480 bytes). The fifth
parameter actually allocates the buffer — pass a nil pointer to let the Sound
Manager handle buffer allocation.

To play the entire sound rather than a part of it, pass a nil pointer as
the sixth parameter. For synchronous sound play (as described in this
chapter), pass a nil pointer for the seventh parameter — the completion
routine pointer. Pass a value of false in the final parameter to tell the
Sound Manager that this will be synchronous play.

OPENING A FINDER SOUND FILE (SYSTEM 7 SOUND FILE)

After creating an `FSSpec` for a Finder sound file, open the file's resource fork in preparation for the playing of the sound data.

CurResFile( )

Opening the resource file of a Finder sound file will result in two resource files being open at once — the application's resource fork and the Finder file's fork. Before making the Finder file's fork the current fork, save a reference number to the application's fork.

```
short   appResNum;
appRefNum = CurResFile();
```

After playing the Finder file's sound, call `UseResFile()` to restore the application resource fork as the current fork.

UseResFile( )

After calling `CurResFile()` to save a reference number to the application resource fork, open the Finder file's resource fork with a call to `FSpOpenResFile()`. Then make that fork current by calling `UseResFile()`.

```
short   finderFileRefNum;
UseResFile( finderFileRefNum );
```

Use the reference number returned by `FSpOpenResFile()` as the parameter to `UseResFile()`. After playing the Finder sound file, again call `UseResFile()` to restore the application resource fork as the current fork.

FSpOpenResFile( )

Before playing a Finder sound file, open its resource fork by calling `FSpOpenResFile()`.

```
short    finderFileRefNum;
FSSpec   theFSSpec;
finderFileRefNum = FSpOpenResFile( &theFSSpec, fsRdPerm );
```

After calling `CurResFile()` to get a reference number to the current resource fork, call `FSpOpenResFile()` to open the resource fork of a Finder sound file and to get a reference number to the sound file. The first parameter to `FSpOpenResFile()` is a pointer to an `FSSpec`. You can use either `FSMakeFSSpec()`, `StandardGetFile()`, or `StandardGetFilePreview()` to obtain this file system specification. The second parameter is a permission level; use the Apple-defined constant `fsRdPerm` to indicate that the resource fork is to be opened with read permission only. After opening the resource fork, the File Manager will return a reference number that can be used in subsequent Toolbox calls.

PLAYING A FINDER SOUND FILE (SYSTEM 7 SOUND FILE)

After opening the resource fork of a Finder sound file, play the sound data by calling `SndPlay()`. Because the sound data is kept as a `snd` resource in a Finder sound file, you'll use the same code to play a Finder file sound as you would to play a `snd` resource found in your application's resource fork. For a description of `SndPlay()`, refer to the "Playing a Sound Resource" section earlier in this reference.

ADJUSTING THE SPEAKER VOLUMES

Sound Manager 3.0 enables you to adjust the speaker volume level for the system alert sound. You can also adjust the volume at which all other sounds are played, without affecting the volume of the system alert sound.

GetDefaultOutputVolume( )

You can determine the current volume level at which calls to `SndPlay()` will play sound resources and at which `SndStartFilePlay()` will play sound files by calling `GetDefaultOutputVolume()`. Call `GetDefaultOutputVolume()` to store the current volume level before changing it:

```
long  theOriginalVol;
GetDefaultOutputVolume( &theOriginalVol );
```

The parameter to `GetDefaultOutputVolume()` is a pointer to a hexadecimal `long` that will be filled by the routine. When the routine has executed, this parameter will hold both the right and left speaker volumes

within it. An example of a returned value for `theOriginalVol` might be
`0x02000080`. This value represents a right speaker volume that is two times
the normal high volume and a left speaker volume level that is one-half the
normal high volume. The high word of the parameter (the first four digits
following `0x`) is the right volume; the low word (the last four digits) is the
left volume. Refer to the description of `SetDefaultOutputVolume()` for a
complete description of this parameter format.

TIP

`GetDefaultOutputVolume()` returns the current volume level for
sounds played by calls to `SndPlay()` and `SndStartFilePlay()`. To
determine the current level at which `SysBeep()` plays sounds, call
`GetSysBeepVolume()`.

SetDefaultOutputVolume( )

You can set the speaker volume level at which `SndPlay()` plays sound
resources and at which `SndStartFilePlay()` plays sound files by calling
`SetDefaultOutputVolume()`.

```
long  theNewVolume = 0x04000400;
SetDefaultOutputVolume( theNewVolume );
```

Before changing the volume level, call `GetDefaultOutputVolume()` to
preserve the current volume level. The parameter to
`SetDefaultOutputVolume()` is a hexadecimal long that embeds both the
right and left speaker volumes within it. The above snippet sets both
speakers to four times the normal highest Mac speaker volume level (see
explanation below).

The high word of the parameter (the first four digits following `0x`) is the
right volume; the low word (the last four digits) is the left volume. Each hex
word has a decimal range of 0 to 256 decimal (`0x0000` to `0x0100` hexadecimal). A value of 256 decimal (`0x0100` hexadecimal) represents full volume.
Fractional values of 256 represent proportionate lower volumes. Thus a
decimal value of 128 (`0x0080` hexadecimal) would represent half of full
volume (128 is half of 256). Table 13-2 lists several speaker volumes and the
hexadecimal numbers that provide these volumes. To set the volume level
of both speakers, you must combine two hexadecimal numbers from the list
into a single number. For example, to set the right speaker to full volume
and the left speaker to half volume, pass `0x01000080` to
`SetDefaultOutputVolume()`.

Table 13-2:
Hexadecimal Values for Setting Volume Levels

Hex Value	% of Full Volume
0x0600	600
0x0500	500
0x0400	400
0x0300	300
0x0200	200
0x0100	100
0x00E6	90
0x00CC	80
0x00B3	70
0x0099	60
0x0080	50
0x0066	40
0x004C	30
0x0033	20
0x0019	10
0x0000	0

SysBeep() — which plays the system alert sound — will be unaffected by SetDefaultOutputVolume(). Use SetSysBeepVolume() to change the speaker volume for SysBeep() calls.

GetSysBeepVolume( )

You can determine the current volume level at which calls to SysBeep() will play the system alert sound by calling GetSysBeepVolume(). Call GetSysBeepVolume() to store the current volume level before changing it.

```
long  theOriginalVol;
GetSysBeepVolume( &theOriginalVol );
```

The parameter to GetSysBeepVolume() is a pointer to a hexadecimal long that will be filled by the routine. When the routine has executed, this parameter will hold both the right and left speaker volumes within it. An example of a returned value for theOriginalVol might be 0x01000040. This value represents a right speaker volume that is the normal high volume and a left speaker volume level that is twice the normal high volume. The high word of the parameter (the first four digits following 0x) is the right volume; the low word (the last four digits) is the left volume. Refer to the description of SetDefaultOutputVolume() for a complete description of this parameter format.

GetSysBeepVolume() returns the current volume level for sounds played by calls to SysBeep(). To determine the current level at which SndPlay() and SndStartFilePlay() play sounds, call GetDefaultOutputVolume().

SetSysBeepVolume( )
You can set the speaker volume level at which SysBeep() plays the system alert sound by calling SetSysBeepVolume().

```
long  theNewVolume = 0x02000200;
SetSysBeepVolume( theNewVolume );
```

Before changing the volume level, call GetSysBeepVolume() to preserve the current volume level. The parameter to SetSysBeepVolume() is a hexadecimal long that embeds both the right and left speaker volumes within it. The above snippet sets both speakers to twice the normal highest Mac speaker volume level. For an explanation of the format of the parameter, as well as a table of parameter values, refer to the description of the function SetDefaultOutputVolume().

SndPlay() (which plays sound resources) and SndStartFilePlay() (which plays sound files) will be unaffected by SetSysBeepVolume(). Use SetDefaultOutputVolume() to change the speaker volume for calls to these routines.

14 QuickTime

*M*ultimedia can mean text, graphics, and sound, all rolled into one dynamic presentation. Apple recognized the importance of multimedia for Macintosh users — thus the emergence of QuickTime. QuickTime is a *system extension,* software that Mac owners can add to the existing system software on their computers. Once QuickTime is added to a Macintosh, that machine is capable of playing movies in standard Macintosh windows.

On its own, QuickTime doesn't play movies. Instead, it enables applications that are written with QuickTime in mind to play movies. To give programmers the ability to add movie-playing features to their applications, Apple has added a number of new movie-related functions to the system software. So many, in fact, that Apple gave this set of routines its own Toolbox, the Movie Toolbox. In this chapter you'll see how to take full advantage of many of the routines so that your own applications can play movies.

QuickTime and QuickTime Movies

QuickTime isn't an application — it's an extension. A QuickTime movie is stored in a QuickTime movie file on disk. When an application plays a QuickTime movie, it loads the movie from the file to memory, then uses QuickTime extension code to play the movie.

THE QUICKTIME EXTENSION

Part of the Macintosh operating system is programmed into ROM chips, another part is stored in the System file found in the System Folder, and still other parts reside in system software extensions in the Extensions folder of the System Folder. Extensions allow Apple and developers to distribute code that acts as if it were a part of the user's operating system — even though it isn't a part of ROM or a part of the System file. QuickTime is such an extension. As with other extensions, you don't run QuickTime; its code is loaded into memory when you start up your Mac. Programs that properly interface with the QuickTime code then gain the ability to play QuickTime movies.

QUICKTIME MOVIE FILES

Macintosh files consist of two parts, or *forks*. Unsurprisingly, the data fork holds data, and the resource fork holds resources. While a file is usually thought of as a document, it doesn't have to be; applications are also files.

 The description of file forks here is a quick summary. You should refer to Chapter 2 for an introduction to forks.

An application typically has all of the program's executable code and resources stored in the application file's resource fork. The data fork goes empty. Document files are created and read by application files. The format of a document file is usually the opposite of an application file — the data fork contains all of the document information, while the resource fork is empty. Figure 14-1 illustrates. On the left of this figure is an application file with several resource types in its resource fork, including CODE resources that hold the program's executable code. On the right of the figure is a document file. The document file's data fork is filled with 1s and 0s to represent the data that could be text, graphics, or both.

 Figure 14-1 shows the format of an application file for a 68K program. A program that is built using a PowerPC compiler is said to be a native PowerPC application, and has its code stored in the data fork rather than in CODE resources.

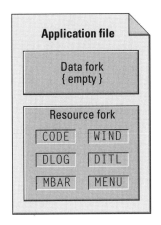 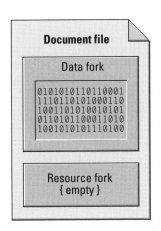

Figure 14-1
The file formats for an application file and a document file.

All Macintosh files have a file type. An application is a file of type
'APPL', a text file is of type 'TEXT', a file that holds a picture is of type
'PICT'. A file that holds a QuickTime movie is a movie file of type 'MooV'.
Because a QuickTime movie file is a document that holds information used
by an application (such as a QuickTime movie player), you might guess that
the file's movie information is held in the file's data fork. That guess is
partially correct. A movie file has information stored in both its resource
fork and its data fork.

Stored within a movie file's resource fork is a moov resource. This movie
resource holds a description of the movie. The description consists of
information such as the movie's default volume setting and the duration of
the movie. The movie resource doesn't hold the movie itself; the data that
makes up a movie is held in the movie file's data fork. Figure 14-2 shows
the format of a movie file.

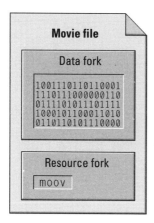

Figure 14-2
The file format for a QuickTime movie file.

Note the difference in capitalization between the movie file type ('MooV') and the movie resource (moov) that is in the resource fork of a movie file.

When an application such as a QuickTime movie player plays a movie, it loads information from both forks of a `movie` file into memory.

The Movie Toolbox

A keen understanding of file types and resource types is often necessary when working with certain Macintosh programming topics. Fortunately, this isn't the case when programming with QuickTime. As short as the preceding section is, it provides more information than you'll likely ever need regarding QuickTime files and resources. The reason for this is the existence of the Movie Toolbox.

THE MACINTOSH TOOLBOX AND THE MOVIE TOOLBOX

The Macintosh Toolbox is a collection of several thousand routines that provide you with the means to give your programs the features expected to be found in any Mac application, elements such as windows, dialog boxes, and menus. The Movie Toolbox is another set of functions that Apple provides to help Macintosh programmers. The routines found in the Movie Toolbox are all QuickTime-related — they enable the programmer to open, play, edit, and close QuickTime movies.

If you have an older Mac, you may wonder if you even have the Movie Toolbox on your machine. The routines that make up the Movie Toolbox are a part of the QuickTime extension. So if you have QuickTime installed, you have the Movie Toolbox.

MOVIE INITIALIZATION

If your program is to make use of QuickTime, you'll need to make two checks near the start of your code. First, you'll verify that the user has QuickTime installed on his or her Macintosh. Because it's an extension, QuickTime may not be a part of each user's system. Second, you'll initialize the Movie Toolbox, just as you now initialize the original Macintosh Toolbox.

To verify that the QuickTime extension is present, call the Toolbox function Gestalt(). You'll recall from Chapter 1 that when one of the many Apple-defined selector codes is passed as the first parameter, Gestalt() fills in the second parameter with information about the topic of the selector code. In this instance, the selector code is gestaltQuickTime. The returned result will be the version of QuickTime that is on the user's Mac. Of more interest to you than the particular version number is whether or not any version of QuickTime is present. For this information, you'll look at the OSErr value returned by Gestalt(), not the result. If the user doesn't have QuickTime, Gestalt() will have a value other than the Apple-defined constant noErr. Here's the QuickTime-checking code:

```
#include <Gestalt.h>
OSErr   theError;
long    theResult;

theError = Gestalt( gestaltQuickTime, &theResult );
if ( theError != noErr )
   ExitToShell();
```

You can see in the above snippet that if the user doesn't have QuickTime installed, Gestalt() will return an error (theError will not equal noErr). You can also see that this situation is handled by abruptly ending the program. You might want to be a little friendlier and instead post an alert with a descriptive message for the user, then exit the program.

Once you're satisfied that the user has QuickTime, you'll initialize the original Macintosh Toolbox and then initialize the Movie Toolbox. As you know, before using the original Macintosh Toolbox, you have to make calls to a few select Toolbox initialization routines such as InitGraf(), InitFonts(), and InitWindows(). Initializing the Movie Toolbox is easier — it only takes a single call to EnterMovies().

The Movie Toolbox function EnterMovies() allocates a block of memory that the Movie Toolbox will use exclusively for your program. The EnterMovies() routine returns an OSErr value that lets you know if the memory allocation was successful. If it wasn't, you'll exit the program. If allocation went smoothly, you'll carry on with your program. The following is an example of a call to EnterMovies(). Make sure to include the Movies.h universal header file at the top of your source file — it provides the function prototypes for each of the Movie Toolbox routines:

```
#include <Movies.h>
OSErr  theError;
theError = EnterMovies();
if ( theError != noErr )
   ExitToShell();
```

The Movie Toolbox is a part of the QuickTime extension. If the user doesn't have QuickTime, then any call your program makes to a Movie Toolbox function, including EnterMovies(), will fail. That's why you'll make the call to Gestalt() early in your source code. In fact, you might want to combine the check for QuickTime and the Movie Toolbox initialization call to EnterMovies() with your routine that initializes the original Macintosh Toolbox. Here's how this new routine, which is aptly named InitializeToolboxes(), might look:

```
void  InitializeToolboxes( void )
{
   OSErr  theError;
   long   theResult;
   InitGraf( &qd.thePort );
   InitFonts();
   InitWindows();
   InitMenus();
   TEInit();
```

```
InitDialogs( 0L );
FlushEvents( everyEvent, 0 );
InitCursor();
theError = Gestalt( gestaltQuickTime, &theResult );
if ( theError != noErr )
   ExitToShell();

theError = EnterMovies();
if ( theError != noErr )
   ExitToShell();
}
```

Once you've initialized the Macintosh Toolbox, verified the presence of QuickTime, and initialized the Movie Toolbox, you're all set to make use of any of the hundreds of routines in the Movie Toolbox.

Loading a Movie File

Before playing a movie, an application must open the QuickTime file in which the movie resides. The movie is then loaded into memory, where the application can work with it.

ESTABLISHING THE PATH TO THE MOVIE FILE

As stated earlier, a QuickTime movie is stored in a file on disk. Usually that file has the distinctive movie film icon, like the two QuickTime movie files shown in Figure 14-3.

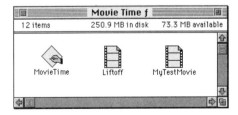

Figure 14-3
QuickTime movies generally have a filmstrip icon.

If you aren't familiar with file pathnames, the FSSpec data type, and the FSMakeFSSpec()
routine, take a side trip to Chapter 15. If you just need a refresher on these topics, continue
reading this sidebar.

FSMakeFSSpec() accepts a volume reference number (designating which disk the file is on), the
file's parent directory (the folder it is housed in), and the file's name (as a Str255 string). In return,
FSMakeFSSpec() fills in the values of the fields of the FSSpec variable that gets passed to it.

By passing a volume reference number of 0, and a parent directory of 0, you tell FSMakeFSSpec()
that the movie file in question is on the default drive (the startup drive) and in the same directory
(folder) as the application that is about to use it. Chapter 15 describes how to access a file that is
in a directory other than the one the application resides in.

Before a program can play a movie, the movie's file needs to be
opened. To let the Movie Toolbox know where the movie file to open is
located, you need to create a file system specification, or FSSpec, for the file.
Use the Toolbox routine FSMakeFSSpec() to do this. Here an FSSpec for a
movie named MyTestMovie is created:

```
OSErr   theError;
FSSpec  MooVFSSpec;
theError = FSMakeFSSpec( 0, 0, "\pMyTestMovie", &MooVFSSpec );
```

OPENING A MOVIE FILE

Before playing a movie, you need to open its file. To do this, make a call to
the Movie Toolbox routine OpenMovieFile(). Pass OpenMovieFile() the
previously created FSSpec for the movie. Also pass a pointer to a short
variable. The Movie Toolbox will fill in this variable with a file reference
number that will be used by other Movie Toolbox routines later in your
program. This variable will serve as a reference to the file fork that holds the
movie resource, the movie's moov resource. The final parameter to
OpenMovieFile() designates a permission level. When a QuickTime movie

is open, you can let the user play the movie (read it), edit the movie (write to it), or both. The three Apple-defined constants for these permission levels are `fsRdPerm`, `fsWrPerm`, and `fsRdWrPerm`. The following snippet opens a movie with a permission level that allows the user to play the movie:

```
FSSpec   MooVFSSpec;
OSErr    theError;
short    moovRefNum;

theError = OpenMovieFile( &MooVFSSpec, &moovRefNum, fsRdPerm );
```

LOADING A MOVIE FILE

The `OpenMovieFile()` routine readies a file for your program's use, but it doesn't load the file's movie into memory. To do that, call the Movie Toolbox routine `NewMovieFromFile()`. Below is a snippet that makes the call to `NewMovieFromFile()`. Following this snippet is a description of the half dozen parameters that get passed to `NewMovieFromFile()`:

```
OSErr    theError;
Movie    theMovie = nil;
short    moovRefNum;
short    moovResID = 0;
Str255   movieName;
Boolean  wasChanged;

theError = NewMovieFromFile( &theMovie, moovRefNum,
                             &moovResID, movieName,
                             newMovieActive, &wasChanged );
```

The call to NewMovieFromFile( ) creates a movie in memory that is much smaller than the combined moov resource and data found in a movie file. That's because all of the movie's data isn't loaded into memory at once. Once a movie starts playing, more of its data will be loaded into memory.

After the `NewMovieFromFile()` routine is completed, the first parameter will hold a movie identifier — a pointer to the memory block that holds the new movie. This variable, of type `Movie`, helps you keep track of a movie in an application that allows more than one movie to be open at a time. When you declare the Movie variable, set its initial value to nil. After the call to NewMovieFromFile() you can check to see if this variable still has a value of nil. If it does, you know that the attempt to load the movie failed.

The second parameter in NewMovieFromFile() is the movie reference number returned by OpenMovieFile(). Here it's used to locate the resource fork of the file that holds the movie to load. Then, based on this resource, it creates a movie in memory.

The third parameter in NewMovieFromFile() is the resource ID of the movie's moov resource. The second parameter told NewMovieFromFile() where to find the moov resource, but it didn't tell the routine which moov to use. A movie file can hold more than one movie. While most don't, there is still this possibility that must be taken into account. If a file does hold more than one movie, it will have more than one moov resource. If this third parameter is set to 0, as in the above snippet, the first movie resource in the file is used. If there is only one movie in the file, as is usually the case, that movie will be used. After locating the moov resource, NewMovieFromFile() will fill in this third parameter with the movie's moov resource ID.

The fourth parameter in NewMovieFromFile() is the name of the movie. NewMovieFromFile() will fill in this parameter with the name of the moov resource from which the movie is created. That means the name of a movie is not the name of the movie file, but rather it is the name of the moov resource in the movie file. Because a file can hold more than one movie, a movie's name comes from its moov resource. If the moov resource doesn't have a name, NewMovieFromFile() will return a value of nil in the fourth parameter. In Figure 14-4 you can see that the movie that is loaded from the MyTestMovie movie file has the name The Test.

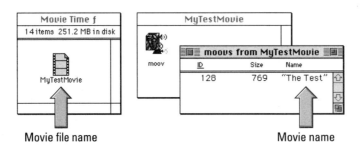

Movie file name   Movie name

Figure 14-4
A movie file in the Finder, and viewed in the resource editor ResEdit.

The fifth parameter to `NewMovieFromFile()` gives the programmer some additional control over how the `NewMovieFromFile()` operates. In almost all cases you'll pass the Apple-defined constant `newMovieActive`. This value tells `NewMovieFromFile()` to activate the newly created movie. A QuickTime movie must be active before it can be played.

The sixth and last parameter to `NewMovieFromFile()` tells whether the Movie Toolbox had to alter any data as it loaded it into memory. The Movie Toolbox will fill in this parameter with a value of `true` or `false`. This value indicates whether changes were made to the movie. The variable wasChanged is filled in by the Movie Toolbox.

CLOSING A MOVIE FILE

If your program allows the user to make changes to an open movie, you'll want to keep the file that the movie came from open. That will allow you to save any changes back to the file. If, however, your program doesn't give the user write permission, you can close the file right after the new movie is created from its contents.

Use the Movie Toolbox routine `CloseMovieFile()` to close an open movie file. To let `CloseMovieFile()` know which movie file to close, pass the routine the reference number of the movie to close. You'll recall that the Movie Toolbox function `OpenMovieFile()` returned this reference number to your program. Here's a call to `CloseMovieFile()`:

```
short   moovRefNum;
CloseMovieFile( moovRefNum );
```

Before moving on to the displaying of a movie in a window, take a look at how the opening of a movie file and the loading of its movie can be packaged in a single routine. When it comes time to load a movie, the `GetMovieFromFile()` function that appears below can be called from anywhere in your source code. You'll declare a `Movie` variable, then invoke the routine, like this:

```
Movie  theMovie;
theMovie = GetMovieFromFile();
```

As you look at the `GetMovieFromFile()` routine, notice that it is limited to opening only one particular movie, the one that's held in the movie file named in the call to `FSMakeFSSpec()`. By setting the first two parameters to `FSMakeFSSpec()` to 0, the routine also makes the assumption that the movie file named MyTestMovie appears in the same folder as the application that calls `GetMovieFromFile()`. Later in this chapter you'll see an improved version of `GetMovieFromFile()`. The modified version will use the standard Open dialog box to let the user select the movie that gets loaded:

```
Movie  GetMovieFromFile( void )
{
    OSErr    theError;
    FSSpec   MooVFSSpec;
    Movie    getMovie = nil;
    short    moovRefNum;
    short    moovResID = 0;
    Str255   movieName;
    Boolean  wasChanged;
    theError = FSMakeFSSpec( 0, 0, "\pMyTestMovie", &MooVFSSpec );
    if ( theError == noErr )
    {
        theError = OpenMovieFile( &MooVFSSpec, &moovRefNum, fsRdPerm );
        if ( theError == noErr )
        {
            theError = NewMovieFromFile( &getMovie, moovRefNum,
                                         &moovResID, movieName,
                                         newMovieActive, &wasChanged );
            CloseMovieFile( moovRefNum );
        }
    }
    return ( getMovie );
}
```

Notice that the local Movie variable getMovie is assigned an initial value of nil. If the call to FSMakeFSSpec(), OpenMovieFile(), or NewMovieFromFile() fails (for whatever reason), getMovie will still have this nil value. It's up to the routine that calls GetMovieFromFile() to check the returned Movie to ensure that it is anything but nil. If it is nil, the calling code should either post an error alert, quit the application, or both. The NoControlMovie program in this chapter provides an example of this.

Once you have a Movie variable that points to a movie in memory, you don't need the movie file that held the movie to be open. The movie file can be closed after its movie is loaded, provided the application won't be allowing the user to edit the movie and save the changes. You'll be using the Movie variable, not the movie file, to access the movie. Since this version of GetMovieFromFile() opens the movie without write permission, it's okay for it to close the file.

Displaying a Movie in a Window

The steps that you've taken so far have led to the creation of a movie in memory, but not to the display of the movie. For that you need to open a window and adjust its size to that of the movie that will appear in it.

THE MOVIE GRAPHICS WORLD: PAIRING A WINDOW WITH A MOVIE

A movie makes use of a *graphics world* — a drawing environment that holds display information for that movie. Before a movie is first played, you'll set the movie's display coordinate system to that of the window in which the movie is to be played. A QuickTime movie is displayed in a standard Macintosh window. You can use either the GetNewCWindow() or the NewCWindow() Toolbox function to create a color window to hold the movie. Assuming a window has been created, a call to the Movie Toolbox function SetMovieGWorld() can be made to set the movie's display coordinate system to that of the window:

```
Movie      theMovie;     // obtain from NewMovieFromFile()
WindowPtr  theWindow;    // obtain from GetNewCWindow()
SetMovieGWorld( theMovie, (CGrafPtr)theWindow, nil );
```

The first parameter to SetMovieGWorld() is the movie that is to have its display coordinate system set. The second parameter can be a pointer to one of three data structures: a graphics port, a color graphics port, or a graphics world. SetMovieGWorld() will know what to do with a variable of any of these types. Here, a WindowPtr is typecast to a CGrafPtr, a pointer to a color graphics port. The WindowPtr variable theWindow is the window that was sized just for this movie. The final parameter is a handle to the movie's graphics device structure. Passing a value of nil here results in the current device being used.

> This section, and the "Playing a Movie" section that follows, discuss the setup and playing of a movie that doesn't have a movie controller. If your program will attach a movie controller to the bottom of a movie window, you should still read the following text. It provides background material that applies to a movie that uses a controller. And why would a program play a movie without a controller? Usually, you won't; you'll want to give the user the ability to control movie playing. There are, however, applications that will take the initiative of opening and playing a movie without the user's intervention. A game, for instance, might open, play, and close movies at different points in the game. A noninteractive program that advertises or promotes a product might also play movies at different points in the presentation.

A WindowPtr points to the first field of a WindowRecord — which happens to be a GrafPort. A GrafPtr (and a CGrafPtr) also point to a GrafPort. That's why a WindowPtr can be typecast to a CGrafPtr.

After the call to SetMovieGWorld(), the movie *could* be displayed in the window. At this point, however, the window is invisible. You'll see why as you continue reading.

OPENING AND SIZING A MOVIE DISPLAY WINDOW

As just mentioned, a movie is displayed in a standard Macintosh window. The examples in this chapter each use a call to GetNewCWindow(), with a WIND resource providing window descriptive information. The alternative method is to make a call to NewCWindow(), with the window description provided in the parameters to this Toolbox function.

Whether you set up the window's placement on the screen with a WIND resource (if using GetNewCWindow()) or a call to SetRect() (if using NewCWindow()), your concern will be with the window's top left corner only. As you'll see, the window's size is unimportant; your program will resize the window to the exact size of the movie that it will hold. The top left corner of the window, however, will remain at the same coordinates that you initially provide. In Figure 14-5 you can see that the window's top left corner has been set to (100, 100). The bottom and right values have been arbitrarily chosen, and give the window a width and height of 100 pixels. Notice that the window has been set to be initially invisible. To prevent the user from seeing the window changing size on the screen, keep the window hidden until resizing is finished. Here's the call that loads the window information into memory:

```
WindowPtr  theWindow;
theWindow = GetNewCWindow( 128, nil, (WindowPtr)-1L );
```

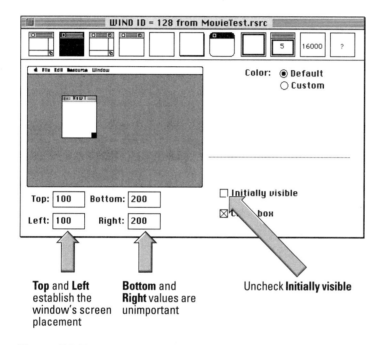

Top and **Left**
establish the
window's screen
placement

Bottom and
Right values are
unimportant

Uncheck **Initially visible**

Figure 14-5
A standard window, created from a WIND *resource, can be used to hold a QuickTime movie.*

Once your program makes a Toolbox call to create the window, you'll resize and then display the window. To do this, first call the Movie Toolbox routine GetMovieBox(). This function determines the size of a box that would perfectly surround the movie that is to be displayed. Pass GetMovieBox() the Movie variable that NewMovieFromFile() returned to your program, and a rectangle in which GetMovieBox() can place the movie box values. Here's how a call to GetMovieBox() looks:

```
Movie  theMovie;  // obtain from NewMovieFromFile()
Rect   movieBox;

GetMovieBox( theMovie, &movieBox );
```

After the call to GetMovieBox(), the Rect variable movieBox will hold the coordinates of the movie. You can't, however, make the assumption that the left and top values will each be 0, and that the left and bottom values then provide you with the width and height of the movie. In Figure 14-6 you can see that for a movie that is 300 pixels wide by 230 pixels high, GetMovieBox() returned the following movieBox coordinates:

```
movieBox.left      100
movieBox.top        50
movieBox.right     400
movieBox.bottom    280
```

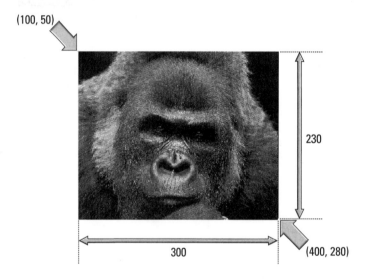

Figure 14-6

GetMovieBox() *returns the size of a movie, but not with a reference point of (0, 0).*

The box that holds the movie should have left and top coordinates of 0. That way, when the movie is placed in a window, it will appear in the window's upper left corner without any white space surrounding it. To make this adjustment, call the Toolbox routine OffsetRect(). If you pass this routine negative values of the movieBox left and top coordinates, you'll offset, or shift, the movie so that its upper left corner starts at (0, 0). After the shift you'll end up with a Rect with the desired coordinates. As far as your program is concerned, you've just set the coordinates of a local Rect variable named movieBox. The Movie variable won't know of the change. To remedy this situation, call the Movie Toolbox routine SetMovieBox() to provide the Movie variable with these adjusted coordinates:

```
Movie  theMovie;    // obtained from NewMovieFromFile()
Rect   movieBox;    // obtained from GetMovieBox()
OffsetRect( &movieBox, -movieBox.left, -movieBox.top );
SetMovieBox( theMovie, &movieBox );
```

Remember that when you load a movie into memory, there is no window associated with it. That's why you have to do a little tinkering to get a movie to fit snugly in a new window that you open.

Now the Movie variable knows where in the window to place the movie. But there's still one more adjustment to make. The window that was created with the call to GetNewCWindow() or NewCWindow() has coordinates that were arbitrarily selected — the window will most likely not be the same size as the movie. A call to the Toolbox function SizeWindow() will take care of that discrepancy. Now that the movie box has been offset to start at (0, 0), you can pass the movie box right and bottom coordinates as the right and bottom coordinates for the window. Figure 14-7 shows the placement of a window and the area it would occupy both before the call to SizeWindow() and after. In this figure, the WIND coordinates from Figure 14-5 and the movie coordinates from Figure 14-6 were used. With the window properly sized, follow up with a call to ShowWindow() to finally display the window on the user's screen:

```
WindowPtr  theWindow;    // obtained from GetNewCWindow()
Rect       movieBox;     // obtained from GetMovieBox(), repositioned
                         // using OffsetRect()
SizeWindow( theWindow, movieBox.right, movieBox.bottom, true );
ShowWindow( theWindow );
```

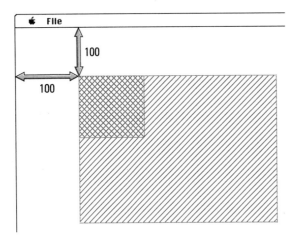

⊠ Area of window after call to `GetNewCWindow()`

⧄ Area of window after call to `SizeWindow()`

Figure 14-7
Placement and area of a window before and after resizing it.

BY THE WAY

You might think it's strange that the upper left coordinate of a movie isn't automatically and conveniently set at (0, 0), so that the right and bottom give the movie width and height. But if you've ever used the Toolbox function `GetPicture()` to obtain a handle to a `PICT` resource, you've encountered a similar situation. To get the picture's size you dereference the handle to access the `picFrame` field. The `picFrame` field is a rectangle that holds the dimensions of the picture. You can't, however, assume that the rectangle's right coordinate holds the picture's width and the bottom coordinate holds the picture's height. Instead, you have to subtract the left side from the right, and the bottom from the top — as in the following snippet:

```
PicHandle   thePicture;
Rect        pictRect;
short       pictWidth;
short       pictHeight;
thePicture = GetPicture( 128 );
pictRect = (**thePicture).picFrame;
pictWidth  = pictRect.right - pictRect.left;
pictHeight = pictRect.bottom - pictRect.top;
```

The previous section ended with a snippet of code that grouped the window resizing code together. The application-defined function `AdjustMovieWindow()` now packages that same code together. After setting the movie graphics world, the function resizes the passed-in window to the dimensions of the passed-in movie:

```
void  AdjustMovieWindow( Movie theMovie, WindowPtr theWindow )
{
   Rect  movieBox;
   SetMovieGWorld( theMovie, (CGrafPtr)theWindow, nil );

   GetMovieBox( theMovie, &movieBox );
   OffsetRect( &movieBox, -movieBox.left, -movieBox.top );
   SetMovieBox( theMovie, &movieBox );
   SizeWindow( theWindow, movieBox.right, movieBox.bottom, true );
   ShowWindow( theWindow );
}
```

You'll see `AdjustMovieWindow()` used in an example program a little later in this chapter. Until then, the following snippet shows how this function would be invoked. The snippet makes use of the `GetMovieFromFile()` function that was developed earlier in this chapter:

```
Movie     theMovie = nil;
WindowPtr theWindow;

theMovie = GetMovieFromFile();

theWindow = GetNewCWindow( 128, nil, (WindowPtr)-1L );

AdjustMovieWindow( theWindow, theMovie );
```

Playing a Movie

The setup of the movie is complete. Now it's finally time to play the movie. Well, *almost* time.

PREPARING A MOVIE FOR PLAYING

With the preliminary steps out of the way, it's time to play the movie. There's no guarantee that when a movie is opened, it will be set to its first frame. To rewind the movie, call the Movie Toolbox routine `GoToBeginningOfMovie()`. Then call `StartMovie()`. Each routine accepts the movie to play as its only parameter:

```
Movie theMovie;     // obtain from NewMovieFromFile()
GoToBeginningOfMovie( theMovie );
StartMovie( theMovie );
```

`StartMovie()`, contrary to its name, doesn't start the movie playing. Instead, it readies the movie for playing by ensuring that it is active and that the movie playback rate is correct. Once `StartMovie()` has been called, you can go ahead and play the movie.

MOVIE PLAYING

To play a movie you'll call the Movie Toolbox routine `MoviesTask()` — not once, but repeatedly from within a loop. The `MoviesTask()` function *services* a movie. That is, it handles whatever processing is needed for that movie. Processing includes the loading of movie data from the movie file, the displaying of movie frames, and the playing of the movie's soundtrack. Here's a typical call to `MoviesTask()`:

```
Movie theMovie;     // obtain from NewMovieFromFile()
MoviesTask( theMovie, 0 );
```

The first parameter to `MoviesTask()` is the movie to service. If your application allows more than one movie to be open at a time, pass `nil` as this first parameter. That tells the Movie Toolbox to service each active movie. The second parameter to `MoviesTask()` is the time (in milliseconds) given to the Movie Toolbox to perform the servicing. A value of 0 tells the Movie Toolbox to take as much time as required to service each active movie. A nonzero value tells the Movie Toolbox to service as many movies as it can in the allotted time.

MoviesTask() will always complete servicing a movie once it starts, even if it has to exceed the time value passed to it. As an example, consider an application that has three open movies, each requiring 10 milliseconds to service. If MoviesTask() is passed a time value of 15 milliseconds, the function will use 10 milliseconds to service one movie. Since it still has time remaining, MoviesTask() will begin servicing a second movie. MoviesTask() will complete servicing the movie, even though it will require the Movie Toolbox to go beyond the 15 milliseconds allotted to it. The third movie will go unserviced.

Your application should call MoviesTask() repeatedly until the specified movie (or movies) has completed playing. You can determine if a movie has completed by calling the Movie Toolbox routine IsMovieDone(). Pass the movie to this function, and the Movie Toolbox will return a value of true if the movie has completed, false if it hasn't. Here's the loop that plays a movie:

```
Movie  theMovie;   // obtain from NewMovieFromFile()
do
{
   MoviesTask( theMovie, 0 );
}
while ( IsMovieDone( theMovie ) == false );
```

Once a movie is open and in a window, you can play it by calling a routine like the PlayOneMovie() function listed below. The application needs to do all of the previously discussed setup work (such as opening and resizing the window, and loading a movie) only once. The Movie Toolbox routines discussed in this section (and that appear in PlayOneMovie()), however, must be called each time a movie is to be played:

```
void  PlayOneMovie( Movie theMovie )
{
   GoToBeginningOfMovie( theMovie );
   StartMovie( theMovie );
   do
   {
      MoviesTask( theMovie, 0 );
   } while ( IsMovieDone( theMovie ) == false );
}
```

The PlayOneMovie() function plays a single movie from start to finish. If your program uses a movie controller, as discussed later in this chapter, you'll give the user the option of playing only a part of the movie.

Closing a Movie

When the user closes a movie window, whether by clicking on the movie window's close box or by selecting a Close menu item, you'll want to deallocate the memory that holds both the movie and the window. You free the memory occupied by the movie by calling the Movie Toolbox routine `DisposeMovie()`. After you have freed the movie memory, you call the Toolbox function `DisposeWindow()` to free the memory occupied by the window. The following simple function takes care of these two tasks. `CloseMovie()` closes both the movie and the window that are passed to it as parameters:

```
void  CloseMovie( Movie theMovie, WindowPtr theWindow )
{
    DisposeMovie( theMovie );
    DisposeWindow( theWindow );
}
```

Example Program: NoControlMovie

The NoControlMovie program is an example of how an application can open and play a QuickTime movie without the use of a movie controller. When you run NoControlMovie, the program will open a QuickTime movie file named MyTestMovie and load the file's movie into memory. You will then see a window like the one in Figure 14-8. The movie (which, incidentally, was made from a series of photographs by the nineteenth-century action photographer Eadweard Muybridge) will play from start to finish. When the movie ends, so will the application.

Figure 14-8
The movie played by the NoControlMovie program.

You can have NoControlMovie play any movie you want. First, move the current MyTestMovie to a different folder for safekeeping (or give it a new name). Then select a movie of your choice, rename it MyTestMovie, and place it in the same folder as the NoControlMovie application.

RESOURCES FOR NOCONTROLMOVIE

NoControlMovie requires just one resource, the WIND in which the movie will be displayed. Figure 14-9 shows this resource. Remember, the program will change the size of the window to match the size of whatever movie is to be played in it, so the size you specify in the WIND resource is unimportant.

If you substitute the program's call to GetNewWindow() with a call to NewWindow(), the WIND resource — and the resource file — won't be necessary.

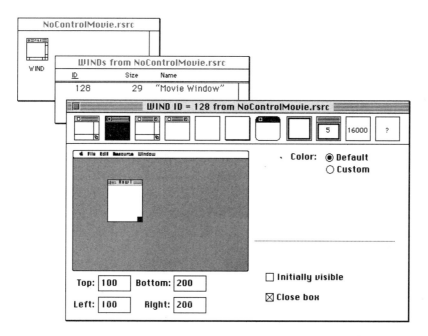

Figure 14-9
NoControlMovie requires only one resource — a WIND.

If your program displays a movie that the user can interact with (such as a movie with a movie controller, as discussed later in this chapter), you will want that movie to appear in a window with a drag bar (a title bar). If your program displays a movie that doesn't allow user interaction, then that movie's movie window doesn't have to have a title bar. Figure 14-10 shows how to define a window that is simply a frame. This approach lets you inset a movie window within another window to create a picture-in-picture effect, as shown in Figure 14-11. In that figure, a movie of a roulette wheel is displayed in a window that opens over the upper left corner of a modeless dialog box. The application could play the movie as soon as the roulette window opened.

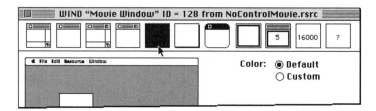

Figure 14-10
To create an immovable movie that will appear in a different Mac window, select the window type shown here.

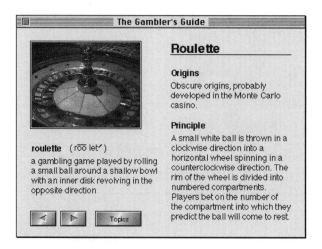

Figure 14-11
An example of an application that displays a movie within a different window.

SOURCE CODE FOR NOCONTROLMOVIE

NoControlMovie uses the five routines that were developed in this chapter. Each routine is called from the program's `main()` routine. The first, `InitializeToolboxes()`, which is from this chapter's "The Movie Toolbox" section, initializes both the original Toolbox and the Movie Toolbox. The next routine, `GetMovieFromFile()`, which is from the "Loading a Movie File" section of this chapter, opens a QuickTime movie file, loads the file's movie, and then closes the file. Then a color window is opened, but not shown. The next routine, `AdjustMovieWindow()`, from the "Displaying a Movie in a Window" section, resizes the window to match the size of the movie. The `PlayOneMovie()` function, discussed in this chapter's "Playing a Movie" section, plays the movie. Finally, the `CloseOneMovie()` routine, from the "Closing a Movie" section, closes the movie:

```
//_____
#include <Movies.h>
//_____
void  InitializeToolboxes( void );
Movie GetMovieFromFile( void );
void  AdjustMovieWindow( Movie, WindowPtr);
void  PlayOneMovie( Movie );
void  CloseOneMovie( Movie, WindowPtr );
//_____
void  main( void )
{
   WindowPtr   theWindow;
   Movie       theMovie = nil;
   InitializeToolboxes();

   theMovie = GetMovieFromFile();
   if ( theMovie == nil )
      ExitToShell();

   theWindow = GetNewCWindow( 128, nil, (WindowPtr)-1L );

   AdjustMovieWindow( theMovie, theWindow );

   PlayOneMovie( theMovie );
   CloseOneMovie( theMovie, theWindow );
}
//_____
void  InitializeToolboxes( void )
{
   OSErr  theError;
   long   theResult;
   InitGraf( &qd.thePort );
   InitFonts();
```

```
    InitWindows();
    InitMenus();
    TEInit();
    InitDialogs( 0L );
    FlushEvents( everyEvent, 0 );
    InitCursor();
    theError = Gestalt( gestaltQuickTime, &theResult );
    if ( theError != noErr )
        ExitToShell();

    theError = EnterMovies();
    if ( theError != noErr )
        ExitToShell();
}
//_____
Movie  GetMovieFromFile( void )
{
    OSErr     theError;
    FSSpec    MooVFSSpec;
    Movie     getMovie = nil;
    short     moovRefNum;
    short     moovResID = 0;
    Str255    movieName;
    Boolean   wasChanged;
    theError = FSMakeFSSpec( 0, 0, "\pMyTestMovie", &MooVFSSpec );
    if ( theError == noErr )
    {
        theError = OpenMovieFile( &MooVFSSpec, &moovRefNum, fsRdPerm );
        if ( theError == noErr )
        {
            theError = NewMovieFromFile( &getMovie, moovRefNum,
                                         &moovResID, movieName,
                                         newMovieActive, &wasChanged );
            CloseMovieFile( moovRefNum );
        }
    }
    return ( getMovie );
}
//_____
void  AdjustMovieWindow( Movie theMovie, WindowPtr theWindow )
{
    Rect  movieBox;

    SetMovieGWorld( theMovie, (CGrafPtr)theWindow, nil );
    GetMovieBox( theMovie, &movieBox );
    OffsetRect( &movieBox, -movieBox.left, -movieBox.top );
    SetMovieBox( theMovie, &movieBox );
    SizeWindow( theWindow, movieBox.right, movieBox.bottom, true );
    ShowWindow( theWindow );
```

```
   }
   //_____
   void  PlayOneMovie( Movie theMovie )
   {
      GoToBeginningOfMovie( theMovie );
      StartMovie( theMovie );
      do
      {
         MoviesTask( theMovie, 0 );
      } while ( IsMovieDone( theMovie ) == false );
   }
   //_____
   void  CloseOneMovie( Movie theMovie, WindowPtr theWindow )
   {
      DisposeMovie( theMovie );
      DisposeWindow( theWindow );
   }
```

The Standard Open File Dialog Box

If a program will open movies on its own — without user interaction —
then the technique of calling FSMakeFSSpec() and then passing the returned
FSSpec to the Movie Toolbox routine OpenMovieFile() works fine. This is
because the program will know the name of each movie file. It's just as
likely, however, that an application will allow the user to select a movie to
open and play. In this instance, your program should display the standard
Open dialog box to present the user with a list of movies to select from.

THE STANDARD OPEN DIALOG BOX AND PREVIEWING MOVIES

The standard Open dialog box, which the screen displays after a call to the
Toolbox routine StandardGetFile(), displays a list of files that the user can
open. The standard Open dialog box isn't new to QuickTime; it's been
around as long as the Macintosh itself. Figure 14-12 shows a typical version
of this dialog box, as displayed in response to a user's selecting Open from
the File menu of ResEdit.

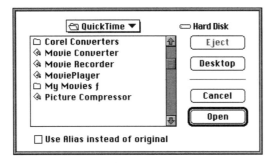

Figure 14-12
The standard Open dialog box..

If you haven't used the standard Open dialog box in any of your own programs, refer to Chapter 15. There you will find all the details of the StandardGetFile() function (including information about the function's parameters) and an example program that makes use of this Toolbox routine. In this chapter I'll only offer a summary of StandardGetFile().

The Movie Toolbox offers a new version of the StandardGetFile() function, named StandardGetFilePreview(). While the dialog box that results from a call to this function looks very similar to the one displayed by a call to the older StandardGetFile() routine, there is one key difference. The StandardGetFilePreview() dialog box includes a Show Preview check box not found in the older dialog box. Figure 14-13 shows this dialog box.

Figure 14-13
The standard Open preview file dialog box, collapsed.

When checked, the Show Preview check box expands the left side of the standard Open dialog box (see Figure 14-14). When unchecked, the check box collapses it (as shown in Figure 14-13). When expanded, the left side of the dialog box displays a small version, or *thumbnail*, of the first frame of the movie that is currently selected in the dialog box list. This thumbnail gives the user an idea of what a movie looks like without having to open the movie.

Figure 14-14
The standard Open preview file dialog box, expanded to show a movie preview.

Some movies won't display a file preview. When that happens, the user can click on the Create button and a thumbnail of the currently selected movie will be created. Figure 14-15 shows that the user will be informed that this action is taking place.

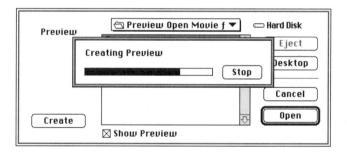

Figure 14-15
Clicking the Create button will cause the system to add a thumbnail preview for a movie.

If a movie displays a file preview, then that movie's file holds both a PICT resource and a pnot resource (in addition to a moov resource). If a movie doesn't display a file preview, clicking on the Create button will add these two resources to the movie file.

DISPLAYING THE STANDARD OPEN PREVIEW FILE DIALOG BOX

The Movie Toolbox routine StandardGetFilePreview() accepts the same four parameters that the Toolbox routine StandardGetFile() uses. Here is a typical call to the Movie Toolbox routine:

```
SFTypeList         typeList = { MovieFileType, 0, 0, 0 };
StandardFileReply  theReply;
StandardGetFilePreview( nil, 1, typeList, &theReply );
```

Like its companion Toolbox routine StandardGetFile(), the Movie Toolbox function StandardGetFilePreview() is the kind of routine that programmers dream about. Once called, this routine displays the standard Open preview file dialog box and then takes over and handles all of the user's actions. Whether the user switches folders with the pop-up menu, opens a movie by double-clicking on its file name, expands or collapses the dialog box with a click on the Show Preview check box, or clicks on any of the buttons in the dialog box, it is the StandardGetFilePreview() routine that handles things. Only when the user finally selects a file or clicks the Cancel button will the call to StandardGetFilePreview() be complete.

The file list in the standard Open dialog box doesn't display all the files in a folder, only the files of a type or types that you specify. Files of any other type will be filtered out. StandardGetFilePreview() enables you to easily display up to four different file types (such as 'TEXT', 'PICT', and so on). If you want to display more than four types, you will need to use the first parameter to StandardGetFilePreview() to pass a pointer to an optional filter function. Since you'll only be displaying one type of file (type 'MooV'), you won't need a filter function. Pass a nil pointer here. The second parameter tells how many file types will be in the list. As just mentioned, your program will only display one file type, so you should set this second parameter to 1.

The third parameter to StandardGetFilePreview() specifies which file types to include in the dialog box list. Any file type not mentioned in the SFTypeList variable will be excluded from the list. In the above snippet you can see that only QuickTime movie files will be shown. The Apple-defined constant MovieFileType represents the 'MooV' file type, as you can see from its definition in the Movies.h Universal Header file:

```
enum
{
   MovieFileType   = 'MooV'
};
```

The last parameter to StandardGetFilePreview() is a pointer to a
variable of type StandardFileReply. After the user dismisses the standard
Open dialog box, the Movie Toolbox will fill in the fields of this parameter.
Typically, you'll only be interested in two of the many StandardFileReply
fields. The sfGood field is a Boolean that will have a value of true if a file
was selected and a value of false if the Cancel button was clicked. The
sfFile field is a file system specification, an FSSpec, for the selected file.
Recall from earlier in this chapter that if a file's name and location are
known, you can use the Toolbox routine FSMakeFSSpec() to obtain an
FSSpec for a file.

Earlier in this chapter you saw an application-defined routine named
GetMovieFromFile(). That function used a call to FSMakeFSSpec() to create an
FSSpec for a QuickTime movie named MyTestMovie. With little modification,
GetMovieFromFile() can be altered so that it lets the user select the movie to
open. In the following version of the function, unneeded code from the
NoControlMovie version has been commented out and replaced with code
in bold type:

```
Movie  GetMovieFromFile( void )
{
   OSErr               theError;
// FSSpec              MooVFSSpec;
   SFTypeList          typeList = { MovieFileType, 0, 0, 0 };
   StandardFileReply   theReply;
   Movie               getMovie = nil;
   short               moovRefNum;
   short               moovResID = 0;
   Str255              movieName;
   Boolean             wasChanged;
// theError = FSMakeFSSpec( 0, 0, "\pMyTestMovie", &MooVFSSpec );
   StandardGetFilePreview( nil, 1, typeList, &theReply );
// if ( theError == noErr )
   if ( theReply.sfGood == true )
   {
//    theError = OpenMovieFile( &MooVFSSpec, &moovRefNum, fsRdPerm );
      theError = OpenMovieFile( &theReply.sfFile, &moovRefNum, fsRdPerm );
      if ( theError == noErr )
```

```
        {
            theError = NewMovieFromFile( &getMovie, moovRefNum,
                                         &moovResID, movieName,
                                         newMovieActive, &wasChanged );
            CloseMovieFile( moovRefNum );
        }
    }
    return ( getMovie );
}
```

Here is a quick summary of the changes to GetMovieFile(). Because the sfFile field of the StandardFileReply variable theReply is an FSSpec, the MoovFSSpec variable is no longer needed. In its place are two variables used as parameters to StandardGetFilePreview(). The call to FSMakeFSSpec() has been replaced with a call to StandardGetFilePreview(). To see if a movie file was selected, the sfGood field of theReply is examined. And when it's time to open the movie file, the sfFile field of theReply is passed to OpenMovieFile(). Here's a "clean" listing of the new version of GetMovieFromFile() — the commented code and bold type have been removed:

```
Movie  GetMovieFromFile( void )
{
    OSErr              theError;
    Movie              getMovie = nil;
    short              moovRefNum;
    short              moovResID = 0;
    Str255             movieName;
    Boolean            wasChanged;
    SFTypeList         typeList = { MovieFileType, 0, 0, 0 };
    StandardFileReply  theReply;
    StandardGetFilePreview( nil, 1, typeList, &theReply );
    if ( theReply.sfGood == true )
    {
        theError = OpenMovieFile( &theReply.sfFile,
                                  &moovRefNum, fsRdPerm );
        if ( theError == noErr )
        {
            theError = NewMovieFromFile( &getMovie, moovRefNum,
                                         &moovResID, movieName,
                                         newMovieActive, &wasChanged );
            CloseMovieFile( moovRefNum );
        }
    }
    return ( getMovie );
}
```

Example Program: PreviewOpenMovie

You've just read a very detailed explanation of how to alter the application-defined function `GetMovieFile()` so that it displays the standard Open preview file dialog box. Why such a thorough walk-through? Because the changes to that routine are the only differences between this chapter's NoControlMovie example program and the PreviewOpenMovie example that you'll also find in the Chapter 14 folder on the CD that accompanies this book.

When you launch PreviewOpenMovie you'll see the standard Open preview file dialog box. When you select a movie from the dialog box, the dialog box will be dismissed and the movie will open and play, and then the application will terminate, exactly as it did in the NoControlMovie example.

QuickTime Movie Controllers

To play a movie you can use the Movie Toolbox function `MoviesTask()`. While this routine is useful for playing a movie from start to finish, it robs the user of control of the movie. If your application allows user interaction, you'll want to add a movie controller to each movie that opens.

THE MOVIE CONTROLLER COMPONENT

A Toolbox manager is nothing more than a conceptual grouping of related Toolbox routines. For instance, the Window Manager is the set of Toolbox functions that work with windows. While you're familiar with managers such as the Window Manager, the Dialog Manager, and the Menu Manager, you're probably much less knowledgeable about the Component Manager. The Component Manager is the set of Toolbox and Movie Toolbox routines that work with *components*. A component is a code resource that is dedicated to one service, and can be used by many applications. While QuickTime is a primary user of components, a component doesn't have to be QuickTime-related.

QuickTime uses image-compression components to provide compression services for movies. Applications that are capable of receiving digitized data from an external source (such as Apple's Movie Recorder, which captures images from a VCR or camcorder) use sequence grabber components. The most commonly used component that QuickTime applications make use of is the movie controller component. This component makes it easy for programmers to add a movie controller to the bottom of any open movie, as shown in Figure 14-16.

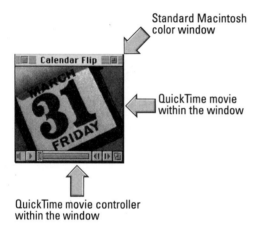

Standard Macintosh color window

QuickTime movie within the window

QuickTime movie controller within the window

Figure 14-16
A QuickTime movie appears in a standard Macintosh window, and can have a movie controller attached to it.

When a movie controller is added to a window that holds a QuickTime movie, it is said to be *attached* to the movie. Attaching a movie controller to a movie provides the user with a standardized means of playing the movie. Once attached, the movie controller and the Movie Toolbox do most of the work of playing a movie. By adding a call to a single Movie Toolbox routine, you let the user of your program use the buttons of a movie controller (shown in Figure 14-17) to play a movie, step through the movie one frame at a time, or adjust the movie's volume.

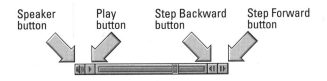

Figure 14-17
The parts of a QuickTime movie controller.

ATTACHING A MOVIE CONTROLLER TO A MOVIE

A movie that uses a movie controller is opened in the same way as a movie that doesn't use a controller. The following list summarizes the process of opening and displaying a movie:

1. Call `FSMakeFSSpec()` or `StandardGetFilePreview()` to obtain movie file information in the form of an `FSSpec`.
2. Pass the `FSSpec` to `OpenMovieFile()` to open the movie file.
3. Call `NewMovieFromFile()` to load the movie into memory.
4. Open (but don't make visible) a color window in which to display the movie.
5. Call `SetMovieGWorld()` to set the movie's coordinate system to that of the window.
6. Resize the window to the size of the movie.
7. Call `ShowWindow()` to display the resized movie window.

Each of the above steps, with the exception of Step 6, include the name of the specific Toolbox or Movie Toolbox routine necessary to execute the step. Step 6 is intentionally vague because the routines you'll use to resize a movie with a movie controller differ from those you'll use with a movie that doesn't attach a controller.

For a movie without a controller, you call `GetMovieBox()` to get a `Rect` that holds the movie's dimensions. The coordinates in the Rect may not include the point (0, 0), so you'll next call `OffsetRect()` to shift the rectangle to the origin, without changing its overall size. Next, a call to `SetMovieBox()` assigns this shifted rectangle to the movie:

```
Movie  theMovie;    // obtained from NewMovieFromFile()
Rect   movieBox;
GetMovieBox( theMovie, &movieBox );
OffsetRect( &movieBox, -movieBox.left, -movieBox.top );
SetMovieBox( theMovie, &movieBox );
```

For a movie with a controller, you'll again begin with a call to
GetMovieBox(). Here, however, you'll make the call so that you can get the
width of the movie. The Rect that is filled by GetMovieBox() should be
passed to the Movie Toolbox function NewMovieController(). This routine
creates a new movie controller and attaches it to a movie. The height of a
movie controller is always the same. The width of the controller is dependent on the width of the movie, as shown in Figure 14-18.

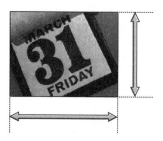

GetMovieBox() returns a Rect that
holds the dimensions of a movie

Pass the GetMovieBox() Rect to
NewMovieController() so that the width
of the controller can be calculated

Figure 14-18
*A movie controller has a fixed height, but its width varies with the width of
a movie.*

Here's a snippet of code that creates a movie controller and attaches it
to a movie. The name of the MovieController variable is prefaced with a *g*
to show that it will be a global variable. The reason for making this one
variable global will become evident in this chapter's "Using a Controller to
Play a Movie" section:

```
MovieController  gController;
Movie            theMovie;
Rect             movieBox;
GetMovieBox( theMovie, &movieBox );
gController = NewMovieController( theMovie, &movieBox, mcTopLeftMovie );
```

The first parameter to `NewMovieController()` is the movie to which the controller will be attached. The second parameter is the rectangle that holds the dimensions of the movie. The `left` and `right` fields of this rectangle will be used by the Movie Toolbox to establish the width of the movie controller. The final parameter to `NewMovieController()` specifies where within the window the movie should be placed. When a movie *doesn't* have a controller, it's a call to `OffsetRect()` that shifts the movie to a window's upper left corner. When a movie *does* have a controller, it's the Apple-defined constant `mcTopLeftMovie` that does the trick (see Figure 14-19).

The `mcTopLeftMovie` constant tells
`NewMovie Controller ()` to assemble
the movie/controller in the top left corner
of the movie's window

Figure 14-19

The `NewMovieController()` function creates a controller and shifts it to line up with the movie.

At this point the window that holds the movie (and the controller) is still invisible. So the creating and attaching of a controller won't be observable by the user.

With the movie and controller in place, it's time to resize the window. You'll recall that the initial size of the window is unimportant; it may be smaller or larger than the movie that it will eventually hold. *Without* a movie controller, a call to `SetMovieBox()` sets the movie's bounding rectangle to the rectangle that was shifted to (0, 0). *With* a movie controller, you will rely on the Movie Toolbox routine `MCGetControllerBoundsRect()` to supply your program with the correct size of the movie. Further, if mcTopLeftMovie was used in the call to NewMovieController(), MCGetControllerBoundsRect() will return the movie's dimensions, offset to (0, 0). This is shown in Figure 14-20.

The following snippet calls GetMovieBox() to get the size of a movie. It then passes these dimensions (in variable movieBox) to NewMovieController() to create a properly sized controller and attach that controller to a movie. Finally, a call to MCGetControllerBoundsRect() returns the overall dimensions of both the movie and its now-attached controller:

```
MovieController  gController;
Movie  theMovie;
Rect    movieBox;
Rect    windowRect;
GetMovieBox( theMovie, &movieBox );
gController = NewMovieController( theMovie, &movieBox, mcTopLeftMovie );
MCGetControllerBoundsRect( gController, &windowRect );
```

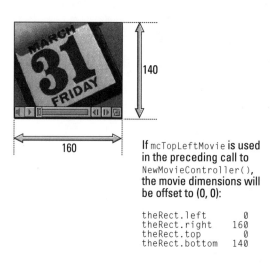

If mcTopLeftMovie is used in the preceding call to NewMovieController(), the movie dimensions will be offset to (0, 0):

```
theRect.left      0
theRect.right    160
theRect.top       0
theRect.bottom   140
```

Figure 14-20
MCGetControllerBoundsRect() returns the size of a movie and its controller.

The call to MCGetControllerBoundsRect() returns a rectangle that holds the size of the movie, including the attached controller. To resize the movie's window, use that rectangle in a call to SizeWindow(). Figure 14-21 illustrates this. Finally, call ShowWindow() to make the window visible.

To resize the window, pass
`SizeWindow()` the `Rect` returned by
`MCGetControllerBoundsRect()`

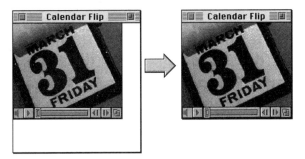

Figure 14-21

SizeWindow() resizes a window to match the size of a movie and its controller.

Earlier in this chapter you saw a version of an application-defined routine named `AdjustMovieWindow()`, which was used for a movie that didn't use a controller. Here is a new version of that function, adapted for use with a movie that does have a controller. The main difference between the two versions of `AdjustMovieWindow()` is that the old version's calls to `OffsetRect()` and `SetMovieBox()` have been replaced by calls to `NewMovieController()` and `MCGetControllerBoundsRect()`:

```
void  AdjustMovieWindow( Movie theMovie, WindowPtr theWindow )
{
   Rect   movieBox;
   Rect   windowRect;

   SetMovieGWorld( theMovie, (CGrafPtr)theWindow, nil );
   GetMovieBox( theMovie, &movieBox );
   gController = NewMovieController( theMovie, &movieBox,
                                     mcTopLeftMovie );
   MCGetControllerBoundsRect( gController, &windowRect );
   SizeWindow( theWindow, windowRect.right, windowRect.bottom, true );
   ShowWindow( theWindow );
}
```

Using a Controller to Play a Movie

To give your program's users the ability to play a movie to which you've attached a controller, you will only need to add a single Movie Toolbox routine to your program. However, you will also have to modify your program's main event loop.

THE OLD MAIN EVENT LOOP

Most Macintosh programs have a main event loop routine that gets called from main(). The program will then remain in the main event loop routine until the program terminates. The following is an abbreviated main() that does just that:

```
void  main( void )
{
    InitializeToolboxes();

    EventLoop();
}
```

The format of the main event loop routine (EventLoop() in this example) is as follows:

- Call WaitNextEvent() to get information about the next event in the event queue.
- Use a switch statement to compare the type of the event with some or all of the Apple-defined event type constants.
- Take action appropriate to the event type.

The following version of EventLoop() handles two types of events (a click of the mouse button and a window update) and complies with the above format:

```
Boolean  gDone = false;
void  EventLoop( void )
{
    EventRecord  theEvent;

    while ( gDone == false )
    {
```

```
         WaitNextEvent( everyEvent, &theEvent, 0, nil );
         switch ( theEvent.what )
         {
            case updateEvt:
               // handle an update event
               break;
            case mouseDown:
               // handle a mouse down event
               break;
            // include a case section for each
            // event type that the program handles
         }
      }
   }
```

MCISPLAYEREVENT() AND THE NEW MAIN EVENT LOOP

If your program is capable of displaying a QuickTime movie with an attached controller, you'll want to slightly modify the program's main event loop so that it can intercept and act upon events that involve a movie controller. Here is a version of EventLoop() that shows, in general terms, how that would be done:

```
void  EventLoop( void )
{
   EventRecord  theEvent;

   while ( gDone == false )
   {
      WaitNextEvent( everyEvent, &theEvent, 0, nil );
      // Pass a controller and the EventRecord to a Movie Toolbox
      // routine for handling. If the event is controller-related,
      // consider it handled and skip the following switch statement.
      // If the event isn't controller-related, execute the switch
      // statement to handle the event in the normal fashion.
      switch ( theEvent.what )
      {
         case updateEvt:
            // handle an update event
            break;
         case mouseDown:
            // handle a mouse down event
            break;
         // include a case section for each
         // event type that the program handles
      }
   }
}
```

The Movie Toolbox routine that handles a controller-related event is
`MCIsPlayerEvent()`. You'll call this routine at each pass through the event
loop. If the event is controller-related, `MCIsPlayerEvent()` will take control
and handle the event. That means that all the handling of mouse clicks on
the Play button, either Step button, the Speaker button, and the controller's
slide bar is taken care of for you — you won't need to write any code to
make a movie controller function properly. Here is a typical call to
`MCIsPlayerEvent()`:

```
EventRecord       theEvent;        // obtained from WaitNextEvent()
MovieController   gController;      // obtained from NewMovieController()
ComponentResult   movieRelatedEvent;
movieRelatedEvent = MCIsPlayerEvent( gController, &theEvent );
```

Many Movie Toolbox routines return a `ComponentResult`. For most
routines, this result is unimportant and can be disregarded.
`MCIsPlayerEvent()` is one of the Movie Toolbox routines that returns a
`ComponentResult` that you'll be interested in. If `MCIsPlayerEvent()` handled
the event that is passed to it, the returned `ComponentResult` will be 1. If
`MCIsPlayerEvent()` didn't handle the event, the `ComponentResult` will be 0.
Your event loop should examine the `ComponentResult` to determine if further
processing of the current event is necessary. A value of 0 means that the
event is not controller-related, and should be handled by traditional means;
that is, by the code in the body of the event loop's `switch` statement. If the
event was already handled by `MCIsPlayerEvent()`, then the `switch` statement
can be skipped. The following version of `EventLoop()` shows how
`MCIsPlayerEvent()` fits into an event loop. The changes from the previous
version of `EventLoop()` appear in bold type:

```
void  EventLoop( void )
{
   EventRecord        theEvent;
   ComponentResult    movieRelatedEvent;
   while ( gDone == false )
   {
      WaitNextEvent( everyEvent, &theEvent, 0, nil );
      movieRelatedEvent = MCIsPlayerEvent( gController, &theEvent );

      if ( movieRelatedEvent == 0 )
      {
         switch ( theEvent.what )
         {
```

```
                case updateEvt:
                   // handle an update event
                   break;
                case mouseDown:
                   // handle a mouse down event
                   break;
                // include a case section for each
                // event type that the program handles
             }
          }
       }
    }
```

CLOSING A MOVIE THAT HAS A CONTROLLER

Earlier you saw how to close a movie. You simply include a call to a Movie Toolbox routine and a call to a Toolbox routine to free the movie memory and the movie window memory:

```
void  CloseOneMovie( Movie theMovie, WindowPtr theWindow )
{
   DisposeMovie( theMovie );
   DisposeWindow( theWindow );
}
```

For a movie that includes a controller, the above rule also applies. However, you will also want to free the memory associated with the controller. Here's the new listing for CloseOneMovie(). Note the order of the function calls; you don't want to dispose of a window before you dispose of its contents, and you don't want to dispose of a movie before you dispose of the controller that is attached to it:

```
void  CloseOneMovie( Movie           theMovie,
                     WindowPtr       theWindow,
                     MovieController theController )
{
   DisposeMovieController( theController );
   DisposeMovie( theMovie );
   DisposeWindow( theWindow );
}
```

Example Program: ControlMovie

When ControlMovie is launched, the standard Open preview file dialog appears on the screen. Selecting a movie from the dialog box list opens that movie, just as it did in the OpenPreviewMovie example. Unlike the OpenPreviewMovie program, however, ControlMovie opens the movie with a controller attached to it, as shown in Figure 14-22. The movie window will be frozen on the screen; clicking on it will have no effect. The movie's controller, however, is functional. Click on the Play button to run the movie, and again to pause it. You can click on either the Step Forward or Step Backward buttons to step through the movie frame-by-frame. If the movie includes sound, the Speaker button will be enabled and you can click on it to adjust the sound volume level. To end the program, press any key on the keyboard.

Figure 14-22
*The ControlMovie program displays a movie
that includes an attached controller.*

RESOURCES FOR CONTROLMOVIE

The ControlMovie project requires just one resource, a WIND in which the movie will be displayed. This is the same resource used by the previous two examples in this chapter.

SOURCE CODE FOR CONTROLMOVIE

To use a movie controller, the user needs to be able to use the mouse button. So unlike the other simple example programs in this chapter, ControlMovie can't get by with just playing a movie and quitting. ControlMovie replaces the call to PlayOneMovie(), which was used in the NoControlMovie example, with a call to the EventLoop() routine developed in this section. Here's the new main() function. This one difference from the main() function found in NoControlMovie is shown in bold type:

```
void  main( void )
{
   WindowPtr  theWindow;
   Movie      theMovie = nil;

   InitializeToolboxes();

   theMovie = GetMovieFromFile();
   if ( theMovie == nil )
      ExitToShell();

   theWindow = GetNewCWindow( 128, nil, (WindowPtr)-1L );

   AdjustMovieWindow( theMovie, theWindow );
   EventLoop();  // replaces PlayOneMovie()

   CloseOneMovie( theMovie, theWindow, gController );
}
```

EventLoop() is similar to the version you saw earlier in this section. The only event type this version watches for is a press of a key. When that happens, the program sets the global variable gDone to true to end the loop and end the program:

```
void  EventLoop( void )
{
   EventRecord      theEvent;
   ComponentResult  movieRelatedEvent;
   while ( gDone == false )
   {
      WaitNextEvent( everyEvent, &theEvent, 0, nil );
      movieRelatedEvent = MCIsPlayerEvent( gController, &theEvent );

      if ( movieRelatedEvent == 0 )
      {
         switch ( theEvent.what )
```

```
            {
                case keyDown:
                    gDone = true;
                    break;
            }
        }
    }
}
```

The remaining functions in ControlMovie are all identical to the versions discussed in this section. If you'd like to see the entire listing, refer to the source code file found on this book's CD.

Movie Controller Actions

When a movie controller is created and attached to a movie, it displays a default action. For instance, clicking on a the controller's Play button causes a movie to play once, from start to finish. By using the Movie Toolbox routine MCDoAction(), you can change many of a controller's actions.

MOVIE ACTIONS AND MCDOACTION()

The Movie Toolbox routine MCDoAction() has three parameters. The first parameter is the movie controller that will be affected. The second parameter is one of several Apple-defined constants that specifies what action is to take place. The final parameter is always a pointer. What it points to depends on the action being taken. The specific looping examples that follow will clarify how this last parameter should appear.

MOVIE LOOPING

To cause a movie to loop continuously, call MCDoAction() with an action of mcActionSetLooping. The third parameter to MCDoAction() should be a pointer to a Boolean value: true if looping is to be turned on for the controller specified in the first parameter, false if looping is to be turned off. Because of the requirement that the last parameter be a pointer, you will need to typecast the Boolean value to a generic Ptr type, as shown in this snippet that turns looping on:

```
MovieController   gController;
MCDoAction( gController, mcActionSetLooping, (Ptr)true );
```

Once looping is turned on, the controller is set to loop. Once the user clicks on the controller's Play button, the movie will continuously play until he or she clicks on the controller's Stop button. Each time the user plays the movie, it will loop until the user stops it. To turn looping off so that the Play button reverts to its default setting of "one press, one play," again call MCDoAction(). Again use the mcActionSetLooping action, but pass a pointer to false:

```
MovieController   gController;
MCDoAction( gController, mcActionSetLooping, (Ptr)false );
```

If your program needs to check to see if looping is turned on or off for a movie controller, pass MCDoAction() an action of mcActionGetLooping. The third parameter should again be a pointer to a Boolean. This time, however, pass in the address of a Boolean variable and let the Movie Toolbox supply the value of true or false to let your program know the current looping status:

```
MovieController   gController;
Boolean           loopOn;
MCDoAction( gController, mcActionGetLooping, &loopingOn );
```

Palindrome looping is a special kind of looping that causes a movie to loop back and forth. When a movie set to normal looping completes its first play, it starts back at the beginning and plays again. When a movie set to palindrome looping completes its first play, it doesn't wrap back to the start. Instead, it plays backwards from the end to the start. To set a movie controller to play a movie in palindrome mode, call MCDoAction() with an action parameter of mcActionSetLoopIsPalindrome. Before making this call, turn looping on by calling MCDoAction() with an action of mcActionSetLooping. Here's how to turn palindrome looping on for one movie:

```
MovieController   gController;
MCDoAction( gController, mcActionSetLooping, (Ptr)true );
MCDoAction( gController, mcActionSetLoopIsPalindrome, (Ptr)true );
```

BY THE WAY

Figure 14-23 hints at another use for `MCDoAction()` — playing movies at different rates. Here is an example that plays a movie at double speed:

```
MCDoAction( gController,
    mcActionPlay, (Ptr)0x00020000 );
```
You'll find details about the `mcAction` play action at the end of this chapter, in the reference section.

A movie controller's looping mode can be set via a menu item. At the top of the Play menu in Figure 14-23 are two looping-related items.

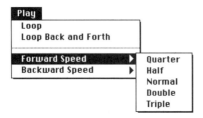

Figure 14-23

Use menu items in conjunction with calls to `MCDoAction()` *to play a movie at different rates.*

The following snippet of code shows how a program should respond to a user selecting **Loop** from the Play menu:

```
#define    mPlay      131    // MENU resource ID of Play menu
#define    iLoop        1    // first item in the Play menu
void  HandlePlayChoice( short theItem )
{
    MenuHandle  playMenuHandle;
    Boolean     loopOn;

    switch ( theItem )
    {
        case iLoop:
            MCDoAction( gController, mcActionGetLoopIsPalindrome, &loopOn );
            playMenuHandle = GetMHandle( mPlay );
            if ( loopOn == true )
            {
                // looping is on, toggle it off and uncheck it
                MCDoAction( gController, mcActionSetLooping, (Ptr)false );
                CheckItem( playMenuHandle, iLoop, false );
```

```
            }
         else
            // looping is off, toggle it on and check it
            MCDoAction( gController, mcActionSetLooping, (Ptr)true );
            CheckItem( playMenuHandle, iLoop, true );
            }
         break;
      // case sections for other Play menu items here
      }
   }
}
```

In the above code `MCDoAction()` is called with the
`mcActionGetLoopIsPalindrome` action to determine the current state of
looping for the `gController` movie controller. If looping is on, `MCDoAction()`
is again called, to turn looping off. The Loop menu item is then unchecked.
If the first call to `MCDoAction()` instead reveals that looping is off, looping is
set to on and the Loop menu item is checked.

Refer to Chapter 6 if you need a refresher on menu handling or adding
a checkmark to a menu.

Example Program: LoopingMovie

When you run the LoopingMovie program, you'll see the standard Open
preview file dialog box. After the selected movie opens, click on the Play
button of its controller. The movie will play continuously until you again
click the Play button to stop it.

The LoopingMovie example is identical to the preceding program,
ControlMovie, with the exception of a single line of code in the program's
`main()` routine. A call to `MCDoAction()` has been added with the action of
`mcActionSetLooping`. Here is the LoopingMovie `main()` routine, with the
single addition appearing in bold type:

```
void  main( void )
{
   WindowPtr   theWindow;
   Movie       theMovie = nil;

   InitializeToolboxes();

   theMovie = GetMovieFromFile();
   if ( theMovie == nil )
      ExitToShell();
```

```
        theWindow = GetNewCWindow( 128, nil, (WindowPtr)-1L );

        AdjustMovieWindow( theMovie, theWindow );
        MCDoAction( gController, mcActionSetLooping, (Ptr)true );
        EventLoop();

        CloseOneMovie( theMovie, theWindow, gController );
    }
```

Working with Multiple Movies

The NoControlMovie program opens a single movie, plays it, and quits. Not a terribly powerful application, but a satisfactory first demonstration of playing a movie. The OpenPreviewMovie application lets the user choose the movie to play — an example of how to implement the standard Open preview file dialog box. The ControlMovie program demonstrates how to attach a controller to a movie. While all of these example programs serve a particular purpose, they are not typical of real-world Macintosh applications. Mac programs usually open more than one window, and often those windows are of different types.

Chapter 7 provides the details of how to implement multiple windows in a single program. If you haven't read that chapter, do so now. Implementing multiple windows is a troubling topic for many programmers, so it warrants further investigation. Because many programs that play QuickTime movies allow several movies to be open at once, now is a good time to reinforce the ideas presented back in Chapter 7.

After referring to this chapter's Reference section, try using other MCDoAction() calls in LoopingMovie. For example, you can play the movie backwards once by replacing the current MCDoAction() call with this call:

```
MCDoAction( gController, mcActionPlay, (Ptr)0xFFFF0000 );
```

WINDOW RECORDS AND WINDOW INFORMATION

In Chapter 7 you saw that a variable of type WindowPtr points to the first field of a WindowRecord: the port field, which is of type GrafPort. You also saw that a variable of type WindowPeek also points to this field. The difference between these two pointer types is not in what they point to, but in how much memory access each is allowed. A variable of type WindowPtr can only access the first field of the WindowRecord, the GrafPort. The GrafPort holds information about the drawing environment of a window, so its information is of the most importance to a programmer. A variable of type WindowPeek can access any and all fields of the WindowRecord, including the GrafPort field. Figure 14-24 (which you saw in Chapter 7) serves as a review of these data types.

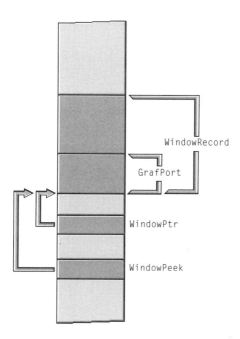

Figure 14-24
A WindowPtr *accesses a* GrafPort, *while a* WindowPeek *accesses a* WindowRecord *(which includes a* GrafPort*).*

Every window has its own WindowRecord, and every window is modeled after information found in that WindowRecord data structure. For all windows, the fields of the WindowRecord data structure are of course the same, though the values of the fields differ. For instance, whether or not a window is visible on the screen is determined by the value (true or false) of the visible field of that window's WindowRecord. If you want to store additional application-specific information about each window in your program, you can create your own type of window pointer that accesses not only a window's GrafPort and the rest of the window's WindowRecord, but also other information that is stored in memory just after the WindowRecord. Figure 14-25, again from Chapter 7, illustrates. Note that the WindowPtr, WindowPeek, GrafPort, and WindowRecord are all Macintosh data types, while the MyWindRecPeek and MyWindRec are application-defined data types.

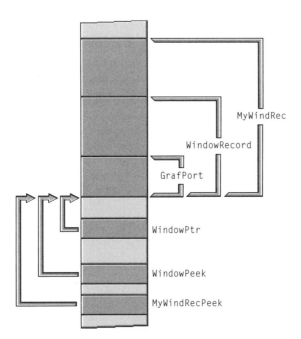

Figure 14-25
Your own application-defined data type, such as MyWindRec, can be used to hold both Apple-defined window data and your application-defined window data.

How is an application-defined data type written so that a pointer to the data type points to a GrafPort, a WindowRecord, and additional data? By defining the data structure such that its first field is a WindowRecord. Because a pointer to a data structure points to the first field of the data structure, a pointer to such an application-defined data type points to a WindowRecord (and, in turn, to the first field of the WindowRecord, its GrafPort). The following is the application-defined data type that will be used in the remainder of this chapter:

```
typedef  struct
{
    WindowRecord      theWindowRecord;
    short             theWindowType;
    Movie             theMovie;
    MovieController   theController;

}  MyWindRec, *MyWindRecPeek;
```

This new structure has a type of MyWindRec, and a pointer type of MyWindRecPeek. Figure 14-26 shows that the Apple-defined WindowPtr and WindowPeek types, as well as the application-defined MyWindRecPeek, all point to the start of the window's GrafPort. A variable of type WindowPtr can access the GrafPort, a variable of type WindowPeek can access both the GrafPort and WindowRecord, and a variable of type MyWindRecPeek can access the entire MyWindRec data structure, including the window's *private data* — the application-defined fields that follow the WindowRecord field (theWindowType, theMovie, and theController).

BY THE WAY

If a program has several types of windows, then the MyWindRec might contain fields for the other types. For instance, if a program opens both a QuickTime movie window and a window that displays a still picture, MyWindRec might also include a PicHandle field to hold a handle to the picture that the picture window uses:

```
typedef  struct
{
    WindowRecord      theWindowRecord;
    short             theWindowType;
    Movie             theMovie;
    MovieController   theController;
    PicHandle         thePicture;

}  MyWindRec, *MyWindRecPeek;
```

QuickTime windows would ignore (or set to nil) the PicHandle field, while picture windows would ignore (or set to nil) the Movie and MovieController fields.

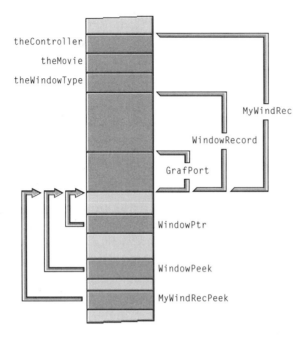

Figure 14-26
Though three data types all point to the same address, each accesses different amounts of memory.

USING THE APPLICATION-DEFINED WINDOW RECORD

To open a window that uses the application-defined window record, rather than an Apple-defined WindowRecord, reserve storage the size of the application-defined window record and use that storage in a call to GetNewCWindow():

```
Ptr        windStorage;
WindowPtr  theWindow;

windStorage = NewPtr( sizeof( MyWindRec ) );
theWindow = GetNewCWindow( 128, windStorage, (WindowPtr)-1L );
```

You'll recall that when you set the second parameter to `GetNewCWindow()` to `nil`, as you typically do in small programs that don't use mulitple window types, the Window Manager reserves the memory for you. When that happens, the Window Manager reserves just enough memory for a `WindowRecord`.

At this point you have a `WindowPtr` that points to the new color window. But you've seen that a `WindowPtr` only allows access to a window's `GrafPort`. To move beyond that field to the application-defined data members, you will need to typecast the `WindowPtr` variable to a `MyWindRecPeek` pointer type. Once you do that, you can access any of the `MyWindRec` fields by dereferencing this cast pointer. In the following snippet, the window's `theWindowType` field — a `short` — is set to 1:

```
MyWindRecPeek  windPeek;
windPeek = ( MyWindRecPeek )theWindow;
windPeek->theWindowType = 1;
```

If a program has different types of windows, it can place a value that identifies the window's type in the `theWindowType` field of the window. Assuming the program can display QuickTime movie windows and another window with a text message in it, then a value of 1 in the `theWindowType` field could mark a window as a QuickTime movie window, and a value of 2 in that field could identify a window as a message window.

Figure 14-27 shows two application-defined window records in memory. A `WindowPtr` variable has been cast to a `MyWindRecPeek` and points to the start of one of the window records. In previous figures memory has been labeled, but no values have been shown in memory. Figure 14-27 also shows a few values. From the figure you can see that because the cast pointer points to a window record that has a `theWindowType` of 1, the pointer points to a window record that represents a QuickTime movie window. Because the `Movie` and `MovieController` data types are pointers, the movie and movie controller fields hold pointers to the window's QuickTime movie and movie controller.

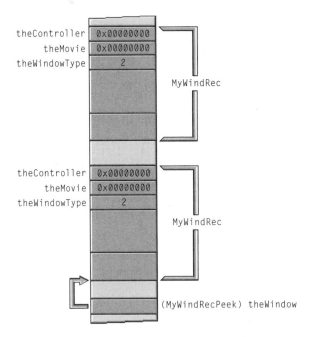

theController   0x00000000
theMovie   0x00000000
theWindowType   2

MyWindRec

theController   0x00000000
theMovie   0x00000000
theWindowType   2

MyWindRec

(MyWindRecPeek) theWindow

Figure 14-27
A WindowPtr *variable, cast to a* MyWindRecPeek *type, points to one of two* MyWindRec *data structures in memory.*

SETTING AND RETRIEVING WINDOW RECORD DATA

In Chapter 7 you saw that two functions should be written for each field of application-defined data in a structure such as MyWindRec. One function sets the value of a field; the other retrieves the current value of that field. For the theWindowType field of MyWindRec, the function to set the fields data would look like the one listed below. The first function requires two parameters — a WindowPtr and a short. The function will typecast the WindowPtr so that the application-defined data can be accessed, then set the theWindowType field to the value of the short parameter:

```
void  SetWindowType( WindowPtr theWindow, short type )
{
   MyWindRecPeek  windPeek;
   windPeek = ( MyWindRecPeek )theWindow;
   windPeek->theWindowType = type;
}
```

To retrieve the current value of theWindowType for a window, pass GetWindowType() a pointer to the window in question. The routine will first typecast the pointer so that the window's private data can be accessed, then it will return the value of the theWindowType field:

```
short  GetWindowType( WindowPtr theWindow )
{
   MyWindRecPeek  windPeek;
   windPeek = ( MyWindRecPeek )theWindow;
   return ( windPeek->theWindowType );
}
```

Knowing a window's type is important in determining how to deal with a window. For instance, a QuickTime movie window and a window that simply displays a text message should be closed in different ways. When the user clicks on a window's close box, your code should determine the type of window, then close it in a way appropriate for that window type. Here's how this section's MoreMovies program handles a mouse-click in the close box of a window:

```
if ( TrackGoAway( whichWindow, theEvent.where ) )
{
   if ( GetWindowType( whichWindow ) == kQuickTimeWindowType )
      CloseOneMovie( whichWindow );
   else
      CloseOneWindow( whichWindow );
}
```

In the above code, the Toolbox routine TrackGoAway() returns a value of true if the mouse button is released while the cursor arrow is over the close box of whichWindow. If that happens, the application-defined function GetWindowType() then determines if whichWindow is a QuickTime movie window or a message window. If the window holds a movie, the application-defined routine CloseOneMovie() is called to dispose of the controller, the movie, and the window. If the window is a message window, a call to a different application-defined routine, CloseOneWindow(), is made.

The above snippet is shown below in the context of the routine it came from, HandleMouseDown(). HandleMouseDown() gets called from the MoreMovies event loop when a mouse click unrelated to a movie controller occurs:

```
void  HandleMouseDown( EventRecord theEvent )

{
   WindowPtr  whichWindow;
   short      thePart;
   thePart = FindWindow( theEvent.where, &whichWindow );
   switch ( thePart )
   {
      case inDrag:
         DragWindow( whichWindow, theEvent.where, &qd.screenBits.bounds );
         break;
      case inGoAway:
         if ( TrackGoAway( whichWindow, theEvent.where ) )
         {
            if ( GetWindowType( whichWindow ) == kQuickTimeWindowType )
               CloseOneMovie( whichWindow );
            else
               CloseOneWindow( whichWindow );
         }
         break;
      case inContent:
         SelectWindow( whichWindow );
         break;
   }
}
```

WINDOWS, MOVIES, CONTROLLERS, AND THE WINDOW RECORD

A program that uses the multiple window scheme presented in this chapter doesn't need to declare global variables to keep track of a movie controller, as the previous example did. The program won't need to keep track of window pointers or movie variables either. Instead, this information can be obtained from the application-defined window record that is associated with each window that opens.

When a new window is to open, your program will reserve a block of memory for it. As you saw a few pages back, this block of memory will be the size of the application-defined window record:

```
Ptr        windStorage;
WindowPtr  theWindow;
```

```
windStorage = NewPtr( sizeof( MyWindRec ) );
theWindow = GetNewCWindow( 128, windStorage, (WindowPtr)-1L );
```

Next, you'll use application-defined routines to set the window's data. Continuing with the preceding example, that means that for a QuickTime window the theWindowType field would be set to 1. Additionally, a QuickTime window would set the window's theMovie and theController fields. When the program opens a movie with the application-defined routine GetMovieFromFile(), it returns a Movie. This is the Movie that should be passed to a function that sets a window record's theMovie field:

```
Movie  theMovie = nil;

theMovie = GetMovieFromFile();
if ( theMovie == nil )
   ExitToShell();
SetWindowMovie( theWindow, theMovie );
```

A movie's controller is created by a call to the Movie Toolbox routine NewMovieController() in the application-defined AdjustMovieWindow() routine. In past examples, a global variable was used for the controller. Here, the variable can be local to AdjustMovieWindow(). Once the controller is created, it can be returned to the routine that called AdjustMovieWindow(). In the MoreMovies example, a routine named OpenQuickTimeMovie() groups together the code for opening a movie, a window, and a controller:

```
void  OpenQuickTimeMovie( void )
{
   Movie            theMovie = nil;
   WindowPtr        theWindow;
   MovieController  theController;
   Ptr              windStorage;

   theMovie = GetMovieFromFile();
   if ( theMovie == nil )
      ExitToShell();

   windStorage = NewPtr( sizeof ( MyWindRec ) );
   theWindow = GetNewCWindow( 128, windStorage, (WindowPtr)-1L );

   theController = AdjustMovieWindow( theMovie, theWindow );
   SetWindowType( theWindow, kQuickTimeWindowType );
   SetWindowMovie( theWindow, theMovie );
   SetWindowController( theWindow, theController );
   ++gNumWindows;
}
```

When a call to OpenQuickTimeMovie() completes, a new movie window, with a controller, will be on the screen. A block of memory will hold the window's type, and pointers to the movie and the controller.

With the potential for several windows to be open at once, how does MoreMovies know which window data to use? By calling GetWindowType().The following snippet shows a part of the MoreMovies routine HandleMouseDown(). When a mouse-click occurs, HandleMouseDown() uses the Toolbox routine FindWindow() to ascertain which window received the click. Once the window is known, its WindowPtr can be passed to any of the program's "get" routines to get any of the window's data. In HandleMouseDown(), the type of movie is obtained with a call to GetWindowType():

```
void  HandleMouseDown( EventRecord theEvent )
{
    WindowPtr   whichWindow;
    short       thePart;
    thePart = FindWindow( theEvent.where, &whichWindow );
    switch ( thePart )
    {
        case inGoAway:
            if ( TrackGoAway( whichWindow, theEvent.where ) )
            {
                if ( GetWindowType( whichWindow ) == kQuickTimeWindowType )
                    CloseOneMovie( whichWindow );
                else
                    CloseOneWindow( whichWindow );
            }
            break;
        // case inDrag, inContent, etc
    }
}
```

Figure 14-28 shows how a Toolbox routine that returns a WindowPtr, as FindWindow() does, can be used to access a window's private data. The returned WindowPtr is passed to one of the application-defined routines that retrieves window data. This routine typecasts the WindowPtr to a MyWindRecPeek pointer, then returns the desired information.

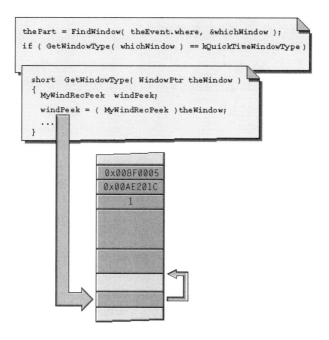

Figure 14-28

A WindowPtr, *once cast to the application-defined window pointer type, can be used to access application-defined window data.*

In the previous snippet you see that if a window's theWindowType is a QuickTime movie window, CloseOneMovie() is called. In previous versions of this routine a window and its movie and controller were all passed as parameters. Now, only the window need be passed. From there, CloseOneMovie() calls "get" routines to get the movie and the controller that are both associated with the window:

```
void  CloseOneMovie( WindowPtr theWindow )
{
   MovieController   theController;
   Movie             theMovie;

   theController = GetWindowController( theWindow );
   theMovie = GetWindowMovie( theWindow );

   DisposeMovieController( theController );
   DisposeMovie( theMovie );
   DisposeWindow( theWindow );
   —gNumWindows;
}
```

Example Program: MoreMovies

MoreMovies is a program that opens three windows: two QuickTime movie windows and one window that displays a line of texts. Figure 14-29 shows the program in action.

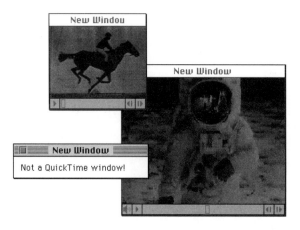

Figure 14-29
The MoreMovies program displays two QuickTime movie windows and one non-QuickTime movie window.

Because QuickTime movies can occupy large amounts of memory, you'll want to increase your application's heap size. In Figure 14-30 you can see that the MoreMovies program will get a preferred heap size of 1MB (1024K) rather than the default size of 384K. This figure shows the Project panel of the CodeWarrior preferences dialog box. If you use a Symantec compiler, you will use the Set Project Type dialog box (see Figure 14-31) to set the partition size.

To keep the code to a minimum, MoreMovies doesn't use menus. Your program will. Look back to Chapter 7 to see the source code listing for an example that makes use of menus and multiple windows.

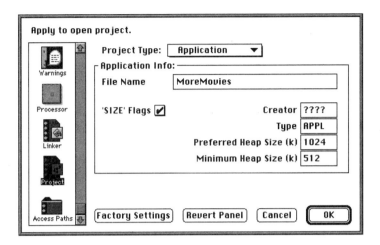

Figure 14-30
Setting the size of the MoreMovies application heap using the Metrowerks CodeWarrior compiler.

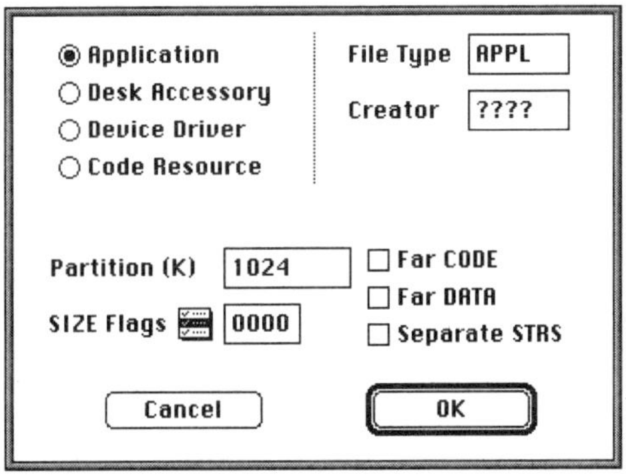

Figure 14-31
Setting the size of the MoreMovies application heap using the Symantec C++/THINK C compiler.

OPENING DIFFERENT TYPES OF WINDOWS

As you know from previous discussion, MoreMovies uses the strategy of using an application-defined data structure to hold information about each window. When a window is opened, memory is reserved for the structure,

and the private window data (the window type, movie, and controller)
values are set. A global variable (gNumWindows) is then incremented so that
the program can keep track of the total number of windows that are on the
screen. To open a QuickTime movie window, MoreMovies uses two
application-defined routines with which you are already familiar:
GetMovieFromFile() and AdjustMovieWindow(). Here is that routine:

```
#define      kQuickTimeWindowType   1
#define      kMessageWindowType     2
void  OpenQuickTimeMovie( void )
{
    Movie            theMovie = nil;
    WindowPtr        theWindow;
    MovieController  theController;
    Ptr              windStorage;

    theMovie = GetMovieFromFile();
    if ( theMovie == nil )
        ExitToShell();

    windStorage = NewPtr( sizeof ( MyWindRec ) );
    theWindow = GetNewCWindow( 128, windStorage, (WindowPtr)-1L );

    theController = AdjustMovieWindow( theMovie, theWindow );
    SetWindowType( theWindow, kQuickTimeWindowType );
    SetWindowMovie( theWindow, theMovie );
    SetWindowController( theWindow, theController );
    ++gNumWindows;
}
```

To open a message window, MoreMovies again reserves memory and
opens a window. Of the three private data fields, only the window type
field is of importance — it's set to a constant that identifies the window as a
message window, while the other two fields are simply set to nil:

```
void  OpenNonQuickTimeWindow( void )
{
    Ptr        windStorage;
    WindowPtr  theWindow;

    windStorage = NewPtr( sizeof ( MyWindRec ) );
    theWindow = GetNewCWindow( 129, windStorage, (WindowPtr)-1L );

    SetWindowType( theWindow, kMessageWindowType );
    SetWindowMovie( theWindow, nil );
    SetWindowController( theWindow, nil );
    ++gNumWindows;
}
```

WINDOW UPDATING

Updating of the text window is handled in the program's event loop:

```
case updateEvt:
   whichWindow = (WindowPtr)theEvent.message;
   BeginUpdate( whichWindow );
      EraseRect( &(whichWindow->portRect) );
      if ( GetWindowType( whichWindow ) == kMessageWindowType )
      {
         SetPort( whichWindow );
         MoveTo( 10, 20 );
         DrawString( "\pNot a QuickTime window!" );
      }
   EndUpdate( whichWindow );
   break;
```

When an update event occurs, MoreMovies checks to see if the window is the text window. If it is, a string is drawn to the window. A more sophisticated program, one that had several types of windows, might handle updating by calling a different application-defined updating routine for each window type:

```
case updateEvt:
   whichWindow = (WindowPtr)theEvent.message;
   BeginUpdate( whichWindow );
      EraseRect( &(whichWindow->portRect) );
      theType = GetWindowType( whichWindow );
      switch ( theType )
      {
         case kMessageWindowType:
            UpdateMessageWindow();
            break;
         case WIND_TYPE_PICT:
            UpdatePictureWindow();
            break;
         case WIND_TYPE_CONTROL:
            UpdateControlWindow();
            break;
      }
   EndUpdate( whichWindow );
   break;
```

Window updating and the BeginUpdate() and EndUpdate() Toolbox routines are discussed in Chapter 7.

Notice that the MoreMovies updateEvt event handling code does not update the QuickTime movie windows. Recall that normal event handling, such as updates and mouse clicks, will only be handled by the event loop if the event is not related to a movie window. If the event *is* QuickTime-related, the Movie Toolbox routine `MCIsPlayerEvent()` handles it. In previous examples you saw `MCIsPlayerEvent()` called from the event loop, as shown here:

```
movieRelatedEvent = MCIsPlayerEvent( gController, &theEvent );
```

`MCIsPlayerEvent()` requires the controller for one movie as a parameter. In a program that allows more than one movie window to be open at a given time, this controller might not be the one that is attached to the movie window that experienced an event. For this reason, the `MCIsPlayerEvent()` routine must be called from the event loop once for every open movie. Because of this requirement, MoreMovies uses a slightly different strategy from that of previous example programs — it calls an application-defined routine to determine how many times to call `MCIsPlayerEvent()`:

```
movieRelatedEvent = HandleOpenMovies( theEvent );
```

`HandleOpenMovies()`, which is shown below, employs a loop to check the window type of every open window. If the window is a QuickTime movie, the movie's controller is obtained and passed to `MCIsPlayerEvent()`. If the window isn't a movie window, it is ignored. If `MCIsPlayerEvent()` is called and returns a value of 1 for the movie it is working with, the event is considered handled and the routine ends. If you imagine the scenario of a user who clicks on the Play button on the controller of the first controller examined in the loop, this technique should make sense. In that case, `MCIsPlayerEvent()` would handle the playing of that movie and the event would be considered handled; there would be no need to call `MCIsPlayerEvent()` for the second movie. If the second movie needs some kind of processing (such as updating), that will be a new event handled by the next pass through the program's event loop.

If every window gets examined in the `HandleOpenMovies()` loop, and if `MCIsPlayerEvent()` returns 0 for all of the movie window controllers, a value of 0 will be returned to the event loop. This tells the event loop that the event was not related to any open movie window, and was thus not handled by `HandleOpenMovies()`. That means the event loop should handle the event using its traditional comparison of the event type to the constants `mouseDown`, `keyDown`, `updateEvt`, and so on:

```
long  HandleOpenMovies( EventRecord theEvent )
{
   int i;
   MovieController    theController;
   WindowPtr          windowFromList;
   WindowPeek         windPeek;
   ComponentResult    eventHandled;

   windowFromList = FrontWindow();
   for (i = 0; i < gNumWindows; i++)
   {
      if ( GetWindowType( windowFromList ) == kQuickTimeWindowType  )
      {
         theController = GetWindowController( windowFromList );
         eventHandled = MCIsPlayerEvent( theController, &theEvent);
         if ( eventHandled == 1 )
            return ( 1 );
      }
      windPeek = ((WindowPeek)windowFromList)->nextWindow;
      windowFromList = (WindowPtr)windPeek;
   }
   return ( 0 );
}
```

One of the fields of the Apple-defined `WindowRecord` data structure is the `nextWindow` field. This field holds a pointer to the next window in the window list. The window list is a list of all open windows in an application, and is maintained by the system; your program normally doesn't have to be concerned with it. Here, `HandleOpenMovies()` relies on this `nextWindow` field of the `WindowRecord` of each window to cycle through every open window. A call to `FrontWindow()` returns a pointer to the foremost window on the screen. After looking at the front window, the window's `WindowPtr` is typecast to a `WindowPeek` so that the window's `nextWindow` field can be accessed. That enables `HandleOpenMovies()` to get a pointer to the next open window. There's more information about the window list back in Chapter 7.

CLOSING DIFFERENT TYPES OF WINDOWS

Just as the handling of more than one open window requires extra effort, so does the closing of multiple windows. The MoreMovies program uses the application-defined routine `CleanUpAndQuit()` to close all open windows and set the global quit flag. `CleanUpAndQuit()` uses a loop in much the same way as HandleOpenMovies(): the front window is first checked, then the window list is used to cycle through every open window. If a window has a theWindowType of 1 (kQuickTimeWindowType), the CloseOneMovie() routine is called to dispose of the controller, movie, and window. If the window's type is 2 (kMessageWindowType), the CloseOneWindow() routine is called to dispose of just the window.

Regardless of a window's type, the gNumWindows variable is decremented by the routine that closes the window. For this reason, the loop test doesn't rely on gNumWindows (as HandleOpenMovies() does) to determine how many iterations to perform. Instead, the number of open windows is saved in the local variable windowsToCheck at the start of the CleanUpAndQuit() routine:

```
void  CleanUpAndQuit( void )
{
    int         i;
    int         windowsToCheck;
    WindowPtr   windowFromList;
    WindowPeek  windPeek;
    WindowPtr   theNextWindow;

    windowsToCheck = gNumWindows;
    windowFromList = FrontWindow();
    for (i = 0; i < windowsToCheck; i++)
    {
        windPeek = ((WindowPeek)windowFromList)->nextWindow;
        theNextWindow = (WindowPtr)windPeek;
        if ( GetWindowType( windowFromList ) == kQuickTimeWindowType )
            CloseOneMovie( windowFromList );
        else
            CloseOneWindow( windowFromList );
        windowFromList = theNextWindow;
    }
    gDone = true;
}
```

TIP If the gDone assignment is removed, CleanUpAndQuit() could become a CloseAllWindows() routine that gets called in response to a Close All menu item in the File menu of a program.

RESOURCES FOR MOREMOVIES

MoreMovies requires two `WIND` resources — one for a QuickTime movie and another for a text, or message, window (see Figure 14-32). A call to `GetNewCWindow()`, with a `WIND` resource ID of 128, will be used for QuickTime movies:

```
theWindow = GetNewCWindow( 128, windStorage, (WindowPtr)-1L );
```

To open a non-QuickTime movie, `GetNewCWindow()` will be called again, this time with a `WIND` resource ID of 129:

```
theWindow = GetNewCWindow( 129, windStorage, (WindowPtr)-1L );
```

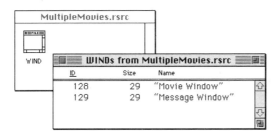

Figure 14-32
MoreMovies uses two `WIND` resources, one for each type of window.

SOURCE CODE FOR MOREMOVIES

Because MoreMovies has several routines new to this chapter, the entire source code listing is provided here:

```
//_____
#include <Movies.h>
//_____
void            InitializeToolboxes( void );
void            EventLoop( void );
void            HandleMouseDown( EventRecord );
void            OpenQuickTimeMovie( void );
Movie           GetMovieFromFile( void );
MovieController AdjustMovieWindow( Movie, WindowPtr );
long            HandleOpenMovies( EventRecord );
void            CloseOneMovie( WindowPtr );
void            OpenNonQuickTimeWindow( void );
void            CloseOneWindow( WindowPtr );
```

```
void            SetWindowType( WindowPtr, short );
void            SetWindowMovie( WindowPtr, Movie );
void            SetWindowController( WindowPtr, MovieController );
short           GetWindowType( WindowPtr );
Movie           GetWindowMovie( WindowPtr );
MovieController GetWindowController( WindowPtr );
void            CleanUpAndQuit( void );
//_____
#define   kQuickTimeWindowType      1
#define   kMessageWindowType        2
//_____
typedef   struct
{
   WindowRecord      theWindowRecord;
   short             theWindowType;
   Movie             theMovie;
   MovieController   theController;

} MyWindRec, *MyWindRecPeek;
//_____
Boolean   gDone = false;
short     gNumWindows = 0;
//_____
void  main( void )
{
   InitializeToolboxes();
   OpenQuickTimeMovie();
   OpenQuickTimeMovie();

   OpenNonQuickTimeWindow();

   EventLoop();
}
//_____
void  InitializeToolboxes( void )
{
   OSErr   theError;
   long    theResult;
   InitGraf( &qd.thePort );
   InitFonts();
   InitWindows();
   InitMenus();
   TEInit();
   InitDialogs( 0L );
   FlushEvents( everyEvent, 0 );
   InitCursor();
   theError = Gestalt( gestaltQuickTime, &theResult );
   if ( theError != noErr )
     ExitToShell();

   theError = EnterMovies();
   if ( theError != noErr )
     ExitToShell();
```

```
   }
//_____
void  EventLoop( void )
{
   EventRecord   theEvent;
   long          movieRelatedEvent;
   WindowPtr     whichWindow;
   while ( gDone == false )
   {
      WaitNextEvent( everyEvent, &theEvent, 0, nil );
      movieRelatedEvent = HandleOpenMovies( theEvent );

      if ( movieRelatedEvent == false )
      {
         switch ( theEvent.what )
        {
           case updateEvt:
               whichWindow = (WindowPtr)theEvent.message;
               BeginUpdate( whichWindow );
                  EraseRect( &(whichWindow->portRect) );
                  if ( GetWindowType( whichWindow ) == kMessageWindowType )
                  {
                     SetPort( whichWindow );
                     MoveTo( 10, 20 );
                     DrawString( "\pNot a QuickTime window!" );
                  }
               EndUpdate( whichWindow );
               break;
            case mouseDown:
               HandleMouseDown( theEvent );
               break;
            case keyDown:
               CleanUpAndQuit();
               break;
        }
      }
   }
}
//_____
void  HandleMouseDown( EventRecord theEvent )
{
   WindowPtr  whichWindow;
   short      thePart;
   thePart = FindWindow( theEvent.where, &whichWindow );
   switch ( thePart )
   {
      case inDrag:
         DragWindow( whichWindow, theEvent.where, &qd.screenBits.bounds );
         break;
      case inGoAway:
         if ( TrackGoAway( whichWindow, theEvent.where ) )
         {
```

```
                    if ( GetWindowType( whichWindow ) == kQuickTimeWindowType )
                        CloseOneMovie( whichWindow );
                    else
                        CloseOneWindow( whichWindow );
                }
                break;
            case inContent:
                SelectWindow( whichWindow );
                break;
        }
    }
}
//_____
void  OpenQuickTimeMovie( void )
{
    Movie             theMovie = nil;
    WindowPtr         theWindow;
    MovieController   theController;
    Ptr               windStorage;

    theMovie = GetMovieFromFile();
    if ( theMovie == nil )
        ExitToShell();

    windStorage = NewPtr( sizeof ( MyWindRec ) );
    theWindow = GetNewCWindow( 128, windStorage, (WindowPtr)-1L );

    theController = AdjustMovieWindow( theMovie, theWindow );
    SetWindowType( theWindow, kQuickTimeWindowType );
    SetWindowMovie( theWindow, theMovie );
    SetWindowController( theWindow, theController );
    ++gNumWindows;
}
//_____
Movie  GetMovieFromFile( void )
{
    OSErr             theError;
    SFTypeList        typeList = { MovieFileType, 0, 0, 0 };
    StandardFileReply theReply;
    Movie             getMovie = nil;
    short             moovRefNum;
    short             moovResID = 0;
    Str255            movieName;
    Boolean           wasChanged;
    StandardGetFilePreview( nil, 1, typeList, &theReply );
    if ( theReply.sfGood == true )
    {
        theError = OpenMovieFile( &theReply.sfFile, &moovRefNum, fsRdPerm );
        if ( theError == noErr )
        {
            theError = NewMovieFromFile( &getMovie, moovRefNum,
                                         &moovResID, movieName,
                                         newMovieActive, &wasChanged );
            CloseMovieFile( moovRefNum );
        }
```

```
   }
   return ( getMovie );
}
//_____
MovieController  AdjustMovieWindow( Movie theMovie, WindowPtr theWindow )
{
   Rect            movieBox;
   Rect            windowRect;
   MovieController theController;

   SetMovieGWorld( theMovie, (CGrafPtr)theWindow, nil );
   GetMovieBox( theMovie, &movieBox );
   theController = NewMovieController( theMovie, &movieBox,
                                       mcTopLeftMovie );
   MCGetControllerBoundsRect( theController, &windowRect );
   SizeWindow( theWindow, windowRect.right, windowRect.bottom, true );
   ShowWindow( theWindow );

   return ( theController );
}
//_____
long  HandleOpenMovies( EventRecord theEvent )
{
   int i;
   MovieController theController;
   WindowPtr       windowFromList;
   WindowPeek      windPeek;
   ComponentResult eventHandled;

   windowFromList = FrontWindow();
   for (i = 0; i < gNumWindows; i++)
   {
      if ( GetWindowType( windowFromList ) == kQuickTimeWindowType )
      {
         theController = GetWindowController( windowFromList );
         eventHandled = MCIsPlayerEvent( theController, &theEvent);
         if ( eventHandled == 1 )
           return ( 1 );
         }
         windPeek = ((WindowPeek)windowFromList)->nextWindow;
         windowFromList = (WindowPtr)windPeek;
   }
      return ( 0 );
}
//_____
void  CloseOneMovie( WindowPtr theWindow )
{
   MovieController theController;
   Movie           theMovie;

   theController = GetWindowController( theWindow );
   theMovie = GetWindowMovie( theWindow );
```

```
      DisposeMovieController( theController );
      DisposeMovie( theMovie );
      DisposeWindow( theWindow );

      -gNumWindows;
}
//_____
void  OpenNonQuickTimeWindow( void )
{
   Ptr        windStorage;
   WindowPtr  theWindow;

   windStorage = NewPtr( sizeof ( MyWindRec ) );
   theWindow = GetNewCWindow( 129, windStorage, (WindowPtr)-1L );

   SetWindowType( theWindow, kMessageWindowType );
   SetWindowMovie( theWindow, nil );
   SetWindowController( theWindow, nil );
   ++gNumWindows;
}
//_____
void  CloseOneWindow( WindowPtr theWindow )
{
   DisposeWindow( theWindow );

   -gNumWindows;
}
//_____
void  SetWindowType( WindowPtr theWindow, short type )
{
   MyWindRecPeek  windPeek;
   windPeek = ( MyWindRecPeek )theWindow;
   windPeek->theWindowType = type;
}
//_____
void  SetWindowMovie( WindowPtr theWindow, Movie theMovie )
{
   MyWindRecPeek  windPeek;
   windPeek = ( MyWindRecPeek )theWindow;
   windPeek->theMovie = theMovie;
}
//_____
void  SetWindowController( WindowPtr theWindow, MovieController theController
     )
{
   MyWindRecPeek  windPeek;
   windPeek = ( MyWindRecPeek )theWindow;
   windPeek->theController = theController;
}
//_____
short  GetWindowType( WindowPtr theWindow )
{
```

```
    MyWindRecPeek  windPeek;
    windPeek = ( MyWindRecPeek )theWindow;
    return ( windPeek->theWindowType );
}
//_____
Movie  GetWindowMovie( WindowPtr theWindow )
{
    MyWindRecPeek  windPeek;
    windPeek = ( MyWindRecPeek )theWindow;
    return ( windPeek->theMovie );
}
//_____
MovieController  GetWindowController( WindowPtr theWindow )
{
    MyWindRccPeek  windPeek;
    windPeek = ( MyWindRecPeek )theWindow;
    return ( windPeek->theController );
}
//_____
void  CleanUpAndQuit( void )
{
    int        i;
    int        windowsToCheck;
    WindowPtr  windowFromList;
    WindowPeek windPeek;
    WindowPtr  theNextWindow;

    windowsToCheck = gNumWindows;
    windowFromList = FrontWindow();
    for (i = 0; i < windowsToCheck; i++)
    {
        windPeek = ((WindowPeek)windowFromList)->nextWindow;
        theNextWindow = (WindowPtr)windPeek;
        if ( GetWindowType( windowFromList ) == kQuickTimeWindowType )
            CloseOneMovie( windowFromList );
        else
            CloseOneWindow( windowFromList );
        windowFromList = theNextWindow;
    }
    gDone = true;
}
```

TURNING MOREMOVIES INTO A FULL-FEATURED PROGRAM

If you added menus and combined the multiple movie handling techniques
from this section with this chapter's movie-playing code, you could turn
MoreMovies into a full-featured movie viewing program. Table 14-1 lists
several menu commands that could appear in the program. Next to each

command is the name of a routine that's included in the chapter, which you can use (sometimes with sight modification) to implement the command. The table also includes the name of the chapter section where you'll find a discussion of each routine.

Table 14-1

Suggested Menu Commands for the MoreMovies program

Menu	Command	Routine to Use	Chapter Section
File	Open Movie...	OpenQuickTimeMovie()	Example Program: MoreMovies
	Open Text	OpenMessageWindow()	Example Program: MoreMovies
	Close	HandleMouseDown()	Example Program: MoreMovies
	Close All	CleanUpAndQuit()	MoreMovies program
Play	Loop	HandlePlayChoice()	Movie Looping
	Palindrome	HandlePlayChoice()	Movie Looping
	Play Double	MCDoAction()	QuickTime Reference
	Play Backwards	MCDoAction()	QuickTime Reference

QuickTime Reference

Any function that is a part of the original Macintosh Toolbox is prefaced by the word *Toolbox*, while any function that is a part of the new Movie Toolbox is prefaced *Movie Toolbox*. If you need to refer to other texts for more information on a function, this information may help you narrow your search.

INITIALIZING THE MOVIE TOOLBOX

Don't make the assumption that all users who try your program have QuickTime installed on their Macintosh.

Gestalt( )

Before using any Movie Toolbox functions, call the Toolbox function
Gestalt() with a selector code of gestaltQuickTime to verify that the
user has QuickTime installed. If theError equals noErr, assume
QuickTime is present:

```
#include <Gestalt.h>
OSErr   theError;
long    theResult;

theError = Gestalt( gestaltQuickTime, &theResult );
```

If interested in the version of QuickTime that the user has, check the
value of theResult. The version number will be returned as a hexadecimal
value. The second, third, and fourth digits hold the version, and the last four
digits will be 8000. Here are a few examples:

- For QuickTime version 1.5:   theResult will be: 0x01508000
- For QuickTime version 1.6.1: theResult will be: 0x01618000
- For QuickTime version 2.0:   theResult will be: 0x02008000

EnterMovies( )

Before calling any other Movie Toolbox routine, call the Movie Toolbox
routine EnterMovies() once to initialize the Movie Toolbox. If theError
equals noErr, your program may use the Movie Toolbox:

```
#include <Movies.h>
OSErr   theError;
theError = EnterMovies();
```

LOADING A MOVIE INTO MEMORY

After opening a QuickTime movie file, load the file's movie into memory in
preparation for playing.

FSMakeFSSpec( )

Some Movie Toolbox functions need to know where on disk a movie file is located. This path must be provided in the form of an FSSpec variable. To create an FSSpec for a movie that has both a file name and path that are known in advance, call the Toolbox function FSMakeFSSpec():

```
OSErr    theError;
short    volRefNum = 0;
long     dirID = 0;
Str255   movieFileName = "\pFlying Fish";
FSSpec   MooVFSSpec;
theError = FSMakeFSSpec( volRefNum, dirID,
                         movieFileName, &MooVFSSpec );
```

A volume reference number of 0 indicates that the file is on the startup hard drive. A parent directory ID of 0 indicates that the file is in the same folder as the application. The movie file name, Flying Fish, is the QuickTime movie file name as it appears in the Finder. FSMakeFSSpec() fills in the fields of the last parameter. Use this last parameter in subsequent Movie Toolbox functions that require an FSSpec.

To create an FSSpec for a movie that is selected by the user, call the Toolbox routine StandardGetFilePreview() rather than FSMakeFSSpec().

StandardGetFilePreview( )

The Movie Toolbox routine StandardGetFilePreview() displays the standard Open preview file dialog box that lets the user open a movie:

```
SFTypeList           typeList = { MovieFileType, 0, 0, 0 };
StandardFileReply    theReply;
FileFilterProcPtr    procPtr = nil;
short                numFileTypes = 1;
StandardGetFilePreview( procPtr, numFileTypes, typeList, &theReply );
```

The first parameter is used only if you want the standard file dialog box to display more than four types of files. To display one file type, pass 1 as the second parameter. The typeList variable defines up to four file types to display; you'll only display one type (movie files, designated by the Apple-defined constant MovieFileType). The last parameter is filled in by the Toolbox after the user selects a movie from the standard Open dialog box. The sfFile field of the StandardFileReply variable theReply is of type

FSSpec. After the user selects a movie, the sfFile field will hold the FSSpec of the movie. Use theReply.sfFile in subsequent Movie Toolbox functions that require an FSSpec.

OpenMovieFile( )

Before playing a movie you must call the Movie Toolbox function OpenMovieFile( ) to open the QuickTime movie file that holds the movie:

```
OSErr    theError;
FSSpec   MooVFSSpec;
short    moovRefNum;

theError = OpenMovieFile( &MooVFSSpec, &moovRefNum, fsRdPerm );
```

Pass OpenMovieFile( ) the movie file's FSSpec that was obtained from either a call to FSMakeFSSpec( ) or a call to StandardGetFilePreview( ). Use one of three Apple-defined constants (fsRdPerm, fsWrPerm, fsRdWrPerm) to define the user's level of movie interaction: read (play), write (alter), or both. OpenMovieFile( ) will return a movie resource reference number that will be used in subsequent Movie Toolbox routines. If theError has any value other than noErr, the attempt to open the movie file failed.

NewMovieFromFile( )

After opening a movie file, call the Movie Toolbox function NewMovieFromFile( ) to load the movie into memory:

```
OSErr    theError;
Movie    theMovie = nil;
short    moovRefNum;
short    moovResID = 0;
Str255   movieName;
Boolean  wasChanged;

theError = NewMovieFromFile( &theMovie, moovRefNum,
                             &moovResID, movieName,
                             newMovieActive, &wasChanged );
```

When supplied a movie resource reference number (obtained from a call to OpenMovieFile( )), NewMovieFromFile( ) loads the file's movie into memory and returns a Movie — a pointer to the memory that holds the movie. To use the first (and usually the only) movie in a movie file, set the `moovResID` to 0. Pass the Apple-defined constant `newMovieActive` to activate the movie. `NewMovieFromFile()` will return the name of the movie (the name of the `moov` resource) and a `Boolean` value that tells whether the Movie Toolbox had to change any data as it was loaded. If the attempt to load the movie fails, `theError` will have a value other than `noErr`.

CloseMovieFile( )

After opening a movie file and loading its movie into memory, you can close the file with a call to the Movie Toolbox function `CloseMovieFile()`. The `moov` resource reference number that is this routine's only parameter was obtained in a call to OpenMovieFile():

```
short   moovRefNum;
CloseMovieFile( moovRefNum );
```

DISPLAYING A MOVIE IN A WINDOW

Once a QuickTime file has been opened and its movie loaded into memory, create a window in which to display the movie.

GetNewCWindow( )

A movie is displayed in a standard color window. You can use a `WIND` resource and a call to the Toolbox routine `GetNewCWindow()` to create this window. The size of the window is unimportant; it will be altered before the movie is placed in it. Be sure to set the window to invisible so that user doesn't see the resizing of the window:

```
#define    rMovieWindow    128
WindowPtr  theWindow;
Ptr        windStorage = nil;
theWindow = GetNewCWindow( rMovieWindow, windStorage, (WindowPtr)-1L );
```

Pass `GetNewCWindow()` the resource ID of the `WIND` resource that holds the window information. Pass a `nil` pointer to let the Toolbox allocate memory for the window (as opposed to your supplying a pointer to a memory block). Type cast -1L to a `WindowPtr` as the last parameter to tell the Toolbox to place the window in front of all others.

If your program displays more than one window at a time, you may want to create a data structure that holds a `WindowRecord` and additional application-specific window information. If you do, then you will make use of the second parameter to `GetNewCWindow()`. The following snippet defines a data structure, then creates a window pointer that points to a block of memory the size of this structure:

```
typedef  struct
{
    WindowRecord    theWindowRecord;
    short           theWindowType;
    PicHandle       thePicture;
    Str255          theString;

} MyWindRec, *MyWindRecPeek;
#define    rMovieWindow    128
Ptr        windStorage;
WindowPtr  theWindow;

windStorage = NewPtr( sizeof( MyWindRec ) );
theWindow = GetNewCWindow( rMovieWindow, windStorage, (WindowPtr)-1L );
```

GetMovieBox( )

Before displaying a movie in a window, resize the window to match the dimensions of the movie. To get the size of the movie, call the Movie Toolbox routine `GetMovieBox()`:

```
Movie  theMovie;
Rect   movieBox;

GetMovieBox( theMovie, &movieBox );
```

The `Movie` variable should be obtained from a call to `NewMovieFromFile()`. After calling `GetMovieBox()`, the `Rect` variable will hold the boundaries of the movie. Because the movie coordinates are not guaranteed to start at the point (0, 0), as desired, follow the call to `GetMovieBox()` with calls to `OffsetRect()` and `SetMovieBox()`.

OffsetRect()

Before displaying a movie in a window, resize the window to match the dimensions of the movie. First call the Movie Toolbox function `GetMovieBox()` to obtain a `Rect` that holds the movie's boundaries. Then call the Toolbox routine `OffsetRect()` to reposition this rectangle to the (0, 0) coordinate:

```
Rect  movieBox;
OffsetRect( &movieBox, -movieBox.left, -movieBox.top );
```

The `Rect` variable comes from a call to the Movie Toolbox routine `GetMovieBox()`. Because the movie coordinates are not guaranteed to start at the point (0, 0), as desired, follow the call to the Movie Toolbox routine `GetMovieBox()` and the Toolbox function `OffsetRect()` with a call to the Movie Toolbox function `SetMovieBox()`.

SetMovieBox()

Before displaying a movie in a window, resize the window to match the dimensions of the movie. First call the Movie Toolbox routine `GetMovieBox()` to obtain a `Rect` that holds the movie's boundaries. Then call the Toolbox function `OffsetRect()` to reposition this rectangle to the (0, 0) coordinate. Finally, set the movie coordinates to the shifted values by calling the Movie Toolbox routine `SetMovieBox()`:

```
Movie  theMovie;
Rect   movieBox;
SetMovieBox( theMovie, &movieBox );
```

The `Movie` variable should be obtained from a call to the Movie Toolbox function `NewMovieFromFile()`. The `Rect` variable initially comes from a call to the Movie Toolbox routine `GetMovieBox()`. Before calling `SetMovieBox()`, the `Rect` variable's coordinates are shifted using a call to the Toolbox function `OffsetRect()`.

SizeWindow()

After adjusting the size of the movie box, call the Toolbox function `SizeWindow()` to set the display window to the same size as the movie:

```
WindowPtr   theWindow;
Rect        movieBox;
Boolean     updateFlag = true;
SizeWindow( theWindow, movieBox.right, movieBox.bottom, updateFlag );
ShowWindow( theWindow );
```

The `WindowPtr` variable was obtained from a call to Toolbox function `GetNewCWindow()`. The `Rect` variable was initially obtained from a call to the Movie Toolbox function `GetMovieBox()`. Before its use here, the `Rect` variable was shifted to the origin using a call to the Toolbox routine `OffsetRect()`. The last parameter to `SizeWindow()` indicates whether any new area that was added to the window (if `SizeWindow()` enlarges the window) should be updated. Typically this should be set to `true`. Follow the call to `SizeWindow()` with a call to the Toolbox function `ShowWindow()`.

ShowWindow( )

After adjusting the size of the window that will display the movie, make the window visible by calling the Toolbox function `ShowWindow()`:

```
WindowPtr   theWindow;
ShowWindow( theWindow );
```

SetMovieGWorld( )

After creating a movie and opening and sizing a window, establish the movie's display coordinate system by setting the graphics world:

```
Movie       theMovie;
WindowPtr   theWindow;
GDHandle    graphicsDeviceH = nil;
SetMovieGWorld( theMovie, (CGrafPtr)theWindow, graphicsDeviceH );
```

The first parameter is the movie to work with. The second parameter should be a pointer to either a graphics port, a color graphics port, or a graphics world. The last parameter is a handle to the movie's graphics device structure. A value of `nil` results in the current device being used.

PLAYING A MOVIE

With a movie loaded in memory and a window opened and sized to match the movie dimensions, play the movie.

GoToBeginningOfMovie()

When a movie is loaded into memory, it may or may not be set to begin play at its first frame. To ensure that the movie will in fact begin at the beginning, call the Movie Toolbox routine GoToBeginningOfMovie():

```
Movie  theMovie;
GoToBeginningOfMovie( theMovie );
```

StartMovie()

Contrary to its name, the Movie Toolbox routine StartMovie() doesn't start a movie playing. Instead, it prepares for the start by making the movie active (if it isn't already) and setting the movie's playback rate:

```
Movie  theMovie;
StartMovie( theMovie );
```

MoviesTask()

To play a movie, call the Movie Toolbox routine MoviesTask(). This function services a movie; that is, it updates the display of the movie:

```
Movie  theMovie;
long   maxMillisecondUpdate = 0;
MoviesTask( theMovie, maxMillisecondUpdate );
```

The first parameter to MoviesTask() is the movie to update. The second parameter is the amount of time (in milliseconds) the Movie Toolbox will be given to service the movie. Passing a value of 0 for this parameter tells the Movie Toolbox to update the movie completely, regardless of how much time it takes. The MoviesTask() function must be called repeatedly until the movie has finished playing. To do this, embed a call to MoviesTask() within a loop. End the loop when the movie has completed. The Movie Toolbox routine IsMovieDone(), discussed next, will indicate to your program when the movie has finished playing.

```
do
{
    MoviesTask( theMovie, 0 );
}
while ( IsMovieDone( theMovie ) == false );
```

IsMovieDone( )

To check to see if a playing movie is done, call the Movie Toolbox routine
IsMovieDone(). When passed a movie, this routine returns a value of true if
the movie has completed, false if it has not. This function is typically used
to determine when to stop calling the Movie Toolbox function
MoviesTask(), as shown in the following loop:

```
Movie   theMovie;
do
{
    MoviesTask( theMovie, 0 );
}
while ( IsMovieDone( theMovie ) == false );
```

CLOSING A MOVIE

When the user closes the window that holds a movie, clean up by releasing
the memory occupied by both the movie and the window.

DisposeMovie( )

To free the memory that holds a movie, call the Movie Toolbox routine
DisposeMovie(). Because you'll want to free the memory occupied by
something *in* a window before releasing the memory *of* the window, call
this function before calling the Toolbox routine DisposeWindow().
DisposeWindow(), described next, frees the memory occupied by a window.

```
MovieController   theController
Movie             theMovie;
WindowPtr         theWindow;
DisposeMovieController( theController );
DisposeMovie( theMovie );
DisposeWindow( theWindow );
```

DisposeWindow( )

To free the memory that holds a window, call the Toolbox routine
`DisposeWindow()`. If the window holds a movie controller, call
`DisposeMovieController()` first. If the window has a movie, then call
`DisposeMovie()` to release the memory that holds the window's movie.
Finally, call `DisposeWindow()` to release the window memory:

```
MovieController   theController
Movie             theMovie;
WindowPtr         theWindow;
DisposeMovieController( theController );
DisposeMovie( theMovie );
DisposeWindow( theWindow );
```

MOVIE CONTROLLERS

To give the user the power to work with a movie, attach a movie controller
to the movie.

NewMovieController( )

The Movie Toolbox routine `NewMovieController()` creates a new movie
controller component and attaches it to a movie. The height of a standard
movie controller is always the same — 16 pixels. The controller's width is
dependent upon the size of the movie it is attached to. To determine the
width of the controller, call `GetMovieBox()` to get the width of the movie:

```
MovieController   theController;
Movie             theMovie;
Rect              movieBox;
long              sizeFlag = mcTopLeftMovie;
GetMovieBox( theMovie, &movieBox );
theController = NewMovieController( theMovie, &movieBox, sizeFlag );
```

The first parameter to `NewMovieController()` is the movie that the
controller is to attach to. The second parameter is a `Rect` that is used by the
Movie Toolbox to determine the width of the controller. The final parameter
is a constant that tells the Movie Toolbox where in the window the movie
(and the controller) should be placed. Generally you'll want to place the top
left corner of the movie in the top left corner of the window; that's what the
Apple-defined constant `mcTopLeftMovie` does.

To create a movie that is of a size other than its original size, use the Apple-defined constant `mcScaleToFit` in place of `mcTopLeftMovie`. If you set a `Rect` to a size other than the dimensions of `movieBox`, then pass `NewMovieController()` this `Rect` as the second parameter and `mcScaleToFit` as the third parameter; the Movie Toolbox will scale the movie to fit this new rectangle.

MCGetControllerBoundsRect( )

The Movie Toolbox routine `MCGetControllerBoundsRect()` returns a rectangle that holds the dimensions of a movie and its attached controller. To properly resize the movie's window, use the rectangle returned by this routine in a call to `SizeWindow()`:

```
MovieController   theController;
Rect              windowRect;
WindowPtr         theWindow;
ComponentResult   compResult;
Boolean           updateFlag = true;
compResult = MCGetControllerBoundsRect( theController, &windowRect );
SizeWindow( theWindow, windowRect.right, windowRect.bottom, updateFlag );
```

MCIsPlayerEvent( )

Call the Movie Toolbox routine `MCIsPlayerEvent()` at each pass through your program's event loop. At each pass, call this routine once for each open movie that has an attached controller. `MCIsPlayerEvent()` will handle a mouse-click on any of the buttons of a movie controller:

```
EventRecord       theEvent;
MovieController   theController;
ComponentResult   compResult;
compResult = MCIsPlayerEvent( theController, &theEvent );
```

The first parameter is the movie controller that the second parameter may effect. If the event held in `theEvent` is controller-related and is handled by `MCIsPlayerEvent()`, the function will return a `compResult` value of 1. The remainder of the current pass through your program's event loop should then be skipped. If the event turns out to be unrelated to the controller, `compResult` will have a value of 0 and your program should execute the remainder of the current pass through the event loop.

DisposeMovieController( )

Call the Movie Toolbox routine `DisposeMovieController()` when the
window that holds a movie and its attached movie controller is to be closed.
Follow the call with calls to the Movie Toolbox routines `DisposeMovie()` and
`DisposeWindow()`:

```
MovieController  theController
Movie            theMovie;
WindowPtr        theWindow;
DisposeMovieController( theController );
DisposeMovie( theMovie );
DisposeWindow( theWindow );
```

MCDoAction( )

The Movie Toolbox routine `MCDoAction()` changes the properties of a movie
controller. For instance, this function can set a controller to play a movie in
normal or looping mode:

```
MovieController  theController;
short            theAction = mcActionSetLooping;
MCDoAction( theController, theAction, (Ptr)true );
```

The first parameter to `MCDoAction()` is the movie controller that will be
effected. The second parameter is one of several Apple-defined constants
that specifies what action is to take place. The final parameter varies, but it
is always typecast to a generic pointer.

Action constants

This section describes some of the action constants. Each constant includes
a description and an example function call.

mcActionSetLooping

This constant turns looping on if the third parameter to `MCDoAction()`is `true`,
off if `false`. Calling `MCDoAction()`with this constant does not play the movie.
Looping goes into effect the next time the user clicks the Play button and
remains in effect until `MCDoAction()` is again called — this time with
`(Ptr)false` passed to it:

```
Boolean loopOn = true;
MCDoAction( theController, mcActionSetLooping, (Ptr)loopOn );
```

mcActionGetLooping

This constant tells your program if looping is currently on or off. If looping is on, the Movie Toolbox will set `loopOn` to `true`. If looping is off, `loopOn` will be set to `false`:

```
Boolean  loopOn;
MCDoAction( theController, mcActionGetLooping, (Ptr)loopOn );
```

mcActionSetLoopIsPalindrome

This constant turns palindrome looping on if the third parameter to `MCDoAction` is `true`, off if `false`. A call to `MCDoAction()` with this constant does not play the movie. Looping goes into effect the next time the user clicks the Play button and remains in effect until `MCDoAction()` is again called, this time with `(Ptr)false` passed to it. For this action to work, looping must first be turned on. Therefore you must make sure that the call to `MCDoAction()` with the `mcActionSetLoopIsPalindrome` action is preceded by a call to `MCDoAction()` with the action `mcActionSetLooping`:

```
Boolean  palLoopOn = true;
MCDoAction( theController, mcActionSetLoopIsPalindrome, (Ptr)palLoopOn );
```

mcActionGetLoopIsPalindrome

This constant tells your program if palindrome looping is currently on or off. If on, the Movie Toolbox will set `palLoopOn` to `true`. If off, it will be set to `false`:

```
Boolean  palLoopOn;
MCDoAction( theController, mcActionGetLoopIsPalindrome, &palLoopOn );
```

mcActionPlay

This constant sets the rate of play for a movie and then plays the movie. After the movie has ended, the rate returns to normal speed. The third parameter to `MCDoAction()` is a fixed point number that holds the play rate. If you are not familiar with fixed points, use one of the values in Table 14-2 to set the play rate.

Table 14-2

Fixed point values and their corresponding play rates

Play Rate	Parameter Value
forward, one-eighth speed	0x00002000
forward, one-quarter speed	0x00004000
forward, one-half speed	0x00008000
forward, normal speed	0x00010000
forward, double speed	0x00020000
forward, triple speed	0x00030000
forward, quadruple speed	0x00040000
backwards, one-half speed	0xFFFF8000
backwards, normal speed	0xFFFF0000
backwards, double speed	0xFFFE0000

For example:

```
Fixed  playRate = 0x00020000;  // play movie once at double speed
MCDoAction( theController, mcActionPlay, (Ptr)playRate );
```

MCGetMovie( )

To retrieve a Movie from a movie controller, call the Movie Toolbox routine
MCGetMovie(). Pass this routine a MovieController and it will return the
movie that the controller is attached to:

```
MovieController  gController;
Movie            theMovie;
theMovie = MCGetMovie( gController );
```

Files
and Printing

*Y*our program should be able to allow users to create interesting things. It should also allow users to save and print the results of their work. After you've implemented the features that have been described in the other parts of this book, you'll want to add the two features covered in this section: file handling and printing.

15

Files

*M*any Macintosh applications make good use of graphics, movies, and sound. Programs such as games and interactive tutorials use sound and movies by opening predetermined files and playing their contents. Such programs need to know how to find these files before they can be opened and played. In this chapter, you will see how a Mac program uses a file's pathname to find and open a file.

If your program doesn't know in advance which file should be opened, it can let the user make the selection. This chapter shows how your program can display the standard Open dialog box — the dialog box that allows the user to move from folder to folder to find and select a file to open.

A resource file may be the most important file type for a Macintosh programmer; it holds the data that defines what a Mac program looks like. The resource file is also very important to many Macintosh users as well, although most users may not ever be aware that they're using a file of this type. That's because a resource file can be used to save application data, such as program preferences or user-entered data records. In this chapter you'll see how your application can prompt a user for data input, create a new resource file, save that data into a record in that file, and then close the new file. Because the data has been saved to a file on disk, your program can reopen the new file at any time and use the saved data.

Selecting Files

Before your application can work with a file — that is, read from it or write to it — the application needs to open the file. However, before the application can open the file, the application needs to know the location of the file on the disk.

FILE SYSTEM SPECIFICATION

A file system specification is the means by which the system locates any file or directory (folder). By using file system specification structures, structures of type FSSpec, your program can easily access a file. An FSSpec holds three pieces of information about a file. The first is the *volume reference number,* a reference number for the volume that a file is on. The word *volume* refers to the floppy disk or hard drive on which the file resides. An FSSpec also keeps an ID number for the *parent directory* of a file. The parent directory is the folder in which the file resides. Finally, an FSSpec keeps track of a file's *name,* the name that appears under the file's icon on the desktop. Here is a look at the definition of the FSSpec data type:

```
struct FSSpec
{
    short   vRefNum;
    long    parID;
    Str63   name;
};
```

MAKING AN FSSPEC FOR A FILE

To open a file, your program needs an FSSpec for that file. To create a FSSpec, call the Toolbox routine FSMakeFSSpec(). This function accepts a volume reference number, a parent directory ID, and a file name for the file that requires an FSSpec. FSMakeFSSpec() combines the information in these three parameters to form a single FSSpec and then returns that file system specification in the FSSpec variable that was passed in as the fourth parameter.

```
Str255  theFileName;
short   theVolRef;
long    theDirID;
FSSpec  theFSSpec;
OSErr   theError;
theError = FSMakeFSSpec( theVolRef, theDirID, theFileName, &theFSSpec );
```

Some applications come with a set of support files that the application uses. Such support files may include sound files, QuickTime movie files, or resource files. For example, a game may store sound effects in several sound files, while an educational program may keep short instructional film clips in a set of QuickTime movie files. These files are generally stored within the same folder as the application that uses them. To create an FSSpec for such a file, set the first two parameters in a file to 0 to call FSMakeFSSpec(). Values of 0 for the volume reference number and for the parent directory ID tell the File Manager that the file in question resides in the default directory, the directory that holds the application. The file name should be the name of the file as it appears on the desktop. Optionally, the file name may be preceded by a colon. Because the name is in the format of a Pascal string, it needs to be preceded by /p and appear between quotation marks. The following declarations both produce a valid name for a file named Doorbell that is in the same folder as the application that uses the file:

```
Str255  theFileName = "/pDoorbell";    // valid name
Str255  theFileName = "/p:Doorbell";   // also a valid name
```

To create an FSSpec for a file named Doorbell that resides in the same folder as the MyKillerApp program that will use the file, use the code that follows. You should refer to Figure 15-1 as you look over the following snippet:

```
Str255  theFileName = "/pDoorbell";
short   theVolRef   = 0;
long    theDirID    = 0;
FSSpec  theFSSpec;
OSErr   theError;
theError = FSMakeFSSpec( theVolRef, theDirID, theFileName, &theFSSpec );
```

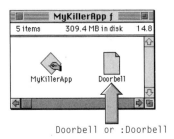

```
Doorbell or :Doorbell
```

Figure 15-1
A file that is located in the same folder as the application that uses it has the same name as that used by the Finder. The name may optionally be preceded by a colon.

Rather than keeping support files loose in the application folder, you may want to keep them in their own folder within the application folder. Accessing such a file is again done via an FSSpec. Because this new subfolder will still reside in the application folder, you can again use a volume reference number of 0 and a parent directory ID of 0. Here, however, the file name should now include a *partial pathname.* That is, the name should include the directory path from the parent directory to the file. The folder names between the parent directory and the file need to be preceded by a colon, and the file name itself should also be preceded by a colon. The following snippet again creates an FSSpec for the Doorbell file:

```
Str255  theFileName = "\p:Support Files ƒ:Sound Files ƒ:Doorbell";
short   theVolRef   = 0;
long    theDirID    = 0;
FSSpec  theFSSpec;
OSErr   theError;
theError = FSMakeFSSpec( theVolRef, theDirID, theFileName, &theFSSpec );
```

In the above snippet, the Doorbell file is held in a folder named Sound Files *ƒ*. This folder is located in another folder named Support Files *ƒ*. Figure 15-2 shows the partial pathname to the Doorbell file.

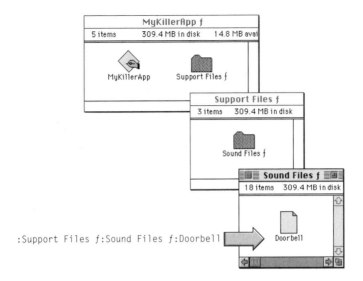

Figure 15-2
If a file appears in a subdirectory of the folder in which the application that uses it resides, the file's name should include the names of the folders in its path.

If the call to FSMakeFSSpec() is successful, your application will have a filled-in FSSpec structure in the variable theFSSpec. This variable can then be used in subsequent calls to File Manager or Resource Manager routines that work with files — routines that are covered later in this chapter. In general, your program should check the outcome of the call to FSMakeFSSpec(). If the path or file name isn't correct or if the file is missing, FSMakeFSSpec() will return an OSErr value other than noErr (most likely fnfErr, file not found).

```
Str255  theFileName = "\p:Support Files ƒ:Sound Files ƒ:Doorbell";
short   theVolRef   = 0;
long    theDirID    = 0;
FSSpec  theFSSpec;
OSErr   theError;
theError = FSMakeFSSpec( theVolRef, theDirID, theFileName, &theFSSpec );
if ( theError == noErr )
   // use theFSSpec to open file
else
   // post alert: file not found
```

As the above snippet shows, if `FSMakeFSSpec()` is successful, your program should open the file. If the call is unsuccessful, post an error message such as the one shown in the alert in Figure 15-3.

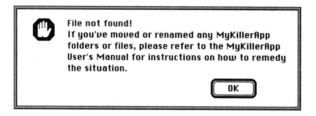

Figure 15-3
The type of error message your application should display if the user changes the name of a file or moves a file.

USING THE STANDARD OPEN DIALOG BOX

Calling `FSMakeFSSpec()` to create an `FSSpec` for a file is useful when your application knows in advance the name and location of the file to open. While this is the case for many programs — such as tutorials, games, and other programs that use support files — other applications may not be privy to this information ahead of time. Instead, some programs, such as text editors, sound players, or movie viewers, let the user select a file to open. Such programs can use the *standard Open dialog box* both to let the user select a file and to let the system create the FSSpec for that file. Figure 15-4 shows the standard Open dialog box.

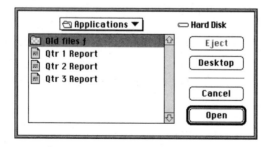

Figure 15-4
The standard Open dialog box.

Posting the standard Open dialog box requires a call to just a single Toolbox routine, `StandardGetFile()`. The following call to `StandardGetFile()` causes the standard Open dialog box to appear on the screen, with only text files and folders shown in the dialog box list:

```
SFTypeList          typeList = { 'TEXT', 0, 0, 0 };
StandardFileReply   theReply;
StandardGetFile( nil, 1, typeList, &theReply );
```

The first of the four parameters to `StandardGetFile()` is a pointer to a filter function. The standard Open dialog box normally displays all files of a certain type or types. For instance, when a text editor uses the standard Open dialog box, all text files in a folder will be displayed. If an application needs to limit the display of files to only some of the files of a given type, the optional filter function is used. Since this is seldom the case, you'll generally pass a value of `nil` as this first parameter rather than a pointer to a filter function.

The second parameter to `StandardGetFile()` is the number of file types to be displayed in the dialog box list. The standard Open dialog box normally displays up to four different file types, such as `'TEXT'` or `'PICT'`. The second parameter should thus be a value between 1 and 4. In the above example, the dialog box list will hold only text files, and as such the second parameter to `StandardGetFile()` is a 1.

The third parameter to `StandardGetFile()` is directly related to the second parameter; it names the file types that are to be displayed in the dialog box list. The type of this parameter, `SFTypeList`, is defined to be an array of four `OSTypes`. Each `OSType` is a four-character name of a file type that is surrounded by single quotes. The `SFTypeList` variable used for this third parameter can be initialized when the variable is declared. List the file types between braces, with 0 for any of the four types that go unused.

The last parameter to `StandardGetFile()` is a pointer to a `struct` variable, a `StandardFileReply` variable. After `StandardGetFile()` posts the standard Open dialog box and the user has made a file selection from the dialog box list, `StandardGetFile()` fills the `StandardFileReply` variable with information about the selected file. You will probably be most interested in the `sfFile` member of the `StandardFileReply` structure; it is an `FSSpec` structure. The following snippet defines the `StandardFileReply` data type and includes comments by the two most commonly referenced members of the structure:

```
struct StandardFileReply
{
   Boolean      sfGood;        // true if user did NOT cancel
   Boolean      sfReplacing;
   OSType       sfType;
   FSSpec       sfFile;        // file system specification
   ScriptCode   sfScript;
   short        sfFlags;
   Boolean      sfIsFolder;
   Boolean      sfIsVolume;
   long         sfReserved1;
   short        sfReserved2;
};
```

After the user dismisses the standard Open dialog box (by either selecting a file or clicking on the Cancel button), your program should check the sfGood member of the now filled-in StandardFileReply variable. If sfGood is true, a file was selected. The user either double-clicked on a file name in the standard Open dialog box list or clicked on a name once and then clicked on the Open button. If sfGood is true, your program should go ahead and open the selected file. The sfFile member of the StandardFileReply variable will hold an FSSpec (created by the system) for the selected file. You use this FSSpec to open the file. If sfGood is false, your program can assume that the Cancel button was clicked on and should instead handle that scenario. The following snippet provides a general approach to using StandardGetFile() to display the standard Open dialog box with a list that includes both text and picture files. Later in this chapter you will see the specifics of how to open these file types.

```
SFTypeList           typeList = { 'TEXT', 'PICT', 0, 0 };
StandardFileReply    theReply;
StandardGetFile( nil, 2, typeList, &theReply );
if ( theReply.sfGood == true )
   // use the FSSpec found in theReply.sfFile to open a file
else
   // handle case of user canceling the dialog box
```

You should refer to the Chapter 13 example program PickSoundFile and the Chapter 14 example program PreviewOpenMovie for source code listings that make use of the StandardGetFile() function.

Application Data and Files

Applications can save data in a number of ways. One of the most convenient methods is to group related data together into a data structure and
then save that structure as a single resource in a resource file.

RESOURCES AS RECORDS

All Macintosh programmers are familiar with some of the many standard
resource types, such as the WIND, MENU, and DLOG types. The resources a
program uses don't have to be limited to the dozens of predefined types.
You can use a resource editor to create your own resource type and then
write a Mac application that is capable of using the data stored in resources
of this new type. If you use ResEdit as your resource editor, all resource
types that are not recognized by ResEdit will have a generic icon like the
one shown in Figure 15-5. In the figure you can see how the Microsoft
Word application has its own resource types — the MSWD, PCOD, and RFIL
resource types all use the generic icon. In the Microsoft Word preferences
file, the ICst resource type is also a nonstandard resource type.

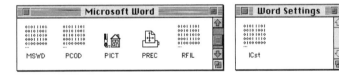

Figure 15-5
*Resources that are application-defined display a generic icon consisting of 1s
and 0s.*

Programmers know about the standard resource types — and so does
the code that makes up the Macintosh Toolbox. When an application makes
a call to GetNewWindow(), for instance, the Window Manager knows the
format of the data it will find in the WIND resource that is uses to load a
window into memory. The same is not true for nonstandard resource types.
If you create your own resource to hold program data, you'll have to
describe the format of this new resource type to the program that uses these
resources. This topic is covered next.

SAVING APPLICATION DATA AS A RESOURCE RECORD

An application that is to save data to a resource in a resource file will first save that data to heap memory in the application's partition. As discussed in Chapter 3, this can be done by defining a data structure that consists of a member for each item to be saved. The following code could be used in a game. The code defines a structure that holds a user's name and score.

```
typedef  struct
{
    Str31   theName;
    long    theScore;

} ScoreRecord, *ScorePtr, **ScoreHandle;
```

After the user plays the game, his or her name and score can be saved by first allocating a block of memory the size of a ScoreRecord structure. In Chapter 3 you learned that the Toolbox function NewHandle() is used for this task. In the following snippet, the Toolbox function NewHandleClear() is used. It allocates a block of memory in the heap and returns a handle to it, which is similar to the way NewHandle() works. NewHandleClear() takes the extra step of clearing this block by filling each byte with a 0.

```
Handle  dataHandle;
dataHandle = NewHandleClear( sizeof( ScoreRecord ) );
```

Figure 15-6 shows the results of calling NewHandleClear().

To assign a value to one of the fields of the ScoreRecord data structure, dereference the handle twice and then use the dot operator with the name of the field to access. This snippet assigns a value of 3500 to the theScore field:

```
Handle  dataHandle;
dataHandle = NewHandleClear( sizeof( ScoreRecord ) );
(**(ScoreHandle)dataHandle).theScore = 3500;
```

The value that is assigned to a member of the structure in memory can also come from a variable, of course.

```
long    winnersScore = 3500;
Handle  dataHandle;
dataHandle = NewHandleClear( sizeof( ScoreRecord ) );
(**(ScoreHandle)dataHandle).theScore = winnersScore;
```

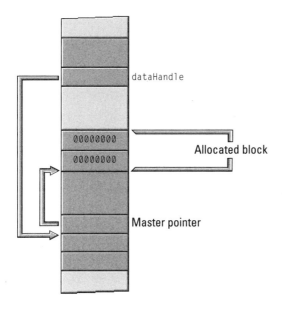

Figure 15-6

NewHandleClear() can be used to allocate a block of memory that is the size of an application-defined data structure.

Of course in your program a value such as 3500 won't come from the source code, as is shown here. It's more likely that a global variable would be keeping track of the user's score, and when the game ends, this variable would hold the value that is assigned to theScore. The user's name wouldn't appear in the source code either. It would probably be entered by the user and read from an edit box in a dialog box.

The effects of the following snippet are illustrated in Figure 15-7.

Numerical values can be assigned to memory in a simple assignment statement, as shown above. Working with strings requires a little extra effort. Because a string is an array of characters rather than a single value, you need to use a Toolbox routine that copies a block of data from a source to a destination. To copy the contents of a string variable to memory, use the Toolbox routine BlockMoveData(). Pass this routine a string to copy, a pointer to the area in memory where the string should be copied to, and the number of bytes to copy (in a variable of type Size, which is defined to be a long). Here is an example:

```
Handle   dataHandle;
Str31    winnersName = "\pJohnny";
```

```
Size     numBytes;
dataHandle = NewHandleClear( sizeof( ScoreRecord ) );
numBytes = winnersName[0] + 1;
BlockMoveData( winnersName, (**(ScoreHandle)dataHandle).theName, numBytes );
```

In the above snippet, the length of the winnersName string is found in the first element of the Str31 array. Element winnersName[0] provides the number of characters in the winnersName string. Then the first element, the length character, needs to be added. In the above example numBytes would have a value of 7. The string length is held in winnersName[0], and the characters that make up the "\pJohnny" string are held in winnersName[1] through winnersName[6].

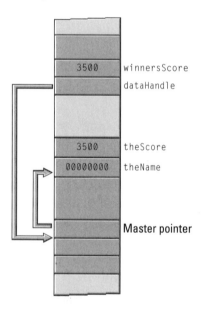

Figure 15-7
To assign a value to a member of a data structure in memory, dereference the data's handle.

With the length of the string known, BlockMoveData() can be called to copy the winnersName string to the theName member of the structure that the dataHandle handle references.

At this point you may well wonder what saving data to a structure in memory has to do with saving data to a resource. The previous steps were taken so that the information that is to be written to a resource is grouped together in memory and referenced by a single handle. A call to the Toolbox routines AddResource() and WriteResource() are then made to write the data from memory to a resource, as shown in Figure 15-8.

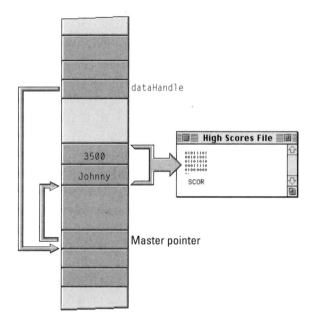

Figure 15-8
The data in a block of memory can be written to disk as a single resource.

In Figure 15-8 the resource type that the data is being written to is SCOR. You won't find the SCOR type listed in your resource editor — it's a type being defined by your application. You can use any four-character name that isn't already defined by Apple. Here, SCOR was selected to hint at what a resource of this type holds, the score of a game.

To turn the data in memory to a resource, first call AddResource(). This Toolbox routine will write the handle, a resource type, a resource ID, and a resource name to the resource map in memory. Follow the call to AddResource() with a call to the Toolbox routine WriteResource(). This call immediately writes to disk the data referenced by the handle. The following code would create a resource like the one shown in Figure 15-9:

```
AddResource( dataHandle, 'SCOR', 1000, "\pScore Record" );
WriteResource( dataHandle );
```

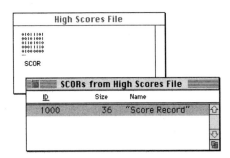

Figure 15-9
An application-defined resource created and saved from an application.

Rather than risk using a duplicate ID number by including a particular resource ID in a call to AddResource(), use the Toolbox function Unique1ID() to let the Resource Manager select an ID. Once it is given a resource type, Unique1ID() will check the current resource file for all resources of that type. Based on the IDs of the resources in the current file, Unique1ID() will return an ID guaranteed to be unique. The following snippet is an improvement on the previous code for writing a resource. It uses Unique1ID(), as well as a couple of #define directives.

```
#define    kResTypeSCOR               'SCOR'
#define    kResNameSCOR        "\pScore Record"
short  resID;
resID = Unique1ID( kResTypeSCOR );
AddResource( dataHandle, kResTypeSCOR, resID, kResNameSCOR );
WriteResource( dataHandle );
```

Before writing a resource, you'll want to open the correct resource file, which is the topic of the next section. Once the file is open, call NewHandleClear() to allocate the memory block that will hold the data that will become the resource. Before working with the handle returned by NewHandleClear(), lock it — you'll want to prevent memory compaction from moving your memory block while your program accesses it. After the resource has been written, unlock the handle and release the memory block that the handle references. The following snippet covers the code described in this section, with the exception of the opening and closing of a resource file:

```
#define     kResTypeSCOR              'SCOR'
#define     kResNameSCOR    "\pScore Record"
Str31       winnersName  = "\pJohnny";
long        winnersScore = 3500;
Handle      dataHandle;
short       resID;
Size        numBytes;
// open a resource file

dataHandle = NewHandleClear( sizeof( ScoreRecord ) );
HLock( dataHandle );
    numBytes = winnersName[0] + 1;
    BlockMoveData( winnersName, (**(ScoreHandle)dataHandle).theName, numBytes
    );
    (**(ScoreHandle)dataHandle).theScore = winnersScore;

    resID = Unique1ID( kResTypeSCOR );
    AddResource( dataHandle, kResTypeSCOR, resID, kResNameSCOR );
    WriteResource( dataHandle );
HUnlock( dataHandle );
ReleaseResource( dataHandle );

// close the resource file
```

BY THE WAY

A Resource Manager routine that includes a 1 in its name, like Unique1ID( ), looks only in the current resource file. In this case, that is exactly what you want. If there are SCOR resources in the application fork or some other open file, the Resource Manager shouldn't be considering their IDs as it determines an ID. The ID need only be unique for the file that the resource is being written to.

If you would like the Resource Manager to consider all open resource files in its search, use the same routine without the 1, UniqueID( ). The same applies to other Resource Manager routines discussed later in this chapter, such as Get1IndResource( ) and Count1Resources( ).

OPENING AND CLOSING A RESOURCE FILE

Before writing application data to a resource, your program will need to open the resource file that is to serve as the data file. While a data file can be kept in any folder, the Preferences folder in the System Folder is a popular choice. This is especially true for data that is to be hidden from the user. This chapter's high score data is just such an example. A game application will save a player's name and score as a resource in a file. At the user's request (through a menu item selection), the application can open the data file, read in the data, and display the information in a window or dialog box. The user never needs to directly access the data file; only the application does. Hiding the data file in the System folder minimizes the chances of the file's being inadvertently discarded by the user.

Regardless of where the data file is kept, an FSSpec is needed if the file is to be opened. The techniques for creating an FSSpec appear earlier in this chapter. If the data file is kept in the Preferences folder, your application can make a call to the Toolbox function FindFolder() to obtain both the volume reference number and the parent directory ID for the file. Pass the FindFolder() function three parameters that hold information regarding which folder the file appears in, and FindFolder() will fill in the values of the last two parameters.

```
#include <Folders.h>
short   theVolRef;
long    theDirID;
OSErr   theError;
theError = FindFolder( kOnSystemDisk, kPreferencesFolderType,
                       kDontCreateFolder, &theVolRef, &theDirID );
```

The first parameter that is passed to FindFolder() is a reference number of the volume that holds the parent folder. Since the Preferences folder is in the System Folder, the volume will be the system, or startup, disk. The Apple-defined constant kOnSystemDisk can be used here. The second parameter that is passed to FindFolder() describes the parent directory. Use the Apple-defined constant kPreferencesFolderType here. The third parameter specifies whether a new parent folder should be created if such a folder isn't found. You can assume that any System Folder does contain a Preferences folder, so pass the Apple-defined constant kDontCreateFolder as the third parameter.

If you want the resource file created in a folder other than the Preferences folder, skip the call to FindFolder(). To create an FSSpec for a nonexistent file that will soon be created in the same folder as the application, just call FSMakeFSSpec():

```
Str255   theFileName = "/pHigh Scores File";
short    theVolRef   = 0;
long     theDirID    = 0;
FSSpec   theFSSpec;
OSErr    theError;
theError = FSMakeFSSpec( theVolRef, theDirID, theFileName, &theFSSpec );
```

FindFolder() is a function that is available only to Macintosh owners who have a version of System 7 (or beyond) as their operating system. With Copland (System 8) on the horizon (or possibly, available as you read this), any version of System 6 is fast becoming outdated. Apple encourages System 6.x users to upgrade to System 7.

After a call to FindFolder(), your program will have a volume reference number and a parent directory ID that can be used in a subsequent call to FSMakeFSSpec(). Here it is assumed that the data file to open is named High Scores File.

```
#define     kHighScoreFileName     "\pHigh Scores File"
FSSpec      theFSSpec;
theError = FSMakeFSSpec( theVolRef, theDirID, kHighScoreFileName, &theFSSpec
    );
```

The FSSpec that is returned by FSMakeFSSpec() should now be used in a call to the Toolbox function FSpOpenResFile(). Pass this routine the FSSpec and a permission level, and the Resource Manager will open the specified resource file and return a file reference number for the file. The permission level should be the Apple-defined constant fsRdWrPerm, which gives your application permission to both read from and write to the file.

```
FSSpec  theFSSpec;
short   fileRefNum;
fileRefNum = FSpOpenResFile( &theFSSpec, fsRdWrPerm );
```

An application can have more than one resource file, or fork, open at any given time. Because the application's resource fork is always open, as soon as a resource file is opened there will be two open resource forks. To direct subsequent calls to Resource Manager routines to the newly opened resource file, call UseResFile(). Pass this routine the reference number of the data file:

```
UseResFile( fileRefNum );
```

Chapter 2 discusses how more than one resource file can be open at a time. That chapter also discusses the Toolbox routines UseResFile() and CurResFile().

There may be instances when a data file that needs to be opened doesn't exist. For instance, you may choose not to distribute an empty data file with your application. Or the user may have intentionally or inadvertently deleted the data file from the Preferences folder. To handle such cases, check the value of the file reference number that gets returned by FSpOpenResFile(). If the reference number has a value of –1, then the call to FSpOpenResFile() has failed. In that case, assume that the data file doesn't exist and create a new one. A call to the Toolbox routine FSpCreateResFile() will handle that chore. After the file is created, again call FSpOpenResFile() to open the file.

```
if ( fileRefNum == -1 )
{
    FSpCreateResFile( &theFSSpec, 'RSED', 'rsrc', smSystemScript );
    fileRefNum = FSpOpenResFile( &theFSSpec, fsRdWrPerm );
}
```

For the first parameter to FSpCreateResFile(), pass the file system specification for the file that is to be created. This is simply the FSSpec for the file that your program was attempting to open. The second parameter to FSpCreateResFile() should be the file creator, and the third parameter should be the file's type. If you'd like a double-click on the file to launch ResEdit, use 'RSED' as the creator and 'rsrc' as the file type. If you would rather use Resorcerer to launch and open the file, use 'Doug' as the creator and 'RSRC' as the file type.

If you don't intend for a user of your application to ever open the data file, the choice of creator and type will probably depend on which resource editor *you* use. For purposes of examining a data file and testing your application, choose the creator and type that match the resource editor that you're accustomed to using. When your application is complete, you can change the creator to one that *doesn't* match either ResEdit or Resorcerer. That provides a bit of file security — the user can't open the file by double-clicking on it. The file can, however, still be opened from within a resource editor.

The final parameter that is passed to `FSpCreateResFile()` is a script code. The script code is used by the Finder in the display of the file's name. The Apple-defined constant `smSystemScript` is suitable for this parameter.

The following application-defined function makes use of the Toolbox routines covered in this section. When the `OpenFileInPreferencesFolder()` routine is passed the name of a resource file in the Preferences folder, the routine opens the folder, makes it the current resource file, and returns a reference number to the file.

```
short   OpenFileInPreferencesFolder( Str255 theFileName )
{
   short   theVolRef;
   long    theDirID;
   FSSpec  theFSSpec;
   short   fileRefNum;
   OSErr   theError;
   theError = FindFolder( kOnSystemDisk, kPreferencesFolderType,
                          kDontCreateFolder, &theVolRef, &theDirID );

   theError = FSMakeFSSpec( theVolRef, theDirID, theFileName, &theFSSpec );

   fileRefNum = FSpOpenResFile( &theFSSpec, fsRdWrPerm );

   if ( fileRefNum == -1 )
   {
      FSpCreateResFile( &theFSSpec, 'RSED', 'rsrc', smSystemScript );
      fileRefNum = FSpOpenResFile( &theFSSpec, fsRdWrPerm );
   }
   UseResFile( fileRefNum );
   return ( fileRefNum );
}
```

To call the above function, pass it the name of the file to open:

```
#define    kHighScoreFileName    "\pHigh Scores File"
short      fileRefNum;
fileRefNum = OpenFileInPreferencesFolder( kHighScoreFileName );
```

To close an open resource file, pass the file's reference number to the Toolbox routine `CloseResFile()`.

```
CloseResFile( fileRefNum );
```

READING DATA FROM A RESOURCE RECORD

After saving application data to a resource, your program may want to read the data back at a later point, or even at a later execution of the application. To do this, call the Toolbox routine `Get1IndResource()`.

```
#define      kResTypeSCOR       'SCOR'
Handle  dataHandle;
dataHandle = Get1IndResource( kResTypeSCOR, 1 );
```

The `Get1IndResource()` function loads into memory the data from a single resource of a specified type. After loading the data to a block of memory in the heap, `Get1IndResource()` returns a handle to the block (as shown in Figure 15-10).

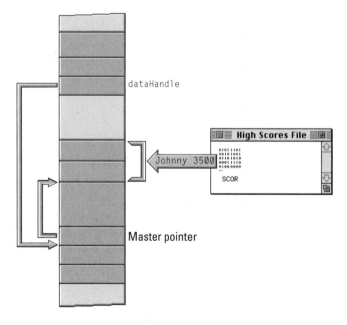

Figure 15-10
The data from an application-defined resource can be read into a single block of memory.

You'll recall from Chapter 3 that a Toolbox routine that loads a resource and returns a pointer or a handle to the resource data takes care of allocating the memory block for you. That's why the above snippet doesn't need a call to `NewHandle()` or `NewHandleClear()` before using the `dataHandle` variable. `GetNewWindow()`, `GetPicture()`, and `GetResource()` are a few other examples of such Toolbox functions.

The `Get1IndResource()` routine accepts a resource type as its first parameter. The second parameter is an index that tells the routine which individual resource to load into memory. In the above snippet, `Get1IndResource()` will use the data found in the first `SCOR` resource in the current resource file. The first `SCOR` resource is defined to be the first `SCOR` resource added to the resource file, not the `SCOR` resource with the lowest resource ID. As you'll see later in this chapter, a program can include a call to `Get1IndResource()` in the body of a loop. At each pass through the loop, the value of the second parameter to `Get1IndResource()` can be incremented. In this way the program can access all of the resources of a given type in a given file.

When the data from memory was originally saved to a resource, it was done so in the order in which it appeared in memory. Now when the data is loaded from the resource back into memory, it will again be copied in order. After the call to `Get1IndResource()`, a block of memory matching the `ScoreRecord` structure will be present in the heap, and the program will have a handle that references that memory. As a reminder, here's a second look at the `ScoreRecord` data structure:

```
typedef  struct
{
   Str31  theName;
   long   theScore;

} ScoreRecord, *ScorePtr, **ScoreHandle;
```

To copy heap data to a local or global variable, dereference the handle that leads to the data and assign the value in the desired field to the variable. Figure 15-11 illustrates how the following code works:

```
long  dataScore;
dataScore = (**(ScoreHandle)dataHandle).theScore;
```

> Notice that the procedure for copying data from a heap block to a variable is simply the reverse of the procedure used to copy heap data to a variable. Earlier in this chapter the data in a `long` variable named `winnersScore` was moved into a heap block as follows:
>
> ```
> long    winnersScore = 3500;
> (**(ScoreHandle)dataHandle).theScore = winnersScore;
> ```

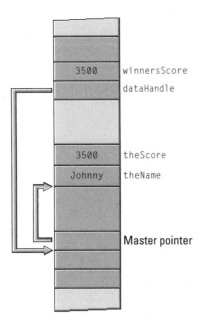

Figure 15-11

Any one member of the resource data can be copied to an application variable.

> You'll recall that `BlockMoveData()` was used to copy a string *into* the heap. In the above snippet it's used to copy a string *from* the heap. Compare the first two parameters to `BlockMoveData()` in the above snippet to those in the snippet used earlier in this chapter to copy the string in `winnersName` to the heap:
>
> ```
> Size    numBytes;
> Str31   winnersName = "\pJohnny";
> numBytes = winnersName[0] + 1;
> BlockMoveData( winnersName, (**(ScoreHandle)dataHandle).theName, numBytes );
> ```

Once data has been copied from a resource to a heap block, and a structure member has been copied to a variable, neither the resource data nor the heap data is needed for that member. In the above example, the theScore data is now stored in variable dataScore. Henceforth the dataScore variable can be used when working with score data. Here 10 points are added to the score, and then the score is converted to a string and drawn to a window.

```
Str255  scoreString;
dataScore += 10;
NumToString( dataScore, scoreString );
MoveTo( 20, 30 );
DrawString( scoreString );
```

To work with a string, determine the length of the string in the heap and then call BlockMoveData( ) to copy the heap string to a string variable.

```
Size    numBytes;
Str31   nameString;
numBytes = (**(ScoreHandle)dataHandle).theName[0] + 1;
BlockMoveData( (**(ScoreHandle)dataHandle).theName,
               nameString, numBytes );
```

EXAMPLE PROGRAM: FILEWRITEANDREAD

The FileWriteAndRead example program performs all the critical tasks discussed in this chapter. The program creates a resource file if one isn't already present, writes data to application-defined SCOR resources in that file, and later reads back the data in those resources.

To continue with the high score program examples that have been discussed in this chapter, FileWriteAndRead begins by displaying a dialog box like the one shown in Figure 15-12. The dialog box displays a number score and an edit box that lets the user enter a name. A different score appears each time in the dialog box. The score is generated by the Random( ) Toolbox function. In a full-featured game, the score would of course be determined by the user's playing skills.

Figure 15-12
The user-input dialog box from the FileWriteAndRead program.

When the user clicks on the Save to File button, the information in the dialog box is saved to a new SCOR resource and the dialog box is dismissed. After that, the program opens a second dialog box. This one displays the information from the SCOR resource. Because a new SCOR resource is created each time the program runs, this dialog box won't always show the same number of entries. Figure 15-13 shows the dialog box during the second running of the FileWriteAndRead program.

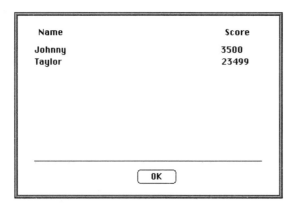

Figure 15-13
The score display dialog box from the FileWriteAndRead program.

 If you're writing a game, display a dialog box like the user input dialog box when the game ends. Make the score display dialog box available from a menu item, such as Show High Scores. You're not writing a game? Examine the code closely — these techniques apply to any type of program that needs to save data from one execution to another.

The FileWriteAndRead project requires a resource file that holds two DLOG resources and two DITL resources. Figures 15-14 and 15-15, respectively, provide a look at the two DITLs in ResEdit, including the item numbers of each item.

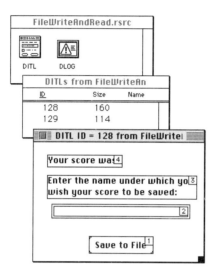

Figure 15-14
The user-input DITL from the resource file for the FileWriteAndRead project.

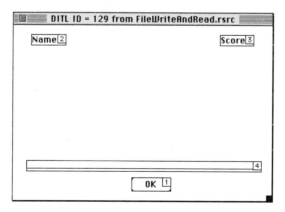

Figure 15-15
The score display DITL from the resource file for the FileWriteAndRead project.

After you run FileWriteAndRead one time, a new file will be added to the Preferences folder of your Mac's System Folder. The file holds a single SCOR resource. A new SCOR resource is added each time you run the FileWriteAndRead program. Figure 15-16 shows how ResEdit displays one of two SCOR resources that are found in a typical High Scores File.

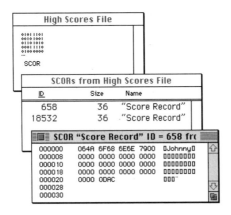

Figure 15-16

Viewing an application-defined SCOR resource from within ResEdit.

 The SCOR resource isn't easy to read. For a program like FileWriteAndRead, where neither you nor the user ever has to look at the resource itself, this isn't a problem. If you would like to view the contents of an application-defined resource, create a template for the resource type. Templates are discussed later in this chapter.

The FileWriteAndRead program uses the same ScoreRecord data structure that you've seen throughout this chapter.

```
typedef  struct
{
    Str31  theName;
    long   theScore;

} ScoreRecord, *ScorePtr, **ScoreHandle;
```

After the user enters his or her name in the edit box of the user input dialog box, the program calls the application-defined routine SaveScoreInfoToRecordInFile(). This function first opens the High Scores File by using the OpenFileInPreferencesFolder() routine that was developed in this chapter. A call to NewHandleClear() is made to allocate memory for a `ScoreRecord`, and then the data from the user input dialog box (which is stored in global variables `gHighScore` and `gNameString`) is copied to this memory.

```
#define      kResTypeSCOR              'SCOR'
#define      kResNameSCOR     "\pScore Record"
Str31   gNameString;
long    gHighScore;
Handle  dataHandle;
short   resID;
Size    numBytes;
dataHandle = NewHandleClear( sizeof( ScoreRecord ) );
HLock( dataHandle );
   numBytes = gNameString[0] + 1;
   BlockMoveData( gNameString, (**(ScoreHandle)dataHandle).theName, numBytes
     );
   (**(ScoreHandle)dataHandle).theScore = gHighScore;

   resID = UniqueIID( kResTypeSCOR );
   AddResource( dataHandle, kResTypeSCOR, resID, kResNameSCOR );
   WriteResource( dataHandle );
HUnlock( dataHandle );
```

To demonstrate how to delete a resource, FileWriteAndRead allows only ten SCOR resources to be saved. On the 11th running of FileWriteAndRead, the program will delete the first SCOR resource that was added to the High Scores File. From that point on, each running of the program will result in one resource being deleted and one being added.

BY THE WAY

If you want your program to make use of a preferences file — a file that keeps track of user preferences such as volume settings, window sizes, and so on — you'll use the techniques described in this chapter and in this program. A preferences file writes data to a resource in a resource file, just as the FileWriteAndRead program does.

You say you *would* like to make use of a preferences file? You now know how to work with one. Just modify the FileWriteAndRead code and incorporate it into your own program. Create a resource file (like the High Scores File in FileWriteAndRead), and save it in the Preferences folder. Include a menu item that displays a dialog box (like the user name dialog box in FileWriteAndRead) that requests user preferences information. Save this information as data in an application-defined record (like the `ScoreRecord` structure in FileWriteAndRead) and then to a resource (like the SCOR resource in FileWriteAndRead). Each time the program starts, read the application-defined resource and make use of the information in it (like the score display dialog box in FileWriteAndRead).

The following snippet is from the `SaveScoreInfoToRecordInFile()` routine. A call to the Toolbox routine `Count1Resources()` returns the number of SCOR resources in the open High Scores File. If this number is equal to the maximum number of score records that FileWriteAndRead allows, one resource is deleted in preparation for the adding of one new resource. A call to the Toolbox routine `Get1IndResource()`, with an index value of 1, loads the first SCOR resource from the resource file and returns a handle to the resource data. While the program isn't interested in using this data, a handle to it is needed for the next Toolbox call — a call to `RemoveResource()` removes the resource from the resource map in memory. The memory occupied by the data is no longer considered resource-related, so call the Toolbox function `DisposeHandle()` rather than `ReleaseResource()` to free the memory occupied by the resource data.

```
#define    kMaxScoreRecords      10
define     kResTypeSCOR        'SCOR'
short      theNumSCORresources;
Handle     dataHandle;

theNumSCORresources = Count1Resources( kResTypeSCOR );
if ( theNumSCORresources == kMaxScoreRecords )
{
    dataHandle = Get1IndResource( kResTypeSCOR, 1 );
    RemoveResource( dataHandle );
    DisposeHandle( dataHandle );
}
```

That covers writing a SCOR resource using application data. The `WriteScoresToWindow()` function handles the reading of a SCOR resource. Just as in writing a resource, reading one requires that the resource file is opened first. `WriteScoresToWindow()` calls the same application-defined function that `SaveScoreInfoToRecordInFile()` called, `OpenFileInPreferencesFolder()`. The function then calls the Toolbox routine `Count1Resources()` to determine how many SCOR resources there are in the High Scores File. The number serves as a loop index. Each iteration of the loop reads in the data from one SCOR resource and writes that data to the score-displaying dialog box. Here is the loop used in `WriteScoresToWindow()`:

```
#define    kResTypeSCOR      'SCOR'
short    theNumSCORresources;
int      i;
```

```
Handle   dataHandle;
Size     numBytes;
Str31    nameString;
long     dataScore;
Str255   scoreString;
for ( i = 1; i <= theNumSCORresources; i++ )
{
    dataHandle = Get1IndResource( kResTypeSCOR, i );

    numBytes = (**(ScoreHandle)dataHandle).theName[0] + 1;
    BlockMoveData( (**(ScoreHandle)dataHandle).theName,
                   nameString, numBytes );
    MoveTo( 20, 35 + ( i * 15 ) );
    DrawString( nameString );
    dataScore = (**(ScoreHandle)dataHandle).theScore;
    NumToString( dataScore, scoreString );
    MoveTo( 300, 35 + ( i * 15 ) );
    DrawString( scoreString );

    ReleaseResource( dataHandle );
}
```

Yes, the function could just as well have been named
WriteScoresToDialog(). More appropriate still, the function could be
named WriteScoresToPort(). That's because the routine writes to
whichever port is current, whether it's a window or a dialog box.

Here's one other topic that's worth mentioning before presenting the
source code listing for FileWriteAndRead. The FileWriteAndRead program
consists of code that might be used in a game, but the program isn't a
game. The user doesn't achieve any score that can be written to a resource.
FileWriteAndRead simulates a score by generating a random number and
storing that value in the global variable gHighScore. A call to the Toolbox
function Random() does the work of generating the random number. To
guarantee that a positive number is returned, the result of Random() is used
as the parameter to the ANSI function labs(). This routine, defined in the
stdlib.h ANSI header file, returns a long absolute value of the parameter.

```
long  gHighScore;
gHighScore = labs( Random() );
```

Random() doesn't actually return a true random number. It returns one
value from a sequence of numbers. Each time Random() is called, it returns
the next number from the sequence. The sequence is based on a *seed*
value, a number that sets the starting point for the sequence of numbers

used by the Random( )function. If the same seed value is used each time the program is run, the same sequence of random numbers will be generated. And guess what? The same seed value will be used every time you run a program — unless you change the seed. This seed value is held in the randSeed member of the QuickDraw global structure qd. The FileWriteAndRead program chooses a new randSeed each time the program is run, basing the seed on the current Macintosh clock value, a value that will always be different.

```
unsigned long  theSeconds;
GetDateTime( &theSeconds );
qd.randSeed = theSeconds;
gHighScore = labs( Random() );
```

Here is the complete listing for the FileWriteAndRead program:

```
//_____
#include <Folders.h>
#include <stdlib.h>
//_____
void    InitializeToolboxes( void );
void    OpenGetInfoDialog( void );
void    SaveScoreInfoToRecordInFile( void );
short   OpenFileInPreferencesFolder( Str255 );
void    OpenShowInfoDialog( void );
void    WriteScoresToWindow( void );
//_____
#define        rGetInfoDialog              128
#define        kSaveButton                 1
#define        kNameEditBox                2
#define        rShowInfoDialog             129
#define        kOKButton                   1
#define        kMaxScoreRecords            10
#define        kResTypeSCOR                'SCOR'
#define        kResNameSCOR          "\pScore Record"
#define        kHighScoreFileName    "\pHigh Scores File"
//_____
typedef    struct
{
    Str31   theName;
    long    theScore;

} ScoreRecord, *ScorePtr, **ScoreHandle;
//_____
Str31  gNameString;
long   gHighScore;
short  gAppResForkRefNum;
//_____
```

```
void  main( void )
{
    InitializeToolbox();

    gAppResForkRefNum = CurResFile();

    OpenGetInfoDialog();

    OpenShowInfoDialog();
}
//_____
void  OpenGetInfoDialog( void )
{
    unsigned long  theSeconds;
    Str255         scoreString;
    DialogPtr      theDialog;
    Boolean        done = false;
    short          theItem;
    Handle         itemHandle;
    short          itemType;
    Rect           itemRect;
    GetDateTime( &theSeconds );
    qd.randSeed = theSeconds;
    gHighScore = labs( Random() );
    NumToString( gHighScore, scoreString );

    theDialog = GetNewDialog( rGetInfoDialog, nil, (WindowPtr)-1L );
    ShowWindow( theDialog );
    SetPort( theDialog );

    MoveTo( 140, 30 );
    DrawString( scoreString );

    while ( done == false )
    {
        ModalDialog( nil, &theItem );

        switch ( theItem )
        {
            case kOKButton:
                GetDialogItem( theDialog, kNameEditBox,
                               &itemType, &itemHandle, &itemRect );
                GetDialogItemText( itemHandle, gNameString );
                done = true;
                break;
        }
    }

    SaveScoreInfoToRecordInFile();

    UseResFile( gAppResForkRefNum );

    DisposeDialog( theDialog );
}
```

```
//_____
void  SaveScoreInfoToRecordInFile( void )
{
   short    fileRefNum;
   short    theNumSCORresources;
   Handle   dataHandle;
   short    resID;
   Size     numBytes;
   fileRefNum = OpenFileInPreferencesFolder( kHighScoreFileName );

   theNumSCORresources = Count1Resources( kResTypeSCOR );
   if ( theNumSCORresources == kMaxScoreRecords )
   {
      dataHandle = Get1IndResource( kResTypeSCOR, 1 );
      RemoveResource( dataHandle );
      DisposeHandle( dataHandle );
   }

   dataHandle = NewHandleClear( sizeof( ScoreRecord ) );
   HLock( dataHandle );
      numBytes = gNameString[0] + 1;
      BlockMoveData( gNameString, (**(ScoreHandle)dataHandle).theName,
    numBytes );
      (**(ScoreHandle)dataHandle).theScore = gHighScore;

      resID = Unique1ID( kResTypeSCOR );
      AddResource( dataHandle, kResTypeSCOR, resID, kResNameSCOR );
      WriteResource( dataHandle );
   HUnlock( dataHandle );
   ReleaseResource( dataHandle );

   CloseResFile( fileRefNum );
}
//_____
short  OpenFileInPreferencesFolder( Str255 theFileName )
{
   short    theVolRef;
   long     theDirID;
   FSSpec   theFSSpec;
   short    fileRefNum;
   OSErr    theError;
   theError = FindFolder( kOnSystemDisk, kPreferencesFolderType,
                        kDontCreateFolder, &theVolRef, &theDirID );

   theError = FSMakeFSSpec( theVolRef, theDirID,
                            theFileName, &theFSSpec );

   fileRefNum = FSpOpenResFile( &theFSSpec, fsRdWrPerm );

   if ( fileRefNum == -1 )
   {
      FSpCreateResFile( &theFSSpec, 'RSED', 'rsrc', smSystemScript );
      fileRefNum = FSpOpenResFile( &theFSSpec, fsRdWrPerm );
   }
```

```
   UseResFile( fileRefNum );

   return ( fileRefNum );
}
//_____
void   OpenShowInfoDialog( void )
{
   DialogPtr   theDialog;
   Boolean     done = false;
   short       theItem;
   theDialog = GetNewDialog( rShowInfoDialog, nil, (WindowPtr)-1L );
   ShowWindow( theDialog );
   SetPort( theDialog );
   WriteScoresToWindow();

   while ( done == false )
   {
      ModalDialog( nil, &theItem );

      switch ( theItem )
      {
         case kOKButton:
            done = true;
            break;
      }
   }

   DisposeDialog( theDialog );
}
//_____
void   WriteScoresToWindow( void )
{
   short   fileRefNum;
   short   theNumSCORresources;
   int     i;
   Handle  dataHandle;
   Size    numBytes;
   Str31   nameString;
   long    dataScore;
   Str255  scoreString;
   fileRefNum = OpenFileInPreferencesFolder( kHighScoreFileName );
   theNumSCORresources = Count1Resources( kResTypeSCOR );
   for ( i = 1; i <= theNumSCORresources; i++ )
   {
      dataHandle = Get1IndResource( kResTypeSCOR, i );

      numBytes = (**(ScoreHandle)dataHandle).theName[0] + 1;
      BlockMoveData( (**(ScoreHandle)dataHandle).theName,
                     nameString, numBytes );
      MoveTo( 20, 35 + ( i * 15 ) );
      DrawString( nameString );
      dataScore = (**(ScoreHandle)dataHandle).theScore;
      NumToString( dataScore, scoreString );
```

```
        MoveTo( 300, 35 + ( i * 15 ) );
        DrawString( scoreString );

        ReleaseResource( dataHandle );
    }
    CloseResFile( fileRefNum );
}
```

RESOURCE RECORDS

After running the FileWriteAndRead program, you'll find that a file named High Scores File now exists in the Preferences folder found in the System Folder on your Mac. Double-click on this file to launch ResEdit, and open the High Scores File. After you double-click on the SCOR icon in the file, double-click on one of the SCOR resources. You'll see the data for that resource. Figure 15-17 shows one such SCOR resource.

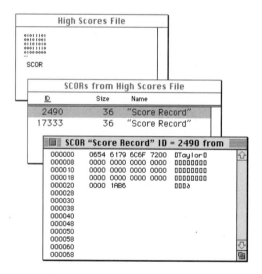

Figure 15-17

Viewing an application-defined SCOR resource from within ResEdit.

Figure 15-17 shows that while an application-defined resource is easily read by a Mac application, it isn't so easily understood by a person. To remedy this, you can create a template, a resource of type TMPL, that will add formatting to an application-defined resource type.

CREATING TEMPLATES

To create a template using ResEdit, open the Select New Type dialog box by selecting Create New Resource from the Resource menu. Scroll to the TMPL type in the list, and click once on that name, as shown in Figure 15-18. Alternatively, you can just type TMPL in the edit box of the dialog box. In either case, click on the OK button when finished.

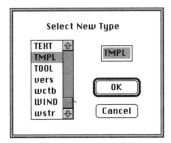

Figure 15-18
Creating a new TMPL, *or template, resource in ResEdit.*

After you click the OK button, a TMPL icon, a list of templates, and a template editor will all appear in the High Scores File, as shown in Figure 15-19.

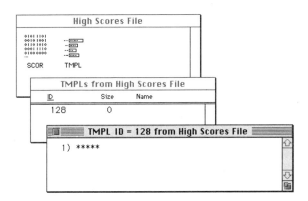

Figure 15-19
The TMPL *editor in ResEdit.*

ResEdit lets you create a separate template resource for each application-defined resource type that your program uses. Because the FileWriteAndRead program uses just one resource type, only one template resource is needed. Before proceeding with the filling in of the template, highlight the template resource by clicking once on the number 128 in the window that displays the templates, and then select Get Resource Info from the Resource menu. In the dialog box that opens, type in the name of the resource type that this template will be used with, SCOR. Figure 15-20 shows this dialog box with the correct name typed in. After typing in the name, close the Get Resource Info dialog box.

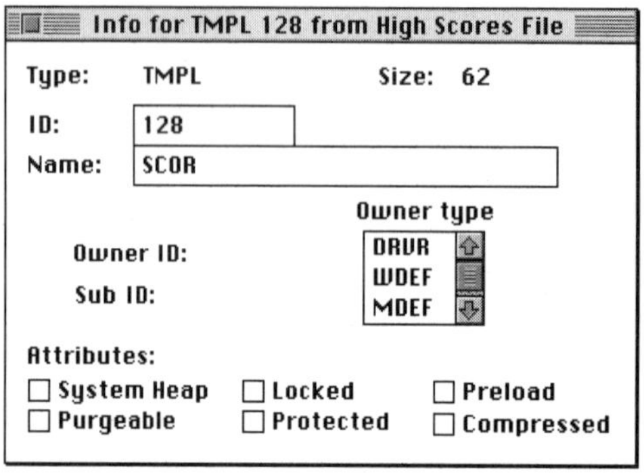

```
Info for TMPL 128 from High Scores File

Type:    TMPL              Size:  62

ID:      128

Name:    SCOR

                    Owner type
    Owner ID:       DRVR  ⬆
                    WDEF
    Sub ID:         MDEF  ⬇

Attributes:
☐ System Heap  ☐ Locked     ☐ Preload
☐ Purgeable    ☐ Protected  ☐ Compressed
```

Figure 15-20
Setting the TMPL name to the name of the resource type the template will be used with.

The name of the template *must* match the name of the resource type the template is to be used with. If you forget this step, the template will have no effect on resources of type SCOR.

Now it's time to add items to the TMPL resource. For every structure member in the application-defined ScoreRecord structure, there should be a corresponding template item. Each item will tell ResEdit how to display a structure member in the SCOR resource. Here is another look at the ScoreRecord struct:

```
typedef  struct
{
    Str31  theName;
    long   theScore;

} ScoreRecord, *ScorePtr, **ScoreHandle;
```

Each SCOR resource holds a string and a long value, in that order. The template used by the SCOR resource should thus have two items. To create the first item, click on the row of asterisks in the template editor and then select Insert New Field(s) from the Resource menu. When you do that, ResEdit will add a Label edit box and a Type edit box to the template editor. Type in playerName for the label and P01F for the type. Note that the second character in the type is a 0. Click on the next row of asterisks, select Insert New Field(s) from the Resource menu, and enter the information for the second item. Here you should type highScore for the label and DLNG for the type. Refer to Figure 15-21 to see how the template editor should look.

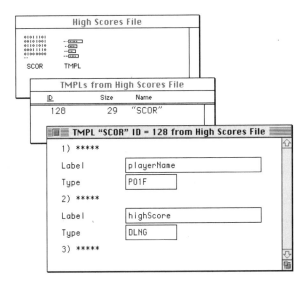

Figure 15-21
The TMPL template in ResEdit, after two items have been added.

The labels that you have entered are descriptive names that help you identify the fields in a SCOR resource. The types tell ResEdit how to display the data in a SCOR resource. The P0xx type is used to display strings. Replace the xx with the hexadecimal value for the string length. Because 31 in decimal is 1F in hexadecimal, a Str31 string uses a type of P01F. The second field of the ScoreRecord is of type long. In a template, a long is represented by DLNG — the D is for "data," the LNG is for "long." Figure 15-22 shows how the application-defined structure corresponds with the ResEdit template.

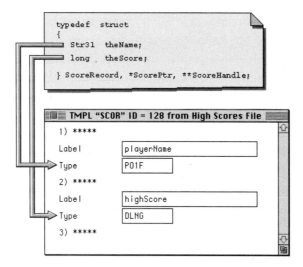

Figure 15-22
The items in a template correspond to the members of the application data structure that was used in writing the data to a resource.

That completes the TMPL resource. Close it, and then double-click on the SCOR icon in the High Scores File window. Double-click on any of the SCOR resources in the window that opens. When you do, the data will be displayed in a format that matches the template. Compare the ResEdit view of the SCOR resource in Figure 15-23 with the view without the template back in Figure 15-17.

If you need to view application-defined resources, create a template for each resource type. ResEdit offers a wealth of item types that allow you to pair template items with just about any data structure member type. The following structure definition uses several common data types. Beside each type is the ResEdit template item type for that application data type.

```
typedef   struct
{
    Str31    the31String;     // P01F
    Str63    the63String;     // P03F
    Str255   the255String;    // P0FF
    char     theChar;         // CHAR
    Byte     theByte;         // DBYT
    short    theShort;        // DWRD
    long     theLong;         // DLNG
    Boolean  theBool;         // BOOL
```

```
        Rect        theRect;            // RECT

    } MyBigRecord, *MyBigRecPtr, **MyBigRecHandle;
```

High Scores File
SCOR
TMPL
SCORs from High Scores File
ID
Size
Name
2490
36
"Score Record"
17333
36
"Score Record"
SCOR "Score Record" ID = 2490 from High Scores Fi
playerName
Taylor
highScore
6838

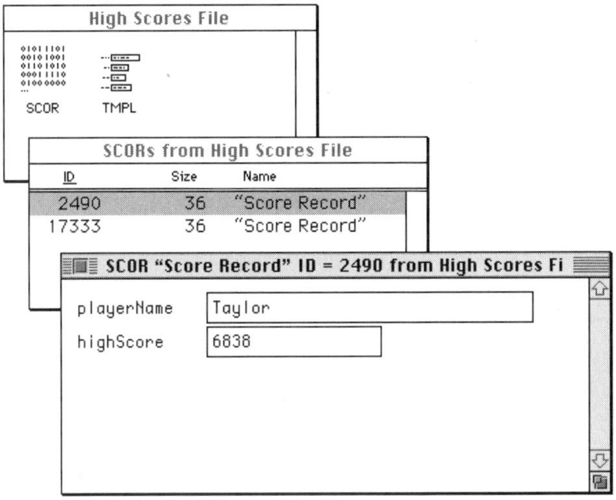

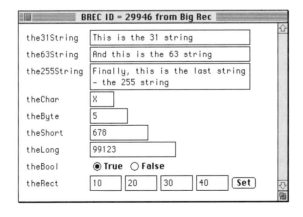

Figure 15-23

Viewing an application-defined `SCOR` resource from within ResEdit after a template has been created.

Figure 15-24 shows what the data from such a structure would look like if it were saved to a resource and then viewed using a template.

BREC ID = 29946 from Big Rec
the31String
This is the 31 string
the63String
And this is the 63 string
the255String
Finally, this is the last string
- the 255 string
theChar
X
theByte
5
theShort
678
theLong
99123
theBool
True
False
theRect
10
20
30
40
Set

Figure 15-24

Viewing an application-defined resource when a template exists for that resource type.

File Reference

This section summarizes the Toolbox functions that are used to work with files. While the emphasis here is on resource files, many of the routines work for other file types as well.

THE FILE SYSTEM SPECIFICATION DATA TYPE

A file is identified by a file system specification, which is represented by an FSSpec data structure that holds information about the file's pathname. The information includes the drive where the file is located, the directory where the file resides, and the name of the file.

FSSpec

The FSSpec is the data structure a program uses to identify where a particular file resides.

```
struct  FSSpec
{
    short   vRefNum;
    long    parID;
    Str63   name;
};
```

MAKING AN FSSPEC FOR A FILE

Before an application can work with a file, an FSSpec for that file is needed. Once an application has an FSSpec for a file, that file can be opened, accessed, and closed.

FSMakeFSSpec( )

To create an FSSpec for a file with a known pathname, call FSMakeFSSpec(). Typically FSMakeFSSpec() is used for files that are distributed with an application — resource, sound, or movie files that are used by the application.

```
Str255  theFileName = "/p:Movies ƒ:BlackJack";
short   theVolRef   = 0;
```

```
long     theDirID    = 0;
FSSpec  theFSSpec;
OSErr   theError;
theError = FSMakeFSSpec( theVolRef, theDirID, theFileName, &theFSSpec );
```

When FSMakeFSSpec() is passed a volume reference number, a parent directory ID, and a file name, it returns a filled-in FSSpec. If the file is located in a the same folder as the application or within a folder that is in the same folder as the application, set the volume reference number and the parent directory ID to 0, as you saw in the above snippet. If the file is in the same directory as the application, theFileName can be the file name as it appears on the desktop. If the file is in a subdirectory (a folder within the folder the application resides in), precede the file name with the subdirectory name. In the above snippet, the file BlackJack is in a folder named Movies ƒ, which resides in the same folder as the application.

FindFolder( )

The FindFolder() function doesn't create an FSSpec. It determines the volume reference number and the parent directory ID for a file that is to be kept in a particular folder. These two returned values can then be used in a subsequent call to FSMakeFSSpec().

```
#include <Folders.h>
short    desiredVolume = kOnSystemDisk;
OSType   desiredDir    = kPreferencesFolderType;
Boolean  createFolder  = kDontCreateFolder;
short    theVolRef;
long     theDirID;
OSErr    theError;
theError = FindFolder( desiredVolume, desiredDir,
                       createFolder, &theVolRef, &theDirID );
```

The first two parameters specify where a new file should be placed. The first is a volume reference number constant; the second is a parent directory constant. FindFolder() will use these two constants to find the path to the desired parent directory and will then return a volume reference number in theVolRef and a parent directory ID in theDirID. To specify a directory on the startup drive, use the Apple-defined constant kOnSystemDisk as the first parameter. To specify the Preferences folder as the parent directory, use the Apple-defined constant kPreferencesFolderType as the second parameter. To determine the pathname for a file that is to go in a different system folder, use one of the following constants for the second parameter:

```
kSystemFolderType       // fill will appear in the System Folder
kDesktopFolderType      // file will appear on desk top.
kStartupFolderType      // file will be a startup item
kAppleMenuFolderType    // file will appear in the apple menu
kPreferencesFolderType  // file will appear in the Preferences folder
```

The third parameter that is passed to FindFolder() tells the File Manager whether or not to create a new parent directory if the specified directory doesn't exist. Using the Apple-defined constant kCreateFolder here creates a new directory; kDontCreateFolder doesn't create a new directory.

USING THE STANDARD OPEN DIALOG BOX

The standard Open dialog box provides the user with the ability to open a file of his or her choice.

StandardFileReply

After the user makes a selection from the list in the standard Open dialog box, the File Manager creates an FSSpec for the file and places it in the sfFile field of a StandardFileReply data structure.

```
struct StandardFileReply
{
    Boolean      sfGood;
    Boolean      sfReplacing;
    OSType       sfType;
    FSSpec       sfFile;
    ScriptCode   sfScript;
    short        sfFlags;
    Boolean      sfIsFolder;
    Boolean      sfIsVolume;
    long         sfReserved1;
    short        sfReserved2;
};
```

StandardGetFile( )

The StandardGetFile() function displays the standard Open dialog box that lets the user open a text file.

```
SFTypeList          typeList = { 'TEXT', 0, 0, 0 };
StandardFileReply   theReply;
FileFilterProcPtr   procPtr = nil;
short               numFileTypes = 1;
StandardGetFile( procPtr, numFileTypes, typeList, &theReply );
```

The first parameter is used only if you want to mask out the display of certain files. If you're using StandardGetFile() to display sound files, you can refer to Chapter 13 for details. If you're using the routine to display movie files, refer to Chapter 14. To display a single file type, pass 1 as the second parameter. The typeList variable defines up to four file types to display. The last parameter is filled in by the Toolbox after the user selects a file from the standard Open dialog box. The sfFile field of the StandardFileReply variable theReply is of type FSSpec. After the user selects a file, the sfFile field will hold the FSSpec of the file. Use theReply.sfFile in subsequent Toolbox functions that require an FSSpec. If the user clicks the Cancel button, the sfGood field of the StandardFileReply will be false.

CREATING, OPENING, AND CLOSING RESOURCE FILES

Before a resource file can be worked with, it must be open. If a resource file doesn't already exist, a new one needs to be created.

FSpOpenResFile( )

The FSpOpenResFile() function opens an existing resource file in preparation for reading from or writing to the file.

```
FSSpec  theFSSpec;
short   fileRefNum;
fileRefNum = FSpOpenResFile( &theFSSpec, fsRdWrPerm );
```

Pass the function an FSSpec for the file to be opened. This FSSpec should have been filled in prior to the call to FSpOpenResFile(). Use either FSMakeFSSpec() or StandardGetFile() to create an FSSpec for the file to open. The second parameter is a permission level that specifies what types of operations can be performed on the file. Use one of the Apple-defined constants here: fsRdPerm to allow read-only access, fsWrPerm to allow write-only access, or fsRdWrPerm to allow both read and write operations to take place. After FSpOpenResFile() is finished, the function returns a reference number for the opened file. Use this reference number in subsequent calls to File Manager routines that require such a value. If FSpOpenResFile() returns a reference number of –1, then the attempt to open the resource file failed.

CloseResFile( )

To close an open resource file, pass the file's reference number to the Toolbox routine CloseResFile(). The reference number comes from the call that opened the file: FSpOpenResFile().

```
short   fileRefNum;
CloseResFile( fileRefNum );
```

FSpCreateResFile( )

To create a new, empty resource file, call FSpCreateResFile().

```
FSSpec      theFSSpec;
OSType      theCreator = 'RSED';
OSType      theType    = 'rsrc';
ScriptCode  theScript  = smSystemScript;
FSpCreateResFile( &theFSSpec, theCreator, theType, theScript );
```

Pass the function an FSSpec for the file to be created. This FSSpec should have been filled in prior to the call to FSpCreateResFile(). You can use FSMakeFSSpec() to create an FSSpec for a nonexistent file. If the file is to be saved in the Preferences folder, use the Toolbox function FindFolder().

The second and third parameters to FSpCreateResFile() are the file creator and file type for the new file. A creator of 'RSED' and a type of 'rsrc' will create a file that when double-clicked will be opened by ResEdit. A creator of 'Doug' and a type of 'RSRC' will create a file that when double-clicked will be opened by Resorcerer. Note that the creator and type only indicate which resource editor will be launched when a file is double-clicked. Both resource editors can open a file created by a different editor by using the Open menu item.

The final parameter is a script code. The script code is used by the Finder in the display of the file's name. The Apple-defined constant `smSystemScript` is suitable for this parameter.

After the file is created, it won't be open. Call `FSpOpenResFile()` to open the newly created file.

SAVING AND REMOVING RESOURCES

After copying data to a data structure in the application heap, the handle to that data can be used to write the data to a resource in a resource file.

BlockMoveData( )

The `BlockMoveData()` function copies bytes from one area in memory to another. You can use this function to copy the value of a string variable to a member of a structure in memory. Once the structure in memory is filled, it can be saved as a resource using calls to `AddResource()` and `WriteResource()`.

```
Str255   theSourceString;
Str255   theDestinationString;
Size     numBytes;
numBytes = theSourceString[0] + 1;
BlockMoveData( theSourceString, theDestinationString, numBytes );
```

The first parameter to `BlockMoveData()` is a pointer to the memory that is to be copied. A string of any type can be used here. The second parameter is a pointer to the memory that is to serve as the destination. Again, a string can be used for this parameter. The final parameter is the number of bytes to copy. The length (in bytes) of a string is found in the first element of the string. To get the total size of the string, add 1 byte to account for this length byte.

AddResource( )

The `AddResource()` function writes resource information to the resource map in memory and reserves disk space for a resource.

```
Handle   dataHandle;
ResType  theResType = 'RCRD';
short    theResID   = 2000;
Str255   theResName = "\pRecord";
AddResource( dataHandle, theResType, theResID, theResName );
```

The first parameter to `AddResource()` is a handle to a block of data in memory. This is the data that is to become a resource. Before calling `AddResource()`, call `NewHandleClear()` to allocate a block of memory the size of an application-defined data structure type and then fill the fields of that structure with values. The remaining parameters specify the type, ID, and name for the resource. The above snippet is used to create a resource of type `RCRD` with an ID of 2000 and a name of Record. All of the information in the `AddResource()` call gets added to the resource map in memory. `AddResource()` reserves disk space for the writing of the resource to disk but doesn't actually write the resource to disk. To perform that step, call `WriteResource()` after a call to `AddResource()`.

WriteResource( )

The `WriteResource()` function writes data from a block in the application heap to a resource in the current resource file.

```
Handle  dataHandle;
WriteResource( dataHandle );
```

Pass `WriteResource()` a handle to a block of memory. This block should hold the data that is to become a resource. The handle is originally obtained from the call to `NewHandleClear` — it's that call that reserves the memory for the data.

When an application calls `CloseResFile()` to close a resource file, the resource fork of that file is updated. Updating a fork includes writing to disk any new resources found in the resource map. Thus a call to `WriteResource()` isn't always necessary to save a resource — the closing of the file will accomplish the same task. If a resource fork is to be left open for any length of time, you should consider calling `WriteResource()`, which saves the resource immediately.

RemoveResource( )

The `RemoveResource()` function removes resource information from the resource map in memory.

```
Handle    dataHandle;
RemoveResource( dataHandle );
```

Passing this function a handle to resource data that has been loaded into memory removes the resource information from the resource map. To free the memory occupied by the data, call `DisposeHandle()` after the call to `RemoveResource()`. If you don't call `DisposeHandle()`, the memory will be released when the resource file is closed by a call to `CloseResFile()`.

Unique1ID( )

The `Unique1ID()` checks the IDs of all resources of a given type in the current resource file. Using this information, the function determines an ID that is unique for this resource type and returns it to the calling program.

```
short   theResID;
ResType theResType = 'RCRD';
theResID = Unique1ID( theResType );
```

Pass the `Unique1ID()` function a resource type, and the function will return a number that can be used as a resource ID for a new resource of that type. Calling `Unique1ID()` to select an ID for a new resource is safer than picking a number yourself. That's because a call to `Unique1ID()` is guaranteed to return an ID that is unused by any existing resources of the specified type. In the above snippet, all `RCRD` resources in the current resource fork will be examined in order to return an ID that is unique.

To determine a resource ID that is unique to *all* open resource forks, call the Toolbox `UniqueID()`. This function uses the same parameter as `Unique1ID()`.

RETRIEVING A RESOURCE FROM DISK

After saving a resource to disk, your application may need to use the resource data at a later time. To make that possible, load the data back into memory.

Get1IndResource( )

The `Get1IndResource()` function loads the data from a resource into memory. By including a call to this function in the body of a loop, your program can easily recall the data from all resources of a given type.

```
Handle    dataHandle;
ResType   theResType = 'RCRD';
short     index = 2;
dataHandle = Get1IndResource( theResType, index );
```

Pass this routine a resource type and an index that specifies one of the possible many resources of this type. In return, Get1IndResource() will load the data from this resource and return a handle to the data block. In the above snippet, the routine will load the data from the second RCRD resource in the current resource file.

To make use of *all* open resource forks, pass the same parameters to the Toolbox routine GetIndResource(). To load all resources of a type, first call the Toolbox function Count1Resources() to determine the number of resources of a type. Then use this value as a loop index, calling Get1IndResource() each pass through the loop.

Count1Resources( )

The Count1Resources() function counts the number of resources of a given type and returns that value to the calling program.

```
ResType   theResType = 'RCRD';
short     theNumRes;
theNumRes = Count1Resources( theResType );
```

Pass the Count1Resources() routine a resource type and the routine will count the number of resources of that type. Only the current resource fork will be examined for resources of the specified type. To count the number of resources of a given type in *all* open resource forks, call CountResources().

16

Printing

*M*any programmers who write Macintosh programs assume incorrectly that it's difficult to give an application the capability to print. Consequently, such a feature is usually left out of programs. In this chapter, you'll learn that adding just a few Printing Manager functions is all that's needed to give your Mac programs printing capabilities. You don't have to include code that handles various printer models differently; you can take advantage of printer driver software that's specific to the users' various printers to handle sending output to a printer.

In this chapter, you'll learn about opening a printer driver in preparation for printing. Then you'll see how any standard QuickDraw drawing commands can easily be directed to send their output to a printer rather than to a window. By the end of the chapter you'll understand how your programs can incorporate the standard printing style and job dialog boxes. These two dialog boxes give your program the uniform printing user interface that's found in all commercial Macintosh software applications.

Printing Basics

An application prints by first obtaining information about a printer and about the document to print. After that, a few calls to Printing Manager functions are all that's needed to print text and graphics.

THE PRINT RECORD

The first step in printing from a Mac application is the creation of a *print record,* which stores information about the printer and the user's printing job preferences. Printer information includes such factors as the printer's resolution and the margin that the printer will always use. The printing job preferences are used the next time the user prints something — that is, during the next printing job. This information includes the number of copies to print and the range of pages to print.

The TPrint data structure defines a print record. The THPrint data type is a handle to a print record. Because a program accesses this record through a handle, NewHandleClear() is called when a new print record is being created:

```
THPrint thePrintRecord;

thePrintRecord = (THPrint)NewHandleClear( sizeof( TPrint ) );
```

The above snippet allocates a block of memory the size of a TPrint structure, casts the resulting handle to a handle of type THPrint, and then returns that handle to the program.

A user of a program will indirectly set the values of the fields of a TPrint record. When a user chooses either the Page Setup or Print item found in the File menu of a program, the settings he or she selects get placed in the print record. Until that happens, the program will rely on a set of default values that can be placed in the new print record with a call to PrintDefault():

```
PrintDefault( thePrintRecord );
```

The one parameter to PrintDefault() is the THPrint print record handle returned by the call to NewHandleClear().

PREPARING A PROGRAM FOR PRINTING

All printers come with driver software, an extension that gets added to the Extensions folder. This driver software holds the code that converts

QuickDraw function calls into commands understood by the printer. Before your program calls any Printing Manager functions, it must open a printer's driver file:

```
PrOpen();
```

Most Mac users have more than one printer driver in the Extensions folder. A call to PrOpen() opens whichever driver was most recently selected by the user. The user makes this driver choice by running the Chooser program, found in the Apple menu.

After PrOpen() has been called, a program can call any Printing Manager function, including the previously mentioned PrintDefault(). When the program is through with a print driver, the file must be closed. A call to PrClose() takes care of that:

```
THPrint thePrintRecord;

thePrintRecord = (THPrint)NewHandleClear( sizeof( TPrint ) );
PrOpen();
PrintDefault( thePrintRecord );
// print something
PrClose();
```

The above snippet allocates memory for a print record, opens a printer driver, fills the print record with default values, prints something, and then closes the printer driver.

The "print something" comment in the above snippet is somewhat vague. Here's a snippet that provides a few of the details of how printing takes place:

```
THPrint  thePrintRecord;
TPPrPort thePrinterPort;

thePrinterPort = PrOpenDoc( thePrintRecord, nil, nil );

PrOpenPage( thePrinterPort, nil );
// QuickDraw commands
PrClosePage( thePrinterPort );

PrCloseDoc( thePrinterPort );
```

Just as drawing takes place in a port, so too does printing. A call to SetPort() tells QuickDraw to send drawing to a graphics port. A call to PrOpenDoc tells QuickDraw to send drawing to a printing graphics port.

When PrOpenDoc() has executed, a TPPrPort, a pointer to a new printing graphics port, will be returned. As you can see in the above snippet, this pointer is used by other Printing Manager routines. The first parameter in PrOpenDoc() is a handle to a print record. The second parameter is used when working with an existing printing graphics port. The third parameter is used to specify an area in memory that can be used as a printing buffer. You'll normally pass nil for both the second and third parameters. When finished with a printing graphics port, call PrCloseDoc() to close it.

PrOpenDoc() creates and initializes a new printing graphics port. PrOpenPage() starts the printing of a single page. Pass PrOpenPage() the printing graphics port pointer that was returned by PrOpenDoc(). The second parameter is for delaying printing (a feature generally used only by older printers); pass a value of nil here.

Once PrOpenPage() is called, printing begins. Each call to a QuickDraw function is now directed to a printer rather than to a window. After a page's worth of drawing has been sent to the printer, call PrClosePage() to stop printing. Pass PrClosePage() the same pointer used in the call to PrOpenPage().

QUICKDRAW AND PRINTING

You've just read that all the QuickDraw calls subsequent to a call to PrOpenPage() result in drawing taking place on a printer. Once PrOpenPage() is called, there's nothing special you need to do to the QuickDraw calls. Instead, just write the code as if the output were going to a window:

```
TPPrPort thePrinterPort;
Rect     theRect;

PrOpenPage( thePrinterPort, nil );
  SetRect( &theRect, 100, 50, 150, 70 );
  FrameRect( &theRect );
  MoveTo( 110, 65 );
  DrawString("\pFish!");
PrClosePage( thePrinterPort );
```

The preceding snippet draws a rectangle 50 pixels wide by 20 pixels high. In it the word "Fish!" is written. Notice that the four QuickDraw calls (SetRect(), FrameRect(), MoveTo(), and DrawString()) all appear just as you've seen them in the past. Figure 16-1 shows what a part of the resulting printed page would look like.

The QuickDraw calls that lie between the calls to PrOpenPage() and PrClosePage() don't need to be indented, as they are in the above snippet. That's done here only to emphasize what function calls are being used for printing and to make the code more readable.

Figure 16-1
QuickDraw commands can be sent to a printer.

Printers all leave a small margin on each side of a printed page. This margin differs from the margin that some programs, such as word processors, provide control over. Typically, this printer margin is about one-quarter of an inch on all sides of the paper. As Figure 16-2 shows, it is from these margins that the graphics pen measures come.

Your program can package the page-drawing QuickDraw calls in an application-defined function, rather than placing them all directly between the calls to PrOpenPage() and PrClosePage():

```
void UpdateFishWindow( void )
{
   SetRect( &theRect, 100, 50, 150, 70 );
   FrameRect( &theRect );
   MoveTo( 110, 65 );
   DrawString("\pFish!");
}
```

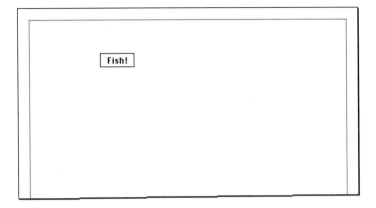

Figure 16-2
Pixel coordinates are measured from a page's border, or printer margin, not from the edge of the page.

Now, to print a page, just call the new function:

```
PrOpenPage( thePrinterPort, nil );
    UpdateFishWindow();
PrClosePage( thePrinterPort );
```

The application-defined `UpdateFishWindow()` function provides the commands that will be used to print one page — yet its name implies something else. As you may have already guessed, this function is capable of serving a dual purpose. You'll read about that later in this chapter, in the section titled "Windows and Printing."

EXAMPLE PROGRAM: PRINTINGINTRO

The PrintingIntro program prints the page shown back in Figure 16-1. When you run PrintingIntro you won't see a window, and you won't have to interact with the program. Instead, the program will briefly display a dialog box that tells you that spooling or printing is taking place. The application will quickly terminate, and after a few moments your printer will print out a single page.

You've already seen most of the code that makes up PrintingIntro. One addition that has been made is to the `UpdateFishWindow()` function. The PrintingIntro version of this application-defined routine uses a call to the

Toolbox function TextFont() to set the font to the Chicago, or system, font. It then makes a call to the Toolbox function TextSize() to set the font's size to 12 points:

```
TextFont( systemFont );
TextSize( 12 );
```

To keep most of the numbers from being scattered about the source code listing, PrintingIntro defines four constants: kFrameLeft, kFrameRight, kFrameTop, and kFrameBottom. These constants are used in setting up the rectangle and in centering the text within that rectangle.

As you look over the PrintingIntro source code, notice that no Printing Manager routines are called until PrOpen() is invoked — as required. Also notice that each call to an "Open" function has a corresponding call to a "Close" function — again, as required:

```
//_____
#include <Printing.h>

//_____
#define    kFrameLeft      100
#define    kFrameRight     150
#define    kFrameTop        50
#define    kFrameBottom     70

//_____
void main( void )
{
   THPrint   thePrintRecord;
   TPPrPort thePrinterPort;
   InitializeToolbox();
   thePrintRecord = (THPrint)NewHandleClear( sizeof( TPrint ) );
   PrOpen();
   PrintDefault( thePrintRecord );
   thePrinterPort = PrOpenDoc( thePrintRecord, nil, nil );

   PrOpenPage( thePrinterPort, nil );
    UpdateFishWindow();
   PrClosePage( thePrinterPort );
   PrCloseDoc( thePrinterPort );

   PrClose();
}

//_____
void UpdateFishWindow( void )
```

```
{
    Rect theRect;
    SetRect( &theRect, kFrameLeft, kFrameTop, kFrameRight, kFrameBottom );
    FrameRect( &theRect );
    TextFont( systemFont );
    TextSize( 12 );
    MoveTo( kFrameLeft + 10, kFrameBottom - 5 );
    DrawString("\pFish!");
}

//_____
void InitializeToolbox( void )
{
    InitGraf( &qd.thePort );
    InitFonts();
    InitWindows();
    InitMenus();
    TEInit();
    InitDialogs( 0L );
    FlushEvents( everyEvent, 0 );
    InitCursor();
}
```

The Printing Style and Printing Job Dialog Boxes

As you just saw in the PrintingIntro example, a program can print a page at any time. It's more likely, however, that you'll want to give the user control of how much to print and when printing should take place. The Printing Manager enables you to do just that. In this section you'll see an easy way to integrate two standard printing dialog boxes into your programs.

THE PRINTING STYLE DIALOG BOX

The printing style dialog box is the dialog box that is displayed when a user selects the Page Setup command found in the File menu of most applications. While the exact look of this dialog box varies with the printer driver used, all versions of it include a means of changing such printing style features as page orientation and paper size. Figures 16-3 and 16-4 show two of the many versions of the printing style dialog box.

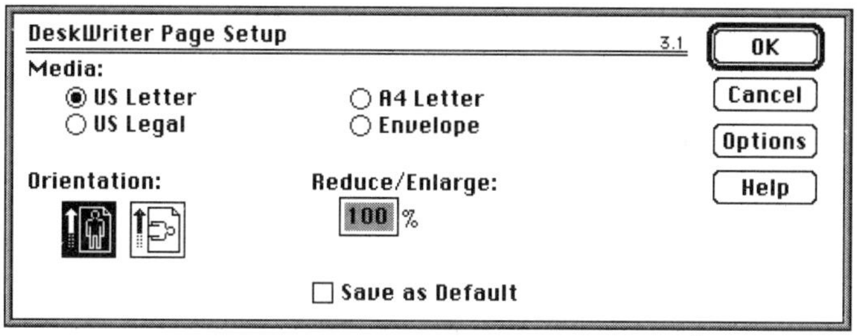

Figure 16-3

A typical printing style dialog box.

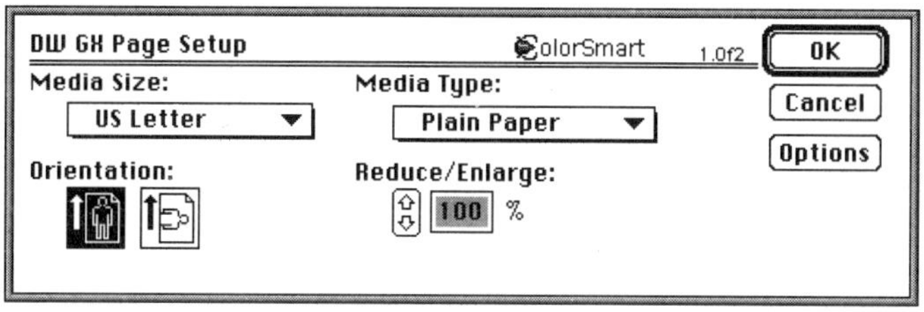

Figure 16-4

A second example of a printing style dialog box.

Your application can bring up the printing style dialog box by calling PrStlDialog(), as shown here:

```
THPrint   thePrintRecord;
Boolean   userClickedOK;

userClickedOK = PrStlDialog( thePrintRecord );
```

PrStlDialog() requires a parameter that is a handle to a print record; you should use the one returned by the call to NewHandleClear(). After the user chooses the desired settings and clicks on the OK button, PrStlDialog() updates the print record to reflect the user's preferences. PrStlDialog() then returns a value of true to let your program know that the user clicked on the style dialog box's OK button. If the user cancels his or her changes by clicking on the Cancel button, a value of false will be returned. Your program won't need to check this return value — the user's decision as to whether to keep or cancel his or her page setup changes won't affect your program's printing. The decision to print or not to print comes in the form of the printing job dialog box, which is discussed next.

THE PRINTING JOB DIALOG BOX

Most Macintosh programs make the display of the printing style dialog box
an option the user can pass on. Displaying the printing job dialog box,
however, is usually a requirement that precedes the printing of a document.
Figure 16-5 shows a typical job dialog box. As with the style dialog box, the
exact look of the job dialog box is dependent on the printer driver that the
user has selected.

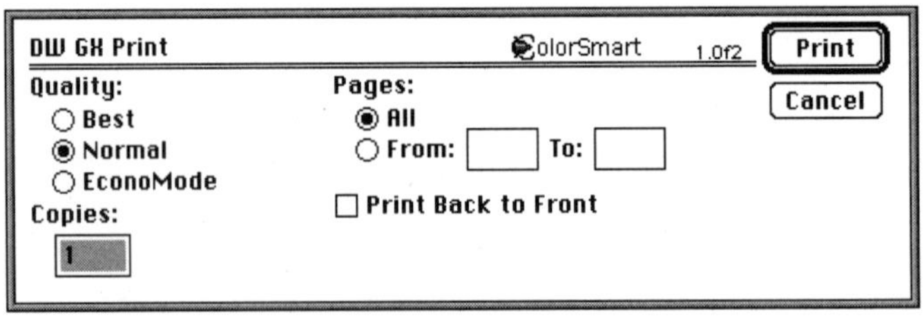

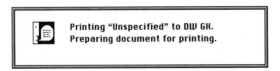

Figure 16-5
A typical printing job dialog box.

After the user has clicked on the OK or Print button in the printing job
dialog box (as with the printing style dialog box, printing job dialog boxes
differ), an alert message similar to the one shown in Figure 16-6 will appear.
As with the style and job dialog boxes, the look of this informative alert
varies depending on the printer driver being used.

> **Printing "Unspecified" to DW GX.**
> **Preparing document for printing.**

Figure 16-6
Printer drivers display a message after the user confirms printing.

To display the printing job dialog box, call `PrJobDialog()`. As shown
in this snippet, the one parameter used by `PrJobDialog()` is a handle to a
print record — the print record that was set up with an earlier call to
`NewHandleClear()`:

```
THPrint  thePrintRecord;
Boolean  userClickedOK;

userClickedOK = PrJobDialog( thePrintRecord );
if ( userClickedOK == true )
  // execute printing code
else
  // skip printing code
```

The PrJobDialog() function, like the PrStlDialog() function, returns a Boolean value that tells whether the user clicked on the OK button. In this chapter's snippet that used PrStlDialog(), this Boolean value wasn't checked after the call to PrStlDialog() completed. Whether the user clicks on the OK button or the Cancel button, the program will carry on in the same manner. The job dialog is handled differently, however. If the user clicks on the Cancel button in that dialog box, your program will have to skip the printing code that follows.

EXAMPLE PROGRAM: PRINTINGDIALOGS

The PrintingDialogs program demonstrates how a program can display both the printing style dialog box and the printing job dialog box. When you run PrintingDialogs you'll see the printing style dialog box. Make changes to the settings in this dialog box (switch the page orientation, for example), or leave everything as it is. Then click on the OK button or the Cancel button. The style dialog box will be dismissed, and in its place the job dialog box will appear. Click on the OK button to print out a rectangle with "Fish!" written in it.

If the user clicks on the Cancel button in the job dialog box, PrintingDialogs will end without printing. Because PrOpen() was called earlier in the program, it is necessary to call PrClose() to close the open printer driver file before quitting. You'll notice that whether or not the user chooses to print, a call to PrClose() will be made.

PrintingDialogs was developed by adding just a few lines of code to this chapter's PrintingIntro program — the new code is shown in bold type in the listing that follows:

```
//_____
void main( void )
{
  THPrint  thePrintRecord;
  TPPrPort thePrinterPort;
  Boolean  userClickedOK;

  InitializeToolbox();

  thePrintRecord = (THPrint)NewHandleClear( sizeof( TPrint ) );

  PrOpen();

  PrintDefault( thePrintRecord );

  userClickedOK = PrStlDialog( thePrintRecord );

  userClickedOK = PrJobDialog( thePrintRecord );
  if ( userClickedOK == true )
  {
   thePrinterPort = PrOpenDoc( thePrintRecord, nil, nil );

   PrOpenPage( thePrinterPort, nil );
     UpdateFishWindow();
   PrClosePage( thePrinterPort );

   PrCloseDoc( thePrinterPort );
  }

  PrClose();
}
```

EXAMPLE PROGRAM: PRINTPICTURE

The motto for Macintosh printing could be: If you can draw it, you can print it. Whatever QuickDraw commands you have used to draw to a window can be used to draw to a printer. The PrintPicture program adds a few lines of code to the UpdateFishWindow() function so that program now loads a PICT resource and draws the fish picture stored in that resource. Figure 16-7 shows what a printed page from PrintPicture looks like.

The resource file for the PrintPicture project holds a single PICT resource, as shown in Figure 16-8.

The source code for PrintPicture is very similar to the code for the previous example, PrintingDialogs. In fact, the main() functions used in the two programs are identical. For that reason, the PrintPicture listing shows only the three new constants and the new version of UpdateFishWindow():

Figure 16-7
The printed output generated by the PrintPicture program.

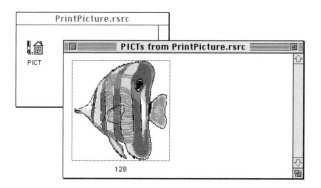

Figure 16-8
The one resource used by the PrintPicture project.

```
//_____
#define    rFishPicture    128
#define    kPictureLeft     20
#define    kPictureTop     100

//_____
void UpdateFishWindow( void )
```

```
{
    Rect       theRect;
    PicHandle thePicture;
    short      theWidth;
    short      theHeight;

    SetRect( &theRect, kFrameLeft, kFrameTop, kFrameRight, kFrameBottom );
    FrameRect( &theRect );

    TextFont( systemFont );
    TextSize( 12 );
    MoveTo( kFrameLeft + 10, kFrameBottom - 5 );
    DrawString("\pFish!");

    thePicture = GetPicture( rFishPicture );
    if ( thePicture == nil )
        ExitToShell();
    theRect = (**thePicture).picFrame;
    theWidth = theRect.right - theRect.left;
    theHeight = theRect.bottom - theRect.top;
    SetRect( &theRect, kPictureLeft, kPictureTop,
        kPictureLeft + theWidth, kPictureTop + theHeight );

    DrawPicture( thePicture, &theRect );

    ReleaseResource( (Handle)thePicture );
}
```

 If you need a refresher on working with pictures, refer to Chapter 10.

Windows and Printing

Up to this point, none of this chapter's example programs have displayed a window. Instead, they have just printed text and graphics and then quit. Macintosh programs don't normally print things that the user doesn't first view in a window, of course.

WINDOWS, PRINTERS, AND PORTS

Earlier you read that the motto for Macintosh printing could be: If you can draw it, you can print it. A more succinct version of that same motto might be: A port is a port. You can use the same QuickDraw commands to draw to a window and to a printer because the Macintosh treats both a window and a printer as a port. If you precede a QuickDraw function call with a call to SetPort(), the results of the QuickDraw function will end up in a window. If you precede the same QuickDraw function call with a call to PrOpenDoc(), the results of the QuickDraw function will end up on a sheet of printer paper. The following snippet provides an example. It draws a string to a window, then draws that same string to a printer:

```
WindowPtr  theWindow;
TPPrPort   thePrinterPort;
THPrint    thePrintRecord;

// open a window
// prepare for printing

SetPort( theWindow );
MoveTo( 10, 20 );
DrawString( "\pDrawing to a port" );
thePrinterPort = PrOpenDoc( thePrintRecord, nil, nil );
MoveTo( 10, 20 );
DrawString( "\pDrawing to a port" );
```

Of course, good programming style dictates that code shouldn't be needlessly repeated, as it is above. So you'll want to write a single function that can be used to draw to a window initially, update the window when necessary, and draw the window contents to a printer:

```
void UpdateTestWindow( void )
{
  MoveTo( 10, 20 );
  DrawString( "\pDrawing to a port" );
}
```

The next snippet substitutes the MoveTo() and DrawString() code used in the previous printing snippet with calls to the UpdateTestWindow() function:

```
WindowPtr  theWindow;
TPPrPort   thePrinterPort;
THPrint    thePrintRecord;

// open a window
// prepare for printing

SetPort( theWindow );
UpdateTestWindow();
thePrinterPort = PrOpenDoc( thePrintRecord, nil, nil );
UpdateTestWindow();
```

By now you should understand why this chapter's printing examples made use of a function named `UpdateFishWindow()`. From your readings in Chapter 7 you're familiar with window updating. By now you've probably written at least a small program of your own that draws to a window and handles the redrawing to that window in response to update events. No doubt your program employs functions with names similar to `UpdateWindow()`. Now that you're about to incorporate printing into your programs, there's no need to change your programming practices. To handle the printing of a window, first prepare for printing as described in this chapter. Then call the window's update routine, as done in the above snippet.

EXAMPLE PROGRAM: PRINTWINDOW

The PrintWindow program prints the same graphics as the PrintPicture program: a rectangle, a short string, and a picture of a fish. The PrintWindow program also displays those graphics in a window, as shown in Figure 16-9.

Figure 16-9
The window displayed by the PrintingWindow program.

After the window appears on the screen, the printing style dialog box opens. After that dialog box is dismissed, the job dialog box opens (see Figure 16-10). Clicking on the OK or Print button sends the contents of the window to the printer. The job dialog box will be dismissed, but the window will remain on the screen. To end the program, click the mouse button.

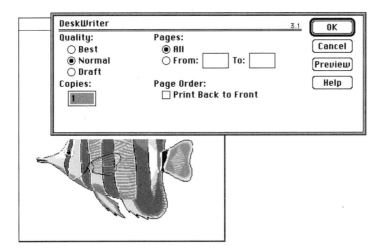

Figure 16-10
The printing job dialog box obscures part of the window, like the printing style dialog box, necessitating an update.

PrintWindow calls `UpdateFishWindow()` three times. The first call is made to initially draw the graphics to the newly opened window. The second call is made from within an application-defined printing routine named `PrintFishWindow()`. The last call is made to update the window. In Figure 16-10 you can see that the printing job dialog box obscures a part of the window. When the job dialog box is dismissed, the part of the window that was obscured needs to be redrawn. The third call to `UpdateFishWindow()` takes care of that:

```
InitializePrinting();

theWindow = GetNewWindow( rFishWindow, nil, (WindowPtr)-1L );
SetPort( theWindow );
UpdateFishWindow();

PrintFishWindow();

SetPort( theWindow );
UpdateFishWindow();
```

BY THE WAY

Your own full-featured programs won't have printing dialog boxes that mysteriously pop out at users. Instead, they will appear in response to File menu commands that you'll name Page Setup and Print.

In response to a Page Setup selection, your program should simply call PrStlDialog(). Handling the Print menu item takes a little extra work—but not a lot. You've already seen the code for displaying the printing job dialog box. The extra work comes into play if your program allows more than one window to be open at a time. If it does, you'll need to call the correct update routine to make sure the correct window contents go to the printer.

The Print menu item should print the contents of the frontmost window. You can call FrontWindow() to get a WindowPtr to that window. If you're using the multiple window handling technique described in Chapter 7, you'll then find out what type of window is to be printed. After that, call the correct update function. That code might look something like this:

```
switch ( theWindowType )
{
  case kTextWindow:
    UpdateTextWindow();
    break;
  case kPictureWindow:
    UpdatePictureWindow();
    break;
}
```

PrintWindow handles the creation of the program's print record a little differently from the preceding examples. Because a program needs only one print record and because that print record needs to be allocated and initialized only one time, the program handles these tasks in a short application-defined routine. The program also makes the print record handle a global variable so that it can be used outside of this function:

```
THPrint gPrintRecord;

void InitializePrinting( void )
{
  gPrintRecord = (THPrint)NewHandleClear( sizeof( TPrint ) );
  PrOpen();
  PrintDefault( gPrintRecord );
  PrClose();
}
```

The `InitializePrinting()` routine serves as a good reminder that `PrOpen()` must be called before a Printing Manager function can be invoked. It also shows that a call to `PrOpen()` must be paired with a call to `PrClose()`. While the program could wait until a later time to make the call to `PrClose()`, it's best to call this routine immediately after the current print-related task is complete. Both `PrOpen()` and `PrClose()` can be called again when the program performs another printing chore. This is in fact what the PrintingWindow program does in its `PrintFishWindow()` routine:

```
//_____
#include <Printing.h>
//_____
#define     rFishWindow      128
#define     rFishPicture     128
#define     kFrameLeft       100
#define     kFrameRight      150
#define     kFrameTop         50
#define     kFrameBottom      70
#define     kPictureLeft      20
#define     kPictureTop      100

//_____
THPrint gPrintRecord;

//_____
void main( void )
{
  WindowPtr theWindow;

  InitializeToolbox();

  InitializePrinting();

  theWindow = GetNewWindow( rFishWindow, nil, (WindowPtr)-1L );
  SetPort( theWindow );
  UpdateFishWindow();

  PrintFishWindow();

  SetPort( theWindow );
  UpdateFishWindow();

  while ( !Button() )
    ;
}

//_____
void PrintFishWindow( void )
{
  TPPrPort thePrinterPort;
  Boolean  userClickedOK;
```

```
    PrOpen();
    userClickedOK = PrStlDialog( gPrintRecord );

    userClickedOK = PrJobDialog( gPrintRecord );
    if ( userClickedOK == true )
    {
     thePrinterPort = PrOpenDoc( gPrintRecord, nil, nil );

     PrOpenPage( thePrinterPort, nil );
       UpdateFishWindow();
     PrClosePage( thePrinterPort );
     PrCloseDoc( thePrinterPort );
    }

    PrClose();
}

//_____
void UpdateFishWindow( void )
{
  Rect     theRect;
  PicHandle thePicture;
  short    theWidth;
  short    theHeight;

  SetRect( &theRect, kFrameLeft, kFrameTop, kFrameRight, kFrameBottom );
  FrameRect( &theRect );

  TextFont( systemFont );
  TextSize( 12 );
  MoveTo( kFrameLeft + 10, kFrameBottom - 5 );
  DrawString("\pFish!");

  thePicture = GetPicture( rFishPicture );
  if ( thePicture == nil )
     ExitToShell();
  theRect = (**thePicture).picFrame;
  theWidth = theRect.right - theRect.left;
  theHeight = theRect.bottom - theRect.top;
  SetRect( &theRect, kPictureLeft, kPictureTop,
      kPictureLeft + theWidth, kPictureTop + theHeight );

  DrawPicture( thePicture, &theRect );

  ReleaseResource( (Handle)thePicture );
}

//_____
void InitializePrinting( void )
{
  gPrintRecord = (THPrint)NewHandleClear( sizeof( TPrint ) );
  PrOpen();
  PrintDefault( gPrintRecord );
  PrClose();
}
```

Printing Reference

This section describes the most commonly used Printing Manager routines. These functions prepare a program for printing and display the two standard printing dialog boxes.

INITIALIZING PRINTING

Before printing, create a print record. The print record holds information about printer features and information about the user's preferences for the current print job.

NewHandleClear( )

Call NewHandleClear() to allocate memory for a print record — a TPrint structure:

```
THPrint thePrintRecord;

thePrintRecord = (THPrint)NewHandleClear( sizeof( TPrint ) );
```

PrintDefault( )

To initialize the fields of a new print record, call PrintDefault(). These default values will be changed by the user when he or she sets options in the printing style and printing job dialog boxes:

```
THPrint thePrintRecord;

PrintDefault( thePrintRecord );
```

The one parameter to PrintDefault() is a handle to a print record. This is the handle returned by NewHandleClear() when the print record was created.

PrOpen( )

Before calling any Printing Manager functions, open the current printer driver by calling `PrOpen()`. The current driver is the one that was last selected in the Chooser. Each call to `PrOpen()` must be balanced with a call to `PrClose()`:

```
PrOpen();
```

PrClose( )

When through with a printer driver, call `PrClose()`. A call to `PrClose()` must be preceded somewhere in your code by a call to `PrOpen()`:

```
PrClose();
```

PRINTING GRAPHICS PORTS

All printing takes place via a printing graphics port. Your program needs to create such a port before printing can take place.

PrOpenDoc( )

To create and initialize a new printing graphics port, call `PrOpenDoc()`. This routine tells the system to send the results of all subsequent calls to QuickDraw routines to a printer rather than a window:

```
TPPrPort  thePrinterPort;
THPrint   thePrintRecord;
TPPrPort  theExistingPort = nil;
Ptr       theIOBuffer = nil;

thePrinterPort = PrOpenDoc( thePrintRecord, theExistingPort, theIOBuffer );
```

The first parameter to `PrOpenDoc()` is a handle to a print record. This is the handle returned by `NewHandleClear()` when the print record was created. The second parameter is used when working with an existing printing graphics port. The third parameter is used to specify an area in memory that can be used as a printing buffer. You'll normally pass a value of `nil` for both of these parameters. Balance a call to `PrOpenDoc()` with a call to `PrCloseDoc()`.

PrCloseDoc( )

When finished with a printing graphics port, call `PrCloseDoc()`. The one parameter is the pointer to the printing graphics port that was returned by the prior call to `PrOpenDoc()`:

```
TPPrPort thePrinterPort;

PrCloseDoc( thePrinterPort );
```

PRINTING

Printing of a page takes place when the Printing Manager function `PrOpenPage()` is called. A call to `PrClosePage()` terminates the printing of the page.

PrOpenPage( )

To begin printing a page, call `PrOpenPage()`. Once this call has been made, the results of all subsequent QuickDraw commands will appear on a printed page:

```
TPPrPort thePrinterPort;

PrOpenPage( thePrinterPort, nil );
```

The first parameter in `PrOpenPage()` is the pointer to the printing graphics port that was returned by `PrOpenDoc()`. The second parameter is used only with older printers that support delayed printing. You'll generally pass a value of `nil` here. To end the printing of a page, call `PrClosePage()`. Balance a call to `PrOpenPage()` with a call to `PrClosePage()`.

PrClosePage( )

When a page has been printed, call `PrClosePage()`. The parameter in `PrOpenPage()` is the pointer to the printing graphics port that was returned by `PrOpenDoc()`:

```
TPPrPort thePrinterPort;

PrClosePage( thePrinterPort );
```

THE STANDARD PRINTING DIALOG BOXES

The Printing Manager provides two standard dialog boxes that let Mac programmers add a uniform printing interface to their applications.

[3]PrStlDialog( )

To display the standard printing style dialog box, call PrStlDialog(). This dialog box offers the user a chance to change printer settings such as page orientation and paper size. Changes made by the user will be applied in subsequent print jobs:

```
THPrint thePrintRecord;
Boolean userClickedOK;

userClickedOK = PrStlDialog( thePrintRecord );
```

The one parameter in PrStlDialog() is a handle to a print record. You should pass PrStlDialog() the THPrint variable that was returned by NewHandleClear(). After the user dismisses the style dialog box, PrStlDialog() will return a value of true if the user clicked on the OK button or false if the Cancel button was clicked.

PrJobDialog( )

To display the standard printing job dialog box, call PrJobDialog(). This dialog box offers the user the chance to change document printing settings such as the number of copies to print and the quality at which the pages should be printed. Clicking on the OK or Print button in this dialog will start the print job:

```
THPrint thePrintRecord;
Boolean userClickedOK;

userClickedOK = PrJobDialog( thePrintRecord );
if ( userClickedOK == true )
  // execute printing code
else
  // skip the printing code
```

The one parameter used by PrJobDialog() is a handle to a print record. You should pass PrJobDialog() the THPrint variable that was returned by NewHandleClear(). After the user dismisses the style dialog box, PrJobDialog() will return a value of true if the user clicked on the Print button or false if the Cancel button was clicked. If the user cancels the print job, your code should avoid making the call to PrOpenPage() that normally starts the print job.

A PowerPC Programming

You've seen that the CD that accompanies this book holds four project versions for each example program. For every example, there are two Symantec projects and two Metrowerks projects. That means that whether you have the Symantec IDE or the Metrowerks IDE, you will be able to build both a 68K application and a PPC (PowerPC) application for each of the dozens of example programs. You may have also noticed that for any given example program, both the 68K project and the PPC project use the same source code file and the same resource file — so it may seem unnecessary for you to create two versions of any one program. In this appendix you'll see why a developer might want to create these two versions. More important, you'll see how you can easily combine these two versions into a single application that satisfies owners of both 68K-based and PPC-based Macs.

Native PowerPC Code and Backward Compatibility

As mentioned in Chapter 1, before 1994 all Macintosh computers used one of the Motorola 680x0 microprocessors: the 68000, 68020, 68030, or 68040. Starting in 1994, Macintosh models began to appear that used one of the new PowerPC 601 microprocessors.

After source code is compiled and linked, the resulting program, or *stand-alone application,* consists of computer instructions. Different microprocessors recognize different sets of instructions. That's why a program built for a Macintosh won't run on a PC-compatible computer, and vice versa. So how is it that older programs, built to run on Macs driven by one of the 680×0 microprocessors, can run on newer PowerPC-based Macs? And how do newer programs, applications using PowerPC instructions, remain *backward-compatible* with older Macs? The answer is twofold, involving *emulation* and *fat binary applications.*

68K EMULATION

Each PowerPC-based Macintosh has emulation software, software that enables the computer to understand instructions from the instruction set of the 680×0 microprocessors. When a PowerPC-based Mac runs a program that consists of 680×0 instructions, it funnels the instructions through the emulation software. The emulation software, in effect, converts 680×0 instructions to PowerPC instructions and then passes the converted instructions on to the PowerPC microprocessor.

While emulation enables a program built to run on a 680×0-based Macintosh to also run on a PowerPC-based Macintosh, the program will not take advantage of the enhanced speed of the PowerPC microprocessor. The instruction conversions that the emulator is responsible for take time. The time spent converting instructions from one instruction set to the other offsets the speed difference between the old 680×0 microprocessors and the new PowerPC microprocessors.

NATIVE POWERPC CODE

If you'd like to compile your source code so that the resulting application does take advantage of the fast PowerPC-based Macs, you'll want to use an integrated development environment, or IDE, that generates *native* PowerPC code. Such an IDE produces a program that consists of instructions from the PowerPC instruction set rather than the 680×0 instruction set. The result? A program that runs on a PowerPC-based Mac without the assistance — and subsequent delays — of the emulator software. If you own a Metrowerks CodeWarrior IDE, you're all set. Every version of

CodeWarrior includes a compiler that generates 680×0 code and a compiler that generates native PowerPC code. If you use the Symantec IDE, you'll need to use version 8.0 or later; prior versions didn't include a compiler that produces native PowerPC code.

The advantage of producing a program that consists of native code is that it runs faster on a PPC-based Mac than a program generated from a compiler that produces 680×0 code does. The disadvantage is that a PowerPC native program can't run on 680×0-based Macintosh. This limits its usefulness, since owners of older Macs can't use it. This potential dilemma can be solved by creating a *fat binary application.*

FAT BINARY APPLICATIONS

A fat binary application, also referred to as a fat binary or fat app, is a Macintosh application that holds two versions of a single program. Within the application are both native PowerPC code and 680×0 code. When this one program is launched on an older 68K-based Mac, the section of the program that holds the 680×0 code gets loaded into memory. If this same program is instead launched on a PPC-based Mac, the PowerPC code gets loaded into memory.

The advantage of making an application a fat app is that not only owners of both old and new Macs can run the program (after all, that's also true for an older 68K-based application), but also owners of PPC-based Macs get to enjoy the speed gains of their fast PowerPC microprocessor. That's because the fat app will run the fast PowerPC native version of the code on a PPC-based Macintosh.

The only disadvantage of making an application a fat app is that it occupies more disk space because it holds two versions of the application code. With the falling prices for large hard drives, this disadvantage is becoming a trivial one.

Creating a fat app

To create a fat application, you first create a 68K project and generate a 680×0 version of a program. That is, you build a 68K program just as you normally would. After that, you create a PPC project, just as if you were instead generating a PPC version of the same program. The PPC project has one new addition to it, however: You'll add the 68K application to the PPC project. When you then generate the PPC version of the program, your IDE will embed the code and resources from the 68K program into the PPC program. The result will be a single application that holds two versions of code — a fat app.

The next two sections use the SimpleMovie example from Chapter 1 to provide a specific example of how you can build a fat app using either Metrowerks CodeWarrior or the Symantec IDE.

Creating a fat app using Metrowerks CodeWarrior

If you're using CodeWarrior, first create a 68K version of the program you wish to turn into a fat app. On this book's CD you will find a folder named XA PowerPC, which holds an example that uses the SimpleMovie program. The project shown at the top of Figure A-1 shows how the 68K project looks using the CW6 version of CodeWarrior.

After building and testing the 68K version of the program, create a PPC project. Add the same source code file you used for the 68K version, as shown in the project at the bottom of Figure A-1. Again, this figure is from the CW6 version of CodeWarrior. Next, add the 68K application to this PPC project. CodeWarrior lets you add an application to a project just as you'd add a source code file, resource file, or library.

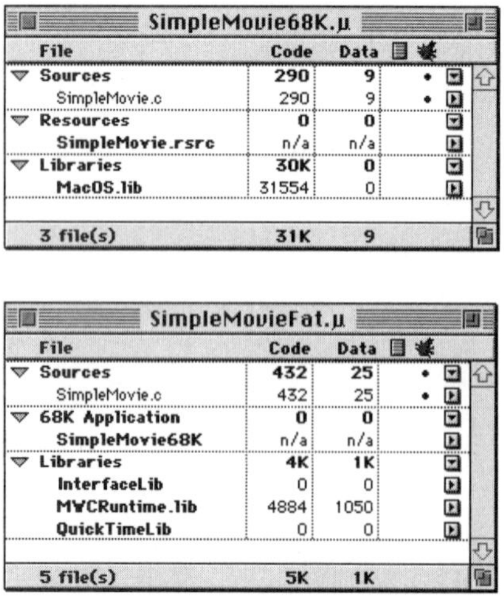

SimpleMovie68K.µ

File	Code	Data		
▽ Sources	290	9	•	▣
SimpleMovie.c	290	9	•	▣
▽ Resources	0	0		▣
SimpleMovie.rsrc	n/a	n/a		▣
▽ Libraries	30K	0		▣
MacOS.lib	31554	0		▣
3 file(s)	31K	9		

SimpleMovieFat.µ

File	Code	Data		
▽ Sources	432	25	•	▣
SimpleMovie.c	432	25	•	▣
▽ 68K Application	0	0		▣
SimpleMovie68K	n/a	n/a		▣
▽ Libraries	4K	1K		▣
InterfaceLib	0	0		▣
MWCRuntime.lib	4884	1050		▣
QuickTimeLib	0	0		▣
5 file(s)	5K	1K		

Figure A-1
CodeWarrior 68K and PPC projects used in the creation of a fat app.

Because the application holds the resources for the program, there's no need to add the resource file to the PPC version. The fat app needs only one set of resources, and it gets it from the 68K program that CodeWarrior merges into the application.

When you select Make from the Project menu, CodeWarrior will create a single application that holds both the 68K code and the PPC code.

Creating a fat app using Symantec C++

If you're using the Symantec C++ 8.0 IDE, you actually have two development environments: the THINK Project Manager, which is used to generate 68K applications, and the Symantec Project Manager, which is used to generate PPC applications. You can build a fat app as follows: First, run the THINK Project Manager and create a 68K version of the program. On this book's CD you will find a folder named XA PowerPC that contains an example that uses the SimpleMovie program. The project shown at the top of Figure A-2 shows how the 68K project looks using the THINK Project Manager that is included on the Symantec C++ 8.0 CD.

After building and testing the 68K version of the program, quit the THINK Project Manager and launch the Symantec Project Manager. Create a PPC project. Add the same source code file you used for the 68K version, as shown in the project at the bottom of Figure A-2.

SimpleMovie68K.π	
Name	**Code**
▽ **Sources**	**250**
SimpleMovie.c	246
▽ **Resources**	**4**
SimpleMovie.rsrc	0
▽ **Libraries**	**7110**
MacTraps	7106
Totals	**7942**

✓ SimpleMovieFat.π		
Headers ▼ Options SimpleMovieFat.π ▼		
✓ ⇩**Name** ※		**Code**
▽ ▢ **Libraries**		**2120**
◇ ▦ InterfaceLib.xcoff		0
◇ ▦ MathLib.xcoff		0
◇ ▦ PPCRuntime.o		2120
◇ ▦ QuickTimeLib.xc...		0
◇ ▤ SimpleMovie.c ◇		424
Totals		**2544**

Figure A-2
Symantec 68K and PPC projects used in the creation of a fat app.

As shown in Figure A-2, at the time of this writing the two Symantec development environments have a different look. Soon, Symantec will release a version of its IDE that will provide a more uniform look to the two types of projects, 68K and PPC.

Because you'll be merging the 68K application, which holds the resources for the program, into the PPC version, there's no need to add the resource file to the PPC version. The fat app needs only one set of resources, and it gets it from the 68K program that Symantec C++ merges into the application.

Next, select Options from the Project menu. Click on the Project Type icon at the left of the Project Options dialog box, and then check the Merge checkbox. Click on the Select application button to bring up a dialog box that lets you select a 68K application to merge with the PPC application you're going to build from this project. Figure A-3 shows that the SimpleMovie68K application will be merged.

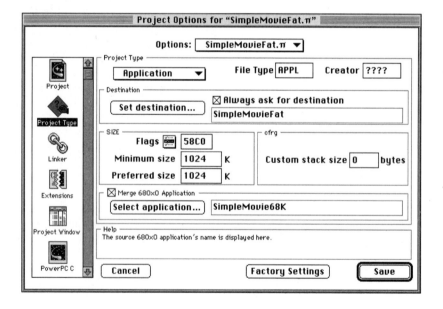

Figure A-3
Using the Symantec Project Manager to specify that a 68K application be merged with a PowerPC application.

After dismissing the Project Options dialog box, select Build Application from the Project menu. The Symantec Project Manager will then create a single application that holds both the 68K code and the PowerPC code.

B

Copland Programming

*A*ppendix A, PowerPC Programming, discusses compatibility across microprocessors. This appendix deals with compatibility across operating systems. At the time of this writing, Apple's much-anticipated new System 8 operating system — better known by its original code name, Copland — has not been released. When it does become available, it will offer Macintosh users an interface with a whole new look and a host of new features. A few of those features are:

- More visual and behavioral consistency among interface elements such as windows, menus, and controls.
- Improved, more flexible file management.
- Better memory protection.
- On-screen assistance to aid users in setting up and performing complex tasks.

When Copland is released, it will offer the Macintosh developer a large set of new Toolbox routines with which this added functionality can be incorporated into newly developed programs. While the details of the routines that will be in the new Copland Toolbox have yet to be made public, there are still some steps you can take to ensure that your program will work well with Copland.

Copland Code and Backward Compatibility

Apple is going to great lengths to see to it that existing programs don't "break" when run on the Copland operating system. In doing so, Apple is doing much of the work for you — programs like the ones in this book should all work well now and when System 8 arrives. If you write a Mac program now, however, there are a few things you can watch for to ensure that your program makes a smooth transition to Copland. Because Copland hasn't been released at the time of this writing, there are many unknowns regarding what it will do and just how it will do it. Apple has, however, provided several hints for Macintosh developers.

Rather than dealing with how to take advantage of the new features that will be added to the operating system, most of the tips Apple has supplied are aimed at keeping current programs compatible with Copland. The following sections describe some of the key points to watch for as you program the Mac.

SYSTEM 7.5 AND COPLAND

If you write programs that behave well on a machine running System 7.5, you're on your way to programming for Copland. That's because besides adding new Toolbox routines, Copland supports the Toolbox routines used under System 7.5.

All of the example programs included in this book — and on the CD — were developed on Macs running System 7.5.

EXTENSIONS

Included in the Copland operating system will be many of the features that are now available only as system software extensions. That means extensions like QuickTime and QuickDraw 3D will disappear. It also means that all Macintosh users who have Copland on their machines will have access to these dynamic elements of the Macintosh. Programs that currently make use of extensions — like the QuickTime movie examples in this book — will still work when run under Copland.

If you create a program that is "Copland only" — that is, requires Copland in order to run — you can assume that all users of your program will be able to take advantage of any parts of your program that make use of the features now supported by system software extensions. If your program is to be backward-compatible with System 7.5, it will still need to check to see if the user has the necessary extension or extensions on his or her Macintosh.

The development of extensions is beyond the scope of this book and isn't discussed in this text. While system software extensions are usually thought of as being supplied by Apple, any knowledgeable programmer can write an extension. Obviously, now is not the time to write your own extension because Copland is imminent.

USER-DEFINED INTERFACE

Copland will enable users to personalize their computers by changing the look of the interface. This may seem to contradict the previously mentioned Copland goal of improving interface consistency. The degree to which users can make changes, however, will be limited by a number of *themes*. Each theme is a set of designs. Users will be able to choose an interface design set that provides a certain desired look to the desktop and applications. At any time, a user can switch to a different theme. While different themes will provide different interface looks, the interface functionality — the way windows, menus, and controls operate — will remain constant for each.

Because the user will be able to change the look of interface elements, your programs shouldn't make assumptions about certain aspects of these elements. For example, while the default background color for all windows is now white, under Copland your program shouldn't make this assumption. If currently your program for some reason clears a window by filling it with a white pattern, you'll want to change this behavior. If the user chooses an interface design set that uses nonwhite windows, your application's white window will look out of place. It also won't update properly when the user obscures the window and then again brings the window to the forefront. If you don't make the change now, at least comment your source code so that you can easily make the change when you modify your program for Copland:

```
// ** Copland note: change the following "white-out" code
SetRect( &theRect, 0, 0, kWindowWidth, kWindowHeight );
FillRect( &theRect, &qd.white );
```

DATA STRUCTURE ACCESS

In this book you've seen emphasis placed on accessing Apple data structure fields through the use of accessor functions. Consider the changing of the fill pattern used by the graphics pen as an example. Rather than changing the pnPat field of a window's GrafPort data structure directly, you use the PenPat() function:

```
WindowPtr   theWindow;

SetPort( theWindow );
theWindow->pnPat = qd.ltGray;    // works, but improper!
PenPat( &qd.ltGray );            // works, and is proper
```

The use of Toolbox functions such as PenPat() free you, the programmer, from memorizing the fields of Apple-defined data structures such as the GrafPort. Using these functions also gives Apple the freedom to make changes to the fields of a data structure should the need arise. In doing this, Apple would make corresponding changes to the definition of Toolbox functions used to access fields of the structure. All these changes would be hidden from the programmer; you would go on using the Toolbox functions as you always have.

Because there isn't a Toolbox routine to access every field of every Apple-defined data structure, programmers have occasionally found the need to access a data structure field directly. Knowing this, Apple has been reluctant to make changes to data structures. If they did, the existing code of some programmers would break.

Along with Copland comes a host of new accessor functions. These new Copland Toolbox routines will eliminate the need for any programmer to access Apple-defined data structure fields directly. This affords Apple the luxury of knowing that if improvements warrant the change of data structure fields, these changes can be made safely. To keep your code compatible with Copland, it's more important than ever to avoid directly accessing data structure fields — always use the provided accessor Toolbox functions.

GRAPHICS

QuickDraw graphic routines have been a part of the Mac's system software since the first Macintosh. Recently, two new versions of QuickDraw have been added to the original — QuickDraw GX and QuickDraw 3D. The code that programs use to gain the functionality offered by the two newer QuickDraw versions is found in system extensions. In Copland, those extensions will disappear. The code for the Toolbox routines for all three versions of QuickDraw will henceforth be a part of the system software found on all Macintosh computers.

Copland will use a common code base to implement all versions of QuickDraw. The result will be improved performance: Drawing will be accelerated. Copland will support all current Toolbox graphics routines, so the graphics your programs now use will not only work under Copland, their performance will also improve with no programming effort on your part.

What's on the CD?

On the CD included with this book, you'll find a folder named IDG Sydow Book Examples. Simply double-click on the CD-ROM icon to display the folder and its contents.

About This CD

The IDG Sydow Book Examples folder holds the source code for all of the example programs found in the book. Because IDG Books wants these files to be usable by all readers — regardless of which compiler they own — the examples are provided in a variety of formats. Within the IDG Sydow Book Examples folder you'll find two more folders. If you own Metrowerks CodeWarrior, you'll use the projects and C language source code files found in the Metrowerks Versions folder. If you use a Symantec compiler such as the THINK C or Symantec C++ compiler, you'll use the projects and C language source code files found in the Symantec Versions folder. Additionally, whether you program for the Mac or the new PowerPC Macintosh, you'll find a project that works for you.

Once you've found the appropriate folder that matches the compiler you use, double-click on it to open it. In it you'll find sixteen more folders — one for each chapter in the book. Open one of these subfolders and you'll find that each chapter example has its project and source code in its own folder. Consider the SimpleMovie program — the second example in Chapter 1. The project and source code files for this example can be found in the P02 Simple Movie folder in the C01 Introduction folder. Here, "C01" stands for Chapter 1 and "P02" stands for program 2. This naming convention applies no matter which compiler your using.

Besides the IDG Sydow Book Examples folder, which holds all of the example code, you'll find a Goodies folder. In this folder are a variety of shareware and public domain software that you'll find useful in your programming endeavors. One example is the SoundApp utility. This program allows you to convert sound files from one format to another — a useful trick for turning just about any sound file into one that can be used by your own Mac programs. Chapter 13 provides more details about SoundApp. As you read the book, occasionally browse through the Goodies folder to see if any of the programs apply to the topic your studying.

Index

(continued)

(continued)

(continued)

• Q •

Notes

10/31/95

Title	Author	ISBN	Price
The Internet For Macs® For Dummies® 2nd Edition	by Charles Seiter	ISBN: 1-56884-371-2	$19.99 USA/$26.99 Canada
The Internet For Macs® For Dummies® Starter Kit	by Charles Seiter	ISBN: 1-56884-244-9	$29.99 USA/$39.99 Canada
The Internet For Macs® For Dummies® Starter Kit Bestseller Edition	by Charles Seiter	ISBN: 1-56884-245-7	$39.99 USA/$54.99 Canada
The Internet For Windows® For Dummies® Starter Kit	by John R. Levine & Margaret Levine Young	ISBN: 1-56884-237-6	$34.99 USA/$44.99 Canada
The Internet For Windows® For Dummies® Starter Kit, Bestseller Edition	by John R. Levine & Margaret Levine Young	ISBN: 1-56884-246-5	$39.99 USA/$54.99 Canada

MACINTOSH

Mac® Programming For Dummies®	by Dan Parks Sydow	ISBN: 1-56884-173-6	$19.95 USA/$26.95 Canada
Macintosh® System 7.5 For Dummies®	by Bob LeVitus	ISBN: 1-56884-197-3	$19.95 USA/$26.95 Canada
MORE Macs® For Dummies®	by David Pogue	ISBN: 1-56884-087-X	$19.95 USA/$26.95 Canada
PageMaker 5 For Macs® For Dummies®	by Galen Gruman & Deke McClelland	ISBN: 1-56884-178-7	$19.95 USA/$26.95 Canada
QuarkXPress 3.3 For Dummies®	by Galen Gruman & Barbara Assadi	ISBN: 1-56884-217-1	$19.95 USA/$26.99 Canada
Upgrading and Fixing Macs® For Dummies®	by Kearney Rietmann & Frank Higgins	ISBN: 1-56884-189-2	$19.95 USA/$26.95 Canada

MULTIMEDIA

Multimedia & CD-ROMs For Dummies® 2nd Edition	by Andy Rathbone	ISBN: 1-56884-907-9	$19.99 USA/$26.99 Canada
Multimedia & CD-ROMs For Dummies® Interactive Multimedia Value Pack, 2nd Edition	by Andy Rathbone	ISBN: 1-56884-909-5	$29.99 USA/$39.99 Canada

OPERATING SYSTEMS:

DOS

MORE DOS For Dummies®	by Dan Gookin	ISBN: 1-56884-046-2	$19.95 USA/$26.95 Canada
OS/2® Warp For Dummies® 2nd Edition	by Andy Rathbone	ISBN: 1-56884-205-8	$19.99 USA/$26.99 Canada

UNIX

MORE UNIX® For Dummies®	by John R. Levine & Margaret Levine Young	ISBN: 1-56884-361-5	$19.99 USA/$26.99 Canada
UNIX® For Dummies®	by John R. Levine & Margaret Levine Young	ISBN: 1-878058-58-4	$19.95 USA/$26.95 Canada

WINDOWS

MORE Windows® For Dummies® 2nd Edition	by Andy Rathbone	ISBN: 1-56884-048-9	$19.95 USA/$26.95 Canada
Windows® 95 For Dummies®	by Andy Rathbone	ISBN: 1-56884-240-6	$19.99 USA/$26.99 Canada

PCS/HARDWARE

Illustrated Computer Dictionary For Dummies® 2nd Edition	by Dan Gookin & Wallace Wang	ISBN: 1-56884-218-X	$12.95 USA/$16.95 Canada
Upgrading and Fixing PCs For Dummies® 2nd Edition	by Andy Rathbone	ISBN: 1-56884-903-6	$19.99 USA/$26.99 Canada

PRESENTATION/AUTOCAD

AutoCAD For Dummies®	by Bud Smith	ISBN: 1-56884-191-4	$19.95 USA/$26.95 Canada
PowerPoint 4 For Windows® For Dummies®	by Doug Lowe	ISBN: 1-56884-161-2	$16.99 USA/$22.99 Canada

PROGRAMMING

Borland C++ For Dummies®	by Michael Hyman	ISBN: 1-56884-162-0	$19.95 USA/$26.95 Canada
C For Dummies® Volume 1	by Dan Gookin	ISBN: 1-878058-78-9	$19.95 USA/$26.95 Canada
C++ For Dummies®	by Stephen R. Davis	ISBN: 1-56884-163-9	$19.95 USA/$26.95 Canada
Delphi Programming For Dummies®	by Neil Rubenking	ISBN: 1-56884-200-7	$19.99 USA/$26.99 Canada
Mac® Programming For Dummies®	by Dan Parks Sydow	ISBN: 1-56884-173-6	$19.95 USA/$26.95 Canada
PowerBuilder 4 Programming For Dummies®	by Ted Coombs & Jason Coombs	ISBN: 1-56884-325-9	$19.99 USA/$26.99 Canada
QBasic Programming For Dummies®	by Douglas Hergert	ISBN: 1-56884-093-4	$19.95 USA/$26.95 Canada
Visual Basic 3 For Dummies®	by Wallace Wang	ISBN: 1-56884-076-4	$19.95 USA/$26.95 Canada
Visual Basic "X" For Dummies®	by Wallace Wang	ISBN: 1-56884-230-9	$19.99 USA/$26.99 Canada
Visual C++ 2 For Dummies®	by Michael Hyman & Bob Arnson	ISBN: 1-56884-328-3	$19.99 USA/$26.99 Canada
Windows® 95 Programming For Dummies®	by S. Randy Davis	ISBN: 1-56884-327-5	$19.99 USA/$26.99 Canada

SPREADSHEET

1-2-3 For Dummies®	by Greg Harvey	ISBN: 1-878058-60-6	$16.95 USA/$22.95 Canada
1-2-3 For Windows® 5 For Dummies® 2nd Edition	by John Walkenbach	ISBN: 1-56884-216-3	$16.95 USA/$22.95 Canada
Excel 5 For Macs® For Dummies®	by Greg Harvey	ISBN: 1-56884-186-8	$19.95 USA/$26.95 Canada
Excel For Dummies® 2nd Edition	by Greg Harvey	ISBN: 1-56884-050-0	$16.95 USA/$22.95 Canada
MORE 1-2-3 For DOS For Dummies®	by John Weingarten	ISBN: 1-56884-224-4	$19.99 USA/$26.99 Canada
MORE Excel 5 For Windows® For Dummies®	by Greg Harvey	ISBN: 1-56884-207-4	$19.95 USA/$26.95 Canada
Quattro Pro 6 For Windows® For Dummies®	by John Walkenbach	ISBN: 1-56884-174-4	$19.95 USA/$26.95 Canada
Quattro Pro For DOS For Dummies®	by John Walkenbach	ISBN: 1-56884-023-3	$16.95 USA/$22.95 Canada

UTILITIES

Title	Author	ISBN	Price
Norton Utilities 8 For Dummies®	by Beth Slick	ISBN: 1-56884-166-3	$19.95 USA/$26.95 Canada

VCRS/CAMCORDERS

Title	Author	ISBN	Price
VCRs & Camcorders For Dummies™	by Gordon McComb & Andy Rathbone	ISBN: 1-56884-229-5	$14.99 USA/$20.99 Canada

WORD PROCESSING

Ami Pro For Dummies®	by Jim Meade	ISBN: 1-56884-049-7	$19.95 USA/$26.95 Canada
MORE Word For Windows® 6 For Dummies®	by Doug Lowe	ISBN: 1-56884-165-5	$19.95 USA/$26.95 Canada
MORE WordPerfect® 6 For Windows® For Dummies®	by Margaret Levine Young & David C. Kay	ISBN: 1-56884-206-6	$19.95 USA/$26.95 Canada
MORE WordPerfect® 6 For DOS For Dummies®	by Wallace Wang, edited by Dan Gookin	ISBN: 1-56884-047-0	$19.95 USA/$26.95 Canada
Word 6 For Macs® For Dummies®	by Dan Gookin	ISBN: 1-56884-190-6	$19.95 USA/$26.95 Canada
Word For Windows® 6 For Dummies®	by Dan Gookin	ISBN: 1-56884-075-6	$16.95 USA/$22.95 Canada
Word For Windows® For Dummies®	by Dan Gookin & Ray Werner	ISBN: 1-878058-86-X	$16.95 USA/$22.95 Canada
WordPerfect® 6 For DOS For Dummies®	by Dan Gookin	ISBN: 1-878058-77-0	$16.95 USA/$22.95 Canada
WordPerfect® 6.1 For Windows® For Dummies® 2nd Edition	by Margaret Levine Young & David Kay	ISBN: 1-56884-243-0	$16.95 USA/$22.95 Canada
WordPerfect® For Dummies®	by Dan Gookin	ISBN: 1-878058-52-5	$16.95 USA/$22.95 Canada

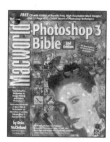

PROFESSIONAL PUBLISHING GROUP

10/31/95

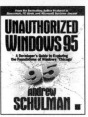

Unauthorized Windows® 95: A Developer's Guide to Exploring the Foundations of Windows "Chicago"
by Andrew Schulman

ISBN: 1-56884-169-8
$29.99 USA/$39.99 Canada

Unauthorized Windows® 95 Developer's Resource Kit
by Andrew Schulman

ISBN: 1-56884-305-4
$39.99 USA/$54.99 Canada

Best of the Net
by Seth Godin

ISBN: 1-56884-313-5
$22.99 USA/$32.99 Canada

Detour: The Truth About the Information Superhighway
by Michael Sullivan-Trainor

ISBN: 1-56884-307-0
$22.99 USA/$32.99 Canada

PowerPC Programming For Intel Programmers
by Kip McClanahan

ISBN: 1-56884-306-2
$49.99 USA/$64.99 Canada

Foundations™ of Visual C++ Programming For Windows® 95
by Paul Yao & Joseph Yao

ISBN: 1-56884-321-6
$39.99 USA/$54.99 Canada

Heavy Metal™ Visual C++ Programming
by Steve Holzner

ISBN: 1-56884-196-5
$39.95 USA/$54.95 Canada

Heavy Metal™ OLE 2.0 Programming
by Steve Holzner

ISBN: 1-56884-301-1
$39.95 USA/$54.95 Canada

Lotus Notes Application Development Handbook
by Erica Kerwien

ISBN: 1-56884-308-9
$39.99 USA/$54.99 Canada

The Internet Direct Connect Kit
by Peter John Harrison

ISBN: 1-56884-135-3
$29.95 USA/$39.95 Canada

Macworld® Ultimate Mac® Programming
by Dave Mark

ISBN: 1-56884-195-7
$39.95 USA/$54.95 Canada

The UNIX®-Haters Handbook
by Simson Garfinkel, Daniel Weise, & Steven Strassmann

ISBN: 1-56884-203-1
$16.95 USA/$22.95 Canada

Learn C++ Today!
by Martin Rinehart

ISBN: 1-56884-310-0
34.99 USA/$44.99 Canada

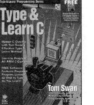

Type & Learn™ C
by Tom Swan

ISBN: 1-56884-073-X
34.95 USA/$44.95 Canada

Type & Learn™ Windows® Programming
by Tom Swan

ISBN: 1-56884-071-3
34.95 USA/$44.95 Canada

Windows is a registered trademark of Microsoft Corporation. Mac is a registered trademark of Apple Computer. UNIX is a registered trademark of AT&T. Macworld is a registered trademark of International Data Group, Inc. Foundations of ----, Heavy Metal, Type & Learn, and the IDG Books Worldwide logos are trademarks under exclusive license to IDG Books Worldwide, Inc., from International Data Group, Inc.

For scholastic requests & educational orders please call Educational Sales, at 1. 800. 434. 2086

FOR MORE INFO OR TO ORDER, PLEASE CALL ▶ 800. 762. 2974

For volume discounts & special orders please call Tony Real, Special Sales, at 415. 655. 3048

IDG BOOKS WORLDWIDE

Order Center: **(800) 762-2974** *(8 a.m.–6 p.m., EST, weekdays)*

Quantity	ISBN	Title	Price	Total

Shipping & Handling Charges

	Description	First book	Each additional book	Total
Domestic	Normal	$4.50	$1.50	$
	Two Day Air	$8.50	$2.50	$
	Overnight	$18.00	$3.00	$
International	Surface	$8.00	$8.00	$
	Airmail	$16.00	$16.00	$
	DHL Air	$17.00	$17.00	$

*For large quantities call for shipping & handling charges.
**Prices are subject to change without notice.

Ship to:

Name _____

Company _____

Address _____

City/State/Zip _____

Daytime Phone _____

Payment: ☐ Check to IDG Books Worldwide (US Funds Only)

☐ VISA   ☐ MasterCard   ☐ American Express

Card # _____ Expires _____

Signature _____

Subtotal _____

CA residents add
applicable sales tax _____

IN, MA, and MD
residents add
5% sales tax _____

IL residents add
6.25% sales tax _____

RI residents add
7% sales tax _____

TX residents add
8.25% sales tax _____

Shipping _____

Total _____

Please send this order form to:

**IDG Books Worldwide, Inc.
7260 Shadeland Station, Suite 100
Indianapolis, IN 46256**

*Allow up to 3 weeks for delivery.
Thank you!*

IDG BOOKS WORLDWIDE LICENSE AGREEMENT

3. **Other Restrictions.** You may not rent or lease the Software. You may transfer the Software and user documentation on a permanent basis provided you retain no copies and the recipient agrees to the terms of this Agreement. You may not reverse engineer, decompile, or disassemble the Software except to the extent that the foregoing restriction is expressly prohibited by applicable law. If the Software is an update or has been updated, any transfer must include the most recent update and all prior versions.

4. **Limited Warranty.** IDG warrants that the Software and disk(s) are free from defects in materials and workmanship for a period of sixty (60) days from the date of purchase of this Book. If IDG receives notification within the warranty period of defects in material or workmanship, IDG will replace the defective disk(s). IDG's entire liability and your exclusive remedy shall be limited to replacement of the Software, which is returned to IDG with a copy of your receipt. This Limited Warranty is void if failure of the Software has resulted from accident, abuse, or misapplication. Any replacement Software will be warranted for the remainder of the original warranty period or thirty (30) days, whichever is longer.

5. **No Other Warranties.** To the maximum extent permitted by applicable law, IDG and the author disclaim all other warranties, express or implied, including but not limited to implied warranties of merchantability and fitness for a particular purpose, with respect to the Software, the programs, the source code contained therein and/or the techniques described in this Book. This limited warranty gives you specific legal rights. You may have others which vary from state/jurisdiction to state/jurisdiction.

6. **No Liability For Consequential Damages.** To the extent permitted by applicable law, in no event shall IDG or the author be liable for any damages whatsoever (including without limitation, damages for loss of business profits, business interruption, loss of business information, or any other pecuniary loss) arising out of the use of or inability to use the Book or the Software, even if IDG has been advised of the possibility of such damages. Because some states/jurisdictions do not allow the exclusion or limitation of liability for consequential or incidental damages, the above limitation may not apply to you.

7. U.S. Government Restricted Rights. Use, duplication, or disclosure of the Software by the U.S. Government is subject to restrictions stated in paragraph (c) (1) (ii) of the Rights in Technical Data and Computer Software clause of DFARS 252.227-7013, and in subparagraphs (a) through (d) of the Commercial Computer — Restricted Rights clause at FAR 52.227-19, and in similar clauses in the NASA FAR supplement, when applicable.

Replacement Disc. If a replacement CD-ROM is needed, please write to the following address: IDG Books Disc Fulfillment Center, Attn: *Foundations of Mac Programming,* IDG Books Worldwide, 7260 Shadeland Station, Indianapolis, IN 46256, or call 800-762-2974.

Disk
Instructions

On the CD-ROM included with this book, you'll find a folder named IDG Sydow Book Examples. Drag the folder to your hard disk to access its contents, or simply double-click on the CD-ROM disc icon to display the folder and then double-click on the folder to display its contents.

The IDG Sydow Book Examples folder holds the source code for all of the example programs found in the book. Because IDG Books wants these files to be usable by all readers — regardless of which compiler they own — the examples are provided in a variety of formats. Within the IDG Sydow Book Examples folder you'll find two more folders. If you own Metrowerks CodeWarrior, you'll use the projects and C language source code files found in the Metrowerks Versions folder. If you use a Symantec compiler such as the THINK C or Symantec C++ compiler, you'll use the projects and C language source code files found in the Symantec Versions folder. Additionally, whether you program for the Mac or Power Mac, you'll find a project that works for you.

Once you've found the appropriate folder that matches the compiler you use, double-click on it to open it. In it you'll find sixteen more folders — one for each chapter in the book. Open one of these subfolders and you'll find the project and source code subfolders for each example program.

IDG BOOKS WORLDWIDE REGISTRATION CARD

RETURN THIS REGISTRATION CARD FOR FREE CATALOG

Title of this book: Foundations of Mac Programming

My overall rating of this book: ❏ Very good [1] ❏ Good [2] ❏ Satisfactory [3] ❏ Fair [4] ❏ Poor [5]

How I first heard about this book:

❏ Found in bookstore; name: [6]

❏ Advertisement: [8]

❏ Word of mouth; heard about book from friend, co-worker, etc.: [10]

❏ Book review: [7]

❏ Catalog: [9]

❏ Other: [11]

What I liked most about this book:

What I would change, add, delete, etc., in future editions of this book:

Other comments:

Number of computer books I purchase in a year: ❏ 1 [12] ❏ 2-5 [13] ❏ 6-10 [14] ❏ More than 10 [15]

I would characterize my computer skills as: ❏ Beginner [16] ❏ Intermediate [17] ❏ Advanced [18] ❏ Professional [19]

I use ❏ DOS [20] ❏ Windows [21] ❏ OS/2 [22] ❏ Unix [23] ❏ Macintosh [24] ❏ Other: [25]_____
(please specify)

I would be interested in new books on the following subjects:
(please check all that apply, and use the spaces provided to identify specific software)

❏ Word processing: [26]

❏ Data bases: [28]

❏ File Utilities: [30]

❏ Networking: [32]

❏ Other: [34]

❏ Spreadsheets: [27]

❏ Desktop publishing: [29]

❏ Money management: [31]

❏ Programming languages: [33]

I use a PC at (please check all that apply): ❏ home [35] ❏ work [36] ❏ school [37] ❏ other: [38] _____

The disks I prefer to use are ❏ 5.25 [39] ❏ 3.5 [40] ❏ other: [41]_____

I have a CD ROM: ❏ yes [42] ❏ no [43]

I plan to buy or upgrade computer hardware this year: ❏ yes [44] ❏ no [45]

I plan to buy or upgrade computer software this year: ❏ yes [46] ❏ no [47]

Name: _____ Business title: [48] _____ Type of Business: [49] _____

Address (❏ home [50] ❏ work [51]/Company name: _____)

Street/Suite# _____

City [52]/State [53]/Zipcode [54]: _____ Country [55] _____

❏ **I liked this book!** You may quote me by name in future
IDG Books Worldwide promotional materials.

My daytime phone number is _____

IDG BOOKS

THE WORLD OF
COMPUTER
KNOWLEDGE

YES!

Please keep me informed about IDG's World of Computer Knowledge.
Send me the latest IDG Books catalog.